Dedication

To my parents for their continuous encouragement;
to my four-year-old son for making each day special;
and to America's youth and children, who face many challenges ahead.

Understanding Contemporary Gangs in America
An Interdisciplinary Approach

❖

REBECCA D. PETERSEN

University of Texas-San Antonio

Foreword by

Joan Moore, Ph.D.
University of Wisconsin-Milwaukee

Prentice
Hall

Upper Saddle River, New Jersey 07458

Library of Congress Cataloging-in-Publication Data

Understanding contemporary gangs in America : an interdisciplinary approach / [edited
by] Rebecca D. Petersen.
    p. cm.
  Includes bibliographical references and index.
  ISBN 0-13-039474-2
    1. Gangs—United States. 2. Juvenile delinquency—United States. I. Petersen, Rebecca
D.

HV6439.U5 U53 2004
364.1'06'608350973–dc21   2002042505

Editor-in-Chief: Stephen Helba
Executive Editor: Frank Mortimer, Jr.
Assistant Editor: Sarah Holle
Production Editor: Janet Kiefer, Carlisle Publishers Services
Production Liaison: Barbara Marttine Cappuccio
Director of Production and Manufacturing: Bruce Johnson
Managing Editor: Mary Carnis
Manufacturing Buyer: Cathleen Petersen
Creative Director: Cheryl Asherman
Cover Design Coordinator: Miguel Ortiz
Cover Designer: Carey Davies
Cover Image: Andrew Brown/Corbis/Stock Market
Editorial Assistant: Barbara Rosenberg
Marketing Manager: Tim Peyton
Formatting and Interior Design: Carlisle Communications, Ltd.
Printing and Binding: Phoenix Book Tech Park

Pearson Education LTD, *London*
Pearson Education Australia PTY, Limited, *Sydney*
Pearson Education Singapore Pte. Ltd.
Pearson Education North Asia Ltd., *Hong Kong*
Pearson Education Canada, Ltd., *Toronto*
Pearson Educación de Mexico, S.A. de C.V.
Pearson Education— Japan, *Tokyo*
Pearson Education Malaysia, Pte. Ltd.

10 9 8 7 6 5 4 3 2 1
ISBN: 0-13-039474-2

Contents

❖

Foreword

---❖---

This book meets a very real need. People who do research on gangs come from many different backgrounds. They include criminologists, sociologists, psychologists, social workers, and anthropologists. Every researcher has his/her own preference for publication outlets, and the result is that literature on gangs is scattered throughout a dozen or more journals. It is difficult enough for professional researchers to keep up with this diverse literature, and it is virtually impossible for students to get a first-hand acquaintance with such literature.

It is particularly important that students interested in gangs be exposed to research because most people's thinking about the topic is based on highly sensationalized media reports. Few people have ever met a gang member face-to-face. We hear about gangs when a particularly heinous crime is committed, and we know enough to avoid certain parts of town because they are "gang territory." However, most people know virtually nothing about the background of gangs or about how youth gang members (who are, after all, mostly adolescents) cope with school, with family, and with their free time; they know very little about how incarceration actually affects gang members.

Dr. Rebecca D. Petersen, an expert on gang research, has compiled readings that draw on a variety of research approaches. If nothing else, students, practitioners, and others who use this book should think seriously about the difficulties of doing research on gangs. Some of our information comes from police reports, for example. What kind of information do the police actually obtain? Some of the information comes from surveys done in schools, detention facilities, and community organizations. What are the strengths and drawbacks of such approaches? What about researchers who go into community settings and interview or observe youth in their "natural" environments?

Doing research on gangs is emphatically not the same as doing research on which brand of potato chips one prefers. Gang members belong to small secret societies that are often at odds with authorities and with parents. Sometimes, the members want to boast about their membership and their bold deeds. At other times, they may feel deeply ashamed of something they have done. Usually, they want to conceal their activities (and the activities of fellow members) from law enforcement or other adults. Sometimes, the gang is a refuge from an appalling family situation, but sometimes gang members victimize each other, too. They live in a complex world, and this book gives an excellent sampling of some of the contradictions in that world. However, don't forget; most research taps into little pieces of that world, but none can represent the totality.

Then again, research is driven by dissatisfaction with what we don't know. Almost every gang researcher has read something that jars with his/her sense of what is really going on. He/she may realize that there is a whole dimension of gang life that has not been touched or a whole population whose gang activities have not been studied. The researcher produces a report, some other researcher finds flaws or omissions in it, and the process begins all over again.

In spite of all these issues, we know more about gangs in the United States than any other nation in the world. So, why haven't we been able to do more about them? In the 1970s, police in only 19 states reported gangs; by the turn of the 21st century, police in all 50 states and in 60 percent of our nation's cities—small and large alike—reported gang problems. This book reports on some efforts to ameliorate these problems. As with research, these program reports can generate dissatisfaction with policy and practice; dissatisfaction often marks the beginning of creativity and progress.

Joan Moore, Ph.D.
Distinguished Professor Emerita
University of Wisconsin-Milwaukee

Preface

❖

Understanding Contemporary Gangs in America: An Interdisciplinary Approach is a unique text-reader providing a comprehensive, understandable, and contemporary perspective on gangs in America.

As I was preparing for a new senior seminar course on youth gangs in 1999, I was surprised there was not a comprehensive text on gangs. I had a difficult time selecting academic research and material that was both understandable and current. Furthermore, much published research included advanced methods and statistical analysis, were narrow in scope, and/or were limited in addressing broader societal implications of the gang problem.

I contend that students need some type of "introductory" book that is comprehensive and interdisciplinary with both empirical and theoretical research, yet not too advanced as far as methods, statistical analysis, or topical coverage is concerned. Most social science majors and practitioners in the field do not have a statistical background nor a clear grasp of statistics, especially at the more advanced level. This is the balance I hope is achieved here in this text-reader.

The main purpose of this text-reader on gangs is to provide for a more comprehensive, interdisciplinary, contemporary, and understandable text accessible for undergraduate and graduate students, academicians, practitioners, policymakers, and the general public. The most important goal is to include a variety of contemporary perspectives on gangs understandable to a wide range of audiences. The articles in this text-reader have been selected for their diversity of perspectives and their contribution to understanding gangs. All articles are from academic, peer-reviewed journal articles or chapters from recent books, which provide the audience with an in-depth examination into gangs.

The book is divided into seven sections based on general themes: 1) Understanding and defining gangs, 2) Gender issues in gangs, 3) Race and ethnicity in gangs, 4) Gangs in prisons and schools, 5) Violence, drugs, and gangs, 6) Gang victimization, and 7) Gang prevention and intervention. Each chapter ends with *Questions for Understanding and Critical Thinking*. These thought-provoking questions are included for the readers to grasp and understand the material presented as well as to address gang issues from a critical thinking perspective.

Acknowledgments

I am indebted to each author and scholar whose works are included in this text-reader. I wish to express my gratitude and thanks to Prentice-Hall for providing me this opportunity, as well as to my freelance editor, Susan Beauchamp, Janet Kiefer at Carlisle Publishers Services and to the following reviewers: Frank M. Afflitto, Arizona State University, Tempe, AZ; Stephen Brodt, Ball State University, Muncie, IN; Patricia O' Donnell Brummett, California State University, Northridge, CA; Scott Decker, University of Missouri, St. Louis, MO; Alexjandro del Carmen, University of Texas at Arlington, Arlington, TX; Janice Joseph, The Richard Stockton College of New Jersey, Pomona, NJ; Barry Sherman, Madonna University, Livonia, MI; Kimberley Tobin, Westfield State College, Westfield, MA; and Stephanie Whitus, California State University Sacramento, CA. I am thankful for my mentors and former professors who have shaped my academic career; most notably Dr. Dennis Palumbo and Dr. Elizabeth (Libby) Deschenes. Finally, I would like to thank my family and my son for their support, encouragement, and patience and, most of all, to thank God who has given me much more than I deserve. I invite all who read this text-reader to send comments about *Understanding Contemporary Gangs in America: An Interdisciplinary Approach,* to me: rpetersen@utsa.edu

Rebecca D. Petersen, Ph.D.
University of Texas-San Antonio

About the Editor

❖

Dr. Rebecca D. Petersen, Assistant Professor of Criminal Justice at the University of Texas-San Antonio, received her Ph.D. in Justice Studies from Arizona State University. Professor Petersen recently completed a major Centers for Disease Control and Prevention-funded study on intimate violence among Mexican American adolescent females in which she was the Co-Principal Investigator. Her recent publications include academic journal articles and book chapters on juvenile justice policy, females and crime, gangs, juvenile corrections, intermediate sanctions and drug courts. Her recent honors include two consecutive years of being included in *Who's Who Among America's Teachers.*

Contributing Authors

Rhonda Braaten-Antrim, Graduate Student of Sociology, North Dakota State University

William B. Brown, Associate Professor of Sociology, University of Michigan-Flint

Scott H. Decker, Curator Professor of Criminology and Criminal Justice, University of Missouri-St. Louis

Elizabeth Piper Deschenes, Professor of Criminal Justice, California State University-Long Beach

Finn-Aage Esbensen, E. Desmond Lee Professor of Youth Crime and Violence, University of Missouri-St. Louis

Jeffrey Fagan, Professor of Biosciences and Director of the Center for Violence Research and Prevention, Columbia University

Mark S. Fleisher, Semi J. and Ruth W. Begun Professor, and Director, Begun Center for Violence Research, Prevention and Education, Case Western Reserve University

John M. Hagedorn, Associate Professor of Criminal Justice, University of Illinois-Chicago

Eric Henderson, Associate Professor of Anthropology, Great Basin College

James C. Howell, Adjunct Researcher, National Youth Gang Center

Geoffrey Hunt, Senior Research Associate, Institute for Scientific Analysis

Karen Joe-Laidler, Associate Professor of Sociology, University of Hong Kong

Stephen J. Kunitz, Professor Emeritus of Community and Preventative Medicine, University of Rochester

Jerrold E. Levy, Professor Emeritus of Anthropology, University of Arizona

Rick Lovell, Associate Professor of Criminal Justice Programs, University of Wisconsin-Milwaukee

Kathleen MacKenzie, Research Associate, Institute for Scientific Analysis

Gregory Yee Mark, Professor of Ethnic Studies, California State University-Sacramento

Jody Miller, Associate Professor of Criminology and Criminal Justice, University of Missouri-St. Louis

Joan W. Moore, Distinguished Professor Emerita of Sociology, University of Wisconsin-Milwaukee

Rebecca D. Petersen, Assistant Professor of Criminal Justice, University of Texas-San Antonio

Edward L. Portillos, Doctoral Candidate in the School of Justice Studies, Arizona State University

Carl E. Pope, Professor of Criminal Justice Programs, University of Wisconsin-Milwaukee

Randall G. Shelden, Professor of Criminal Justice, University of Nevada at Las Vegas

Doug E. Thompkins, Ford Fellow, Department of Criminal Justice, University of Illinois-Chicago

Kevin M. Thompson, Professor of Sociology, North Dakota State University

Sharon K. Tracy, Professor of Political Science, Georgia Southern University

L. Thomas Winfree, Professor of Criminal Justice, New Mexico State University

Marjorie Zatz, Professor of Justice Studies, Arizona State University

PART I

Understanding and Defining Gangs

1

Introduction

Randall G. Shelden, Sharon K. Tracy, and William B. Brown

❖

WHAT IS A GANG?

We must initially consider the problem of defining what exactly constitutes a gang and a gang member. If four youths are standing on a street corner or are simply walking down the street, is this a gang? If this same group of youths hang out together frequently and occasionally engage in some form of deviant activity, does this mean they are a gang? Suppose this same group invents a name for itself and even purchases special shirts or jackets and invents slogans or hand-signs—does this mean it is a gang? If a young person is seen giving special hand signals or heard uttering gang phrases because he thinks it is cool or hip to do so, whether he may fully understand the implications, is he then to be considered a gang member? Or, if a youth living in a neighborhood inhabited by a gang (but no one in the gang considers him a member), just happens to be passing the time on a street corner with a gang member he has known for several years, and is coincidentally questioned by a police officer, who subsequently fills out a field investigation card on him, is he therefore to be counted as a gang member? And how does race enter into the picture in the definition of gangs? If three or four white youths spend a considerable amount of time together, occasionally commit crimes together, and are often seen wearing the kinds of clothes typical of adolescents in general and some gangs in particular, are they considered a gang? We suspect that the average white citizen (and many police officers) would respond to this group differently than if they saw a group of three or four African-American teenagers hanging out together (e.g., at a shopping mall). Perhaps this is one reason why most official estimates

From *Youth Gangs in American Society, 2nd edition,* by R.G. Shelden, S.K. Tracy, and W.B. Brown © 2001. Reprinted with permission of Wadsworth, an imprint of the Wadsworth Group, a division of Thomson Learning. Fax 800-730-2215.

of gangs and gang members tell us that less than 10 percent are white and the majority are African-American or some other minority group (usually Hispanic). In other words, could it not be argued that the very definition of *gang* is racially biased? Even these few examples illustrate the difficulty in defining gangs and gang members.

The term *gang* can have many different definitions. Gil Geis has provided one of the most interesting comments about the etymology of the term, noting that the early English usage of *gang* was "a going, a walking, or a journey" (quoted in Klein, 1995:22). The definition given by the Random House College Dictionary (1975:543) provides similar meanings of a positive or neutral nature, such as "a group or band"; "a group of persons who gather together for social reasons"; "a group of persons working together; squad; shift; *a gang of laborers*"; along with the more negative meanings. The thesaurus of the word processing program used to type these words gives such synonyms as "pack," "group," "company," and "team."

Not surprisingly, there has existed little consensus among social scientists and law-enforcement personnel as to what these terms mean. One writer defined gangs as "groups whose members meet together with some regularity, over time, on the basis of group-defined criteria of membership and group-defined organization" (Short, 1990:3). In many studies researchers have often used whatever definition was used by the police. Many researchers have apparently confused the term *group* with the term *gang* and have proceeded to expand the definition in such a way as to include every group of youths who commit offenses together. One of the most accepted definitions comes from the work of Klein:

> [A gang is] any denotable . . . group [of adolescents and young adults] who (a) are generally perceived as a distinct aggregation by others in their neighborhood, (b) recognize themselves as a denotable group (almost invariably with a group name), and (c) have been involved in a sufficient number of [illegal] incidents to call forth a consistent negative response from neighborhood residents and/or enforcement agencies (Klein and Maxson, 1989:205).

The dominant law-enforcement perspective is that gangs are essentially criminal conspiracies with a few hard-core members (often described as sociopaths) and believe that arrest and imprisonment of these individuals are required as a viable social policy. An example is provided by the California Penal Code (Section 186.22), which gives a definition of a "criminal street gang" as "any organization, association, or group of three or more persons whether formal or informal . . . which has a common name or common identifying sign or symbol, where members individually or collectively engage in or have engaged in a pattern of criminal activity" (Spergel, 1990:18–19). A report from the Los Angeles County Sheriff's Department defines a gang as "any group gathered together on a continuing basis to commit anti-social behavior" (Los Angeles County, 1992:1).

Adding to the ambiguity of the term *gang* is the most recent National Youth Gang Survey (1996) sponsored by the Office of Juvenile Justice and Delinquency Prevention (OJJDP). In this survey of about 5,000 agencies, a *youth gang* was defined as follows: "a group of youths or young adults in your jurisdiction that you or other responsible persons in your agency or community are willing to identify or classify as a 'gang.' " Omitted from this definition were such groups as motorcycle gangs, hate/ideology groups, prison gangs, or "other exclusively adult gangs" (U.S. Department of Justice, 1999:57). In other words, a "gang" is whatever an agency says it is!

Modern researchers have argued that gangs and delinquent groups are significantly different, but most now generally agree that gang offenders are usually older; are more homogeneous with regard to age, sex, race, and residence; and tend to commit more violent crimes than ordinary delinquent groups. Curry and Spergel distinguish among the terms *gang, street gang, traditional youth gang,* and *posse/crew.* They define *gang* as

> a group or collectivity of persons with a common identity who interact in cliques or sometimes as a whole group on a fairly regular basis and whose activities the community may view in varying degrees as legitimate, illegitimate, criminal, or some combination thereof. What distinguishes the gang from other groups is its communal or "fraternal," different, or special interstitial character (Curry and Spergel, 1990:388).

They define *street gang* as "a group or collectivity of persons engaged in significant illegitimate or criminal activities, mainly threatening and violent." The emphasis is placed on the location of the gang and their gang-related activities (ibid.).

The *traditional youth gang*

> refers to a youth or adolescent gang and often to the youth sector of a street gang. Such a group is concerned primarily with issues of status, prestige, and turf protection. The youth gang may have a name and a location, be relatively well organized, and persist over time. [They] often have leadership structure (implicit or explicit), codes of conduct, colors, special dress, signs, symbols, and the like. [They] may vary across time in characteristics of age, gender, community, race/ethnicity, or generation, as well as in scope and nature of delinquent or criminal activities (ibid:389).

Still another variation is the *posse* or *crew,* which, while often used in conjunction with the terms *street* or *youth gang,* is more commonly "characterized by a commitment to criminal activity for economic gain, particularly drug trafficking" (ibid.: 389).

Spergel and Curry also note that there are various kinds of deviant groups, such as "Stoners, punk rockers, neo-Nazi Skinheads, Satanic groups, motorcycle gangs, prison gangs." These may resemble traditional youth gangs or street gangs. They also caution that these gangs should be distinguished from what have often been called *youth groups* and *street groups,* common in an earlier era (e.g., as when Thrasher wrote in the 1920s). These groups are often called *street clubs, youth organizations,* or *athletic clubs.*

Spergel and Curry also note that there are *delinquent groups* and *criminal organizations.* The former are far less organized and criminal than the gangs defined previously and do not have distinctive dress, colors, signs, and so on. The latter refers more to a relatively well-organized and sophisticated group of either youths or adults (often a combination of both) organized mainly around the illegal pursuit of economic gain. Finally, there are gang *cliques* or *sets* that are often smaller versions (or subgroups) of larger gangs, usually based on age (ibid.: 390).

Huff alerts us to another distinction, which has gained more significance in recent years, namely, that existing between gangs and organized crime. As he notes, *youth gangs* historically were largely groups of adolescents (mostly male) who engaged in a variety of deviant activities, especially turf battles and gang fights. Now they are increasingly involved in major crimes, especially those that are violent or drug related. *Organized crime* has meant *adult* criminal enterprises operating businesses. Today such organized activities characterize many youth gangs. Huff defines a *youth gang* as a

> collectivity consisting primarily of adolescents and young adults who (a) interact frequently with one another; (b) are frequently and deliberately involved in illegal activities; (c) share a common collective identity that is usually, but not always, expressed through a gang name; and (d) typically express that identity by adopting certain symbols and/or claiming control over certain "turf" (persons, places, things, and/or economic markets) (Huff, 1993:4).

In contrast, Huff defines an *organized crime group* as a

> collectivity consisting primarily of adults who (a) interact frequently with one another; (b) are frequently and deliberately involved in illegal activities directed toward economic gain, primarily through the provision of illegal goods and services; and (c) generally have better defined leadership and organizational structure than does the youth gang (ibid.).

There are several key differences between these two groups. First, they differ significantly in terms of age, youth gangs being much younger than organized crime groups. Second, whereas the organized crime group exists almost exclusively for the purpose of economic criminal activity, youth gangs engage in a variety of both legal and illegal activities, with their illegal activities usually committed by individuals or small groups of individuals rather than by the entire group.

It is obvious that the majority of these definitions focus almost exclusively on delinquent or criminal behavior as the distinguishing feature that differentiates gangs from other groups. This is consistent with a strictly law-enforcement perspective. Several other researchers disagree and argue that gangs should not be defined as purely criminal or delinquent organizations (i.e., the reason they began in the first place and the reason they continue to exist is the pursuit of delinquent or criminal activity). In this context, it is important to consider one of Huff's most pertinent comments. He notes that

> in analyzing youth gangs, it is important to acknowledge that it is normal and healthy for adolescents to want to be with their peers. In fact, adolescents who are loners often tend to be maladjusted. Because adolescents go to dances together, party together, shop together (and, in many cases, shop *lift* together), it should not be surprising that some of them join together in one type of social group known as a gang. Group experience, then, is a familiar and normative phenomenon in adolescent subculture, and gangs represent an extreme manifestation of that age-typical emphasis on being together and belonging to something (Huff, 1993:5–6, emphasis in the original).

Hagedorn believes that gangs are not merely criminal enterprises or bureaucratic entities with formal organizational structures. Rather, as other researchers have noted (e.g., Moore, 1978; Suttles, 1968), gangs are age-graded groups or cliques "with considerable variation within each age group of friends" (Hagedorn, 1998:86).

It is difficult to conceive of gangs as purely criminal organizations. Most gang members spend the bulk of their time simply hanging out or engaging in other nondelinquent activities. Jackson notes that many researchers, accepting the popular imagery of gangs, have spent a considerable amount of time (perhaps months) "waiting for something to happen" (Jackson, 1989:314).

It should be noted that a new category has been invented recently. According to the most recent National Youth Gang Survey, respondents were asked to identify how many "troublesome youth groups" they had in their jurisdiction. This term apparently is a combination of the term "unsupervised peer groups" and "troublesome youth groups." Citing several sociologists (Sampson and Groves, 1989; Short, 1996; Warr, 1996), the report notes that these adolescent groups typically have three or four members and are not well organized and rather transitory (what adolescent groups are *not?*). Also, they occasionally get involved in delinquent activities (again, what adolescent groups do *not?*) but are not committed to a life of crime (once again, what adolescent groups are any different?). Despite any connection to full-fledged youth gangs, survey respondents were asked to estimate the number of these kinds of adolescent groups (how they were to identify them and what criteria were to be used is not spelled out in this report). Not surprisingly (given that those doing the data collection were all adults), the vast majority of jurisdictions reported the existence of such groups (U.S. Department of Justice, 1999).

An equally difficult task is trying to determine what constitutes a *gang-related offense*. If a gang member kills another gang member in retaliation for the killing of a fellow gang member, few would argue over whether this would be gang related. However, what if a gang member is killed as a result of some sort of love triangle, or if a gang member is killed by someone not in a gang, or if a gang member kills someone while committing a robbery on his own? Decisions about these kinds of incidents must be made, and police officials have procedures for such reporting. However, as Klein and Maxson observe, such procedures are conducted "not always according to reliable criteria, not always with adequate information regarding the motive or circumstances of the crime, not always with extensive gang-membership information on file, and—most clearly—not by the same criteria from city to city" (Klein and Maxson, 1989:206).

Klein and Maxson reviewed this process in five cities around the country and found that each city had somewhat different methods for defining gang-related incidents; for example, in two cities, only violent incidents were counted. In one city the policy was to include only gang-on-gang crimes, but the authors found that robberies where the offenders (but not the victims) were gang members constituted gang-related crimes. In another city any offense committed by a gang member was counted as gang related (Klein and Maxson, 1989:208).

In short, there appears to be little consensus on what a gang-related crime is. Given the complexity of the problem, it is highly unlikely that such a consensus will ever be achieved. Quite often we will find that a gang member is engaging in offending behavior by himself, without any assistance from his fellow gang members. Also, rarely will one find an entire gang (if, for example, there are 100 members) involved in a single incident. A method used by the Chicago Police Department seems as good a solution as any that has been offered or presented.

CHICAGO'S USE OF DESCRIPTORS TO DEFINE GANG-RELATED CRIME

Based on the definition of gang-related crime provided by Bobrowski, the Chicago Police Department uses the term *descriptors* to aid in their recording of data on gang crimes. These descriptors Bobrowski defines as "certain features which serve to distinguish street gang related cases from those which are not." Based on the research by this police department, there "emerges a finite set of descriptors which can be thought of as trademarks of the street gang crime" (Bobrowski, 1988:15).

The term *descriptors* implies more than just motives, as it suggests a certain "commonality of circumstances" of street-gang crime. The Gang Crimes Section of the Chicago Police Department chose seven specific descriptors "which serve to categorize the event data found in case narratives." The seven are representing, retaliation, street fighting, vice related, recruitment, turf violations, and other. The first four descriptors together constituted about 94 percent of all street gang-related crimes during the period under study

(January 1, 1987, through July 31, 1988). The seven descriptors are summarized as follows (Bobrowski, 1988:17–29):

1. *Representing.* This term is used to denote any incident in which, in the process of committing a crime, the offender represents himself as being a member of a particular gang. This can be a verbal statement, a hand-sign, a display of colors, or any other similar symbolic gesture. In a recent period of time (January 1, 1987, through July 31, 1988) Chicago police noted that this descriptor was found in 32 percent of all street-gang-related cases.

2. *Retaliation.* This term denotes when one gang resorts to some form of violence to solve certain conflicts with one or more other gangs. Examples include attempts to protect its own interests, uphold its interests, and seek revenge (for example, for a harm done to one of its own members). Such behavior arises out of insults, chance altercations, and infringements on one's criminal activities. This descriptor was found in about 8 percent of gang-related activities in Chicago.

3. *Street Fighting.* This is similar to the classic rumble, whether it be spontaneous or planned, an execution or hit, or simply a fair fight. The most common are "spontaneous assaultive engagements among small groups (three to five persons), random encounters among antagonistic rivals, and small bands of two or three persons assaulting non-gang victims" (Bobrowski, 1988:22). These actions constituted 24 percent of gang-related crimes in Chicago.

4. *Vice-Related.* This category accounted for 30 percent of all the street-gang-related offenses. About 92 percent of these were narcotics, liquor-law violations, gambling, and prostitution offenses. It should be noted that less than 1 percent of all nonvice offenses involved drug activities (for example, evidence of vice activity was found in only 2 out of 82 homicides during the period under study).

5. *Recruitment.* This refers to activities in which a gang member in some way attempts to force a nonmember to join the gang. Usually it is a type of "join or continue to pay" situation. Recruitment is probably grossly underrepresented in these statistics. Victims are often fearful of further actions against them by the gang and simply distrust the police; therefore, reporting does not occur. Also, if the youth joins the gang, the likelihood of the incident's being reported to the police is almost nil. Statistically, recruitment efforts constitute only 3 percent of the reported gang crimes.

6. *Turf Violations.* These include the defacing of gang graffiti and passing through a designated gang territory, frequently a favorite hangout of a particular gang (for example, a restaurant, street corner, or bar). These events are also woefully underreported for basically the same reasons as noted in recruitment. Officially, these violations accounted for only 1.5 percent of all street-gang crimes in Chicago.

7. *Other Descriptors.* These include such crimes as extortion (mostly forcing people to pay turf tax to cross into and through gang territory), personal conflicts among gang members, and prestige-related crimes, which may be greater than reported. These offenses "may include acts committed to satisfy membership initiation; to establish a special reputation, a position of responsibility, or a leadership role; to respond to challenges or avoid reproach; or to prevail in internal

power struggles" (Bobrowski, 1988:27). Together all of these constituted only 4 percent of the officially reported gang crimes in Chicago.

Reiner notes that there are two different ways of defining gang crimes. On the one hand there are *gang-related crimes,* and on the other hand there are *gang-motivated crimes.* The former is the broader definition that states if either the criminal or the victim is a gang member, then the crime is gang related. This is known as the *member-based* definition. This makes it a lot easier for law-enforcement authorities to count gang crime. However, some believe that it will tend to overstate the amount of crime attributed to gangs because many, if not most, of the individuals involved would probably commit crimes and/or be a victim whether or not they were in a gang (Klein, 1995:15).

Some believe that focusing on motivation is using a more narrow view. From this perspective, gang-related crime is caused by *gang activity.* Supporters of this view claim that one of the main virtues of using the *motive-based* definition is that it eliminates unrelated kinds of crime and focuses on crimes that are "clearly due to the presence of gangs" (e.g., drive-by shootings), although it may understate the gang problem (Reiner, 1992:95–96).

Using the *motive-based* definition may in effect obscure the extent of the gang problem in an area, perhaps hoping that the problem will "just go away" (Knox, 1991:343). Indeed, there are significant differences in the amount of "gang-related" crime, depending on which definition one uses. Klein compared homicide rates in Los Angeles and Chicago. In Los Angeles, with a member-based definition there were about twice as many gang-related homicides as in Chicago, which uses a motive-based definition (Klein, 1995).

STEREOTYPES OF GANGS

Part of the problem in arriving at a consensus definition of *gang* and *gang-related crime* is that we are dealing with widely accepted stereotypes of gangs, most of which are derived from the biased information of law enforcement and the media. From many years of research, Joan Moore has compiled the following list of the most common stereotypes: (Moore, 1993:28–29):

> (1) They are composed of males (no females) who are violent, addicted to drugs and alcohol, sexually hyperactive, unpredictable, and confrontational; (2) They are either all African-American or all Hispanic; (3) They thrive in inner-city neighborhoods where they dominate, intimidate, and prey upon innocent citizens; (4) They all deal heavily in drugs, especially crack cocaine; (5) "A gang is a gang is a gang"—in other words, they are all alike or "you see one and you see them all"; (6) There is no good in gangs, it is all bad (a corollary to this is that anyone who would want to join a gang must be stupid or crazy); (7) Gangs are basically criminal enterprises and that youths start gangs in order to collectively commit crimes; in other words, there is a tendency to confuse individual and group criminality; (8) The "West Side Story" image of aggressive, rebellious, but nice kids has been replaced in recent years by the "gangster" image of a very disciplined criminal organization complete with "soldiers."

According to Moore, stereotypes shape the definitions of gangs and therefore determine policies structured to deal with gangs. Especially important is the stereotype of gangs as criminal enterprises, which confuses individual and collective criminal activity. Quite often the police, as well as the media and the public, will label as gang related criminal behavior that is individually motivated. It should also be noted that stereotypical thinking is a common phenomenon in the world. To stereotype is to think in terms of rigid and inflexible categories. Most of the time such thinking is normal and harmless, but when it is associated with anxiety or fear, it is very different. "Stereotypes in such circumstances are commonly infused with attitudes of hostility or hatred towards the group in question" (Giddens, 1990:303). As was stated earlier, it is not uncommon for white citizens, for example, to have a completely different response when they see a group of three or four young African-American males together in a shopping mall as opposed to a group of three or four young white males, even when each group is wearing clothing and/or colors that are stereotypically associated with gang attire.

Stereotypes have a great deal to do with what researchers have called *moral panics*. This term was originally popularized by British criminologist Stanley Cohen when describing the reaction to various youth disturbances (by youths called "mods and rockers") in Britain during the 1960s (Cohen, 1980; see also Goode and Ben-Yehuda, 1994). Cohen defined a moral panic as a "condition, episode, person or group of persons" that "emerges to become defined as a threat to societal values and interests." The nature of this problem "is presented in stylized and stereotypical fashion by the mass media," while the "moral barricades are manned by editors, bishops, politicians and other right thinking people" (Cohen, 1980:9). These kinds of threats are "far more likely to be perceived during times of widespread anxiety, moral malaise, and uncertainty about the future" (McCorkle and Miethe, 2001:19).

These panics build on already-existing divisions in society, usually based on race, class, and age. (Typically the most visible crime is the focus of attention, which just happens to be the outrageous and, it should be noted in the case of gangs, the rare "drive-by" shootings.) The moral panics typically focus on youth because they always represent the most serious challenge to conventional values held by adults. The recent growth of the underclass—consisting disproportionately of minorities and the young—in an isolated and deteriorating inner city is where the greatest concentration and growth of gangs have been.

Moral panics have three distinguishing characteristics (McCorkle and Miethe, 2001:19–20). First, there is a focused attention on the behavior (either real or imagined) of certain groups, who are in turn transformed into sort of "folk devils" with the corresponding emphasis on negative characteristics over any positive one. There is an "evil" in our midst, and it must be eliminated. Second, there is quite a gap between the concern over a condition or problem and the objective threat that it poses. Typically, as in the case of gangs, the objective threat is far less than popularly perceived. Third, there is a great deal of fluctuation over time in the level of concern over a problem. The threat is "discovered," then concern reaches a peak, and subsequently subsides—but perhaps reemerging once again.

Besides gangs, there have been many examples of such moral panics during the 1980s, when gangs emerged as a "problem." One was the panic over "satanic cults" in the 1980s, and another was the problem of "missing" or "stolen" children around the same time. Also, there was the "crack epidemic" around the same time, which corresponded with the antigang hysteria. Still another panic was that over "serial killers." All of these panics were eventually proven, through careful research, to far exceed the objective nature of the threats alleged by the media and law-enforcement officials (McCorkle and Mieche, 2001:22–32).

HOW MANY GANGS AND GANG MEMBERS ARE THERE?

Gangs can be found in all cities with populations of 100,000 or more. Gangs are also found within both the federal and the state prison systems and in most juvenile correctional systems. Gangs are found within practically every major urban high school in the country (Camp and Camp, 1985; Curry and Decker, 1998:125–132; Howell, 1998:4; Klein, 1995:168–170; Shelden, 1991; Spergel, 1995:116–127).

Exactly how many gangs and how many gang members there are in the country is presently not known with any degree of certainty. In fact, there are as many estimates as there are estimators![1] In the 1920s, Thrasher estimated that there were 1,313 gangs in Chicago alone (Thrasher, 1927). Miller's nationwide survey in the 1970s estimated anywhere from 700 to almost 3,000 gangs in the largest cities in the country (Miller, 1975, 1982). The most recent estimate is that there are more than 30,000 gangs and over 800,000 gang members (Howell, 1998; U.S. Department of Justice, 1999). What is especially interesting about estimates is that over the past 20 years during which such surveys have been conducted, the number of gangs and gang members increases every year. What is also interesting is that in almost every case the estimates come almost exclusively from law-enforcement sources (especially the most recent surveys, such as the latest National Youth Gang Survey). Moreover, during all these years the amount of money going to police departments keeps increasing as well, in addition to the number of "gang units" and police officers assigned to these units. As noted earlier, in virtually every survey in recent years the definition of *gang* and *gang member* has been left entirely up to the reporting law-enforcement agencies.

Estimates from individual cities and states have been provided throughout the years and may be used for comparative purposes. Spergel (1990:26–27, 31–33) provided some estimates from the 1980s in several major urban areas. These estimates show how the gang problem increased during this decade, according to law-enforcement sources. For example, in Dade County, Florida, the number of gangs in 1980 was estimated to be only 4, but by 1988 there were 80; in Los Angeles County in 1988 there were about 800 gangs, up from 239 in 1985, whereas estimates of the number of gang members range from 50,000 to 70,000 (one estimate said there were about 25,000 Crips and Bloods gang members alone); in 1975, in San Diego County, there were only three gangs with about 300 members total, but by 1987 there were between 19 and 35 gangs with a total membership of about 2,000. In some cities, the numbers have been fluctuating: Phoenix in 1974 reported about 34 gangs but 31 in 1986 (however, these numbers have recently increased again); in New York City, the number of gangs declined from 315 (with about 20,000 members) in 1974 to 66 in 1987 (with only about 2,500 members); Louisville reported about 15 gangs in 1985 but only one gang in 1988; and in Fort Wayne, Indiana, six gangs existed in 1986 (with more than 2,000 members), but only three gangs and about 50 members were noted in 1988.

The 1995 national survey noted that California reported the largest number of gangs at 4,927, with Texas having 3,276, followed by Illinois with 1,363 and Colorado with 1,304. Not surprisingly, California topped the list for the number of gang members, with an estimated 254,618, with Illinois a distant second with 75,226 and Texas third with 57,060. It should be no surprise to find that Los Angeles had the largest number of gang members at 60,000 (county estimate; the city estimate was 58,197), followed by Chicago with 33,000 (U.S. Department of Justice, 1997).

A reporting system known as GREAT (Gang Reporting Evaluation and Tracking) was established in the early 1990s by the Los Angeles Police Department. Reportedly this has become one of the most sophisticated gang-reporting systems in the country. As of October 1991 this system listed a total of 936 gangs in Los Angeles County. Of this number, there were 298 African-American gangs (213 Crips, 85 Bloods), 467 Chicano gangs, 63 Asian gangs (plus 16 Samoan gangs), 61 Stoner gangs, and 18 Anglo gangs. In the early 1990s it was estimated that there were in excess of 100,000 gang members in Los Angeles County. Of this number, 94 percent are male, and just 6 percent are female. About 57 percent are Chicano, while 37 percent are African-American, and about 4 percent are Asian (Reiner, 1992:109–110). The more recent estimate of 60,000 gang members suggests one of two conclusions: There has been an actual decline in the number of gang members in Los Angeles County, or improved reporting techniques account for the "decline." We are not certain which of these reasons is correct, but we are inclined to support the second interpretation.

These differing estimates may reflect many factors, including how local criminal justice officials define *gang* and *gang member.* Some agencies provide conservative estimates (sometimes to preserve a safe image of their city or to promote tourism), while others highly exaggerate the numbers (often in hopes of obtaining more funding). The changing numbers noted above may reflect changing perspectives and definitions.

Some comments about the sources of the above statistics are in order at this juncture. The fact that those providing most of these estimates are law-enforcement bureaucracies and the amount of federal dollars flowing into these bureaucracies should arouse the curiosity of any critical reader. And naturally so, given the vested interest in producing high numbers. It is also curious that every year a national survey is done there seem to be more gangs and more gang members identified. Moreover, it is certainly no surprise to find gangs and gang members in just about every suburb and rural hamlet in every part of the country since federal dollars will certainly flow to these small departments (according to the 1996 survey, 25 percent of all rural counties and 57 percent of all suburban counties reported having gangs). As noted earlier, a new category was invented for this most recent survey, called "troublesome youth groups." Almost three-fourths of large cities reported having these groups, while just over half of all rural counties have them (U.S. Department of Justice, 1999:15). Given the vagueness of the definition of "troublesome youth groups," is this not surprising? It should not come as any surprise to the reader that the authors are very skeptical of the above numbers. What really bothers us is the existence of this new category of "troublesome youth groups." Why? Simply because almost any youth (especially a minority youth) can be identified as belonging to such a group! (How many groups of three or four adolescents will not be perceived as "troublesome" to some adults?) Once so identified, it may be easy to eventually classify them as a gang and thus more easily controlled. The civil libertarian in each of us raises some alarms, as it should for all of us.

As this is being written (April, 2000) one of the biggest police scandals in the history of Los Angeles has emerged (*Los Angeles Times,* 2000; *Washington Post,* 2000). It is important to note that the scandal involves a group of officers affiliated with an anti-gang unit known as Community Resources Against Street Hoodlums (CRASH), who has been accused of making false arrests, extorting money from drug dealers, unjustified shootings, and, most importantly for the subject at hand, falsely accusing many individuals of being "gang members." One report noted that these accusations (corroborated by several police officers) cast doubt about the authenticity of the gang data based in Los Angeles. The report claims there are 112,000 gang members in Los Angeles County—62,000 of whom have been identified by the CRASH unit that was disbanded. Police officials and police gang "experts" claim that the data are accurate, but we wonder. So far, at least 100 convictions of "gang" members have been overturned and 20 officers have been fired or have quit (Jablon, 2000; O'Connor, 2000).

According to self-report studies (most often a random sample of youths in high school or junior high asked about their delinquent behavior), the percentage of youths who report being in a gang or engaging in gang-related behavior has not changed significantly during the past two decades. Typically, no more than 10 to 15 percent of all youths report being in a gang (and this estimate includes areas with a high rate of crime and gang membership) (Johnstone, 1981; Sampson, 1986; Savitz, Rosen, and Lalli, 1980). However, in certain areas the numbers are still quite large, especially for minorities. For example, the previously cited estimate for Los Angeles County Crip and Blood members means that over 25 percent of the total African-American male population between 15 and 24 in Los Angeles County are members of these two gangs. In Chicago, there are estimates ranging from 12,000 to 120,000 gang members. Spergel (1990) provided the following percentages of those within a particular school population in the Chicago area who reportedly are in gangs: 5 percent of the elementary school youths, 10 percent of all high school youths, 20 percent of those in special school programs, and, more alarmingly perhaps, 35 percent of those between 16 and 19 years of age who have dropped out of school!

Even higher numbers are found when we consider those who are on probation or elsewhere in the criminal justice system. A 1990 survey of juvenile correctional institutions found that more than three-fourths had a gang problem inside these institutions. Another survey found that two-thirds of the inmates reported belonging to a gang, likewise in detention centers (Howell, 1998).

Regardless of the numbers, there is some evidence that gang members commit a disproportionate amount of crime, especially violent crime. Yet this aspect of the problem may be exaggerated because the violence captures the public imagination and makes the headlines. Also, the violence is heavily concentrated within certain neighborhoods or within certain schools in large cities. If we consider an entire city or county we find that gang members do not contribute that much to the overall crime problem. In Chicago, for example, it has been estimated that gang crime constituted less than 1 percent of all Part I crimes between 1986 and 1988.[2] More recent estimates suggest the same, although in certain neighborhoods gangs contribute a lot to the overall crime problem (Howell, 1998). Most of the offenses committed by gang members continue to be property crimes (often these are committed by gang members independently rather than as part of an organized gang activity).

Many believe that gang members commit a disproportionate number of homicides, but this may be distorted. Some recent estimates indicate that gang homicide accounts for a disproportionate share of the violence committed in some areas (Howell, 1998). In many cities, such as Los Angeles, the problem of gang homicide has grown worse. For example, Klein reports that the number of gang homicides in Los Angeles County increased dramatically during the late 1980s, going from 271 in 1985 to 803 in 1992 (Klein 1995:120). Since 1992, however, there has been a significant decrease in gang homicides, with about 400 in 1997. In 1992 gang-related homicides constituted about 45 percent of all homicides but just 25 percent in 1997.[3]

GANG MIGRATION

Quite a bit of controversy revolves around the issue of "gang migration" with suggestions that gangs have engaged in a nationwide "franchising" operation. The term *migration* often gets confused with a similar term known as *proliferation*. The latter term signifies the increase in the number of communities in the nation reporting that they have gang problems. While it is true that more communities report having gang problems in recent years, this is usually the result of social conditions within the communities themselves that have caused gangs to grow. On the other hand, we would also suggest that such an increase may stem from changing definitions of *gang* and *gang member* and the tendency for law-enforcement agencies to exaggerate the problem in order to obtain more funding. We are not the only researchers who have raised this issue, for Cheryl Maxson argues that some of the increase in gang proliferation may stem from a "heightened awareness of gang issues, redirection of law enforcement attention, widespread training, and national education campaigns" (Maxson, 1998:2).

On the other hand, the term *gang migration* suggests something entirely different. This term suggests "the movement of gang members from one city to another." Maxson's study of gang migration defined migration rather broadly to include (1) "temporary relocations" (e.g., visits to relatives); (2) "short trips to sell drugs or develop other criminal enterprises"; (3) "longer stays while escaping crackdowns on gangs or gang activity"; (4) "residential moves (either individually or with family members)"; and (5) "court placements" (Maxson, 1998:2).

Much research has documented the "proliferation" of gangs in many communities and even noted some "connection" to gangs in other cities, but for the most part the exact nature of this "connection" has not been explored often, until Maxson and her colleagues began to study the issue in depth (Maxson, 1998; Maxson, Woods, and Klein, 1996; See also Curry, Ball, and Decker, 1996; NDIC, 1996).

What emerges from more recent studies is a very complex picture of gang migration. First, according Maxson's survey, out of 1,000 cities, 710 had experienced gang migration by 1992. Second, gang migration has been concentrated in just a few large cities, especially in the San Francisco Bay Area, Southern California, Chicago, and southern Florida. In fact, almost half (44 percent) of the migration was in the western part of the country. Third, almost all of the cities that have experienced gang migration also have gangs that have been "homegrown" (only 45 of the 710 cities had no homegrown gangs). Fourth, most cities already had a gang problem before new gang migration began, which clearly contradicts the notion that gang problems are the result of "franchising." (Maxson notes that the majority of those interviewed, 81 percent, disagreed with the statement "Without migration, this city wouldn't have a gang problem." Most reported that migration was not the major cause of the gang problem, contradicting reports by the media and by politicians.) Fifth, "emergent" gang problem cities (gang problems have emerged during the past 20 years or so) and "chronic" gang problem cities (those with gangs dating back several decades) are about equally as likely to report gang migration.

What is most important from Maxson's study was what she found when she asked law-enforcement officials what they thought were the major reasons why gang members move to their cities from another area. The most common reason (stated by 39 percent) was that the gang member simply moved with their families. Another major reason was to stay with relatives and friends. Combined, these "social" causes of migration constituted more than half (57 percent) of the cases. Drug market expansion was cited in 20 percent of the cases, with another 12 percent citing other criminal opportunities (for a total of 32 percent), what Maxson calls "pulls." Finally, in about 11 percent of the cases, the reason given was that the gang member was forced out in some way—either by police crackdowns, court order relocation, or simply a desire to escape gangs. It was also discovered that these gang members are about equally as likely to join already existing gangs in their new city as remain with their original gang (Maxson, 1998:7–9).

This complex picture suggests that gang members move mostly for the same reasons that others move—moving with their families or to be closer to friends or relatives. What is also clear is that most of these moves are by individual gang members rather than large segments of one particular gang. Clearly, there is little evidence to suggest that gangs migrating from one city to another are the major source of the gang problem. Nor is there any evidence of "franchising" or the "outside agitator" hypothesis. Maxson (and many other researchers) suggests that the popular perception of gang "franchising" stems mostly from "the diffusion of gang culture in the media." The nation's youth "are hardly dependent on direct contact with gang members for exposure to the more dramatic manifestations of gang culture, which is readily accessible in youth-oriented television programming, popular movies, and the recent spate of 'tell-all' books from reputed urban gang leaders" (Maxson, 1998:9). What is perhaps most interesting from Maxson's study is the fact that the only sources are those in law enforcement. Perhaps a more complex picture will emerge when others are interviewed about such moves, especially the gang members themselves, their families, school officials, and so on.

SUMMARY

Gangs are not something new to the social arena. They existed in fourteenth- and fifteenth-century Europe and colonial America. Throughout the twentieth century social researchers have devoted extensive time and resources to the understanding of youth gangs in America. First, many studies point out that discriminatory policies and practices by the government have contributed to the emergence of gangs in various parts of America. These policies and practices include the promotion of social disorganization in Chicago, the deportation of immigrants in Southern California during the Great Depression, and police brutality in Watts during the 1960s, among others.

Second, we have pointed out that public perception (and fear), crucial to policy development, is shaped largely by the mass media. It is clear that the media have done little to differentiate fact from fiction in their portrayal of youth gangs. Moreover, the media, over the past few years, have capitalized on the incidents of gang activities by significantly increasing their coverage of youth gangs between 1983 and 1994. The media have contributed to the stereotypical images of how we think about gangs and gang members.

Third, the only agreement about what constitutes a gang, its members, and its activities is disagreement. Often, this discord is linked to location (e.g., type of neighborhood), age (e.g., adolescent versus young adult), and purpose (e.g., play group, organized crime, drugs). We have found that one of the major problems associated with the study of gangs is the identification of gang-related crime. Each jurisdiction seems to create its own criteria to determine whether a crime is gang related.

Fourth, this chapter addressed the issue of *how many*. How many gangs are currently active in America? How many individuals are in these groups? There are a significant number of projections and estimates related to these questions. Frequently, the argument is raised that because gangs come and go, it is difficult to determine accurately the number of gangs and gang members. It is our contention, however, that in order to determine how many gangs or gang members are active in America, we must first determine what exactly a gang or gang member is.

Finally, the subject of "gang migration" was explored, especially the suggestion that there is a sort of "franchising" method working here. Contrary to popular belief, gang members who move do so for the same general reasons that young people in general move—with their families.

QUESTIONS FOR UNDERSTANDING AND CRITICAL THINKING

1. Why is it so difficult to arrive at a universal definition of gangs, especially when compared to a delinquent peer group?
2. To what extent is a universal definition of a gang needed or necessary?
3. What are the pros and cons of having a universal definition of gangs as applied to criminal justice-related policy?
4. How do gang-related and gang-motivated crimes differ? What impact do such terms have on defining and measuring "gang crime"?
5. To what extent have gangs created a moral panic?

NOTES

1. This apparent obsession over how many gangs and gang members there are is typical of the positivistic orientation in the social sciences, and in the larger society in general, which too often gets reduced to a mere numbers game. Part of this obsession is the need to "control" or "manage" gangs. For this to be done it is apparently important to know the exact size of the "problem." What is lost in this procedure are people, both the victims and the victimizers, of social disadvantage and oppression. What is also lost are the various social conditions that create gangs.
2. Spergel (1990:34). *Part I* crimes include homicide, rape, robbery, aggravated assault, burglary, larceny, motor vehicle theft, and arson.
3. Personal communication with Cheryl Maxson.

REFERENCES

BOBROWSKI, L. J. 1988. *Collecting, Organizing and Reporting Street Gang Crime.* Chicago: Chicago Police Department, Special Functions Group.

CAMP, G. M., AND C. G. CAMP. 1985. *Prison Gangs: Their Extent, Nature and Impact.* Washington, DC: U.S. Department of Justice.

COHEN, S. 1980. *Folk Devils and Moral Panics: The Creation of the Mods and Rockers.* 2d ed. New York: St. Martin's Press.

CUMMINGS, S., AND D. J. MONTI, EDS. 1993. Gangs: *The Origins and Impact of Contemporary Youth Gangs in the United States.* Albany, NY: SUNY Press.

CURRY, G. D., AND S. H. DECKER. 1998. *Confronting Gangs: Crime and Community.* Los Angeles: Roxbury Press.

_____, and I. A. SPERGEL. 1988. "Gang Homicide, Delinquency, and Community." *Criminology.* 26:381–405.

_____, and S. DECKER. 1996. "Estimating the National Scope of Gang Crime From Law Enforcement Data." In Huff, *Gangs in America,* 2d ed.

GIDDENS, A. 1990. *Introduction to Sociology.* New York: Norton.

GOLDSTEIN, A. P., AND C. R. HUFF, EDS. 1993. *The Gang Intervention Handbook.* Champaign, IL: Research Press.

GOODE, E., AND N. BEN-YAHUDA. 1994. *Moral Panics: The Social Construction of Deviance.* Cambridge, MA: Blackwell.

HAGEDORN, J. M. 1998. *People and Folks: Gangs, Crime and the Underclass in a Rustbelt City.* 2d ed. Chicago: Lakeview Press.

HOWELL, J. C. 1998. "Youth Gangs: An Overview." Office of Juvenile Justice and Delinquency Prevention. Washington, DC: U.S. Department of Justice.

HUFF, C. P. 1993. "Gangs in the United States." In Goldstein and Huff, *The Gang Intervention Handbook.*

_____, ed. 1996. *Gangs in America,* 2d ed. Thousand Oaks, CA: Sage.

JABLON, R. 2000. "L.A. Prepares for Worst as Police Scandal Grows." *Associate Press,* Feb. 19.

JACKSON, P. G. 1989. "Theories and Findings About Youth Gangs." *Criminal Justice Abstracts.* June:313–329.

JOHNSTONE, J. C. 1983. "Youth Gangs and Black Suburbs." *Pacific Sociological Review.* 24:355–373.

KLEIN, M. 1995. *The American Street Gang.* New York: Oxford University Press.

KLEIN, M., AND C. MAXSON. 1989. "Street Gang Violence." In Wolfgang and Weiner, *Violent Crime, Violent Criminals.*

MAXSON, C. L. 1998. *Gang Members on the Move.* Bulletin. Washington, DC: U.S. Department of Justice, Office of Justice Programs, Office of Juvenile Justice and Delinquency Prevention.

_____, WOODS, K. J., AND M. W. KLEIN. 1996. "Street Gang Migration: How Big a Threat?" *National Institute of Justice Journal.* 230:26–31.

MCCORKLE, R. AND T. MIETHE. 1998. "The Political and Organizational Response to Gangs: An Examination of a Moral Panic." *Justice Quarterly.* 15:41–64.

MILLER, W. B. 1975. *Violence by Youth Gangs and Youth Groups as a Crime Problem in Major American Cities.* Washington, DC: U.S. Department of Justice.

_____. 1982. *Crime by Youth Gangs and Groups in the United States.* Washington, DC: U.S. Department of Justice.

MOORE, J. W. 1978. *Homeboys: Gangs, Drugs, and Prisons in the Barrio of Los Angeles.* Philadelphia: Temple University Press.

_____. 1993. "Gangs, Drugs, and Violence." In Cummings and Monti, *Gangs: The Origins and Impact of Contemporary Youth Gangs in the United States.*

NATIONAL DRUG INTELLIGENCE CENTER. 1996. *National Street Gang Survey Report.* Johnstown, PA: National Drug Intelligence Center.

O'CONNOR, A. 2000. "Police Scandal Clouds List of Gang Members." *Los Angeles Times,* March 25.

REINER, I. 1992. *Gangs, Crime and Violence in Los Angeles: Findings and Proposals from the District Attorney's Office.* Arlington, VA: National Youth Gang Information Center.

SAMPSON, R. J. 1986. "Effects of Socioeconomic Context on Official Reaction to Juvenile Delinquency." *American Sociological Review.* 5:876–885.

_____, and B. W. GROVES. 1989. "Community Structure and Crime: Testing Social-Disorganization Theory." *American Journal of Sociology.* 94:774–802.

SAVITZ, L. D., L. ROSEN, AND M. LALLI. 1980. "Delinquency and Gang Membership as Related to Victimization." *Victimology.* 5:152–160.

SHORT, J. F. 1990. "Gangs, Neighborhoods, and Youth Crime." *Criminal Justice Research Bulletin.* 5.

_____. 1996. "Gangs and Adolescent Violence." Unpublished report. Boulder, CO: Center for the Study and Prevention of Violence.

SPERGEL, I. A. 1990. *Youth Gangs: Problem and Response*. Chicago: University of Chicago, School of Social Service Administration.

_____. 1995. *The Youth Gang Problem: A Community Approach*. New York: Oxford University Press.

SUTTLES, G. 1968. *The Social Order of the Slum*. Chicago: University of Chicago Press.

THRASHER, F. 1927. *The Gang*. Chicago: University of Chicago Press.

U.S. DEPARTMENT OF JUSTICE, OFFICE OF JUSTICE PROGRAMS. 1999. *1996 National Youth Gang Survey*. Washington, DC: Office of Juvenile Justice and Delinquency Prevention.

WARR, M. 1996. "Organization and Instigation in Delinquent Groups." *Criminology*. 34:11–37.

WOLFGANG, M. E., AND N. A. WEINER, EDS. 1989. *Violent Crime, Violent Criminals*. Newbury Park, CA: Sage.

2

Definitions of a Gang and Impacts on Public Policy

Rebecca D. Petersen

Abstract

At the turn of the 21st century, the U.S. prison population is at an all-time high. In large part, this is due to the punitive response, by policymakers, of locking up offenders. Incarceration is not the solution to crime. This country needs more prevention and intervention programs to tackle the problem of crime before it spreads, especially with regard to the rapid increase of gangs. Gang prevention programs should be based upon the knowledge of those who have some insight into such issues, that is, those most affected by the policies. This is the only way to ascertain a more holistic understanding of gangs and crime. The present study examines the perspectives of thirty-four incarcerated young women—some involved with gangs and some not—by analyzing their definitions of gangs. It is hoped that their insights might be incorporated into more effective policies while simultaneously empowering a marginalized population. © 2000 Elsevier Science Ltd. All rights reserved.

INTRODUCTION

"... criminologists have preached to one another about the futility of the get tough movement, but they have done precious little to articulate alternatively, politically feasible, crime-control policies." (Cullen et al., 1998, p. 201)

Juvenile gangs have become widespread and are at the forefront of America's consciousness. In the wake of the "get tough on crime" movement, punitive criminal and juvenile

Reprinted from Journal of Criminal Justice, Vol. 28, No. 2, 2000, pp. 137–149, Petersen, R.D. "Definitions of a gang and impacts on public policy," with permission from Elsevier Science.

justice policies are popular responses to crime, and gangs are frequently incorporated into such policies. Some common policy responses include aggressive gang suppression programs by the police, and sentence enhancements by the courts for crimes committed by alleged gang members. What appears to be lacking in policy is the focus on combating crime and delinquency before it occurs. To proactively eliminate or reduce the prevalence of gangs, prevention is key. The concept of prevention, however, is hard to sell in the current punitive political climate where both major political parties capitalize on getting tough on crime and gangs, often advocating incarceration. Prevention and even intervention policies to delinquency appear to be not only unpopular in the press but also in practice. If this country is to ever become less violent, prevention policies must be at the top of the nation's criminal justice policy agenda.

Prevention programs need to be based on realistic measures and goals rather than idealistic ones. It is easy to preach "just say no," "stay out of gangs," or "get out of your gang." These approaches are often impossible to implement or achieve. Many policymakers do not understand the context of offenders' everyday lives. For example, they often do not realize that many youth are born into gangs, see the gang as their real family, and/or know of no other way of life. Just saying no to gangs does not work and is not the defining answer. Going to the source for explanations of gang problems instead of simply addressing the symptoms is the answer.

Ordinary citizens, such as young offenders or youth gang members, are not involved in the policy process, yet they are the ones toward whom the policy is directed. "The end result is detrimental for youths and ultimately to society, in that people without power often become more alienated from democracy and from further 'buying into' society" (Petersen, 1995, p. 648). It is, therefore, important to look to the ones most affected by such policies (i.e., young offenders and gang members), not only to ask them for their input but also to involve them in the framing of criminal justice policies.

According to Dryzek (1990), Lindbloom and Woodhouse (1993), and Petersen (1995), in order for policies to encourage citizenship and democracy, clients of a policy need to become empowered and made part of the policy-making process. It is hoped that by seeking answers to "the crime problem" from them, we as a society may develop a better understanding of how to prevent such atrocities from occurring again or at least, to reduce the amount of crime and delinquency. To make any type of positive changes at either the macro or micro level, it is necessary to go to the source for insightful answers. According to Hagedorn, "just as programs need to include gang members, so should research" (1988, p. 169). Policy is, therefore, best informed by those closest to the problem and it is these individuals who need to be involved in the policy-making *process* (Petersen, 1995).

Gang Policy

Contemporary criminal justice policy decisions are made by experts, who think they know what is best for everyone (Petersen, 1995), and by a small group of politicians and experts who have a self-interest in the policies they promote. Policies are frequently developed without ever seeking answers from the source. This is antithetical to democracy. Ordinary citizens are not involved in the policy process, yet they are the ones at whom policies are directed. The optimal goal of creating policy is for people to be represented and empowered. If people do not become involved, the process may lead to further alienation from society as illustrated by Petersen: "Groups receiving policy may feel neglected in the policy *process,* which leads to alienation" (1995, p. 646, author's emphasis). The voices of disadvantaged groups, such as those youths who are in gangs or who are incarcerated, will rarely be heard. This is disheartening because criminal justice policy is based on a system of segregation and control of many disadvantaged Americans (Petersen & Palumbo, 1997; Tonry, 1990).

More time and resources need to be invested to reduce future gang involvement rather than to simply react to gangs. Policymakers have implemented anti-gang policies without having a clear understanding of actual gang members and others closely affected by such policies and programs. Shelden, Tracy, and Brown were right on point when they stated: ". . . the legal response [to gangs] demonstrates that practitioners, with few exceptions, do not *listen to gang members*" (1997, p. 221; original emphasis). It is, therefore, of crucial importance to question gang members and to listen to what they have to say so that their perspectives can be integrated into effective policies. A more proactive approach can be partially achieved by asking gang members their views on gangs and crime. This approach not only goes to the source for answers, but is unarguably the best way to discover ways of preventing gang delinquency. Their interpretations, for example, of definitions of gangs and differences between gangs and peer groups can be used as a basis for future gang prevention efforts and policies.

How gang members define gangs, and the utility of such definitions, has been addressed by Miller (1998), and Decker and Van Winkle (1996). A body of contemporary gang research exists, which uses gang members' perspectives in understanding gangs through qualitative, ethnographic methods (Decker & Van Winkle, 1996; Hagedorn, 1988; Moore, 1991; Sanders, 1994). These works underscored the value of such an approach. This article, however, stresses the importance and utility of using such an approach by adding a few critical dimensions. First, the perspectives of the youth in this study are exclusively from thirty-four incarcerated females. A large portion of criminological research, especially gang studies, has been based on the activity of male gang members. Females have long been left out of this type of research. With the exception of Miller's (1998) contemporary research on girls in gangs, few recent studies have wholly examined the perspectives of females in gangs. Second, this research addresses perspectives from both females in gangs and those not in gangs to assess the degree to which views on gangs may differ. Third, all the youth in the present study were incarcerated. The work by Fleisher (1995)[1] on inmates documented the utility of using prisoners' perspectives to understand their lives more holistically. Finally, using young women's perspectives to understand gangs leads to a sense of empowerment. It was hoped that giving the young women a voice would lead not only to an empathetic understanding of the context of their lives, but also to the realization that they can have an impact on future policies.

This study offered insight into the perspectives of thirty-four incarcerated female offenders, many of whom were gang members prior to incarceration. Those who were not in gangs possessed widespread knowledge of gangs and gang issues. This research gave incarcerated female offenders a voice and by doing so, a sense of empowerment as well, while simultaneously learning from them about gangs in order to combat and prevent gangs and gang activity.

Gang Prevention Literature

With the advent of increased gang activity, a variety of prevention and intervention programs have been developed. Some gang literature looked at the tactics for gang prevention. For example, Spergel (1989) identified four different gang prevention strategies used to control gang activity. These included suppression, social intervention, community organization programs, and provision of opportunities. Suppression tactics are the most common approaches to gang prevention. These law enforcement approaches, which typically rely on police crackdowns and curfews, often involve task forces, crime control policies, and local police gang units. The social intervention approach to curbing gang delinquency uses social work strategies such as mentoring programs for gang and at-risk youth and community activity centers. Related to this approach are community organization programs aimed at restoring neighborhoods from the effects of gang activity and often include programs such as cleaning up graffiti and reviving dilapidated houses. Finally, the opportunity model approaches gang prevention through youth job preparation and training. Its ultimate goal is to provide legitimate opportunities for youth with otherwise bleak futures.

Of these four gang prevention approaches identified by Spergel (1989), community organization programs appear to be quite effective in reducing gang activity by mobilizing and empowering citizens of the community. Both youths associated with and not associated with gangs, as well as the other members of the community, become involved in gang prevention. Restoration of communities helps make the neighborhood look and feel safer for everyone and is thus, a prevention mechanism.

Simply *reacting* to the gang problem through suppression programs does not and will not work. The current policy agenda is nearly entirely reactive and dominated by debates over new jails and prisons, longer prison sentences, mandatory prison sentences, and the death penalty. Policymakers spend a great deal of time reacting to the gang dilemma "rather than a subscription to social justice" (Shelden et al, 1997, p. 219). These current, reactive anti-gang efforts are often futile. To illustrate, the national GREAT (Gang Resistance Education and Training) program is a police-administered program targeting ten- to twelve-years olds in grades five, six, and seven. Uniformed police officers go into the classrooms of these students for one class period per week over nine consecutive weeks and speak with them about the consequences of gang behavior, goal setting, and methods for resisting peer pressure and resolving conflicts without violence. The goals of the program are many, but the stated objectives are to reduce gang activity and to educate a population of youth as to the consequences of gang involvement (Esbensen & Osgood, 1999). It is speculated that targeting pre-adolescent youth will help to hinder youth from becoming involved in gangs, especially since much gang recruitment occurs at the middle school level (Johnstone, 1983; Vigil, 1983).

Few studies have evaluated the GREAT program, though evidence has been mixed. For example, Palumbo and Ferguson (1995) found that the GREAT program had a small but positive impact on students' attitudes and resistance skills, but not much on whether or not they joined gangs. Overall, they found that the impact of the program was small in relation to huge expenditure of resources. Esbensen and Osgood (1999), in their national evaluation of eleven GREAT sites, found that students completing the program had more prosocial attitudes and lower rates of some types of delinquent behavior than students who did not participate in the program. One caveat to their research, however, is that they only evaluated the short-term impacts of the program one year after the program was implemented.

This author argued that one significant reason for the skepticism surrounding the GREAT program is that it tries to do too much with too little. Going into student classrooms for a total of nine hours is hardly enough time to break the cycle of gangs. Many people are born into gangs or are born into the gang lifestyle. They may see no other way of life. The GREAT approach is ideal, although it is not practical in many communities and cultures.

Another reason why gang prevention programs fall short is that many do not target young children, but rather teenagers instead. This is too late in the game. Research has shown that antisocial and delinquent behaviors emerge by the age of nine (Geismar & Wood, 1986; Loeber & Stouthamer-Loeber, 1986; Snyder & Patterson, 1987). In order for the cycle of gang activity to diminish, earlier ages must be addressed.

Another important dimension that appears to be lacking in many gang prevention programs is the *direct influence that youth have in establishing policy,* which forms these programs. This author contends that such an absence may be another reason why prevention and intervention programs have often been deemed unsuccessful. They are developed by those in power who often do not incorporate the insights of future participants or target groups into policies. In doing so, they are missing the complete picture. By asking youth—for example, "What are gangs?"—policymakers could develop a much more holistic understanding of what gangs really are and how best to work with and combat them. If gang life is to be understood on its own terms, developing policies and future programs should be geared toward such needs and concerns. Then, perhaps, one may be more optimistic and hopeful of gang prevention programs and of saving endangered youth.

Definition of Gangs

"Legislators struggle with the troublesome question 'What constitutes a gang' " (Shelden et al., 1997, p. 219). Despite numerous research attempts to answer this question, no consensus exists regarding what constitutes gang activity, nor agreement among researchers on the "true" definition of a gang (Campbell, 1984; Covey et al., 1992; Curry & Spergel, 1988; Fagan, 1989; Hagedom, 1988; Klein & Maxson, 1989; Kornhauser, 1978; Moore, 1978; Morash, 1983; Spergel, 1984; Vigil, 1983). Miller's (1980) analysis of the composition of various youth groups found many different types of law violating youth groups, but the problem was deciding which ones should be defined as gangs. He came to a baseline definition that has been adopted extensively by academicians and practitioners:

> A youth gang is a self-formed association of peers, bound together by mutual interests, with identifiable leadership, well-developed lines of authority, and other organizational features, who act in concert to achieve a specific purpose or purposes, which generally include the conduct of illegal activity and control over a particular territory, facility, or type of enterprise. (Miller, 1980, p. 121)

Illegal behavior and territory form two crucial elements of this definition of youth gangs. Miller also conceded that organizational structure and territory are the major factors separating gangs from other groups of people. Not all the characteristics in the definition given by Miller fit the groups that many academicians and practitioners consider gangs.

To be considered a gang, nonetheless, it has usually been accepted that the group be involved in some type of organized illegal activity, often of a violent nature. Decker and Van Winkle's ethnographic research on gangs in St. Louis, Missouri found violence *the* defining feature and the central value of gang life: "Whether for protection or for the opportunity to engage in violence, the members of our sample attached considerable importance to the role of violence in their definition of a gang" (1996, p. 254). Despite disagreement on what constitutes a gang, many researchers argued that a uniform definition of a gang and gang behavior is both needed and necessary (Esbensen & Huizinga, 1993; Klein & Maxson, 1989; Mitler, 1980; Spergel & Chance, 1991). According to Esbensen and Huizinga, "a uniform definition of gangs and gang behavior would be a point of departure for a better understanding of a phenomenon that may well be substantially distorted because of a lack of a common means for studying, describing, and regulating gang behavior" (1993, p. 581). Decker and Kempf-Leonard further stressed the importance in understanding gang definitions:

> Public perception of the seriousness and magnitude of the gang problem is based in large part on the definition of gangs used. . . . This is significant, especially if a substantial portion of the knowledge policymakers use as a basis for action comes from media sources. In a very real sense, the response of policymakers to gangs defines them as a social problem. (1995, p. 14)

From these perspectives, having a clear definition, may be useful in understanding gang life in all facets of society, and can be said to have both a research and policy impact.

Others, however, question the futility of having such a definition. Horowitz argued that obtaining a universal definition of a gang is neither necessary nor desirable. "Agreement will never be achieved, and definitions often obscure problematic areas and may not encourage the development of new questions" (Horowitz, 1990, p. 38). She also maintained that each gang study uses its own definitional terms, questions, and methodologies and that keeping the definition pluralistic would adhere to different contexts and study sites as well as uncover issues previously unseen or unexplored. Conley (1993) also advocated abandoning the term altogether as the definition is a meaningless label constructed by politicians, policymakers, and government officials.

The author of this present study maintained that gang activity and membership constantly change within a community, just as the definition of crime does. Revised definitions are necessary because of the continuous changes in the context, diversity, and complexity of gangs. As Ball and Curry suggested, "even when older definitions [of gangs] have proved acceptable, new definitions often become necessary, either because of changes in the phenomenon itself or changes in the purposes for which definition is required" (1995, p. 239). They continued to argue that "as the relative visibility of various phenomenal features changes with research progress, and the salience of these various features shifts with new perspectives and purposes, redefinition often becomes necessary" (Ball & Curry, 1995, p. 239).

Knowledge about gangs should not be limited to a *universal* definition per se, since it may exclude other unknown or misunderstood elements of gang life. Obtaining definitions on a more contextual or microlevel approach can aid not only the understanding of various types of gangs and gang activity but also the development of some baseline commonalities. It should be noted that not all gangs are alike and therefore, programs that work in one setting may not work in another. Policies should be geared toward the individuality and diversity of such gang groups and should not be applied universally. Doing so will only lead to failure, a common evaluation of delinquency prevention programs.

It is important, nevertheless, to uncover the perspectives of gang activity through both youth involved in gangs and those who are not, to understand the various dimensions of gang activity and gang life. The definitions elucidated from the young women in this study may not be better or different than other definitions, but they are taken from the youths' points of view. A major strength of such in-depth interviewing is the ability to shed light on this aspect of the social world (Adler & Adler, 1987) while highlighting individuals' meanings based on their experiences.

In addition, Ball and Curry (1995) have addressed some problems in defining gangs by examining the logic of definition and by offering insights into different methodological approaches to the definition of gangs in terms of various purposes. They argued that one problem of defining gangs and comparing definitions is that people use different methods of definition. For example, a lexical definition involves the popular, dictionary definition of a concept. This may be useful for standardizing a term universally, though concepts vary from one segment of society to another and as such, the actual meaning may be misconstrued. The stipulatory definition, however, offers a more contextual approach. The process of arriving at these definitions would include contributions from different people in society approaching gangs from different perspectives, experiences, and views. It is this latter stipulatory definition that was used throughout this article.

METHODS AND SAMPLE

The research design of this study proposed to capture the perspectives and elucidate the context of the youths being studied. Interviewing is best used to access the perspective of the interviewee with relatively few structural guidelines or restrictions based upon the search for *Verstehen,* that is, empathetic understanding and meaning. Such interviewing can yield rich data for building theories that describe or explain social events. Interviews framed for these purposes result in one-to-one casual conversations where the interviewer listens closely to the context of what is being said.

For this research the goal of in-depth interviewing was to gain a greater understanding of the nature and meanings of gang life from the points of view of the females themselves. As Esbensen & Winfree eloquently wrote, "it is time for a conscientious inclusion of females in the study of gangs—not only for academic reasons, but also for identifying and designing gang prevention programs that include girls in the target population" (1998, p. 521). The current study aimed to do just that.

Establishing rapport with subjects was crucial for this study as it strengthens reliability and validity. Rapport enhances the researcher's ability to convey empathy and understanding without judgment and it elicits more truthful responses, which build detailed answers to questions. Incarcerated young women may feel intimidated that an adult stranger, whom they may perceive negatively as an "authoritarian figure" or an "intruder" in their lives, is asking them personal questions especially while they are incarcerated. It was, therefore, important to underscore the importance of rapport in this study.

It should be noted that since the author was a volunteer at the institution, many of the girls had established a good rapport, and a certain amount of trust already existed. Volunteers are usually perceived differently than correctional staff and are often thought of as wanting to help the population without monetary compensation or particular political agendas. It was hoped that the young women recognized and respected this attribute about the interviewer in this study. In addition, after some youth were interviewed, it was assumed that other youth inquired about their experiences and the researcher.

Since in-depth, unstructured interviews were the method used for this research, little notes were taken while conducting the interviews, since they would limit the ability to record verbatim responses. Note taking can prove disruptive, since the interviewee may become self-conscious about what is being written down. Taking notes also minimizes the informal nature of the unstructured interview and diminishes eye contact and interactive conversations. It was therefore essential to use a tape recorder during the interviews. Recording interviews increases the accuracy of data collection, because it is systematically transcribed at a later date, allowing the interviewer to be more attentive to each respondent.

Instead of assigning a pseudonym, each participant in the study was given an identifying number (i.e., Youth 14) to organize data analysis and to examine differences and similarities among perspectives. Each youth was quoted *at least once* throughout the analysis.

This research was primarily a qualitative study, therefore, numeric accounts and frequencies of perspectives were not calculated quantitatively, with the exception of demographic information. Categorized responses of thirty-four youth were collectively enumerated through qualitative descriptions based upon the following frequency continuum: none, one, a few, some, several, about half, over half, many, the majority, most, nearly all, and all. Arranging responses using this method of analysis permitted further understanding of respondents' perspectives both collectively and individually.

The research took place at a juvenile correctional institution in the Southwest, henceforth referred to as SWI.[2] By law, if organizations receive federal subsidies, parental/guardian consent is required for the study of minors and as such, parental consent was needed. According to the supervisory staff at SWI, the best way to contact parents/guardians for consent was through the mail, since many of the youth's parents/guardians did not have working telephones. Letters were sent to each parent/guardian during a seven-month timeframe, from July 1996 to January 1997.

A self-addressed stamped envelope to the researcher was included in the letter to increase the response rate. If a response or a signed parental consent form was not received within three weeks, a follow-up letter was sent. Of the total 103 letters mailed, 4 notices from the youths' parents were received indicating that they did not want their youth to participate in the study. A total of thirty-six signed parental consent forms were mailed back. Two of these youth had been incarcerated less than a month and were dropped from the study.[3] All thirty-four remaining girls was asked to participate in the study. *All* thirty-four agreed to participate, constituting the total sample number of youths interviewed.[4] The time-length of each interview varied with the individual and ranged from forty-five minutes to over four hours, however, the average length of time for each interview was approximately ninety minutes.

DATA ANALYSIS

When discussing gang prevention, the points of view of gang members are seldom given much, if any, consideration. The images of gang members are determined primarily by the stigma of crime, based largely on media representations. "Gangsters" are hardly thought of as people who have anything constructive to say, especially with regard to social policy. Much can be learned and incorporated into policy from gang members and prisoners. The true effect of delinquency prevention policies and programs becomes evident in the impact they have on the individual lives and communities of such members.

Personal Definitions of a Gang

The youth had various perspectives about what constitutes a gang, and their perspectives on "What is the difference between a gang and a peer group?" were found to be of significant importance in this study. Regardless of whether the youths were or were not gang members before incarceration, each youth was asked what her own personal opinion of a gang was[5] to ascertain a more global understanding of the gang phenomenon. A similar methodology was applied in the study by Winfree et al. (1997), who allowed youth to self-report their levels of gang involvement. Others have suggested that self-report data provide comparatively reliable and valid measures of gang membership (Bjerregaard & Smith, 1993; Fagan, 1990; Thornberry et al., 1993; Winfree et al., 1992).

Girls not Affiliated with Gangs

Some girls who were not part of gangs believe that gangs were nothing but a bunch of scoundrels. To illustrate: Youth 19 said that, "[A gang] is a bunch of wimps that can't fight for themselves, so they have to have a whole bunch of people do it for them." This view was further illustrated by Youth 20; "[Joining a gang] is trying to take the easy way out. It's a cop-out for life and it's not gonna get you anywhere." Youth 6 also believed that gangs were "a bunch of stupid people who go out making their own [family and friends] in the wrong ways. They're out to prove something and they're out to have others supposedly love them and have their backing on everything."

Others, however, thought that gangs were an outlet for acceptance and belonging: "I think a gang is somewhere people think they belong" (Youth 31). Several young women further indicated that gangs are formed by groups of people with unconditional loyalty and strong bonds. The following were responses from young women not affiliated with gangs: "[A gang is] a group of people that is like one person that fights for what's right for them" (Youth 5); "Gangs are people that stick together, are there for you" (Youth 18); "A gang, they're down for their color, down for their side, down for their friends" (Youth 21).

Another described a gang as "a power struggle for a neighborhood or territory" (Youth 9). In this context, she believed that the way a gang establishes power is through a particular territory or area. Youth 13 explained that a gang is "a bunch of kids that like to cause trouble and nothing else." In her eyes the gang was an outlet for deviant activity.

These perspectives from youth (not involved in gang activities) demonstrated that a gang is comprised of wimps, people with strong bonds to one another, those who fight over particular turfs, and those who cause some type of trouble. How these viewpoints contradicted or supported those affiliated with gangs was then examined.

Girls Involved in Gangs

The youth affiliated with gangs also discussed bonding and loyalty with their gang member friends and often perceived a family-like quality. In this sense the gang may act like a substitute family for some gang members. To illustrate, one gang member described a gang as: "A family thing. We do things together. We socialize. We walk around. We just do things together and have fun" (Youth 7). Another female gang member also believed that a gang acts like a family: "It's like a second family. Because I don't have my dad, I know my homeboys are there for me . . . and always will be 'cause that's just the way it is" (Youth 3). Youth 15 claimed that a gang is "a group of friends that just want to have fun." Another youth similarly revealed that a gang is "a group of people who stick together for you, they have nobody else" (Youth 33). These viewpoints illustrate that for a few, the gang is the primary group with whom they have the most social contact.

A few young women, who participated with gangs, suggested that a gang involves a type of color and/or territory based on some strong belief. Youth 14 said, "[Gangs are] members who fight over a color or race or a territory. What they believe in." Still another youth claimed that "[A gang is] a group of people with certain colors and certain beliefs" (Youth 26).

As noted from the respondents' definitions, gangs mean a lot of different things to a lot of different people. For girls not affiliated with gangs, their definitions included peer pressure, familial loss, power, excitement/boredom, and protection. Those involved in gangs had slightly different perspectives. These included a group of individuals who act as a primary group in lieu of a family, who have fun together, and who bond together through loyalty and territory. These conclusions supported much of the literature indicating that gangs are not monolithic (Campbell, 1984; Covey et al., 1992; Curry & Spergel, 1988; Fagan, 1989; Hagedorn, 1988; Klein & Maxson, 1989; Kornhauser, 1978; Moore, 1978; Morash, 1983; Spergel, 1984; Vigil, 1983), though perspectives varied depending upon the individuals' involvement with gangs. Those not in gangs sometimes viewed their counterparts as wimps and troublemakers, often involving some type of fighting over particular geographic areas. Those who were affiliated with gangs often viewed gangs as their primary reference groups whom they spent the most time with.

Differences Between a Gang and a Peer Group

All the youths were further asked to elaborate on individual perceptions of a gang and discuss differences between a gang and a group of people getting into trouble. On almost every occasion, the girls had a difficult time answering this question. For several, puzzled looks formed on their faces as if they were really baffled about an answer. Many indicated that there was not much of difference between a gang and a group of youth getting into trouble. One youth said that, "I don't think there is much of a difference" (Youth 2—affiliated with a gang). This response was further echoed by another gang member who said, "There's not always a difference. A gang does not have to commit criminal activity. It is just something to do. We end up getting into trouble 'cause there's nothing to do, and it's fun to go do bad things." A similar response was given by a nongang member: "It's the same thing" (Youth 22). Individuals affiliated with gangs as well as those not affiliated, suggested that there might not always be much of a difference.

When probed to elaborate on this, many believed that in a gang, there is an assumption of criminal activity and that this may be what separates the gang from a group of youth getting into trouble. According to many young women, what ties and holds the gang together may be the assumption of criminal activity. The following quotes from youth not involved with gangs illuminate this point:

> A gang does more crimes. (Youth 5)
> What gangs do you know that do not do any crimes? (Youth 18)
> A peer group might get into trouble together, but I seriously doubt they'd be willing to shoot down somebody for you for something stupid or petty, like wearing red when they should be wearing blue. (Youth 6)
> Gangs have a purpose. People [nongang members] that just hang out and sometimes cause trouble don't intend to commit crimes. (Youth 24)

Interviewees affiliated with gangs, however, had similar types of responses:

Not all gangs have to participate in crimes and drugs, but most of them do. (Youth 12)

[A gang] does three, four times over what a bunch of normal kids would do, like speeding, getting high, causing trouble. (Youth 4)

[Nongang members] don't go out on drive-bys. They don't have enemies. They don't fight against other people or fight for a territory. (Youth 7)

Gangs always cause trouble. People who are not in gangs may do crimes, but we always do [commit crimes]. (Youth 30)

The responses from the young women showed that committing crimes might be what separates a gang from a peer group. Both gang members and nongang members reified this point. Many researchers have found that gang membership increases the prevalence, frequency, and seriousness of crime and that leaving the gang leads to reductions in such activities (Esbensen & Huizinga, 1993; Esbensen & Winfree, 1998; Fagan, 1990: Shelden et al., 1993; Thornberry et al., 1993).

A few other youth regarded gangs as more protective of their members and more protective of their territories than groups of youth causing trouble. One gang member stated, "I think the difference is that we're [gangs] more violent and we're more protective and will do anything for our barrio" (Youth 16). A youth—not affiliated with gangs—suggested that the difference may be that people who are not associated with gangs can have friends from all walks of life while those in gangs can only have certain friends: "Gangs only have certain people to hang out with and cannot hang out with other people" (Youth 27). In addition, a nongang member believed that gangs are not true friends as groups of peers may be: "The gang really don't care about you. If you got shot, they will find somebody to take your place. But peers [who are not in gangs] support you and would care and be there for you" (Youth 13).

The issue of dress and demeanor also ensued when examining the differences between a gang and a peer group. A gang member explained that, "We [gang members] look the same, act the same, and have a color we would die for" (Youth 26). Nongang members illustrated this perspective further. Youth 19 stated that, "Gang members wear one certain color and throw up signs." And another said, "The only difference is that the nongang members just dress differently and act differently and they don't throw up their hoods" (Youth 9).

CONCLUSION AND POLICY IMPLICATIONS

A primary purpose of this research was to *understand* more holistically the gang phenomenon by asking incarcerated juvenile gang members and those familiar with gangs, their insights into gangs in hopes of integrating their perspectives into proactive policy. It is known, although infrequently practiced, that the best, most effective, and democratic policies are those developed, at least in part, by the people most effected (Dryzek, 1990; Ingram & Schneider, 1993; Lindbloom & Woodhouse, 1993; Petersen, 1995; Stone, 1993). It was hoped that by allowing youth to express themselves, they would become mobilized and develop a greater sense of belonging to society. Only broader social justice will reduce or prevent crime and with the route this country is taking, crime will continue on its ill path.

Policymakers need to know what tools work best for each target population. This study may give them such insight. In addition, most contemporary criminological research is theoretical rather than applied. Such research builds a knowledge base, but it is not purposely used to inform or effect criminal justice policy (Petersen & Palumbo, 1997).

The issues of "What is a gang?" and "What is the difference between a gang and a peer group?" are important ones and need to be examined more extensively in gang literature. Some researchers have addressed this issue but not for the purpose of empowering young women in the policy-making process. The majority of the young women in this study did not know how to respond when they were asked to discuss the actual differences and most did not believe that major differences existed. It was only after they were asked to elaborate, that they further discussed how criminal activity might be what separates a gang from a peer group.

It was found that perspectives, gleaned from both the responses of girls involved with gangs and those not involved, vary as to what a gang is and the differences between a gang and a peer group. For example, some common responses from gang members were that gangs: act as pseudo-families, offer a means of power, supply a sense of protection, and render outlets of excitement. For those affiliated with gangs, criminal activities were sometimes used as a means of protection, that is, to defend their turfs and to protect their identities. A popular misconception of gangs was that all participate in criminal activities "for the hell of it" or because they are "bad, dangerous" people. Those not affiliated with gangs, however, had slightly different views citing that gangs are for "wimps," those who fight over turfs, and those who get into trouble. It can be stated that perspectives vary as to what constitutes a gang (or gang characteristics) by virtue of those who belong to gangs and those who do not.

According to many youth, the main difference between a gang and a peer group was the illusion of criminal activity. From the voices of the youth in this study, a major difference between a gang and a peer group was criminal activity. It can be stated that gang members commit more criminal activities than those not associated with gangs but this study did not clearly substantiate that. The young women suggested that it may be the *illusion* that separates a gang from a peer group.

This study found a great diversity in the way gangs are defined both by gang members and nongang members. This would seem to suggest that no coherent policy recommendations can be developed if such diversity exists. Esbensen and Deschenes, in their national, multisite evaluation of the GREAT program, stated that "finding somewhat different patterns in the prediction models for each site reaffirms the belief that delinquent gangs may well have underlying similarities but have local differences that should be considered in the development of prevention programs for younger juveniles" (1998, p. 820). One universal definition of a gang will never exist since gangs are different in each society and each person has a different perception of the definition. It is critical, however, to underscore the importance of giving the youth a voice. "Authentic democratic participation is key to ameliorating the conditions of society" (Petersen, 1995, p. 648).

Qualitative research of this kind can help policymakers conceptualize gang issues and anti-gang strategies. Gang prevention policies can be developed from these perspectives. For example, the issues of family, power, protection, and excitement were illustrated by those involved with gangs as reasons for gang attraction.

The findings of this research can enlighten policymakers with a clearer understanding of how youth perceive gangs, and provide the basic tools necessary for conceptualizing and building anti-gang programs. It may be difficult, if not impossible, for the findings of this study to reach the policy agenda. It should also be noted that programs, which target gangs, may have a cohesion-building effect (Klein, 1995). This may make them more difficult to dissolve in the long run, and as such, involving them in the policy-making process could lead to negative, latent consequences. This, however, does not make this research any less important. It does suggest, however, that criminologists should make themselves better known to state and national policymakers. By giving these young women in this study a voice, it was hoped that their perspectives would lead to positive change, and that their involvement would give them a sense of empowerment.

From the perspectives of the youth, what appears to be needed is individually based family programs (i.e., family intervention strategies from young ages through adolescence). Some young women see gangs as attractive because they offer opportunities for power. If youth, however, contributed more in decision making (i.e., involvement in studies such as this) and issues that affected their lives, maybe gang life would becomes less appealing. These constant battles over gang turfs must be resolved. Several youth commented that they were "fighting over a street corner that belongs to the government." Perhaps other gang members feel this way. By gathering youth together in their communities and mobilizing them to be productive citizens, society might better understand their needs and concerns, and develop ways to ensure that youth feel protected without having to join gangs. The excitement that makes gangs attractive could be best combated by offering more conventional activities for at-risk youth to be involved in via school, the community, or both.

Multiple prevention strategies are needed to reduce the factors associated with gangs, and they can be complementary to one another (Ohlin, 1998). A major way to help alleviate gangs is through social and educational programs for young children and adolescents. This, however, cannot be done effectively without support from the communities. It also cannot be achieved until members of communities know the best ways of combating gangs and crime. This can be achieved by going to the source for the answers, that is the youth, to understanding their needs more holistically. There may also be a need for special prevention and intervention programs aimed specifically at females to help reduce gang association and involvement. Future research could address this in more detail.

In an era of the get-tough movement, prevention policies will be difficult to sell and implement. "However, we need to attack the problems of crime and delinquency with a much more proactive policy approach, bringing together and encouraging as many voices as possible, with the goal of each having an equal participatory vote" (Petersen, 1995, p. 647). In the end policies need to improve the lives of children and youth in our society and such policies must be wholly integrated into practice.

QUESTIONS FOR UNDERSTANDING AND CRITICAL THINKING

1. How can those directly involved with gangs (i.e., actual gang members, parents and teachers of gang members, and communities with gang problems) be given a voice to impact public policies relating to gangs?
2. How might these such perspectives differ from those formulating public policy?
3. To what extent can proactive, preventative gang policies be implemented?
4. How can personal definitions of gangs by incarcerated female gang members enlighten policymakers?
5. How might such personal definitions of gangs by females be different than male accounts?

NOTES

1. Fleisher's ethnographic research on inmates did not address gang membership or views on gangs.
2. The author and the correctional institution both agree that SWI would be the pseudonym used for the study.
3. The rationale behind dropping these two from the study was based on the premise that since they had only been incarcerated a few days or weeks, their insights into gangs in prison would be naive and incomplete.
4. Demographic information for the sixty-nine nonparticipants was incomplete and therefore, not included.
5. Both the youth in gangs before incarceration and those who were not were asked questions about gang life. It appeared that those not affiliated with gangs were very familiar with the gang life.

REFERENCES

ADLER, P. A., & ADLER, P. (1987). *Membership Roles in Field Research.* Newbury Park, CA: Sage Publications.

BALL, R. A., & CURRY, G. D. (1995). The logic and definition of criminology: purposes and methods for defining "gangs." *Crim 33,* 225–245.

BJERREGAARD, B., & SMITH, C. (1993). Gender differences in gang participation, delinquency, and substance use. *J Quant Crim 4,* 329–355.

CAMPBELL, A. (1984). *Girls in the Gang.* New York: Basil Blackwell.

CONLEY, C. H. (1993). *Street Gangs: Current Knowledge and Strategies.* Washington, DC: National Institute of Justice.

COVEY, H. C., MENARD, S., & FRANZESE, R. J. (1992). *Juvenile Gangs.* Springfield, IL: Charles C. Thomas Publishers.

CULLEN, F. T., WRIGHT, J. P., BROWN, S., MOON, M. M., BLAKENSHIP, M. B., & APPLEGATE, B. K. (1998). Public support for early intervention programs: implications for a progressive policy agenda. *Crime & Del 44,* 187–204.

CURRY, G. D., & SPERGEL, I. A. (1988). Gang homicide, delinquency, and community. *Crim 26,* 381–405.

DECKER, S., & KEMPF-LEONARD, K. (1995). Constructing gangs: the social definition of youth activities. In M. W. Klein, C. W. Maxson & J. Miller (Eds.), *Modern Gang Reader* (pp. 14–23). Los Angeles, CA: Roxbury Publishing.

DECKER, S. H., & VAN WINKLE, B. (1996). *Life in the Gang: Family, Friends and Violence.* New York: Cambridge University Press.

DRYZEK, J. S. (1990). *Discursive Democracy.* Cambridge, UK: Cambridge University Press.

ESBENSEN, F., & DESCHENES, E. P. (1998). A multisite examination of youth gang membership: does gender matter? *Crim 36,* 799–828.

ESBENSEN, F., & HUIZINGA, D. (1993). Gangs, drugs, and delinquency in a survey of urban youth. *Crim 31,* 565–589.

ESBENSEN, F., & OSGOOD, D. W. (1999). Gang resistance education and training (GREAT): results from a national evaluation. *J Res in Crime & Del 36,* 194–225.

ESBENSEN, F., & WINFREE, L. T. (1998). Race and gender differences between gang and nongang youth: results from a multisite survey. *Just Quar 15,* 505–526.

FAGAN, J. (1989). The social organization of drug use and drug dealing among urban gangs. *Crim 27,* 633–669.

FAGAN, J. (1990). Social processes of delinquency and drug use among urban gangs. In C. R. Huff (Ed.), *Gangs in America* (pp. 183–219). Newbury Park, CA: Sage Publications.

FLEISHER, M. S. (1995). *Beggars and Thieves: Lives of Urban Street Criminals.* Madison, WI: University of Wisconsin Press.

GEISMAR, I. L., & WOOD, K. M. (1986). *Family and Delinquency: Resocializing the Young Offender.* New York: Human Sciences Press.

HAGEDORN, J. M. (1988). *People and Folks: Gangs, Crime, and the Underclass in a Rustbelt City.* Chicago, IL: Lakeview Press.

HOROWITZ, R. (1990). Sociological perspectives on gangs: conflicting definitions and concepts. In C. R. Huff (Ed.), *Gangs in America* (pp. 37–54). Newbury Park, CA: Sage Publications.

INGRAM, H., & SCHNEIDER, A. (1993). Constructing citizenship: the subtle messages of policy design. In H. Ingram & S. R. Smith (Eds.), *Public Policy for Democracy* (pp. 68–94). Washington, DC: Brookings Institution.

JOHNSTONE, J. W. (1983). Recruitment into a youth gang. *Pac Soc Rev 24,* 355–375.

KLEIN, M. C. (1995). *The American Street Gang: Its Nature, Prevalence, and Control.* New York: Oxford University Press.

KLEIN, M. C., & MAXSON, C. M. (1989). Street gang violence. In N. A. Weiner & M. E. Wolfgang (Eds.), *Violent Crime, Violent Criminals* (pp. 136–159). Newbury Park, CA: Sage Publications.

KORNHAUSER, R. R. (1978). *Social Sources of Delinquency.* Chicago, IL: University of Chicago Press.

LINDBLOOM, C. E., & WOODHOUSE, E. J. (1993). *The Policy-Making Process.* Englewood Cliffs, NJ: Prentice-Hall.

LOEBER, R., & STOUTHAMER-LOEHER, M. (1986). Family factors as correlates and predictors of juvenile conduct problems and delinquency. In M. Tonry and N. Morris (Eds.), *Crime and Justice: An Annual Review of Research* (pp. 29–19). Chicago, IL: University of Chicago Press.

MILLER, J. (1998). Gender and victimization risk among young women in gangs. *J Res in Crime & Del 35,* 429–453.

MILLER, W. B. (1980). Gangs, groups, and serious youth crime. In D. Shichor & D. Kelly (Eds.), *Critical Issues in Juvenile Delinquency* (pp. 115–138). Lexington, MA: Lexington Books.

MOORE, J. W. (1978). *Homeboys: Gangs, Drug, and Prison in the Barrios of Los Angeles.* Philadelphia, PA: Temple University Press.

MOORE, J. W. (1991). *Going Down to the Barrio: Homeboys and Homegirls in Change.* Philadelphia, PA: Temple University Press.

MORASH, M. (1983). Gangs, groups, and delinquency. *Br J Crim 23,* 309–331.

OHLIN, L. E. (1998). The future of juvenile justice policy and research. *Crime & Del 44,* 143–153.

PALUMBO, D. J., & FERGUSON, J. L., (1995). Evaluating gang resistance education and training (GREAT): is the impact the same as that of drug abuse resistance education (DARE)? *Eval Rev 19,* 591–619.

PETERSEN, R. D. (1995). Expert policy in juvenile justice: patterns of claimsmaking and issues of power in a program construction. *Policy Stud J 23,* 636–651.

PETERSEN, R. D., & PALUMBO, D. J. (1997). The social construction of intermediate punishments. *Prison J 77,* 77–91.

SANDERS, W. (1994). *Drive-bys and Gang Bangs: Gangs and Grounded Culture.* Chicago, IL: Aldine de Gruyter.

SHELDEN, R. G., SNODGRASS, T., & SNODGRASS, P. (1993). Comparing gang and nongang offenders: some tentative findings. *Gang J I,* 73–85.

SHELDEN, R. G., TRACY, S. K., & BROWN, W. B. (1997). *Youth Gangs in American Society.* Belmont, CA: Wadsworth Publishing Company.

SNYDER, J., & PATTERSON, G. (1987). Family intervention and delinquent behavior. In H. C. Quay (Ed.), *Handbook of Juvenile Delinquency* (pp. 216–243). New York: John Wiley & Sons.

SPERGEL, I. (1989). *Youth Gangs: Problems and Responses. A Review of the Literature.* (Tech. Rep 1, National Youth Gang Suppression and Intervention Project). Chicago, IL.: University of Chicago, School of Social Service Administration.

SPERGEL, I. A. (1984). Violent gangs in Chicago: in search of social policy. *Soc Ser Rev 58,* 199–226.

SPERGEL, I. A., & CHANCE, R. L. (1991). National youth gang suppression and intervention program. *NIJ Rep 224,* 21–24.

STONE, D. A. (1993). Clinical authority in the construction of citizenship. In H. Ingram & S. R. Smith (Eds.), *Public Policy for Democracy* (pp. 45–67). Washington, DC: Brookings Institution.

THORNBERRY, T., KROHN, M. D., LIZOTTE, A. J., & CHARD-WIERSCHERN, D. (1993). The role of juvenile gangs in facilitating delinquent behavior. *J Res in Crime & Del 30* 75–85.

TONRY, M. (1990). *Race, Crime, and Punishment in America.* New York: Oxford University Press.

VIGIL, I. D. (1983). Chicago gangs: one response to Mexican urban adaptation in the Los Angeles area. *Urban Anth 12,* 45–75.

WINFREE, L. T., FULLER, K., VIGIL, T., & MAYS, G. L. (1992). The definition and measurement of "gang status": policy implications for juvenile justice. *Juv & Fam Ct J 43,* 29–37.

WINFREE, L. T., FULLER, K., VIGIL, T., & MAYS, G. L. (1997). The logical definition in criminology: purposes and methods for defining "gangs." In G. L. Mays (Ed.), *Gangs and Gang Behavior* (pp. 3–21). Chicago, IL: Nelson Hall Publishing.

PART II
Gender Issues in Gangs

3

What Happens to Girls in the Gang?

Joan W. Moore and John M. Hagedorn

Anne Campbell (1984) laid the groundwork for the study of gang women in her classic *Girls in the Gang*. She argued convincingly that gang girls have rarely been studied as seriously as have gang boys. Instead, they have been stereotyped as promiscuous sex objects— segregated in "ladies' auxiliary" gangs—or as socially maladjusted tomboys, vainly trying to be "one of the boys." The stereotypes appeared in the social work literature and were also strongly embedded in much of the research literature.[1]

Both stereotypes—tomboy and slut—rest on the contrast between gang girls' behavior and that of "decent" girls. The implicit scenario is straight out of the 1950s—that adolescent girls who fail to conform to gender norms will jeopardize their futures. The premise is that marriage is the only serious career option for women and that improper behavior will alienate the kind of man who could be a good husband and provider. This is in sharp contrast with admonitions for boys. Even though gang membership also jeopardizes boys' futures, it's not because they are sexually promiscuous and fight but because they risk acquiring criminal records.

Most recent researchers on gang girls find that the stereotypes are greatly exaggerated. There is substantial variation both between gangs and within gangs in the ways in which girls behave, and girls are considerably more oriented to their gang girlfriends than the male-oriented early literature suggested. What, then, does happen to gang girls? How do their adult careers reflect the gang experience? Is the gang a temporary career diversion or a major turning point?

There is no single answer to these questions. One study showed that gang membership stigmatizes women on several levels and may seriously interfere with their later-life

Moore, J.W. & Hagedorn, J.H. What happens to girls in the gang? In *Gangs in America*, (1996, 2nd edition), Ed. Huff, C. R. pp. 205–218. Reprinted by permission of Sage Publications, Inc.

options—depending on how they come into and how they act in the gang, and on what kind of community they live in. Another study suggested that gang membership opens up opportunities for careers in drug dealing. Much of the answer depends on the time, the place, and the local culture of the community. And beyond this is the microculture of the particular gang and the initiative of the individual girl.

TIME AND PLACE: VARIATIONS IN WHAT HAPPENS TO GANG GIRLS

Levels of Labeling in Los Angeles

In an effort to understand the later lives of Los Angeles gang women, we analyzed interviews with random samples of 51 female and 106 male members of two long-standing Chicano gangs. All were adults when they were interviewed in 1986–1987. As teenagers, half had been active in the gangs in the 1950s and half in the 1970s.[2] The gangs were well established in very poor Mexican and Mexican American communities. Those communities, at that time, held very conservative values, particularly about how young women should behave. (See Moore, 1991, and cf. Campbell, 1990a, for Latina gang members in New York; and Horowitz, 1983, for Latinas in a Mexican community in Chicago).

Earlier we had found that gang members exhibited three major adult adaptations: (a) about 40% of the men and fewer of the women matured out of the gang into a "square" lifestyle; (b) more than a quarter of the men and fewer of the women became deeply involved with the lifestyle surrounding heroin—the climax drug in those communities at the time; and (c) the remainder followed an unstable, street-oriented lifestyle (Moore, 1991, pp. 125ff.). Although many gang girls did become "square" when they grew up, they were more likely than gang boys to fall into the third, street-oriented lifestyle—"just hanging out."

We were primarily interested in exploring the careers of women who had become at all involved with heroin. Forty-one percent of the gang women had used heroin at one time or another, as compared with 70% of the men. Whether or not they became addicted to the drug, any use of heroin represented extremely risky behavior for these women. We examined several points in their lives: their families of origin, their behavior in the gang, and their behavior in adulthood. It became evident that gang women who became involved with heroin had been largely confined to a street-oriented world throughout their lives. The gang was part and parcel of that life experience. (See Moore, 1994, for details.)

To begin with, girls who joined the gangs tended to come from different kinds of families than boys. Because it was more acceptable for boys to be "out on the streets," boys were more likely to come from conventional working-class families, whereas girls were more likely to come from "underclass" families and also from abusive families. Thus, if we take running away from home as some measure of problems in the family, we find that almost a third of the gang boys ran away from home—but fully three quarters of the girls ran away at least once. To put it succinctly, there was a self-selection process in gang recruitment that revolved around gender.

This selectivity was exaggerated for girls who wound up using heroin. Their families were even unhappier and more violent than those of other female gang members. Family members made sexual advances to a third of the girls who became heroin users and more than a quarter of those who did not, whereas such experiences were almost unknown among men. Girls were also more likely to have alcoholic or heroin-using parents.[3]

"Bad" families—including the children—were stigmatized in these communities, and respectable families would not allow their children to play with such children. In addition, street-oriented families may have been more likely than conventional families to be permissive with their daughters and to provide street-oriented opportunities and role models (Giordano, Cernkovich, & Pugh, 1978; Moore, 1990b). In effect, many of the girls may have been propelled by community and family dynamics to join a gang: this was a group that could sympathize with them, welcome them, and in some cases shelter them.

This initial selectivity is fateful, because membership in the heavily stigmatized gang further narrows a young woman's horizons and social opportunities, especially if she turns to heroin.[4] Traditional Mexican American gender norms tend to differentiate between "bad" and "good" girls, and *any* girl who joins a gang is defined as bad, no matter what her family is like. Labeling of boys in gangs is much less harsh.

Labeling happened even within the gang: Gang boys usually didn't consider themselves to be deviant just because they were in a gang, but many of them did consider the girls who joined a gang to be deviant. This was particularly true for the rowdier girls who fought, drank, or used drugs heavily. Not surprising, women who used heroin were more likely to have indulged in those behaviors. This meant that the more conventional boys wanted nothing to do with them and the girls were confined largely to the wilder boys in the gang—those who used heroin and often wound up in prison.

The experience in the gang was pivotal, channeling these girls' "deviant" careers ever more narrowly. The influence of the gang persisted into the heroin-using women's adult lives. Women heroin users were more likely to live with a male gang member at a very early age (16 or under), they were less likely to have been married formally, and they were less likely to work.

Milwaukee: Another Time, Other Ethnic Groups

In the early 1990s, we mounted a study of gangs in Milwaukee, Wisconsin, a large Rustbelt city that like many others in the East and Midwest began to experience serious gang problems in its inner-city neighborhoods as factory jobs faded from the scene.[5] We interviewed both African American and Latino (predominantly Puerto Rican) gang members—90 males and 64 females—when they were in their middle 20s. How did women's gang experiences relate to their later-life adaptations in Milwaukee? In many ways, they were very different from those of women in Los Angeles.

In contrast to the gangs in Los Angeles, which had long-standing, quasi-institutionalized traditions, the Milwaukee gangs were new. All of the men and women had been among the founding members of the gangs when they developed in the 1980s. The gangs adopted symbols and traditions from Chicago gangs (Hagedorn, 1988), which were very meaningful for the men, but for the women members—especially the African Americans—had little relevance. This meant that for the women—but not for the men—the gang was almost completely an adolescent experience. None of the African American women were involved in any way with the gang as adults, and fewer than 10% of the Latinas had any involvement. Almost all of the African American members, male and female, had moved out of the gang's old neighborhood, whereas a third of the Latinas still lived in the old neighborhood and the rest lived nearby.

The fact that the women had no gang ties in adulthood doesn't mean that gang membership had been a casual matter to these women when they were teenagers. Like the gang women studied in Los Angeles, female gang members in Milwaukee generally came from more troubled families than male gang members, and sexual abuse was far more prevalent. Thus, for many, the gang represented an alternative family.

Ethnic differences between Latina and African American gangs were important. Drug use differed dramatically, largely for historical reasons. Cocaine, the climax drug in these gangs, had been prevalent in the Latino neighborhood 5 to 10 years before it became popular in the African American neighborhoods, even though the neighborhoods were separated by only a mile. This meant that cocaine use was widespread among Latina gang members during their teens (with 89% using the drug), but nonexistent among the African Americans at the same age. In adulthood, though few were directly involved with the gang, a majority of the Latinas continued to use cocaine, and a third were reported to be heavy users. Cocaine use among African American women was much lower.

Drug dealing also differed. Many more of the Latinas (72% of the women and 81% of the men) than of the African Americans (31% of the women and 69% of the men) reportedly sold cocaine at some time in their lives. In at least one African American neighborhood two drug houses were run independently by women whose brothers or cousins were in the gang, and independent female-run drug houses were found elsewhere as well. At the time of the interview, however, none of the gang women was reported as supporting herself by selling drugs.

Several factors explain why Latinas were more active in the drug trade than African Americans. Of primary importance was the fact that the Latino drug markets were much more lucrative than the African American markets. Latino dealers served an affluent Anglo clientele from the adjacent downtown area, as well as a set of local customers, whereas most customers for African American dealers were also African American and many were from the local community (Hagedorn, 1994b). One Latina described the first male and the first female in her gang to sell drugs, and her account shows how the work was divided by gender:

> Bobby was the leader. Armida was a runner. She went places to go pick up large quantities. She'd go out of state for the dope and she'd bring it back. Yes, she was part of the group. She was a runner, a pick-up person.

At times, gang drug dealing led to severe sexual exploitation. One Latina explained that although the gang was a source of great support for her from a troubled family life, she was also ashamed of certain things. She nervously told the interviewer how she was offered to drug distributors to induce them to lower their wholesale price to a local gang dealer:

> He used me, to, you know . . . even thinking about it disgusts me, but it was, you know, I had to do it just to prove myself. . . . [It was] prostitution. . . . do extra favors, you know, starting the guys. You know, their drugs would be a lot cheaper [for the gang dealer].

Thus, comparing the Milwaukee women with the Los Angeles women suggests that ethnicity counts, but so do opportunities. For Latinas in both cities, gang membership tended to have a significant influence on their later lives, but for African American women in Milwaukee, the gang tended to be an episode. There is much less sense in Milwaukee that gang girls of any ethnicity were as heavily labeled in their community as were Chicana gang girls in Los Angeles. For Latinas in both cities, gangs tended more to be a family matter than they were for African Americans. In Milwaukee, Latinas tended to continue living in or near the gang neighborhood, cocaine tended to be more widely available, and there were better opportunities in drug marketing than there were for Latinas in Los Angeles or African Americans in Milwaukee.

HAVING CHILDREN: A CONSTANT FOR WOMEN

No matter what the cultural context, and no matter what the economic opportunity structure, there seems to be one constant in the later life of women in gangs. Most of them have children, and children have more effect on women's lives than on men's.

Gang men also have children, but for women the consequences are very much stronger. For women, but rarely for men, new responsibilities associated with child rearing may speed up the process of maturing out of the gang.

Part of this process has to do with reputation. Horowitz (1983) argues that a Chicana who has been labeled as "loose" has a chance to retrieve her reputation when she bears a child. If she becomes a "good mother," staying away from gang hangouts, her past is forgiven, but if she neglects her children and continues to hang out with her buddies, her bad reputation is simply confirmed. More important, perhaps, is that her relationship with her parents changes. Teenaged gang mothers usually find that they get more deeply involved with their parents, who may exert "ownership" rights over the children if they don't approve of their daughters' lifestyle (cf. Moore & Devitt, 1989).

But childbearing also generates internalized identity changes. For example, when we asked Mexican American gang members in Los Angeles what had been the major turning points in their lives, the differences between males and females were striking. In their teens, the most significant turning points for males usually had something to do with the gang, with drugs, and with being arrested and going to jail—all "tough-guy" stuff. For females, the significant turning points had to do with marriage and childbearing, with parents, and—a distant third—drugs.

Most of these women were primarily responsible for raising their children, often on their own, without the help of either stable husbands or their parents. Only a minority of the men, by contrast, raised their own children. (Differences between males and females are shown in Table 3–1.) Furthermore, because of the handicaps that gang girls in these communities faced in the marriage market, they were more likely to be encumbered with an alcoholic or heroin-using spouse. On the positive side, women with children have been able

TABLE 3–1   Who Raised Your Children? Gang Women and Gang Men in Los Angeles

	Female	Male
Respondent alone	50%	2%
Respondent with spouse	23	38
Respondent and other relative	12	2
"The children's mothers"	NA	50
Other relative	15	7
Total *N* (=100%)	(48)*	(86)*

NOTE: *These numbers include only those gang members with children. In the total sample of gang members, 94% of the women and 84% of the men had children.

to secure income through the welfare system, and this source of income has helped keep many of them from extensive involvement in drug selling. Drug dealing is a dangerous business with an ever-present hazard of prison. Women may be less willing to risk the violence or the chance of being separated from—or losing—their children through incarceration.

THE CAREERS OF FEMALE ADDICTS

Gang members usually use a wide variety of drugs, in addition to alcohol. Heroin and cocaine are "climax" drugs—the "hard" drugs—which take a greater toll on their users. What are the lives of heroin- and cocaine-using gang women like?

The Los Angeles Chicana heroin addicts who were active a generation ago tended to take one of three routes (Moore, 1990b). More than a third (39%) became "street people," completely and degradingly immersed in the heroin lifestyle. As one woman put it,

> We were, like, in a separate group of people. We were using, ripping, running. People didn't let us go in their houses that knew us. . . . My family . . . I was considered like dead to them. . . . My friends . . . they didn't consider me like a human being any more.

More of the women—approximately half—were less intensely involved with the street lifestyle. They tended to alternate between dependence on a man—for their heroin supply and for protection, as well as for daily sustenance—or on their gang homeboys and homegirls. Some were able to conceal their addiction from their parents, and many were able to avoid involvement with the police; they were sheltered, at home.

A much smaller proportion of the women—perhaps 10%—fell into a third category. They grew up in families that were established in the drug trade. These women had much less stressful access to heroin, because they got it through family-member dealers, and they tended to be more restrained in their heroin use. They were less likely to become hog-wild addicts. Ironically, even though their families may have introduced them to this dangerous drug in the first place, their families had also given them a head start in coping with some of the most serious dangers of heroin.

The introduction of crack cocaine in the 1980s has often been portrayed in the media as leading to the ultimate in women's degradation. "Crack whores," trading sex for drugs, mothers deserting their children for cocaine—all of these are part of the new stereotype about women and drugs that echoes the old "slut" stereotype of the past. We found no support for this stereotype. Although male gang members in Milwaukee talked about the ease with which drug house workers could exchange cocaine for sex, nearly every female gang member we interviewed was indignant when we asked her whether she had "dope dated." Gang women in Milwaukee were not the primary customers of gang drug dealers and were not selling themselves for crack. Thus, they did not match the stereotype of the crack whore, nor were they regularly involved in prostitution.

GETTING INTO DEALING

Drug dealing is probably the most important illicit income-generating activity of male gang members. (Some also become sporadically involved in robberies or property crimes, but few rely on such work for a steady source of income in the way they rely on drug dealing.)

Drug dealing, as a group enterprise, has been assumed to be particularly easy for gang members because the gang already provides established networks with proven mutual loyalty, willingness to use violence, and a degree of secrecy (Padilla, 1992; Steffensmeier, 1983).

Is that also true for gang women? After all, (unlike many conventional girls) they have the same kind of opportunities as gang boys to establish reputations in networks that would "qualify" them for more responsible roles. Many of them fight, stand up for the gang, and form intense loyalties to the gang as a whole. Some have argued that the intense sexism of the male underworld severely limits women's chances to rise above very narrow roles that emphasize their gender (Steffensmeier, 1983). Miller (1973) found that gang girls knew "their place," "actively" sought dependency on a male, and, moreover, that they "gloried in it" (p. 35). They were accomplices in their own dependency, and this accommodation may make the whole system of male domination work more smoothly.

It would thus seem that gang women's chances for a career in dealing drugs are limited by the intragang labeling of women and their reactions to it. Some data from Los Angeles corroborate this view. Even though almost half of a sample of Chicana heroin addicts "had the bag" (i.e., did some heroin dealing) at some time during their careers in the 1970s, most of those women were "employees," rather than entrepreneurs.[6] Only a small minority (perhaps 10%) were career dealers. But not every woman accepted a subordinate status— even then (Moore & Mata, 1981).[7]

Several authors argue that times have changed since the 1970s. Carl Taylor (1993), studying African American women in Detroit in the 1990s, asserted that "females have moved beyond the status quo of gender repression" (p. 118), and he went on to describe women's penetration into drug-dealing "corporate" gangs, some of which are independent of male domination altogether. Lauderback and his colleagues in San Francisco found that although in the late 1980s Latina gang members played a wide range of roles, very similar to those found in Los Angeles among Chicanas in the 1970s, at least one gang of African American women, resentful because they were not getting enough of the profits, had broken away from male-dominated selling activities altogether. Their gang was completely independent, operating out of several crack houses (Lauderback, Hanson, & Waldorf, 1992).

We have presented ample evidence from Milwaukee that gender repression has not disappeared, however. In all studies comparing male and female gangs, the level of women's dealing is reported as being lower than that of the men. The Milwaukee data show how much women's participation in drug dealing depends on opportunities (which were much greater for Latinas than for African American gang women), but also how much gender norms continue to shape most women's participation. Times may have changed, but gender exploitation persists. Cities may vary, and in each city, there are exceptional women who attain independent status as drug dealers of substance. But the norm is for a lower level of dealing, and for a general pattern of subordination to men.

CONCLUSION

In this chapter, we have focused on the variety of ways in which girls in gangs grow up in different ethnic communities and at different times. At the beginning, we asked whether the experience in the gang is a major turning point. What happens to girls in the gang does depend on time, place, ethnicity, the local culture, and economic opportunities. But girls who get into gangs are even more likely than gang boys to come from families in trouble, and this means that joining a gang does not necessarily result in their lives taking a sharp U-turn for the worse: They are not leaving the Brady Bunch for the Hell's Angels. Nonetheless, for most women, being in a gang does have a real impact on later life.

What about differences in time and place? What, in particular, has changed? Most of the changes occurred at the level of the broader society.

Changes Over Time and Place

First, and perhaps most important, the 1950s scenario that held out marriage and family as the ultimate ideals is much more difficult to obtain. Most gangs live in the nation's inner cities. The economies of these communities have been seriously damaged in the past generation. Even when a city has generally recovered from the crisis of deindustrialization, inner cities often continue to suffer critically high unemployment rates.

This means that most young males no longer have much of a future to look forward to, and it is much more difficult for women in most gang neighborhoods to look forward to marriage as a predictable aspect of their future. For example, Robin Jarrett (1994) cites one young African American woman in Chicago who sadly commented that marriage has become "a little white girl's dream." And in Milwaukee, a young Latina, marginal to a gang, in 1995 expressed the problem when she said she really wanted "a good husband." But then she added, "'Course if they are like the rest of these jerks right now, well I don't want one. I'll take care of myself and my kids" (Thomsen, 1996).

Second, there have been changes in gender ideologies corresponding to changes in opportunities for men and for women. Young women like the ones just quoted are now considerably more likely to see themselves as potentially independent, and young men's attitudes have also changed. In poorer neighborhoods, young males are likely to take on what Majors and Billson (1992) call the "cool pose," a facade of aloofness and control, which "counters the . . . damaged pride [and] shattered confidence . . . that come from living on the edge of society" (p. 8). The cool pose inhibits the formation of nurturant relationships with women and children. As those who listen to some rap music know, it can be very disparaging of women.

Third, the economy of many inner-city communities has become informalized, with a heavy illicit component. In Milwaukee's gang neighborhoods we found a drug-dealing business operating in virtually every other block of gang neighborhoods. The drug economy is much more important in the 1990s than it was in the 1970s, and immeasurably more important than in the 1950s.

There are also differences by place. Special traditions and patterns develop in particular communities. Los Angeles gangs will never be quite like those in Detroit or Milwaukee. The gang traditions are different and the cities are different in too many ways to be reduced to a few pat statements.

Differences by Ethnicity

In addition to changes over time, there are clearly differences between ethnic communities, largely having to do with the expected role of females. Women in Latino—especially Mexican American—communities are subject to more traditional expectations than those in African American communities, where for generations more women have been forced to assume independent roles, both economically and in the family. For example, when we asked Milwaukee gang women what they thought of the following statement: "The way men are today, I'd rather raise my kids by myself," we found sharp ethnic differences. Seventy-five percent of the African American but only 43% of the Latina gang members in Milwaukee agreed with that sentiment. In a similar vein, 29% of the Latinas—but *none* of the African Americans—believed that "All a woman needs to straighten out her life is to find a good man." And two thirds of the African American women thought that women should have as much sexual freedom as men, whereas only 39% of the Latinas agreed.

Both in Los Angeles and in Milwaukee, we found that when women were asked to assess their gang experiences, they were more negative than the men, but there were interesting ethnic differences, as well. When we asked what they thought of the statement that "Gangs are not all bad," we found that 8% of the African Americans *dis*agreed—meaning that they thoroughly rejected the thought that there was any good in gangs. A much larger proportion of Latinas—57%—disagreed. This supports the notion that, at least in Milwaukee, the gang may well have more long-range effects on Latinas than on African American women.

Unfortunately, the future prospects for women at the bottom of the economic heap are not very promising. Gangs have been proliferating throughout the country, accurately reflecting a declining economy and a growing sense in many inner-city communities that there is no worthwhile future for most adolescents. More young women may now be involved in gangs than at any time in the past. Programs directed at gangs rarely consider the special needs of female members, and the media continue to be fascinated by these women's sexual experiences and to perpetuate the myth of the "new violence" of women's gangs. Ironically, the most important influence on gang women's future may be the dismantling of the nation's welfare system in the 1990s. This system has supported women with children who want to stay out of the drug marketing system and in addition has provided a significant amount of cash to their communities.[8] Its disappearance will deepen poverty and make the fate of gang women ever more problematic.

QUESTIONS FOR UNDERSTANDING AND CRITICAL THINKING

1. How do gender stereotypes of "gang girls" shape their acceptance, involvement, and respect in the gang and onto when they become adults?
2. How do adult lives and careers of females reflect their gang experience?
3. What happens to girls in the gang as far as a career in dealing drugs?
4. Review and discuss the variations in what happens to gang girls in Los Angeles and Milwaukee, taking into consideration their respective contexts.
5. How does race/ethnicity influence expected roles of such females?

NOTES

1. In the 1990s, the tomboy stereotype was embellished, at least in journalistic accounts, by the notion that female gangs had moved into a new and violent phase, emulating their male counterparts. Chesney-Lind (1993) saw this wave of coverage as exaggerating the evidence for increased violence and continuing the tradition of "demonizing" the young women. (See also Bowker and Klein, 1983, for an early refutation of the maladjustment approach.)

2. Research was supported by Grant #DA03114 from the National Institute on Drug Abuse, which bears no responsibility for opinions expressed in this chapter.
3. A quarter of the heroin-using women had an addicted father, and 14% an addicted mother, compared with 3% of the nonusing women's fathers and mothers. By contrast, only 7% of the heroin-using men had addicted fathers, and none had an addicted mother. No nonusing men had parents who were addicted to heroin.
4. Rosenbaum (1988) developed the concept of "a career of narrowing options" to understand the lives of women heroin addicts.
5. Research was supported by Grant #DA07128 from the National Institute on Drug Abuse, which bears no responsibility for opinions expressed in this chapter.
6. There were several routes to drug dealing. A third of the women had established good relationships with their connections, which led the latter to set them up as dealers. Another 16% had a stock of heroin on consignment. Almost 21% first got the bag through relatives, another 12% by dealing for a friend. Only 12% got the bag when their heroin-dealing husband went to prison. Another 9% got the bag by means that were too varied to be categorized. Other studies report that between 15% and 34% of women in gangs as far apart as New York, Los Angeles, and Detroit sold drugs (Fagan, 1990; Harris, 1988; Taylor, 1990a).
7. In Los Angeles, the gang was particularly important for women in making connections to obtain drugs for personal use. Thirty-two percent in the "Heroin" study (Moore & Mata, 1981) said that their connections were homies from the same gang, and an additional 28% connected through their boyfriends (who were often fellow gang members). A smaller fraction—11%—made their connections through relatives. Only 3% developed connections outside of these networks. As for dealers, most frequently (in a third of the cases) they obtained their stock of heroin through their connections. Another 16% first got it on consignment. Twenty-one percent first got their heroin from relatives, and 12% by selling for a friend. Only 12% got the bag when their dealer-husbands went to prison.
8. Almost a quarter of the income (21%) in Milwaukee's African American communities was provided by welfare.

REFERENCES

BOWKER, L., & KLEIN, M. (1983). The etiology of female juvenile delinquency and gang membership: A test of psychological and social structural explanations. *Adolescence, 13,* 739–751.

CAMPBELL, A. (1984). *The girls in the gang.* New York: Basil Blackwell.

CAMPBELL, A. (1990a). Female participation in gangs. In C. R. Huff (Ed.), *Gangs in America* (1st ed.). Newbury Park, CA: Sage.

CHESNEY-LIND, M. (1993). Girls, gangs and violence: Anatomy of a backlash. *Humanity and Society, 7,* 321–344.

FAGAN, J. (1990). Social processes of delinquency and drug use among urban gangs. In C. R. Huff (Ed.), *Gangs in America* (1st ed.). Newbury Park, CA: Sage.

GIORDANO, P., CERNKOVICH, S., & PUGH, M. (1978). Girls, guys and gangs: The changing social context of female delinquency. *Journal of Criminal Law and Criminology, 69*(1), 126–132.

HAGEDORN, J. M. (1994b). Neighborhoods, markets, and gang drug organization. *Journal of Research in Crime and Delinquency, 32,* 197–219.

HAGEDORN, J. M. (with Macon, P.). (1988). *People and folks: gangs, crime, and the underclass in a rustbelt city.* Chicago: Lake View Press.

HARRIS, M. G. (1988). *Cholas: Latino girls and gangs.* New York: AMS.

HOROWITZ, R. (1983). *Honor and the American dream: Culture and identity in a Chicano community.* New Brunswick, NJ: Rutgers University Press.

JARRETT, R. (1994). Living poor: Family life among single parent, African-American women. *Social Problems, 41,* 30–49.

LAUDERBACK, D., HANSEN, J., & WALDORF, D. (1992). Sisters are doin' it for themselves: A black female gang in San Francisco. *Gang Journal, 1*(1), 57–72.

MAJORS, R., & BILLSON, J. M. (1992). *Cool pose: The dilemmas of black manhood in America.* New York: Touchstone.

MILLER, W. B. (1973). Race, sex and gangs: The Molls. *Society, 11,* 32–35.

MOORE, J. W. (1990b). Mexican-American women addicts: The influence of family background. In R. Glick & J. Moore (Ed.), *Drugs in Hispanic communities.* New Brunswick, NJ: Rutgers University Press.

MOORE, J. W. (1991). *Going down to the barrio: Homeboys and homegirls in change.* Philadelphia: Temple University Press.

MOORE, J. W. (1994). *The chola life course: Chicana heroin users and the barrio gang. International Journal of the Addictions, 29*(9), 1115–1126.

MOORE, J., & DEVITT, M. (1989). Addicted Mexican-American mothers. *Gender & Society, 3,* 53–78.

MOORE, J., & MATA, A. (1981). *Women and heroin in Chicano communities* (Final Report for NIDA). Los Angeles: Chicano Pinto Research Project.

PADILLA, F. (1992). *The gang as an American enterprise.* New Brunswick, NJ: Rutgers University Press.

ROSENBAUM, M. (1988). *Women on heroin.* New Brunswick, NJ: Rutgers University Press.

STEFFENSMEIER, D. (1983). Organization properties and sex-segregation in the underworld, *Social Forces, 61,* 1010–1032.

TAYLOR, C. S. (1990a). *Dangerous society.* East Lansing: Michigan State University Press.

TAYLOR, C. S. (1990b). Gang imperialism. In C. R. Huff (Ed.), *Gangs in America* (1st ed.). Newbury Park, CA: Sage.

TAYLOR, C. S. (1993). *Girls, gangs, women, and drugs.* East Lansing: Michigan State University Press.

THOMSEN, G. (1996). Perceptions of school and the future: A case study of 12th grade Latino students' perceptions of their adult opportunities and their current school experiences. Unpublished doctoral dissertation, University of Wisconsin-Milwaukee.

4

"I'm Calling My Mom"

The Meaning of Family and Kinship Among Homegirls[*]

Geoffrey Hunt, Kathleen MacKenzie, and Karen Joe-Laidler

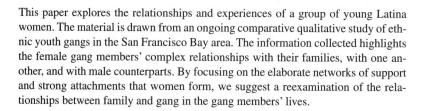

This paper explores the relationships and experiences of a group of young Latina women. The material is drawn from an ongoing comparative qualitative study of ethnic youth gangs in the San Francisco Bay area. The information collected highlights the female gang members' complex relationships with their families, with one another, and with male counterparts. By focusing on the elaborate networks of support and strong attachments that women form, we suggest a reexamination of the relationships between family and gang in the gang members' lives.

Public concern about crime has centered increasingly on the rise of female participation in crime, especially by young women. For example, females involved in delinquency cases between 1985 and 1994 increased by 54 percent, compared with a 38 percent increase for males (Chesney-Lind 1997; FBI 1995, 1996). Women's involvement in perpetrating violence has also raised national concern. During the 1985–1994 period, according to FBI data, female arrests for homicide increased by 60 percent and by 137 percent for aggravated assault.[1]

*Collection of data for this article was made possible by funding from the National Institute on Alcohol Abuse and Alcoholism (RO1-AA10819), administered by Susan Martin, Ph.D. The authors wish to acknowledge Jacqueline Martinez for her work in interviewing the respondents.

G. Hunt, K. Mackenzie, & K. Joe-Laidler. (2000). "I'm calling my mom" The meaning of family and kinship among homegirls. *Justice Quarterly,* 17, 1–31. Reprinted by permission of the Academy of Criminal Justice Sciences.

---

[1] See Chesney-Lind (1997) for a discussion of possible ways of interpreting these figures.

Some of the increasing concern about female crime focuses on girls' participation and role in youth gangs. Some researchers argue that girl gang membership is increasing; others are more cautious, believing that participation has remained relatively stable over time. Estimates of female membership today range from 10 to 30 percent of all gang members (Campbell 1984; Chesney-Lind 1993; Curry, Ball, and Fox 1994; Esbensen and Huizinga 1993; Fagan 1990; Klein 1995; Moore 1991).

Researchers traditionally have minimized females' roles in street gangs as well as the social processes and consequences of their involvement in gangs. With the exception of feminist work (Bowker and Klein 1983; Brotherton 1996; Brown 1977; Campbell 1984, 1991; Fishman 1988; Harris 1988; Joe and Chesney-Lind 1995; Moore 1991; Quicker 1983), male gang researchers typically have characterized female members as maladjusted tomboys or sexual deviants who, in either case, were no more than appendages to male gang members (Joe and Chesney-Lind 1995). This traditional view contrasts sharply with recent public discussions about female gang members, which indicate that these females are no longer simply male gang members' "molls" but are establishing their own ground, taking an active, independent role in crime and violence (Joe and Chesney-Lind 1995).

This most recent image of gang girls has created much public alarm because it highlights more than the problems of adolescent maladjustment or teenage rebellion. For male gang members, being on the streets is a natural, legitimized social activity governed by rules of masculinity (Campbell 1986; Kennedy and Baron 1993). Girls on the street, however, are less typical (McRobbie and Garber 1976; Moore 1990) and are somewhat less of a problem than boys, because they are more likely to be regulated within the home. As Nava (1984) points out, "[O]n the whole parental policing over behaviour, time, labour and sexuality of girls has not only been more efficient than over boys, it has been different. For girls, unlike for boys, the principal site and source for the operation of control has been the family" (p.11). The family thus plays a central role in the structure and process of "gender as social control" (Bottcher 1995).

Consequently, young women's involvement in gangs is disquieting precisely because females in gangs are perceived to be outside the traditional arena of family control. More specifically, female gang participation generates alarm because it signifies, yet again, fears about the decline of the "traditional family." We emphasize *again* because the family has been the target of both praise and condemnation in America since early colonial days, and has been defined clearly in class and culturally biased terms.

On the one hand, the family has been and still is portrayed as an "ideal" socializing and control agent. As early as the 1640s, the state gave parents the authority to instill discipline over the "stubborn child," including the use of corporal and capital punishment (Sutton 1988). Throughout the 1980s, in their more general call for a "return to traditional family values," the Reagan-Bush administrations promoted the notion that parents know best (Joe 1991). Scholars, most notably Hirschi (1969), have emphasized both the salience of family as a mechanism of social control and the corrupting influences of peer groups.

On the other hand, and at the same time, politicians and policy analysts have regularly pointed at the family, and inevitably at minority working- and lower-class families, as the primary arena for many of society's ills.[2] A century ago, in the search for the causes of

---

[2] See, for example, Herrnstein and Murray (1994); Murray (1984).

delinquency and troublesome behavior, child savers were led to argue that vulnerable and impressionable children (in those days, immigrant youths) were being subjected to a "poor family environment." The progressive era's "cure" was state intervention and "parentship" to instill discipline and obedience—first through houses of refuge and reform, and eventually through the juvenile court (Platt 1969). For girls in particular, this meant "correcting" their sexual (mis)conduct and "training" them in "women's work." More recently, however, the state has taken a less paternalistic and less empathetic position than a century ago; instead it has adopted a more punitive, more intolerant stance toward delinquency, as evidenced by the increase in waivers to adult court.

Today the search for reasons within the family remains attractive in attempts to explain girls' involvement in gangs. "Normal" girls would not become involved in gangs or on the street; therefore the reasons why certain young women join gangs lie within deeply troubled families. The existence of the female gang member, like that of the sexually promiscuous girls of the early twentieth century, calls into question the authenticity of societal notions of femininity. Then and now, blame has been attributed to individuals who have broken with family traditions rather than to the larger social factors that shape and disrupt people's everyday lives and aspirations. Accordingly, the female gang member is viewed within the larger framework of family disintegration and violence. From this viewpoint, aggression and violence in the family are regarded, by definition, as dysfunctional and deviant forms of family disintegration. Consequently, young gang women adopt a lifestyle of violence only as a result of an early and damaging experience, and in compensation for such an experience.[3]

In this paper, then, we begin to look more critically at female gang members' relationships and experiences with their families and with their peers. Unlike many researchers studying gang members, we take the family as our starting point. We do not seek to blame the family for society's social problems, nor for the increase in female adolescents' involvement in gangs; instead we want to illuminate the complexities, paradoxes, and ambiguities of day-to-day relations between adolescent women, their parents, other family members, and gang members.

Many studies of gang members, whether male or female, have focused primarily on gang members' behavior and activities, partly divorced from their relationships with their families. Here, following the lead of such writers as Campbell (1984), Decker and Van Winkle (1996), and Moore (1991), we attempt to construct a perspective that joins family and gang, in which these two arenas are viewed as interrelated rather than as distinct social realms. We try to illustrate the continuity that exists for these homegirls between the two most important social groups in their lives: family and gang. In doing so, we examine the following questions: What types of relationships exist between female gang members and their families? Is gang involvement associated with a detachment from family relations? In what ways are family and gang interconnected, and what really is the meaning of family in these young women's lives?

In addressing these questions, we try to illuminate two important points about the relationship between family and girl gang members. First, our data suggest that gang girls maintain relatively strong ties to particular family members, predominantly their mothers

---

[3] See Burbank (1994) for a discussion of female aggression as acceptable, not as pathological.

and also (to a lesser extent) their sisters, aunts, and other female kin. Second, gang and family for many young women intersect; this intersection raises questions about the influence and control of the family versus that of peers in delinquency.

THE RESEARCH ON FAMILY AND GANGS

As Decker and Van Winkle note, "[T]here is little systematic research that examines the link between family characteristics, values and processes and gang membership" (1996:230). Still, a number of gang researchers observe that problems within contemporary families contribute to young people's turning to their peers on the street for refuge. The absence of a strong and vibrant sense of belonging or attachment to family members, combined with an authoritarian, disciplinary, traditional attitude on the part of "unacculturated" immigrant parents, can lead to stress in family relationships, creating a lack of attachment between parent and child. This void ultimately is filled by the gang (Harris 1988). Vigil (1988) highlights the role of family stress and emotional problems within the family in providing an environment that leads a young person to identify with street and gang life. Family stress and a disorganized family encourage adolescents to become "involved with a gang [and] seek the kind of support that they were lacking from family sources" (Vigil 1988:44).

Some researchers point out that "the problem" is not only due to a generation gap or parental indifference, but also is connected intimately to broader political and economic changes that have altered contemporary family structures and everyday life. Campbell (1984), Fishman (1988), and Joe and Chesney-Lind (1995) indicate that many female gang members live in chaotic, often violent families that face practical everyday problems in their communities such as poverty, unemployment, inadequate housing, high rates of alcohol and drug use, high crime rates, and urban neglect. Harris (1988) and Vigil (1988) also suggest that structural factors such as immigration, poverty, and the industrialization of modern society have created social circumstances which have "weakened" family controls over the young and have encouraged them to develop a support system among their peers. In essence, gang members and their families live in bleak environments with little to offer to adults and young people.

In this context, researchers have highlighted how the gang acts as a surrogate family for both male and female members (Campbell 1984; Fleisher 1998; Harris 1988; Joe and Chesney-Lind 1995; Joe-Laidler and Hunt 1997; Moore 1991). In a study on Latino male gang members, Vigil notes that "the gang is a force of attraction that provides many family-type functions" (1988:90). Campbell (1984), Harris (1988), Joe and Chesney-Lind (1995), and Moore (1991) also emphasize the importance of the gang's family characteristics for female members. As Messerschmidt (1997) observes in summarizing these approaches, "[T]he gang is where many lower working class girls and boys of color develop strong 'family' ties with members of their neighborhood" (p.71).

Decker and Van Winkle (1996) recently set out both to examine the family structure and characteristics of male gang members and to contrast "the perceptions of active gang members about ties to their family with the perceptions of family members" (p. 231). One issue to emerge from this research, which is especially interesting in light of our own work, is the extent to which an overwhelming majority of gang members, when asked whether they would choose the gang over the family, chose the family. As Decker and Van Winkle point out, this finding suggests that "despite its problems and despite the many attractive features of gang affiliation, the family retains its role (if not function) in the lives of gang members" (1996:251).

We follow these authors' lead and borrow from feminist discussions in exploring the complexity of female gang members' relationships. Chodorow (1978) and Taylor, Gilligan, and Sullivan (1995) contend that the ties between mothers and daughters may change over the life course and may entail generational stress and conflict; yet the intimacy remains. This strong bond is related to at least two distinctive dimensions of families and parenting. First, beginning at an early age, the daughter, unlike her male counterpart, defines herself in connection with her mother. Accordingly "the basic feminine sense of self is connected to the world," therefore is relational (Chodorow 1978:169). Second, mothers are ever-present for their daughters, as they are not for their sons.

The intimacy between mothers and daughters differs significantly across ethnicities. Taylor et al. (1995) found that as black girls become adolescents, they develop a distinctive openness and closeness with their mothers. By contrast, white girls are increasingly less open than in their childhood, and their own ideas and needs clash with those of their mothers. Latina and Portuguese girls are less revealing with their mothers in their childhood, partly to mask their own feelings and partly because they have not yet "accepted" their fate of living in a family whose culture stresses a gender double standard. All of these girls perceive their mothers' restrictions and authority as understandable and protective (Taylor et al. 1995:75).

Other studies indicate strong but tension-filled relationships between mothers and daughters as the girls try to negotiate their own expectations and desires with those of their mothers (Cauce et al. 1996; Taylor 1996). Relationships between fathers and daughters, however, tend more often to be sporadic and estranged. Still, Way and Stauber (1996) indicate that though daughters have less contact with their fathers, many "absent fathers" are not really absent from the daughters' point of view. Other research, however, emphasizes the "non-relational" quality of father-daughter relationships (Apter 1993; Youniss and Smollar 1985).

Some researchers have pointed out that gang life is not merely a substitute for family life and familial relationships. In addition, specific gangs reflect or incorporate the traditional family culture of individual gang members' dominant ethnicity. For instance, Padilla suggests that the collectivist nature of the gang "is an extension of the traditional Puerto Rican family" (1992:105). Traditional ties of *compadrazco* and blood ties produce "an intricate network of reciprocal obligations" (p.105). Harris (1988) similarly argues that values of Latino culture, such as a sense of belongingness, are part of "familism" and are clearly exhibited in gang life. Horowitz believes that notions of honor, normally located within the family, have become "encapsulated in the gang and . . . increasingly linked to an exaggerated notion of toughness and aggressiveness" (1983:227). Although these theories examine the cultural specificities of particular ethnic and minority groups, some scholars question the extent to which "traditional" family notions embody norms and values, and disregard change and variations, in these cultures (Zavella 1987). For example, Bean, Russell, and Marcum (1977), who examine notions of "familism" in Chicano families, conclude that "there is little evidence that familism is an over-ridingly important factor in Mexican American family life" (p.766).

Still, the cultural traditions of family may be important in other ways for female gang members. For example, the Latino cultural emphasis on extended family may play an important role in the support system for these gang members as they negotiate womanhood in a patriarchal environment at home and on the street. Scholars have shown that African American families develop strong real and fictive kinship networks for both emotional and practical support (Martin and Martin 1978; Stack 1974). This extended kinship system has endured over time, but the familial ties have become increasingly complex in the last 15 years because of the destruction of inner-city life by crack cocaine, crime, unemployment, and government neglect (Dunlap 1992; Wilson 1989). Joe-Laidler (1997) underscores the significance of extended-family systems among Asian Pacific American female drug users: Relatives provide shelter, food, child care, financial assistance, and emotional support. This type of complexity also may be reflected in the intricate and elaborate networks that female gang members form on the streets as well as in their families.

In the following sections, we attempt to show that although joining a gang may create tension within the family, especially when parents disapprove, gang members do not necessarily sever all ties with the family. In many cases, the gang members and their parents, or other significant adults, maintain their relationships in spite of these tensions and conflicts. Furthermore, although a significant number of gang members express negative feelings toward particular family members, they often call on those persons when they need help. Female gang members, at least in our sample, exhibit complex ongoing and changing relationships with their parents, especially their mothers, as well as with other female relatives, with nonrelated women in the gangs, and (in many cases) with family members in the gangs. We present findings that explore a broader understanding of family, which extends beyond kinship and into the streets.

RESEARCH DESIGN AND SAMPLE

Methodology

The data for this analysis are drawn from an ongoing larger comparative qualitative study of ethnic youth gangs in the San Francisco Bay area. We conducted face-to-face interviews with 47 Latina gang members during 1997. These gang members belonged to 23 different groups; we located them using the snowball sampling approach (Biernacki and Waldorf 1981). The total number of young women involved in gangs in this area is unknown; our sample is exploratory.

The interview process consisted of two stages, both of which we tape-recorded. In the first stage, the respondent answered questions from a quantitative interview schedule covering topics such as basic sociodemographic data, work and criminal histories, patterns of alcohol and drug use, activities of gang members, and violence experienced by gang members. The second stage was an in-depth focused interview that explored topics such as the respondent's background and early life, including her relationships with important people in her family and at school; history of her involvement in the gang, including gang activities, both social and criminal; relationships with gang members, both homeboys and homegirls; and finally her experiences of violence within the gang. This combination of qualitative and social survey methodology enabled us to focus on the group's history, its organization and activities, personal demographics, alcohol and drug use, individual history and involvement with the group, and prior contact with the justice system. We also asked the young women about power relations and gender expectations within the group, with the various males in their lives, and with their families.

The interviews were conducted by a Latina social scientist, who previously had been a gang member and was generally familiar with the gang scene. Given this background and knowledge, although the interviewer did not know the girls personally before the interviews, she had few difficulties in establishing rapport and trust. She conducted the interviews in a variety of settings such as the respondent's or a peer's residence, parks, church youth centers, and coffee shops. The interviews were held mainly in English, although respondents occasionally answered questions in Spanish. In those cases, the interviewer translated the responses. Interviews lasted from 90 minutes to three hours, and respondents received a $65 honorarium for their participation and time.

We took several steps to address validity and reliability issues. Because the interviewer was familiar with the scene and with some of the respondents, the respondents were less likely to exaggerate or minimize their experiences. During the interview, she rephrased and repeated questions at different times to detect inconsistencies and to ensure truthfulness. As in all our gang interviews, the interviewer was required to make judgments about the veracity of individual gang members' responses. In doing so, she assessed both each respondent's general truthfulness and the extent of inconsistencies. This latter characteristic was also assessed by our research assistants; in addition, they checked the accuracy of the completed quantitative schedule against the answers given by the respondent. Finally, the interviewer conducted periodic field observations as a further cross-check on respondents' veracity.

Sample Characteristics

The young women's mean age was 19.1 years. The majority (41) had been born in the United States, and the remainder were born in Mexico (see Table 4–1). This connection with Mexico was strong in that the majority of those born in the United States were of Mexican descent; their families had emigrated one or two generations previously. The respondents lived primarily in one of the sprawling urban areas surrounding the San Francisco Bay, home to an ethnically diverse population.

Three-quarters of the respondents had been born in the area. All of them lived in east San Jose, where the population is young, family-oriented, poor, and undereducated. More than 40 percent had grown up in female-headed single-parent families. Just over one-third came from families with either a mother and a father or a mother and a stepfather; two other respondents lived with only their fathers. The remaining nine respondents had grown up in a variety of other family situations: Two were raised in foster homes and three by their grandmothers. The rest moved between different homes and family groupings. One-third of the participants mentioned other extended-family members, most often aunts, grandmothers, and uncles, who lived with them or were important adult figures in their lives. More than half spoke about close relationships with cousins.

Sixty-five percent of the respondents[4] provided information on their current living situation. Eighteen percent had established their own households and were living with their child and/or their husband/boyfriend. Nearly one-third were still living with both parents or with their mother and a stepfather. Twenty-nine percent lived with only one parent, the ma-

---

[4] A smaller percentage of respondents replied on issues of current living situation because neither the quantitative nor the qualitative schedule included a specific question about that situation. Our only direct question on domestic arrangements was contained in the quantitative schedule: "Whom did you live with the most up to your 16th birthday?" Consequently, information on the respondents' current living situation was gained only by default from the more general information obtained in the qualitative interview.

TABLE 4–1   Personal Characteristics of Homegirls (N= 47)

	Frequency	%
Place of birth		
California	40	85.1
Other U.S.	1	2.1
Mexico	6	12.8
Domestic unit before age 16		
Mother and father	13	27.6
Mother and stepfather	3	6.3
Mother only	20	42.6
Father only	2	4.3
Other relative	5	10.6
Other	4	8.5
Current living arrangements		
On own	5	10.6
With both parents	10	21.3
One parent only	9	19.1
Other relatives	6	12.8
Unknown	17	36.2
Education		
Less than 9 years	13	27.7
High school dropout	6	12.8
Still in school	9	19.1
High school graduate	11	23.4
GED	1	2.1
Adult education program	4	8.5
College	3	6.4
Main source of income		
Working	12	25.5
Family, spouse, or boyfriend	14	29.8
Public assistance	7	14.9
Combination: hustle/family/friends	13	27.7
Unknown	1	2.1

jority with their mother. Finally, one-fifth lived with other family members including siblings, aunts, cousins, or (in one case) a grandmother.

Nearly 60 percent of our respondents had graduated or were still in school. Twenty-three percent of these were high school graduates, and 15 percent were in higher education. Twenty-one of the young women had children, and 19 of these had their children living with them. Ten of the women with children lived with a spouse or boyfriend, though not necessarily with the fathers of their children. For the most part, the women were very proud and protective of their children. Children were often cited as the most important people in the lives of those home-girls who were mothers. One 19-year-old mother of two said about motherhood, "I don't re-gret my kids. I love my kids with all my heart." One 23-year-old woman with three children, however, when asked what she would have done differently in her life if she could have done so, replied "I would have went to college and never had so many fucking kids." Not all of those who had children had established their own households; many lived with family members who assisted with child rearing, and a few had completely relinquished the care of their children to relatives.

For one-quarter of the women, the major source of income was work, most often in the service sector or in child care. Four of these women supplemented this income through their families or by some sort of hustle such as drug dealing. Almost one-third of the young women were supported by their families, husbands, or boyfriends, and seven were on pub-lic assistance. Of the remaining 13, three supported themselves solely by various hustles, including drug sales, and 10 by a combination of hustles and family and friends. Their par-ents' occupations included cannery work, construction, and shop ownership; the electron-ics industry was the largest category of employment. The parents of two respondents were on public assistance.

FAMILY RELATIONS

Latina gang members' relationships with their parents and other family members are var-ied and complex. Some reported strong family ties; others described violent confrontations, and sexual and physical abuse; still others expressed extreme hatred (Moore and Hagedorn 1996). Three significant relationships emerged from the homegirls' discussions of family: relations with their mothers, relations with fathers and stepfathers, and relations with other significant family members.

Mothers

For the majority of the young women, the most significant relationship was with their moth-ers. Most described generally positive ties, seeing their mothers in "traditional terms" as well as accommodating to changes in the mother's role and position in the family. One respon-dent, for example, stated that her mother "is a very nice woman, family oriented. . . . When she divorced my dad, she took care of us kids and always worked and was a good role model."

As the respondents grew older, many began to consider their relationships with their mothers in a new light. A change was noted by one-quarter of those respondents who clas-sified their relationships as good. Some of the respondents assessed their mothers and their own relationships with them more even-handedly. One respondent emphasized how her mother had "put up with all my things." Another suggested that although her relationship with her mother was still not perfect, it was improving. In some cases, a more realistic and more practical perspective on their mothers emerged, occasionally furthered by their own experiences as they began to raise children of their own.

Even among the more positive accounts, we heard many references to disruptive features in the family. One 15-year-old respondent, who described her relationship with her mother as good, remarked, as though in passing, that she currently lived with her sister. When asked why, she replied "'Cause my mom got locked up. . . . 'Cause of drugs. Shooting up." Many respondents described intense conflict between their mothers and their fathers, and found themselves siding with their mothers. One 16-year-old respondent remarked that her parents fought a lot and that "my sister doesn't talk to my dad. I talk to my sister. I talk to my mom."

Disruptions to their relationships surfaced in other ways over which the girls felt they had little control. A few respondents found their relationship with their mothers altered because their mothers had commenced a relationship with a new boyfriend:

> Me and my mom always had a good relationship, but for like a year, I moved away from her and we stopped talking 'cause she got with this other guy and . . . I just didn't like it. . . . I felt that this guy was . . . just using her, and . . . I couldn't stand it 'cause it was my mom . . . and I've always . . . had a good relationship (with my mother).

In contrast to these more positive relationships, many homegirls described conflictual relationships with their mothers, often with the same intensity of expression. Nearly three-quarters blamed the poor relationship on their mothers. Over half of these attributed it to their mothers' drinking or drug use. Even so, some of the girls accepted their mothers' problems and assumed the parental role over the mother as well as over younger siblings. One 20-year-old married respondent described her mother's drinking in this way:

> My mom drank every chance she got, but she was always at home doing it. And . . . we always used to take care of her, and put her to sleep when she had too much . . . she would get real emotional, she cried about everybody and how she couldn't help us when we had our problems . . . After a while, I got used to it. . . . I'd have to be there to watch her.

Two respondents' criticisms of their mothers stemmed from their mothers' failure to take their side when they were raped or sexually molested by their stepfathers. The respondents reported that their trust in their mothers had been undermined and that a "lot of hatred" now existed in the home, which made living there impossible. In almost all cases, however, even when the women reported hostile and negative relations with their mothers, some interaction still occurred. Contact was completely severed in only two cases.

In all these negative accounts, only one respondent admitted that her own behavior had contributed to the quality of the relationship with her mother:

> My mom . . . she's done a lot for me so it's time for me to . . . show her what I can do. That I can do a lot for myself and I just don't want to disappoint her anymore . . . I've been in too many problems. And the way she sees it, I have no reason to be in these problems. So . . . I guess she just wants me to straighten out and I just can't seem to do it . . . I know she won't kick me out but I guess it's really gotten to her 'cause it's like she tells me . . . I ain't no little girl no more. I should know what I'm doing.

In spite of these respondents' negative feelings towards their mothers, they felt and maintained ties, partly out of familial loyalty and love, but also for instrumental reasons. They relied on their mothers when they needed assistance. Although a few respondents expressed strong animosity toward their mothers for past behaviors, they called on them for help in looking after their children, providing shelter, and even supplying protection. This seemingly contradictory behavior was highlighted strikingly in one case: The respondent, who had described her mother in the early part of the interview as "a fuckin' bitch" and "a fuckin' drunk," later described proudly how, having been in a fight with an older woman, she telephoned her mother to come and defend her. Her mother "hunted down" the older woman and "kick(ed) her ass":

> I went and called my mom. I said the bitch wants to fuck with me. I said "Mom, drop off my son and come and look at my face 'cause she got two hits on me . . . " and I said "Mom, get over here. I just fought this bitch and she's as old as you." . . . She came . . . and said "Where's this bitch at?" . . . . Everybody . . . thought I was going to go snitch . . . and call the cops. I said "Nah, I'm calling someone better. I'm calling my mom."

The intricacy of these relations and the intensity of these young women's feelings towards their mothers was also evident when the respondents recounted situations in which they had physically defended their mothers. One 22-year-old respondent, in detailing her attitude towards anyone who attempted to hurt anyone in her family, described one such incident:

> A woman beat up my mom really bad, and I went back and I beat that lady to the point of death. I beat her, I took her out of the bar—well, she came out of the bar—and I took her and I grabbed her and I set her up at the back, and I beat her for like 20 minutes nonstop . . . and my mom was standing right there just watching me do it, . . . and that was 'cause [that woman] hurt something of mine, and you don't hurt what's mine.

The young women's defense of their mothers, and their sense of loyalty, also were clear in their home lives, as they often witnessed conflict between their parents or between the mother and the mother's boyfriend or spouse. Forty percent of the women reported such incidents of violence in the home; most of the time they sided with their mothers.

Fathers and Stepfathers

Just as the respondents' relationships with their mothers were varied, so were their relationships with their fathers, although these were less intense and less complex. We found one significant difference, however, in comparing respondents' relationships with their mothers and with their fathers: Respondents had much less to say about their fathers. Nearly one-fourth provided little or no information about these relationships. In some cases they mentioned their fathers only in passing; in others, their fathers appeared to be nonexistent. This feature is not surprising when we consider the small proportion of respondents (32%) who had lived with their fathers for most of the time before their sixteenth birthday. Other respondents complained that their fathers suddenly reappeared after a period of absence, stayed for a short time, and then disappeared again:

> My dad came back when I was nine—my ninth birthday. That fucked me up. 'Cause before that I seen him when I was five, going on six. And then he popped up . . . out of nowhere . . . came for a surprise, and that fucked me up. You know, "What the fuck are you doing here?" Then I figured he was staying. . . . And then he left without even saying goodbye. So one morning I wake up and he's gone.

Only two of the women who lived with both parents described the relationships with their fathers as normal or unproblematic. One of these, a recent immigrant from Mexico, stated "We don't have any problems in our family . . . I don't think anybody has parents like me . . . Cuz I have my love in my dad, and they are always there for us even if we're doing bad." In addition, both of the respondents who lived only with their fathers described the relationships as strong and positive. One recalled how her father helped look after her daughter. She had a high regard for her father, whom she considered "funny and smart." This young woman had little or no contact with her mother, saying "I don't really talk to her." Although she allowed her daughter to see her, she herself didn't visit.

A few respondents described growing up as "just normal" and reported good relationships with their fathers, but many recounted situations of tension and disruption in the family. One 20-year-old woman, while describing her father as the most important person in her life, went on to explain how her father began using cocaine, which ultimately led to her parents' divorce: "We really didn't have problems, till my dad . . . had a drug problem, so my mom left my dad and they just divorced." After the divorce she, her mother, and her brothers and sisters moved in with her grandmother and aunt. Unfortunately her mother, unlike her father, was unable to control her: "My dad was real strict with rules. . . . Whatever he said . . . that's what we did." Consequently, in the respondent's view, her father's cocaine use had catastrophic effects on her and her family. Her father ended up in prison (he was currently serving a 10-year sentence), her sister was "locked up . . . [because] she was under the influence of some drug," and her brother had been locked up since October. Tragically, the respondent blamed herself for the situation, especially her father's imprisonment, commenting that if "I would have talked to my dad better, um . . . more, he wouldn't be locked up now."

Alcohol and drug consumption and alcohol-related violence also played a much more significant role in the respondents' accounts of their relationships with their fathers than with their mothers, a characteristic also evident in the discussions of their stepfathers. Accounts of the latter were generally more negative than those of their fathers. Of the 12 respondents who had grown up with stepfathers, only three described the relationships in positive terms. Like the fathers, the majority of the stepfathers were described either in passing or in harsh terms such as "He disgusts me" and "I hate him a lot." Sometimes tension resulted in violence, especially between the respondents' mothers and their fathers/stepfathers or between their mothers and the mothers' boyfriends. The matter-of-fact way in which these violent incidents were described suggests that often they were regular occurrences in the family.

As many writers have observed (Campbell 1991; Joe and Chesney-Lind 1995; Moore 1991), violence between parents, between siblings, and between parents and children is commonplace in homegirls' stories of their families. Homegirls are often witness to (and victims of) multiple incidents of abuse in their homes, whether from their fathers/stepfathers, mothers, or siblings. More than two-thirds of the women discussed violence in connection with the family. Most of this violent behavior involving the respondents took place between themselves and siblings or cousins of similar age (27%; see Table 4–2). Violent incidents with spouses or boyfriends were reported next most frequently (19%). Although 40 percent of our respondents said they had witnessed violence between their mothers and their fathers, their stepfathers, or their mothers' boyfriends, far fewer respondents engaged in or suffered violence at the hands of their parents or caregivers. Finally, violence had occurred between 17 percent of the respondents and outsiders, in defense of family members.

TABLE 4–2   Reports of Violence in Family

Family Members Involved	Frequency	%
Self with mother	6	12.8
Self with father/stepfather/mother's boyfriend	3	6.4
Self with sister	3	6.4
Self with brother	3	6.4
Self with cousin	7	14.9
Self with outsider (defending family)	8	17.0
Self with spouse/boyfriend	9	19.1
Self with other family member	3	6.4
Mother with father/stepfather/mother's boyfriend	19	40.4
Father or mother with other family member	5	10.6
Other family member	4	8.5

When the respondent was the victim of family violence, it usually involved fathers or stepfathers. The most extreme form of violence described by the young women was rape or sexual molestation: In two of the three cases where this had occurred, stepfathers were the perpetrators; and the father's best friend was the offender in the third case.

In the case involving the father's best friend, the young woman described how she hated her father not only because she blamed him for his best friend's raping her, but also because of his violence towards her: He often pointed a gun at her head. Finally, she observed that these events explain why she is violent today:

> I would get . . . hate for my dad 'cause he didn't take care, he left me alone when he was supposed to take care of me and his best friend raped me when I was seven . . . that's why I got so violent, . . . where I could just kill somebody . . . 'cause that anger that was inside of me . . . I feel a lot of that frustration . . . those people hurt me, man, they hurt me when they do that to me, and that's why I guess I got to a point where I said nothing's gonna hurt me no more, nobody's gonna see me shed a tear for nothing that they did to me. I remember when my dad used to put a gun to my head, it took all fear away from me from dying . . . everything was always stripped from me, I didn't have nothing no more . . . something in me was already taken away as a little girl.

Other young women remembered violent events with their mothers' boyfriends. In the following example, the respondent describes her attempts to protect her mother, whom she says was beaten up regularly:

> He would always beat up on my mom, and I was the one that would call the police because my sister would get scared and go and run and put herself in a corner. They were usually at night. We are trying to go to sleep and we always wake up to my mom screaming. I would wake up and my sister would be all scared and I would be like, "It is okay. I will call the police." Every single time I would try and help my mom. Try to beat him with something. I would always grab some shit and . . . throw it at him or something, and try to get him off her. That motherfucker was strong.

Despite the ups and downs in the young women's relationships with their mothers, they maintained emotional and instrumental ties. In many cases, the relationship was reciprocal in the sense that sometimes the mothers provided the nurturing and protective role for their daughters, while at other times the daughters assumed the motherly role of caregiver and protector. This intimacy and reciprocal caregiving was largely absent from the young women's relationships with their fathers, where interaction was characterized most accurately as distant, periodic, and strained. That relationship was essentially nonrelational. Only a few of the female gang members described feelings of affection and warmth toward their fathers.

Other Significant Family Members

Although relationships with parents, stepfathers, and mothers' boyfriends dominated many of our respondents' accounts of their family experiences, they were not the only prominent family relationships in their lives. When both parents were absent from the family home, for whatever reason, parental responsibility fell to the grandparents, specifically to the grandmothers. In three cases, respondents referred to their grandmothers as significant people in their lives. In one of these, although the mother was alive and living with the respondent, the grandmother nevertheless was the primary mother figure. Her death, when the respondent was 14, was particularly difficult for the respondent because as she said, "I didn't really like my mom. My grandmother was like my mom." In the other two cases, because their mothers were absent from the family home, the grandmothers acted as the real mothers. The grandmother's role as mother had such a lasting effect on one young woman that even when her mother returned home, that event hardly changed the respondent's feelings towards her mother and her grandmother: "With my grandma, it's more mother and daughter . . . but (with) my mom, it's just like sisters."

Significantly, in these three accounts, references to grandfathers are different from references to grandmothers. As in the descriptions of their fathers, the respondents' grandfathers are largely absent from these accounts, with the exception of one homegirl's description of her grandfather's drinking and violence:

> My grandpa had an alcoholic problem while we were young. He used to spank us a lot when he used to get drunk. He'd come home angry, right after drinking at bars. I never remember him hitting [my grandmother], but my aunt told me that he used to hit her when they were young. But when all three of us were there, then he'd come home and get mad at every little thing, and just go off.

Relationships with siblings are also a significant feature in the homegirls' lives. Ninety-five percent of the respondents had grown up with other siblings. Only two respondents were the only children in the family. The young women described their sisters, particularly older ones, as supportive, both in the past and at present. Caregiving featured prominently in sister relationships; like homegirls' relationships with their mothers, it was often reciprocal. Support extended not only from siblings to respondents, but also from respondents to siblings. One respondent, for example, who had a child, had set up a home on her own, and looked after her daughter and her younger sister and brothers. Parenting was not unusual for the homegirls: One respondent described how she had stayed away from school for two years in order to look after her four younger brothers, while her father was working in Washington State and her mother worked in a restaurant.

Homegirls' relationships with brothers seemed much less significant than those with sisters. Brothers, however, were important to the respondents when they described their relationships within the gangs. Other than those instances in which the homegirl acted as surrogate mother, the brothers played a significant role in only two accounts of family relationships, one positive and one negative. In the former case, the respondent described a caring relationship: "[H]e was always there for me and everything. I always looked up to him. Like whenever I needed money or like whenever I needed . . . somebody to talk to, he was always there." In the latter case, the respondent described how she had been sexually abused by her elder brother. The homegirl agreed to his request to remove her clothes because even though she knew it was wrong, she was "used to doing what he said." Fortunately the grandmother discovered them before anything else occurred.

Family disruption was a major reason for running away. The homegirls cited problems with their mothers or stepfathers, or parental drug use. Sixty-three percent had run away from home at least once, some for only a day; others left home for as long as two years, and some left as often as 20 times. Yet the desire to escape family conflict was not the only reason for leaving the family, for whatever length of time. Other reasons included a desire to be independent, the attraction of life outside the family, and (in one case) simply the desire to attend a rave.

A few respondents were adamant that far from running away, they had been "kicked out." As one respondent said wryly,

> My mom tried to report me as a runaway. But I said "No, the bitch kicked me out." So it was like her word against mine. But they had her on file as child-abusing me, 'cause one time she beat me up so badly that I had welts on my legs and I wore shorts to school and the teacher said: "Where'd you get them bruises?" I was like: "Oh! I didn't know I had those." . . . She said "Does your mom hit you?" and I [said] "Yeah, so what?" You know, it was normal.

Even those women who were physically separated from their families described ongoing and caring interaction with them. One 17-year-old respondent, who had left home to live with her homeboys and homegirls, and in spite of feeling estranged from her mother, still telephoned her mother regularly to let her know that she was okay: "I always like to let my mom know where I am at. At least I let her know if I'm doing good and everything, that I'm safe."

The homegirls exhibited a wide range of relationships and feelings towards their parents and other significant family members. The diversity of their accounts underscores the ongoing interaction with family members and the crucial role of family in their lives, even when they lived outside the family unit. At no time in the accounts did we find a sense of separation from ties with the family. Thus, in spite of these periods of conflict and tension, and in some cases even physical separation, the female gang members' relationships with their families continued both inside and outside the gang.

FROM FAMILY TO GANG: EXPANDING THE FAMILY CIRCLE

Despite homegirls' problems with various family members at different times in their lives, they generally viewed their mothers, sisters, and extended kin as a support system. They also found a strong, stable source of emotional and practical support in other gang members. Initially we had assumed that the girls' families and their gang were two distinct and separate associations, but we found that these two seemingly disconnected groups were intimately linked. Far from choosing a sharply different alternative to the family, the homegirls in effect were joining an extension of their families. Homegirls did not relinquish one for the other; they were not thrust into gang membership because of family dysfunction, nor were they necessarily looking for a youth gang to join as a rebellion against their families. Doing so was unwarranted because the gang already was part of their daily lives. Gangs were present in their schools, next door, in the park, on the bus, and, most important, in their families. Many of the homegirls did not formally join a gang; they were already hanging out with their siblings, extended-family members, and other gang members. As one respondent explained, when asked how she came to choose a particular gang,

> Well, I had my cousins that used to live around here, and I used to go over there, and then from there . . . I started meeting all the guys around there. I always wanted to be going over there, and that's how I got into it.

Nearly all (96%) of the respondents had family members who had been in gangs or currently were involved in gangs. For many, growing up in the family was the same as growing up in the gang. Nearly 40 percent of our respondents admitted current or previous gang involvement by either their fathers or their mothers (see Table 4–3). A similar percentage (nearly 40%) had brothers in a gang, more than one-third had sisters in a gang, and 11 percent had both. Extended-family members were also active in gang activities: 22 of the 47 women had cousins who were involved, as well as 11 with uncles and seven with aunts who were gang members. Moreover, family involvement did not include only single members of the family: 66 percent of our respondents had more than one family member in gangs, and nearly one-fifth of our sample had three or more. Connections between family and gang have not gone unnoticed by gang researchers. Harris (1988) and Moore (1991) highlighted this connection, and we observed this striking characteristic even in our own previous research. In our own study (Joe-Laidler and Hunt 1997) we found that 63 percent of our female respondents had family ties to gangs.[5]

The extension of family into the gang was also evident in our respondents' reasons for belonging to a gang. Eighty percent stated that the primary reason for being a gang member

TABLE 4–3   Family Members Who Are or Were Gang Members

Family Member	Frequency	%
Father	10	21.3
Mother	8	17.0
Brother	18	38.3
Sister	15	31.9
Uncle	11	23.4
Aunt	7	14.9
Cousin	22	46.8

---

[5] The percentage of family members involved in gangs varies with ethnicity. For example, although 71 percent of Latinas had immediate family members involved in gangs, this was the case for only 2.4 percent of African-American female gang members (Joe-Laidler and Hunt 1997).

was the sense of "family feeling" that membership gave them. Overall this complex inter-weaving of family and gang may support the idea, recently suggested by Kandel (1996), that the family/peer dichotomy may be too simplistic for examining accurately the countervailing influences of family and of peers on future adolescent behavior. This is not to suggest that friends were not also important in encouraging our respondents to join a gang. In fact, equal numbers of respondents noted that friends as well as family had influenced their involvement.

Nevertheless, whether family or friends provided the most encouragement, one feature was absolutely clear: Other girls and women were by far the most direct influence when these young women became involved in the gangs. Almost one-third were influenced by girlfriends, either a best friend or a group of friends that they hung out with. Only seven respondents were influenced by male friends; three of these were boyfriends. Three of the young women had sisters and two had brothers who introduced them to the gang. Seven said they had learned about the gangs through their cousins, mostly female cousins. Thus, although friends may have exerted a more immediate effect or influence when these girls began to hang out with other gang members, a web of family influences also operated both inside the family and in their peer groups.

GANG RELATIONS

Many of the characteristics of family life continued in the young women's associations within their gangs. Notions of family, including attachment, pride, loyalty, protection, solidarity, safety, and familiarity, as well as conflict, were replicated in relationships with homeboys and boyfriends, and with other homegirls. Sometimes these relations involved real family members; in other cases, familylike relationships or "fictive kin" relations developed in addition to the family bonds already in place.

Relations with Homeboys/Boyfriends

Whether their homeboys were actual relatives or fictive kin, the girls valued the respect and protection embedded in their relationships with the males; these features sometimes were absent from their relationships with their parents. Respect in the male-dominated gang included characteristics such as not letting a fellow gang member down, loyalty, the ability to fight, the ability to protect oneself and others, "backing up your shit," and being prepared to follow through with what you say you will do. Of these features, a homeboy's street prowess and fighting ability are key attributes. We heard the most glowing accounts in some of the homegirls' descriptions of their older brothers and uncles.

Earlier we noted the predominance of negative accounts of male family members, particularly fathers who were absent or exploitative, or who failed to assume the protective paternal role. By comparison, the respondents' discussions of male family members in the gang were predominantly positive. In these accounts we witness, for the first time, homegirls' consistent expression of admiration for their brothers and uncles, and for their reputations as impressive gang fighters:

> My brother Ernesto is crazy. Ernesto is what I call a warrior 'cause that homeboy has seventeen, eighteen, nineteen stab wounds, and two bullet shots. He's got two facial disfigurements. They shot at his cheekbone . . . and they busted the bridge to his nose all the way down to the jawbone. They had to reconstruct his face.

Later in the interview the respondent described how both of her brothers saved her and her homegirls from being caught in the middle of a major gang fight:

> Me and my girlfriends were walking up on Story Road, it was like a hot August night. We were on foot. . . . Anyway my brother Ernesto, he had seen me and he was yelling from across the street for me to turn around. My brother starts running across the street, and then I remember looking . . . and then my brother Carlos came from behind and he jumped and tackled us to the ground, [saying] "Stay down." Anyway, shit broke down quick, right. . . . Ernesto came up on the ground like a grunt, and he . . . crawls to the back of that building . . . "Don't look back. Don't look back." He said it like that. . . . So we did it. Four of us just stuck together like dogs. We were running through the streets, right, crawling like Ernesto said.

In other cases, brothers and homeboys were admired because they had come to the rescue when the respondents were drunk and could not fend for themselves, or when they were involved in one-sided fights. Some of the respect and admiration given to older male family members in the gang reflects the extent to which age and experience in the gang also provided status, even though the gangs generally had no explicit organizational structure.

Although almost half of the women (45%) claimed that everyone was equal, the protective nature of their relationships with their brothers and homeboys often resulted in too much protection and too many restrictions:

> Some of the older guys try to keep us from doing things, like with the younger guys. 'Cause the younger guys . . . they're like . . . who gives a shit . . . get high or whatever. But the older guys say "Hey, why you giving her that shit, you know, she's gonna get all fucked up." They . . . give us their little lectures and then we're like "Okay, yeah, now go away so I can do what I want to do."

The homeboys' "brotherly" protection, support, and respect were often interspersed with control, especially from older, more protective homeboys. Although none of the respondents acknowledged that the older homeboys were in charge, they regularly described circumstances in which the men told them what to do, ordered them around, or restricted them from participating in certain activities.

Relations with Homegirls

In choosing an existence on the street, homegirls found themselves under the control of homeboys and boyfriends. They used a variety of strategies to avoid being regulated by homeboys, such as disagreeing, agreeing but then ignoring the control, or (as in the following case) waiting until the homeboys were absent before engaging in a taboo activity: "[I]f I were to do any other drug besides weed, I wouldn't do it in front of the guys." They also formed alliances with each other as a way of countering this control and potential regulation. To a large extent, these relationships both reflected and extended the important relations in their families. As we discussed earlier, many of the respondents had cousins and sisters in their gangs. All of these relations, whether created by blood, family, or by friendship, were amalgamated into sisterhood. In this process the homegirls created a new family and a new kin group: fictive kin, or kin-in-gang.

Twenty-one of the women claimed that they got together with their homegirls every day. Another 19 said that they met on weekends. When queried about the amount of time they spent with their group, almost one-quarter of the women used the term *twenty-four/seven* (24 hours a day, seven days a week) to describe the extent and strength of their connection. The majority of the respondents said that some contact with their homegirls occurred regularly, and the activities were similar to those among the males: hanging out, going to the mall, walking around, talking, partying, and fighting.

In spite of their attempts to counter homeboys' controls by forming their own connections with their homegirls, the respondents found themselves under another system of control, one imposed and enforced by their own homegirls and implicitly by themselves. A key part of a homegirl's behavior on the street, especially in her relationships with other homegirls, was the notion of *respect*. The image of the tough, independent homegirl on the streets, portrayed increasingly in the media and in popular culture, is one to which many working-class Latinas can relate. In aspiring to live up to this image, these women sought an alternative to their role within the family. In the context of gang membership, the image provided homegirls with an opportunity to achieve respect, a feature they perceived to be relatively rare in their home lives. Forty-two of the 47 respondents had particular ideas about what constituted respect. Within the gang, respect and disrespect are ideological expectations and often are the pivotal base for gang relationships, both positive and negative (Bourgois 1996). Although all the respondents were familiar with the notion, and all knew that they aspired to gain respect, some had difficulty in specifying its components. This is not surprising because respect and the construction of respect within the gang were frequently contradictory and changing.

A number of elements constituted respect. More than one-quarter of the young women said that restraint, especially from excessive drug and alcohol use, was a feature of gaining and maintaining respect. Overindulgence was not respectable behavior. The women were directly responsible for the respect they received. Respect had to be earned and maintained; many women believed that this began with self-respect. As one homegirl remarked,

> Well, it's not how the homeboy is going to treat the homegirl. The homegirls gotta put in their two cents [if] . . . they wanna be respected. They got to respect themselves first. . . . You know, don't be fucked up . . . 'cause that's real bad and shit, 'cause you know girls have different feelings than what guys do. You know, guys can take it. But girls don't take shit like that, they become drug addicts, hoes, and shit, 'cause that brings them down . . . they got to learn how to respect themselves.

To ensure that homegirls maintained respect, the women used a number of different strategies to regulate and control behavior. Gossip, "talking shit," and exclusion were all tools for punishing other women who they felt had stepped out of line. More than one-third of the respondents discussed the power of "talking shit," which one respondent succinctly defined as "putting down my reputation."

Even though these young women spent time on the streets in the pursuit of respect, especially in their relations with their homegirls, they were often disappointed in these relations. As in their real families, where they had high expectations of their mothers and looked up to their sisters, grandmothers, and female cousins, so in their fictive families the respondents expected much more from their homegirls than from their homeboys and boyfriends. They held other homegirls to higher standards than men, and when important women in their lives failed to live up to their expectations, they reacted with surprise, a sense of betrayal, and sometimes even violence. One young woman was placed in juvenile detention for assault and battery on a homegirl who disrespected her by becoming involved with her man:

> It is like I found out she was a banging on my boyfriend. She was supposed to be my friend. And I was like, well, she is my friend. Why is she doing this? . . . And I would be talking to her

on the phone, and it is like . . . "What are you doing?" "Oh nothing." And his sister told me . . . "Yeah, the night you were talking on the phone she be kissing on him and everything." She told me everything. And after I found out, I was like to mad. . . . I just started beating on her. And she had like three kids. . . . And my friend put her kids in the other room so they wouldn't see anything. . . . And you know I just started beating on her.

CONCLUSION

In our analysis we have tried to illuminate the relationships and meaning of family among homegirls. In doing so, we have tried to dispel popular conceptions about the disintegration of contemporary inner-city families of color, and about the pushing of young minority youths onto the streets. Family relationships, particularly homegirls' ties to mothers, sisters, grandmothers, and other extended kin, are based on reciprocal and mutual forms of emotional and practical support. Not surprisingly, we have found, like Decker and Van Winkle (1996), that although homegirls make a heavy investment of time in gang friendships, related activities, and loyalty to the gang, almost all of the women named family members as the most important people or role models in their lives. Of the 33 young women who spoke about the most important people in their lives,[6] 13 mentioned their mothers along with other family members, 12 mentioned their sisters, nine spoke of their fathers, seven mentioned their brothers, and nine made reference to other relatives. Only 3 referred to either their homegirls or homeboys, and two mentioned their boyfriends.

When they spoke of their mothers and sisters, our respondents often stated that "they're the ones I can count on" and "those are the people who are there for me." As one respondent said forcefully, ". . . Those are the ones that are there for me right now, and if I didn't have them, I wouldn't have nothing." Even those who described the most turbulent and most contentious relations with their mothers mentioned (sometimes very surprisingly) moments of pride and respect. As we saw previously, as much as some of the respondents were critical toward their mothers and expressed these criticisms in harsh and derogatory ways, they felt it was legitimate to call on their mothers when they were in need. For the majority of the homegirls, she was there, she could be relied on when necessary, and she would remain "there" during this transitional period in their lives and beyond. As the young women began to mature, they increasingly valued and prized their relationships with their mothers for the quality of caring. This finding is consistent with feminist studies of girls (Taylor et al. 1995).

Many of these women had a fairly elaborate and strong extended-family structure. Many of the other women whom the homegirls admired were to be found in their immediate and extended families and among their homegirls. In their accounts, these two groups were frequently intertwined: Blood sisters, female cousins, and aunts doubled as homegirls

---

[6] Of the 14 respondents who did not answer this question, in five cases the answer was so inaudible that our transcribers were unable to decipher it; two respondents never completed the qualitative component of the interview; and the remaining seven were never asked this question specifically. The latter occurred either because the interviewer forgot to ask this question or, as is more likely, because the respondents gave such lengthy responses to the initial questions about their families and their lives that the interviewer decided not to ask the question.

and "gang sisters." Such loyalties and bonds call into question the standard and traditional notions about what constitutes family. In the homegirls' formation of their domestic and family units, we may be witnessing a pragmatic process encouraging survival in what may be less than ideal environments and situations.

In looking up to these women, homegirls respected independence over all other characteristics. This is not surprising, given their attempts to seek some life outside the family. In one case, a cousin who was also a homegirl was admired because she was successful at being independent and raising her child on her own despite the lack of support from her father, who had kicked her out of the family home. In another case, a homegirl admired her aunt, also an ex-homegirl, who had become an independent, famous, successful interior designer.

These young women may choose to look up to female family members because of their childhood dependence and reliance on the female support networks in their families. (In their accounts, the family is women-centered; see Yanagisako 1977.) Most of the important relationships in their lives are those with the women in their families and extended kin networks, whether their mothers, sisters, aunts, grandmothers, or cousins. These homegirls' relationships with their mothers were by the far the most significant.

Our respondents discussed these relationships with intensity, and far more intensely than their relations with their fathers. This suggests that they expected much more from their mothers, and consequently from other women, than from their fathers and other males. Although they discussed their relationships with male family members, these men played a much less prominent role in our respondents' accounts. The women expressed much less confidence in the men, who had not been consistently present in their lives. Only six respondents designated their fathers as among the most important people in their lives; six cited their boyfriends. Some observers may interpret these findings as an argument favoring the prevailing view that the dysfunctional family or absentee fathers are key factors in encouraging young women to join gangs. To the homegirls, however, as revealed in their narratives, the gaps are less relevant than the relations that operated.

Although these networks were modified during the respondents' lives, they continued to operate even within the gang. It appears that no sharp disjuncture occurred when these young women began to spend less time in the family home and more time on the streets with the gang. The strong family ties continued when the women became involved in gang activities. The absence of any disjuncture may be due to the abundance of family/gang ties in their lives. If gang ties already existed within the family, whether in the past (for mothers, fathers, uncles, and aunts) or in the present (for brothers, sisters, and cousins), then the movement to joining the gang, whether officially or unofficially, should be viewed as a natural progression for a teenager growing up in a working-class minority neighborhood.

This analysis calls into question current policy discussions about the demise of the "traditional family" and its negative effects on young people. Many of today's policy debates are based on idealistic notions about parenthood, particularly motherhood. As Taylor et al. point out, "the idealization of motherhood finds expression in a sentimental political rhetoric about mothers and children and families that goes hand in hand with a denigration of mothers and motherhood and an economic squeeze on families . . . mothers in general are held responsible for many of society's ills" (1995:73–74).

As we and other observers try to emphasize, many of today's popular assumptions about gangs, working-class youths, their families, and their home lives oversimplify and underestimate the salience and the positive dimensions of immediate and extended kinship. Among our respondents, for instance, the domestic unit cannot be equated with the family. Nor can working-class culture continue to be viewed as a male-dominated arena in which women are peripheral members. Women as heads of household and primary providers are a growing trend; many of the homegirls work, as do most of their mothers. Also, although the home may be considered to be a locus of negative forces and stresses for these women, it also has positive qualities and offers support. The same can be said of the streets; this may tell us a great deal about the ease with which these women navigate between these two environments. Moreover, their experiences highlight the extent to which the gang may be an extension of the family rather than a distinct or even an opposing influence. We should not underestimate the salience and flexibility of family relationships, particularly those involving women.

It may be, however, that the prominence of family relations in the accounts of these Latina gang members reflects the importance of family ties in women's lives more generally. Until we examine the importance of family, both for male gang members and for other ethnic groups, we cannot be sure how fully the findings discussed in this report are applicable to other gang members. In any case, the data from this research call into question the conservatism in public policy attacks on contemporary families, as well as assumptions about the dichotomous nature of the peer-versus-family debate. Certainly our findings highlight several new avenues for contemplating gang issues from a more contemporary perspective, in consideration of the complexity of the environments in which these young women are growing up.

QUESTIONS FOR UNDERSTANDING AND CRITICAL THINKING

1. What are the various ways in which young women are involved in gangs?
2. What types of relationships exist between girl gang members and their families? How might such relationships be different between male gang members and their families?
3. How can the family relationship act as both a risk and protective factor for gang involvement?
4. The participants in this research were Latinas. To what extent do you think the authors' findings would be similar and/or different from other racial/ethnic groups?

REFERENCES

APTER, T. 1993. "Altered Views: Fathers' Closeness to Teenage Daughters." Pp. 163–90 in *The Narrative Study of Lives,* vol. 1, edited by R. Josselson and A. Lieblich. London: Sage.

BEAN, F. D., L. RUSSELL, AND J.P. MARCUM. 1977. "Familism and Marital Satisfaction among Mexican Americans: The Effects of Family Size, Wife's Labor Force Participation, and Conjugal Power." *Journal of Marriage and the Family* 39:759–67.

BIERNACKI, P. AND D. WALDORF. 1981. "Snowball Sampling." *Sociological Methods Research* 10:141–63.

BOTTCHER, J. 1995. "Gender as Social Control: A Qualitative Study of Incarcerated Youths and Their Siblings." *Justice Quarterly* 12:33–57.

BOURGOIS, P. 1996. *In Search of Respect: Selling Crack in El Barrio.* Cambridge, UK: Cambridge University Press.

BOWKER, L.H. AND M.W. KLEIN. 1983. "The Etiology of Female Juvenile Delinquency and Gang Membership: A Test of Psychological and Social Structural Explanations." *Adolescence* 18:739–51.

BROTHERTON, D.C. 1996. " "Smartness," "Toughness," and "Autonomy": Drug Use in the Context of Gang Female Delinquency." *Journal of Drug Issues* 26(1):261–77.

BROWN, W.K. 1977. "Black Female Gangs in Philadelphia." *International Journal of Offender Therapy and Comparative Criminology* 21(3):221–28.

BURBANK, V.K. 1994. *Fighting Women: Anger and Aggression in Aboriginal Australia.* Berkeley: University of California Press.

CAMPBELL, A. 1984. *The Girls in the Gang.* New Brunswick: Rutgers University Press.

_____. 1986. "Self-Report of Fighting by Females." *British Journal of Criminology* 26:28–46.

_____. 1991. *The Girls in the Gang.* 2nd ed. Cambridge, MA: Basil Blackwell.

CAUCE, A.M., Y. HIRAGA, D. GRAVES, N. GONZALES, K.R. FINN, AND K. GROVE. 1996. "African American Mothers and Their Adolescent Daughters: Closeness, Conflict and Control." Pp. 100–16 in *Urban Girls: Resisting Stereotypes, Creating Identities,* edited by B. Leadbeater and N. Way. New York: New York University Press.

CHESNEY-LIND, M. 1993. "Girls, Gangs and Violence: Anatomy of a Backlash." *Humanity and Society* 17:321–44.

_____. 1997. *The Female Offender: Girls, Women, and Crime.* Thousand Oaks, CA: Sage.

CHODOROW, N. 1978. *The Reproduction of Mothering.* Berkeley: University of California Press.

CURRY, G.D., R.A. BALL, AND R.J. FOX. 1994. *Gang Crime and Law Enforcement Record Keeping.* Washington, DC: National Institute of Justice.

DECKER, S.H. AND B. VAN WINKLE. 1996. *Life in the Gang: Family Friends and Violence.* Cambridge, UK: Cambridge University Press.

DUNLAP, E. 1992. "Impact of Drugs on Family Life and Kin Networks in the Inner City African American Single Mother Household." Pp. 181–207 in *Drugs, Crime, and Social Isolation,* edited by A. Harrell and G. Peterson. Washington, DC: Urban Institute Press.

ESBENSEN, F.A. AND D. HUIZINGA. 1993. "Gangs, Drugs, and Delinquency in a Survey of Urban Youth." *Criminology* 31:565–89.

FAGAN, J. 1990. "Social Processes of Delinquency and Drug Use among Urban Gangs." Pp. 183–222 in *Gangs in America,* edited by C.R. Huff. London: Sage.

FEDERAL BUREAU OF INVESTIGATION (FBI). 1995. *Crime in the United States—1994.* Washington, DC: U.S. Department of Justice.

_____. 1996. *Crime in the United States—1995.* Washington, DC: U.S. Department of Justice.

FISHMAN, L. 1988. *The Vice Queens: An Ethnographic Study of Black Female Gang Behavior.* Burlington, VT: American Society of Criminology, University of Vermont.

FLEISHER, M.S. 1998. *Dead End Kids: Gang Girls and the Boys They Know.* Madison: University of Wisconsin Press.

HARRIS, M. 1988. *Cholas: Latino Girls and Gangs.* New York: AMS Press.

HERRNSTEIN, R.J. AND C. MURRAY. 1994. *The Bell Curve.* New York: Free Press.

HIRSCHI, T. 1969. *Causes of Delinquency.* Berkeley: University of California Press.

HOROWITZ, R. 1983. *Honor and the American Dream: Culture and Identity in a Chicano Community.* New Brunswick: Rutgers University Press.

JOE, K. 1991. "Milk Carton Madness: The Heart of the Missing Children's Crisis." Doctoral dissertation, University of California, Davis.

JOE, K. AND M. CHESNEY-LIND. 1995. "Just Every Mother's Angel: An Analysis of Gender and Ethnic Variations in Youth Gang Membership." *Gender and Society* 9:408–31.

JOE-LAIDLER, K. 1997. "The Life and Times of Asian American Women Drug Users: An Ethnographic Study." *Journal of Drug Issues* 26(1):199–218.

JOE-LAIDLER, K. AND G. HUNT. 1997. "Violence and Social Organization in Female Gangs." *Social Justice* 24(4):148–69.

KANDEL, D.B. 1996. "The Parental and Peer Contexts of Adolescent Deviance: An Algebra of Interpersonal Influences." *Journal of Drug Issues* 26:289–315.

KENNEDY, L.W. AND S. BARON. 1993. "Routine Activities and a Subculture of Violence: A Study of Violence on the Street." *Journal of Research in Crime and Delinquency* 30:88–112.

KLEIN, M.W. 1995. *The American Street Gang. Its Nature, Prevalence, and Control.* New York: Oxford University Press.

MARTIN, E. AND J. MARTIN. 1978. *The Black Extended Family.* Chicago: University of Chicago Press.

McROBBIE, A. AND J. GARBER. 1976. "Girls and Subcultures: An Exploration." Pp. 209–22 in *Resistance through Rituals,* edited by S. Hall and T. Jefferson. London: Hutchinson.

MESSERSCHMIDT, J.W. 1997. *Crime as Structured Action: Gender, Race, Class, and Crime in the Making.* Thousand Oaks, CA: Sage.

MOORE, J. 1990. "Gangs, Drugs, and Violence." Pp. 160–76 in *Drugs and Violence: Causes, Correlates, and Consequences,* edited by M.D.L. Rosa, E. Lambert, and B. Gropper. Washington, DC: U.S. Government Printing Office.

_____. 1991. *Going Down to the Barrio: Homeboys and Homegirls in Change.* Philadelphia: Temple University Press.

MOORE, J. AND J. HAGEDORN. 1996. "What Happens to Girls in the Gang?" Pp. 205–18 in *Gangs in America,* edited by C.R. Huff. Thousand Oaks, CA: Sage.

MURRAY, C. 1984. *Losing Ground: American Social Policy 1950–1980.* New York: Basic Books.

NAVA, M. 1984. "Youth Service Provision, Social Order and the Question of Girls." Pp. 1–30 in *Gender and Generation,* edited by A. McRobbie and M. Nava. London: Macmillan.

PADILLA, F.M. 1992. *The Gang as an American Enterprise.* New Brunswick, NJ: Rutgers University Press.

PLATT, A. 1969. *The Child Savers.* Chicago: University of Chicago Press.

QUICKER, J.C. 1983. *Homegirls: Characterizing Chicana Gangs.* Los Angeles: International University Press.

STACK, C. 1974. *All Our Kin: Strategies for Survival in a Black Community.* New York: Harper and Row.

SUTTON, J. 1988. *Stubborn Children: Controlling Delinquency in the U.S., 1640–1981.* Berkeley: University of California Press.

TAYLOR, J.M. 1996. "Cultural Stories: Latina and Portuguese Daughters and Mothers." Pp. 117–31 in *Urban Girls: Resisting Stereotypes, Creating Identities,* edited by B. Leadbeater and N. Way. New York: New York University Press.

TAYLOR, J.M., C. GILLIGAN, AND A. SULLIVAN. 1995. *Between Voice and Silence: Women, Girls, Race, and Relationship.* Cambridge, MA: Harvard University Press.

VIGIL, J.D. 1988. *Barrio Gangs: Street Life and Identity in Southern California.* Austin: University of Texas Press.

WAY, N. AND H. STAUBER. 1996. "Are 'Absent Fathers' Really Absent? Urban Adolescent Girls Speak Out about Their Fathers." Pp. 132–48 in *Urban Girls: Resisting Stereotypes, Creating Identities,* edited by B. Leadbeater and N. Way. New York: New York University Press.

WILSON, M. 1989. "Child Development in the Context of the Black Extended Family." *American Psychologist* 44:380–85.

YANAGISAKO, S.J. 1977. "Women-Centered Kin Networks in Urban Bilateral Kinship." *American Ethnologist* 4:207–26.

YOUNISS, J. AND J. SMOLLAR. 1985. *Adolescent Relations with Mothers, Fathers, and Friends.* Chicago: University of Chicago Press.

ZAVELLA, P. 1987. *Women's Work and Chicano Families: Cannery Workers of the Santa Clara Valley.* Ithaca: Cornell University Press.

5

Differences Between Gang Girls and Gang Boys

Results From a Multisite Survey

Finn-Aage Esbensen, Elizabeth Piper Deschenes, and L. Thomas Winfree Jr.

During the past decade, a growing body of literature examining gang girls and the involvement of girls in violence has appeared. In this article, we contribute to this developing literature by using data from a multisite evaluation to explore the extent to which gang girls are similar to or different from gang boys in terms of their attitudes, perceptions of their gangs, and their involvement in ganglike illegal activities. Findings indicate that gang girls are involved in a full array of illegal gang activities, although not as frequently as the gang boys. Whereas similarities exist in behavioral

AUTHORS' NOTE: This research is supported under award No. 94-IJ-CX-0058 from the National Institute of Justice, Office of Justice Programs, U.S. Department of Justice. Points of view in this document are those of the authors and do not necessarily represent the official position of the U.S. Department of Justice. An earlier version of this article was presented at the 1998 annual meeting of the Academy of Criminal Justice Sciences, Albuquerque, NM. We would like to thank our colleagues Drs. Fran Bernat, Michelle Hughes Miller, Wayne Osgood, Chris Sellers, Ron Taylor, and Ron Vogel for their contributions to this research enterprise. We wish to acknowledge the diligent efforts of the following research assistants: Karen Arboit and Lesley Harris from California State University at Long Beach; Danette Sandoval Monnet and Dana Lynskey from New Mexico State University; Lesley Brandt, T. J. Taylor, Jennifer West, and Annette Miller from the University of Nebraska at Omaha; and Leanne Jacobsen from Temple University. Thanks also are extended to Jody Miller and the anonymous reviewers who provided valuable suggestions.

YOUTH & SOCIETY, Vol. 31 No. 1, September 1999 27-53 © 1999 Sage Publications, Inc.
Esbensen, F. A., Deschenes, E. P., and Winfree, L. T. Differences between gang girls and gang boys: results from a multisite survey. *Youth and Society,* 31 (1999), pp. 27–53. Reprinted by permission of Sage Publications, Inc.

activities and in reasons for joining gangs, gang girls report greater social isolation from family and friends than do gang boys. The gang girls also report lower levels of self-esteem than do the boys. These gender differences are discussed in terms of differential developmental trajectories for boys and girls.

The past 100 years have produced volumes of research describing gangs, gang members, and gang activity. Although the U.S. violent crime rate has declined during each of the past 5 years, some criminologists are concerned by the fact that the juvenile violent crime rate has not mirrored this general trend (Fox, 1996; Sickmund, Snyder, & Poe-Yamagata, 1997). Increased access to firearms (Sheley & Wright, 1995) and the resurgence of youth gangs in American society have been hailed as explanations for the increase in juvenile violence (Spergel, 1995).

Until recently, the role of girls in youth violence largely was ignored. Violence and gang membership were viewed primarily as male-dominated phenomena. During the past decade, however, a growing body of literature examining gang girls and the involvement of girls in violence has appeared (e.g., Campbell, 1991; Chesney-Lind, 1997; Curry, 1998; Deschenes & Esbensen, 1999b; Esbensen & Deschenes, 1998; Fleisher, 1998; Joe & Chesney-Lind, 1995; Miller, 1998a, 1998b; Moore, 1991). In this article, we contribute to this developing literature by using data from a multisite evaluation to explore the extent to which gang girls are similar to or different from gang boys in terms of their attitudes, perceptions of their gangs, and their involvement in ganglike illegal activities. Specifically, we address the following four questions:

1. What is the prevalence of girls in gangs in a general sample of adolescents?
2. How similar to gang boys are gang girls in terms of their illegal activity?
3. Are there organizational or structural differences in the gangs described by gang boys and gang girls?
4. Do gang girls report lower levels of self-esteem and higher levels of social isolation than do gang boys?

GENDER AND GANG MEMBERSHIP

Historically, girl gang members either have been overlooked or stereotyped as "tomboys" or "sex objects." During the past decade, a growing number of researchers have concentrated their efforts on understanding the nature and extent of female delinquency and gang membership (e.g., Bjerregard & Smith, 1993; Chesney-Lind & Shelden, 1992; Chesney-Lind, Shelden, & Joe, 1996; Esbensen & Winfree, 1998; Triplett & Meyers, 1995). Estimates concerning the prevalence of females in gangs, however, vary greatly, as do descriptions of their involvement in gang activities (e.g., Cohen, Williams, Bekelman, & Crosse, 1995; Curry, Ball, & Fox, 1994; Esbensen & Huizinga, 1993; Goldstein & Glick, 1994; Huff, 1997; Klein & Crawford, 1995). Most estimates place the figure in the single digits (e.g., Curry et al., 1994; Goldstein & Glick, 1994; Huff, 1997)[1] and thus perpetuate the stereotype of girls being auxiliary members and relegated to gender-specific crimes (i.e., seducing males, concealing weapons, and instigating fights between rival male gangs). For example, a study of 61 large and small police departments yielded a total of 9,092 female gang members, representing less than 4% of the total (Curry et al., 1994). Similarly,

Goldstein and Glick (1994) state that "males continue to outnumber female gang members at a ratio of approximately 20 to 1" (p. 9).

Contrary to these single-digit estimates of girls in gangs, results of recent self-report surveys place the figure well above 20%. Bjerregard and Smith (1993) indicate that 22% of girls in their high-risk sample (i.e., socially disorganized neighborhoods) were gang members. These 60 girls accounted for 31% of the self-reported gang members in that survey. Cohen and her colleagues (1995) interviewed approximately 520 youth (10 to 18 years of age) as part of their evaluation of 13 drug- and gang-prevention projects and found that girls accounted for approximately 21% of self-proclaimed gang members. Esbensen and Huizinga (1993) report girls comprising 20% to 46% of the gang members during 4 years of interviews with high-risk youth included in the Denver Youth Survey. When this longitudinal sample was aged 11 to 15 years, 46% of the gang members were female. By the time the sample had reached the age range of 13 to 19 years, girls accounted for only 20% of the gang members. These findings provide some evidence for the belief that girls age-in and age-out of gangs earlier than do boys. As suggested by some authors, different developmental trajectories may well be operative for these boys and girls (e.g., Brown & Gilligan, 1992; Fleisher, 1998; Lees, 1993; Matsueda & Heimer, 1997; Thorne, 1993).

Two methodological issues contribute to the emergence of these two rather disparate estimates of the prevalence of girls in gangs: (a) the research methodology used to produce the data and (b) the age of the sample members studied. The case study method has been the primary tool used by researchers to study gangs (e.g., Asbury, 1927; Campbell, 1991; Decker & Van Winkle, 1996; Hagedorn, 1988, 1994; Moore, 1978; Puffer, 1912; Spergel, 1966; Thrasher, 1927; Vigil, 1988). This observational approach provides a wealth of information about specific gangs and their members. Its goal has been description, not generalization, and thus these researchers have not attempted to discuss the prevalence of males and females in gangs.

More recently, social scientists have turned to two types of quantitative data. One approach uses law enforcement records to describe gang offenses and gang members (e.g., Curry, Ball, & Decker, 1996; Curry et al., 1994; Maxson & Klein, 1990; Spergel, 1990). This body of research reinforces the stereotypical picture of gang members being disproportionately male and from ethnic or racial minorities, an image often echoed by the popular press. Given enforcement strategies that tend to target individuals with these characteristics, in conjunction with a tendency to discredit the notion that girls possibly can be gang members, this finding is not surprising. An example of differential enforcement practices affecting perceptions of gangs is found in the Los Angeles Sheriff Department's operating manual, which states that youths are classified as gang members when they admit to gang membership. The same manual, however, questions the validity of female self-nomination and encourages officers to disregard females' claims to gang membership. "These same females will say they are members of the local Crip gang; however, evidence has shown that this is not so" (Operation Safe Streets, 1995, p. 40).

A second quantitative approach employs survey methods to study gang behavior (e.g., Esbensen & Huizinga, 1993; Esbensen, Huizinga, & Weiher, 1993; Fagan, 1989; Thornberry, Krohn, Lizotte, & Chard-Wierschem, 1993; Winfree, Backstrom, & Mays, 1994). These surveys tend to include larger, more general samples of youth, allowing comparisons to be made between gang and nongang youth. With larger samples, the researchers also have been able to examine gang characteristics among a variety of gangs. In summary, case studies provide a depth of information but little breadth in coverage, that is, information about a limited number of gangs or their members. Surveys, on the other hand, provide a breadth of information about a larger number of gangs and their members but little depth. It becomes crucial for results from these divergent methods to be compared and contrasted.

A second methodological issue involves sampling design. Despite recent exceptions (e.g., Fleisher, 1998; Miller, 1998a), field research historically has tended to be conducted by male researchers on male individuals, thereby failing to identify and describe female participants, other than through the eyes of male gang members (Campbell, 1991). This shortcoming has posed problems not only in terms of identifying gang girls but also in describing the role of girls in gangs. Older adolescents and young adults frequently serve as objects of field studies. Hagedorn (1988), for example, studied the "top dogs" in the formation of Milwaukee gangs. Campbell (1991) reports on case studies of three gang girls, one of whom did not join the gang until her late 20s. Vigil's (1988) gang boys were 16 to 23 years of age. These older samples fail to identify gang girls captured in general surveys of younger samples. Decker and Van Winkle (1996) include a much wider age range of gang members in their St. Louis study (from 13 to 29 years, with a mean of 16.9 years). Their snowball approach, however, produced only seven female gang members, compared with 92 males. And these gang girls "were often recruited in groups of two or through their boyfriends" (p. 57). Field studies, through a combination of relying on older respondents and reliance on snowball sampling techniques, we suspect, have systematically excluded younger girls from field studies.[2]

Surveys of gang members generally have concentrated on high-school-aged samples, considerably younger than field studies. The Rochester Youth Survey (Bjerregard & Smith, 1993; Thornberry et al., 1993) and the Denver Youth Survey (Esbensen & Huizinga, 1993; Esbensen et al., 1993) included adolescents in their early and middle teens. This discrepancy in age of the samples may be a more salient factor than is the data collection method in accounting for the very disparate findings reported by field studies and general surveys. There is reason to believe that girls age-in and age-out of gangs at earlier ages than do boys. Esbensen and Huizinga (1993), for instance, reported a lower percentage of girl gang members as the sample aged. Additional evidence suggesting that girls mature out of gangs at an earlier age than do males is found in the works of Fishman (1995), Harris (1994), Moore and Hagedorn (1996), and Swart (1995). According to Harris (1994), girls are most active in gangs between 13 and 16 years of age. She suggests that "by 17 or 18, interests and activities of individual members are directed toward the larger community rather than toward the gang, and girls begin to leave the active gang milieu" (p. 300). Thus, gang samples consisting of older adolescents or gang members in their 20s are apt to produce a substantially different picture than studies focusing on middle and high-school-aged youth.

Adding to the confusion is the absence of a common definition of what constitutes a gang or being a gang member. Field researchers generally rely on self-identification corroborated through hours, days, and even years of observation. Law enforcement and survey researchers rely on a range of factors that may well shape the nature of the gang problem. Maxson and Klein's (1990) study highlights the importance of definition (i.e., applying the Chicago Police Department definition of gang affiliation to Los Angeles resulted in a 50% reduction in classifications of gang-related homicides). Some survey researchers have relied on responses to a single item (Bjerregard & Smith, 1993); others have invoked additional criteria, including the requisite that the gang be involved in delinquent activity (Esbensen & Huizinga, 1993; Esbensen et al., 1993) and have some organizational characteristics (Winfree, Backstrom et al., 1994; Winfree, Mays, & Vigil-Backstrom, 1994).

Clearly, such disparate criteria may well affect study results. With these methodological and definitional issues in mind, we now turn to a review of recent research examining the role of girls in gangs.

Gang Membership and Female Delinquency

Are girls as delinquent as boys, especially within the gang context? The prevailing impression is that girls account for very little of the violent crime in society, and this also applies to gang crime. Law enforcement data continue to report female delinquency as considerably less prevalent and less violent than male delinquency. In 1995, for example, girls under 18 years of age accounted for only 14.6% of juvenile arrests for violent crimes and 26% of juvenile property crime arrests (Department of Justice, 1996, p. 217).

Recent results from the Denver Youth Survey reveal that, from a policy perspective, even though they account for only a small percentage of all active offenders, girl gang members account for more violent crimes than do nongang boys (Huizinga, 1997). The stereotype of the girl as primarily a sex object, with limited participation in the delinquent activity of the gang, apparently requires reexamination. Rosenbaum's (1991) study of 70 female gang members who were wards of the California Youth Authority is instructive in this regard. Not one of the females mentioned sex as playing a role in her gang involvement. Huff (1997), however, reported that several of the girls in his study indicated that they were forced to engage in sexual activity with male gang members. Adding clarity to these opposing positions, Miller (1998a) indicates that it is the girl's status within the gang that determines if she will be sexually victimized by gang boys. Thus, it may be that this stereotype of gang girls as sex objects is more an artifact of the data collection technique and of the age of the youth sampled than it is of the actual distribution of the behavior in the targeted population. Furthermore, it may be that the traditional focus on girls and their sexual activity has distracted attention from their "other" delinquent activity.

Recent anecdotal observations in the mass media have suggested that females have become more violent and crime oriented in the recent past. Evidence to support such increases, however, is largely missing (see the critique of the media construction of girl gangs by Chesney-Lind et al., 1996). In an attempt to address this issue of a "new violent female offender," Huizinga and Esbensen (1991) compared self-report data from the 1978 National Youth Survey with 1989 data from the Denver Youth Survey. They did not find any evidence of an increase in female violent offending. Moreover, in his comprehensive review of the literature, Spergel (1995) concludes that "there is no clear evidence that female gang members are increasingly involved in serious gang violence" (p. 58). Likewise, Chesney-Lind and colleagues (1996) note that the "rise in girls' arrests more or less parallels increases in arrests of male youth" (p. 189).

Gang Members: Reasons for Joining the Gang

Who joins gangs, and are gang members different from other similarly situated adolescents? And, are girls who join gangs different from boys who join? These questions are of significant theoretical and practical interest and numerous other researchers have addressed one or more of these questions (e.g., Bjerregard & Smith, 1993; Esbensen et al., 1993; Giordano, 1978; Harris, 1988; Joe & Chesney-Lind, 1995; Winfree, Backstrom et al., 1994;

Winfree, Mays et al., 1994). In a recent publication, we compared demographic and behavioral characteristics of gang and nongang youth (Esbensen & Winfree, 1998). In this article we turn our attention to why adolescents join gangs.

Prior research has indicated that youth join gangs for a multitude of reasons, ranging from protection against victimization to obtaining emotional fulfillment (i.e., a sense of belonging). Do boys and girls differ in the affective need that is met by group membership? The findings reported by, among others, Campbell (1991), Chesney-Lind, Shelden, and Joe (1996), Fleisher (1998), and Harris (1988), indicate that girls join gangs because they are seeking a "familial" peer group. In his account of the Fremont Hustlers, a Kansas City gang, Fleisher (1998) provides vivid descriptions of the lives of gang girls and boys. His 21 months of observations confirmed that the girls tended to seek emotionally fulfilling relationships within the gang, whereas the boys were more drawn to the "action" associated with gang affiliation. To what extent, however, are the differences in gang girls and gang boys an artifact of the gang, rather than a more general gender difference? Fleisher (1998) addresses this issue in an endnote:

> If we don't understand the full range of cross-cultural adolescent female behavior, how are we to pinpoint those behaviors which are unique deviant responses to a range of family and environmental stimuli? In short, we don't understand how much of what we are measuring in female (and male) delinquent and gang behavior is within the range of predictable adolescent behavior in complex urban settings. (p. 257)

Developmental theorists have documented gender differences in children's play (Thorne, 1993), in the organization of peer groups (Thorne & Luria, 1986), and in development of sexual identities (Lees, 1993). Given these differences between boys and girls in general, should we not expect to find differences between gang girls and gang boys?

Research Questions

From this brief review, we can conclude that disagreement permeates the gang literature. There is a lack of consensus concerning not only the extent of female gang participation, but also the nature of that participation and the reasons for why youth join gangs. We organized our analyses around the following four questions:

1. What is the prevalence of girls in gangs in a general sample of adolescents?
2. How similar to gang boys are gang girls in terms of their illegal activity?
3. Are there organizational or structural differences in the gangs described by gang boys and gang girls?
4. Do gang girls report lower levels of self-esteem and higher levels of social isolation than do gang boys?

RESEARCH DESIGN

This investigation of gang girls and gang boys is part of a larger study, the National Evaluation of the Gang Resistance Education and Training (G.R.E.A.T.) program. Site selection and sampling procedures were dictated by that evaluation's design. Because the G.R.E.A.T. program is a seventh-grade curriculum, eighth-grade students were surveyed to allow for a

1-year follow-up and at the same time guarantee that none of the sample was currently enrolled in the program. This multisite, multistate cross-sectional survey was completed during the spring of 1995. Site selection was limited to cities in which the G.R.E.A.T. program
had been delivered in school year 1993–1994 (when the targeted students were seventh
graders).[3]

Site Selection

Records provided by the Bureau of Alcohol, Tobacco, and Firearms, the federal agency
with oversight of the G.R.E.A.T. program, were used to identify prospective sites meeting
two criteria. First, only those agencies with two or more officers trained prior to January
1994 to teach G.R.E.A.T. were considered eligible. Second, to enhance the geographic and
demographic diversity of the sample, some potential cities were excluded from consideration.[4] The 11 sites selected for this phase of the evaluation (Las Cruces, NM; Omaha, NE;
Phoenix, AZ; Philadelphia, PA; Kansas City, MO; Milwaukee, WI; Orlando, FL; Will
County, IL; Providence, RI; Pocatello, ID; and Torrance, CA) provide a diverse sample.

Within the selected sites, schools that offered G.R.E.A.T. during the previous 2 years
were selected and questionnaires were administered in group settings to all eighth graders
in attendance on the specified day. Attendance rates varied from a low of 75% at one Kansas
City middle school to a high of 93% at several schools in Will County and Pocatello. This
resulted in a final sample of 5,935 eighth-grade students representing 315 classrooms in
42 different schools.[5]

This public-school-based sample has the standard limitations associated with school-
based surveys (i.e., exclusion of private school students, exclusion of truants, sick, and/or
tardy students, and the potential underrepresentation of high-risk youth). With this caveat in
mind, the current sample is composed of all eighth-grade students in attendance on the days
questionnaires were administered in these 11 jurisdictions. The sample includes primarily 13-
to 15-year-old students attending public schools in a cross-section of communities within the
continental United States. This is not a random sample and generalizations cannot be made
to the adolescent population as a whole. However, students from these 11 jurisdictions do represent the following types of communities: large urban areas with a majority of students belonging to a racial or ethnic minority (Philadelphia, Phoenix, Milwaukee, and Kansas City);
medium-sized cities (population ranges between 100,000 and 500,000) with considerable
racial and/or ethnic heterogeneity (Providence and Orlando) and medium-sized cities with a
majority of White students but a substantial minority enrollment (Omaha and Torrance); a
small city (less than 100,000 inhabitants) with an ethnically diverse student population (Las
Cruces) and a small racially homogeneous (i.e., White) city (Pocatello); and a rural community in which more than 80% of the student population is White (Will County). This diversity
in locations and in sample characteristics allows for exploration of the distribution of gang
affiliation and delinquent activity in an age group generally excluded from "gang research."

Measures

The student questionnaire consisted of demographic, attitudinal, and behavioral measures.
We report first on the demographic composition of the sample (gender, age, race or ethnicity, and family composition) and then focus on attitudes and behaviors associated with gang

membership. Even though there is a lack of consensus about what constitutes gang membership, and numerous definitional issues arise, we chose to use a self-nomination procedure.[6] This self-definition method has become the standard not only in survey research but is widely accepted in law enforcement practice. In the current research, two filter questions introduce the gang-specific section of the questionnaire: "Have you ever been a gang member?" and "Are you now in a gang?" Given the current sample, with almost all the respondents under the age of 15, even affirmative responses to the first question followed by a negative response to the second may still indicate a recent gang affiliation. In an attempt to limit our sample of gang members to "delinquent gangs," we employed a restrictive definition of gang status. Thus, only those youth who reported ever having been in a gang and who reported that their gangs engaged in at least one type of delinquent behavior (fighting other gangs, stealing cars, stealing in general, or robbing people) were classified as gang members.

This large sample provides us the opportunity to examine the extent to which gang girls are similar to gang boys. Inasmuch as gang membership remains a relatively rare phenomenon, most general surveys do not contain adequate numbers of gang members to make such comparisons. Thus, our emphasis here is to provide a descriptive account of gang girls and gang boys drawn from a general survey of middle school students. With respect to behavioral comparisons, we examine two separate measures of self-reported delinquency and victimization: "ever" prevalence (i.e., have you ever . . .) and "annual" frequency[7] (i.e., how many times in the past 12 months have you . . .). We then turn our attention to an examination of attitudes about gangs and whether gender differences exist.

The self-identified gang members were asked to describe their gang in terms of structural and organizational components, membership, and behavioral characteristics. In addition, respondents indicated how they felt being gang members, why they joined, and where they fit into the gang. To explore the extent to which gang members are socially isolated or suffer from low self-esteem, we examine responses to a six-item self-esteem scale and responses to three questions tapping social isolation.[8]

RESULTS

The focus of this investigation is on differences between gang girls and gang boys. To put the results in perspective, we first provide a description of the demographic composition of the entire sample. Approximately half of the sample is female (52%) and most of the respondents live in intact homes (62%), that is, they indicated that a mother and father (including stepparents) were present in the home. The sample is ethnically diverse, with a sizable number of White (40%), African American (27%), and Hispanic (19%) respondents. As would be expected with an eighth-grade sample, most of the respondents were between 13 and 15 years of age, with 60% being 14 years old. Comparisons of gender differences within the total sample revealed some slight differences: the girls are somewhat younger than the boys and are less likely to live in intact homes.

Table 5–1 reveals, among other things, that there are considerably more girls in gangs than is commonly assumed or than official reports suggest. Of the 623 gang members, representing 10.6% of the sample, 237 are female and 380 are male. Six of the gang members failed to provide information about their sex. Consistent with much of the emerging gang research, but contrary to prevailing stereotypes that gangs are predominantly male, these 237 girls represent 38% of the gang members in this eighth-grade sample. Even though this figure

TABLE 5–1 Demographic Characteristics (in percentages) of Gang Youth by Gender

	Total Sample		Gang Youth Only	
	Male	Female	Male	Female
Total n	2,808	3,043	380	237
Total percentage	48	52	62	38
Race				
White	42[1]	40	26	22
	49[2]	51	65	35
African American	26	27	33	27
	48	52	66	34
Hispanic	19	18	23	28
	49	51	56	44
Asian	6	6	4	5
	45	55	56	44
Other	7	9	14	17
	42	58	55	45
Family Structure**				
Single parent	30	32	40	41
	47	53	61	39
Intact	64	60	50	43
	50	50	65	35
Other	6	8	11	16
	40	60	51	49
Age**				
13 and younger	26	32	14	21
	42	58	50	50
14 years	60	60	59	63
	48	52	60	40
15 and older	14	7	27	16
	63	37	73	27

[1] Column percent.

[2] Row percent.

** $p < .01$ for total sample and for gang youth.

still indicates that females are proportionately underrepresented among gang members, it is to a far lesser extent than is commonly assumed when older samples are studied.

Contrary to popular perception, results from this survey indicate a greater level of gang participation by White youth than most recent research has suggested: 25% of the gang members are White. Although White youth in this sample are less likely to be involved in gangs than are African American and Hispanic youth, it is not to the extent that prior research has suggested.

Consistent with earlier assessments of the demographic characteristics of gangs, this sample reveals that younger youth are underrepresented in gangs and gang members are more likely to live with a single parent. Within this limited age sample, the youth who were 13 years and younger account for only 17% of gang members whereas they represent 29% of the total sample. At the other extreme, 23% of gang members are 15 years old or older whereas only 10% of the total sample is this old. Furthermore, among the gang members, 27% of the males are 15 years old compared to 16% of the females. Although the girls in the entire sample are younger than the boys, this age difference among gang members is more pronounced than in the total sample. This finding is consistent with previous research suggesting that females age-out of gangs at younger ages than do males.

Ethnographic researchers have described family disorganization and dissolution as factors associated with gang involvement. In this sample, we find that gang members are less likely than nongang members to live in intact homes. Whereas the majority of youth in our sample report living in intact homes, only half of the gang boys and 43% of the gang girls report living with both parents. In additional analyses not reported in the tables, we controlled for respondent race. We found no differences in family living status for African American (half of gang and nongang youth resided in single-parent families) or Asian (three fourths of these youth reported living with both parents) gang and nongang youth. For White, Hispanic, and other youth, however, gang members were more likely than nongang youth to live in single-parent homes.

Illegal Activities

Elsewhere we have reported on the rates of male and female involvement in delinquent activity, noting that gang girls are considerably more delinquent than nongang boys (Esbensen & Winfree, 1998). In fact, gang girls are very similar to gang boys in the types of illegal acts they commit. They do differ, however, in the volume of crime committed: Girl gang members commit fewer crimes than do gang boys. Of concern in this analysis is the extent to which gang girls are involved in illegal activities commonly attributed to gang members. Recall that some commentators maintain that gang girls are primarily involved in auxiliary behaviors (i.e., sexual promiscuity) and do not engage in "normal" gang crime. Table 5–2 reports the ever prevalence and annual frequency rates for boys and girls who reported being in a gang. Although a smaller percentage of the gang girls report engaging in these illegal acts and at lower frequencies, it is clear that these girls are more than mere appendages to the gang boys. They are involved in assaults, robberies, gang fights, and drug sales at substantial rates.

The gang boys are more delinquent than the girls, but the girls are far from innocent bystanders. Fewer gang girls admit to ever committing the offenses listed in Table 5–2 than do the gang boys, yet 39% of the girls report attacking someone with a weapon, 21% indicate

TABLE 5–2   Self-Reported Delinquency and Victimization of Gang Members: Ever
Prevalence and Annual Frequency

	Males		Females		
	Ever Prevalence[a]	Annual Frequency[b]	Ever Prevalence[a]	Annual Frequency[b]	Ratio of Male to Female Offending
SRD Item					
Carried hidden weapon[cd]	83%	17.67	65%	7.35	2.4:1
Illegally spray painted[cd]	63%	9.39	46%	3.62	2.6:1
Hit someone to hurt[d]	84%	12.05	81%	8.23	1.5:1
Attacked someone[cd]	57%	5.12	39%	2.48	2.1:1
Robbed someone[cd]	34%	3.53	17%	1.29	2.7:1
Been in a gang fight	85%	9.57	78%	7.67	1.2:1
Shot at someone[c]	34%	2.38	21%	1.06	2.2:1
Sold marijuana	63%	10.76	53%	6.57	1.6:1
Sold other drugs	36%	6.15	26%	2.99	2.1:1
Victimization item					
Been hit[c]	71%	5.88	64%	2.65	2.2:1
Been robbed[cd]	33%	2.09	10%	0.41	5.1:1
Been attacked[cd]	50%	2.94	27%	0.83	3.5:1

NOTE: SRD = self-reported delinquency.
[a] Respondents were asked: "Have you ever . . . ?"
[b] Respondents were asked: "How many times in the past 12 months have you . . . ?" Responses were truncated at 52 to reduce the effect of extreme scores.
[c] $p < .01$, based on chi-square test for ever prevalence.
[d] $p < .01$, based on t-test for annual frequency.

that they have shot at someone because they were told to by someone else, 78% have been involved in gang fights, and 65% have carried hidden weapons. And it is not that they have engaged in these behaviors only once. The gang girls attacked someone an average of 2.48 times in the previous 12 months, participated in more than seven gang fights each, and hit someone with the intention of hurting him or her an average of more than eight times. On the whole, the girls report committing about half as many crimes as do the boys, with ratios ranging from a low of 1.2 for involvement in gang fights to a high of 2.7 for robbery.

The gang girls are less likely than the gang boys to be victims of crime. Whereas the majority of gang girls have been hit in the past, only 10% have ever been robbed and 27%

TABLE 5–3   Characteristics of the Gang

	Males (n = 380)		Females (n = 237)		Total (N = 617)	
	n	%	n	%	n	%
Can join before age 13	308	81	199	84	507	82
Initiation rites	274	72	178	75	452	73
Established leaders[*]	277	73	200	84	477	77
Regular meetings	207	54	134	57	341	55
Specific rules[*]	267	70	191	81	458	74
Specific roles[*]	237	62	173	73	410	66
Roles for each age group	147	39	82	35	229	37
Symbols or colors	340	89	219	92	559	91
Specific roles for girls	200	53	122	51	322	52
Helps out in community	90	24	53	22	143	23
Fights other gangs	349	92	225	95	574	93
Provides protection	349	92	221	93	570	92
Steals things	271	71	172	73	443	72
Robs other people	232	61	127	54	359	58
Steals cars	260	68	153	65	413	67
Sells marijuana	299	79	194	82	493	80
Sells other illegal drugs	237	62	146	62	383	62
Damages or destroys property	294	77	180	76	474	77

[*]$p < .05.$

have been attacked by someone trying to seriously hurt them. The boys report substantially higher levels of victimization in the past, with one third having been robbed and half of them having been attacked. Their annual victimization rates are two to five times greater than those of the girls.

Characteristics of Gangs

Gang members were asked a series of questions about their gangs. Interestingly, as summarized in Table 5–3, there were virtually no differences between the girls' and boys' descriptions of their gangs. With respect to the organizational structure of the gangs, the gang girls indicated a slightly greater level of organization than did the boys; the girls were more likely to report that their gang had established leaders, specific rules, and role specialization. With the exception of these differences, the gang girls and gang boys seemed to describe very similar gangs, whether describing gang organization or gang activities. Two thirds or more of the gang members attributed the following characteristics to their gangs: being able to join prior to age 13; having initiation rites and established leaders; having specific rules and some degree of role specialization; having symbols or colors; providing protection for each other; and engaging in illegal activities, including fighting other gangs, stealing, selling marijuana and other drugs, and destroying property.

With regard to the gender composition of the gangs, only 10 (4.2%) girls stated that their gang was composed of girls only, whereas 39 (10.3%) of the gang boys indicated their gangs were unisex (data not shown). The remaining 536 (92%) gang youth indicated that girls and boys belonged to their gangs. When questioned about their location in the gang, the boys and girls were equally likely to state that they were core members. Respondents were asked to think of their gang as a circle, with a 1 being in the middle and a 5 being on the outside. Forty-five percent of boys and girls circled a 1 or a 2, our definition of core membership.

Reasons for Joining and Attitudes about the Gang

The gang youth also were asked to indicate why they joined their gang. They were presented a list of eight common reasons for joining gangs and asked to circle those reasons that contributed to their joining. Table 5–4 provides a summary of these results. With the exception of boys being more likely to join to get money, there were no gender differences. Approximately half of all the gang members joined for one of the following reasons: for fun, for protection, to get respect, to get money, or because a friend was in the gang. Only 6% or 7% of either gender indicated that they had been forced to join their gang.

Gang members were asked a series of seven questions tapping their gang attitudes. Response categories for the attitudinal items ranged from *strongly disagree* (1) to *strongly agree* (5) such that the higher the score, the more they agreed with the statement. Table 5–5 lists these questions and the mean score for gang girls and gang boys. As can be seen, there is considerable similarity between males and females, although the girls express an overall

TABLE 5–4   Reasons for Joining the Gang by Gender

	Males (n = 380)		Females (n = 237)		Total (N = 617)	
	n	%	n	%	n	%
For fun	165	43	122	51	289	47
For protection	184	48	128	54	312	51
A friend was in the gang	157	41	104	46	266	43
A brother or sister was in the gang	100	26	75	32	175	28
Forced to join	27	7	15	6	42	7
To get respect	180	47	109	44	284	46
For money[*]	180	47	91	38	271	44
To fit in better	98	26	69	29	167	27

[*]$p < .05.$

TABLE 5–5   *t*-Test Comparisons of Gang Attachment by Gender

	Male	Female
Gang makes me feel important.*	3.33	3.54
	(1.24)	(1.06)
Gang members provide support and loyalty.	3.81	3.96
	(1.27)	(1.12)
Being in a gang makes me feel respected.	3.51	3.66
	(1.23)	(1.08)
Being a gang member makes me feel useful.	3.36	3.47
	(1.25)	(1.09)
Being a gang member makes me feel that I belong somewhere.*	3.25	3.53
	(1.29)	(1.16)
I really enjoy being a member of my gang.	3.59	3.67
	(1.34)	(1.13)
My gang is like a family to me.*	3.51	3.87
	(1.38)	(1.16)

NOTE: Standard deviations appear in parentheses.
*$p < .05$.

higher level of attachment to the gang. It is worth noting that on these five-point Likert items, the average score of approximately 3.5 indicates a relatively modest level of attachment to the gang.

The three questions that tap an emotional or affective aspect of gang membership were answered more favorably by girls than boys. That is, the girls agreed more strongly with the following three statements than did the boys: "My gang is like a family to me," "Being a gang member makes me feel like I really belong somewhere," and "Being in a gang makes me feel important." These gender differences do suggest that there is a qualitative difference between the gang girls and gang boys. When it comes to being attached to gangs, girls indicate a greater affective bond than do boys. Of interest, however, is the extent to which this difference in attachment represents a more general gender difference as opposed to a gang girl/gang boy difference. We will return to this issue in the discussion section.

To further explore these differences and to address the impression that gang girls are more socially isolated than gang boys, responses to nine questions measuring self-esteem and social isolation were examined. Table 5–6 provides a summary of the comparison of responses by gang boys and gang girls. The larger the mean response to these questions, the greater is the perception of social isolation. The gang youth generally disagree with statements that they are lonely in school, when with their friends, or with their families. That is, as a group, the gang members do not indicate that they are isolated from their family or friends. The gang girls, however, express lower levels of disagreement with the statements than do the gang boys. This finding configures well with the previous finding about the affective nature of gang

TABLE 5–6   *t*-Test Comparisons of Social Isolation and Self-Esteem by Gender

	Male	Female
Social isolation		
Even though there are lots of students around, I often feel lonely at school.	2.17	2.56
	(1.20)	(1.35)
Sometimes I feel lonely when I'm with my friends.	1.97	2.39
	(1.10)	(1.20)
Sometimes I feel lonely when I'm with my family.	2.59	3.33
	(1.39)	(1.31)
Self-esteem		
I am a useful person to have around.	3.74	3.63
	(1.14)	(1.17)
I feel that I am a person of worth, at least as much as others.	3.85	3.72
	(1.20)	(1.18)
As a person, I do a good job these days.[*]	3.75	2.98
	(1.16)	(1.18)
I am able to do things as well as most other people.[*]	4.09	3.84
	(1.09)	(1.12)
I feel good about myself.[*]	4.09	3.55
	(1.22)	(1.51)
When I do a job, I do it well.[*]	3.94	3.62
	(1.19)	(1.18)

Note: Standard deviations appear in parentheses.
[*]$p < .05$.

membership for girls—an issue we will address in the next section. This is especially the case with the statement, "I sometimes feel lonely when I'm with my family."

Four of the six questions measuring self-esteem reflect lower levels of self-esteem among gang girls than gang boys. The gang boys appear to have quite positive self-assessments. For the most part, the gang girls also indicate positive self-assessments but not at the same level as the boys. The girls are less likely than the gang boys to feel good about themselves and to feel competent in things they do. Multivariate analyses (not reported here) confirmed the ability of the social isolation and self-esteem measures to distinguish between gang boys and gang girls. Elsewhere (Deschenes & Esbensen, in press) we compare gang girls to nongang girls. As with the comparison to gang boys, the gang girls report significantly lower self-esteem and greater isolation from their families than do the nongang girls. We will now turn to a discussion of these gender differences in behavior and attitudes.

DISCUSSION AND SUMMARY

In this article we have attempted to provide a descriptive account of young gang members and to compare the gang experiences of boys and girls. Most gang research has been restricted to single gangs, single sites, or a small sample of gang members, making comparisons between male and female gang members difficult. In the study reported here, almost 6,000 middle school students in 11 different cities across the United States were surveyed. A total of 623 of these students met our restricted definition of being a gang member, with 62% being male and 38% female. Gang girls are clearly not as rare as law enforcement estimates indicate. As we have discussed elsewhere (Esbensen & Winfree, 1998), however, the disparate estimates of female gang participation may be more an artifact of methodological differences and sampling issues than of any real difference. It is our hope that the descriptive information about the gangs to which these youth belong will contribute to the growing body of research examining gender issues in youth gangs (e.g., Bjerregard & Smith, 1993; Cohen et al., 1995; Esbensen & Huizinga, 1993; Thornberry et al., 1993).

Limitations of the current data should be remembered as we discuss the four research questions posed at the outset of this article. The eighth-grade sample may exclude some high-risk students (i.e., truants and expelled students) that bias the estimates of gang membership provided in our analyses. In addition, given some evidence that girls exit gangs at an earlier age than boys, this young sample may overstate the actual distribution of girls in gangs. Our purpose is not to claim that one method or one estimate is better than the other. Rather, our purpose is to bring clarity to the quite disparate estimates of female participation in gangs. In this light, we encourage future research to include not only multiple methods but diverse age groups as well and to consider the possibility that gangs are not the exclusive domain of young males.

Our main objective in the research reported here was to examine the differences and similarities of the gang experience for boys and girls, as measured through survey methods. These findings do not support the notion that gang girls are ancillary members or that they are excluded from the illegal and violent activities in which male gang members are involved. The gang girls commit a wide variety of offenses, similar to the pattern exhibited by gang boys, only at a slightly lower frequency. These findings bolster other recent reports (e.g., Chesney-Lind, 1997; Huizinga, 1997) that claim female involvement in violent crime is substantial, at least greater than commonly believed. We suggest it is high time for a conscientious inclusion of females in the study of gangs and violence in general, not just for academic reasons but also to identify and design gang- and violence-prevention programs that include girls in the target population.

Another question posed at the outset concerned the perceived organization and structural aspects of gangs. Interestingly, there were virtually no gender differences with regard to the following areas of inquiry: reasons for joining gangs, activities in which the gang members were involved, and organizational aspects of the gangs. Overall, the gang experience, in terms of involvement in criminal activity and perceptions of the gang, is remarkably similar for boys and girls.

Gender differences, however, were found when we compared responses to questions measuring social isolation and self-esteem. It appears that the gang girls do differ from gang boys in terms of their perceived social isolation, their self-esteem, and the emotional fulfillment that they receive from their gangs. Although the girls experience the same structural aspects of the gangs, there appear to be qualitative differences between the gang boys and girls. As is the case in other contexts (e.g., educational institutions, workplace, and family), males and females may well describe the organizational context in the same manner, but their reactions and experiences in these settings are different.

These observed differences between gang girls and gang boys, when viewed within adolescent developmental literature should not be unexpected. As noted previously, distinct gender differences have been observed in elementary school playground behavior (Thorne, 1993), in peer interactions (Thorne & Luria, 1986), and in group dynamics (Lees, 1993). Thorne and Luria, for instance, observed elementary schoolchildren in a variety of supervised and unsupervised situations. They concluded that,

> Groups of boys experience shared excitement and bonding focused on public rule transgression. Girls are organized in friendship pairs linked in shifting coalitions and bond more through mutual self-disclosure; they teach and learn strategies for maintaining and ending intimacy. (p. 176)

Similarly, Lees (1993) notes that,

> The contrast between the girls' and boys' groups was startling. The girls interacted and were introspective, talked about relationships and feelings, worries and concerns. The boys all talked at the same time, interrupted each other, rarely listened to what other boys said and vied for attention and dominance; they were very lively. (p. 9)

To what extent, however, do such gender differences affect self-assessments and perceptions of social isolation? Are the gang girls represented in this study different from gang boys, or are girls simply different from boys? Brown and Gilligan (1992) suggest that girls traversing adolescence adapt survival strategies different from those of boys, often becoming disconnected from themselves and others. The girls they studied tended to become withdrawn and less outspoken as they entered adolescence.

> Open conflict and free speaking that were part of girls' daily living thus gave way to more covert forms of responding to hurt feelings or disagreements with relationships so that some girls came to ignore or not know signs of emotional or physical abuse. (p. 218)

Analyses of nongang youth found that the girls reported significantly higher levels of social isolation than did the boys and lower levels of self-esteem on three of the six self-esteem items. In an earlier publication in which we examined predictors of gang membership, we found separate effects of gender and gang membership, as well as an interaction effect of these two measures on perceptions of social isolation (Esbensen & Deschenes, 1998). For self-esteem, we found no direct gang effect but did find a gender and a gender/gang interaction effect. It does appear that whereas girls report lower levels of self-esteem and higher levels of social isolation than do boys, this difference is more pronounced among gang girls.

QUESTIONS FOR UNDERSTANDING AND CRITICAL THINKING

1. How are gang girls similar to and different from gang boys in terms of criminal activity?
2. Do girls and boys join gangs for similar reasons?

3. How do gang girls and boys differ in terms of social isolation and self-esteem?
4. Given the findings of this study, how might gang prevention and intervention programs be better designed to reflect such differences?

NOTES

1. In the Curry, Ball, and Fox (1994) survey, however, they note that law enforcement records may provide substantial underestimates of the number of gang girls, due to idiosyncratic recording practices. They state that "in a number of cities females, as a matter of policy, were never classified as gang members. In other jurisdictions, females were relegated to the status of 'associate' members" (p. 8).
2. Recent ethnographic work by Fleisher (1998) and Miller (1998a) has begun to address the paucity of information about young gang girls. Their research has included a wider array of females, including girls as young as 13 years in their samples.
3. In another article, Esbensen and Osgood (1997) examined program effects. As part of those analyses, preexisting differences between the G.R.E.A.T. program students and comparison group were examined. No systematic differences on demographic characteristics were found between the two groups.
4. With the program's origin in Phoenix, cities in Arizona and New Mexico were overrepresented in the early stages of the G.R.E.A.T. program. Thus, cities such as Albuquerque, Tucson, Scottsdale, and other smaller cities in the Southwest were excluded from the eligible pool of potential sites.
5. Passive consent procedures (i.e., a procedure that requires parents to respond only if they do not want their child to participate in a research project) were approved in all but the Torrance site. The number of parental refusals at each school ranged from zero to 2% at one school. Thus, participation rates (the percentage of students in attendance on the day of administration actually completing questionnaires) varied between 98% and 100% at the passive consent sites. Participation rates in Torrance, where active consent procedures were required, ranged from 53% to 75% of all eighth-grade students in each of the four schools. Five weeks of intensive efforts to obtain active parental consent in Torrance produced an overall return rate of 90% (72% affirmative and 18% refusals). Despite repeated mailings, telephone calls, and incentives, 10% of parents failed to return the consent form. Ninety percent of those students with parental permission completed the questionnaires. For a discussion of active parental consent procedures and its effect on response rates, see Esbensen et al., 1996.
6. For further discussion of this definitional issue, see Decker and Kempf-Leonard (1991); Maxson and Klein (1990); or Winfree, Fuller, Vigil, and Mays (1992). We concur with Klein (1995) that it is the illegal activities of gangs that is of research and policy interest. For that reason, we restrict our definition of gangs to include only those youth who report that their gangs are involved in illegal activities.
7. The skewness of self-report frequency data presents analysis problems. Various approaches can be used in attempts to remedy this problem, including transforming the data using the natural log, truncating at the 90th percentile (Nagin & Smith, 1990), or truncating the high-frequency responses according to some conceptual reasoning. We chose to truncate items at 52. Our premise is that commission of most of these acts on a weekly basis constitutes high-frequency offending. We are thus able to examine these high-frequency offenders without sacrificing the detail of open-ended self-report techniques.
8. The social isolation, self-esteem, and gang attachment items are Likert-type statements with response categories ranging from *strongly disagree* (1) to *strongly agree* (5).

REFERENCES

ASBURY, H. (1927). *The gangs of New York.* New York: Capricorn.

BJERREGARD, B., & SMITH, C. (1993). Gender differences in gang participation, delinquency, and substance use. *Journal of Quantitative Criminology, 4,* 329–55.

BROWN, L. M., & GILLIGAN, C. (1992). *Meeting at the crossroads; Women's psychology and girls' development.* Cambridge, MA: Harvard University Press.

CAMPBELL, A. (1991). *The girls in the gang* (2nd ed.). Oxford, UK: Basil Blackwell.

CHESNEY-LIND, M. (1997). *The female offender: Girls, women, and crime.* Thousand Oaks, CA: Sage.

CHESNEY-LIND, M., & SHELDEN, R. G. (1992). *Girls: Delinquency and juvenile justice.* Pacific Grove, CA: Brooks/Cole.

CHESNEY-LIND, M., SHELDEN, R. G., & JOE, K. A. (1996). Girls, delinquency, and gang membership. In C. R. Huff (Ed.), *Gangs in America* (2nd ed., pp. 185-204). Thousand Oaks, CA: Sage.

COHEN, M. I., WILLIAMS, K., BEKELMAN, A. M., & CROSSE, S. (1995). Evaluation of the national youth gang drug prevention program. In M. W. Klein, C. L. Maxson, & J. Miller (Eds.), *The modern gang reader* (pp. 266-275). Los Angeles: Roxbury.

CURRY, G. D. (1998). Female gang involvement. *Journal of Research in Crime and Delinquency, 35,* 100–118.

CURRY, G. D., BALL, R. A., & DECKER, S. H. (1996). *Estimating the national scope of gang crime from law enforcement data Research in brief.* Washington, DC: Department of Justice.

CURRY, G. D., BALL, R. A., & FOX, R. J. (1994). *Gang crime and law enforcement record keeping. Research in brief.* Washington, DC: Department of Justice.

DECKER, S. H., & KEMPF-LEONARD, K. (1991). Constructing gangs: The social definition of youth activities. *Criminal Justice Policy Review, 5,* 271–291.

DECKER, S. H., & VAN WINKLE, B. (1996). *Life in the gang: Family, friends, and violence.* New York: Cambridge University Press.

DEPARTMENT OF JUSTICE. (1996). *Crime in the United States, 1995.* Washington, DC: Author.

DESCHENES, E. P., & ESBENSEN, F.-A. (1999). Violence and gangs: Gender differences in perception and behavior. *Journal of Quantitative Criminology, 15,* 53-96.

DESCHENES, E. P., & ESBENSEN, F.-A. (in press). Violence among girls: Does gang membership make a difference? In M. Chesney-Lind & J. M. Hagedorn (Eds.), *Girls and gangs in America.* Chicago: Lakeview.

ESBENSEN, F.-A., & DESCHENES, E. P. (1998). A multisite examination of youth gang membership: Does gender matter? *Criminology, 36,* 799–828.

ESBENSEN, F.-A., DESCHENES, E. P., VOGEL, R. E., WEST, J., ARBOIT, K., & HARRIS, L. (1996). Active parental consent in school-based research: An examination of ethical and methodological issues. *Evaluation Review, 20,* 737–753.

ESBENSEN, F.-A., & HUIZINGA, D. (1993). Gangs, drugs, and delinquency in a survey of urban youth. *Criminology, 31,* 565–589.

ESBENSEN, F.-A., HUIZINGA, D., & WEIHER, A. W. (1993). Gang and non-gang youth: Differences in explanatory variables. *Journal of Contemporary Criminal Justice, 9,* 94–116.

ESBENSEN, F.-A., & OSGOOD, D. W. (1997). *National evaluation of G.R.E.A.T.: Research in brief.* Washington, DC: Department of Justice.

ESBENSEN, F.-A., & WINFREE, L. T., JR. (1998). Race and gender differences between gang and non-gang youth: Results from a multi-site survey. *Justice Quarterly, 15,* 505–526.20

FAGAN, J. (1989). The social organization of drug use and drug dealing among urban gangs. *Criminology, 27,* 633–669.

FISHMAN, L. T. (1995). The vice queens: An ethnographic study of Black female gang behavior. In M. W. Klein, C. L. Maxson, & J. Miller (Eds.). *The modern gang reader* (pp. 83–92). Los Angeles: Roxbury.

FLEISHER, M. (1998). *Dead end kids: Gang girls and the boys they know.* Madison: University of Wisconsin Press.

FOX, J. A. (1996). *Trends in juvenile violence: A report to the United States Attorney General on current and future rates of juvenile offending.* Washington, DC: Department of Justice.

GIORDANO, P. (1978). Girls, guys, and gangs: The changing social context of female delinquency. *Journal of Criminal Law and Criminology, 69,* 126–132.

GOLDSTEIN, A. P., & GLICK, B. (1994). *The prosocial gang: Implementing aggression replacement training.* Thousand Oaks, CA: Sage.

HAGEDORN, J. M. (1988). *People and folks: Gangs, crime and the underclass in a rustbelt city.* Chicago: Lakeview.

HAGEDORN, J. M. (1994). Homeboys, dope fiends, legits, and new jacks. *Criminology, 32,* 197–219.

HARRIS, M. C. (1988). *Cholas: Latino girls and gangs.* New York: AMS.

HARRIS, M. C. (1994). Cholas, Mexican-American girls, and gangs. *Sex Roles, 30,* 289–301.

HUFF, C. R. (1997, February). *The criminal behavior of gang members in Ohio, Colorado, and Florida.* Paper presented at the annual meeting of the Western Society of Criminology, Honolulu, HI.

HUIZINGA, D. (1997, February). *Gangs and the volume of crime.* Paper presented at the annual meeting of the Western Society of Criminology, Honolulu, HI.

HUIZINGA, D., & ESBENSEN, F.-A. (1991, November). *Are there changes in female delinquency and are there changes in underlying explanatory factors?* Paper presented at the annual meeting of the American Society of Criminology, San Francisco, CA.

JOE, K. A., & CHESNEY-LIND, M. (1995). Just every mother's angel: An analysis of gender and ethnic variations in youth gang membership. *Gender and Society, 9,* 408–430.

KLEIN, M. W. (1995). *The American street gang: Its nature, prevalence, and control.* New York: Oxford University Press.

KLEIN, M. W., & CRAWFORD, L. Y. (1995). Groups, gangs, and cohesiveness. In M. W. Klein, C. L. Maxson, & J. Miller (Eds.), *The modern gang reader* (pp. 160–167). Los Angeles: Roxbury.

LEES, S. (1993). *Sugar and spice: Sexuality and adolescent girls.* New York: Penguin.

MATSUEDA, R. L., & HEIMER, K. (1997). A symbolic interactionist theory of role-transitions, role-commitments, and delinquency. In T. P. Thornberry (Ed.), *Developmental theories of crime and delinquency* (pp. 163–213). New Brunswick, NJ: Transaction Publishers.

MAXSON, C. L., & KLEIN, M. W. (1990). Street gang violence: Twice as great or half as great? In C. R. Huff (Ed.), *Gangs in America* (pp. 71–100). Newbury Park, CA: Sage.

MILLER, J. (1998a). Gender and victimization risk among young women in gangs. *Journal of Research in Crime and Delinquency, 35,* 429–453.

MILLER, J. (1998b). Up it up: Gender and the accomplishment of robbery. *Criminology, 36,* 37–66.

MOORE, J. W. (1978). *Homeboys: Gangs, drugs, and prison in the barrios of Los Angeles,* Philadelphia, PA: Temple University Press.

MOORE, J. W. (1991). *Going down to the barrio: Home boys and home girls in change.* Philadelphia, PA: Temple University Press.

MOORE, J. W., & HAGEDORN, J. M. (1996). What happens to girls in the gang? In C. R. Huff (Ed.), *Gangs in America* (2nd ed., pp. 205–220). Thousand Oaks, CA: Sage.

NAGIN, D. S., & SMITH, D. A. (1990). Participation in and frequency of delinquent behavior: A test for structural differences. *Journal of Quantitative Criminology, 6,* 335–365.

OPERATION SAFE STREETS (OSS) STREET GANG DETAIL. (1995). L. A. style: A street gang manual of the Los Angeles County Sheriff's Department. In M. W. Klein, C. L. Maxson, & J. Miller (Eds.), *The modern gang reader* (pp. 34–45). Los Angeles: Roxbury.

PUFFER, J. A. (1912). *The boy and his gang,* Boston: Houghton Mifflin.

ROSENBAUM, J. L. (1991). *The female gang member: A look at the California problem,* Unpublished manuscript, California State University at Fullerton.

SHELEY, J. F., & WRIGHT, J. D. (1995). *In the line of fire: Youth, guns, and violence in urban America.* Hawthorne, NY: Aldine.

SICKMUND, M., SNYDER, H. N., & POE-YAMAGATA, E. (1997). *Juvenile offenders and victims: 1997 Update on violence.* Washington, DC: Department of Justice.

SPERGEL, I. A. (1966). *Street gang work: Theory and practice.* Reading, MA: Addison-Wesley.

SPERGEL, I. A. (1990). Youth gangs: continuity and change. In N. Morris & M. Tonry (Eds.), *Crime and justice: An annual review of research* (pp. 171–275). Chicago: University of Chicago Press.

SPERGEL, I. A. (1995). *The youth gang problem.* New York: Oxford University Press.

SWART, W. J. (1995). Female gang delinquency: A search for "acceptably deviant behavior." In M. W. Klein, C. L. Maxson, & J. Miller (Eds.), *The modern gang reader* (pp. 78–82). Los Angeles: Roxbury.

THORNBERRY, T. P., KROHN, M. D., LIZOTTE, A. J., & CHARD-WIERSCHEM, D. (1993). The role of juvenile gangs in facilitating delinquent behavior. *Journal of Research in Crime and Delinquency, 30,* 55–87.

THORNE, B. (1993). *Gender play: Girls and boys in school.* New Brunswick, NJ: Rutgers University Press.

THORNE, B., & LURIA, Z. (1986). Sexuality and gender in children's daily worlds. *Social Problems, 33,* 176–190.

THRASHER, F. M. (1927). *The gang: A study of one thousand three hundred thirteen gangs in Chicago.* Chicago: University of Chicago Press.

TRIPLETT, R., & MEYERS, L. (1995). Evaluating contextual patterns of delinquency: Gender-based differences. *Justice Quarterly, 12,* 59–84.

VIGIL, J. D. (1988). *Barrio gangs: Street life and identity in southern California.* Austin: University of Texas Press.

WINFREE, L. T., JR., BACKSTROM, T. V., & MAYS, G. L. (1994). Social learning theory, self-reported delinquency, and youth gangs: A new twist on a general theory of crime and delinquency. *Youth and Society, 26,* 147–177.

WINFREE, L. T., JR., FULLER, K., VIGIL, T., & MAYS, G. L. (1992). The definition and measurement of "gang status": Policy implication for juvenile justice. *Juvenile and Family Court Journal, 43,* 29–37.

WINFREE, L. T., JR., MAYS, G. L., & VIGIL-BACKSTROM, T. (1994). Youth gangs and incarcerated delinquents: Exploring the ties between gang membership, delinquency, and social learning theory. *Justice Quarterly, 11,* 229–56.

PART III

Race and Ethnicity in Gangs

6

Voices from the Barrio

Chicano/a Gangs, Families, and Communities[*]

Marjorie S. Zatz and Edwardo L. Portillos

❖

Based on in-depth interviews with 33 youth gang members and 20 adult neighborhood leaders and youth service providers, we explore the complicated relationships among gang members, their families, and other residents of poor Chicano/a and Mexicano/a barrios in Phoenix. Listening to the multiple voices of community members allows for a multifaceted understanding of the complexities and contradictions of gang life, both for the youths and for the larger community. We draw on a community ecology approach to help explain the tensions that develop, especially when community members vary in their desires and abilities to control gang-related activities. In this exploratory study, we point to some of the ways in which gender, age, education, traditionalism, and level of acculturation may help explain variation in the type and strength of private, parochial, and public social control within a community.

Criminologists have long been fascinated with the problems posed by youth gangs. In recent years, community ecology approaches to gang-related crime and social control have become popular. One strand of research has focused on macrosocial patterns of crime and inequality among the urban underclass (e.g., Sampson and Laub, 1993; Sampson and Wil-

[*]We wish to thank Nancy Jurik, Richard Krecker, and the anonymous reviewers for helpful comments on an earlier draft of this paper. We also wish to thank the study participants who so willingly gave of their time. This research was supported by a partnership grant between Arizona State University and the Arizona Department of Juvenile Corrections.

Zatz, M. S. and Portillos, E. L. Voices from the barrio: Chicano/a gangs, families, and communities. *Criminology,* 38, 369–401. Reprinted by permission of the American Society of Criminology.

son, 1996; Wilson, 1987). A second strand has examined the "dual frustrations" facing inner-city parents who fear both gang- and drug-related crime *and* police harassment of young men of color (Meares, 1997:140; see also Anderson, 1990; Madriz, 1997). These concerns converge in research that examines the connections between and among the structural causes and community-level effects of economic deprivation, institutional and personal networks within a community, the capacity of local networks to garner human and economic resources from outside the community, and gang-related crime (Anderson, 1990; Bursik and Grasmick, 1993a,b; Hagedorn, 1998; Moore, 1991; Spergel, 1986; Sullivan, 1989). Bursik and Grasmick (1993a) take this approach the farthest theoretically, incorporating Hunter's (1985) three tiers of local community social control into a reformulation of Shaw and McKay's (1942) social disorganization framework. Their theory of community relations recognizes the relevance of long-term economic deprivation and institutional racism for community-based social control at the private, parochial, and public levels.

Bursik and Grasmick suggest that traditional social disorganization theory, sometimes in combination with subcultural theories, placed an emphasis on the private level of systemic control, as reflected in family and friendship dynamics. In underclass neighborhoods characterized by stable, high levels of delinquency, however, parochial (e.g., churches and schools) and public (e.g., police) forms of social control become more apparent. A few researchers, most notably Hagedorn (1998) and Decker and Van Winkle (1996), have applied Bursik and Grasmick's theory to inner-city gang research. Yet, these studies have been limited to midwestern cities. We also draw on this theory of community social control, but focus our research in a Chicano/a and Mexicano/a community in the southwest.[1] As we will demonstrate, our research site reflects a pocket of poverty in the midst of an almost unprecedented economic boom. Also, the community is close to the Mexican border, allowing perhaps for a greater range of traditionalism than might be found in midwestern cities.

Informed by the gang studies noted previously and by other scholarship on the urban poor (e.g., Hernández, 1990; Moore and Pinderhughes, 1993; Wilson, 1996), we see gang members as integral parts of their communities, engaging in some actions that hurt the community and in some that help it. At the same time, we are particularly attentive to the ways in which gender, age, educational status, and degree of traditionalism differentiate the adults' perceptions of the gangs and choice of private, parochial, or public forms of social control.

CONTEXTUALIZING THE PHOENIX GANG PROBLEMS: POCKETS OF POVERTY IN A BOOMING ECONOMY

Our research is set in Phoenix, Arizona, a large, thriving, sunbelt city close to the Mexican border. As we will show, many of our findings parallel those reported by gang researchers in Chicago and Los Angeles, where most of the prominent theories about Chicano gangs were developed (e.g., Moore, 1978, 1985, 1991, 1998; Spergel, 1986; Vigil, 1988). Like those earlier researchers, we find that youths join neighborhood gangs for a variety of reasons, includ-

---

[1] For purposes of this paper, Chicano/a refers to men (Chicano) and women (Chicana) of Mexican descent living in the United States. Mexicano/a refers to men (Mexicano) and women (Mexicana) who were born in Mexico. While the Mexicano and Mexicana youths must be living in the United States to become part of our sample, they may or may not be U.S. citizens or permanent residents.

ing friendship networks; access to alcohol, drugs, and parties; and wanting to feel included and protected by a group. Some of the youths come from multigenerational gang families, whereas others do not. The adult men we interviewed, as well as the youths, also talked about gangs and gang-barrio relations in terms similar to those reported by other scholars.

Unlike the other cities, however, Phoenix has experienced a spectacular economic boom in recent years. Phoenix is the sixth largest city in the United States and ranks number one nationally for its job growth. As we discuss later in this paper, the city and state have received high marks on a number of economic indicators, yet parts of the city remain severely depressed. Indeed, South Phoenix, where we conducted our research, was one of President Clinton's stops during his four-day national tour of impoverished sites in July 1999, along with Appalachia, Watts, the Mississippi Delta, and the Oglala Sioux reservation in Pine Ridge, South Dakota. As the White House stated, it is "a classic example of a fast-growing region where some residents are being left behind" (Barker, 1999:A1).

This situation of poverty in the midst of plenty contextualizes our research. For example, the youths and adults we interviewed lamented that the schools in their communities are in terrible states of disrepair. Yet, the state legislature was unwilling to commit resources to poor school districts until the courts intervened, ordering development of a new system for school funding. Similarly, respondents spoke of the need for better public housing, basic city services such as more street lights and paved roads, and accessible public transportation. Just a mile away from their poverty-stricken neighborhoods, they can see the beautiful new housing developments being built on scenic South Mountain to the south, and the new ballpark to the north, constructed in part out of state and local funds. As a consequence, many residents of South Phoenix barrios feel isolated and alienated, excluded from the boom that surrounds their community. As we will demonstrate, some community members blame gangs for businesses not coming into the barrios. Other residents blame the city for not investing in the barrios, recognizing that economic, educational, and recreational resources might entice businesses *and* give young people something to do besides hang out in gangs. These sometimes divergent perspectives contribute further to tensions within the community. Yet, it is interesting to note that although gangs in other cities have become entrepreneurial, selling drugs as a way for the gang to make money (e.g., Jankowski, 1991; Padilla, 1993), Chicano gangs in Phoenix have not organized around the drug industry. That is not to say that gang members do not use or sell drugs—many do, but the gangs themselves are not organized around drug sales.

A second key factor that distinguishes our study from earlier work on Chicano gangs in Chicago, Milwaukee, and other large cities aside from Los Angeles is Phoenix's proximity to the Mexican border. This factor has a dual effect, contributing both to cultural replenishment and to tensions between Chicanos and Mexican immigrants and migrants. Many of the adults we interviewed commented that the Mexican culture flourishes in Phoenix, although it has been heavily commercialized. Yet, conflicts also develop because many Chicanos and Chicanas are embarrassed by the apparent provincialism of immigrants from rural Mexico and angered that their willingness to work for low wages depresses pay scales for all Latinos. Rivalry between Chicanos and Mexicanos also plays out among the youths, with Chicano/a and Mexicano/a gangs often fighting one another. Finally, as our interview data demonstrate, the degree of traditionalism and immigration status are also key elements in explaining men's and women's views about gangs and, perhaps more importantly, their abilities to tap parochial and public resources.

The prominence of the Chicano and Mexicano population in Phoenix is a related factor that distinguishes Phoenix from other major sites for gang research. Chicago and Los Angeles, for example, have large African-American and Asian/Asian-American populations. Moreover, in Chicago, the Latino population is divided between Puerto Ricans and Chicanos. In Phoenix, however, the Chicano and Mexicano population is the single largest racial/ethnic minority group, far larger than the African-American, Asian-American, or American Indian populations. This fact, we suggest, alters the urban dynamics considerably. For instance, in Arizona (and California, which has a larger number of immigrants), fierce political attacks on immigrants have occurred, aimed primarily at Latinos (e.g., English Only, Proposition 187). Yet, these attacks were ultimately foiled because the Latino population and supporters had sufficient political clout at the state level and in the courts. Nevertheless, this clout does not extend to poor Latino neighborhoods or individuals; on the contrary, barrio residents seem to have very little ability to challenge economic and political decisions unless a higher court intervenes on their behalf, as was seen in the school-funding situation. We suspect that the relative deprivation felt by individual Latinos is probably aggravated because only one major racial/ethnic minority exists, and thus the comparisons between their economic plight and that of wealthier whites becomes especially stark.

DATA AND METHODS: OUR YOUTH AND ADULT SAMPLES

If we are to understand the complexities of gang life, it is important that diverse voices and perspectives are heard. Accordingly, we interviewed teenagers involved in gangs and adults active in neighborhood associations or working with local teenagers. Snowball sampling was used to obtain both samples. For the youths, we began with a sample of teenagers on parole and who were participating in a partnership project between our university and the juvenile correctional system. For the adults, we began with a listing of youth services providers and neighborhood association leaders. At the conclusion of each interview, we asked the respondent for names of others whom we might interview to gain a full picture of gang life and of gang and community relations. Given the small samples and our dual focus on youths' and adults' perceptions of gangs and the larger community, this study must be considered exploratory.

Semistructured interviews lasted from 45 minutes to about 2 hours. The youths were interviewed in the summer and fall of 1995, and the adults in the summer of 1995. All of the interviews were taped and transcribed. Thematic content analysis was conducted to explore major themes in the data, as described in later sections (Lofland and Lofland, 1995).

Consistent with our theoretical interest in exploring multiple stand-points, we used an insider-outsider approach in our interviews. This strategy enhances validity and encourages reciprocity between researchers and the people asked to share their lives and thoughts (Baca Zinn, 1975; Frankenburg, 1993; Zavella, 1996). Although ideally both authors would have interviewed the youths and the adults, we recognized that the youths would be very reluctant to talk frankly with the first author, a white, middle-class, middle-aged female professor, seeing her as too removed from their lives. Based on prior experiences in the field, however, we expected that they would be very willing to talk with the second author, a Chicano graduate student in his mid-twenties. Similarly, we expected that the adults might not be willing to carve out much time from their schedules to talk with a graduate student, but would be willing to discuss their work with a university professor. Accordingly, we employed two strategies. First, we wanted to situate ourselves to minimize social distances along racial/ethnic, educational, and professional lines, which meant that the first author interviewed the adults and the second author interviewed the youths. Second, we were cognizant of and worked with our insider-outsider statuses, discussing our findings as we went along and offering one another insights and suggestions.

Interviews were conducted with 33 self-identified current or former gang members: 24 males and 9 females. They ranged between 14 and 18 years of age, although they were between 9 and 15 when they joined their gangs. Thus, our focus was on the youths, not the older *veteranos*. Five of the youths were born in Mexico; the other 28 are of Mexican or mixed descent but were born in the United States.[2] Interviews took place in restaurants, their homes, the neighborhood, an alternative school for juvenile parolees, and locked institutions. The second author had already worked with some of the youths and their friends for more than a year in a related ethnographic project and was able to quickly establish rapport with them. Another factor facilitating both rapport and validity was his knowledge of Spanish and of *calo* (Chicano gang slang); otherwise, certain phrases might have been misinterpreted (Marin, 1991).

Very few of the youths had managed to avoid entanglement with the juvenile justice system, and most of them were under parole or probation supervision or incarcerated at the time of the interviews. Respondents were given a choice of receiving $10 or lunch at a restaurant of their choice. For the 12 incarcerated youths, $10 was placed in their account. Youths were asked to discuss their relationships with their families and friends, their own involvement with the gang, and their perceptions of gang life. Some bias could result from respondents' concerns that their comments might be relayed to their parole officers or caseworkers. They might exaggerate the extent to which they are easing out of gang activities and other changes in their lives that caseworkers would view positively. To reduce this risk, we made every effort to convince them that the interviews were confidential and that the transcripts would be anonymous.

Interviews were also conducted with 20 adults. They included youth service providers and social workers active in the Chicano/a and Mexicano/a communities, neighborhood association leaders and other neighborhood activists, city neighborhood services representatives from selected neighborhoods, a parish priest, a paid activist from Mothers Against Gangs, and a representative of the Phoenix Police Department. Seven of the adults self-identify as Chicano or Chicana, four as African American, two as Puerto Rican, four as White, one as Hispanic, and one as mixed Hispanic-African American. Our final respondent was born in Mexico. All but one of the adults spoke at least some Spanish. Two interviews were conducted solely in Spanish; in others, the conversations wove between languages. Most of the interviews were conducted in the respondents' offices, although one took place in a cemetery, next to the grave where the respondent's son was buried.

---

[2] Of the 33 youth, 11 self-identified as Mexican, 2 as "wetback," 1 as "wetback" and Indian, 7 as Chicano or Chicana, 2 as Chicano and American Indian, 1 as Chicano and white, and 7 as Hispanic. Two respondents, both of whom were born in the U.S., did not self-identify their ethnicity. It is worth noting that "wetback" has two meanings in this context. It is a derogatory term for an undocumented Mexican immigrant, yet it is also used with pride by members of the Wetback Power gang. Similarly, some of the youth who call themselves "Hispanic" are members of Hispanic Barrio Homeboys, and thus may have selected this term as both an ethnic and a gang identifier.

None of the adults saw the South Phoenix community as simply a site where they worked. Ten of the adults grew up in South Phoenix. Some still reside there; others have moved across town but continue to work with neighborhood youths and visit family and friends in the community. Most of those adults who have moved now live in more affluent areas, but a few made economically lateral moves to other, equally depressed, neighborhoods. For example, five of the adult respondents live on the Westside, a largely African-American area bordering South Phoenix. Eleven of the respondents lived in South Phoenix when we interviewed them.

All of the adult respondents living in South Phoenix or Westside see the very real possibility of death for their children, as well as for their nieces, nephews, and neighbors. This possibility had become a reality for three of the respondents, whose children had died in gang-related incidents in recent years. The three children are buried near one another, in the same section of a local cemetery. The adults had been active in neighborhood affairs before their children's deaths and continue this work, sometimes being paid for it and sometimes as volunteers. Thus, the issues of gangs and violence touched their lives in special ways.

In addition to offering their own impressions, the adults were asked for their expert opinions about how others in the community perceived gangs and efforts to control gang-related crime within the barrio. They were asked to consider variation within the community along lines of gender, age, number of generations the family had lived in the United States, and nationality. Thus, the adult respondents were also both insiders and outsiders, speaking in their own voices in some instances, and for other adults in the neighborhoods where they lived and worked at other times. These multiple standpoints allowed us to explore the intersection of race, class, and gender within the community, and then to take the analysis a step further to tease out the ways in which acculturation and traditionalism cross-cut nationality and age in gendered ways.

Finally, we should note that the validity of qualitative research rests on the researchers' abilities to accurately and fully understand the phenomena under study. Although it is always possible that individuals have lied in telling their stories, we are confident that the 53 interviews we conducted, in combination with the ethnographic research and interviews with juvenile justice officials in the larger study of which this is a part, have afforded us a reasonably nuanced understanding of the relationship between gang youths and their communities. Respondents present a multitude of perspectives on this relationship. Some respondents reinforce popular images of gangs as terrible and support police efforts to rid the neighborhoods of organized gang activity. Other respondents tell what Ewick and Silbey (1995) have called more "subversive" tales about police brutality, politicians ignoring poor parts of town, and lack of resources. Among and within these voices lies a complex set of experiences, fears, and hopes.

THEORETICAL FRAMEWORK: A SYSTEMIC APPROACH TO NEIGHBORHOOD AND GANG DYNAMICS

Most gang research in the United States has been grounded in social disorganization theory, subcultural theories, or, most recently, economic marginalization theories derived from Wilson's (1987) work on the underclass. Bursik and Grasmick (1993a) offer a theoretical framework that combines key elements of Shaw and McKay's (1942) social disorganization theory with recent work on gangs in underclass communities. The central problem with social disorganization theory for gang research, they suggest, is that it overemphasizes family dynamics, focusing on individualized resources and constraints to the exclusion of larger structural concerns. Accordingly, social disorganization approaches cannot adequately account for ongoing patterns of gang behavior in stable neighborhoods where families may live in the same houses or on the same block for many years, often spanning several generations. The gangs in these neighborhoods are often multigenerational, with several members of the extended family belonging to the gang in each generation.

Although initially subcultural theories became popular because of the inability of traditional social disorganization approaches to explain these multigenerational gangs, Moore (1978, 1985, 1991, 1998), Vigil (1988), Hagedorn (1991, 1998), and Sullivan (1989), among others, have offered an alternative explanation that refocuses attention at structural factors, including, especially, the economic marginalization of underclass communities. These scholars point to the crucial importance of whether, and to what extent, residents of poor but stable neighborhoods have access to public resources. Bursik and Grasmick (1993a) weave these concerns into a larger, more encompassing framework that examines access to private, public, and parochial resources. Drawing from Hunter's (1985) typology of local community social control, they suggest that these three dimensions operate simultaneously and that gang activity is most likely to emerge "in areas in which the networks of parochial and public control cannot effectively provide services to the neighborhood" (Bursik and Grasmick, 1993a:141).

Private social control refers to the influences and actions of family and close friends, which could be the nuclear family, the extended family, or the interwoven networks of family and friends that characterize stable barrio communities. Through the family's actions supporting or disdaining particular behaviors, social control is exerted. Parochial social control reflects "the effects of the broader local interpersonal network and the interlocking of local institutions, such as stores, schools, churches and voluntary organizations" (Bursik and Grasmick, 1993a:17). Control is exerted through residents supervising activities within the neighborhood and the integration of local institutions into many aspects of everyday life. Individuals and neighborhoods will vary in the extent to which they can harness parochial forms of social control. For example, monolingual Spanish-speaking parents may encounter difficulties and be easily intimidated when they try to communicate with their children's teachers or school authorities. Public social control, in turn, focuses "on the ability of the community to secure public goods and services that are allocated by agencies located outside the neighborhood" (Bursik and Grasmick, 1993a:17). As Moore and Hagedorn have noted most pointedly, poor barrio communities often do not have access to or alliances with key urban institutions. For instance, although many barrio residents must interact regularly with health care, education, welfare, criminal justice, and immigration authorities, they do so from a position of little or no individual or institutional power. The absence of people who might serve as power brokers, interceding between community residents and institutional authorities, means that residents of economically marginal communities cannot effectively use public systemic control. One example that surfaced often in our interviews was access to police. Although many residents perceived the police to be omnipresent, the same residents complained that the police did not respond quickly when they called for help.

Combining these three forms of social control into a fully systemic model enables a more complete understanding of gang-community dynamics. Following Bursik and Grasmick (1993a), we apply this model to Chicano/a and Mexicano/a gangs in Phoenix. We draw from interviews with gang youths and with adults active in the communities to explore how they perceive gang-neighborhood dynamics. One of the unique contributions of our research to this theoretical agenda is our recognition that access to parochial and public resources is very much gendered. Moreover, as we shall show, recent immigrants and parents with more traditional Mexicano beliefs and values may be more intimidated by key societal institutions and by their children. Thus, we suggest that gender and traditionalism cross-cut age, educational level, and income to influence the extent to which individual parents and neighborhoods can draw on private, parochial, and public social control.

The Phoenix Economy and Public Social Control in Latino/a Communities

Most of the research on gangs that draws from political economic and community ecology perspectives has been conducted in cities that have experienced severe economic decline (e.g., Anderson, 1990; Decker and Van Winkle, 1996; Fagan, 1996; Hagedorn, 1998; Horowitz, 1987; Spergel, 1986; Sullivan, 1989). Chicago, St. Louis, and Milwaukee, for example, all faced structural dislocations with the movement of factories out of central cities. The political, social, and economic plight of poor blacks in these urban ghettos led to Wilson's (1987) depiction of them as the "underclass." We draw from this theoretical and empirical body of research to explore gang-community dynamics in a very different context, that of a pocket of poverty within spectacular economic growth. From 1993 to 1998, Arizona had the nation's second highest job growth rate, and the Phoenix area ranked first in the nation among the 22 largest metropolitan areas, with a 5.8% job growth rate in 1997–1998. The years 1993–1997 were the strongest five-year period of job growth in Arizona history, with more than 400,000 private sector jobs created during these years. Unemployment rates in Arizona are consistently among the lowest in the nation, and in the 1990s they were at their lowest levels since the early 1970s. By September, 1998, unemployment in metropolitan Phoenix had dropped to 2.9% (Arizona Economic Development Update, 1998; Arizona Department of Economic Security, 1998).

In the midst of this economic boom sits South Phoenix. The unemployment rate for 18 census tracts in the South Phoenix area in 1990 was 13.34, almost triple the unemployment rate of 5.3 for Arizona and 5.6 for the United States (U.S. Council of Economic Advisors, 1998), and quadruple that of the rest of metropolitan Phoenix. Elementary schools in the inner city are woefully underfunded. In 1998, the Arizona Supreme Court finally intervened, declaring Arizona's system of school funding to be unconstitutional. The high school serving South Phoenix had a 51.9% graduation rate in 1994 (White, 1995:Appendix A). Broken down by race/ethnicity, 66% of the white youths attending this high school graduated, compared with 48% of the Latino students (White, 1995:Appendix D).

Between 1980 and 1990, the percentage of the county's children living in poverty increased from 12.9% to 17.5%, rising to 19.1% in 1993 (Morrison Institute for Public Policy, 1994:69). In 1993, 20.7% of the families in the county received food stamps, up from 12.7% in 1990. Although only 26% of the county's juvenile population was Latino/a, 40% of the children in Aid to Families with Dependent Children in 1993 were Latino (Morrison Institute for Public Policy, 1994:69, 73), indicating that Latino youths participate in poverty programs at about double their population rate. Also, although 24% of the children 19 years or younger in the state were enrolled in its indigent health care program (up from 19.1% in 1991), 43% of the children enrolled in the program were Latino (Morrison Institute for Public Policy, 1994:69, 73). Finally, Latinos composed 46% of the firearm-related deaths of youths aged 0–19 years, and 32% of juvenile arrests (aged 8–17 years). These statistics paint a bleak picture for Latinos and Latinas in the Phoenix metropolitan area, particularly in South Phoenix. The pockets of poverty appear especially stark, given the strong economic indicators for the state and for the city as a whole.

Like the neighborhoods Hagedorn (1998, 1991) studied in Milwaukee, South Phoenix is a "checkerboard" of stable working class families living next door to crack houses and abject poverty. Some houses are nicely maintained with fresh paint and flowers growing in the gardens, but others are shacks lacking such basic services as electricity and running water. Air conditioning is unusual, although temperatures in the summer regularly rise above 110 degrees Fahrenheit. The barrio receives few municipal resources. Public transportation is practically nonexistent, and roads are poorly maintained. Few streetlights illuminate the darkness at night, lending an eeriness to the neighborhood that exacerbates residents' fears of crime.

The war on drugs waged across the nation can be felt here as well. Grandparents and aunts are often left raising children when their parents are incarcerated for drug offenses, or too strung out to care for their children (see further Donziger, 1996; Lusane, 1991; Mann and Zatz, 1998; Miller, 1996). Drugs are commonplace, especially marijuana, glue, and paint, and drug houses appear to be doing a thriving business.

Yet, the blight cannot be blamed solely on drugs and the drug business. Few economic resources have been invested in the community. No factories or other large businesses are located in the area. Convenience stores and liquor stores abound, but residents must go elsewhere if they want to shop at major chain grocery stores or retail outlets. No shopping malls, movie theaters, or skating rinks are nearby, leaving the streets as the only viable place for teens to hang out.

Thus, in the midst of a remarkable economic boom caused by the surge in the computer microprocessor industry and tourism, residents of South Phoenix have been excluded, marginalized, and isolated. They have been excluded from participation in the mainstream labor market because they lack the necessary training and skills for the jobs that do exist and because public transportation is woefully inadequate; marginalized politically because they have little clout and fewer resources that might make politicians listen to them; and isolated socially because of cultural and linguistic barriers (see, similarly, Moore, 1998:7). As we have noted, poverty and unemployment are rampant in South Phoenix, schools are underfunded, and graduation rates for Latino/a students are horrid. Residents have minimal access to political and economic power brokers, and little exists for young people to do except hang out on the streets. In this context, Bursik and Grasmick's (1993a, b) attention to the possibilities and difficulties of parochial and public social control contributes substantially to our understanding of gang-community dynamics (see, similarly, Hagedorn, 1998; Spergel, 1986).

ADULT PERSPECTIVES ON GANGS AND THE COMMUNITY

The adults expressed a wide range of views, from seeing gangs as a normal part of adolescence to viewing them as social parasites that must be routed from the neighborhoods. This contrast is not surprising, given the heterogeneity of life experiences among barrio residents. Jankowski (1991), Moore (1991), Hagedorn (1998), Decker and Van Winkle (1996), Sullivan (1989), Padilla (1993), and Venkatesh (1996) also report contradictory or ambivalent stances toward gangs in the communities they studied. In the discussion that follows, we attempt to tease out these different perspectives and to account for some of the divergent opinions.

Gangs, The Neighborhood, and The Local Economy

According to a neighborhood specialist for the city, the major problems that surfaced in a survey of South Phoenix residents were crime, homes and landscaping not being well maintained, graffiti, and a shortage of streetlights, followed by the lack of recreational opportunities for young people. Similarly, community leaders repeatedly voiced the fear that graffiti, combined with the threat of drugs and violence, contributes to urban decay by making the neighborhood less attractive to businesses.[3] Yet, gang activity is only one factor affecting the local economy and can as easily be seen as an outcome of economic dislocation as its cause. The weak linkages to centers of economic and political power, in turn, reduce residents' abilities to exercise public systemic control very effectively (Bursik and Grasmick, 1993a:146; Moore, 1985; Moore and Pinderhughes, 1993). It is in precisely such contexts that Bursik and Grasmick suggest gang activity is most likely to develop.

One of the most important and visible forms of public social control is the police. Although a substantial portion of the community is very willing to work with local police in at least some limited ways to eradicate gangs and crime, another portion sees the police, courts, and similar institutions as unable or unwilling to adequately protect them. Tensions between Latino community members and the police have historically been high, the result of years of institutionalized racism in police and court processing (Escobar, 1999; Mirandé, 1987; National Minority Advisory Council on Criminal Justice, 1980; U.S. Commission on Civil Rights, 1970; Vigil, 1988). Allegations of police use of excessive force often lie at the heart of these strained relations. In Phoenix, community anger with the police has centered around the violent deaths of three young men: Rudy Buchanan, Jr., Edward Mallet, and Julio Valerio. Buchanan was African American and Latino. A member of the Crips gang who had reputedly threatened that he was going to kill a police officer, Buchanan was shot at 89 times in January of 1995, with 30 bullets entering his body. His family was awarded $570,000 in a settlement with the City of Phoenix in March 1998. Edward Mallet was a 25-year-old African-American double amputee who died in 1994 after being placed in a neck hold by police officers. In March 1998, a jury awarded Mallet's parents $45 million, finding that the police used excessive force that resulted in his death. The city later settled with Mallet's family, paying about $5 million. Finally, 16-year-old Julio Valerio's case is still pending. He was holding a butcher knife when he was pepper sprayed and then shot at 25 times in 1996 by police (Fiscus and Leonard, 1999).

Access to public social control goes beyond policing to encompass the range of agencies and actors who can provide public goods and services. The South Phoenix community did not perceive itself as well situated with regard to such access. Respondents criticized state and local politicians and other city officials for reducing the community's resource base and for placing it low on the priority list for revitalization, and businesses for taking

---

[3] Neighborhood vehemence against gangs defacing the community was highlighted in October of 1995, while we were conducting our field work. More than 40 angry residents appeared at a juvenile court hearing, hoping to convince the judge that two 16-year-olds should be prosecuted in adult court. The youths had gone on a rampage, spray painting 32 houses and some cars (Whiting 1995).

money from the community but not investing in it. Finally, 19 of the 20 adults condemned sensationalist and biased reporting by the television and print media, particularly, exaggerated reports of gang violence that create the impression that violence is rampant in South Phoenix. Many of the adult respondents pointed out that much of the violence occurs north of the Salt River bed, in what is *not* formally South Phoenix. Nevertheless, South Phoenix continues to bear the stigma of a violent part of town, making it less attractive to businesses that might otherwise relocate there. This reputation, in turn, contributes further to the economic devastation of the community. A local resident and neighborhood activist whose son died in a gang-related shooting described the contradiction

> It's a chicken and egg thing. What do we need first? Jobs and businesses that really care, or to clean up our community of drugs and gangs? How do we do this without jobs and educational opportunities?

Some neighborhood residents work directly with the youths to curtail gang activities. Exercising both private and parochial social control, some residents tutor neighborhood teens with their studies and help them to find jobs; other residents work with voluntary organizations and local churches, organizing block watches to prevent violence, burglaries, graffiti, and drug sales in the neighborhood. One youth service provider criticized block watches, however, for excluding gang members. She argued that neighborhood organizations would be far more effective if they brought the youths in, saying, "What are you going to do?" rather than making them feel like outcasts with little stake in the community. In her words

> The community refuses—*will not*—include them in organizing block watches [and] neighborhood associations for the betterment of the community. Instead, the strategy is to attack them, so gang kids become meaner, more defensive. They claim ownership of the community, and we need to make them a part of it, and instead they're pushed off. Gangs are defined as the enemy, not as part of the community. We need to say to kids, 'Hey, we need you to help with the block watch. What's your part going to be?' They could clean up graffiti, whatever.

In the past, our respondents noted, "Mexican gangs were tied closely to the community. This has changed." Today, gangs "rob people of their sense of security. They barricade themselves in their homes because they feel so vulnerable." Another adult respondent told us

> If a gang is neighborhood based, they protect their neighborhoods and one another, and to the extent they can, their families and the families of other gang members. But that doesn't always work.

These quotes reinforce one of the central contradictions inherent in neighborhood gangs. The youths see themselves as protectors of their communities and the police as abusive interlopers, regardless of whether this imagery appears exaggerated to outsiders. The protection gangs offer may be reduced today to simply making sure that competing gangs do not gain a foothold in the neighborhood, but the youths are adamant that protection of the community is still one of their primary responsibilities. In this sense, they are an integral component of parochial social control. Nevertheless, gangs also wreak havoc in their communities, both by their actions and by the lure they present to rival gangs. In particular, neighborhood residents are at greater risk of injury today than they were a generation ago because of the increase in drive-by shootings. A youth service provider expressed the views of many adults

> A lot of innocent people get hurt in drive-bys. They're just there in the wrong place at the wrong time and get killed or shot when they don't have anything to do with the problem.

Similarly, a Chicano social worker commented

> Neighbors feel they can't go out at night, can't sit on the porch. There's violence and crime. Many gang members may hang out in the neighborhood and not be involved in violence, but they're targets. Somebody will drive by and verbally abuse them, throw things in their yard, or shoot them.

Thus, two different, though interrelated, perspectives surface within the community. Some residents blame the gangs, seeing "the stigma of having gang problems" as contributing to businesses and middle-class families leaving the neighborhood. Other residents focus on the city's and the media's willingness to ignore economic problems in parts of town where poor people of color live. When city officials and reporters do pay attention to the area, they focus only on the negative aspects of life there, without doing much to improve the infrastructure. To better understand these varied perspectives, we looked for structural patterns in the data. As we will demonstrate, much of the variation can be explained by gender, age, number of generations in the United States, educational level, traditionalism, and the extent to which the person's family is gang identified.

The Men's Voices

We asked all of the adult respondents to tell us not only their own opinions about the relationships among gang kids, their families, and the community, but also how they thought other adults in the community perceived these issues. We expected men and women to differ somewhat in their views, consistent with the extant literature on fear of crime and neighborhood-based crime control efforts (Bursik and Grasmick, 1993a:91; Madriz, 1997; Skogan and Maxfield, 1981). Considering first how men in South Phoenix viewed gangs, the neighborhood activists and service providers saw men's opinions as determined primarily by whether they are gang identified. For example, one women observed

> Fathers don't have a big problem with gangs. They were involved in one way or another when they were younger. They always had a homie-type camaraderie.

Other respondents tied acceptance of gangs to prison life, and pointed to the difficulty of private, familial social control of youths with incarcerated parents. From this perspective

> [some men] are accepting of [gangs] and are in prison gangs themselves. We have a gang problem because the adult male population is in prison, so the kids are in street gangs.

Regardless of whether they ever formally joined gangs themselves, adults whose families belong to multigenerational gangs appear to be more accepting of their children's involvement in them, may gain prestige from their children's acts, and see the gang as a barrio institution through which cultural norms of personal and family honor are played out. This finding is consistent with similar research in other cities (Harris, 1994; Horowitz, 1983; Horowitz and Schwartz, 1974; Moore, 1978, 1991; Padilla, 1993; Vigil, 1988). A neighborhood specialist for the city said

> It's multigenerational. The grandfather may have been in a gang. Grandfathers of 40 could still have ties with the gang. You could have a great-grandfather with ties to old gangs!

As they get older, the men ease out of gang life. Yet, as a Latina director of a youth service center commented

> The oldsters, old gangsters, sit back and watch what's happening. They are very aware. They are learning they have to pull away if they want to live, but those are strong friendships that last forever.

An African-American male police officer expressed a similar opinion

> In areas with multi-generational gangs, it is difficult for older males to understand why society comes down so hard on the young ones. The degree of criminal activity has not hit them upside the head until they lose a loved one to a shooting. . . . If the men get a reality slap, they see the differences over time. Or they'll say to the kids, 'Why don't you have a gang like we had? We had a good gang.'

Yet, some differences of opinion surface among the men. The neighborhood specialist quoted above continued

> Some men view the gangs with disdain, seeing them as a blight on the community and a threat to community life, and others feel it provides a sense of fraternity, an opportunity to become involved with others who think and act like they'd like to; it provides them with an outlet.

An African-American woman working closely with neighborhood residents drew similar distinctions

> Some of them are from multigenerational gang families. The parents are hardcore members supportive of the life, and they're raising their kids in it. Others are very hardcore in opposition to it, saying to make prisons tougher. They are harder, more judgmental, saying, 'if you do the crime, do the time.'. . . They say, 'I'm gonna stop it by buying a .45 and blowing away the first motherfucker who comes in my door.'

Thus, for some adult men in the community, gangs are perfectly normal, acceptable parts of life. They take pride in their children following in their footsteps. Other adult men abhor today's gangs. Key factors accounting for these differences of opinion include the extent to which the men hold traditional Mexican values, the length of time they have spent in the United States, and educational achievements. A man born in South Phoenix, still living in the area, and working with local teens both as a volunteer and in his job as a probation officer sees these factors as intertwined

> The first generation, the traditionalists, see the second generation as lazy, as not pursuing the education and opportunities they are seeking for their children. . . . They try to prevent their children from getting involved. . . . The Chicanos who are traditional and have held ground (in the neighborhood) don't see the gangs as so much of a threat. They have raised their children to be successful. They can see the other folks and say, 'Hey, there's a problem there and I wish they'd take care of it!'. . . Of those in the second generation of gangs, the dads have limited educations. They take care of things physically, instead of rationally. They are starting to be supportive of changing

the system, though, because they are seeing too much violence. For the second generation, bicultural men, and I count myself as one, success depends on how much education they have.

According to the adults we interviewed, men born in Mexico generally hold the most traditional values and tend to disapprove of the gang life. Yet, they are stymied by their inability to control their children or grandchildren, and if public resources exist that they might employ to better control the youths, these immigrant men do not know how to access them. They are also uncomfortable requesting help from parish priests, school teachers, or social workers. The women, as we shall see, are somewhat more willing to reach out for these parochial forms of social control.

A middle-aged woman directing a neighborhood association providing educational and employment-related services and training for youths noted, "Grandfathers disapprove, see them as lazy and shiftless." A Puerto Rican social worker stated similarly

> A grandfather will say, 'I worked in the fields, why can't you?' Kids killing one another is not readily understood by the more traditional older generation.

Yet, another man working closely with boys in the neighborhood said

> For the *abuelos* (grandfathers), they have a firm grasp of life, they've lived through many tragedies so they appreciate life and the foolish wasting of it in gangs.

Our data indicate that substantial changes have occurred over time in the perceived extent to which gangs protected the larger community, the dangers to gang members and others in the community posed by today's more lethal weapons, and, generally, the respect with which gang members were and are held by others in the community. We were told.

> The general consensus is gangs are negative. This is especially from grandparents who are used to gangs, from the Zoot Suits. They were respected, they were not a danger to the community. They say, 'I don't understand these punks, why are they doing these things, not taking care of us, of the neighbors. They talk all the time about being part of the neighborhood but they don't take care of us.'
>
> [What about the fathers?]
>
> When I was a kid we had gangs, but we never used guns. We used chains. When we had a problem and fought, it was one-on-one, or a gang on a gang, but never three, five, six to one. That sounds cowardly to them [the fathers]. This generation gap is a problem. The kids say, 'Your way wasn't better, it didn't work. I have more money than you, so how can you tell me it's not right, that your way is better?' This is a big issue. They make money! And they [fathers] can't make money in society.

Another local social worker also reminisced about the "old days" when he was involved in gangs

> In the past, we weren't out to kill each other. Maybe there'd be fist fights or knives, but we weren't out to kill each other. Guns and drugs are the problem, and they're easily bought on the streets.

Thus, educational level, age, and the recency of their family's immigration to the United States structure barrio men's views about gangs and the range of resources they see as available to them. Grandfathers and fathers who immigrated to the United States may be leery of public forms of social control, such as the police and the juvenile justice system, and more hesitant than their wives to call on the Catholic Church for aid. They rely most heavily on the extended family to control youths, often unsuccessfully. In contrast, men raised in the gang life and still tied to it are more accepting of their children's involvement. Finally, the men raised in the barrio but now successful in local businesses and social services (e.g., probation, clinical psychology) have greater access to political and economic brokers in the metropolitan area and, perhaps for this reason, are more willing to rely on public as well as parochial and private forms of social control. Our data suggest that less variation exists within women's perspectives, with the key distinguishing factor being whether they were raised in a traditional Mexican family, either in the United States or in Mexico.

The Women's Voices

The consensus among our adult respondents was that most women disapprove of gangs. A Puerto Rican male working with families of gang members had the impression that "nine out of ten mothers despise gangs." Some of the women were members themselves when they were younger and may remain at least peripherally involved, but as they become mothers many grow increasingly fearful that their children could die in a gang-related shooting.

Gendered cultural expectations of child-rearing responsibilities appear to have contributed to mothers becoming more active than fathers in opposing gang activities. Also, many of the barrio's adult men are incarcerated, or for other reasons do not interact much with their children. Neighborhood leaders, both male and female, commented that it is primarily the women who come forward to work with them. One neighborhood activist said

> [The women] are pretty fed up with it. . . 60% of those who come to community meetings are female. They are very vocal, fed up, afraid to lose their children. Some have already lost their children, or their nephews and nieces, at the hands of guns. They want to bring the neighborhood back under control.

Some of these mothers take a very strong line and "won't let daughters date boys who look like cholos." Neighborhood women are also well represented at funerals. A parish priest with the dubious honor of burying the neighborhood's children told us, "At wakes you will see 400 kids, 50 mothers, and maybe 10 fathers." Mothers Against Gangs, a grassroots organization begun by a mother after her 16-year-old son died in a gang shooting, is a prime example of women organizing to reduce gang violence. Again, we see a link between private and parochial forms of social control. When parents and grandparents are not able to control the youths, they often turn to community organizations, such as Mothers Against Gangs (see, similarly, Fremon, 1995). Moreover, we see that these examples of private and parochial social control are very much gendered.

Mothers and grandmothers raised with traditional values were less likely to be out on the streets and so did not themselves live the gang life. These traditional women often do not know what to do about their children's involvement with gangs. As an activist knowledgeable about gangs said of the mothers who moved here from Mexico

> [They] feel helpless. It's something new for them. Many of them have problems with language. The kids speak English better than they [the mothers] do and better than they speak Spanish,

so the parents can't communicate with the kids. It's not like in Mexico, where the *abuelos* can say and do things. Here, it depends on the parents.

Similarly, a Chicano social worker stated that for mothers

> The general feeling is powerlessness. They have to care for them and love them and wish they weren't involved. They may feel guilty. It must be their fault, what did they do wrong. . . . It is *very* painful if the girls are in the gangs.

The sense of individual, rather than societal, responsibility for gang violence was stressed by many of our respondents. Specifically, they suggested that young mothers often have inadequate parenting skills. A probation officer raised in the barrio commented

> These kids intimidated their parents way before this. The hardline mothers and grandmothers who really push their kids to stay out [of gangs] are winning the battle. Those who are afraid, and they're mostly the 18–20 year olds, are afraid because they didn't put their foot down enough. It comes down to parenting skills, taking a hard line.

Social workers and neighborhood activists suggest that some mothers are unwilling to believe that their children are involved in gangs, even when signs are all around them. We were told that traditional women, in particular

> [See gangs as] a danger to the family unit. They don't want their kids involved in it, are very protective. But they also may have blinders when it comes to their own kids, saying, 'My kid isn't into that' when he is.

A South Phoenix parish priest related a story about a mother who wanted her son to be buried in a red shirt and the pallbearers to wear red, claiming it was always her son's favorite color. Another mother insisted that her son was not involved with gangs, until the priest turned to the young man and asked him to explain the significance of his red shoelaces to his mother.

In conclusion, then, our data suggest that whether and when adults rely on private, parochial, or public forms of social control depends on their access to economic and political resources and their position within the family and neighborhood power structures. One of our contributions to this literature is to show that this access may also be gendered, with women evidencing more indicators of powerlessness, such as not speaking English, and less experience dealing with businesses, courts, and the like. These women are most likely to advocate for a mix of parochial and public social control. They fear for their children's lives, but they tend to be among the most intimidated by their sons and daughters. Many of these women have organized within their communities and work with the police to at least a limited extent, hoping that these efforts will help to keep their children alive. This combination of private, parochial, and public social control is the premise of groups such as Mothers Against Gangs. In contrast, women who were in gangs as teenagers and who maintained that identity are generally the most accepting, and perhaps the least fearful, of gang violence and the least willing to let the police into their communities. Even these women, however, express fears of losing their children to gang violence and may draw on parochial forms of social control within the community.

The perceptions held by adult service providers and residents may be plagued by faulty, perhaps romanticized, recollections of what gangs were like in earlier generations. Also, many of the adults we interviewed had vested interests in the gang problem. Reliance solely on their perceptions ignores how young people see their own lives and the relationship between their gangs and other community members. Consistent with our emphasis on multiple standpoints, we turn now to the thoughts and concerns of the youths.

YOUTH PERSPECTIVES ON GANGS AND THE COMMUNITY

Historically, gangs have been important neighborhood institutions offering disenchanted, disadvantaged youths a means of coping with the isolation, alienation, and poverty they experience every day (Decker and Van Winkle, 1996; Hagedorn, 1991, 1998; Horowitz, 1983; Jackson, 1991; Joe and Chesney-Lind, 1995; Moore, 1978, 1985, 1991; Padilla, 1993; Sullivan, 1989; Vigil, 1988). Yet, gangs are dynamic, responding to transformations in the larger social order. Sometimes, changes in the social and economic structures also cause cracks in what we call the gang-family-barrio equality. It is not so unusual today to find families living in two different neighborhoods and, thus, often participating in two or more gangs. When this situation occurs, fissures appear in the cement bonding the community's social structure together.

Gangs as Neighborhood Institutions

Regardless of what other neighborhood residents may think of them, the youths identify strongly with their neighborhoods, consider themselves to be integral parts of their barrios, and view their gangs as neighborhood institutions. They see themselves as protectors of their neighborhoods, at least against intrusion by rival gangs. A few youths take pride in their care of elderly residents. However, most youths acknowledge that they do not contribute much to their neighborhoods, excluding community service stipulated as part of their probation or parole agreements.[4] For example, one youth stated

> We spray paint the walls and stuff like that, stealing cars, shooting people when we do drive-bys and stuff like that.

Moreover, some youths recognize that innocent bystanders are occasionally shot in drive-bys or other revenge killings

> People are getting smoked everyday and you don't even hear about it on the news, only if it is crazy and shit.

Chicano/a gangs often take the name of their barrio as their gang name. With few exceptions, the youths must live in the neighborhood and be of Mexican origin to become a member of the neighborhood gang.[5] These membership requirements hold whether the youth is "born into" the gang or "jumped" in. Some, particularly the young women, are simply "born" into the gang because they live in the neighborhood. They do not need any more formal initiation rites: It is their neighborhood, so it is their gang. If they want to be taken seriously as a gang member, though, being "born" in is not enough. The youths—male

---

[4] Members of the gangs we studied sell drugs, steal cars, and commit other crimes as both individual and gang-related activities. Unlike the gangs discussed by Padilla (1993) and Jankowski (1991), however, these gangs are not organized as criminal enterprises.

[5] The major exception is a predominantly Mexicano gang that accepts some white youths as members.

and female—must endure a serious beating by a group of their homeboys or homegirls (Portillos, 1999).

Beyond feeling ties to the physical boundaries of the barrio, the youths feel strong emotional ties because neighbors are often family members. If we contextualize the term "family" more broadly to include the nuclear family, the extended family, and the fictive family (*compadres* and *comadres*), gang-family ties become even stronger. All of the youths in our sample claimed that at least one other family member was involved in gangs. For example, a youth informed us

> I got two aunts that were in a gang, my dad was in a gang, my grandpa was in a gang, and I got a lot of cousins in gangs. Most of them are in my barrio but some of them aren't.

Siblings, cousins, and family friends so close as to be considered cousins are frequently members of the same gang, resulting in what often appears to be a gang-family-barrio equality. Although these overlapping social relationships have characterized Chicano/a gangs in the past (Moore, 1991; Vigil, 1988; Zatz, 1987), and in large part continue to define them today, we find that geographic dispersion has altered the tight bonds among the gang, the family, and the barrio.

Communities in Turmoil: Family Fighting Family

Family mobility was another issue that came up frequently in our interviews and provides insights into some of the ways in which public social control and, to a lesser extent, parochial control shape and constrain private forms of social control. Sometimes, families moved because of divorce or job opportunities elsewhere in the valley. Other times, they moved because the parents were so fearful of gang activity in the neighborhood. Children also went to live with grandparents or aunts when their parents were incarcerated. Finally, teenagers unable to get along with their parents sometimes moved in with relatives. An unfortunate and ironic side effect of this mobility is that it may lead to gang rivalries crosscutting families. That is, if gang warfare erupts between these different neighborhoods, families may literally be caught in the cross-fire. This phenomenon of family fighting family is anathema to more traditional Chicanos/as and Mexicanos/as, challenging existing notions of private, familial social control.[6] A 15-year-old female commented that more than 50 members of her extended family are or were in gangs

> We can't have family reunions or anything because they are always fighting, like my *tíos* (uncles) fight. At the funerals they fight, or at the park, or at a picnic when we get together, they just fight. So sometimes the family don't get together, only for funerals, that's the only time.

Similarly, a 16-year-old male reported that his dad was mad because

---

[6] The theme of inter-gang conflicts within families arose during the course of our interviews with the youths. Because interviews with adults were taking place at the same time, we were not able to systematically ask the adults for their perceptions of how extensive this problem had become. We did, however, ask samples of probation officers and juvenile court judges whom we later interviewed for a related project to discuss this issue, and we incorporate their views here.

> I am from westside; they are from eastside. See, I was supposed to be from eastside, but I didn't want to be from there. He don't want me to be his son because I'm not from eastside.

For the family that is split across two feuding gangs, cycles of revenge killings are particularly devastating. A 17-year-old male described the conflicts within his family

> And it's crazy because we are like from different gangs, only me and my cousin are from the same gang. Like my brother, I always disrespect him because he's from Camelback and shit, they did a drive-by on my house and shit, and then he called me. I was like, 'Fuck you, motherfucker, fuck your barrio and shit,' and he was like, 'Don't disrespect,' and I was like, 'Fuck you'. That's the only thing bad about it if you decide to join the wrong gang.[7]

Similarly, a young Mexicano-Indian clarified his relationship with his uncles

> They are from different gangs, though . . . but I don't care about them because they be trying to shoot at us all the time. My own uncle shot at me, one of them tried to kill me already, but that's all right.

He explained further that although most members of his family, including brothers, sisters, aunts, uncles, his dad, his mom, his grandfather, and numerous cousins were in the same gang, a few claimed different neighborhoods. He noted rather matter-of-factly

> I got about two uncles in a gang. I had four of them, but one is dead. My uncles killed him for some reason, I don't know, different barrio maybe.

As this youth noted, it is sometimes difficult to assess the basis for fighting within and across gang families. He was not certain why his uncle was killed, whether it was over gang issues or identities or for some other reason unrelated to gang membership. Yet, his assumption, perhaps because of the centrality of gangs in his own life, was that the intrafamilial homicide was gang related. When family feuds become entwined with gang rivalries, it is clear that the private system of social control has broken down. Family and friendship dynamics are no longer able to keep peace within a community. Under these conditions, parochial and public forms of social control typically come into play. Because one of the major public institutions of social control is the juvenile court, in a related study, we asked a sample of juvenile court judges and probation officers whether they perceived gang-related violence within families to be a significant problem. Most of the court officials responded that intrafamily gang conflicts were not a problem in their courts, although a few had seen such conflicts within extended families. Where intrafamily conflicts developed, the judicial officials attributed them either to the gang becoming a stronger psychological force than the family for particular youths or to youths moving into neighborhoods with strong gangs. As one judicial officer stated

> I think it would depend on the neighborhood that you live in and who was in control of that neighborhood. . . . A lot of these kids join gangs for their own protection. And if this is the gang that is going to afford me the most protection, I don't care what gang José on Oak St. belongs to just because he's my cousin. I don't live over there. I live over here, and I have to do what's best for me.

---

[7] With the exception of the gangs named in note two, pseudonyms are used in place of individual and gang names throughout this analysis. Street names have also been changed so as not to identify particular neighborhoods.

Not to Die For

Gang members are supposed to be willing to do anything for their homeboys and homegirls, even to die for them. The importance of demonstrating one's "heart," or willingness
to be "down" for the gang, is the major reason for jumping in new members and the basis for extolling acts of bravery and craziness (*locura*) by gang members (Portillos et al.,
1996). To assess the relative importance of gangs and families as predominant institutions
in the youths' lives, Decker and Van Winkle (1996) explicitly asked gang members to
choose between their family or the gang. The overwhelming majority, 89%, of the youths
chose their families. As Decker and Van Winkle explain their finding, "For most gang
members, the gang was a place to find protection, companionship and understanding.
Their family, however, represented something deeper, a commitment that most saw as
transcending life in the gang" (1996:251). As we have shown, often gang members *are*
family members.

Given the assumed importance of gangs and historically close ties among the
gang, the family, and the barrio, one of our most interesting findings was that more than
half of the youths would *not* willingly die for all of their homeboys and homegirls.
About a third were willing to die for specific individuals who were in their gang, but not
for everyone. Another third straightforwardly stated that they would not willingly die for
their gangs. The reason, they said, was "because I know they wouldn't die for me, they
ain't that stupid."

In response to the direct query, "For whom would you willingly die?" all of the youths
claimed that they would die for their families. When probed, they named their mothers, their
children, their siblings, maybe an aunt or grandmother, and specific friends and relatives.
Some of these family members belonged to the gang, but others did not. The distinction between someone who is simply a member of one's gang and someone who is family (including fictive kin) was clarified for us by a 16-year-old male who, a few days previously,
had been struck by a bullet that, had he not gotten in the way, would have hit a friend's
grandmother. He said, "I will die for my *true* homeboy; he would die for me."

We suggest that affirming one's willingness to die for a friend takes on new meaning when easy access to guns makes death a real possibility. When asked about the bad
parts of gang life, "death" was typically the first factor named by both the gang members
and adults. Probing indicated that the youths have a very real sense that they could die if
they remain in *la vida loca*.[8] In earlier generations of gangs, when death was not so common a feature, it may have been far easier to claim, with plenty of bravado, that one would
die for one's gang.

The responses to our question reinforce the gendered nature of gang life. Even though
female gang members prided themselves on their fighting skills, none of the young women
declared a willingness to die for her gang. A few confessed that they might have done so
when they were younger, but their tone suggested that this was a phase they had outgrown.
These gendered responses are consistent with the general findings in the literature of lower
rates of violence and lesser acceptance of violence among females than males (Chesney-

---

[8] According to one of our respondents, a machine gun cost about $35 in 1996, when we were
collecting our data. While guns may have been used in the past, in recent years they have become
exceedingly cheap and easy for teenagers to obtain.

Lind and Sheldon, 1998; Curry, 1998; Joe and Chesney-Lind, 1995), but they may also reflect the greater relevance of the family and private social control for young women than for young men.

It is difficult to determine at this point whether we are simply seeing an aging or maturation effect, in which as youths become older and perhaps leave the gang life behind, they see the gang in less romantic terms. They may be maturing into a more adult way of taking care of the barrio, which as we have maintained *is* their extended family, or we may be seeing evidence of a crack in the gang-family-barrio equality.

Of particular interest to our thesis, we suggest that the apparent contradiction between intrafamily fighting and a willingness to die only for one's family may be explained by a more careful analysis of variation in the forms that private social control may take. That is, family fighting family suggests a *reduction* in the amount of private social control, but when youths report that they would die for their families, but not for their gangs (excepting gang members who are family or close family friends), this indicates that the family remains a potent force in their lives. Thus, we do not see a complete breakdown in private social control, but rather what appear to be some changes in the form that private social control takes as we move from more traditional families to more acculturated families. When we add economic stresses and political disenfranchisement, we also see few opportunities for courting public social control on the community's terms. In the section that follows, we return to our earlier theme of economic and political dislocations and what these imply for local youths.

GANGS, MULTIPLE MARGINALITIES, AND URBAN DISLOCATIONS

The final theme that emerged from interviews with the youths brings us back to Vigil's concept of multiple marginalities and urban dislocations. The immediate world within which these youths live is marked by poverty, racial discrimination, cultural misunderstandings, and gendered expectations. As one young man stated, "We are a bunch of project kids, always on the move."

All of the youths in our sample were either kicked out or dropped out of school, and many had not completed ninth grade. This lack of education makes it exceedingly difficult to leave their marginal positions in the inner city and the gang life in their neighborhoods behind (see, similarly, Anderson, 1990; Padilla, 1993; Spergel, 1986). They spoke at length about problems they faced in school. For example

> I use to go to Lincoln Middle School. The teachers, fuckin' white teachers. The gym teacher, you know just because I was messin' around, threw me up against the locker and I reported him. And nobody said shit about it. I told them, 'fuck that, I ain't coming to this school no more' and they didn't even call the damn police. When they did call the police, they said they were going to take me to jail. So I just took off, I was like what the fuck, the motherfucker, he was the one pushing me.

It is interesting to note that the only times when the youths spoke about what we might call parochial and public forms of social control, it was to complain about them. As the previous quote indicates, teachers were not viewed as a resource by most of these youths, but rather as authority figures who reinforced their daily experiences of racism, marginality, and alienation. Moreover, their sense was that the police regularly sided with the teachers, rather than protecting the youths against what they perceived to be assaults and other forms of aggression on the part of the teachers.

The teens we interviewed are cognizant of the barriers confronting them. They recognize that their criminal and academic records make it almost impossible for them to move up the socioeconomic ladder. Yet, they still hold very mainstream aspirations. They see themselves as settling down to life with a steady partner or spouse and children, and they hope to be able to find a decent job. They want to become jet pilots, police officers, and firefighters, and they aim someday to purchase their own homes. For example, a young man expressed high hopes for his future but recognized the sad reality of life in the barrio

> I want to become an Air Force pilot, that wouldn't be a bad thing to be. The only fucked up thing is that I can't become a pilot because I have already been convicted of a felony in adult court.

Thus, although these youths may aspire to very mainstream futures, they recognize that poor schooling, inadequate job training, felony records, and racial/ethnic discrimination limit their potential for success.

CONCLUSIONS

In closing, we must stress that ours is an exploratory study, and our conclusions are based on only 53 interviews. Also, we did not set out to test Bursik and Grasmick's thesis; thus, our study does not constitute a full test of their model. We found, however, that attention to private, parochial, and public social control helped us to better understand the complexities of the relationship between gang members and other community residents.

We urge further research examining the perspectives of adults living and working with the youths. They know a lot about the youths' lives. Some adults are very sad and jaded, having watched their own children die in gang-related incidents. Other adults remain hopeful of making small changes in their worlds, with or without the help of police, business leaders, or politicians. Many adults are themselves former gang members and can shed light on historical shifts in the relationship between the gang, the family, and the neighborhood. Their insights, we suggest, should be incorporated into future studies of neighborhood-based gangs.

In conclusion, our study contributes to the growing body of research on gangs as situated socially and politically within poor urban communities of color. Like many other gang researchers (e.g., Curry and Decker, 1998; Curry and Spergel, 1988; Decker and Van Winkle, 1996; Hagedorn, 1991, 1998; Horowitz, 1983, 1987; Jankowski, 1991; Joe and Chesney-Lind, 1995; Klein, 1995; Moore, 1978, 1985, 1991; Padilla, 1993; Vigil, 1988), we assert that the social, economic, and political contexts within which gang life is set help to explain the complex and often contentious relations among gang members, their families, and the larger communities of which they form a part.

The gang was, and is, composed of brothers, sisters, cousins, and neighbors. The gang gives them a sense of community, a place where they belong. Kicked out of school, assumed to be troublemakers, looking tough and feeling scared, these young people are well aware that their options in life are very much constrained by poverty, racial discrimination, cultural stereotyping, and inadequate education.

Within this context, we suggest that Bursik and Grasmick's (1993a) theory of neighborhood dynamics helps explain the complex and often contradictory relations among the gang, the family, and the barrio. Their attention to private, parochial, and public levels of community-based social control are evident in the barrio we studied, and they point further to the difficulties facing community residents when they try to garner political and economic resources from outside their communities. It is, perhaps, to these political and economic linkages and disconnections that gang researchers and others concerned with crime in poor urban communities should look next.

QUESTIONS FOR UNDERSTANDING AND CRITICAL THINKING

1. What makes the Mexican American population in Phoenix different than other cities with similar racial/ethnic compositions? How do these ethnic factors play into gang research?
2. How can an integrated approach using social disorganization, subcultural theories, and economic marginalization provide for a more holistic understanding of gangs, families, and communities?
3. To what extent are men's and women's views on gangs different and similar?
4. Why are these perspectives important to know and understand?
5. What might be some policy implications of this study?

REFERENCES

ANDERSON, ELIJAH
1990   Street Wise. Chicago, Ill.: University of Chicago Press.

ARIZONA DEPARTMENT OF ECONOMIC SECURITY
1998   Arizona Economic Indicators. Spring. Tucson, Ariz.: The University of Arizona.

ARIZONA ECONOMIC DEVELOPMENT UPDATE
1998   The Gold Sheet. http://www.commerce.state.az.us/genderal/gold.shtml

BACA ZINN, MAXINE
1975   Political familism: Toward sex role equality in Chicano families. Aztlan 6:13-26.

BARKER, JEFF
1999   Phoenix forgotten get Clinton's notice; prosperity's shortfall to be focus of visit. Arizona Republic (June 29):A1.

BURSIK, ROBERT J. JR. AND HAROLD G. GRASMICK
1993a   Neighborhoods and Crime: The Dimensions of Effective Community Control. New York: Lexington Books.
1993b   Economic deprivation and neighborhood crime rates, 1960-1980. Law and Society Review 27(2):263-283.

CHESNEY-LIND, MEDA AND RANDALL G. SHELDON
1998   Girls, Delinquency, and Juvenile Justice. 2d ed. Belmont, Calif.: Wadsworth.

CURRY, G. DAVID
1998   Female gang involvement. Journal of Research in Crime and Delinquency 35(1):100-118.

CURRY, G. DAVID AND SCOTT H. DECKER
1998   Confronting Gangs: Crime and Community. Los Angeles, Calif.: Roxbury Publishing Co.

CURRY, G. DAVID AND IRVING A. SPERGEL
1988   Gang homicide, delinquency, and community. Criminology 26:381-405.

DECKER, SCOTT H. AND BARRIK VAN WINKLE
1996   Life in the Gang: Family, Friends, and Violence. New York: Cambridge University Press.

DONZIGER, STEVEN R. (ED.)
1996   The Real War on Crime: The Report of the National Criminal Justice Commission. New York: HarperPerennial.

ESCOBAR, EDWARD J.
1999   Race, Police, and the Making of a Political Identity: Mexican Americans and the Los Angeles Police Department, 1900-1945. Berkeley, Calif.: University of California Press.

EWICK, PATRICIA AND SUSAN S. SILBEY
1995   Subversive stories and hegemonic tales: Toward a sociology of narrative. Law and Society Review 29(2):197-226.

FAGAN, JEFFREY
1996   Gangs, drugs, and neighborhood change. In Ronald C. Huff (ed.), Gangs in America. 2d ed. Beverly Hills, Calif.: Sage.

FISCUS, CHRIS AND CHRISTINA LEONARD
1999   Phoenix, Buchanans settle suit. Arizona Republic (March 18):B1-B2.

Frankenberg, Ruth
1993   The Social Construction of Whiteness: White Women, Race Matters. Minneapolis, Minn.: University of Minnesota Press.

FREMON, CELESTE
1995   Father Greg and the Homeboys. New York: Hyperion.

HAGEDORN, JOHN M.
1991   Gangs, neighborhoods, and public policy. Social Problems 38(4):529-542.
1998   People and Folks: Gangs, Crime and the Underclass in a Rustbelt City. 2d ed. Chicago, Ill.: Lake View Press.

HARRIS, MARY G.
1994   Cholas, Mexican-American girls, and gangs. Sex Roles 30(3/4):289-301.

HERNÁNDEZ, JOSÉ
1990   Latino alternatives to the underclass concept. Latino Studies Journal 1:95-105.

HOROWITZ, RUTH
1983   Honor and the American Dream. New Brunswick, N.J.: Rutgers University Press.
1987   Community tolerance of gang violence. Social Problems 34:437-450.

HOROWITZ, RUTH AND GARY SCHWARTZ
1974   Honor, normative ambiguity and gang violence. American Sociological Review 39:238-251.

HUNTER, ALBERT J.
1985   Private, parochial and public school orders: The problem of crime and incivility in urban communities. In Gerald D. Suttles and Mayer N. Zald (eds.), The Challenge of Social Control: Citizenship and Institution Building in Modern Society. Norwood, N.J.: Ablex Publishing Co.

JACKSON, PAMELA IRVING
1991   Crime, youth gangs, and urban transition: The social dislocations of postindustrial eco-
         nomic development. Justice Quarterly 8:379-398.

JANKOWSKI, MARTÍN SANCHÉZ
1991   Islands in the Street: Gangs and American Urban Society. Berkeley, Calif.: University of
         California Press.

JOE, KAREN AND MEDA CHESNEY-LIND
1995   Just every mother's angel: An analysis of gender and ethnic variation in youth gang mem-
         bership. Gender and Society 9:408-430.

KLEIN, MALCOLM W.
1995   The American Street Gang: Its Nature, Prevalence, and Control. New York: Oxford Uni-
         versity Press.

LOFLAND, JOHN AND LYN H. LOFLAND
1995   Analyzing Social Settings: A Guide to Qualitative Observations and Analysis. Belmont,
         Calif.: Wadsworth.

LUSANE, CHARLES
1991   Pipe Dream Blues: Racism and the War on Drugs. Boston, Mass.: South End Press.

MADRIZ, ESTHER
1997   Nothing Bad Happens to Good Girls: Fear of Crime in Women's Lives. Berkeley, Calif.:
         University of California Press.

MANN, CORAMAE RICHEY AND MARJORIE S. ZATZ (EDS.)
1998   Images of Color, Images of Crime. Los Angeles, Calif.: Roxbury Publishing Co.

MARIN, MARGUERITE D.
1991   Social Protest in an Urban Barrio: A Study of the Chicano Movement, 1966-1974. Lan-
         ham, Md.: University Press of America.

MEARES, TRACEY L.
1997   Charting race and class differences in attitudes toward drug legalization and law
         enforcement: Lessons for federal criminal law. Buffalo Criminal Law Review
         1:137-174.

MILLER, JEROME G.
1996   Search and Destroy: African-American Males in the Criminal Justice System. New York:
         Cambridge University Press.

MIRANDÉ, ALFREDO
1987   Gringo Justice. South Bend, Ind.: Notre Dame Press.

MOORE, JOAN W.
1978   Homeboys: Gangs, Drugs, and Prison in the Barrios of Los Angeles. Philadelphia, Pa.:
         Temple University Press.
1985   Isolation and stigmatization in the development of an underclass: The case of Chicano
         gangs in East Los Angeles. Social Problems 33:1-10.
1991   Going Down to the Barrio: Homeboys and Homegirls in Change. Philadelphia, Pa.: Tem-
         ple University Press.
1998   Introduction. Gangs and the underclass: A comparative perspective. In John Hagedorn
         (ed.), People and Folks. 2d ed. Chicago, Ill.: Lake View Press.

MOORE, JOAN W. AND RAQUEL PINDERHUGHES (EDS.)
1993   In the Barrios: Latinos and the Underclass Debate. New York: Russell Sage.

MORRISON INSTITUTE FOR PUBLIC POLICY
1994   Kids Count Factbook: Arizona's Children 1994. Tempe: Arizona State University.

NATIONAL MINORITY ADVISORY COUNCIL ON CRIMINAL JUSTICE
1980   The Inequality of Justice. Washington, D.C.: U.S. Department of Justice.

PADILLA, FELIX
1993   The Gang as an American Enterprise. New Brunswick, N.J.: Rutgers University Press.

PORTILLOS, EDWARDO L.
1999   Women, men and gangs: The social construction of gender in the barrio. In Meda
          Chesney-Lind and John Hagedorn (eds.), Female Gangs in America: Girls, Gangs and
          Gender. Chicago, Ill.: Lake View Press.

PORTILLOS, EDWARDO L., NANCY C. JURIK, AND MARJORIE S. ZATZ
1996   Machismo and Chicano/a gangs: Symbolic resistance or oppression? Free Inquiry in Cre-
          ative Sociology 24(2):175-183.

SAMPSON, ROBERT J. AND JOHN H. LAUB
1993   Structural variations in juvenile court processing: Inequality, the underclass, and social
          control. Law and Society Review 27(2):285-311.

SAMPSON, ROBERT J. AND WILLIAM J. WILSON
1996   Toward a theory of race, crime and urban inequality. In John Hagan and Ruth D. Peterson
          (eds.), Crime and Inequality. Stanford, Calif.: Stanford University Press.

SHAW, CLIFFORD R. AND HENRY D. MCKAY
1942   Juvenile Delinquency and Urban Areas. Chicago, Ill.: University of Chicago Press.

SKOGAN, WESLEY G. AND MICHAEL G. MAXFIELD
1981   Coping with Crime: Individual and Neighborhood Reactions. Beverly Hills, Calif.: Sage.

SPERGEL, IRVING A.
1986   The violent gang problem in Chicago: A local community approach. Social Service Re-
          view (March):94-131.

SULLIVAN, MERCER
1989   "Getting Paid:" Youth Crime and Work in the Inner City. Ithaca, N.Y.: Cornell University
          Press.

U.S. COMMISSION ON CIVIL RIGHTS
1970   Mexican Americans and the Administration of Justice in the Southwest. Washington,
          D.C.: U.S. Government Printing Office.

U.S. COUNCIL OF ECONOMIC ADVISORS
1998   Economic Indicators. July. Prepared for the Joint Economic Committee. Washington,
          D.C.: U.S. Government Printing Office.

VENKATESH, SUDHIR ALLADI
1996   The gang in the community. In Ronald C. Huff (ed.), Gangs in America, 2d ed. Beverly
          Hills, Calif.: Sage.

VIGIL, JAMES DIEGO
1988   Barrio Gangs: Street Life and Identity in Southern California. Austin, Tx.: University of
            Texas Press.

WHITE, JONATHAN B.
1995   Dropout Rate Study 1993-94: Annual Dropout Rates in Arizona Public Schools Grades
            Seven Through Twelve. Phoenix, Ariz.: Arizona Department of Education.

WHITING, BRENT
1995   Adult justice sought for two teenage 'taggers'. Arizona Republic (October 19): B1-B6.

WILSON, WILLIAM JULIUS
1987   The Truly Disadvantaged. Chicago, Ill.: University of Chicago Press.
1996   When Work Disappears: The World of the New Urban Poor. New York: Random House.

ZATZ, MARJORIE S.
1987   Chicano youth gangs and crime: The creation of a moral panic. Contemporary Crises
            11:129-158.

ZAVELLA, PATRICIA
1996   Feminist insider dilemmas: Constructing ethnic identity with Chicana informants. In D.L.
            Wolf (ed.), Feminist Dilemmas in Fieldwork. Boulder, Colo.: Westview Press.

7

The Origins of Navajo Youth Gangs

Eric Henderson, Stephen J. Kunitz, and Jerrold E. Levy

In recent years, much attention has been given to the proliferation and emergence of street gangs among ethnic groups in locations formerly gang-free.[1] Navajo tribal members and officials have expressed strong concerns over both the presence of male youth gangs and what has been perceived as growing levels of violence.[2] Such concern is reasonable in a society in which accidents, suicide, homicide, and alcoholism are among the top ten causes of death for males.[3] Thus, "injury mortality" is "the single most important health problem of the Navajo.[4]

In 1997, the Navajo Nation estimated that approximately sixty youth gangs[5] existed in Navajo country. Through the Peacemaker Division of the judicial branch of the Navajo Nation, the tribe secured federal funding to study gangs.[6] The tribe has since been actively pursuing means to ameliorate the conditions that lead to gang formation.

Gang values encourage risky behavior. Many of these behaviors are taken to extremes, such as heavy drinking and drug use. Mortality from injuries and alcohol "occur most frequently in young adult males.[7] Thus, an examination of the history of gang formation, and the extreme forms of risky behavior associated with gang activity holds importance for both law enforcement and public health policy.

Although newspaper accounts[8] of Navajo gangs often stress the gulf between gang behavior and that of youths in earlier times, the origins of Navajo gangs in the early 1970s has some connection to Navajo adolescent male peer groups in the nineteenth century. More importantly, however, recent gang formation has been stimulated by off-reservation mod-

Reprinted from The American Indian Culture and Research Journal, v23, n3, by permission of the American Indian Studies Center, UCLA, Regents of the University of California.

els and changing social and demographic factors within Navajo country. It appears that gangs have formed around core members who were socially marginal members of their communities. Membership in a gang, although limited to a small minority of Navajo youths, represents one significant contemporary path followed in the transition from childhood to adulthood.

The relative contribution of nature and nurture in the transition from youth to adult has been one of the more persistent controversies in anthropology. It has been asserted that some societies develop social and cultural values that ease the transition, while others make the transition far more painful and difficult. Within a single society, individuals adjust differently to conditions of adolescence,[9] and the material conditions of life influence practice within and between cultures. Among the Navajo, the transition to adulthood often has been difficult, especially for males. Injury mortality among the Navajo has exceeded national levels throughout the century, and young Navajo males suffer higher rates of accidental deaths, suicides, and homicides than do Navajo women.[10] In addition to psychosocial factors, environmental hazards (such as poor roads and old vehicles) contribute to these elevated rates.[11]

Terrie Moffitt has developed a dual taxonomy to account for the relationship of age to antisocial behavior.[12] She distinguishes a small set of individuals with "life-course-persistent antisocial behavior" from a much larger number of adolescents who mimic the actions of these most deviant peers. She argues that "temporary versus persistent antisocial persons constituted qualitatively distinct types of persons"[13] based on differences in both nature and nurture. The behavior of persistent antisocial persons roots itself in theology and early socialization, which is grounded in neuropsychological deficits and exacerbated by developmental events.[14] This type of behavior peaks during adolescence,[15] and, according to Moffitt, the major cause of this rise is "adolescent-limited delinquents" engaging in "'social mimicry' of the antisocial style of life-course persistent youths."[16] Her theory of adolescence-limited delinquency views most adolescent "deviance" as "an adaptive response to contextual circumstances."[17]

Moffitt links her theory to the type of society in which these people live or, to use Julian Steward's term, the level of socio-cultural integration.[18] In industrialized nations most adolescent males commit some delinquent acts and only "a small minority abstains completely."[19] Delinquency increases with "modernization" because "[t]eens are less well-integrated with adults than ever before. What has emerged is an age-bound ghetto . . . from within which it seems advantageous to mimic deviant behavior."[20]

Moffitt's theory is useful in examining the emergence of male youth gangs in Navajo country. For the past one hundred years, male youths frequently have forged partying groups at ceremonies or other events. The expansion of Navajo participation in the boarding school system after World War II isolated youths from parents and community. This probably intensified peer group identification and the formation of loosely structured groups of males seeking a good time, so to speak. In general, Navajo males often have difficulty attaining "role and status satisfaction"[21] given their generally subordinate positions in a wage work economy. Given this situation, a young "Navajo male appears more prone to anomie and to frustration than does the female."[22] This observation, combined with Moffitt's view that delinquency is perceived by youths as providing access to the desirable resource of "mature status"[23] helps to explain the emergence of Navajo youth gangs in the 1970s.

In the classic formulation, "delinquent gangs" are a subtype of an urban street corner group of peers of one sex[24] whose most frequent activities are generally "sleeping, eating and hanging around."[25] Even among members, commitment to and identification with gang life varies,[26] being greatest among those who are socially the most marginal. For instance, in discussing Chicano gangs in Southern California, James Diego Vigil and John Long stress the importance of the *cholo* subculture—a subculture at the fringe of Hodigenous, Hispanic, and mainstream *Norte Americano* cultures.[27] Cholo subculture thus is defined as "marginal," and "core participants" in Chicano gangs are "among the most marginalized of these cholo youths."[28]

Similarly, informants who were core members in Navajo gangs were more marginal to both Navajo and Anglo culture than most other Navajo males. As hypothesized by Moffitt, these numbers displayed elevated levels of behaviors associated with conduct disorder. Both social marginalization and the nature and extent of antisocial behavior among core members are important in understanding the emergence of Navajo gangs.

Adolescent male groups array themselves along a continuum of group cohesiveness from spontaneous aggregations of young males through what Carl Taylor terms "organized/ corporate gangs."[29] Malcolm Klein, seeking some minimal criteria to distinguish gangs from other groups of youths, has identified "two useful signposts" to distinguish gangs from less formal "play groups;" (1) a "commitment to a criminal orientation" and (2) "the group's self-recognition of its gang status."[30] Navajo informants also recognize these minimal "signposts" as essential to gang mentality. Some locally designated gangs in the 1970s were relatively benign, while others were more organized and violent.

Informants applied the term *gang* primarily to groups of kin-related age mates residing in the same community. In addition, most of these named groups were viewed as prone to committing delinquent acts such as theft, vandalism, violence, and minor drug sales. However, as with many non-Navajo gangs, the primary focus of the first Navajo youth gangs appears to have been partying" (or "hanging-around").[31] Such emphasis differed little from other young and informal male drinking groups that were common during the years of the reservation livestock economy when most Navajos lived in scattered rural "camps."[32] During these times, young men often gathered at ceremonies to gamble, drink, and meet women. Such groups were ephemeral, dissolving at the end of the ceremony as participants returned to live and work within their extended families.

METHODS

The data for this paper are drawn from extensive interviews with about fifty Navajo men between ages twenty-one and forty-five. Most resided in reservation communities or a border-town along the eastern portion of the Navajo Reservation, although about a half dozen key informants resided in an agency town in the interior of the reservation. The informants constitute a sub-sample of the more than 1,000 individuals who participated in a case-control study of Navajo alcohol use. During the field interviews, several individuals mentioned the importance of their gang in their young drinking experiences. This subset of individuals was questioned at length about their gang involvement. A larger number of individuals was asked about gangs in schools and communities during adolescence. Through these informants we gained a substantial amount of qualitative data concerning the emergence of gangs in the two areas, as well as statements regarding gang activities and structures (or lack thereof).

Several caveats must be borne in mind. First, this is a preliminary survey. Researchers asked individuals if they knew of any gangs in the area when they were younger. The topic was rarely pursued if individuals responded negatively. Second, a number of people knew of gangs but had little contact with gang members or gang activities. Some could not provide gang names, while others provided estimates of gang size and activities.[33] Third, if a person had been affiliated with a gang in some fashion, we asked about gang activities and structure. In general, former members were open about their own involvement in the gang but were reluctant to name and discuss the activities of others. Since we encountered only about a dozen self-identified members, the data presented provide only a preliminary sketch of early gangs. Some interviewees minimized their experiences, while others exaggerated their gang involvement. Four members of one gang were interviewed[34] and provided relatively extensive—and basically consistent—information. Four other individuals who grew up in the same community also provided information regarding this gang and its members.

NAVAJO COUNTRY AND CULTURE CHANGE

The Navajo, an Athabaskan-speaking people, began settling in the San Juan River drainage prior to 1500 and had settled throughout their current land holdings by the mid-nineteenth century. Subsistence patterns changed as they spread across the land. From the Pueblos they adopted horticulture and from the Spaniards they gained livestock through trading and occasional raiding.[35] By the 1800s sheep pastoralism was the mainstay of Navajo subsistence. A few Navajo—primarily young men seeking livestock to establish the nucleus of a flock—launched raids on neighboring groups (primarily Spanish settlements along the upper Rio Grande). Beginning in the late 1840s, the U.S. Army responded to these raids. Between 1863 and 1868, the army incarcerated most Navajo on a reservation at Fort Sumner, New Mexico. Under the terms of the Treaty of 1868, the Navajo returned to a portion of their homeland. As the Navajo population (and their flocks) rapidly expanded, the United States enlarged the reservation through executive orders and congressional acts.[36]

An extensive network of trading posts gradually spread across the territory, progressively involving Navajo pastoralists in market relations.[37] In addition, the federal government established administrative centers at several locations across Navajo country, thus creating the nucleus for the growth of agency towns.

> The agency town in each case was the seat of governmental buildings and activities, whether hospital, school, or administrative office, or some combination of these. As the place through which federal money flowed for expenditure and as the seat of administrative authority and operations they were sources of jobs for Indians. Consequently they attracted Indians who built houses at the edges of the areas where governmental buildings were placed.[38]

Agency towns grew slowly through most of the twentieth century. The vast majority of Navajos continued to live in dispersed, semi-nomadic, extended family groups (primarily matrilocal) focused on pastoral pursuits.[39] Children helped in these tasks and only a small proportion of them attended school.[40] As late as 1950, less than half of the school-age population attended school.[41]

In the 1930s, the federal government's livestock reduction program destroyed the Navajo pastoral economy and altered Navajo social structures.[42] World War II drew many

Navajo further into the wage economy, but Navajo fortunes declined during the postwar recession. The government again intervened. Congress passed the Navajo Hopi Long-Range Rehabilitation Act in 1950 to expand schooling and develop reservation infrastructure.[43] By the late 1950s, nearly 90 percent of Navajo children were attending school, many in distant federal boarding schools.[44] Federal policy also encouraged the relocation of younger tribal members to distant urban areas.[45]

After the 1950s, portions of Navajo country witnessed a boom in natural resource exploitation (uranium, coal, gas, oil, and timber). The agency towns grew more rapidly over the ensuing decades as a result of increasing provisions from the government in the forms health, education, and welfare. Today about a quarter of the reservation's population resides in these administrative and service centers. Moreover, both the Indian and non-Indian populations of towns bordering the reservation also increased.[46]

By the 1970s there were at least four distinct types of communities in Navajo country: (1) rural communities where settlement remained dispersed and in which livestock pastoralism continued as a central activity (even if not remunerative); (2) a few densely settled communities of small family farms; (3) the agency towns; and (4) border towns (urban places near the reservation primarily populated and politically dominated by non-Navajos). While most Navajos continued to reside in rural communities, the other community types were growing and were conducive to the formation of youth gangs.

To understand the life chances of young Navajo males, several factors must be taken into consideration: (1) an end to raiding with the establishment of the reservation; (2) the waning of the livestock-based economy; (3) increased participation in the formal educational system; (4) the growth of the agency towns; and (5) increasing linkages between Navajos and urban areas (both border towns and distant cities). Changes in economic strategies, settlement patterns, and extended family residence arrangements during the past four decades have affected the extent and nature of kinship obligations.[47] For younger males, intergenerational cooperation declined as the live-stock economy waned and participation in schooling increased. In densely settled areas, there was daily contact with a greater number of peers. Such shifts typically diminished the opportunity for adolescents to share in the daily lives of older relatives.[48]

The emergence of a youth culture, comprised of age mates among Navajos in agency towns, is reflected in kinship terminology changes—the recent and widespread use of the English term *cousin-brother* to designate a set of relatives. Kinship terminology generally responds to changes in the sexual division of labor, residence arrangements, and, more directly, descent systems.[49] The rapid diffusion of the English term *cousin-brother* appears to be the result of complex changes in education and residential arrangements. *Cousin-brother* seems to be an informal "age-grade" marker expressed in the kinship idiom.

Navajo language cousin terms are classified by anthropologists as an Iroquoian kin terminology—parallel cousins and siblings are referred to by the same term and cross cousins by another term.[50] Today the term *cousin-brother* has gained currency among both young adults and teenagers and makes sense as a means of reconciliation between the Iroquoian terminology and the Eskimoan terminology of American English. The kin included under the rubric cousin-brother varies depending upon the individual using the term—some young men include all male cousins and siblings, while others limit the term to siblings and parallel cousins of the first degree (consistent with the Iroquoian terminology). Still others extend the term to members of the same clan of approximately the same age, anyone of the same age and somehow related.[51] For most of those who use the term, there is no specific referent to a Navajo linguistic kinship category. Rather, it expresses the solidarity of age-mates and as such has become central to the way Navajos in juvenile groups conceive of their relationships to one another. Members of one's gang frequently are denominated as "cousin-brothers" (and less frequently simply as "bros," or brothers).

A HISTORICAL PERSPECTIVE ON NAVAJO MALE YOUTH GROUPS

In contrast to the elaborate *kinaalda*, giving public recognition to a female's transition to adult status, male puberty is not marked with a rite of passage.[52] Moreover, the Navajo, unlike neighboring Puebloans, lack sodalities for both males and females. There were no warrior societies that typified tribes of the Plains and Prairies.[53]

There are reasons to believe that young Navajo males long have held some values that are distinct from other members of Navajo society. Vogt suggests that the "raiding complex" of the early nineteenth century involved a tension between older men with large flocks ("ricos") and "the young pobres who wanted raids to build up their herds of horses and sheep."[54] Raiding parties generally were comprised of four to ten men who lived in a single locality[55] and were under the command of an experienced man with ritual, war-related knowledge.[56] The establishment of the reservation brought an end to raiding and, hence, to this group activity among Navajo men.

In the pastoral economy of the early reservation years, the ideal behavior for a young Navajo man was to marry and reside with, and work for, his in-laws.[57] Some Navajo youths, of course, did not conform to this ideal, but traveled about, usually alone, seeking out women and forms of excitement such as gambling and drinking.[58] In the course of these travels, young men often congregated at ceremonies to form ephemeral groups. In the late nineteenth century, such groups sometimes engaged in gambling, drinking, and fighting at ceremonies.[59]

Clyde Kluckhohn and Dorothea Leighton, examining Navajo society in the waning years of the pastoral economy, proposed that acculturative pressures resulted in deviance and criminality among groups of younger Navajo males: "Thefts occur chiefly in areas under strongest white influence, especially at 'squaw dances' [Enemyway ceremonies] frequented by ne'er-do-well young men who are souls lost between the two cultures.[60] But these groups should not be confused with the loosely organized street corner gang model that emerges from early gang ethnography.[61] Navajo groups lacked continuity of membership from one event to the next. However, the roots of Navajo gangs may have some connection to these male associations at ceremonies. Some informants refer to young men acting like a gang at Enemyway ceremonies. A man who grew up in a rural community in the 1940s (herding sheep and playing with cousins and other relatives his own age) remembers that, at Enemyways, his group fought with rocks, sticks, and fists against boys from an adjacent community. Within each group the pre-adolescent to young teenage boys were connected both by bonds of kinship and residence in the same community. There were no reports of rivalries or organized fights extending beyond the specific socio-ceremonial occasion.

A strikingly similar description for the early 1970s from two informants involves older teenage boys in another rural pastoral community. A "north side" group would fight a "south side" group at Enemyway ceremonies. The "southsider" said his group was "like a gang" when they came together at Enemyways. They expected fights. The "northsider" recounted a 1973 fight at an Enemyway in another community: "It was like a gang fight."

When he stepped in to defend one of his group who was being beaten, someone in the rival group "hit me with a bottle."

The behavior of such groups at Enemyways and other ceremonies, or, more recently, tribal fairs, often is described as gang-like because groups of related youthful males consorted together. However, the groups were not gang-like in their continuity and cohesion. The youths did not "hang around" together after the gathering or think of themselves as members of an enduring group.[62] Given the rural settlement pattern and subsistence pastoralism dominating Navajo life through the 1940s, there was no opportunity for enduring male youth groups, or gangs, to develop. Most youths worked for their families, herding sheep or working on small farm plots. Often these were solitary chores. There was little time to just hang around. There were few schools or other institutions where youths could congregate away from adult supervision on a consistent and sustained basis. Young men could get together at ceremonies or other events, but these were sporadic occasions.

By the 1950s the majority of school-age Navajos were, for the first time, receiving a formal education, often at off-reservation federal boarding schools.[63] Men attending these institutions generally recall the experience as regimented and disciplined. Sometimes there were problems between Navajo students and students from other tribes. Several informants who attended the boarding school at Ignacio on the Southern Ute Reservation recalled fights between Navajo and Ute students in the 1960s. Individuals who attended Albuquerque Indian School and Sherman Institute reported similar confrontations between Navajo students and members of other tribes. Again, there are indications of gang-like behavior from these reports. One man referred to himself as a member of a "gang of young punks" when he resided at the BIA dormitory in Albuquerque around 1960. He was twelve at the time. With three other Navajo youths at the dorm, he stole from stores—pencils, notebooks, and shoe polish (things he needed for school, he explained). Some of the other kids took things they "didn't need . . . like baloney." Sometimes they "broke into" stores to take things.

The boarding school environment on the reservation also spawned gang-like groups of Navajos from different communities. In one central reservation high school, day students from an agency town banded together in fights with the boarding students from the rural pastoral community. Rural youths not only resided in the same community, but also lived among relatives, an extensive network of extended family members. In fact, in some contexts interviewees used the idiom of kinship rather than territory in referring to people of a rural locality. These groups were like gangs but were explicitly distinguished from more recently named gangs.

Robert Yazzie, chief justice of the Navajo Nation, recently wrote that "traditional" Navajo legal theory stressed the importance of such kinship relations. An offender "is someone who shows little regard for right relationships. That person has no respect for others. Navajos say of such a person, 'He acts as if he has no relatives.' "[64]

The consequences of universal schooling for young Navajo males are difficult to assess. The boarding school experience and the resulting rivalry with other tribes (and with other Navajos from other communities) likely generated greater peer group cohesion. Moreover, some informants report that when young males returned home for the summers, they felt less responsibility to aid kin. Because of the decline in livestock pursuits, there was less need to do so. They could, and did, stay with relatives in agency or border towns, visit relatives in distant rural communities, or gather with school friends to attend rodeos, ceremonies, or simply to "party in the boonies." A youthful male drinking "cohort" (sometimes with a common boarding school experience or ties of kinship) could form "more or less spontaneously at various events and places," especially in agency and border towns.[65]

During and after the 1960s, increasing numbers of Navajo students attended on-reservation schools rather than off-reservation boarding institutions. Each agency town had a growing high school (often with a boarding component). Many rural students were bussed in to these schools. Along the eastern edge of the reservation, many farm community youth attended nearby off-reservation public schools that had a predominately non-Navajo student body. It is in these environments—the agency towns and the border town schools—that the first self-identified Navajo gangs emerged in the early 1970s.

THE ORIGIN AND DISTRIBUTION OF YOUTH GANGS

Early Gangs on the Eastern Edge of the Reservation

The earliest references to self-identified gangs come from about 1970 in an agency town located near the eastern boundary of the reservation. In that year, one interviewee claims to have formed a gang, the Cruisers,[66] with about a dozen other schoolmates between the ages of thirteen and fifteen. Their primary activity consisted of drinking together at the town's drive-in theater on weekends. They shoplifted items "a bunch of times" to pay for liquor, which they got someone older to buy for them.

Other agency town interviewees of the same age cohort engaged in similar behavior but did not identify with a named gang. One person reported going around with about ten "other guys," stealing bicycles. They "hung around all over" the agency town. He recalled his group going to the drive-in to "beat on people for nothing" (for no particular reason), while the Cruiser recalled that his gang was involved primarily in fights with a rival gang called the Renegades, who were located in a border town. While the use of weapons, as well as the targets of violence, differentiated the Cruisers from the more informal group, the main difference between the report of the Cruiser and the non-gang interviewee is self-identification with a *named* group.[67]

Only the Cruiser reported named gangs as early as 1970. Group violence at the agency town drive-in did, however, figure into several other accounts given for the late 1960s and 1970s. In 1975, one individual became aware of gangs in the area when he saw a fight at the agency town drive-in.[68]

Names were obtained for the gangs operating in this agency town—Farm Boys, Spikes, Skulls, and Black Knights. The Metallics, at an adjacent farm community, and the Dead Boys, in a nearby rural community, also operated at this time. These gangs had fifteen to thirty-five members. They used guns, knives, chains, clubs, and other weapons in fights with rival gangs. One Skull reportedly shot himself in the calf with a 22 pistol at the school in 1980.

A non-gang member described the Skulls as a group of agency town high school students who were "from the reservation" (meaning rural reservation communities). Another former student would "just party [and] party with them," in the early 1980s but did not consider himself a member. The Skulls most frequently partied on the periphery of the agency town, drinking beer and smoking marijuana. There was little or no violence at these parties, but sometimes gang members ended up in the agency town jail for public intoxication. According to this informant, there were only fifteen or twenty Skulls and they did not have a leader. "They argued about that and nobody knew who the leader was," he commented.

The gangs of the 1970s, then, emerged in the densely populated agency towns and family farm communities. They were small and loosely structured. Although associated primarily with areas, some noted that the core of the gang consisted of kin living in proximity to one another.

Gangs at an Interior Agency Town

Data from the interior agency town reveal patterns similar to those from the eastern agency town area. A former core gang member, Paddy Lefty, gave relatively extensive descriptions of these gangs for the early 1980s. He identified six named groups (including one by a clan name and another by a family surname), and two unnamed groups (designated by the directions from the center of the agency town).[69] These gangs consisted mostly of relatives—especially cousins and brothers—who referred to each other as "Bro." The gangs were relatively small and lacked internal organizational structure. He could not identify anyone who clearly acted as leader in any of these gangs. These were rival groups that sometimes fought each other with bats, two-by-fours, chains, and knives.

Many of the gang activities Lefty described involved "hang[ing] around," drinking, and vandalism. Sometimes his gang would build a bonfire at a drinking party, but this was rare since fires would attract the attention of the police. Once they burned a large tree on the south side of town "to see what would happen." Often they would bust glass bottles on the highway, again to see what would happen. They spray painted buildings, broke windows, and slashed car tires. The gang members obtained money by robbing people (mostly heavily intoxicated men), bootlegged alcohol, and sold small amounts of marijuana. The gang appears to have disintegrated by the late 1980s as members were incarcerated (including Lefty), left town to seek work (or excitement), or took on family responsibilities.[70]

It may be that interior agency town gangs emerged slightly later in the 1970s than did gangs in the eastern agency town and its environs. Gangs in both areas were rather small and composed mostly of relatives within an age cohort residing primarily in the agency town and nearby farm communities. The gangs associated with adjacent rural communities generally were active only in the school and town.

CHARACTERISTICS OF CORE GANG MEMBERS

Only in the roughest fashion is it possible to estimate the extent of gang membership in these two areas during the 1970s. The information provided by informants indicates that, at most, 15 percent of Navajo male youths in the two areas were affiliated, peripherally or minimally, with gangs. The actual proportion most likely was significantly less than half this figure.[71] A number of individuals identified as gang members during this period had died (most frequently in drinking or violence-related accidents or incidents) or were in prison. Only four core gang members could be interviewed at length. This number is too small for a quantitative analysis, but the life histories of these four former gang members and comparisons with more peripheral members and hangers-on (also interviewed) provide important clues about gang dynamics. The interviews indicate patterns consistent with Vigil's insights concerning marginalization and Moffitt's thesis that many adolescents mimic the relatively few with life-course-persistent antisocial personalities.

All four core gang members were from troubled families. All had fathers who were heavy drinkers and three of the four fathers were physically abusive to their wives and children. One father forced his sons to fight each other because he "didn't want us to be chickenshits, he didn't want us to be pussies." Another core gang member was punished severely by his father, but it was his older brothers who were most abusive—they used to drink and "beat the shit out of me." The fourth informant said his father was not violent but that he had abandoned his family, leaving "my mom [to] grow me up." His mother punished her son "for anything I might do . . . every evening, every day" with "a big belt" or by "twist[ing] my ears." The parents of three of the gang members divorced. The father of the fourth had a second wife and children in a distant community.

None of these core gang members' families were well integrated into their communities. While only one informant came from an extremely poor family, the families of the other three resided away from their home communities (two off the reservation) for several years before the boys reached adolescence. Two of the boys lived for a time with their aunts and one was placed in off-reservation foster care for two years. Navajo was reported as the predominant language in the homes of all these youths. Although none of the families maintained flocks of sheep, two of the youths sometimes herded sheep for grandparents. In sum, these youths were reared on the "margins" of Navajo and white communities.

Prior to puberty and gang membership, all of these youths reported behaviors associated with conduct disorder. Prior to age twelve, all had taken items from stores and two had run away from home. By age thirteen all were frequently skipping school, three of the four had experienced their first sexual encounter, and all but one were already gang members. With gang involvement, delinquent behaviors increased. By age fourteen, all had smoked marijuana and had used at least one other mind-altering substance (usually glue, gas, or paint) and three of the four reported frequent fights and at least one arrest (the fourth was not arrested until age sixteen). By age sixteen, all reported engagement in vandalism and weapon use during fights. These self-reports show early antisocial behaviors which deepened with age and gang involvement.

Lefty, the interior agency town core gang member, described his entry into gang life. His older brother drank with the D.T.s. When Lefty was eleven this brother got him into the D.T.s. Lefty says that he soon assumed the role of "shanker" because "I wouldn't mind stabbing somebody" (and because he was one of the youngest gang members). He claimed he had stabbed several people. Mostly, however, the gang would "roll winos." Sometimes they would shoot dogs, "kill them just for the hell of it." He frequently skipped school and was sent to an off-reservation boarding school as a high school freshman. He was expelled for fighting, returned to the agency town in the mid-1980s, and renewed his gang-related activities. His conduct attracted the attention of social workers who eventually sent him to a state juvenile facility.

When Lefty returned to the agency town, he continued bootlegging, drinking, and marijuana use. The old gang, however, was no longer operating. Lefty was frequently arrested for fighting and for alcohol possession. He made four suicide attempts. At age twenty-two, after an assault arrest, he entered a residential treatment program because he grew "tired of drinking and smoking [marijuana]" and "wanted to make something of myself."

THE METALLICS: A CASE OF GANG FORMATION

In the eastern reservation area, interviews with several informants concerning the Metallics reconstructs gang formation and highlights the interplay among community, marginality, and personality. In the early 1970s, the three eldest Nance brothers formed the gang. These brothers were born in the 1950s in Southern California. The family returned to Mrs. Nance's home community (a reservation farming area) in the late 1960s. The father was described by two of his sons as a heavy drinker who was abusive to the boys and to their mother. Moreover, he was frequently away from home, working, drinking, and engaging in extra-marital affairs.

These brothers were day students at a border town high school after the family returned from California. They gained a reputation for violence and toughness. They were familiar with Southern California gangs and self-consciously set out to create a gang on their own. Apparently, one of the first members was a "clan-brother" who eventually came to be a core member.

At home the brothers frequently fought with their father and younger siblings. One younger brother, Marlin, recalls that when his older brothers drank they "beat the shit out of me." Marlin began shoplifting when he was eight. At thirteen he and some friends burglarized a trading post, taking jewelry and knives. They drank and sniffed glue under a nearby bridge and were apprehended for it. The next year, Marlin and some of these boys joined his older brothers' gang. He stopped sniffing glue and began using marijuana. Later he started drinking alcohol. He helped his older brothers, two of whom had graduated from high school, and other gang members grow and sell marijuana. Marlin also sold a little of the peyote he stole from his father's ceremonial supply. When Marlin was sixteen his father died suddenly of a stroke. "I had what I wanted," Marlin recalled, referring to an end to his father's abuse. Marlin began to engage in acts of vandalism with other gang members and occasionally fought with rival gangs. Mostly, however, the gang got together to drink.

This was consistent with JL's memory. JL was a peripheral member of the gang. A year younger than Marlin, JL was connected to the Metallics primarily through his association with Marlin. When interviewed, JL said his mother was related to Mrs. Nance and while he was not sure of his own clan, he thought (incorrectly) it was the same as the Nance brothers. JL liked to drink and party with the Metallics but did not engage in as much delinquent behavior and was involved, he says, in only one gang fight. Unlike core members of gangs, JL had always lived in the community. His antisocial behaviors began at a later age and were less extensive. He began skipping school about twice a month and shoplifting when he was about thirteen or fourteen and began using tobacco and drinking weekly at fifteen, generally only when he was in the company of the Metallics. JL apparently modeled the behavior of the gang members. His family was more integrated into the community. His parents had more than one hundred head of livestock and his mother was a weaver. JL's father was an unskilled laborer who worked relatively consistently to help support the family (albeit with less income than the parents of the core gang members). There were problems in the home, however. His father drank heavily, although this did not affect his employment or cause him to be mean. When sober, however, JL's father occasionally would whip JL with bailing wire or a leather belt if he disobeyed instructions. JL's mother, on the other hand, would get "mean" and strike JL's father when she drank. JL's older half-brothers also drank and would get "mean," sometimes punching JL. Thus, JL's family situation may have contributed to his seeking out gang members as role models.

In the late 1970s several Metallic leaders killed a rival gang member from the agency town and were sent to prison. As a result, the gang began to dissolve. By the early 1980s, Marlin's two eldest brothers had gotten full-time jobs. JL drifted away from the gang, joined the Jobs Corps and then began working at temporary jobs. JL continued to drink heavily but with less aggressive groups of individuals.

Interviewees estimated that the Metallics included between twenty and thirty-five members.[72] The first members (in the early 1970s) were of approximately the same age and incorporated a somewhat younger group in the late 1970s. The gang was short-lived and lacked cohesion. The Nance brothers seemed to have fought each other as much as members of rival gangs. Marlin reported stabbing an older brother six times during a drunken brawl. Another probable gang member knifed and killed his own half-brother. Moreover, they did not party exclusively with one another or with their own relatives and neighbors (their "cousin-brothers"). In fact, members often partied with strangers and sometimes members of rival gangs. The murder of the rival gang member did not prevent Marlin from subsequently partying at the agency town with the victim's brother. One party ended when the victim's brother broke Marlin's jaw as "pay back" for the murder. This incident indicates that there was little structure to drinking groups, even so-called gangs. Individual group members drank with almost anyone and interest in any party involving alcohol seemed to prevail over group solidarity.

DISCUSSION

During the years of the reservation livestock economy, from the late nineteenth century through the 1930s, Navajos lived in scattered rural camps. Young males sometimes gathered at ceremonies to meet women, gamble, and drink. However, such groups were ephemeral, dissolving with the termination of the ceremony. Young men spent most of their days with their mother's or in-laws' families.

The agency towns provide a striking contrast with the rural dispersed settlement patterns and the lifestyles associated with the livestock economy and the off-reservation boarding schools. In the rural areas, youths only have sporadic contact with more than a handful of age-mates and often spend long hours alone, herding sheep. At the boarding schools, youths were under the (nearly) constant supervision of school personnel. In the towns, families do not care daily for large flocks of sheep and youths do not spend most of their time isolated from others of the same age. Youths are in frequent contact with one another, both at school and in other daily activities. Adult contact and supervision is more intermittent. It is in this context, we have argued, that youth culture has emerged.

That Navajo gangs would first appear in these communities makes sense. Even groups drawing members from rural communities seem to have operated within the high schools of the agency and border towns. In the agency towns hundreds of families live in relative proximity, some in housing projects. Youths attend high schools near their homes. They could easily get together to "party" away from adults and outside of the context of ceremonial gatherings. Most interviewees who spent their high school years in agency towns or communities reported partying in informal groups in the 1960s and 1970s. Agency towns have grown since the turn of the century and many young residents in the 1970s were second- or even third-generation agency town dwellers. Thus, they were surrounded by networks of vaguely defined kin. They often were unaware of the precise nature of these relations and, as is clear from informants' comments adolescent males emphasized connections to peers rather than to their place the complex multi-generational kinship structure. The invention of a new kinship term, cousin-brother, marks this change.

Within this new context in the 1970s, gangs coalesced around core members who came from families that were marginal in the communities to which they returned after living off the reservation or in distant reservation communities. These marginalized Navajo youth at the core of gang formation provide a striking parallel to the importance of "choloization" and marginalization in discussions of Chicano gangs in Southern California.[73] In the case study of the Metallics, the Southern California parallels are especially interesting because the founding members were familiar with Chicano gangs.

These core members were not only socially marginal, but also more deviant at a younger age than peripheral gang members. Core members engaged in more acts of delinquency. They also report behaviors meeting the criteria for conduct disorder prior to their teen years. In later life, many core members continued to exhibit many antisocial behaviors. Peripheral members, on the other hand, report fewer antisocial behaviors. These type behaviors tended to begin later in life, generally corresponding to the time they joined in gang activities. Such data suggest that social mimicry is significant, as peripheral members pattern their behavior to follow the model of their more deviant core member cousin-brothers.

But early Navajo gangs also have roots in the ephemeral drinking groups of young males that spontaneously emerged at ceremonies in previous decades. Drinking parties that sometimes turn violent are not a facet Navajo life limited to gang parties since the 1970s. Fist fights, knifings, occasional shootings occur among the spontaneous partying groups as well as among the gangsters. In fact, no interviewee provided a detailed description of a well-organized gang fight and only a few cases of explicitly gang-related retaliatory attacks were reported. While there may be some undiscovered cases, the lack of information indicates that gang violence was not a central focus of gang identity or activity.

How, then, can we define groups such as the Metallics as gangs? It appears to be limited to self-identification and self-ascription. Indeed, it seems that the gang members of the 1970s and early 1980s had moved only a small step beyond the spontaneous party group by providing a name to a set of age mates who are related through clanship and community and who party frequently together. Some sets of cousin-brothers called themselves a gang, in part to set themselves apart from rivals. Other sets of cousin-brothers, engaging in quite similar activities, never conceived of themselves in this way.

The transition from youth to man is difficult for many Navajos given the paucity of local jobs, the low economic status of many families, and the frequently voiced concerns regarding the maintainance of Navajo tradition. While a number of Navajo youths may become temporary hell-raisers, only a very few, generally the most marginalized individuals—those from abusive or disrupted families living in densely settled communities and attending local schools—become core gang members. The gangs attracted a somewhat largest of peripheral members, apparently "adolescent-limited" delinquents, who modeled the behavior of core members.

Many core members apparently have continued to persist in antisocial acts. Two of the four gang core members interviewed had served prison terms, while the other two were arrested for spousal abuse or disorderly conduct within the two years prior to the interview. Other reputed core members died in accidents or fights, usually involving alcohol. But most former gang members, especially those peripherally involved, "aged-out" of the gang. They follow the life-course pattern that Thomas Hill described as "hell raiser" to "family man" among young Indian men (unaffiliated with gangs) in Sioux City, Iowa, in the 1970s.[74]

Peripheral gang members appear to have differed little in their commitment to anti-social behaviors from males who, prior to the 1970s, frequented ceremonies and other events in dispersed rural communities. However, in the more densely settled communities of the 1970s, these youths were exposed more consistently to more deviant youths who formed delinquent gangs. These core gang members apparently looked to off-reservation models, especially Southern California Chicano gangs, to construct loosely organized and gangs. Although the core members were few in number, they attracted satellite members among peers who were neighbors and kin.

In Navajo country, "the single leading cause of death . . . is accidents."[75] Death rates vary by region and social factors. "Different combinations of employment and domestic and settlement characteristics produce variations in rates and causes of mortality that can be fully explicated only if one understands the local scene."[76] This paper explores one aspect of the local scene in an agency town.

Significantly, "crude mortality is highest in the[se] least remote, most intensely set-tled areas."[77] The social dynamics that have led to the formation of youth gangs in Navajo country help in understanding why this may be so. Navajo gang members exhibit a range of risk-taking behaviors and patterns of alcohol and drug use that significantly contribute to injury-related mortality. Although gang members constitute a very small minority of Navajo youth, drinking parties, assaults, and hell-raising are more widely distributed. Gang behaviors, then, provide an extreme example of the behaviors that generally contribute to leading causes of mortality among young Navajo men.

Since the 1970s, Navajo gangs reputedly have become more common, more institu-tionalized and more closely connected with non-Indian gangs off the reservation.[78] More-over, the antisocial behavior of gang members may be increasingly imitated by other youth in the most densely settled and rapidly growing Navajo communities. Thus, gangs have been added to the repertoire of behavior for some youths making the difficult transi-tion to adulthood within the subordinate socioeconomic conditions that prevail in Navajo country.

Despite the historically limited nature of the data, there may be some important im-plications for gang prevention policy within the Navajo Nation today. First, not all self-identified gang members are alike. The degree of antisocial personality disorder may distinguish core members from peripheral members. This distinction may aid in develop-ing different types of intervention for different types of gang members. Secondly, some gangs may still be little more than street-corner groups while others have hardened. The for-mer may be more amenable to the traditional peacemaking interventions suggested by Chief Justice Yazzie. Third, the socio-demographic conditions, especially in agency towns and within the structure of limited economic opportunities, should be addressed as an ele-ment in gang prevention. It may be that a small number of antisocial individuals will emerge in any community. Given contemporary circumstances, young males with such problems seem to provide the core in the process of gang formation. To the degree that conditions for youths can be improved generally, mimicry of core members should diminish. Thus, gang prevention is not simply, or even fundamentally, a law enforcement issue. It is a public health issue in the broadest sense.

ACKNOWLEDGMENTS

This paper is primarily based on research supported by the United States Public Health Service, National Institute of Alcoholism and Alcohol Abuse (PHS Grant No. RO1 AA09420). We have benefited from the comments on earlier drafts by Jim Zion, Marlene Jasperse, Barbara Mendenhall, Amy Henderson, and Drs. Thomas Hill, Clemens Bartollas, and Troy Armstrong. An earlier version of this paper was presented at the Western Social Science Association Meetings, 39th Annual Conference, Albuquerque, New Mexico (April 1997).

QUESTIONS FOR UNDERSTANDING AND CRITICAL THINKING

1. Review and discuss Moffitt's dual taxonomy of temporary versus life-course-persistent anti-social persons and apply this to the emergence of male youth gangs in the Navajo community.

2. How might gang origins be different from those living on an Indian reservation compared to those living in an inner-city?

3. What are some characteristics of Navajo gang members? Are these similar to other gangs? (Black Hispanic, Asian, White).

4. How can knowledge of the history of Navajo gang formation and their forms of risky behavior be instrumental for both law enforcement and public policy?

NOTES

1. Irving A. Spergel, *The Youth Gang Problem: A Community Approach* (New York: Oxford University Press, 1995), 8, 43–54; Malcolm W. Klein, *The American Street Gang: Its Nature, Prevalence, and Control* (New York: Oxford University Press, 1995), 31–36.

2. Bill Donovan, "Reservation Teens Turn to Youth Groups," *The Arizona Republic* 20 (January 1997); Leslie Linthicum, "Surge of Violence on the Reservation: Gang-Scarred Housing Project Mirrors Growing Menace in Navajo Life," *Albuquerque Journal* 4 (February 1996); Carol Sowers, "Gang Members Stake Out Reservation Turf." *The Arizona Republic* (February 25, 1995).

3. Cheryl Howard, *Navajo Tribal Demography, 1983–1986. A Comparative and Historical Perspective* (New York: Garland Publishing, 1993), 116.

4. Ibid., 185 (Howard includes deaths from accidents, suicide, and homicide under the term "injury mortality").

5. Martin Avery, "Prepared Written Statement." On Behalf of the Navajo Nation Before the House Committee on Appropriations, Subcommittee on Appropriations. . . , Federal News Service, April 17, 1997.

6. Troy Armstrong and Barbara Mendenhall, "On-Reservation vs. Off-Reservation Factors in the Development of Navajo Youth Gangs," Western Social Science Association, Thirty-ninth Annual Conference, Albuquerque, New Mexico Criminal Justice Section (April 1997).

7. Stephen J. Kunitz, *Disease Change and the Role of Medicine: The Navajo Experience* (Berkeley: University of California Press, 1983), 111. In the mid-1980s, injuries accounted for 85 percent of all deaths for Navajo males between ages fifteen and twenty-four. Howard, *Navajo Tribal Demography* 131.

8. Sowers, "Gang Members Stake Out Reservation Turf."

9. Alice Schlegel and Herbert Barry III. *Adolescence An Anthropological Inquiry* (New York: The Free Press, 1991); Martin Orans, *Not Even Wrong: Margaret Mead, Derek Freeman, and the Samoans* (Novato: Chandler and Sharp Publishers, 1996); Derek Freeman, *Margaret Mead and Samoa: The Making of an Anthropological Myth* (Cambridge: Harvard University Press, 1983); Margaret Mead, *Coming of Age in Samoa* (New York: Morrow, 1928).

10. Kunitz, *Disease Change and the Role of Medicine,* 66, 99–111; Howard, *Navajo Tribal Demography,* 128–135.

11. Kunitz, *Disease Change and the Role of Medicine,* 99, 103; A. R. Omran and B. Loughlin, "Epidemiologic Studies of Accidents Among Navajo Indians," *Journal of the Egyptian Medical Association* 55 (1972): 1–22.

12. Terric Moffitt, "Adolescence-Limited and Life-Course-Persistent Antisocial Behavior: A Developmental Taxonomy," *Psychological Review* 100 (1993): 674–701. Moffitt develops her model from a survey of existing literature and from her own empirical work in New Zealand. Antisocial personality disorder (ASP) is defined in the DSM-IV as, "a pervasive pattern of disregard for and violation of the rights of others occurring since age 15 years"; its diagnosis requires "evidence of conduct disorder with onset prior to age 15 years." American Psychiatric Association. *Diagnostic Criteria from DSM-IV* (Washington, DC: American Psychiatric Association, 1994), 279–280. Conduct disorder is defined by the violation of the rights of others but it may also involve violation of "major age-appropriate societal norms or rules." Ibid., 66. Thus, conduct disorder involves some level of antisocial behavior. The type of conduct disorder is determined by whether the onset is before or after age ten. Ibid., 67.

13. Moffitt, "Adolescence-Limited and Life-Course-Persistent Antisocial Behavior: A Developmental Taxonomy," 674.

14. Ibid., 679–685.

15. Ibid., 675–77.

16. Ibid., 686.

17. Ibid., 689.

18. Julian Steward, *Theory of Culture Change: The Methodology of Multilinear Evolution* (Urbana: University of Illinois Press, 1955).

19. Moffitt, "Adolescence-Limited and Life-Course-Persistent Antisocial Behavior: A Developmental Taxonomy," 689.

20. Ibid., 691.

21. Jerrold E. Levy, Stephen J. Kunitz, and Michael Everett, "Navajo Criminal Homicide," *Southwestern Journal of Anthropology* 25 (1969): 124–152.

22. Ibid., 134.

23. Moffitt, "Adolescence-Limited and Life-Course-Persistent Antisocial Behavior: A Developmental Taxonomy," 686, 690.

24. Walter B. Miller, "Lower Class Culture as a Generating Milieu of Gangs: Delinquency," *The Journal of Social Issues* 14 (1958): 5–19.

25. Klein, *The American Street Gang,* 29; James Diego Vigil, "Cholos and Gangs: Culture Change and Street Youth in Los Angeles," in *Gangs in America*, ed. C. Ronald Huff (Newbury Park: Sage Publications, 1990), 124.

26. James Diego Vigil and John M. Long, "Emic and Etic Perspectives on Gang Culture: The Chicano Case," in *Gangs in America,* ed. C. Ronald Huff (Newbury Park: Sage Publications, 1990), 56.

27. Ibid., 56

28. Ibid., 61. Vigil identifies a *cholo* as "an indigenous person who is halfway acculturated to Spanish ways; in short a person marginal to both the original and the more recent European culture." Vigil, "Cholos and Gangs: Culture Change and Street Youth in Los Angeles," 116. He adds that "when generational and status change is throttled, cholization is intensified." Ibid., 121. This view echoes Thrasher's classic comments on the importance of a "cultural frontier" in the genesis of gangs. Frederic M. Thrasher, *The Gang: A Study of 1,313 Gangs in Chicago,* 2d rev. ed. (Chicago: University of Chicago Press, 1927), 217–19.

29. Carl S. Taylor, "Gang Imperialism," in *Gangs in America*, ed. C. Ronald Huff (Newbury Park: Sage Publications, 1990), 108; Carl S. Taylor, *Dangerous Society* (East Lansing: Michigan State University Press, 1990), 7–8.

30. Klein, *The American Street Gang,* 30.
31. Ibid., 29 (for gangs generally); and Vigil and Long, "Emic and Etic Perspectives on Gang Culture: The Chicano Case," 61 (for southern California Chicano gangs).
32. Martin Topper, "Navajo 'Alcoholism': Drinking, Alcohol Abuse, and Treatment in a Changing Cultural Environment," in *The American Experience with Alcohol: Contrasting Cultural Perspectives,* eds. Linda A. Bennett and Genevieve M. Ames (New York: Plenum Press, 1985), 235.
33. This fact is of some interest because it indicates that, at times, self-identified gangs seem to have had little impact on the school or community environment.
34. This gang, designated the Metallics, was the gang for which the greatest amount of information was obtained and is described in some detail in a later section.
35. Garrick Bailey and Roberta Glenn Bailey, *A History of the Navajos: The Reservation Years* (Santa Fe: School of American Research Press, 1986), 18.
36. Lawrence C. Kelly, *The Navajo Indians and Federal Indian Policy: 1900–1935* (Tucson: University of Arizona Press, 1968), 16–36.
37. Frank McNitt, *The Indian Traders* (Norman: University of Oklahoma Press, 1962).
38. Edward H. Spicer, *Cycles of Conquest* (Tucson: University of Arizona Press, 1962), 468.
39. Eric Henderson, "Social Organization and Seasonal Migrations among the Navajo," *The Kiva* 48 (1983): 279–306.
40. Dorothea Leighton and Clyde Kluckhohn, *Children of the People: The Navaho Individual and his Development* (Cambridge: Harvard University Press, 1947).
41. Denis F. Johnston, "An Analysis of Sources of Information on the Population of the Navaho," *Bureau of American Ethnology Bulletin* 197 (Washington, DC: U.S. Government Printing Office, 1966): 48–51.
42. Eric Henderson, "Navajo Livestock Wealth and the Effects of the Stock Reduction Program of the 1930s," *Journal of Anthropological Research* 45 (1989): 379–403.
43. Stephen J. Kunitz, *Disease Change and the Role of Medicine: The Navajo Experience* (Berkeley: University of California Press, 1983), 41–42.
44. Hildegard Thompson, *The Navajos' Long Walk for Education* (Tsaile: Navajo Community College Press, 1975), 127, 137.
45. Eric Henderson and Jerrold E. Levy, "Survey of Navajo Community Studies: 1936–1974," *Lake Powell Research Project Bulletin* Number 6 (Los Angeles: Institute of Geophysics and Planetary Physics, University of California, Los Angeles, 1975), 101–113.
46. Navajo economic development is documented in Philip Reno, *Mother Earth, Father Sky and Economic Development: Navajo Resources and Their Use* (Albuquerque: University of New Mexico Press, 1981). Data on the growth of agency towns and border towns is drawn from United States decennial census volumes for Arizona, New Mexico, and Utah.
47. Leighton and Kluckhohn wrote that "the first and most important lessons which the [Navajo] child learns about human relationships are the approved ways of dealing with various classes of relatives." Leighton and Kluckhohn, *Children of the People,* 44. In the early 1940s, at the agency town of Shiprock, they noted more emphasis on the biological (nuclear) family but in rural communities the extended family was emphasized. Ibid., 126. Shiprock children frequently mentioned parents in response to attitudinal questions but rural children commonly mentioned a wider array of relatives. Ibid., 165–167.
48. Moffitt, "Adolescence-Limited and Life-Course-Persistent Antisocial Behavior: A Developmental Taxonomy," 691.
49. George Peter Murdock, *Social Structure* (New York: The Free Press, 1949), 182–83; Harold Driver, *Indians of North America,* 2d. rev. ed. (Chicago: University of Chicago Press, 1969), 259–68.
50. "The Iroquois terminological system is bilateral in character and is only partially consistent with" unilineal clan groups. Fred Eggan, *The American Indian: Perspectives for the Study of Social Change* (Cambridge: Cambridge University Press, 1966), 8. Nearly thirty years ago, Aberle

showed that historical changes in Navajo economic adaptations "required significant modifications in kinship structure." He noted that some kin term variations suggested that "a shift toward Hawaiian cousin terms . . . may be under way." David F. Aberle, "Navaho," in *Matrilineal Kinship,* eds. David M. Schneider and Kathleen Gough (Berkeley: University of California Press, 1961), 101, 172–75. In the 1970s, when we conducted fieldwork in western rural communities and an agency town, bilingual adults could provide extensive kinship terminologies with ease, but bilingual teenagers sometimes expressed confusion over Navajo terms for collaterals and in-laws. These teenagers were, however, quite familiar with English terms for these relatives. Through the early 1980s we did not learn of any neologisms for kin, and specifically never heard the term *cousin-brother.*

51. A Navajo educator involved in bilingual and multicultural education expressed opposition to the use of the term *cousin-brother*—"I just hate it," she commented. She thought those using the term didn't know what they were talking about or to whom they referred. The use of the term *bro* may be expanding with greater exposure to popular media (such as television and films), participation in pan-Indian events, and connections with urban dwelling family and friends.

52. Joseph G. Jorgensen, *Western Indians* (San Francisco: W. H. Freeman, 1980), 227, 497–98.

53. Robert H. Lowie, *Indians of the Plains* (New York: The American Museum of Natural History, 1954), 106–10.

54. Evon Vogt, "The Navaho," in *Perspectives in American Indian Culture Change*, ed. E. H. Spicer (Chicago: University of Chicago Press, 1961), 306.

55. W. W. Hill, *Navaho Warfare* (New Haven: Yale University Publications in Anthropology, Number 5, 1936), 4.

56. Ibid., 6–7.

57. Aberle, "Navaho," 146–48, 163.

58. These are behaviors that Miller viewed as prime forms of street gang activities. Miller, "Lower Class Culture as a Generating Milieu of Gang Delinquency," 11.

59. Walter Dyk, ed., *Son of Old Man Hat* (Lincoln: University of Nebraska Press, 1967 [1938]), 140–142; Walter Dyk, ed., *A Navaho Autobiography*. Viking Fund Publications in Anthropology, Number 8 (New York: Viking Fund, 1947), 44–45, 54; Left Handed, *Left Handed: A Navaho Autobiography,* eds. Walter and Ruth Dyk (New York: Columbia University Press, 1980), 306.

60. Clyde Kluckhohn and Dorothea Leighton, *The Navaho,* rev. ed. (Cambridge; Harvard University Press, 1974 [1946]), 298.

61. See Thrasher, *The Gang*: and William F. Whyte, *Street Corner Society: The Social Structure of an Italian Slum* (Chicago: University of Chicago Press, 1947).

62. See Klein, *The American Street Gang*, 21.

63. Robert W. Young, compiler, *The Navajo Yearbook* (Window Rock: Navajo Agency, 1961), 20–47.

64. Robert Yazzie, "The Navajo Response to Crime," *Justice as Healing* 3:2 (Summer 1998), from a speech, "Indians, Ant Hills and Stereotypes," delivered at the National Symposium on Sentencing: The Judicial Response to Crime at the American Judicature Society in San Diego, California on November 2–3, 1997. Describing a case that may have implications for male gang activity, Yazzie writes:

In one case, where a non-Indian court intervened and disrupted the negotiations, the families of three young men who raped a young Navajo woman were about to transfer twenty-one head of cows to the victim's family. A state court had jurisdiction, and it refused to enforce the agreement. The woman was shamed by not having a public symbol of her innocence delivered to her home and she got nothing. If the traditional arrangement had been followed, the young men would have been kept on very strict probation by their own families. (I do not know what finally happened).

65. Topper, "Navajo 'Alcoholism': Drinking, Alcohol Abuse, and Treatment in a Changing Cultural Environment," 236.

66. This is a pseudonym. We have used pseudonyms for all individuals and for those gangs that are discussed in some detail. We believe that all of the gangs named ceased to exist well before 1990. We have retained actual gang names, unless otherwise noted, for gangs that are merely mentioned in passing. The actual gang names may be of some intrinsic interest. The names reflect, to some degree, what the youths who formed the gangs saw as appropriate monikers. Almost none of the gang names, so far as we can tell or were told, were adopted directly from off-reservation sources. This situation has apparently changed dramatically in recent years. See Armstrong and Mendenhall, "On-Reservation vs. Off-Reservation Factors in the Development of Navajo Youth Gangs."

67. Both individuals were interviewed about two decades after the events recalled and both were heavy drinkers, had traveled extensively, and were marginally integrated into contemporary agency town society. The Cruiser, especially, seemed to engage in "puffery" and he may have exaggerated the "ganglike" nature of rivalries and violence of his youth to conform it with more contemporary popular media views of gangs.

68. This is consistent with statements by several others concerning gang activity in the agency town in the mid-1970s. Some of those interviewed explicitly denied that gangs existed at this time.

69. He identified the gangs as his gang, the D.T.s (a pseudonym), the Southsiders (also known as SSRs), the LRs (who lived at "low rent" housing), the "Bloods" (the only instance that we have of a gang name known to be cognate with a well-known off-reservation gang but which was not affiliated with that well-known Southern California gang), the M_ (a clan name) Boys, and the J_ (a family surname) Boys (both from an adjacent rural community), and two gangs that did not have names (one composed of "northsiders" and another composed of "westsiders" in the agency town). A second interviewee who lived in this agency town mentioned only the SSRs and LRs. He "ran with" (as a peripheral member) the LRs while in high school in the late 1970s. They would party, drinking whiskey and Budweiser, pass out, wake up, and party some more. He noted that they never drank wine "because of the stigma."

70. Another agency town interviewee confirmed the basic outline of gang activity. He also observed that in the mid-1970s his sister belonged to a small, all-girl gang at the interior agency town high school, but he knew little about the gang. Although the data on the gang scene for the interior agency town are more limited, they conform broadly to data from the eastern area.

71. If informants provided a relatively complete inventory of the gangs of the 1970s and the early 1980s in the two communities and if their rather consistent estimates of the number of gang members are accurate (that gangs had about fifteen to thirty-five members), then there were fewer than 350 gang members in the two communities. It is probable that the number was much lower in any one year. In 1980 the total Navajo population of the two areas was more than 18,000. Males between ten and nineteen, the ages that span the age range of the gang members, account for about 12 to 13 percent of the Navajo population. Thus, perhaps 10 to 15 percent of Navajo male youths were affiliated to some degree with gangs in the 1970s.

72. There was an understandable reluctance to give names and so the characteristics of and relationships among members cannot be determined with precision.

73. Vigil and Long, "Emic and Etic Perspectives on Gang Culture: The Chicano Case," 56; Vigil, "Cholos and Gangs: Culture Change and Street Youth in Los Angeles," 121.

74. Thomas W. Hill, "From Hell-Raiser to Family Man," in *Conformity and Conflict: Readings in Cultural Anthropology,* 2d ed., eds. James P. Spradley and David W. McCurdy (Boston: Little, Brown and Company, 1974).

75. Stephen J. Kunitz, *Disease and Social Diversity* (New York: Oxford University Press, 1994), 156.

76. Ibid., 156.

77. Ibid., 159.

78. Armstrong and Mendenhall, "On-Reservation vs. Off-Reservation Factors in the Development of Navajo Youth Gangs."

8

Oakland Chinatown's First Youth Gang

The Suey Sing Boys

Gregory Yee Mark

❖

Abstract

Research concerned with Chinese gangs in the United States focuses on two sites, San Francisco and New York. This study examines Oakland Chinatown and the development of its first Chinese immigrant youth gang, the Suey Sing boys, during the five years from 1968–1973. I rely heavily on data from primary sources such as interviews with gang members and field observations. Key topics for investigation are the formation of the Suey Sing boys, the relationship of the youth gangs to the Chinatown social structure, and the relationship between gangs in Oakland and San Francisco.

INTRODUCTION

The gang problem is an issue of serious concern to American society. Many people are fearful of, and many are adversely affected by, gangs and their activities. The American public demands tougher police tactics, punishment, and prisons in response. Despite vigorous efforts, crime and gangs continue to be major social problems in the United States. Although most Americans can trace their ancestry to Europe, the literature on youth gangs focuses primarily on African American and Hispanic gangs.

The 1960s witnessed the emergence of contemporary Chinese gangs in the United States. The first nationally known Chinese gang, the Hwa Chings, which means "young Chinese," originated in San Francisco Chinatown in 1964. Eventually, branches of this group and

G.Y. Mark. (1997). Oakland Chinatown's First Youth Gang: The Suey Sing Boys. *Free Inquiry in Creative Sociology*, 25, 41–50. Reprinted by permission of the University of Oklahoma.

other similar types of gangs spread throughout America's Chinatowns. Since the 1970s, due to escalating violence and expanded criminal activities, Chinese gangs have been increasingly viewed as a major social problem in the Chinese American community and as a menace to society-at-large. In government reports and the popular media, these gangs are blamed for the increasing violence in Chinatowns, shiploads of undocumented Chinese immigrants, and the massive smuggling of illegal drugs to the United States. Although these sources frequently exaggerate the criminality of the Chinese gang situation, it is accurate to state that Chinese gangs are involved in a variety of criminal activities, such as extortion, burglary, robbery, assault, and murder, that bring hardship and misery, especially to the Chinese community.

Study of Chinese gangs broadens our knowledge of early gang formation and gang structure, and illustrates how gangs can interface with Chinatown organizations within the context of contemporary social problems. Since the inception of gang studies by researchers Frederick Thrasher (1927) and William Whyte (1943), traditional gang research has paid little or no attention to the Chinese community. Reasons include lack of interest by traditional youth gang researchers, often linked to images of Chinese and other Asian Americans as the "model minority," the difficulty of gaining access to Chinese gang members, especially for non-Chinese researchers, and the political and social isolation of the Asian American community (Joe 1994a, 1994b).

This paper explores the premise that Chinatown gangs are not isolated entities, but are a part of, and connected to, the Chinese community; gangs impact community life and the community impacts gangs. The topics discussed are 1) the historical development of the first contemporary youth gang in the Oakland, California Chinatown community, 2) the "gang perspective" on why they formed a gang, 3) the relationship of the Oakland gang to Chinatown community organizations, and 4) the relationship between Chinese gangs in different sites, San Francisco and Oakland.

METHODOLOGY

I began inquiring about Chinese gangs, in 1968, to understand gang members' experiences and why such gangs form. Oakland, California (1960, population 367,548) was an ideal city in which to document the development of a gang. Chinatown was located in the heart of the city, adjacent to the downtown shopping area and the main police headquarters, and near city hall. There were no deviant Chinese groups operating in the area. Unlike San Francisco Chinatown, with a myriad of social organizations, Oakland Chinatown had only a few, such as the Wong Family Association, the Chinese American Citizen Alliance, and the Suey Sing Tong.

First as a participant observer, my field observations were the foundation to this study. In youth and adult gang studies that utilize observation as the primary methodology (Padilla 1993; Patrick 1973; Whyte 1943), the researchers target a particular community or group to study. In my case, the gang members adopted me as friend and confidant. My father was a well respected tong member who had an excellent rapport with gang members. I was also treated with respect and loyalty by the Suey Sing boys. Though not a gang member, I was looked upon as an educated friend who worked for the members' welfare and needs. I had access to the social benefits of gang membership such as intra-group friendship, but never the responsibilities, such as participating in violent confrontations with other groups. I was marginally a part of the group, who could communicate with its members. I obtained meaningful and valid information as a semiparticipant observer.

Second, I conducted numerous informal interviews with San Francisco and Oakland adult Suey Sing members and the Oakland Suey Sing boys, in a four and a half year period (summer of 1968 to early 1973). Conversations were held at restaurants, bowling alleys, and the Oakland Suey Sing clubhouse. I recorded the gist of these conversations and informal interviews but at that time I was not involved in any active gang research. Since 1993, I have conducted eight interviews with former Oakland Suey Sing boys and their associates. According to the authors count and key informants, there were "officially" 28 Suey Sing boys. Two were considered to be part of the Oakland Suey Sing boys and simultaneously were part of the San Francisco Suey Sing group. One resided and went to school in Oakland but spent a great deal of time in San Francisco and was considered to be an influential gang member. Interviews, which were about 1.5 hours long, were tape recorded (with permission) and transcribed in summary form. Data collection spanned three years (1993–1996). Quality ranged from little useful information to full descriptions of events and community social life.

Third, I examined archival sources in newspapers and governmental reports. From 1970 to 1988, there were articles about Chinese gangs in San Francisco, New York, and Los Angeles. A study of *New York Times* articles on Chinese Americans over an 80-year period showed an abundance of crime coverage (Auman, Mark 1997). The study notes that half of the coverage analyzed was crime-related, followed by political events (25%), routine other news, and culture (Auman, Mark 1997). There were only a few articles on Chinese gangs and crime in Oakland Chinatown. Government criminal intelligence reports or law enforcement conference papers were of little use because of their unreliability and lack of emphasis on Oakland. Government reports do show growing concern of state and federal law enforcement agencies regarding Chinese gangs and heroin smuggling.

Fourth, a few researchers have published books or articles concerning Chinese gangs in San Francisco and New York (Chin 1990; Chin, Fagan, Kelly 1992; Joe 1994; Kwong 1987; Lyman 1970; Sung 1977; Takagi, Platt 1978). No one has studied Chinese gangs in Oakland. Only Gong and Grant (1930) and Chin (1990) examine the tongs to any significant extent.

REVIEW OF LITERATURE

There is a multitude of youth gang studies in the United States, most concerned with ethnic minority communities. However, there has been a death of scholarly research and publications concerning the Chinese gangs in the United States. What little there is falls into two major categories: 1) journalistic accounts, some of which are based upon law enforcement gang task force reports (Bresler 1981; Posner 1988), and 2) descriptive/theoretical studies (Chin 1990; Chin, Fagan 1994; Chin, Fagan, Kelly 1992; Joe 1993, 1994; Lyman 1970; Sung 1977; Takagi, Platt 1978).

Some journalistic accounts glamorize Chinese gangs and heighten the fear of these gangs flooding the U.S. shores with tons of drugs. Two of these accounts, by Bresler (1981) and Posner (1988), state that adult and young Chinese criminals are trafficking in heroin. Bresler believes that there is an international Chinese crime conspiracy that is headquartered in Asia. Posner maintains that the Chinese Triads are the most powerful form of organized crime in the world and consequently pose the most serious threat to law enforcement. Both charge that the Triads in Asia, the tongs in Chinatowns, and the Chinese youth gangs are in close contact and structurally related, posing a serious threat.

Scholarly works on Chinese gangs concern two cities. Lyman's (1970) study focused on San Francisco Chinatown gangs, describing they were due to changing demographics and a tradition of social banditry from China. He examined the development of American born and foreign born San Francisco Chinatown gangs, such as the Hwa Chings and the Red Guards, from the 1950s through the early 1970s.

Sung (1977) examines New York Chinatown gangs using theories of social disorganization, social structure, crime as conformity to explain the nature, and formation of these youth gangs.

Chin's 1990 book, *Chinese Subculture and Criminality*, focuses on New York Chinatown gangs, examining Chinatowns, Chinese secret societies, the development of Chinese gangs nationally, Chinese gang patterns and characteristics, and social sources of Chinese gang delinquency. He studies the relation of adult Chinatown organizations and Chinese criminality, and why and how Chinese gangs formed, claiming that New York Chinatown Chinese gangs and the tongs have a symbiotic relationship that deeply intertwines both bodies.

Karen Joe (1994b) examined the relationships between Asian American gangs and two variables, organized crime and drug distribution (*The New Criminal Conspiracy? Asian Gangs and Organized Crime in San Francisco*). In regard to San Francisco Chinatown gangs, her findings indicate that gang members know little of and have little or no contact with the tongs in Chinatown. Therefore, Joe found no evidence to indicate that the tongs in San Francisco are actually organized crime groups that have incorporated gang members into illegal enterprises. In addition, her findings support the thesis that the gangs as an organized group are not involved in heroin trafficking. Some gang members, as individuals, were involved with drugs, but not the entire gang.

Joe (1994a) *Myths and Realities of Asian Gangs on the West Coast* poses two related questions: are Chinese gangs well-organized with ties to the San Francisco tongs and the Triads in Asia? and Are Asian gangs in Northern California involved in heroin trafficking? Joe refutes the theory, supported by journalistic accounts, that Asian street gangs are part of a larger conspiracy of an "Asian Mafia" and organized crime. She also takes issue with U.S. law enforcement beliefs and policies, in particular, the link between Chinese youth gangs and the Chinese Triads in Hong Kong and Taiwan.

OAKLAND CHINATOWN

Oakland Chinatown has been located in five different sites, each centered around the waterfront and the Oakland downtown/commercial area. By 1880, the location of the present Chinatown was established just a few blocks from where City Hall is today. As in most other cities, Chinatown was restricted to old, undesirable, commercial districts because of racial segregation in both housing and commercial enterprises. Thus, Chinatown was originally established in the midst of warehouses, factories, rooming houses, and junkyards. By 1960, Oakland Chinatown was in a sharp decline due to dispersal of Chinese to other areas in the East Bay and the reduction of residential housing, attributed to construction of the Nimitz Freeway, Laney Community College, the Oakland Museum, and the Bay Area Rapid Transit (BART) (Chow 1976).

An additional and forgotten factor in Chinatown's deterioration was the decline of gambling. This was due to the passage of the 1951 Federal Stamp Act (26 U.S.C. 4401 and 4402), which levied a flat ten percent tax on wagering income and an additional fifty-dollar tax on gambling operators. Violators could receive a $10,000 fine and five years in prison. Thus, gambling in Oakland Chinatown was sharply curtailed, which severely impacted businesses that thrived from the gambling industry (Mark 1989). There were fewer jobs, fewer residents, and a significant decrease in Chinatown business activity.

By the mid-1960s, Oakland Chinatown stabilized and its residential population grew because of the increase in immigrants as a result of the 1965 Immigration Nationalization Act. Families began to reappear, and the local elementary school (Lincoln School), the neighborhood junior high school (West Lake), and the two high schools (Oakland Technical High and Oakland High) enrolled progressively larger numbers of foreign born Chinese students. In 1970, Oakland's Chinese population numbered 11,335 and the Chinatown core area supported a population of 1,607 Chinese (Tracts 4030 and 4033) which represented 570 families (Homma-True 1976). By 1970, the Chinatown community was comprised mostly of immigrants, and 22 percent of Chinatown residents were classified with incomes below the poverty level as compared to 13 percent of the rest of the city. The median income in Chinatown was $6,690 compared to $9,626 for the rest of the city.

"HWA CHINGS" IN SAN FRANCISCO CHINATOWN

San Francisco Chinatown supported 40,000 people in an area of 42 blocks (Takagi, Platt 1978). American-born Chinese street corner groups such as the "Chinos" ("Chinese" in Spanish) became visible in the late 1950s. They raced hot rods and frequented Chinatown bars. One group known as the "Bugs" became involved in burglaries and were identified by their black clothing and raised heel boots. In 1965 over a period of six months, the Bugs committed 48 burglaries worth $7500 cash and $3000 in merchandise (Lyman 1970), but the San Francisco Police Department made key arrests and broke up the Bugs gang.

In 1964–65, the Hwa Chings (Young Chinese) were formed by mainly teen-aged immigrant youths, the majority from Hong Kong. The Chinese population in the United States, and in Chinatowns, in particular were increasing because of the changes in United States immigration laws and policies that permitted an increase in Chinese immigration to the United States. As more Chinese immigrated to San Francisco, the Hwa Chings became larger, more visible, and more powerful. They committed crimes such as burglary and assault. The Hwa Chings had as estimated 300 members in a loosely organized group. In an interview with a reporter, "Tom Tom" declared that the Hwa Chings only wanted jobs, girls, and to be left alone (Lyman 1970). Tom Tom was the gang's main leader, but there were others high in the leadership structure who had many followers.

By 1967, Hwa Ching crimes became more violent, and to the Chinatown establishment, more serious, when they extorted Chinatown businesses for protection money. In the winter of 1968, the Hwa Chings, through their spokesman, George Woo, threatened to burn down Chinatown if their demands for better jobs and educational opportunities were refused. Although the Hwa Chings did not and probably could not follow through on their threats, the Chinatown establishment realized that some action had to be taken (Lyman 1970).

In 1969, the Hwa Chings gained the attention of the national media. In the December 1969 issue of *Esquire* magazine, Tom Tom and the Hwa Chings were part of an article, "The

New Yellow Peril," that centered upon the conflicts and violence that were plaguing Chinatown. Tom Tom was quoted as saying:

> TT: . . . We never marched as a gang. . . . You have to kill us to stop us. You split my head open—I get up, keep fighting. We all been to the hospital. I been three times.
> I: What did you use as weapons?
> TT: Axes and knives.
> I: Axes?
> TT: Yeah. They don't slice but they hurt plenty. (Wolfe 1969)

In 1967/68, San Francisco Chinatown leaders devised a plan to split the Hwa Chings into various factions in order to control the Chinatown gang violence and extortion. The Chinatown establishment leaders turned to one part of the community's social structure, the tongs. Four of Chinatown's five major tongs (Hop Sing Tong, Hip Sing Tong, Bung Kong Tong, Yin On Tong, and Suey Sing Tong) invited gang members to join them and each identified a Hwa Ching leader and recruited him and his followers into the tong. The tongs offered the youth gang members a club house to hang out in, a "slush fund" for bail, and employment opportunities in Chinatown gambling dens which they controlled.

The Hop Sing Tong was initially the most active tong in the recruitment of gang members. Soon their young gang members were demanding protection money from Chinatown gambling dens. However, most of the dens were under the protection of Suey Sing. As a result, the Suey Sing Tong actively recruited Tom Tom and his Hwa Ching followers in order to counteract Hop Sing. The gang situation in Chinatown dramatically changed from one large gang to five smaller ones, the remnants of the Hwa Chings and the four tong youth groups, each vying for power and control over the Chinatown community. Contrary to the intentions of the Chinatown elders, gang violence increased, and the tongs could not control the youth groups. The top gang had the fear and respect of the community. By the end of 1968, the Tom Tom gang, the youth gang affiliated with the San Francisco Suey Sing Tong, emerged as the strongest gang.

SUEY SING TONG

The word *tong* means "hall," or, freely translated, "lodge." The tongs descended from Triad or "secret societies" that originated in China. Formed after the Manchu overthrow of the Ming Dynasty in 1644, the tongs sought to overthrow the Manchus and to restore to power the Mings. The concept of these secret societies was transferred to the United States and the first tong, the Kwong Duck Tong, was founded in San Francisco in 1852. The second was the Hip Sing Tong, the only tong to have branches throughout the United States. Soon after the Hip Sing Tong was founded, Yee Low Dai established the Suey Sing Tong (Hall of Auspicious Victory) (Gong, Grant 1930).

The initial purpose of the tongs was to counteract the larger and wealthier family (surname) associations (Gong, Grant 1930). The early history of the tongs was marked by conflicts with other Chinese societies, especially the family associations. The tongs were most successful in their wars with the clans and by the 1890s gained a great deal of power and wealth. Simultaneously, the tongs gradually lost sight of their original function, which was to seek justice for the weaker groups. Inside Chinatown the secret societies soon took control of gambling and prostitution (Gong, Grant 1930).

Since World War II, the tongs have continued their involvement in the gambling industry (Mark 1989). A tong would either directly operate a gambling den or have it under its protection (Chin 1990). If a gambling den was on a tong's protection list, the den would make weekly contributions to the tong and possibly hire some of its members (Mark 1989).

The Suey Sing Tong national headquarters is located in San Francisco Chinatown. There are nine Suey Sing branches in the western U.S.: Oakland, Stockton, Watsonville, Salinas, Marysville, Monterey, Portland, and Seattle. The ten Suey Sing Tongs elect officers every year. For example, in 1972, eleven officers were elected for the San Francisco headquarters. The top seven positions were occupied by Chinatown business owners.

Chinese New Year is a significant event for the different Suey Sing Tongs. Although all of the branches celebrate this annual event, each year, one Suey Sing Tong hosts the other cities for a large celebration with performances by a Chinese orchestra and singers, banquet dinners and gambling.

By the 1970s, the Suey Sing Tong served four basic functions: 1) It celebrated special occasions such as New Year. 2) It provided assistance such as interpreter services, employment referrals, and burial arrangements; 3) the tong clubhouse provided opportunities for members; 4) the tong protected the business interests of its leaders by providing opportunities for additional business, such as business partnerships.

WHY FORM A GANG?

Only three studies (Chin 1990; Lyman 1970; Takagi, Platt 1978) concerned with Chinatown youth gangs examine why the gangs formed. Lyman (1970) asserts that the gangs were a product of conflict and rebellion, and examines why existing groups such as the Hwa Ching develop in a specific direction.

Takagi and Platt (1978) attribute gang formation and gang violence to the social structure, asserting that the Chinatown structure, specifically the tongs, were the reasons for the violence in Chinatown.

Ko-lin Chin (1990) believed that causative and intervening social factors gave rise to Chinese gang delinquency, including school problems, family problems, and the lack of employment opportunities. These factors alienate immigrants from the Chinatown community and the broader society. Chin asserts that these causative factors, coupled with intervening factors, such as affiliation with and internalization of tong norms and values, contribute to a youth group's development into a Chinatown street gang.

In this section, I look at an earlier stage in Chinatown gang formation than the three other researchers. What I believe is important to explore is just why these youth join or form a group in the first place.

During my five years of association with the Suey Sing boys, I had the opportunity to casually talk to many of the San Francisco and Oakland members. Several, including Tom Tom, were original Hwa Ching members. All of the gang members indicated that after their arrival in the United States, they were verbally harassed and physically abused by many different groups at school and in their neighborhoods. The gang members stated that the people that harassed them the most were the American-born Chinese (ABCs). Regarding this topic, Tom Tom stated in an interview:

> We use to fight the American-born Chinese all the time. They call us 'Chinabugs.' We say 'Who you think you are?' They say, 'We American-born.' That's a joke. They Chinese same as us. (Wolfe 1969).

Another gang leader stated:

> I wanted to go to school. And I tried. But it didn't work. You know what happens; the other Chinese kids say they are not Chinese but Americans. They spit on me. (Allard 1975)

As a result, many Chinese immigrant youths were forced to band together with other Chinese immigrants in order to protect themselves (Thompson 1976).

Why would the ABCs antagonize the Chinese immigrant children, commonly referred to as "FOBs" (Fresh Off the Boat)? Many local-born Chinese respond to this question by stating that the foreign-born Chinese represented everything that they "wanted to get away from" such as speaking Chinese, dressing differently, eating Chinese food, and simply not being "American." Ignatius Chinn, who for 21 years was the primary police officer working in Oakland Chinatown, expresses this sentiment. Chinn grew up in a middle-class family, his father was an Oakland accountant, his mother a secretary. Asked about his youth, Chinn speaks with painful candor.

> When I was young, I was trying to be white. Most of my friends at Westlake Junior High and Oakland High School were white. When I saw Asian immigrants I thought they were geeks. I felt contempt for them because they reminded me of who I didn't want to be. . .

With difficulty, Chinn tells of feeling ashamed when friends visited his house and met his uncle from Canton, who spoke no English.

> I felt uncomfortable because they reminded me of what I was trying so hard not to be. I felt between races, between cultures. I didn't have much background about anything Asian. (Rosenthal 1991)

A method for the ABCs to create a barrier between themselves and the FOBs was to make fun of, put down, and verbally and physically harass their foreign born cousins. In this way the foreign-born would be established as a different and distinct group from the American-born Chinese.

Why did Chinese born in the U.S. feel ashamed of their ethnic background; or, in other words, suffer an ethnic identity conflict? The Chinese were a small ethnic minority numbering only 237,292 in 1960, and 431,583 in 1970. Shortly after the first arrival of Chinese workers to the United States in 1850, racial discrimination and hatred was directed towards the newcomers, culminating in the Chinese Exclusion Acts of 1882, 1888, 1892, and 1902 (Lai, Choy 1972). For over a hundred years, to be Chinese in the United States meant to be slandered, abused, and treated as a third class citizen with few of the rights guaranteed by the Constitution to other Americans. To many young Chinese Americans, to be Chinese was not desirable. What was desirable was to be like mainstream white America; speaking standard English, eating sandwiches, cookies, and milk for lunch, and wearing the latest American teen fashions. As a result, anything associating them with China and being Chinese was rejected.

THE OAKLAND SUEY SING TONG YOUTH GROUP

The Oakland Suey Sing Tong is located on 8th Street, right in the heart of Chinatown. Oakland Chinatown supports several Chinese traditional associations and community service organizations; but Suey Sing is the only tong. In 1966/1967, teenage immigrants began to develop a community reputation as a group of young toughs who frequently got into trouble. One incident occurred in late 1967 when two Oakland youths, "Barry" and "Puki," were beaten up in San Francisco Chinatown by some Hwa Ching members including "Ben Gong" and a youth nicknamed "Big Head." As a result, Tom Tom and his San Francisco followers assisted and befriended the two from Oakland. "Ben Gong" was later murdered in 1970, in an unrelated crime. By 1967/68, approximately 28 young men who hung out on the corner of 8th and Webster started to spend time in the Suey Sing Tong clubhouse. Their ages ranged from 15 to 18 years old and their families had immigrated from Hong Kong. All were fluent in Cantonese and one was completely fluent in English. They wore casual clothes. Only one eventually completed high school. All but four lived at home with their families.

A merger between youth gangs and the old established Oakland tong was brokered by two tong members. They had established rapport with gang members and were willing to take on this risky endeavor. "Uncle Choy" was the Suey Sing Tong member who recruited and advised the San Francisco youth group. At that time, "Uncle Yee," my father, was active in San Francisco, and was also the Oakland Suey Sing President. According to D.F., "Uncle Yee" was the main Oakland Suey Sing contact and worked with "Uncle Choy" to recruit the Oakland Suey Sing group.

The motives for the Oakland Suey Sing boys were different. They simply wanted a place to hang out. They also desired affiliation with the San Francisco Suey Sing group for their protection from other youths. At the same time, Tom Tom and his San Francisco Suey Sing Tong followers believed that the Oakland group could assist them in turf battles in San Francisco Chinatown. By 1968, the group was called the "Oakland Suey Sing boys" or "Sing Sing boys" and the San Francisco group was referred to as the "Tom Tom Gang" (Chin 1990). The Oakland group was relatively small, consisting of eight paid official Suey Sing members and about 20 associates. Unlike the Hwa Chings and, later, Tom Tom's group, the Oakland Suey Sing boys did not have a clearly defined leader. From my observations, between 1968 to 1972, they often deferred to Tom Tom, but by no means was he their acknowledged leader.

One day in August 1968, a Suey Sing member was beaten up by two Hop Sing Tong members. Later that night the former saw "Big Nose" of the Hop Sings driving his car on Grant Avenue in San Francisco, and ran up and shot "Big Nose" in the head. Although "Big Nose" survived and knew who shot him, the assailant was never arrested. The assailant was able to leave San Francisco and flee across the Bay where he stayed for one night at the home of one of the Oakland Suey Sing youths, and then stayed the next three weeks at the Oakland home of a tong elder. After a cooling off period, the Suey Sing member joined the Merchant Marine and left the gang life.

By 1969, the Oakland group faced two major challenges. One was conflict with Chicanos, especially at Oakland Technical High School. When Chinese students were beaten up by Chicano students, older Suey Sing members came to the aid of the high school members and used hatchets as weapons to defend the Chinese students. During the same time period an Oakland-based American born group of Chinese and Japanese, "The Rickshaw

Runners," posed the second challenge. The Runners had numerous altercations with the Suey Sing boys in Oakland Chinatown and at the local bowling alley. In this case, the San Francisco Suey Sing members assisted their Oakland counterparts in fighting the "Rickshaw Runners" in a number of skirmishes. Eventually, the "Rickshaw Runners" were forced to back down and maintain their distance from Chinese immigrants in general, and the Suey Sing boys in particular.

In August 1969, the East Bay Chinese Youth Council (EBCYC) was established in Oakland Chinatown. It was organized by American-born Chinese college students who wanted to bring a progressive voice to the East Bay Chinese community. They lobbied to increase social services for Chinese youth in the East Bay cities of Oakland, Alameda, Emeryville, and Berkeley. Unlike other Chinatown organizations, the founders were a diverse group of young people. Some of the founding members and original EBCYC Board of Directors included three Suey Sing boys from Oakland. Tom Tom from San Francisco was a founding member. I was the organization's founder and first President.

Unfortunately, the goals of the gang members involved in EBCYC was not to bring about community empowerment and social change, but to make "easy money" through government-funded programs the way Tom Tom did in San Francisco. In San Francisco Tom Tom was employed as a gang outreach worker and often worked only 15 minutes per day. His job was to control gang activities and violence. However, this position only further enhanced Tom Tom's ability to recruit new gang members because it demonstrated to potential members that he had the connections and the intelligence to manipulate "the system." In the case of the East Bay Chinese Youth Council, it never became a source of "easy money." The Youth Council never obtained the gang prevention funding that other organizations in San Francisco Chinatown were able to obtain, and the EBCYC staff was interested only in working for the larger community.

The relationship between EBCYC and the gang members had a profound effect upon the latter. Between 1970–1972, new members (ages 14–17) attached themselves to the Oakland Suey Sing youth group and were also participants in EBCYC's programs such as the War on Poverty's Neighborhood Youth Corps Program. Many of the older gang members (ages 18–22) had changed and had adopted the principles of the college students. Those older gang members were now concerned with improving Chinatown community life.

By the end of 1972, Tom Tom's gangs power base eroded because of a change in policy by the San Francisco tongs and increasing competition and conflict with other gangs in Chinatown. First, by the summer of 1972, the San Francisco experiment of incorporating the former Hwa Chings into the tongs was deemed a failure. The tong youth groups were viewed as too big a liability. In San Francisco, both the Hop Sing and Suey Sing tongs, who had the largest youth groups, either expelled many youth members or no longer supported the youth. In San Francisco Suey Sing, only fifteen who actually became tong members remained.

Another factor was the reemergence of the Hwa Chings. In January 1970, one of the old Hwa Ching leaders, Kenny Mack, was discharged from the U.S. army. He maneuvered his way back into power and revitalized the Hwa Chings. One night in August 1972, Tom Tom was severely beaten in a San Francisco Chinatown restaurant. He was hospitalized for six weeks. During that time, the Tom Tom gang dissolved: some joined other gangs, and others left the gang life. Still others had to flee because Tom Tom could no longer protect them, and a few, including Tom Tom himself, moved to Oakland. Thus, the transition of power was made—the Hwa Chings became the strongest gang in San Francisco Chinatown.

Tom Tom and the remnants of the San Francisco Suey Sing group attempted to reestablish themselves as a viable gang in Oakland. Tom Tom approached the Oakland Suey Sing boys and was rejected by the older group that once supported him. As mentioned earlier, EBCYC had positively influenced some of the older gang members and they did not want to follow Tom Tom.

Some of the younger Suey Sing members and their friends followed Tom Tom and initiated a hostile takeover of the EBCYC club house, programs, and staff. I participated in three months of negotiations which resulted in the takeover of the Youth Council by Tom Tom and a few of his followers. By the time the gang members took over the EBCYC, nothing was left to take over except for an empty shell of a club house. The EBCYC Board of Directors and staff had transferred everything to the newly founded organization, East Bay Asians for Community Action, which continued and expanded upon the EBCYC programs.

In 1968, the Oakland Chinese Community Council (OCCC) was established to provide Chinese-speaking referral and social services to the Oakland Chinese community. In 1970, OCCC hired its first full-time salaried Executive Director, Edward K. Chook. Little was known about Chook except that he was active in the local Kuomintang (KMT) Party. In the beginning of his tenure, EBCYC and Edward Chook had a cordial working relationship. By 1972, the relationship had cooled a great deal. According to Tom Tom, Chook had advised him and his followers to take over the Youth Council. Chook even promised Tom Tom that he would help set up youth programs such as the summer Neighborhood Youth Corp program. In 1972/1973, Tom Tom's efforts to remodel EBCYC for his personal benefit had failed and the organization had a quiet end. Tom Tom lost his followers and was shortly afterward deported to Hong Kong because of a felony conviction.

Unlike their San Francisco counterparts, the original Oakland Suey Sing youth group did not extort Oakland Chinatown businesses and community members. However, after the group no longer existed as a Suey Sing Tong sponsored group, some of Tom Tom's young Oakland followers named themselves "Suey Sing boys" and began to extort members of the Oakland Chinese community. In November 1972, a local newspaper reported the arrest and conviction of four Chinese juveniles and two adults who were part of an extortion ring. To their victims they identified themselves as "Suey Sing boys."

The Suey Sing boys took a variety of paths. Four continued their deviant life style and have become involved with drugs and two were incarcerated for serious crimes such as murder. Twenty are married with children, and they have indicated that they do not want them to join any gang. Six own and operate businesses. One is a well known chef and restaurant owner in another city. Approximately 20 are gainfully employed in occupations such as hair stylist and automobile mechanic, and seventeen have moved out of Oakland but still live in the greater San Francisco Bay Area, and are successful in their professional and personal lives.

IMPLICATIONS AND CONCLUSIONS

The findings from this study suggest that early Chinese gangs on the West Coast were not originally a product of mere greed and irrational deviant behavior. Instead, they were initially a group of youths who banded together for protection and survival. Even today, thirty years later, young immigrants still join Chinese gangs, Samoan gangs, Cambodian gangs, and Filipino gangs for mutual-protection (Alegado 1994; Revilla 1996). The implications of this study for public policy makers is that they should look beyond the gangs as the sole problem, and to look inwards towards the broader Asian American community. One obvious question to be addressed is how we can reduce the rift between local-born Asians and our immigrant/refugee cousins.

Oakland Chinatown's Suey Sing boys did not come into existence as a gang because of their association with San Francisco Chinatown gang members nor due to the Oakland Suey Sing Tong. Before their recruitment into Oakland Suey Sing, they already functioned as a gang. However, they were acknowledged as a gang only after they became affiliated with Suey Sing Tong and the nature of their activities were in fact influenced by the San Francisco Tom Tom gang. In other urban centers, the pattern of gang members in one city creating or influencing the development of a new gang in another city has been a major factor in the spread of Chinatown gangs in the United States. This phenomena requires additional study not only for Chinese gangs but other Asian gangs in the United States.

The Asian gang literature does make linkages (Chin 1990) and non-linkages (Joe 1994) with the tongs and Triads. What I discuss in this study that requires further research is the links to other community organizations such as those of the Suey Sing boys to the East Bay Chinese Youth Council. For the Suey Sing boys, the gang's development and also its demise were influenced by a variety of components of the Chinese community. Future gang studies need to address these important issues of gang/social structure relations. Another topic for examination is: can self help community-based organizations positively impact the nature of a gang, gang membership, and violence perpetuated by gang members? If so, should there be more community programs for our youth? And what should these programs look like? These questions have significant public policy implications regarding the control of gangs and related criminal activities.

In 1971, Oakland Chinatown had only one gang, the Suey Sing boys. This group operated as a gang for approximately five years. The situation in Oakland Chinatown is different today. There are now 16 predominantly ethnic Chinese gangs in Oakland and many are based in Chinatown. They have gang names such as the Red Fire, Wo Hop To, Vietnamese Troublemakers, Asian Car Thieves, and Chinatown Rulers (Rosenthal 1991). What can we do?

QUESTIONS FOR UNDERSTANDING AND CRITICAL THINKING

1. In contrast to urban street gangs who are often isolated from their respective communities, how and why are Chinatown gangs connected to their community?

2. Why is it important to examine tongs when discussing gangs in Chinese communities?

3. Based on the author's interviews, why have gangs formed in Oakland's Chinatown?

4. To what extent was the origin of Chinatown gangs in Oakland separate from that of San Francisco?

REFERENCES

ALEGADO D 1994 *Immigrant Youths From the Philippines: Embedded Identities in Hawaii's Urban Community Contexts* December paper presented at First World Congress on Indigenous Filipino Psychology and Culture.

ALLARD WA 1975 Chinatown, the gilded ghetto *National Geographic* November

AUMAN A, GY MARK 1997 From 'heathen Chinee' to 'model minority': the portrayal of Chinese Americans in the U.S. news media. In *U.S. News Coverage of Racial Minorities: A Sourcebook, 1934 to Present* Westport, CT: Greenwood Press

BRESLER F 1981 *The Chinese Mafia* NY: Stein and Day

CHIN K 1990 *Chinese Subculture and Criminality: Nontraditional Crime Groups in America* Westport CT: Greenwood Press

CHIN K, J FAGAN 1994 Social order and gang formation in Chinatown *Advances in Criminological Theory* 6 216–251

CHIN K, J FAGAN, R KELLY 1992 Patterns of Chinese gang extortion *Justice Ortly* 9 625–646

CHOW WT 1976 Oakland Chinatown: the dynamics of inner city adjustment *China Geographer* Spring

GONG YE, B GRANT 1930 *Tong War!* NY: NL Brown

HOMMA-TRUE R 1976 Characteristics of contrasting Chinatowns *Social Casework* March 155–159

JOE KA 1993 Getting into the gang: methodological issues in studying ethnic gangs *Drug Abuse Among Minority Youth: Methodological Issues and Recent Research Advances* 130 234–57

_ 1994a Myths and realities of Asian gangs on the West Coast *Humanity and Society* 18 3–18

_ 1994b The new criminal conspiracy? Asian gangs and organized crime in San Francisco *J Res Crime Delinquency* 31 390–415

KWONG P 1987 *The New Chinatown* NY: Hill and Wang

LAI HM, PP CHOY 1972 *Outline History of the Chinese in America* San Francisco: Chinese Historical Society of America

LYMAN SM 1970 *The Asian in the West* Reno & Las Vegas: Western Studies Center and Desert Research Institute

MARK GY 1989 Gambling in Oakland Chinatown: a case of constructive crime. In *Frontiers of Asian American Studies* Pullman, WA: Washington State U Press

PADILLA FM 1993 *The Gang as an American Enterprise* New Brunswick: Rutger U Press

PATRICK J 1973 *A Glasgow Gang Observed* London: EyreMethuen

POSNER G 1988 *Warlords of Crimes* NY: McGraw-Hill

REVILLA L 1996 Filipino Americans: issues for identity in Hawaii. In *Pagdiriwang 1996: Legacy and Vision of Hawaii's Filipino Americans* Honolulu: SEED and Center for Southeast Asian Studies, U of Hawaii

ROSENTHAL D 1991 Iggy Chinn's last patrol *San Francisco Examiner Image* March 311–321

SUNG B 1977 *Gangs in New York's Chinatown* NY: Department of Asian Studies, City College of New York, monograph No. 6

TAKAGI P, A PLATT 1978 Behind the gilded ghetto: an analysis of race, class, and crime in Chinatown *Crime and Social Justice* Spring-Summer 2–25

THRASHER FM 1927 *The Gang: A Study of 1,313 Gangs in Chicago* Chicago: U Chicago Press

THOMPSON J 1976 Are Chinatown gang wars a cover-up? *San Francisco Magazine* February

WHYTE WF 1943 *Street Corner Society* Chicago: U Chicago Press

WOLFE T 1969 The new yellow peril *Esquire* December 190–199

Gangs in Prisons and Schools

9

An Overview of the Challenge of Prison Gangs

Mark S. Fleisher and Scott H. Decker

A persistently disruptive force in correctional facilities is prison gangs. Prison gangs disrupt correctional programming, threaten the safety of inmates and staff, and erode institutional quality of life. The authors review the history of, and correctional mechanisms to cope with prison gangs. A suppression strategy (segregation, lockdowns, transfers) has been the most common response to prison gangs. The authors argue, however, that given the complexity of prison gangs, effective prison gang intervention must include improved strategies for community re-entry and more collaboration between correctional agencies and university gang researchers on prison gang management policies and practices.

America now imprisons men and women with ease and in very large numbers. At the end of the year 2000, an estimated two million men and women were serving prison terms. The mission of improving the quality of life inside our prisons should be a responsibility shared by correctional administrators and community citizens. Prisons are, after all, public institutions supported by tens of millions of tax dollars and what happens inside of these costly institutions will determine to some degree the success inmates will have after their release. Oddly though, citizens often believe that anyone can offer an intelligent opinion about prison management and inmate programming. In recent years, elected officials have called for tougher punishment in prisons, stripping color televisions, removing weightlifting equipment, and weakening education programs as if doing these rather trivial things will punish inmates further and force them to straighten out their lives and will scare others away from crime. If criminals choose to commit crime, "let them suffer" seems to be the prevailing battle cry of elected officials and citizens alike, who have little formal knowledge of crimogenesis, punishment, and imprisonment.

A parallel argument would let smokers suffer the ravages of cancer because their behavior, above all others, caused their health problem. Similarly, we should allow students who do not choose to study to remain ignorant because their behavior led them to marginal illiteracy. As we sanction cigarette companies for selling a carcinogenic product, as we strive to improve public education, we also should continuously improve prison management and the quality of life inside these costly, tax-supported institutions. We do not advocate coddling inmates but we surely do not advocate allowing millions of imprisoned inmates to live with drug addictions, emotional difficulties, and educational and employment skills so poor that only minimum-wage employment awaits them. These are the disabilities that, to some degree, define the American inmate population, and these same disabilities will damage the quality of life in our communities when these untreated, uneducated, and marginal inmates return home.

Criminologists have argued for decades that persistent criminals often do not have the power to control the destructive forces in their environment, which created their disabilities. Many criminals are, in a real sense, victims of family abuse and neglect, school disciplinary practices that expelled them before they had sufficient education to get a good job, and impoverished neighborhoods well outside the opportunity networks in the dominant community.

Western civilization has used prisons as an experimental site where socially destructive human behavior supposedly is transformed into socially productive behavior. This experiment has yielded consistently poor results. As we begin the next century, we might want to rethink the mission of the prison, shifting the prevailing approach from punishing convicted offenders to using these public institutions as society's last chance to reform men and women who, for whatever reason, have not been able to conform to mainstream community norms.

American history shows prison inmates have, for the most part, been marginal to the dominant economy of the time and were the society's most poorly educated and least well-prepared citizens to hold gainful employment. But now the gap between the social and economic margin and mainstream grows wider and faster than it ever has grown. In the 1950s, a general equivalency diploma (GED) was sufficient to enable employment in America's expanding factory economy, but now the GED affords only minimum-wage employment in the fast-food industry and/or service work in hotels, malls, and restaurants. America's high-tech twenty-first century has decreasing career opportunities for the nearly two million poorly educated American prisoners whose economic future grows more distant from the mainstream economy as the nanoseconds pass. Prisons are our last best chance to help law-breakers find a lawful, economically stable place in mainstream communities.

That is a lofty mission, indeed, especially with tens of thousands of inmates entering prison annually. To accomplish the difficult job of retraining, educating, and treating inmates, prisons must be well-managed public institutions. Every prison cell house that burns in a disturbance burns millions of tax dollars. Managing prisons is difficult and that task should be delegated exclusively to the correctional experts rather than to elected officials pandering to voters. The highest security prisons hold the most violent and disruptive inmates who are most likely to be as disruptive inside as they were outside. In such places and others of lower security, a social force is operating today that will thwart even our best efforts to create and sustain high-quality prison management. That disruptive social force is prison gangs.

A BRIEF HISTORY OF PRISON GANGS

Lyman (1989) defines a prison gang as

> an organization which operates within the prison system as a self-perpetuating criminally oriented entity, consisting of a select group of inmates who have established an organized chain of command and are governed by an established code of conduct. The prison gang will usually operate in secrecy and has as its goal to conduct gang activities by controlling their prison environment through intimidation and violence directed toward non-members (p. 48).

We have only a rudimentary knowledge of prison gangs as social groups operating inside prisons and of the interplay between street gangs and prison gangs. Thus the scope, understanding, and study of prison gangs are broader and somewhat different from street gangs. One thing we do know: prison gangs are gang researchers' final frontier and prison managers' biggest nightmare.

While we debate prison gang demographics and their distribution in American prisons, we know such groups have been in prisons a long time. The first known American prison gang was the Gypsy Jokers formed in the 1950s in Washington state prisons (Orlando-Morningstar, 1997; Stastny & Tyrnauer, 1983). The first prison gang with nationwide ties was the Mexican Mafia, which emerged in 1957 in the California Department of Corrections.

Camp and Camp (1985) identified approximately 114 gangs with a membership of approximately 13,000 inmates. Of the 49 agencies surveyed, 33 indicated that they had gangs in their system: Pennsylvania reported 15 gangs, Illinois reported 14. Illinois had 5,300 gang members, Pennsylvania had 2,400, and California had 2,050. In Texas, there were nine prison gangs with more than 50 members each, totaling 2,407 (Ralph & Marquart, 1991). Fong (1990) reported eight Texas gangs with 1,174 members. Illinois reported that 34.3 percent of inmates belonged to a prison gang, which was then the highest percent of prison gang-affiliated inmates in the nation (Camp & Camp, 1985).

Lane (1989) reported that the Illinois Department of Corrections (IDOC) estimated the inmate gang population to be nearly 90 percent of the entire population, attributing that number to the importation of gangs from Chicago's streets, which is supported by research (Jacobs, 1974). Rees (1996) shows that Chicago police estimated more than 19,000 gang members in that city and a high percent of IDOC inmates were arrested in Cook County. Other correctional agencies, however, report their gang troubles started inside rather than outside prison walls. Camp and Camp (1985) cite that of the 33 agencies surveyed, 26 reported street counterparts to prison gangs.

Knox and Tromanhauser (1991) suggest there are approximately 100,000 or more prison gang members across the nation. Subsequent to Camp and Camp (1985), the American Correctional Association found that prison gang membership doubled between 1985 and 1992 from 12,624 to 46,190 (Baugh, 1993), with relatively few gang members in minimum security units. Later, Montgomery and Crews (1998) argued that Knox and Tromanhauser overestimated the prison gang population and cited the American Correctional Association's 1993 study that reported some 50,000 prison gang members.

Obtaining data on the number of prison gangs and gang membership has been difficult. Most estimates are now 10 to 20 years old. Fong and Buentello (1991) suggest three
major reasons for the lack of prison gang research. First, official documentation on prison
gangs is weak. What documentation exists is generally only for departmental use. Second,
prison managers are reluctant to allow outside researchers into facilities to conduct prison
gang research. Fears over security and concern that research might hamper the welfare of
the prison are the oft-cited reasons for excluding prison researchers. Third, prison gang
members themselves are secretive and likely would not disclose sensitive information about
their prison gang group to outside researchers.

PRISON GANGS: STRUCTURE AND ORGANIZATION

Prison gangs share organizational similarities. Prison gangs have a structure usually with
one person designated as the leader who oversees a council of members who make the
group's final decisions. The rank and file form a hierarchy, making these groups look more
similar to organized crime than their counterparts on the outside (Decker, Bynum, &
Weisel, 1998). The United States Department of Justice (1992) suggests that leaders and
hard-core members are some 15–20 percent of a gang's membership and that the majority
of members do not have a vested interest in the organization leadership.

Prison gangs, like some street counterparts, have a creed or motto, unique symbols
of membership, and a constitution prescribing group behavior. Absolute loyalty to one's
gang is required (Marquart & Sorensen, 1997); as is secrecy (Fong & Buentello, 1991).
Violent behavior is customary and can be used to move a member upward in the prison hierarchy. Prison gangs focus on the business of crime generally through drug trafficking.
Such crime groups have an interest in protecting their membership (Montgomery &
Crews, 1998).

Gang members are the essential capital in crime-oriented social groups; likewise,
when members want to leave the group, such out-group movement jeopardizes group security, thus the so-called blood in, blood out credo, according to Fong, Vogel, and
Buentello (1992). These researchers surveyed 48 former prison gang members who de-
fected and found that the number of gang defectors was proportional to their prison gang's
size. A number of reasons were cited for defecting. Most commonly, former members lost
interest in gang activities; the next most common reason was a refusal to carry out a hit on
a non-gang member; and the least common reason for leaving was a disagreement with the
direction of the gang's leadership. A small number of former members violated a gang rule
and were fearful of a gang violation against them, outgrew a sense of belonging to the
gang, turned informant, or refused to commit gang crimes. We do not know, however, how
many defectors were killed inside and outside prisons as a percentage of the total number
of defectors.

Research suggests there are at least five major prison gangs, each with its own structure and purpose. The Mexican Mafia (La Eme) started at the Deuel Vocational Center in
Tracy, California, in the 1950s and was California's first prison gang (Hunt, Riegel,
Morales, & Waldorf, 1993) composed primarily of Chicanos, or Mexican Americans. En-
trance into La Eme requires a sponsoring member. Each recruit has to undergo a blood oath
to prove his loyalty. The Mexican Mafia does not proscribe killing its members who do not
follow instructions. Criminal activities include drug trafficking and conflict with other

prison gangs, which is common with the Texas Syndicate, Mexikanemi, and the Aryan Brotherhood (AB) (Orlando-Morningstar, 1997).

The Aryan Brotherhood, a white supremacist group, was started in 1967 in California's San Quentin prison by white inmates who wanted to oppose the racial threat of black and Hispanic inmates and/or counter the organization and activities of black and Hispanic gangs (Orlando-Morningstar, 1997). Pelz, Marquart, and Pelz (1991) suggest that the AB held distorted perceptions of blacks and that many Aryans felt that black inmates were taking advantage of white inmates, especially sexually, thus promoting the need to form and/or join the Brotherhood. Joining the AB requires a 6-month probationary period (Marquart & Sorensen, 1997). Initiation, or "making one's bones," requires killing someone. The AB traffics in drugs and has a blood in, blood out rule; natural death is the only nonviolent way out. The Aryan Brotherhood committed eight homicides in 1984, or 32 percent of inmate homicides in the Texas correctional system, and later became known as the "mad dog" of Texas corrections (Pelz, Marquart, & Pelz, 1991).

The Aryan Brotherhood structure within the federal prison system used a three-member council of high-ranking members. Until recently, the federal branch of the Aryan Brotherhood was aligned with the California Aryan Brotherhood, but differences in opinion caused them to split into separate branches. The federal branch no longer cooperates with the Mexican Mafia in such areas as drugs and contract killing within prisons, but as of October 1997, the California branch still continued to associate with the Mexican Mafia. Rees (1996) suggested that the Aryan Brotherhood aligned with other supremacist organizations to strengthen its hold in prisons. The Aryan Brotherhood also has strong chapters on the streets (Valentine, 1995), which allows criminal conduct inside and outside prisons to support each other.

Black Panther George Jackson united black groups such as the Black Liberation Army, Symbionese Liberation Army, and the Weatherman Underground Organization to form one large organization, the Black Guerilla Family, which emerged in San Quentin in 1966. Leaning on a Marxist-Leninist philosophy, the Black Guerilla Family was considered to be one of the more politically charged revolutionary gangs, which scared prison management and the public (Hunt et al., 1993). Recently, offshoots within the Black Guerilla Family have appeared. California reported the appearance of a related group known as the Black Mafia (Orlando-Morningstar, 1997).

La Nuestra Familia ("our family") was established in the 1960s in California's Soledad prison, although some argue it began in the Deuel Vocational Center (Landre, Miller, & Porter, 1997). The original members were Hispanic inmates from Northern California's agricultural Central Valley who aligned to protect themselves from the Los Angeles-based Mexican Mafia. *La Nuestra Familia* has a formal structure and rules as well as a governing body known as *La Mesa,* or a board of directors. Today, *La Nuestra Familia* still wars against the Mexican Mafia over drug trafficking but the war seems to be easing in California (Orlando-Morningstar, 1997).

The Texas Syndicate emerged in 1958 at Deuel Vocational Institute in California. It appeared at California's Folsom Prison in the early 1970s and at San Quentin in 1976 because other gangs were harassing native Texans. Inmate members are generally Texas Mexican Americans, but now the Texas Syndicate offers membership to Latin Americans and perhaps Guamese as well. The Texas Syndicate opposes other Mexican American gangs, especially those from Los Angeles (Hunt et al., 1993). Dominating the crime agenda is drug trafficking inside and outside prison and selling protection to inmates (Landre et al., 1997).

Like other prison gangs, the Texas Syndicate has a hierarchical structure with a president and vice president and an appointed chairman in each local area, either in a prison or in the community (Orlando-Morningstar, 1997). The chairman watches over that area's vice chairman, captain, lieutenant, sergeant at arms, and soldiers. Lower-ranking members perform the gang's criminal activity. The gang's officials, except for the president and vice president, become soldiers again if they are moved to a different prison, thus avoiding local-level group conflict. Proposals within the gang are voted on, with each member having one vote; the majority decision determines group behavior.

The *Mexikanemi* (known also as the Texas Mexican Mafia) was established in 1984. Its name and symbols cause confusion with the Mexican Mafia. As the largest gang in the Texas prison system, it is emerging in the federal system as well and has been known to kill outside as well as inside prison. The *Mexikanemi* spars with the Mexican Mafia and the Texas Syndicate, although it has been said that the *Mexikanemi* and the Texas Syndicate are aligning themselves against the Mexican Mafia (Orlando-Morningstar, 1997). The *Mexikanemi* has a president, vice president, regional generals, lieutenants, sergeants, and soldiers. The ranking positions are elected by the group based on leadership skills. Members keep their positions unless they are reassigned to a new prison. The *Mexikanemi* has a 12-part constitution. For example, part five says that the sponsoring member is responsible for the person he sponsors; if necessary, a new person may be eliminated by his sponsor (Orlando-Morningstar, 1997).

Hunt et al. (1993) suggest that the *Nortenos* and the *Surenos* are new Chicano gangs in California, along with the New Structure and the Border Brothers. The origins and alliances of these groups are unclear; however, the Border Brothers are comprised of Spanish-speaking Mexican American inmates and tend to remain solitary. Prison officials report that the Border Brothers seem to be gaining membership and control as more Mexican American inmates are convicted and imprisoned.

The Crips and Bloods, traditional Los Angeles street gangs, are gaining strength in the prisons as well as are the 415s, a group from the San Francisco area (415 is a San Francisco area code). The Federal Bureau of Prisons cites 14 other disruptive groups within the federal system, which have been documented as of 1995, including the Texas Mafia, the Bull Dogs, and the Dirty White Boys (Landre et al., 1997).

PRISON GANGS AND VIOLENCE

Prison gangs dominate the drug business and many researchers argue that prison gangs also are responsible for most prison violence (Ingraham & Wellford, 1987). Motivated by a desire to make money and be at the top of an institution's inmate power structure, prison gangs exploit the inherent weaknesses resulting from overcrowded, understaffed mega-prisons such as correctional staffers' inability to watch the activities of say, 3,000–5,000 inmates every moment of each day, month after month.

Where profits are at stake, research on street gangs shows that violence is often the outcome. Inside prisons, the same pattern appears. Camp and Camp (1985) noted that prison gang members were on aggregate 3 percent of the prison population but caused 50 percent or more of the prison violence. In a small confined area with a finite number of drug customers as well as customers of other gang-related services, such as gambling and prostitution (Fleisher, 1989), the stage is set for inter-gang competition (Fong, Vogel, &

Buentello, 1992), especially in overcrowded prisons. "Turf wars" occur on the street as well as in prison, where gang members and non-gang members are packed together, leaving few options for retreat to a safe and neutral spot (Gaston, 1996).

CORRECTIONAL RESPONSES TO PRISON GANGS

Prison gangs have had adverse effects on prison quality of life. Those adverse effects have motivated correctional responses to crime, disorder, and rule violations. Many correctional agencies have developed policies to control prison gang-affiliated inmates. Carlson outlines the approaches used by major correctional agencies to handle prison gangs (see article in this issue).

Since the publication of Clemmer's (1958) classic *The Prison Community,* prison scholars have debated the effect that prison has on the formation of inmate groups and individual behavior. Do inmates form disruptive groups as a result of the actions of prison administrators? Will inmates form disruptive groups as a prison extension of their street behavior (Jacobs, 1977) in spite of the best efforts of prison managers to create a positive environment (Hunt et al., 1993)?

Fong and Buentello (1991) argue that inmates' need for social identity and belonging contribute to the formation of inmate prison groups; however, a need for identity and belonging does not explain the importation of outside gang structures, names, and symbols into a prison where security and continuous oversight are among the institution's principal organizational traits. That inmates form groups based on the need for identity, belonging, personal interests, and race/ethnicity conforms to well-known processes in all human groups, and such behavior inside a prison should not be a surprise. To try to suppress human tendencies to form social groups, as was tried in the early days of the Pennsylvania system, would be pointless as a general management strategy (Knox, 2000). In many respects, however, today's super-maximum security institutions attempt to do just that.

In institutions where prison management controls on inmate crime and violence are weak and where prisons routinely violate inmates' civil rights (Fong et al., 1995; DiIulio, 1987; Ralph and Marquart, 1991), it may be understandable that inmates form tips and cliques to ensure their own physical safety. Given this line of argument, if prisons want fewer inmate tips and cliques and by extension prison gangs, management must step forward proactively and offer inmates a meaningful alternative to prison gangs and gang crime and offer inmates treatment for personal issues such as addiction. Scott's article (this issue) focuses on altering the prison environment. He argues that prisons, like mainstream communities, must broaden their approach to dealing with prison gangs. Hardening the environment, Scott argues, may fail as a long-term prison control strategy as law enforcement suppression, to the exclusion of social intervention, has failed to quell the street gang problem.

Adjusting prison environments most often happens in court. Jacobs (1977) argues that the courts weakened the authority of correctional officers to control gangs taking control since the earliest cases on inmates' rights; prison administrators are confined within the limits of case law. In this issue, Federal Bureau of Prisons' lawyer Daniel Eckhart reviews recent federal legal cases on prison gangs. Eckhart's useful article informs correctional administrators who must develop gang control strategies that meet the limits of federal court precedents; such precedents are also useful information to correctional researchers who may evaluate prison control strategies.

Mainline prisons for the most part are expected to house inmates, independent of gang affiliation. Prison suppression and intervention strategies likely will affect gang-affiliated inmates differently from non-gang-affiliated inmates. Why? Shelden (1991) compared 60 gang members (45 black, 15 Hispanic) to 60 non-gang members. There were a number of similarities between the gang and non-gang groups: they shared similar socioeconomic backgrounds, education levels, and marital status; both groups had substance abuse problems. Gang members, however, were more likely to have never been employed, more likely to have a juvenile crime record (30 percent of them had juvenile court records compared with 8 percent of non-gang inmates); 32 percent of the gang members had 15 or more arrests compared with 7 percent of non-members; and gang members also were more likely to have used a weapon than non-members. Krienert and Fleisher show in their article in this issue that new admissions into the Nebraska Department of Corrections who report a prior gang affiliation are significantly different from those who do not report a gang affiliation on many of the same factors Shelden used. Their research documents the growing nature of this problem.

Shelden's contribution also shows that while imprisoned, gang members were twice as likely to have more than five rule violations, were more likely to violate drug use sanctions, were more likely to fight, and were less likely to be involved in treatment programs. Without in-prison treatment, education, and vocational training, the likelihood that gang-affiliated inmates would be prepared for a lawful lifestyle outside prison is low. The article by Davis and Flannery in this issue deals with special challenges that gang-affiliated inmates pose to therapists.

How have prison officials responded to prison gangs? Prisons have tried a variety of overt and covert strategies, including the use of inmate informants, the use of segregation units for prison gang members, the isolation of prison gang leaders, the lockdown of entire institutions, the vigorous prosecution of criminal acts committed by prison gang members, the interruption of prison gang members' internal and external communications, and the case-by-case examination of prison gang offenses. There are, however, no published research evaluations testing the efficacy of these suppression strategies on curbing prison gang violence and/or other criminal conduct inside correctional institutions. Below is a brief summary of some of these anti-prison-gang initiatives.

The Texas state legislature passed a bill in September 1985 that made it a "felony for any inmate to possess a weapon" (Ralph & Marquart, 1991, p. 45). The bill also limited the discretionary authority of sentencing judges: inmates convicted of weapons possession must serve that sentence subsequent to other sentences. Officials believe that laws like this might help to keep inmates, especially those in prison gangs, under control (Ralph & Marquart, 1991).

A popular control procedure is segregation. Inmates are isolated in a cell 23 hours a day, with one hour assigned to recreation and/or other activities. Texas used administrative segregation and put all known prison gang members into segregation in 1985 in the hope of limiting their influence on mainline inmate populations. Violence in the general population decreased, with nine prison gang-motivated homicides from 1985 to 1990; fewer armed assaults were reported as well. By 1991, segregation housed more than 1,500 gang members (Ralph & Marquart, 1991).

By contrast, Knox (2000) reports that more than half of the 133 prison officials interviewed in a national survey on prison gangs believe a segregation policy is not effective because gang activity still occurs. When an order is issued by a prison gang to commit a violent act, it is carried out, even in a segregation unit. Then, too, segregation is expensive and does not solve the problem of developing better prison management to control prison gangs.

Isolating gang leaders has become a popular control strategy. With a prison gang leader locked down, vertical communication within the gang ideally would weaken and the prison gang group's solidarity eventually would deteriorate. One version of isolating prison gang leaders is to transfer them among institutions or keep them circulating between prisons (United States Department of Justice, 1992). There are no published evaluations of isolation and/or "bus therapy."

Another attempt to reduce gang membership is "jacketing." This involves putting an official note in an inmate's file if he is suspected of being involved with a gang. This note follows him in prison and allows authorities to transfer him to a high-security facility. Many find this process inappropriate because it may involve suspected but unconfirmed gang activity, often reported by a snitch, which leads to incorrectly labeling an inmate as a prison gang member or associate. When so labeled, an inmate can be controlled with threats of segregation and transfer. There are no published evaluations of this approach either.

Correctional agencies now use databases to track prison gang members and gang activities. This allows for effective communication between a correctional agency and a state police agency and improves data accuracy because data can be entered as soon as they are gathered (Gaston, 1996). The New York City Department of Correction uses a system that allows for digitized photos that document gang members' marks and/or tattoos. Database searches can be done by a tattoo, scar, or other identifying marks. The speed and capacity to update intelligence information make the use of a shared database an effective tool in prison gang management.

Providing alternative programming could become part of prison gang management strategy; however, prison gang members have not embraced such programming. The Hampden County Correctional Center in Ludlow, Massachusetts, developed a graduated program for prison gang members wanting to leave segregation. The program uses movies, discussion sessions, and homework. At the program's end, participants must write a statement certifying they will no longer participate in gang activities. Two years into the program, 190 inmates were enrolled and 17 were returned to segregation for gang activities (Toller & Tsagaris, 1996). Details of the program's evaluation are not available.

Another control strategy is the use of out-of-state transfers, which send key prison gang members out of state in the hope of stopping or slowing a prison gang's activities. If a gang already has been established, it is hoped that such a transfer would disrupt a gang to the point of its demise; however, there are no data showing the effectiveness of this type of control strategy. In fact, transferring a high-ranking prison gang member could be the impetus to transfer his prison gang to yet another institution (United States Department of Justice, 1992).

Correctional agencies have tried to weaken prison gangs by assigning members of different prison gangs to the same work assignment and living quarters in anticipation of limiting the power of one prison gang over another at a specific place. The Texas Department of Corrections, for instance, assigned prison gang members to two or three high-security lockdown institutions. Illinois tried this approach to no avail because the inmate prison gang population was too large to control effectively within a few locations (United States Department of Justice, 1992). Illinois developed a "gang-free" institution near Springfield, but as yet there are no published evaluations of its effectiveness on reducing gang-related/motivated crime within the Illinois Department of Corrections.

Camp and Camp (1985) surveyed facilities and asked officials which strategies they were most likely to employ against prison gangs. Transfer was cited by 27 of the 33 agencies (such an approach is analogous to schools expelling disruptive students to alternative schools); the use of informers was cited 21 times; prison gang member segregation was cited 20 times; prison gang leader segregation was cited 20 times; facility lockdown was cited 18 times; and vigorous prosecution and interception of prison gang members' communications were cited 16 times.

Knox and Tromanhauser (1991) surveyed prison wardens asking about prison gang control: 70.9 percent advocated bus therapy. Some prison officials tried to quell prison gang disruptions by discussing those disruptions with gang leaders. And another 5.5 percent of the wardens said they ignored prison gangs. These researchers show that fewer than half of the prisons surveyed provided any type of prison gang training; but recently, Knox (2000) shows that correctional officers training has improved, with a finding that more than two-thirds of the 133 facilities surveyed provided some gang training in 1999.

A NEED FOR MORE COLLABORATION

We have little hard data on the demographics of today's prison gangs and the nature and levels of prison gang-related disorder in American prisons. This lack of data is a serious impediment to making progress against a serious and growing problem. The Camp and Camp (1985) inventory of prison gangs describes an earlier era in American corrections. Collaborative research between correctional officials and experienced gang and prison researchers can yield the data needed to develop effective prison gang intervention and suppression strategies as well as the data needed to test the efficacy of current strategies. Collaboration between correctional agencies and university researchers is a key to creating strong solutions to the difficult, persistent problem posed by prison gangs. Such collaboration should create the programs that will increase the likelihood that prison gang members, leaving institutions after decades of doing time, will remain crime free. Imagine how strange today's job market looks to the inmates who were imprisoned in 1980 or even 1990. To be sure, the challenge of beginning a career, even for a college graduate, is daunting. For a former inmate and a prison gang member, searching to find a lawful path will be difficult and alien.

Efforts to control prison gangs must be matched by thoughtful community initiatives. Such initiatives may include carefully designed community reintegration programs offering specialized education and training to meet the expectations of entry-level high-tech employment. Research shows that prison gangs' criminal influence extends into the community (Fong & Buentello, 1991). The important implication of this observation is that prison gangs will gain a stronger hold in communities if communities do not structure intervention to include more than law enforcement suppression. If that happens, street gangs may become better structured and drug gangs may become more powerful forces in the community. The article by Fleisher, Decker, and Curry in this issue urges correctional agencies to unite with communities to provide careful, post-imprisonment programming for gang-affiliated inmates. In this way, the response to gangs both on the street and in prison can be comprehensive and integrated.

QUESTIONS FOR UNDERSTANDING AND CRITICAL THINKING

1. How are prisons gangs structured and organized?
2. What are the five major prison gangs in the United States, and how do each offer unique challenges for corrections officials, administration and staff?

3. What have been correctional responses and mechanisms to manage prison gang problems?

4. The authors argue that effective prison gang intervention must include improved community reintegration programs. Who would design these? Where would the money come from? Who would manage these types of programs? Who would be ultimately responsible for the programs' failure or success?

REFERENCES

BAUGH, D.G. (1993). *Gangs in correctional facilities: A national assessment.* Laurel, MD: American Correctional Association.

CAMP, G.M., & CAMP, C.G. (1985). *Prison gangs: Their extent, nature, and impact on prisons.* Washington, DC: U.S. Government Printing Office.

CLEMMER, D. (1958). *The prison community.* New York: Holt, Rinehart, and Winston.

DECKER, S.H., BYNUM, T.S., & WEISEL, D.L. (1998). Gangs as organized crime groups: A tale of two cities. *Justice Quarterly, 15,* 395–423.

DILULIO, J.J. (1987). *Governing prisons: A comparative study of correctional management.* New York: Free Press.

FLEISHER, M.S. (1989). *Warehousing violence.* Newbury Park, CA: Sage Publications.

FONG, R.S. (1990). The organizational structure of prison gangs: A Texas Case Study. *Federal Probation, 59,* 36–43.

FONG, R.S., & BUENTELLO, S. (1991). The detection of prison gang development: An empirical assessment. *Federal Probation, 55,* 66–69.

FONG, R.S., VOGEL, R.E., & BUENTELLO, S. (1992). Prison gang dynamics: A look inside the Texas Department of Corrections. In P.J. Benekos & A.V. Merlo (Eds.), *Corrections: Dilemmas and directions.* Cincinnati, OH: Anderson Publishing Co. (pp. 57–78).

GASTON, A. (1996). Controlling gangs through teamwork & technology. *Large Jail Network Bulletin,* Annual Issue, 1996, 7–10.

HUNT, G., RIEGEL, S., MORALES, T., & WALDORF, D. (1993). Changes in Prison Culture: Prison gangs and the case of the 'Pepsi Generation.' *Social Problems, 40,* 398–409.

INGRAHAM, B.L., & WELLFORD, C.F. (1987). The totality of conditions test in eighth-amendment litigation. In S.D. Gottfredson & S. McConville (Eds.), *America's correctional crisis: Prison populations and public policy.* New York: Greenwood Press.

JACOBS, J.B. (1974). Street gangs behind bars. *Social Problems, 21,* 395–409.

JACOBS, J.B. (1977). *Stateville. The penitentiary in mass society.* Chicago: University of Chicago Press.

KNOX, G.W. (2000). A national assessment of gangs and security threat groups (STGs) in adult correctional institutions: Results of the 1999 Adult Corrections Survey. *Journal of Gang Research, 7,* 1–45.

KNOX, G.W., & TROMANHAUSER, E.D. (1991). Gangs and their control in adult correctional institutions. *The Prison Journal, 71,* 15–22.

LANDRE, R., MILLER, M., & PORTER, D. (1997). *Gangs: A handbook for community awareness.* New York: Facts On File, Inc.

LANE, M.P. (1989, July). Inmate gangs. *Corrections Today, 51,* 98–99.

LYMAN, M.D. (1989). *Gangland.* Springfield, IL: Charles C Thomas.

MARQUART, J.W., & SORENSEN, J.R. EDS., (1997). *Correctional contexts: Contemporary and classical readings.* Los Angeles, CA: Roxbury Pub.

MONTGOMERY R.H., JR., & CREWS, G.A. (1998). *A history of correctional violence: An examination of reported causes of riots and disturbances.* Lanham, MD: American Correctional Association.

ORLANDO-MORNINGSTAR, D. (1997, October). Prison gangs. *Special Needs Offender Bulletin, 2,* 1–13.

PELZ, M.E., MARQUART, J.W., & PELZ, C.T. (1991). Right-wing extremism in the Texas prisons: The rise and fall of the Aryan Brotherhood of Texas. *The Prison Journal, 71,* 23–37.

RALPH, P.H., & MARQUART, J.W. (1991). Gang violence in Texas prisons. *The Prison Journal, 71,* 38–49.

REES, T.A., JR. (1996, Fall). Joining the gang: A look at youth gang recruitment. *Journal of Gang Research, 4,* 19–25.

SHELDEN, R.G. (1991). A comparison of gang members and non-gang members in a prison setting. *The Prison Journal, 71,* 50–60.

STASTNY, C., & TYRNAUER, G. (1983). *Who rules the joint? The changing political culture of maximum-security prisons in America.* New York: Lexington Books.

TOLLER, W., & TSAGARIS, B. (1996, October). Managing institutional gangs: A practical approach combining security and human services. *Corrections Today, 58,* 100–111.

UNITED STATES DEPARTMENT OF JUSTICE. (1992). *Management strategies in disturbances and with gangs/disruptive groups.* Washington, DC: U.S. Government Printing Office.

VALENTINE, B. (1995). *Gang intelligence manual.* Boulder, CO: Paladin Press.

10

Gang Subcultures and Prison Gangs of Female Youth

Rebecca D. Petersen

Abstract

Inmate violence, disruptions and problems recently have been attributed to the rise of prison gangs. While some research has investigated this phenomenon, studies of female inmates, especially the juvenile population, have been largely ignored. This study examines the role of female gangs and subcultures by giving detailed, firsthand accounts from thirty-four young incarcerated women. The models used for the analysis include both the importation and deprivation views of prison subculture development. Results include interpretations of the nature and extent of prison gangs, gang recruitment, prison gang problems and friendship patterns based on gang alliances. Findings support both subculture models depending upon the contextual question.

Both in media and public discourse, prison gangs have evoked negative reactions. They are viewed as disruptive and violent. For more than two decades, the proliferation of gangs in prison has disrupted many American correctional institutions (Fong, Vogel & Buentello 1996) with prison gangs regarded as a major source of violence and other correctional problems. A comprehensive study conducted by Camp & Camp (1985) identified the presence of 114 male prison gangs nationwide with a total membership of 12,634 in 33 adult prison systems. While these prison gangs accounted for only 3 percent of the country's adult male prison population, they have been found responsible for over 50 percent of prison management problems (Fong, Vogel & Buentello 1996). A study conducted by the American Correctional Association (1993) found similar results. They concluded that prison gang members accounted for 6 percent of the prison population and were responsible

R. D. Petersen. (2000). Gang subcultures and prison gangs of female youth. Free Inquiry in Creative Sociology, 28; 27–42. Reprinted by permission of the University of Oklahoma.

for approximately 20 percent of violent incidences toward prison staff and 40 percent toward other prisoners.

In spite of prison gangs receiving more attention and being partly responsible for inmate problems, little research has been directed toward gangs in prison. Furthermore, to date there has been no comprehensive study looking at prison gangs in state juvenile facilities for either males or females.

How gang involvement may influence the processes of prison subcultural development for females is unknown. While gang involvement in women's prisons may be viewed as the product of importation, that is, females in gangs before incarceration continuing their gang affiliation while incarcerated, it may also be the result of deprivation, i.e., gangs forming to compensate for the lack of close-knit peer groups or for protection, just as in male institutions. It also may be that gangs develop due to a combination of both reasons. Regardless of origin, a primary assumption is that gang membership in prison provides opportunities for achieving power, feeling protected and acquiring a vast array of comforts to make the prison stay more tolerable.

This study attempts to fill the void of both subcultural and prison gang research by examining the role gangs play in inmate subcultures of female adolescents, in particular, one juvenile correctional facility located in the Southwest. The questions of deprivation and importation are examined in the context of adaptation to incarceration while specifically looking at the role of gangs. This research examines to what extent gangs account for how adolescent females react and adapt to imprisonment using the deprivation and importation models. These concepts are measured through in-depth analysis with thirty-four young women to examine individual and collective responses on reactions to confinement and gang life.

POLICY AND INMATE SUBCULTURES

Unfortunately, policymakers have implemented correctional policies without a clear understanding of how gangs impact the correctional experience. Further, policy is best informed by those closest to the problem (Petersen 2000; 1995) and as such, why listening to and understanding these young women is of particular significance.

Some literature has concerned itself with the question of whether gangs are imported into prisons or are an outgrowth of the deprivations of prison life. For example, McConville (1985) seems to suggest the latter is more prominent with mandatory minimum prison sentences a major factor contributing to gangs in prison. However, the recent growth of prison gangs may be the result of more individuals sentenced to prison who are gang members and as such, importation would also be a factor.

The increase of female gang involvement has most likely influenced inmate subcultures by altering the dynamics of power and status. With the increase in girls' participation in gangs, what they import into the institution and their variable effect on inmate subcultures are extremely important issues. The present research investigates how the values and norms of incarcerated gang girls may affect the values and norms of inmates who are not affiliated with gangs. Currently, no research in the literature exists involving juveniles detained in correctional facilities exclusively regarding the issue of gangs. There are also no reported studies of girls and gangs lodged within the network of inmate subcultures. How female gang involvement and affiliation represent the processes of importation or deprivation is unknown.

IMPORTATION AND DEPRIVATION:
FEMALE SUBCULTURES AND GANGS

The most popular belief in the existence of prison gangs can be attributed to importation. This perspective asserts that the inmate's social world is shaped by personal and social characteristics imported into prison (Irwin, Cressey 1962) with gangs in prison one result of such processes. Importation would suggest that gangs in prison are a result of individuals bringing their gangs into the prison. For example, if an individual is part of a street gang prior to incarceration, s/he may bring this mentality and behavior into the prison culture. How s/he adapts to the incarceration experience would be, in part, shaped by his/her prior gang affiliation. They may see prison life as an opportunity for extending their hometown gang.

Conversely, a polarized perspective on the existence of prison gangs is that of deprivation. This model argues that since the social world of inmates is shaped by a variety of prison deprivations (Clemmer 1940), gangs in prison may be the result of "easing the pains of imprisonment" especially if faced with a lengthy prison sentence (McConville 1985). Deprivation would view that individuals are deprived of, for example, companionship, status, power or protection and would form or join a gang to compensate for such losses. Inmates may find it necessary to form into groups for self-protection, power and/or dominance with such groups often developing into "prison gangs." These prison gangs are seen as notorious for incidences of violence, threats, intimidation and other types of disruption within the prison milieu.

It is, however, also possible that prison gangs develop for a combination of both deprivation and importation reasons, something previous literature on subcultures has not adequately addressed. Matthews (1999) contends that an important relationship exists between the social and cultural backgrounds of those who enter prison and that such backgrounds provide a framework for understanding the ways in which the pains of imprisonment are experienced. In fact, both the importation and deprivation models could be intertwined to better understand gang development in prison. For instance, gang subcultures on the outside can be imported to the institution via values, culture, norms, symbols, and language. Moreover, since youth are deprived of intimate peer relationships, they may join a gang or continue affiliation to compensate for their lack of intimacy, power, leadership, or even as a method of survival. These assertions can be applied to the understanding of gangs in prison. Clearly, the lack of knowledge and understanding of the world of female gangs lodged within the inmate social system merits serious examination.

Prior research on both female adult and juvenile subcultures is scant, at best, especially when compared to studies of male prisons (see Ward, Kassebaum 1965; Giallombardo 1966; 1974; Heffernan 1972). These and other investigations of female inmate subcultures often have been based on gender stereotypes with a preoccupation of sexual relations, in particular, homosexuality, and the role of pseudo-family relationships (Otis 1913; Ford 1929; Selling 1931; Kosofsky, Ellis 1958; Halleck, Hersko 1962; Ward, Kassebaum 1965; Konopka 1966; Giallombardo 1974; Carter 1981; Propper 1981). While incarcerated young women may be involved in homosexual relationships and may form pseudo-families, our knowledge of inmate subcultures of female youth virtually stops there. Furthermore, the few studies exclusively focused on inmate subcultures of female adolescents have produced mixed results as to which model explains subculture development accurately (Giallombardo 1974; Propper 1981; Carter 1981; Arnold 1994). It is, therefore, unclear as to the methods of how females adapt to incarceration, i.e., importation and/or deprivation, and how prior gang affiliation may account for their adaptation.

There are generally three types of ways females are involved or affiliated with gangs: (1) membership in an independent, all-female gang, (2) regular membership in a male or mixed-gender gang, and (3) female auxiliaries of male gangs. Research has overwhelmingly found the auxiliary roles most common (for example, Bowker 1978; Brown 1977; Campbell 1984; Flowers 1987; Hanson 1964; Miller 1975; 1980). These girls often are identified as girlfriends, friends, sisters or cousins of male gang members with their role in the gang minimal, i.e., carrying weapons, driving the get-a-way car, partying with the male gang members. It has been suggested that female gang membership has been increasing steadily in all these categories, but this is far from certain and research has not concretely substantiated such claims. As such, considerable ignorance exists concerning the role of females and gangs, especially relating to the impact of such gang affiliation on imprisonment.

Since more young women are being incarcerated every year accompanied by changes in gender roles, it is critical to explore how the various dimensions of social life affect inmate subculture formation. Because the perspective that gang research literature has about girl gang membership may no longer be accurate given contemporary conditions, it is important to understand the importation view of gang culture into the prison experience. It has been speculated that incarcerated gang members are often versions of their hometown gangs who merely have been regrouped in prison. What type of effect this has on subculture formation and inmate adaptation of young female inmates needs closer examination.

The goal of this study is to add to the understanding of the dynamics of gang affiliation among females relating to inmate subcultures. Specifically, I examine (1) whether the youth were involved with gangs before incarceration, (2) if they continued their gang affiliation while committed, (3) the impact of gang affiliation on subculture formation, and (4) if girls who were not in gangs before commitment decided to join while imprisoned and why.

METHODOLOGY

Given the state of the prior research and literature on this topic, the goal is not specifically hypothesis-testing. However, my reading of the literature on the role of females and gangs and on the importation and deprivation models in male prisons leads me to suggest some patterns I would expect to find. Specifically, the gang literature suggests that gangs play a lesser role for females than for males and the prison literature suggests that females feel the pains of family/role deprivation more than males. Thus, this would imply that the deprivation model may be more suitable in explaining the dynamics of gangs for incarcerated young women.

The intent of this study is not to produce a quantitative, statistical account. Rather, it is an exploratory study (Creswell 1994) designed to build constructed descriptions and interpretations of social events by the young women themselves. The findings of this study based solely on the interview responses, are to be understood through Verstehen, that is, empathetic understanding and meaning (Weber 1949) which underscores the importance of the context of the girls' lives. This study is meant to add a holistic understanding to the role of subcultures and gangs in a juvenile correctional facility. Inferences regarding the impact of incarceration on gang membership cannot be universally generalized. However, it is hoped that through this type of methodology, the role of subcultures and gangs can be well-understood, especially pertaining to correctional and public policy.

The interview model used in this research most closely relates to the interpretive approach toward social knowledge and meaning. Interviews framed for these purposes result in one-to-one casual conversations with the interviewer listening closely to the context of what is being said. The interviewee is treated as a conversational partner rather than an object of research (Rubin, Rubin 1995). The interview is very much like an ordinary conversation, but with more depth and detail. Kahn & Cannell (1957:49) describe in-depth interviewing as "a conversation with a purpose."

All accounts must be interpreted in terms of the context in which they were produced. According to Hammersley & Atkinson (1983:126), "Interview data, like any other, must be interpreted against the background of the context in which they were produced." Interpretations of meanings are made by the social actors, in this case, adolescent females, and by the researcher as well as by the audience reading the final study.

METHOD AND SETTING

Establishing rapport with subjects is crucial for this type of study. Rapport enhances the researcher's ability to convey empathy and understanding without judgment, to elicit more truthful responses, and to build detailed answers to questions. Incarcerated young women may feel intimated that an adult stranger, whom they may perceive negatively as an "authoritarian figure" or an "intruder" in their lives, is asking them personal questions while they are incarcerated. Therefore, it is important to underscore the importance of rapport in this study.

It should be noted that since I was a volunteer at the institution for approximately six months before the study commenced, many of the girls and I had established good rapport, and I believe a certain amount of trust already existed. Volunteers are usually perceived differently than correctional staff and are often thought of as wanting to help a population without monetary compensation or a particular political agenda. It was hoped that the young women recognized and respected this attribute. Furthermore, after some youth were interviewed, it was assumed that other youth would ask them about their experience and about the researcher and that this would help to alleviate potential suspicions. In addition each youth was awarded a certificate of appreciation for participation in the study.

Since in-depth, unstructured interviews are the method used for this research, taking notes while conducting the interview would limit the ability of recording verbatim responses. Moreover, note taking can prove disruptive with the interviewee becoming self-conscious about what is being written down. Taking notes also minimizes the informal nature of the unstructured interview and diminishes eye contact and interactive conversations. Recording interviews increases the validity of data collection, which is systematically transcribed at a later time, allowing the interviewer to be more attentive to each respondent. It was, therefore, essential to use a tape recorder during the interview.

Instead of assigning pseudo-names, each participant in the study has been given an identifying number, i.e., Youth #14, to organize data analysis and to examine differences and similarities among perspectives. Since this research is primarily a qualitative study, numeric accounts and frequencies of perspectives are not calculated quantitatively, with the exception of descriptive demographic information. Rather, categorized responses of thirty-four youth are collectively enumerated through qualitative descriptions based upon the following frequency continuum: none, one, a few, some, several, about half, over half, many, the majority, most, nearly all and all. Arranging responses using this method of analysis permits further understanding of their perspectives both collectively and individually.

The research took place at a juvenile correctional institution in the Southwest, henceforth referred to as SWI.[1] By law, if organizations receive federal subsidies, parental/guardian consent is required to study minors. As such, parental consent was needed for this study. According to the supervisory staff at SWI, the best and most common way they reach parents/guardians was through the mail since many of the youth's parents/guardians did not have working telephones. As such, letters were sent to each parent/guardian during a seven-month timeframe, from July 1996 to January 1997. One-hundred-three young women were incarcerated at some point during this study period.

A self-addressed stamped-envelope to the researcher was included in the letter to increase the response rate. If a response or a signed parental consent form was not received within three weeks, a follow-up letter was sent. Of the total 103 letters mailed, four notices from the youths' parents were received indicating that they did not want their daughter to participate in the study. A total of thirty-six signed parental consent forms were returned. Two of these youth had been incarcerated less than a month and were dropped from the study.[2] All thirty-four remaining girls were asked to participate in the study. All thirty-four agreed to participate which constitutes the total sample number of youth's interviewed.[3] The time length of the interview varied with each individual but ranged from forty-five minutes to over four hours with the average length of time approximately ninety minutes.

One final note on parental consent should be mentioned. Thirty-three percent of the girls incarcerated during the study time-frame were interviewed. I did not find it too surprising that over 60 percent of the parents/guardians did not sign and return the consent form. First, other research has shown that response rates for mailings, especially when the subject matter is sensitive and when the subject is a minor, are low and tend to fall between 10 to 50 percent (see Esbensen, Miller, Taylor et al. 1999; Kearney, Hopkins, Mauss et al. 1983; Miller 1991; Moberg, Piper 1990; Neuman, Wiegand 2000; Severson, Ary 1983). Unfortunately, since parental consent results in lower response rates, this invariably carries over to reduced sample sizes which not only increases the probability of subject selection bias but limits the validity and generalizability of study results (Hollmann, McNamara 1999). Second, I would speculate that many of these parents/guardians were suspect of an unknown "outside researcher" not directly connected to the correctional facility to possibly interview their child about personal issues. Finally, I would also contend that parents/guardians would not want a person to pry further into their child's life by asking a serious of sensitive questions. As such, it is difficult to estimate the effect of such nonresponses to this study's overall findings.

DATA ANALYSIS

Central to the analysis is gang importation into the institution, how this influenced subculture formation, and if girls joined gangs or continued gang involvement for either importation and/or deprivation reasons. The issue of gangs is addressed in themes according to perceptions of gangs, the extent of gang activity at SWI, if girls in gangs try to recruit non-gang inmates into their gang and the extent to which the latter is accomplished all within the framework of inmate subcultures. To keep the study and analysis focused, the analysis highlights only those issues that pertain to inmate subcultures.

DEMOGRAPHIC INFORMATION

Of special importance in giving meaning and shaping interpretation of the girls' voices is to profile some demographic information, i.e., age, race, length of disposition, total time served at interview, and previous geographical residence. Such descriptive information aids in understanding the perspectives of youth. Since this researcher was not allowed access to court or other official records, all data and information collected here are gleaned from the youths themselves.[4]

At SWI youth can be committed up until the age of eighteen. Table 10–1 illustrates the average age of the youth was 15.4 years with the range from thirteen to seventeen. Only one youth in the study was younger than fourteen. Table 10–1 indicates the ethnicity of each individual. Fifty-percent of the youth were white, followed by Hispanics (23.5%). The state in which the youth were confined is predominately white, with the largest minority population Hispanic. Hence, these findings tend to mirror the general population.

The length of institutionalization has been found to be related to the formation of inmate subcultures. The table notes the average length of incarceration was approximately nine months with the range from three months to over thirteen. For most of the young women, this was their first time sentenced to SWI. However, four indicated that they had been incarcerated at least one time before the study took place: two indicated that this was their second time at SWI; one said that this was her third time; and one expressed that this was her fourth time.[5] To understand more clearly how the duration of incarceration affects subcultures, the table shows at what time during the sentence the youth were interviewed. As illustrated, over fifty percent of the youth were interviewed within six months of their initial incarceration. Since the average length of sentence was around nine months, these findings are not surprising. Finally, Table 10–1 also indicates the youth's geographic residence prior to incarceration. Urban cities are measured by a population of at least 500,000 people. Suburbs and rural towns in the state are also included. Small cities included in the analysis are areas with approximately 40,000 residents. These findings suggest that a large number of youth previously resided in urban areas.

TABLE 10–1   Demographic Information (n= 34)

Age	13	14	15	16	17	$\overline{X}$
	1 (3%)	8 (23.5%)	9 (26.5%)	8 (23.5%)	8 (23.5%)	15.4
Ethnicity		**White**	**Hispanic**	**Af.Amer.**	**Native Am.**	**Asian**
		17 (50%)	8 (23.5%)	4 (12%)	4 (12%)	1 (2.5%)
Length of Disposition		**3–4 mos.**	**6–9 mos.**	**11–12 mos.**	**13+ mos.**	$\overline{X}$
		7 (22%)	15 (44%)	9 (26%)	3 (8%)	8.7
Total Time Served at Interview		**1–3 mos.**	**4–6 mos.**	**7–9 mos.**	**10+ mos.**	$\overline{X}$
		12 (35%)	12 (35%)	6 (18%)	4 (12%)	5.4
Area of Residence		**Urban**	**Suburban**	**Rural**	**Small City**	
		22 (64%)	6 (18%)	2 (6%)	4 (12%)	

Previous studies profiling females in prison (American Correctional Association 1990; Glick, Neto 1977) have found similar demographic characteristics, especially age and race. However, my study further explores the geographic location of residence before incarceration.

GANGS AT SWI

Analysis of the interview transcripts soon made it clear that a major factor in the girls' pre-prison experiences was their prior involvement with gangs. Gang affiliation was evident among this group of girls with twenty-two of the thirty-four girls indicating that they were involved in gangs[6] before incarceration. In some ways, this seemed to imply that importation, not deprivation, would be a major factor in the development subcultures. However, not all thirty-four girls were members of gangs prior to incarceration. Also, the extent to which subcultures formed in prison based on such gang alliances was further questioned by those young women affiliated with gangs as well as by those not involved with gangs.

Claiming gangs

When a young woman first enters the cottage at SWI, one of the first things that is asked by her peers is, "Where are you from?" As one non gang member noted, "I said that I was from [A City]. But that's not what they meant" (Youth #6). What the girls mean when they ask this crucial question is, "What gang do you claim?" not which part of the state one is from. One youth stated that "When they [the girls] first come in [to SWI], most of the girls let it be known that they are in a certain gang or not in a certain gang" (Youth #10). Moreover, Youth #4 who is associated with a gang stated that "people asked me when I first got here if I was from a gang and I said 'no'. But then they asked me who I 'kicked-back' with, then I told them."

Some girls continued claiming their gang at SWI while others do not. As illustrated by Youth #3, "I told them [peers at SWI] I am affiliated with it [gang] but that I stay away from it because it's not what I want to do with my life." On the other hand, some still identify with and claim their gang throughout their incarceration because, as illustrated by one youth not involved with gangs, "I think a lot of the girls here want out of their gangs but are afraid of being alone when they do leave here. A lot of the girls need something here to help them out and make them feel wanted" (Youth #22). Claiming the gang may not terminate inside the institution, although, their desire to get out of the gang may subside.

These findings seem to suggest that importation may be a factor in inmate subculture formation in that the girls who are affiliated with gangs bring this identity into the institution. At face, the youth still seem interested in knowing who is or is not a gang member and some still claim their gang, which can be interpreted as part of the importation model.

Based on these perspectives, there appears to be four major reasons why prison gang subcultures are not pervasive at SWI. First, many youth affiliated with gangs "do not want to be a part of the gang anymore" (Youth #4). Another young woman suggested that, "I'm trying to get out of it [gang]. I'm really not into it as much as I was. I am getting out, slowly but surely" (Youth #19). Based on the interviews, nearly all the girls involved with gangs did not want to be part of their gang anymore and their desire subsided before entering SWI. As Youth #22 illustrated, "A lot of the girls try to get out of their gangs in here, try to leave them . . . when they walked in the door, leave them there and not pick them up when they leave." Another young woman involved with a gang wanted to get jumped into her gang after release from SWI but was having second thoughts: "The way I see it is a way of getting into more trouble." (Youth #20). Accordingly, getting jumped into a gang would mean more involvement with other gang members and thus, more trouble. Still another youth articulated that "I quit caring about the gang life. Besides, everybody was getting locked up" (Youth #1). Youth #4 mentioned that she started to lessen her involvement with the gang before coming to SWI because "it got stupid to me. I stopped claiming [the gang] 'cause I thought the gang groups was starting to get stupid."

Second, girls affiliated with gangs knew that they would be further sanctioned if indications of gang involvement were present and visible, i.e., claiming their gang, throwing gang signs and talking about their gang. One youth pointed out the dangers of gangs at SWI: "I never throw up my gang sign at the institution 'cause I know you'd get in trouble. Not only that, but because your gang member friends aren't in here with you so, they [rival gang members] can throw it back at you" (Youth #8). A third and related reason is that the SWI administration and staff discourages these activities and rules prohibit such behavior. For example, SWI attempts to restrict gangs through forbidding gang signs and requiring girls to wear only certain colors. To illustrate, the girls wear light colored t-shirts, sweatshirts, sweatpants, shorts and identical state-blue jeans. Youth #10 indicated that "that's why we have these peach and yellow shirts 'cause they are so far off from being gang-related [colors]." Similarly, Youth #30 said that, "You can't wear red or blue here. You can't have nothin' here red or blue. You can't even have toothbrushes red or blue." Similarly, another youth added that, "you can't even have a blue toothbrush in here. That's how bad it is. When God made colors, I'm sure He didn't have in mind that it was going to belong to a gang" (Youth #9). The issue of gangs at SWI has, in part, influenced correctional policies by placing additional restrictions on the dress code and having other rules to curtail gangs.

A fourth reason for the lack of core, prison gang subcultures at SWI is there exists an absence of protection or a defined "turf" in such small living quarters. Some youth involved with gangs may be used to a defined turf on the streets. This is related to the final reason why gangs at SWI are not rampant. Since no gang territory at SWI apparently exists, each youth is forced into the same territorial area. They have no choice but to do their time with other surrounding peers and gang life may be further minimized by personal relationships, many of which are non-voluntary. As such, the minimal presence of gangs in prison may be related to structural and ecological factors in the institution downplaying the effect of both importation and deprivation.

Recruitment at SWI

One major question this research intended to address was the issue of gang recruitment at SWI. Do girls affiliated with gangs try to recruit others into their gang, whether this be a young woman not part of a gang or an individual already associated with another gang? By and large, the answer to this was "no." In the words of Youth #20, "they [gang members at SWI] just mind their own business." In fact, as illustrated previously, several young women in gangs were either slowly getting out of them before institutionalization or realized that "my gang only got me here" (Youth #1). Therefore, recruiting others into a gang appeared to be minimal, at best.

Youth # 8, affiliated with a gang, mentioned that, "There's pressure to join a gang [on the outside], but there's no pressure in here. The ones that are not [part of gangs] don't want to join one." A young woman not involved in gangs explained that, "They [girls in gangs] don't want to talk about getting nobody in it. Pretty much, they talk about getting out" (Youth #24). Still another young woman not involved with gangs illuminated that being in a gang is synonymous with violence and drugs: "I didn't want to be physically involved in drugs. I didn't want to have to carry a gun and look behind my shoulder every ten seconds. That's not my idea of fun. That's basically how gang life is: do or die" (Youth #7). Furthermore, there are dangers of trying to recruit others into a gang at SWI as illustrated by Youth #26: "People really don't try to recruit gang members here 'cause they might end up staying longer." Apparently, there may be sanctions by the institution for trying to recruit gang members and hence, this activity is largely avoided by the young women.

From the various interview responses of both girls affiliated with gangs and those not, it does not appear that gang members try to recruit others into their respective gang. Those who are part of gangs do not try to recruit others into their gang, and those who are not part of gangs do not want to become associated with gangs or gang members. In fact of those young women not affiliated with gangs prior to incarceration, none joined a gang while at SWI. As to how girls in gangs initially became involved on the outside and how this could affect importation, most were not actively recruited into their gang as they seemed to slowly "fall into" the gang lifestyle.

The same can be said to occur at SWI, as the girls involved with gangs do not actively recruit non-gang members and thus, is an illustration of importation. To further demonstrate this assertion, the girls not part of gangs often believed that a gang was nothing but a bunch of scoundrels. To illustrate, Youth #19 said that, "[A gang] is a bunch of whimps that can't fight for themselves, so they have to have a whole bunch of people do it for them." This view was further illustrated by Youth #20: "[Joining a gang] is trying to take the easy way out. It's a cop-out for life and it's not gonna get you anywhere." Youth #6 also believed that gangs were "a bunch of stupid people who go out making their own [family and friends] in the wrong ways. They're out to prove something and they're out to have others supposedly love them and have their backing on everything." Youth #28 suggested that "there's some reasons why people do join gangs 'cause they didn't get the acceptance in their family and they didn't get the love in their family, that's understandable. But there's other ways to get that [besides being in a gang]. You don't need to go out killing people." Youth #25 said "I don't like gangs. I don't have nothin' to do with them . . . I think there is no point to them."

Thus, the young women imported these views into the institution which can be said to be a major reason they would not join a gang if they were approached with the situation in prison. Youth #5, a gang member, suggested that "The [girls] that are not [in gangs] don't want to join one" either in prison or when they are released from prison. In this context of importation, there would be no reason why non-gang girls would join a gang while incarcerated. A notable question would be, why would they join? For those involved with gangs, the prison milieu is completely different than what they are used to in the "real" world. These above reasons tend to suggest that deprivation is not the active factor in subculture formation and that in regards to gang recruitment, importation has some explanatory power.

Gangs as Problems at SWI

Some youth thought gangs were problematic[7] to institutional life but most did not. Furthermore, their opinions did not appear to be formed based on gang membership. In other words, just as many gang girls and non-gang girls thought that gangs were problematic or not problematic at the institution.

The girls who viewed gangs at SWI as causing many problems gave various reasons. For example, Youth #24 said that, "Gangs are a really big thing in here. A lot of people will use their gang signs to get back at people, to put them down." One young woman affiliated with a West Side gang indicated that she purposefully avoids initial contact with rival gang members at SWI to avoid any type of conflict: "At the beginning when the new girls get here, I don't talk to them if they're from the South Side or from the North Side, especially from the North Side 'cause man, I don't get along with them or the South Side at all" (Youth #3). More commonly, gangs appear to be problematic on an individual-level. For example, "If two people get into an argument and it's over something stupid, they'll bring their gang into it . . . they'll throw their gang signs or claim their gang as better" (Youth #19). As such, the girls may try to bring their gangs in for the feeling of being protected or backed-up while incarcerated, an example of importation.

However, others thought that "gang stuff is not used a lot" and that "they usually keep their gangs to themselves." Many youth responded by saying that the girls who are part of gangs "leave it at the door." According to one gang member, "I think some of us [gang members] leave the gang stuff at the door. It's like, we're in jail. What are we supposed to be fighting over? We don't have a street corner here, although, some girls think that they brought it in their pocket or something" (Youth #4). Youth #2, affiliated with the Crips, explained that, "In here, I get along with the Crips, Bloods and Brown Pride. Now, I've had some confrontations with other Bloods [at SWI] but that was no problem." This process was reinforced by Youth #24 who suggested that, "People get along despite their gangs. It really don't matter." Youth #13 added that, "Gangs are an issue in here, but not an everyday one." Similarly, another youth said that, "Gangs are really not a problem here. Everybody hangs out with everybody" (Youth #15).

These findings suggest that most young women, regardless of gang affiliation, did not see gangs as problematic to everyday, institutional living at SWI. However, some believed that gangs can cause trouble on a more micro-level, that is, between two or more people rather than at a macro-level, i.e., the institution. When asked if the gangs were a problem at SWI, most of the girls (both gang members and non gang members) indicated that gangs at SWI did not pose a serious problem and that the girls in gangs "pretty much keep it to themselves." Exceptions to this were when a conflict arose between two or more girls and then they started claiming their gang or throwing their gang signs at each other, which can be said to be a product of importation as they brought this type of defense mechanism with them into the institution. Sometimes, the conflicts were based on friendship alliances while other times, they were not.

Friendships

Friendships often form through some type of commonality between two or more people. How friendships develop for the incarcerated young women and what form they take, especially in relation to gangs, was examined. One youth said that when she first arrived at SWI, she noticed that "two girls, one's a Blood and one's a Crip, are best friends. They're really, really good friends. And I know two others. One's a Crip, one's a Blood, and they're tight . . . they're tight as anything. They don't care about the gangs" (Youth #4). It appears that even though two or more people are from rival gangs in the community, they tend to often get along at SWI. It may also be the case that rival gang members become friends because they have a common bond of gang affiliation. For example, Youth #2 said "I see a lot of Crips talking to Bloods and a lot of Bloods talking to Crips and a lot of Bloods and Crips talking to the Mexican, Brown Pride gangs. It don't really matter in here. We really don't get into fights about it like we would on-the-outs." It appears that some girls in gangs click together even though they may be from different or even rival gangs, and as Youth #31 noted: "Despite their gang differences on-the-outs, they come together real close." The young women seem to form some degree of friendships in spite of being from different or rival gangs and in spite of being of different races. Since the youth reside and work in small areas at SWI, they often form friendships based on whom they have regular contact with.

Thus in these cases, importation does not appear to be a major factor in inmate subculture formation, particularly relating to gangs. This could be due, in part, to the fact that while incarcerated, they do not have much of a choice on whom to befriend. Since the youth live in small living quarters, have three to four roommates and work with other peers, they often are "thrown into" establishing some type of relationship with other peers. While many of the young women were affiliated with gangs before incarceration, this did not appear to have much impact on how they adapted to institutional life. They either wanted to quit the gang or their previous gang affiliation had little impact on the friendships that were made. Thus, the ways girls formed friendships were based on easing the pains of imprisonment or the deprivation model.

Treatment and Punishment

This study proposed to briefly examine if the type of institution (i.e., treatment or punishment) would have any bearing on inmate subcultures, as gleaned from the voices of the young women. Opinions were mixed and some thought SWI practiced both punishment and treatment elements. However, overwhelmingly most believed that SWI was more interested in discipline rather than treatment and/or punishment. "I really don't see it [SWI] as punishment 'cause I see it more as discipline" (Youth #10). As a matter of fact, Youth #19 indicated that, "I enjoy the discipline here." By this, she alluded to the strict schedule and structure at SWI something previously not noted in her life. And another youth added that, "In here we learn how to be structured" (Youth #3).

On the issue of treatment, Youth #3 suggested that "this is more of a treatment place than jail 'cause we do groups and stuff and gotta be positive." Another agreed and indicated that "this place is more like treatment, about issues that you have, if you like, have a drug problem and stuff like that" (Youth #33). Furthermore, one young woman suggested that the group sessions "make you think about what you've done that's wrong and how you can improve" (Youth #9).

Still others believed that treatment was in the form of not only groups but also education, as the young women were required to go to school several hours per day unless they received their GED. Others explained that SWI is treatment if one makes it out to be that way. To illustrate, "I feel it's a place . . . if you want to have treatment and if you want to change yourself. The girls that don't want to change themselves, it's not treatment at all. It's just a place to do your time" (Youth #32). Youth #24 agreed: "You get out of this place what you put into it, pretty much."

Many viewed SWI as a place of punishment and a place to do time. To illustrate, Youth #18 said that, "I think it's punishment being behind these walls, you know." Another young woman believed that "this is real punishment because having my freedom is gone" (Youth #28). One young woman expressed that "I think it's a place of punishment 'cause you're not able to go home and do what you want" (Youth #22). Another youth (Youth #27) described her thoughts on punishment in great detail:

> I think it's punishment for the crimes I have done in the past. But, I mean, when you do something wrong in here, you don't get punished. I mean, you get punished; you go to separation or something like that. But you don't get like, five months added on. You don't get too much taken away from you when you do something wrong. And I think that should happen. That way it might stop you from doing something wrong again.

This particular individual believed if punishment at SWI was implemented fully, it could possibly act as a deterrent to future misbehavior.

Another youth described that, "I feel it's punishment . . . we get absolutely no treatment here. So, I basically feel like our line-movements is more important than our learning how to stay off drugs and getting our act together and figuring out what we want to do with our lives" (Youth #4). As such, this particular individual believed that treatment was virtually non-existent at SWI and that the institution stressed other issues which were not treatment-oriented. Similarly, Youth #7 suggested that, "I think it's more punishment and it all revolves around punishment. We have a point-system here and they tally down mostly the bad things you do, but not the good things." And Youth #34 suggested that, "I look at this place sometimes and 'we're treatment' and I just laugh. I mean, I've only talked to a psychologist once since I've been here [five months]."

From the voices of the youth, it appears that SWI has both treatment and punishment elements with variations based on individual responses. However, many young women indicated that SWI is a place of discipline, rather than punishment, and that it does offer some programs and treatment services. Accordingly, whether or not SWI was treatment or punishment depended upon the attitude of the individual and what she made of the incarceration experience. As such, views were individualized depending upon the perspective of each inmate. I did not find any congruent perspectives on this issue.

SUBCULTURE FORMATION AT SWI

The inmate subculture at SWI that does exist may be explained by the time spent at SWI (with an average of nine months), which may not be long enough for distinct, intense and different subcultures to develop. At the time of the interviews, the young women had been incarcerated for an average of 5.4 months. Wheeler (1961) notes that when inmates become aware of their imminent release, their reference group orientation shifts from within the walls to outside of the walls. This anticipatory socialization illustrates that the youth may not need to make as many adjustments or compensations to prison life knowing that they will soon be released which appears to be the case for many young women at SWI.

Since most studies of prison gangs have been based on adult males, whose sentences are generally longer, prison gangs for young, female inmates may not be omnipresent. These young women may not be sentenced long enough to feel as if they need to join or form a gang and thus, the deprivation model may not be suitable for this particular phenomenon.

It seems as if many youth view SWI as a place of discipline and not necessarily treatment or punishment. On a custody-treatment continuum, SWI leans toward treatment in the types of services actually provided. Many hours are spent in group sessions, thereby employing a type of "therapeutic community" within the institution. Therefore, both the amount of time spent in the institution and the level of custody-treatment influence the extent of inmate subcultures. In this study, the average sentence length was nine months. As such, both the minimal time spent at the institution and the "treatment" characteristics of the institution may help explain the nature and extent of the inmate subculture at SWI. It appears as if most young women want to avoid trouble, finish their sentence and get out as quickly as possible and affiliating with gangs would hinder such goals.

CONCLUSION

A limited amount of empirical research exists on the nature and extent of inmate gangs, let alone female, juvenile prison gangs. This research examined the issue of gangs through a case study involving in-depth interviews of thirty-four incarcerated young women. The interviewing methodology was fitting for this study since it examined perspectives in context, lessened objectivity of the subject-researcher role (Rubin, Rubin 1995) and gave the young women a public voice. This study of a relatively unknown area of investigation began with no pre-defined hypotheses, and the topics, themes and data analysis evolved throughout the research process. Originally, the study planned to examine generally the deprivation and importation models of institutional life. However, after interviewing several youth, it incrementally became apparent that the issues of gangs and peer relationships were extensive. Thus, after analyzing the interview notes, I decided to focus almost exclusively on these two issues and how they relate to the extent of inmate subculture formation. This research examined the extent to which gangs account for the development of inmate subcultures of female youth using the deprivation and importation models.

A major conclusion of this study is that even though twenty-two youth were affiliated with gangs prior to incarceration, most of these young women indicated they no longer desired to be associated with gangs. Many youth involved with gangs appeared to leave their gangs "at the door" and did not want to become involved with them at SWI or upon release. Moreover the majority of females associated with gangs were slowly lessening their activities and contacts with the gang prior to incarceration. Thus, all of these reasons can be said to be a function of the importation model.

Even though over half the inmates were affiliated with gangs, they did not try to recruit non-gang member inmates. Those not affiliated with gangs had virtually no interest in gang life before or during incarceration. None of these women joined gangs while at SWI. The incarcerated young women not part of gangs were even more turned-off by gang life, partly as a result of being incarcerated with many girls who were affiliated with them. These women learned about gang-life in explicit detail by hearing stories of those affiliated with gangs and through living in such close proximity to each other. In the eyes of one youth, "the more people you know, the more people you talk to, the more you get into trouble. The more you stay to yourself, the better off you will be" (Youth #10). These findings support the importation model since while in society, those involved in gangs were not actively recruited themselves. Furthermore, the youth not affiliated with gangs had no desire of being involved with gangs while in society or while incarcerated and as such, could be an illustration of importation.

Nevertheless, this could also be interpreted through deprivation in that girls associated with gangs may not recruit nongang members due to fear of being further sanctioned by the staff at the institution. Most young women appeared to simply be "sitting out" or merely waiting for their sentence to end and thus, did not really form distinct gang subcultures. As Youth #1 illustrated, "I just want to get out [of SWI]." Many youth tried to avoid trouble, find activities to fill their days, make limited friendships and do what they thought was necessary to survive so they could get out as soon as possible. Since several youth indicated that they just wanted to "do their time and get out," this finding was not surprising.

A limitation of this research was that it did not adequately address the extent of the young woman's affiliation or how strong her ties were to the male gang. It could be hypothesized that the more involved they were with the gang or if they were actually a gang member, that they would be more inclined to bring these bonds into the prison and not be as hasty to forget about their prior gang life, especially as the gang relates to whom they befriend.

In society friendships are often formed by some type of common bond that attracts two or more people together. Friendships of incarcerated girls appear to form in a similar way. Those who are affiliated with gangs often develop friendships with those who are also associated with gangs, including rival gangs, as this was the "type" of friendships they made while in society. This context suggests the importance that importation has in the development of friendships along "gang" lines.

This study found both deprivation and importation influential in the development of inmate subcultures at SWI, depending upon the contextual question at hand. However, the importation model appeared to have more influence on the nature and extent of subculture formation particularly relating to gangs. Such findings do not support previous research on inmate subcultures of female youth (Otis 1913; Ford 1929; Selling 1931; Kosofsky, Ellis 1958; Halleck, Hersko 1962; Konopka 1966; Giallombardo 1974; Carter 1981; Propper 1981). One reason may be that SWI is a vastly different context from other sites that theories were founded upon; another reason is that the few previous studies based on female juvenile inmates were done decades ago when the social roles of female youth were different than in contemporary society; yet another important conclusion is that the length of stay at SWI may be too short for subcultures to mature and develop. Studies have found that the more time an inmate spends in prison and custody-level institutions, the greater the inmate's antisocial attitudes, and hence, the greater the prisoner subculture (McConville 1985; Wheeler 1961). It may be that this group of youth, and other juvenile correctional populations serving time, are not committed long enough for any type of formal or distinct subcultures to mature, particularly relating to gangs.

The principal adaptation technique in this study appears to be doing time and avoiding trouble. The young women want to stay out of trouble so they can do their time to get out as quickly as possible. This seems to be the motivating force behind their efforts of conformity and adaptation to prison life. Therefore, new subculture concepts need to be developed or refined for other prison contexts, especially for juveniles often serving shorter sentences than adults. As such, this study concludes that gangs for these young women at SWI have limited influence on adaptation strategies and subculture development.

This study not only is significant to understand the context of subcultures and gangs but also to realize how such responses can effect policy. Correctional and public policy is frequently developed without going to the source for answers (Petersen 2000; 1995). As such, this is antithetical to democracy. Ordinary citizens, such as gang members and young offenders, are not often involved in the policy process, yet they are the ones toward whom policy is directed. "The end result is detrimental for youths and ultimately to society, in that people without power often become more alienated from democracy without further 'buying into' society" (Petersen 1995:648). It is, therefore, crucial to look at the ones most affected by criminal and/or juvenile justice policies, i.e., young offenders and gang members, to not only ask them their input but for them to have a meaningful effect on the way policies are framed.

By giving these thirty-four women a voice, it is hoped that this can lead to empathetic understanding to impact the direction of future policies. The findings of this research could enlighten policymakers with clearer understandings of the nature and extent of gangs in prison which could provide the basic tools necessary to conceptualize and develop gang programs both in prison and in the larger society.

A FINAL NOTE ON PARENTAL CONSENT

Legal and ethical standards require parental consent if the subjects of research are less than eighteen years old. It has been well-documented that parental consent reduces sample size. Moreover, I would argue that parental consent further reduces the sample size of youth who are part of the juvenile or criminal justice system and who are asked to participate voluntarily in a study normally conducted outside the purview of the system, i.e., university-based research, even if advocated by the justice system.

I contend that a major motivation behind refusal of their son/daughter to participate in such study is due to emotional distress that the interview questions, often of a sensitive nature, may inflict upon their child. The parents may perceive that their son/daughter has already "been through enough" and may want to minimize any type of further anguish. Another almost equally valid reason rests on the issue of trust. The parent(s) do not know the person directing the research or conducting the interview. They may have doubts as to the real nature of the study and if the researchers will positively keep their child's name confidential or anonymous. They are suspect of the entire study.

The research environment with adolescents is not "user friendly" especially for incarcerated youth and female adolescents. Getting parents to read the consent form, "buy into" the study, sign the form and return the form is an arduous process. This should not halt researchers from trying to study youth but this is a fact and something that appears not to change anytime in the near future.

QUESTIONS FOR UNDERSTANDING AND CRITICAL THINKING

1. What are the two models in which inmates adapt to the incarceration experience?
2. How and why are these two approaches important when examining gangs in prison?
3. How can gang subcultures at this particular institution be explained using the two models?
4. Why is it of critical importance to include young women's voices in the policy process?

REFERENCES

AMERICAN CORRECTIONAL ASSOCIATION 1990 *The female offender: What does the future hold?* Washington, DC: St. Mary's Press

AMERICAN CORRECTIONAL ASSOCIATION 1993 *Gangs in correctional facilities: A national assessment* US Department of Justice, Office of Justice programs Washington, DC: National Institute of Justice

ARNOLD R 1994 Processes of victimization From girlhood to womanhood in Zinn MB, BT Dill eds *Women of color in American society* pp 10–31 Philadelphia, PA: Temple University Press

BOWKER L 1978 ed *Women, crime and the criminal justice system* Lexington, MA: Lexington Books

BROWN WK 1977 Black female gangs in Philadelphia *International Journal of Offender Therapy and Comparative Criminology* 21 221–228

CAMP GM, CG CAMP 1985 *Prison gangs: Their extent, nature and impact on prisons* US Department of Justice, Office of Legal Policy Washington, DC: US Government Printing Office

CAMPBELL A 1984 *The girls in the gang* New York: Basil Blackwell

CARTER B 1981 Reform school families In Bowker L ed *Women and crime in America* 58–71 New York: Macmillan

CLEMMER D 1940 *The prison community* New York: Holt, Rinehart & Winston

COVEY HC, S. MENARD, RJ FRANZESE 1992 *Juvenile gangs* Springfield, IL: Charles C Thomas

CRESWELL DW 1994 *Research design: Qualitative and quantitative approaches* Thousand Oaks, CA: Sage

ESBENSEN F, MH MILLER, TJ TAYLOR, N HE, A FRENG 1999 Differential attrition rates and active parental consent *Evaluation Review* 23 316–335

FLOWERS RB 1987 *Women and criminality* New York: Greenwood Press

FONG RS, RE VOGEL, S BUENTELLO 1996 Prison gang dynamics: A research update in Miller JM, JP Rush eds *Gangs: A criminal justice approach* pp 105–128 Cincinnati, OH: Anderson

FORD CA 1929 Homosexual practices of institutionalized females *Journal of Abnormal and Social Psychology* 23 442–449

GIALLOMBARDO R 1966 *Society of women: A study of a women's prison* New York: John Wiley & Sons

GIALLOMBARDO R 1974 *The social world of imprisoned girls: A comparative study of institutions for juvenile delinquents* New York: John Wiley & Sons

GLICK R, V NETO 1977 *National study of women's correctional programs* Washington, DC: US Department of Justice

HALLECK SL, M HERSKO 1962 Homosexual behavior in a correctional institution for adolescent girls *Journal of Orthopsychiatry* 32 911–917

HAMMERSLEY M, P Atkinson 1983 *Ethnography: Principles in practice* London: Tavistock

HANSON K 1964 *Rebels in the streets: The story of New York's girl gangs* Englewood Cliffs, NJ: Prentice-Hall

HEFFERNAN E 1972 *Making it in prison: The square, the cool and the life* New York: John Wiley & Sons

HOLLMANN CM, JR MCNAMARA 1999 Considerations in the use of active and passive parental consent procedures *Journal of Psychology* 133 141–156

IRWIN J, DR CRESSEY 1962 Thieves, convicts and the inmate culture *Social Problems* 10 145–147

KAHN R, C CANNELL 1957 *The dynamics of interviewing* New York: John Wiley

KINSEY AC, WB POMEROY, CE MARTIN 1948 *Sexual behavior in the human male* Philadelphia PA: WB Saunders

KEARNEY KA, RH HOPKINS, AL MAUSS, RA WEISHEIT 1983 Sample bias resulting from a requirement for written parental consent *Public Opinion Quarterly* 47 96–102

KONOPKA G 1966 *The adolescent girl in conflict* Englewood Cliffs, NJ: Prentice-Hall

KOSOFSKY S, A ELLIS 1958 Illegal communication among institutionalized female delinquents *Journal of Social Psychology* 48 155–160

MATTHEWS R 1999 *Doing time: An introduction to the sociology of imprisonment* New York: St Martin's Press

MCCONVILLE S 1985 *Prison Gangs: Symposium* Midwestern Criminal Justice Association Annual Meeting Chicago, IL

MILLER, D 1991 *Handbook of research design and social measurement* Newbury Park, CA: Sage

MILLER WB 1975 *Violence by youth gangs and youth groups as a crime problem in major American cities* Washington, DC: National Institute of Justice

MILLER WB 1980 Gangs, groups and serious youth crime in Shichor D, D Kelly eds *Critical issues in juvenile delinquency* pp 56–72 Lexington, MA: Lexington Books

MOBERG DP, DL PIPER 1990 Obtaining active parental consent via telephone in adolescent substance abuse prevention research *Evaluation Review* 14 701–721

NEUMAN WL, B WIEGAND 2000 *Criminal justice research methods* Boston, MA: Allyn & Bacon

OTIS M 1913 A perversion not commonly noted *Journal of Abnormal Psychology* 8 113–116

PETERSEN RD 2000 Definitions of a gang and impacts on public policy *Journal of Criminal Justice* 28 139–149

PETERSEN RD 1995 Expert policy in juvenile justice: Patterns of claims-making and issues of power in a program construction *Policy Studies Journal* 23 636–651

PROPPER A 1981 Lesbianism in female and coed correctional institutions *Journal of Homosexuality* 3 265–274

RUBIN HJ, IS RUBIN 1995 *Qualitative interviewing: The art of hearing data* Thousand Oaks, CA: Sage

SELLING LT 1931 The pseudo family *American Journal of Sociology* 37 247–253

SEVERSON HH, DV ARY 1983 Sampling bias due to consent procedures with adolescents *Addictive Behaviors* 8 433–437

WARD DA, G KASSEBAUM 1965 *Women's prison: Sex and social structure* Chicago: Aldine

WEBER M 1949 *Methodology of the social sciences* New York: Free Press

WHEELER S 1961 Socialization in correctional communities *American Sociological Review* 26 697–706

NOTES

1. It was agreed by both the author and the correctional institution that SWI would be the pseudo-name used for the study.
2. The rationale behind dropping these two from the study was based on the premise that since they had only been incarcerated a few days or weeks, their insight into subculture formation, reactions to confinement and friendship development would be naive and incomplete.
3. Demographic information of the sixty-nine non-participants was either not available to this researcher nor incomplete and therefore, not included.
4. Lack of official data/records and reliance solely on self-reporting may reduce the credibility of findings. However, not only was I restricted from obtaining their official records but the purpose of this study was to obtain information about gangs and subcultures, often not known in official records, from the actual participants to parallel the methodology of interpretivism and Verstehen.
5. This particular individual was seventeen years old and indicated that in each of the three previous times she was incarcerated, she was confined to SWI each time for approximately one week.
6. After interviewing several young women, it became apparent that there were "official" girl gang members (i.e., those who had been "jumped in" to a gang) and those involved/affiliated with gangs (those who "hung out" with gang members or who had friends/close relatives in a gang) but who were not formally initiated into a gang.
7. In this context, a "problem" could mean something to them personally, to their peers or to institutional life. Each youth responded to this in various forms of what she defined and perceived as a problem.

11

School Violence

Gangs and a Culture of Fear

Douglas E. Thompkins

Abstract

Recent media coverage of isolated acts of violence committed by students on school property has increased concern about school violence. Reports documenting higher levels of school violence in the face of a general decline in crime rates, together with several high-profile cases, have resulted in a reactive preventive security response. Congress has passed several initiatives aimed at reducing levels of school violence. Gangs and gang activity within our nation's schools are often linked to increased levels of school violence, but little explanation has been offered for this increase. Greater security measures have been taken by school administrations in response to the problem, and, while these may reduce levels of school violence in some communities, they can also help to perpetuate a culture of fear that has been created by intense media coverage of such violence. The presence of security officers, metal detectors, and security cameras may deter some students from committing acts of violence, but this presence also serves to heighten fear among students and teachers, while increasing the power of some gangs and the perceived need some students have for joining gangs.

In October 1998, I was part of a panel at a criminology conference on school violence held at Valparaiso University. Among the panelists were two local school superintendents who presented us with their plans to combat school violence. Although their presentations received high approval from the audience, I was disturbed. Almost every security measure imaginable had been suggested for implementation. What troubled me most was that these measures were not designed for inner-city schools with serious gang violence but for suburban or rural

Thompkins, D.E. School violence: Gangs and a culture of fear. *Annals of the American Academy of Political and Social Science,* 567(2000). Pp. 54–71. Reprinted by permission of Sage Publications, Inc.

schools. They would make the schools look more like prisons than schools. While I appreciate any attempt to prevent school violence before it develops, too many security measures not only may mask the underlying issues but can create more problems than they solve. How did we arrive at such a reactionary policy?

During the 1980s and early 1990s, there was a dramatic increase in the level of violence in America. Much of this increase was attributed to a rise in the level of violent acts committed by teenagers. Between 1987 and 1991, the number of teenagers arrested for murder around the country grew by an astounding 85 percent. During the same period, the level of school violence increased at an alarming rate (Chase 1993, 20). In 1993, the National Education Association estimated that 100,000 youngsters carried guns to school every day and that some 2000 students and 40 teachers were attacked every hour (Chase 1993, 20). Gangs and gang-related behavior have been blamed for the increase in violent crime rates, specifically the increase in the number of homicides committed. However, since 1991, while crime rates generally, and violence rates in particular, had been declining each year through 1999, reports of high-profile violent victimizations in schools had been dramatized by the news media.

Between October 1997 and April 1999, a rash of school shootings took place across the country. Murders such as those committed by students in Littleton, Colorado; Edinboro, Pennsylvania; and Springfield, Oregon, have been characterized by the media as typical of the kinds of violent acts being committed in our nation's schools. Television news programs, daily newspapers, government reports, and results of public polls bombard us regularly with vivid accounts of the violent acts committed by America's youths (Arnette and Walsleben 1998). These reports have helped to fuel the level of fear within society, regardless of how frequent or probable the acts are or how typical they are of the general level of violence in schools. This greater social sensitivity to school violence has led to calls for more severe penalties for juvenile offenders and the passing of new anti-school violence initiatives by Congress. These proposed state and federal legislative initiatives are intended to provide money for additional school security, which in turn is to provide schools with additional security officers, who are being referred to as "resource officers" (Barlas 1999).

Media coverage of isolated acts of juvenile violence leaves a fearful public with the impression that school violence is a widespread national problem. We are being told that violent acts committed by juveniles are taking an unacceptable toll on the lives, education, and opportunities of our youths (Arnette and Walsleben 1998). Lost, however, in the media dramatization and understandable emotional reaction are important distinctions about the nature of violence in schools and important trends that suggest an alternative reality might be taking shape. First, while the level of school violence might be increasing, there are different types of school violence. A critical question is whether all types of violence are increasing, and, if not, what is the nature of the kind of violence that is increasing. Second, is all juvenile crime increasing or just certain kinds of violent victimization in schools? For example, we are not told that the violent crime arrest rate declined between 1994 and 1996 by 15 percent for juveniles under 15 years of age and 12 percent for those 15 and older (Puzzanchera 1998). Nor are we told that the juvenile arrest rate for murder in 1996 was at its lowest since 1990, which is consistent with the general decline in crime nationwide during the 1990s. Third, is the problem of violent juvenile crime pervasive or concentrated? For example, we are also not told that 56 percent of the country's juvenile homicide arrests have been made in just six states and that four large metropolitan centers accounted for 30 percent of juvenile arrests (Locke and Schiraldi 1996). As a result of these omissions, it is arguable that the intense media coverage of isolated acts of school violence, such as those that occurred between October 1997 and April 1999 in largely rural and suburban school districts, can cause more harm than good. Such reports fuel the level of fear that already exists within society, where school violence is concerned, without adding to our understanding of the problem.

Indeed, even the government statistics on the nature of school violence may be misleading. In response to reports that juvenile violence was rising at alarming rates, the Bureau of Justice Statistics and the National Center for Education Statistics jointly published a report (U.S. Department of Education 1998) that compares student victimization rates in 1989 and 1995. More helpful would have been data for the years 1985 through 1995, since two dates are an inadequate basis on which to establish a trend. Further, as with most publications of this type, the report has little to say about why juveniles are involved in acts of violence, why these acts occur at school, or why the number of violent incidents seems to be increasing. One factor that stands out, however, is a rise in the number of reports of gangs and gang activity within our nation's schools.

The purpose of this article is to examine the data provided by the Bureau of Justice Statistics and the National Center for Education Statistics in their 1998 report and to address the following questions: Has there been dramatic growth in the level of juvenile violence in schools? Is gang presence responsible for this growth, and, if so, what factors are responsible for the increase in the juvenile gang presence in the schools? Could increased school security measures have prevented the tragedies that occurred in Littleton, Colorado, or Springfield, Oregon? Alternatively, is it possible that increases in security measures (the presence of security officers, metal detectors, and security cameras), combined with continuous reports from the media focusing on isolated incidents of school violence, have created a culture of fear among students and teachers? Is it possible that this culture of fear actually enhances the power and attractiveness of gangs for some students? Finally, what measures can be taken to reduce the risk of school violence in this context? Do we need increased security measures that meet students' needs—needs that are currently met for some students by gangs?

LEVEL OF VIOLENCE IN SCHOOLS

In March 1998, the Bureau of Justice Statistics and the National Center for Education Statistics jointly published a report comparing the level of student victimization in 1989 and 1995 (U.S. Department of Education 1998). The report contained the results of two surveys. The first part of the report contained data collected from a survey of 1234 principals or school disciplinarians for the 1996-97 school year (U.S. Department of Education 1997). This survey asked about incidents of school violence reported to the police or other law enforcement representatives occurring during or after school hours. The second part of the report used the School Crime Supplement to the National Crime Victimization Survey, implemented by the Bureau of Justice Statistics, to provide a picture of the types and frequency of the violence that students encountered at school in 1989 and 1995. For both years, the survey used representative samples of approximately 10,000 students whose ages ranged between 12 and 19. The students were interviewed in their homes. The survey asked about crimes that occurred in the school building, on school grounds, or on a school bus during the six-month period prior to the interview (U.S. Department of Education 1998).

In 1996 and 1997, school principals and disciplinarians reported approximately 10.0 incidents of crime per 1000 public school students. Of the 10.0 incidents, 9.5 were categorized

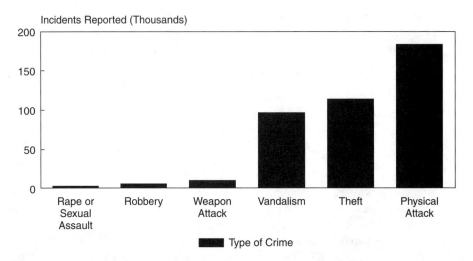

FIGURE 11–1 Types of Crime in Public Schools
Source: U.S. Department of Education 1997.

as less serious or nonviolent crimes. The other 0.5 included serious or violent crimes such as robbery, physical attack, or fighting with a weapon, murder, suicide, and rape or sexual assault. The types of crime most frequently reported to the police were physical attacks or fights without a weapon (U.S. Department of Education 1998) (see Figure 11–1).

In 1996, students between the ages of 12 and 18 were victims of approximately 225,000 incidents of nonfatal violent crime in school and approximately 671,000 incidents outside of school. Importantly, these numbers indicate that students were more than twice as likely to be victimized outside school rather than inside. Also in 1996, students living in urban areas were more likely to be victimized by an act of serious violent crime than students living in suburban and rural areas. In 1996-97, 10 percent of all public schools reported at least one incident of serious violent crime to the police, while 47 percent reported at least one nonviolent crime to the police. Elementary schools were less likely than middle or high schools to report any type of crime (Kaufman et al. 1998).

In the victimization survey of students, there was little or no change in the percentage of students reporting any violent or property victimization at school (14.5 percent in 1989, compared to 14.6 percent in 1995). However, there was a 25 percent increase in the percentage of students who reported violent victimization at school (3.4 percent in 1989, compared to 4.2 percent in 1995) (see Figure 11–2). Further, the greatest increase in victimization was reported to be among female students (see Figure 11–3).

The most noticeable change between 1989 and 1995 was the reported presence of gangs or gang activity within schools. For those attending public schools, the proportion of students who reported that street gangs were present at school increased from 16.4 percent in 1989 to 30.6 percent in 1995 (see Figure 11–4). For students attending private schools, the proportion of those reporting that gangs were present at their schools increased from 4.4 percent in 1989 to 6.8 percent in 1995.

Importantly, reports of an increase in gang activity varied by the ethnicity and family income of the respondent. While all ethnic groups reported an increase in the level of gang ac-

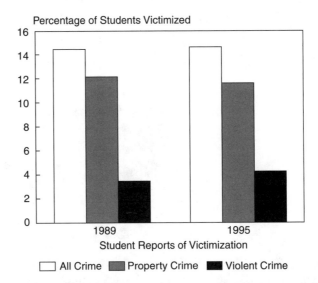

Percentage of Students Victimized

Student Reports of Victimization

☐ All Crime   ▦ Property Crime   ■ Violent Crime

FIGURE 11–2   Victimization of Students Aged 12–19, 1989 and 1995
Source: As reported by students aged 12–19 who were interviewed as part of the U.S.
government's national victimization survey; see U.S. Department of Education 1998.

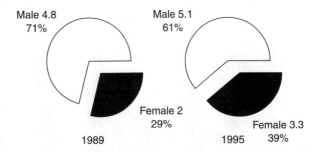

FIGURE 11–3   Victimization by Gender, Students Aged 12–19, 1989 and 1995
Source: As reported by students aged 12–19 who were interviewed as part of the U.S.
government's national victimization survey; see U.S. Department of Education 1998.

tivity between 1989 and 1995, Hispanic students reported the highest rate (see Figure 11–5).
Although reports of gang activity increased across all income groups, it was greatest among
students from families with the lowest incomes (see Figure 11–6). As might be expected, reports of gang presence were greatest among students living in central-city areas, but interestingly the increase between 1989 and 1995 was greater among students living in suburban and
rural areas, which increased by 88 and 155 percent, respectively, compared with the increase
in central cities of 64 percent. This is consistent with the thesis on gang diffusion or migration reported by some researchers (Maxson, Woods, and Klein 1995) (see Figure 11–7).

Finally, in 1989 and 1995, student reports of violent victimization were related to the
reported presence of gangs within the school. In 1995, for those students who reported no
gang activity, only 2.9 percent reported being victims of violent crimes, while 7.5 percent of

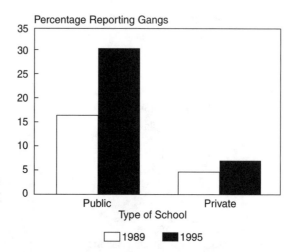

FIGURE 11–4   Gang Presence at School, by Type of School, 1989 and 1995
Source: As reported by students aged 12–19 who were interviewed as part of the U.S.
government's national victimization survey; see U.S. Department of Education 1998.

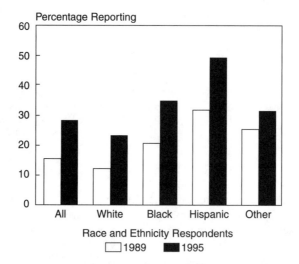

FIGURE 11–5   Gangs Reported in Schools
Source: As reported by students aged 12–19 who were interviewed as part of the U.S.
government's national victimization survey; see U.S. Department of Education 1998.

those students who reported the presence of gangs in their schools were victimized by acts of
violence (U.S. Department of Education 1998). Moreover, while violence was up among
those reporting gangs, it was slightly down among those not reporting gangs (see Figure 11–8).

These data should be interpreted with caution for several reasons. First, the reports by
principals and disciplinarians about crimes may underrepresent the extent of school crime
and violence, since school administrators get to hear about only the more serious incidents;

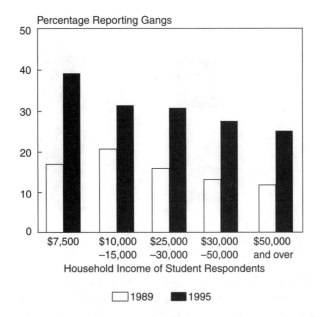

FIGURE 11–6   School Gangs, by Family Income
Source: As reported by students aged 12–19 who were interviewed as part of the U.S.
government's national victimization survey; see U.S. Department of Education 1998.

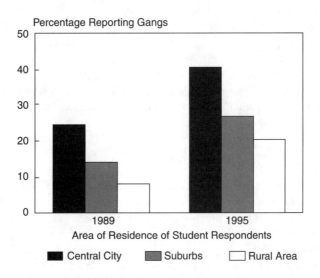

FIGURE 11–7   School Gangs, by Area of Residence 1989 and 1995
Source: As reported by students aged 12–19 who were interviewed as part of the U.S.
government's national victimization survey; see U.S. Department of Education 1998.

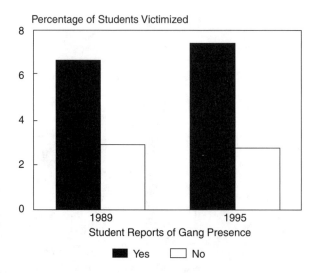

FIGURE 11-8   Violence, by Gang Presence, 1989 and 1995.
Source: As reported by students aged 12–19 who were interviewed as part of the U.S. government's national victimization survey; see U.S. Department of Education 1998.

depend upon reports by teachers and other students, who may filter out some incidents; and may have an interest in minimizing bad publicity for their schools. In many ways, the report based on information from the principals and disciplinarians has all the problems typically associated with official crime statistics. Second, with regard to gang activity, the victimization reports describe students' perceptions of gang activity. To say, for example, that gang presence is reported to be the greatest among Hispanic students does not mean this population was more involved in gangs but merely that it saw more gang activity. Thus societal reaction to gangs and gang activity may reflect more of a fear or cultural stereotype than actual levels of gang activity. With these caveats in mind, we can consider in more detail the relationship between gangs and violence in schools.

GANGS AND SCHOOL VIOLENCE

Gangs and gang activity have plagued our nation since the 1800s (Howell 1998). Based on a 1995 national survey of 4000 local law enforcement agencies, the U.S. Department of Justice estimates that there are as many as 23,000 youth gangs in America. Youth gangs have been reported to exist in all 50 states. Surveys of the extent of gangs in cities have found that 94 percent of U.S. cities with populations of 100,000 have gang problems; the estimated number of gang members is put at 500,000; and there have been both an increase in youth gang activity over previous years and a diffusion of gangs from larger to smaller cities (Klein 1995). In a survey of 700 communities nationwide, 40 percent of the suburban communities and nonmetropolitan towns and cities responded that gangs were a factor in the level of violence within their schools (National League of Cities 1994).

There are several explanations of why gangs may form in neighborhoods, particularly the inner city. These range from the Chicago school theory of social disorganization resulting from transitional neighborhoods and ethnic conflict (Thrasher 1927); the status frustration and fatalism of being a lower-class child in a middle-class educational system (Cohen 1955); youths' blaming the system for not providing viable equal opportunities (Cloward and Ohlin 1961); to the more recent ideas that gangs are a product of the change from a manufacturing to a service economy. This change has resulted in the replacement of high-paying, skilled jobs with low-paying, dead-end jobs. Gangs emerge in areas of economic decline, absent positive role models, community networks, and stable families. Such an environment yields social disorganization and an undermining of informal social controls (Jackson 1991; Padilla 1992).

Whatever the explanation for gang formation, the important point here is that gangs do not form independently of the wider social and cultural forces of a particular era. In each era, there may be different conditions that lead to the same effects that make the time ripe for gangs to appear. These conditions affect youths, and gangs fill the void where family, community, and social acceptance would typically be. Consider the following astute observations on what makes gangs attractive to youths:

> First, youth experience a sense of alienation and powerlessness because of a lack of traditional support structures, such as family and school. This can lead to feelings of frustration and anger, and a desire to obtain support outside of traditional institutions. . . . Second, gang membership gives youth a sense of belonging and becomes a major source of identity for its members. In turn, gang membership affords youth a sense of power and control, and gang activities become an outlet for anger. . . . Third, the control of turf is essential to the well-being of the gang, which often will use force to control both its territory and its members. . . . Finally, recruitment of new members and expansion of territory are essential if a gang is to remain strong and powerful. Both "willing" and "unwilling" members are drawn into gangs to feed the need for more resources and gang members. (Burnett 1994, 102)

It is important to note, however, that, contrary to popular belief, the pressure to join a gang placed on nonmembers by members may have been overstated. Huff (1998) reported that youths who resist joining gangs suffer far less physical harm than those who join and go through the initiation process. In a comparison of 50 gang members with 50 "similarly at-risk" nongang youths in four cities in three states, Huff found that youths began to express an interest in belonging to gangs at ages 12–13 and joined a gang at age 13 or 14, typically after six months of hanging out with the gang. The study also found that gang members were more likely than nongang at-risk youths to sell drugs, and gangs were more likely to sell more frequently to fewer customers and make more money from their sales ($1000 per week compared with $675 per week earned by nongang at-risk youths). The study found that between 19 and 38 percent of gang members admitted selling drugs in school, compared with 8 percent of nongang youths. Drug sales outside school were much higher for both groups, with a greater proportion of gang members (58–75 percent) than nongang youths (17 percent) reporting selling drugs. Between 51 and 66 percent of gang members reported assaulting students, compared to 35 percent of nongang youths. Between 15 and 27 percent reported assaulting teachers, compared to 18 percent of nongang youths. Between 38 and 58 percent reported carrying knives to school, compared to only 10 percent of nongang members. More important for Huff's study, gang members were also much more likely to possess powerful lethal weapons: no less than 40 percent and as much as 53 percent admitted carrying guns to school, compared to 10 percent of nongang members (Huff 1998, 2–4). Clearly, gang membership intensifies crime and violence.

Gangs do not appear within a community or school overnight. There is a distinct process involved in their formation, and part of the problem is that school and law enforcement officials often fail to realize when a gang problem is developing. Some officials are quick to write off certain forms of delinquent behavior committed by students as part of growing up. Another common response by officials is to classify gang members as "wannabes" (Trump 1996). Such responses lead to officials' ignoring the seriousness of the problem. Once a gang problem has developed, it is usually too late to simply put a stop to it. In many cases, by the time officials begin to recognize the existence of a gang problem within their school and attempt to respond to it, the gangs have already established a foothold of power. Students know long before school officials whether there is a gang presence within their school.

Many students are drawn to the gang because it offers them something they are not receiving at home, in their community, or at school (Arnette and Walsleben 1998). Gangs offer excitement, in contrast to the mundane; a challenge to be someone; freedom to those youths who are powerless; love for one's fellow gang members; a mutual loyalty with the intensity and commitment of "blood brothers"; and a clearly identifiable collective identity and protection from a world of fear, alienation, and isolation. In addition, gangs offer the potential of relatively easy money through various criminal activities, not least drug sales.

The response of most officials to the presence of gangs in their schools often creates an atmosphere of "us versus them," which, paradoxically, leads to many gangs' gaining a level of credibility and increased power. As real and suspected gang members are singled out and punished for what is determined to be gang behavior, students may come to fear the gangs even more. Moreover, the "us versus them" relationship has the potential to draw some students to the gangs precisely because they want to be recognized as outsiders, as someone who breaks the rules and challenges authority.

As gangs gain a stronghold in some schools, the level of violence usually increases, since gang activity includes competition for space and respect. Ironically, the response of most officials to gangs actually fuels this competition as students who are associated with gangs begin to see themselves as being different from others. They become special people, a status that is confirmed by the attention that officials give them, and they are celebrated by the media for their exploits. Where else can youths gain such kudos and freedom so quickly? This difference, this special identity, leads to an increased level of bonding between gang members. They have become something, something to be reckoned with. The "us versus them" relationship begins to include not just gang members and school officials, but students who are not gang members as well.

When addressing issues of school violence, it is important to remember the nature and social context in which schools became more violent during the 1980s and early 1990s. Students existed and learned within an environment where violence was as much a reality for them as HIV, MTV, and crack cocaine. Perhaps more than in any other period, some students came to believe that they had to react to violence with violence or at least express a willingness to use violence. In this regard, Anderson (1994) refers to the "code of the streets," which reflects the belief that a person must be able to take care of himself or herself rather than turn to others such as parents, teachers, or the police for help. The code requires that one not interfere in matters that involve other people's problems. Accordingly, with respect to certain forms of violent behavior within inner-city communities, what is important is not that one uses violence or that one wins a fight but that one is willing to resort to violence to deal with situations and challenges. I would argue that today this inner-city "code of the streets" applies equally to the school environment. It would appear that a code of silence has developed among students on many school campuses to the extent that students refuse to provide officials with information and would rather stand by and watch a fight than do anything to stop it. This reluctance to become involved could be due to a fear of retaliation (Futrell 1996), or an acceptance of and respect for the "code of the streets" could have taken hold within the school environment (Anderson 1994).

Schools have always had their resident bullies. Traditionally, bullying has been viewed as some perverse form of the usual interaction between youngsters. The common response has been "Kids will be kids" (Arnette and Walsleben 1998). As gangs begin to appear on school campuses, they become the bullies, and the level of fear and violence escalates. Gang members commit both individual and group acts of violence, and students know, or at least believe, that if they retaliate against an act of aggression committed by one gang member, they will have to deal with the entire gang. This can lead to students' suffering increased levels of fear and stress, which not only disrupt their learning process but can also lead to the formation of new gangs. Previously unaffiliated students have been known to come together or "clique up" and form their own gang for protection against other gangs. Once this occurs, the new gangs begin to adopt standard gang behavior and attitudes and can eventually become a part of the gang problem as they compete for space and respect (2-1 1998).

A CULTURE OF FEAR

The presence of uniformed security staff, metal detectors, and security cameras may help to deter certain types of school crime. However, we must keep in mind that the acts of school violence that have shaken the nation recently are not typical of acts of school violence nationwide and certainly are not typical of the everyday kinds of violence that occur in urban schools. As a result, the effectiveness of standardized security measures is likely to vary across both communities and school types. However, what seems to be constant, regardless of the community or school, is that increased levels of security suggest to students and teachers that they learn and teach in a violent environment where students cannot be trusted and are under suspicion. In schools where there is no history of violence, intense security measures, such as video cameras, can have a chilling effect on the school environment and raise serious privacy issues. Consider the comments of one student, who wrote,

> As I walk through the halls of my school, . . . placed strategically . . . to view every corner, hallway and classroom door in the building are 32 security cameras. Hidden in little black bulges hanging from the ceiling, these video cameras watch everything that goes on during nine hours of my day. In towns where schools are often wrecked and millions of dollars are spent on repairs yearly, security cameras might be warranted. In a town like Munster, they're not. . . . the thinking of school officials . . . seems to ask why give people in society the benefit of the doubt when you can more simply doubt them. . . . Claiming their intentions to be "good and in our best interest," our privacy is lost. (Porta 1999; reprinted with permission of the *Vidette Times*)

In those schools where organized gangs exist, this message of distrust and invasion increases the power of gangs because gang members can play on the fears of both students and teachers. In this context, an isolated incident of violence can heighten the fears, whether the act of violence was gang related or not. Often gang members and wanna-be gang members will take credit for a random act of violence for which they were not responsible. This increases the level of fear that students and teachers have of them. Gangs are able to dominate a community or school only when people are afraid to confront them or afraid to resist their presence and influence. Just how serious is this heightened level of fear?

A 1993 national school-based survey of a representative sample of high school students showed that approximately 4.4 percent of the respondents missed a day of school each month because they feared for their personal safety. In addition to fearing for their personal safety, many students also felt fear in response to violence experienced by other students. A 1994 national survey of parents showed that 40 percent of the respondents were "very or somewhat worried about their child's safety while in school" (Leitman, Binns, and Unni 1994).

Regarding teachers' fears, a survey conducted by the Teachers Union in Boston showed that 43 percent of the 1500 teachers who responded felt their personal safety was in jeopardy. A survey conducted by Metropolitan Life showed that teachers who are characterized as strict are the most likely to be victimized. Of those responding to this survey, 38 percent of teachers and 57 percent of students ranked strict teachers as being more at risk of becoming victims than other members of the teaching staff (Futrell 1996). When the school environment becomes one where teachers are afraid to hold students responsible for their work and for their behavior, the learning process itself has been compromised.

There seems no doubt that the level of fear felt by students, parents, and teachers has increased within the last decade and certainly since the Columbine High incident, which brought forth numerous copycat incidents and threats, resulting in the closing of schools for the day and the refusal of parents to send children to school. Whether increased levels of security fuel these fears is an empirical question. Of course, increased security and the presence of uniformed security officers might make some students and teachers less fearful. We can conclude that the fear of being victimized while at school is preventing many teachers from disciplining students who misbehave or violate school policies. When a teacher refuses to get involved or fails to question a student who has broken a rule or law, the teacher loses credibility with other students. This affects the teacher's ability to teach and his or her ability to stop or prevent acts of violence on the school campus. Once students discover that a teacher is afraid, he or she loses the ability to be effective both as an educator and as a disciplinarian. This is a serious concern because the primary peacekeepers in schools have to be the teachers (Toby 1998). Increased levels of security and security measures cannot be the main instrument for preventing school violence because security officers are not in the classroom with the teachers and students. Indeed, it is likely that there will never be enough security officers to maintain order in hallways, gyms, and cafeterias in order to prevent assaults or other acts of violence. And in many schools, the most feared place with respect to violence is the bathrooms. Increased levels of security may prevent outsiders from entering school premises; however, in terms of preventing school violence, security officers constitute a second line of defense; they cannot, by themselves, provide a disciplined environment (Toby 1998).

ALTERNATIVE SOLUTIONS TO SCHOOL VIOLENCE

If the presence of gangs on school campuses is associated with the rising levels of school violence, officials have to confront the gangs before they gain power within the school environment. Recognition and acceptance that there is a gang presence in and around a school in the early stages is one key factor to successfully managing gang concerns (Trump 1996, 46).

Also, school officials must accept the fact that wanna-be gang members can be more of a threat to safety and school security than actual gang members. Wanna-be gang members often commit more acts of violence than actual gang members because they feel a need to impress others, specifically, persons who are actually involved in gang activity. Wanna-be gang members feel a need to establish a sense of credibility and will often commit acts of violence that confirmed gang members do not feel a need to commit (Trump 1996).

In response to the rash of shootings that took place on school grounds around the country, Congress and President Clinton began to address the issue of school violence. They held a nationally telecast conference in October 1998 and another gathering of experts in May 1999. The 1999 budget approved by Congress includes several initiatives aimed at reducing school violence. Project SERV, which has a budget of $12 million, and the Safe Schools–Safe Communities Initiative, which has a budget of $25 million, will provide funds for the hiring of additional school security personnel (Barlas 1999). These security personnel are being referred to as "resource officers," but how these officers are used is often determined by the orientation chosen by school officials. Some choose to think of these resource officers as school police and emphasize their law enforcement powers. Others choose to think of them as being directly supportive of the educational process and train them in the style of investigators, aides, and counselors (Vestermark 1996).

For resource officers to be effective at reducing levels of school violence, they must function as a resource for the students as well as for school officials. If students feel that resource officers are there to help them and that they are approachable, students will seek them out when they have problems. Such a relationship involves establishing trust and respect. Resource officers who communicate with the students are better equipped to stop trouble before it starts (L. V. 1999). If, however, the resource officers function solely as school police officers and merely enforce the law when they see an infraction, students will usually avoid them.

In order for resource officers to be effective at reducing school violence, they must have access to information. Some police agencies have pushed for greater interagency collaboration, which includes schools' sharing their information and records on students, with all the privacy rights questions that that raises. However, this may be the only way to stop trouble before it starts. If students believe that resource officers are there to function as a resource for them as well as for school officials, students will begin to provide the officers with information concerning gang activity and potentially violent situations. Following the Littleton, Colorado, school murders, it became clear that students on campus were aware of the potential harm those responsible for the murders could possibly cause. Yet school officials seem to have been unaware of any potential danger or warning signals.

A successful program for reducing gang violence

An example of a successful attempt at reducing school violence and the attractiveness that gangs have for some students is the program instituted at Webb Middle School in Austin, Texas (Juarez 1996). Approximately 85 percent of the student body at Webb Middle School qualify for free or reduced-cost lunch, and 65 percent come from single-parent homes. What has proven to be successful is a collective effort involving teachers, parents, students, community volunteers, employees of local businesses, and local professionals in the creation of clubs that provide many of the same opportunities that gangs provide, namely, order, structure, discipline, and a sense of identity.

With the help of students, over 50 clubs have been established. The goal was to create a club that each student on campus would find attractive. Class times were adjusted to allow for club meetings, and members of the community became actively involved in providing for the needs of students. Local organizations began to sponsor sporting events at which every participant walked away a winner. Local business owners, employees, and professionals began to function as mentors. School officials did away with F as a grade, and teachers became creative in their class teaching.

The club program has proven to be very successful. A year after the club program started, truancy and dropout rates fell dramatically, to almost zero, and grades improved. Students began to wear uniforms donated by local businesses, and they took pride in wearing their club colors instead of gang colors. Most important, gangs and gang activity became less attractive.

The program implemented at Webb Middle School has been successful because school officials and community members began to provide for the needs of their students. Gangs became less attractive because students had another source from which they could gain a sense of identity. They were made to feel good about themselves: the clubs were a resource that they cocreated, in which they actively participated, and about which they collaborated with the community. School officials at Webb Middle School confronted the gangs directly by taking back those students who once had sought out gang involvement; until this program was implemented, gangs were the only organized community option for students. Most important, it was a community effort, with students involved in the decision-making process. Indeed, "it takes a village to raise a child," and Webb Middle School made the effort to get the village involved in the lives of its children.

CONCLUSION

As a reaction to a spate of high-profile incidents of school violence, particularly those in suburban and rural schools that resulted in multiple deaths of students and teachers, school administrations, sometimes mandated by the state, have prepared and implemented safe-school plans. These plans typically under-analyze the problem and overemphasize security. Intensive security measures may be necessary within certain schools located in urban communities where the crime rate is already high. These security measures may prove useful at keeping out of the school some persons who do not belong there, and they may provide early detection for extreme but rare cases. But it is questionable whether any school security measure could have prevented the tragedies of 1998 and 1999. School security might, at best, protect schools from lawsuits brought by parents whose children might have been victimized by others. At worst, they will further undermine the education process, making school seem more like a detention center than an education center. Moreover, merely increasing the level of security within a school will not solve the problem of school violence; it is more likely to mask it by allowing administrations to bask in the illusion that they have implemented a solution.

Schools need to consider the negative impact of such measures on the majority of school students. They need to consider the impact of heightened fear, invasion of privacy, and the undermining of the educational mission that result from having hidden cameras, drug-sniffing dogs, metal detectors, and identity tags. What is the message sent by this kind of hidden curriculum? Following the Littleton, Colorado, massacre, school officials around the country began to ban the wearing of black trench coats on school campuses. There were even reports of security officers' calling the police to local malls where young people were seen wearing black trench coats (Russell 1999). Such reactionary policies do nothing to reduce the level of violence within society. What they do is further alienate students who are not a threat to society. Young people who feel alienated and harassed by school officials and law enforcement personnel may be more prone to joining gangs.

Banning the wearing of black trench coats and alleged gang colors on school campuses will not have any appreciable effect on levels of school violence. Increased levels of school security cannot prevent incidents like that at Columbine High from happening again, nor have they prevented them before. However, providing students with alternative opportunities to enjoy the activities, kudos, excitement, community, and challenge that gangs provide will help in reducing the attractiveness that gangs have for some students and may help to reduce the level of so-called normal school violence. However, the reduction of such violence will require a collective effort involving the entire community, and young people must be included in the process. Examples of successful programs should be explored and experimented with. One example is the club program at Webb Middle School, which provided students with a sense of identity, gave them a sense of pride and dignity, and made them feel as though they belonged. Only when students have real alternatives to gangs will they reject what youth gangs have to offer, and the level of violence within our nation's schools will, it is hoped, begin to decline.

QUESTIONS FOR UNDERSTANDING AND CRITICAL THINKING

1. Review and discuss the relationship between violence and gangs *at school.*
2. How might the "us versus them" response to school violence actually attract students to gangs?
3. Likewise, how might increased school security measures create a "moral panic" among students and teachers?
4. What are some alternative solutions to gangs and school violence that could improve rather than exacerbate gang problems at school?

REFERENCES

ANDERSON, ELIJAH. 1994. Violence and the Inner-City Street Code. In *Violence and Childhood in the Inner-City,* ed. Joan McCord. New York: Cambridge University Press.

ARNETTE, JUNE L. AND MARJORIE C. WALSLEBEN. 1998. *Combating Fear and Restoring Safety in Schools.* NCJ 167888. Washington, DC: Department of Justice, Office of Justice Programs, Office of Juvenile Justice and Delinquency Prevention.

BARLAS, STEPHEN. 1999. School Violence Initiatives Debated. *American City & County* Jan.:12.

BURNETT, L. 1994. *Gangs and School.* Holmes Beach, FL: Learning.

CHASE, ANN. 1993. School Violence: Two Ways to Fight Back. *Governing* Mar.:20.

CLOWARD, RICHARD AND LLOYD OHLIN. 1961. *Delinquency and Opportunity.* New York: Free Press.

COHEN, ALBERT. 1955. *Delinquent Boys.* New York: Free Press.

FUTRELL, MARY HATWOOD. 1996. Violence in the Classroom: A Teacher's Perspective. In *Schools, Violence and Society,* ed. Allan M. Hoffman. Westport, CT: Praeger.

GANGSTER DISCIPLES (a Chicago street gang). 1999. Interviews of gang members by author. Chicago, Mar.

HOWELL, JAMES C. 1998. *Youth Gangs: An Overview.* NCJ 167249. Washington, DC: Department of Justice, Office of Justice Programs, Office of Juvenile Justice and Delinquency Prevention.

HUFF, C. RONALD. 1998. Comparing the Criminal Behavior of Youth Gangs and At-Risk Youths. *NIJ Research in Brief* Oct.:1–8.

JACKSON, PAMELA IRVING. 1991. Crime, Youth Gangs, and Urban Transition: The Social Dislocations of Postindustrial Economic Development. *Justice Quarterly* 8:79–97.

JUAREZ, TINA. 1996. Where Homeboys Feel at Home in School. *Educational Leadership* 53(5):30–32.

KAUFMAN, PHILLIP, XIANGLEI CHEN, SUSAN P. CHOY, KATHRYN A. CHANDER, CHRISTOPHER D. CHAPMAN, MICHAEL R. RAND, AND CHERYL RINGEL. 1998. *Indicators of School Crime and Safety.* NCJ 172215. Washington, DC: Department of Education, Office of Educational Research and Improvement.

KLEIN, MALCOLM. 1995. *The American Street Gang, Its Nature, Prevalence and Control.* New York: New York University Press.

LEITMAN, R., K. BINNS, AND A. UNNI. 1994. *The Metropolitan Life Survey of the American Teacher 1994, Violence in America's Public Schools: The Family Perspective.* New York: Louis Harris and Associates.

LOCKE, E. AND V. SCHIRALDI. 1996. *An Analysis of Juvenile Homicides: Where They Occur and the Effectiveness of Court Intervention.* Alexandria, VA: National Center on Institutions and Alternatives.

L. V. (member of Woodbury, MN, Police Department). 1999. Interview by author. Woodbury, MN, Mar.

MAXSON, CHERYL, KRISTI WOODS, AND MALCOLM KLEIN. 1995. *Street Gang Migration in the United States.* Los Angeles: University of Southern California, Center for the Study of Crime and Social Control.

NATIONAL LEAGUE OF CITIES. 1994. School Violence in America's Cities. *Youth Record* 6(19):4.

PADILLA, FELIX. 1992. *The Gang as an American Enterprise.* New Brunswick, NJ: Rutgers University Press.

PORTA, ASHLEY. 1999. Somebody's Watching Me: Cameras Take Privacy from Students. *Vidette Times,* 2 Feb.

PUZZANCHERA, CHARLES M. 1998. *The Youngest Offenders, 1996.* FS-9887. Washington, DC: Department of Justice, Office of Justice Programs, Office of Juvenile Justice and Delinquency Prevention.

RUSSELL, JOHN G. 1999. Black Trench Coats Face Local Bias. *Daily Iowan,* 26 Apr.

THRASHER, FREDERICK. 1927. *The Gang.* Chicago: University of Chicago Press.

TOBY, JACKSON. 1998. Getting Serious About School Discipline. *Public Interest* 133:68–83.

TRUMP, KENNETH S. 1996. Gangs and School Safety. In *Schools, Violence and Society,* ed. Allan M. Hoffman. Westport, CT: Praeger.

2-1 (an Indianapolis youth gang). 1998. Interviews of gang members by author. Indianapolis, Dec.

U.S. DEPARTMENT OF EDUCATION. 1998. *Student's Reports of School Crime: 1989 and 1995.* NCES 98-241; NCJ 169607. Washington, DC: Department of Education, National Center for Education Statistics and Department of Justice, Office of Justice Programs, Bureau of Justice Statistics.

U.S. DEPARTMENT OF EDUCATION. National Center for Education Statistics. 1997. *Violence and Discipline Problems in U.S. Schools: 1996–1997.* 98-030. Washington, DC: Department of Education.

VESTERMARK, S. D., JR. 1996. Critical Decisions, Critical Elements in an Effective School Security Program. In *Schools, Violence and Society,* ed. Allan M. Hoffman. Westport, CT: Praeger.

VICE LORDS (a Chicago street gang). 1999. Interviews of gang members by author. Chicago, Mar.

PART V

Violence, Drugs, and Gangs

12

Youth Gang Homicides

A Literature Review

James C. Howell

This literature review aims to help fill the information void regarding youth gang homicide by summarizing data and results of empirical studies. Information on the topic is summarized in five areas. First, the growth in youth gang homicides is assessed. Second, distinguishing characteristics of gang homicides are reviewed. Third, studies of the relationship between youth gang homicides and drug trafficking are examined. Fourth, promising programs and intervention strategies are reviewed. Program and policy implications are discussed in the final section. Youth gang homicides can be prevented and reduced.

GANG HOMICIDE TRENDS

Youth gang[1] homicide has been a neglected topic in homicide studies in the United States. Unfortunately, national data on youth gang homicides that can be used to document trends precisely have not been available. Several surveys, however, provide data on a large number of cities that give an indication of youth gang homicide trends. Miller (1982) reported the first multicity gang homicide data. He tabulated gang-related killings from 1967 to 1980 for nine of the nation's largest cities (Los Angeles, Chicago, Philadelphia, San Francisco, Boston, Miami, Detroit, San Antonio, and New York) and 50 other cities for which data

---

Howell, J.C. Youth gang homicides: A literature review. *Crime and Delinquency,* 45 (1999).
Pp. 208–241. Reprinted by permission of Sage Publications, Inc.

were available. Reported gang-related killings in the 59 cities increased from 181 in 1967 to 633 in 1980, an increase of 250 percent.

Curry and his colleagues (Curry, Ball, and Decker 1995, 1996a, 1996b; Curry, Fox, Ball, and Stone 1992) surveyed law enforcement agencies in the 72 largest U.S. cities in 1991. Forty-one of them reported youth gang homicides, for a total of 964. Maxson and her colleagues (Klein 1995a, 1995b; Maxson, Woods, and Klein 1995) also asked law enforcement agencies to report gang-related homicides in 1991. Among the 792 cities reporting local street gangs, 40 percent reported gang-related homicides. Law enforcement agencies in these 299 cities reported 2,166 gang-related homicides in 1991 (Maxson 1998). These three surveys indicate that youth gang homicides are no longer confined to a few large cities, although they remain concentrated in large urban areas. Los Angeles and Chicago report a total of 500 gang homicides in 1991—23 percent of the total number (Maxson 1998).

Chicago and Los Angeles are now the youth gang homicide capitals, and the number of gang homicides increased sharply in the late 1980s and early 1990s in both of these cities. The annual number of street gang-motivated homicides in Chicago increased almost fivefold between 1987 and 1994, from 51 to 240, and nearly doubled from 1992 to 1994, then dropped slightly in 1995 (Block, Christakos, Jacob, and Przybylski 1996; Maxson 1998). Gang-related homicides in Los Angeles County more than doubled from 1987 to 1992, from 387 to 803 (Klein 1995a), dropped slightly in 1993, climbed back to the 800 level by 1995, and then dropped by 20 percent in 1996 (California Department of Justice 1998; Maxson 1998).

Admittedly, this is a crude comparison between the total homicide increase and the growth in youth gang homicides for previous historical periods. The number of cities surveyed by Maxson and her colleagues and Curry and his colleagues is much greater than the number surveyed by Miller. However, it appears that youth gang homicides increased at a faster pace than total homicides for the period between 1980 and 1995. During this period, all murders of people between the ages of 14 and 24 increased only 18 percent (Fox and Zawitz 1998).

Studies also show that an increasingly larger proportion of homicides in both Chicago and Los Angeles are gang related in the recent past than a decade ago. The proportion of all Chicago homicides that are gang motivated increased from 9 percent in 1965 to 26 percent in 1994 (Block et al. 1996). In Los Angeles County, 15 percent of all homicides in 1984 were gang related, compared with nearly half (45 percent) in 1995 (Maxson, forthcoming). (It is important to keep in mind that use of the more restricted, gang-motivated definition in Chicago diminishes both the total number of gang homicides and the relative proportion, compared with Los Angeles.)

Although it is apparent that gang-related homicides have increased in the past 30 years, more precise comparisons cannot be made at this time for two important reasons. First, the criteria used to record youth gang homicides vary. Whether one counts only gang-motivated homicides (those that grow out of a gang function) or gang-related events (in which a gang member only need be involved in some capacity) can halve or double the tally (Maxson and Klein 1990, 1996). Using Chicago and Los Angeles data, Maxson and Klein show that Chicago's motive-based police arrest records produce homicide estimates only half as large as when using Los Angeles' member-based arrest data. About equal proportions of large jurisdictions use one or the other of these definitions, whereas small jurisdictions tend to use the narrower gang-motivated definition (Johnson, Webster, and Connors 1995). Therefore, the tabulation of youth gang homicides is affected by police departments' use of these different criteria to classify them. Second, local law enforcement databases are not designed to compile aggregate statistical information; rather, they are designed to track and support apprehension of individual gang members. (For other limitations of law enforcement gang homicide data, see Curry et al. 1996a, 1996b; Maxson 1998.)

More precise gang homicide trend data are forthcoming. The National Youth Gang Center (1997) asked jurisdictions in its 1995 National Youth Gang Survey (see Moore 1997 for a summary) to report gang-related homicides for that year. These data are being analyzed, and a report is in preparation that will provide national-level data and also compare reported homicides for 1995 with Maxson and Curry's 1991 numbers (Maxson, Curry, and Howell, forthcoming).

DISTINGUISHING CHARACTERISTICS OF YOUTH GANG HOMICIDES

Youth gang homicides are unique in several respects. For one thing, Block's (1993) research on Chicago homicides revealed that increases and decreases in gang-motivated homicides occur in spurts and thus do not correspond with the city's overall homicide trend line. Youth gang homicides are also distinct from nongang homicides in terms of settings in which they occur and participant characteristics (Maxson, Gordon, and Klein 1985). Drive-by shootings and the use of firearms also distinguish them from other homicides committed by adolescents and young persons.

Settings and Participants

Maxson and her colleagues (1985) compared gang and nongang homicides that occurred between 1978 and 1982 in sections of the City of Los Angeles and in unincorporated areas of the county. As expected, they found that gang homicides involved more participants: two and one-half times as many. Interestingly, participants in gang homicides were only half as likely to have had a prior relationship. There was no evidence of any prior personal contact in more than half of the gang cases. "In these gang homicides, the relationship between opponents appears to be based on gang affiliation rather than enmity between familiar individuals" (Maxson et al. 1985, p. 215). In sum, they concluded that "it is evident that gang incidents are generally more chaotic, with more people, weapons, offenses, and injuries out in the open, among people less familiar with each other" (p. 220).

This study identified other characteristics that distinguish gang from nongang homicides. "Yet the differences are not so striking as one might expect" (Maxson et al. 1985, p. 212). Tables 12–1 and 12–2 summarize the differences between gang and nongang homicides, as indicated in Los Angeles Sheriff's Department (see Table 12–1) and police (see Table 12–2) data (Klein and Maxson 1989). Not only did gang homicides involve a larger number of participants but they were more likely to take place in public settings, particularly on the street; were somewhat more likely to involve automobiles and shooting out of automobiles; were more likely to involve weapons, particularly guns, in the incident; result in more injuries; and generally involved a larger number of other violent offenses. Gang homicides were also more likely to involve younger participants and minority youth. On average, gang homicide suspects were about 19 years old, and victims averaged nearly 24 years old in Los Angeles (Klein and Maxson 1989). Almost all were males. Maxson's (1998) new study examining 1998-1989 data found comparable differences in the characteristics of gang and nongang homicides in the latter period compared to the 1984-1985 period (Klein, Maxson, and Cunningham 1991), except that the differences between gang and nongang cases diminished slightly in the latter period.

TABLE 12–1   Gang Homicides in the Jurisdiction of the Los Angeles Sheriff's Department

	Gang (N = 226)	Nongang (N = 220)
Setting (Gang homicides . . .)		
More often occur in the street	48%	14%
Less often occur at a residence	24%	53%
More often involve autos	66%	56%
More often involve guns	80%	60%
More often involve other weapons	31%	22%
More often involve a higher average number of weapons	2.23	1.68
More often involve additional offenses	72%	52%
Additional offenses are of a more violent character	45%	22%
More often involve assault with a deadly weapon	57%	39%
Less often include robbery	20%	34%
More often involve injuries to other persons	30%	10%
More often include unidentified assailants	19%	7%
More often include fear of retaliation	33%	10%
Participants (Gang homicides . . .)		
More often involve a higher average number of participants	8.96	3.59
More often involve victims with no prior contact	54%	24%
Are more likely to include clearly gang victims	47%	4%
Suspects are on the average younger	19.16	24.02
Victims on the average are younger	23.50	29.00
Suspects are likely to be all male	97%	87%
Victims are likely to be all male	92%	82%
Suspects are more often Hispanic	74%	30%
Victims are more often Hispanic	83%	39%

Source: Klein and Maxson (1989, p. 223).

Race and Ethnicity

Several studies have shown differences between gang and nongang homicides comparable with those reported by Maxson and Klein (see Block and Block 1993; Block and Christakos 1995; Block, Christakos, Jacob, and Przybylski 1996; Brewer, Damphousse, and Adkinson 1998; Spergel 1984), except for racial and ethnic variations. Racial/ethnic involvement in particular varies from one city to another and among communities in the same city (Block and Block 1993; Block and Christakos 1995; Block et al. 1996; Curry and Spergel 1988). Maxson and her colleagues (1985) found that the over-whelming proportion of gang-related

TABLE 12–2   Gang Homicides in the Jurisdiction of the Los Angeles Police Department

	Gang (N = 135)	Nongang (N = 148)
Setting (Gang homicides . . .)		
More often occur in the street	49%	34%
More often involve autos	64%	49%
More often involve guns	83%	68%
Less often involve knives	24%	37%
More often include unidentified assailants	23%	10%
More often involve fear of retaliation	33%	9%
More often involve injuries to other persons	23%	14%
Participants (Gang homicides . . .)		
Involve a higher average number of participants	6.96	3.77
More often involve victims with no prior contact	49%	27%
More likely to involve clearly gang victims	40%	2%
Suspects on the average are younger	19.40	23.68
Victims on the average are younger	23.67	31.06
Suspects are more likely to be all male	94%	84%
Victims are more likely to be all male	95%	89%
Victims are more often Hispanic	53%	39%

Source: Klein and Maxson (1989, p. 224).

homicides are intraracial and that in sections of Los Angeles where the population is mainly Hispanic, both the perpetrators and victims are Hispanic. The same finding applies to areas in which the population is mainly Black.

To better understand race/ethnicity patterns, Block (1993) examined the residential location of gang-related homicide victims. She developed a Residential Exposure Index, "which measures the probability that someone of a given race/ethnicity will encounter a person of another race/ethnicity in the block where the first person lives" (p. 303). Using this index to examine gang-related homicides, she found that Latino murderers tended to kill other Latino youth in excess of the probability suggested by the Residential Exposure Index. Their choice of Black victims was about equal to the probability suggested by the index, and their choice of White victims was much lower than the suggested probability. Black youth's choice of Black victims exceeded the probability suggested by the index to an even greater extent. Whites committed very few gang homicides, but when they did, they were more likely to kill Hispanics than other Whites or Blacks.

Other comparisons of city gang homicide rates show significant racial/ethnic differences. For example, in Los Angeles during 1989–1991, the homicide victimization rate for Black males between the ages of 15 and 19 was 192, compared with 94 for Hispanic males of the same age (Hutson, Anglin, Kyriacou, Hart, and Spears 1995). In Chicago, at the midpoint of the Los Angeles calculation (1990), the victimization rate for Black males between the ages of 15 and 19 was nearly 250, and for Hispanic males, the rate was slightly more than 100 (Block et al. 1996). Thus, male Hispanic rates were similar in the two cities at that particular point in time, and rates for Black males were significantly higher in Chicago than in Los Angeles. However, in an earlier period (the late 1970s and early 1980s), Hispanic males in Chicago had a higher gang homicide victimization rate than Blacks (see Block et al. 1996, p. 9). In their analysis of Los Angeles gang-related homicides, Hutson and his colleagues (1995) found that the homicide offending rate for Black males between the ages of 15 and 19 increased most dramatically during the study period, from 60 per 100,000 in 1979–1981 to 192 in 1989–1991, an increase of more than 300 percent. In contrast, the rate for Hispanic males between the ages of 15 and 19 increased about 34 percent, from 70 to 94. Thus, racial/ethnic groups' gang homicide rates vary in different cities and at different points in time in the same city.

Drive-By Shootings

Another important characteristic of gang homicides is the use of automobiles. This gang attack style is not new. Klein (1971) tells us that drive-bys originally were called "japping" after the hit-and-run tactics of Japanese soldiers in World War II. Miller (1966, p. 36) initially called mobile attacks "forays." Although most gang drive-by shootings involve shooting from a car (Hutson, Anglin, and Eckstein 1996), they may also take the form of driving to a specific location, finding a target, jumping out of the car, chasing the victim down, and then fleeing in the car after the shooting (Sanders 1994). Killing is a secondary intent in drive-by shootings; promoting fear and intimidation among rival gangs is the primary motive (Hutson et al. 1996), and cars, houses, and abandoned buildings are often targets.

Drive-by shootings have now replaced fair fights. Fair fights, also called "rumbles" or "gangbangs," were a means of establishing community status among gangs from the earliest record of gang fights (Sante 1991) to the 1970s (Miller 1982; Moore 1991). But now, drive-bys are more frequently used in some cities as instruments for establishing gang status and rank. This development is disturbing because of the lethality and impersonality of drive-bys and the fact that innocent bystanders—nongang youth, children, and older persons—are sometimes wounded or killed (Hutson, Anglin, and Pratts 1994) in violation of the gang code that existed in a previous era (see Sweeney 1980). Several factors account for the increasing popularity of drive-by shootings. As Miller (1982) has indicated,

> One reason clearly involves technology. The classic rumble could be . . . executed with combatants proceeding by foot to the battle site and engaging each other with fists, clubs, chains, and possibly knives—logistical and technological means available to combatants throughout recorded history. By contrast, the foray, in one of its major forms, requires two technological devices—the automobile and the gun. While both have been in existence for some time, neither has been readily available in large numbers to urban adolescents until relatively recently. In the 1970s, for reasons not well understood, the conjoint use of guns and cars increased substantially. (P. 117)

Sanders's (1994) explanation for the popularity of drive-by shootings in southern California is that the expansive geographical area

> is not well-suited for treks by a large number of youth to a gang fight. Large groups could be spotted by the police, and if the gang broke up in smaller groups to rejoin for a rumble with a rival, the segment could be attacked en route to the fight. The drive-by shooting is a tactic that lets gangs cope with the spread-out city and survive retaliation. (P. 56)

Other characteristics of southern California that have rendered the area well-suited for drive-bys include the lower population density, little public transportation, and an excellent highway system (Sanders 1994, p. 66).

Drive-by shootings serve several gang purposes. They provide grist for gang status (showing "heart" and courage) and a means of resolving arguments, they facilitate premeditated attacks of members of other gangs, and they help counter competition in illegal businesses (Sanders 1994). Sanchez-Jankowski (1991) has noted a similar purpose of drive-by shootings in Los Angeles: "In a number of the cases, the gangs doing the shooting were attempting to send a message to that community that their local gang branch was not able to protect them" (pp. 205-6). This message was intended to enhance the status of the shooting gang in the community. Few drive-by shootings appear to be related to drug trafficking (Hutson, Anglin, and Pratts 1994). Rather, the most common reasons include turf fights, retaliations for previous shootings, and control over an illegal criminal enterprise.

In Los Angeles County during 1979–1994, 25 percent of gang-related homicides resulted from drive-by shootings (Hutson et al. 1995). In the latter part of this period, from 1989 through 1994, 33 percent of Los Angeles gang-related homicides were drive-bys (Hutson et al. 1996), which resulted in 590 homicides. Nearly half of the people shot at and 23 percent of the homicide victims were innocent bystanders. The proportion of all gang-related homicides that were drive-by shootings increased from about one-tenth in 1986 to about one one-third in 1992. Younger persons tended to be involved in drive-by shootings more than in other types of gang-related homicide (Hutson et al. 1995; see also Hutson, Anglin, Mallon, and Pratts 1994).

Los Angeles police estimate that more than 90 percent of all drive-by shootings involve members of violent street gangs (Hutson, Anglin, Mallon et al. 1994). Hutson, Anglin, and Pratts's (1994) detailed study of drive-by shootings in the City of Los Angeles documented more than 1,500 of them that involved gangs in 1991. Nearly half of the victims were children and adolescents (younger than age 18), of whom 63 percent had gunshot wounds and 5 percent died from their injuries. Nearly one-third of the victims were not gang members. One-fourth of the incidents involved shooting into cars. Juvenile incidents represented 38 percent of all Los Angeles drive-by shootings during 1991 (the remainder of which involved persons older than age 18) and 23 percent of all juvenile homicides in the City of Los Angeles during the year (Hutson, Anglin, and Pratt 1994, pp. 326-7). A later study by Hutson and his colleagues (1995) revealed a decrease in Los Angeles County drive-by shootings in 1994.

Drive-by shootings have not been as prevalent in Chicago as in Los Angeles, but they began increasing in Chicago in 1985 (Block et al. 1996). Chicago saw only 120 drive-by shooting homicides over the 30-year period 1965–1994, which represented just 7 percent of all gang-motivated homicides in the city. Most of the 120 such homicides (59 percent) occurred during the period 1985–1994.

Firearms

The growing use of firearms in gang assaults is a major contributor to the growth of gang murders. The proportion of all youth gang homicides committed with a firearm has been increasing so that at the present time almost all are the result of firearm use (see Zimring 1996 for an analysis of the relationship between guns and homicide trends). However, gang use of firearms is not new. In the 1970s, "more people were shot, stabbed, and beaten to death in gang-related incidents than during any previous decade . . . and the prevalence and sophistication of firearms used was unprecedented" (Miller 1982, p. 142). The growth in youth gang homicides over the past decade is driven mainly by increased access to and use of firearms, particularly more lethal weapons (automatic and semiautomatic firearms).

Increased use of firearms in youth gang homicides is evident in both Los Angeles and Chicago. The proportion of Los Angeles gang-related homicides involving firearms increased from 71 percent in 1979 to 95 percent in 1994, mainly because of the increased use of handguns, particularly semiautomatic handguns (Hutson et al. 1995). Homicides by semiautomatic handguns increased dramatically from 5 percent in 1986 to 44 percent in 1994. Almost all gang-motivated homicides in Chicago (92 percent) over the past 30 years have been committed with a firearm (Block et al. 1996). Most of the significant increase in gang deaths in Chicago from 1990 to 1994 was accounted for by murder with a semi- or fully automatic weapon. The increased use of automatic or semiautomatic handguns in Chicago gang-related homicides, especially from 1987 to 1993, has been reported (Block and Block 1993; Block and Christakos 1995).

Surprisingly, assault weapons are rarely used in gang drive-by shootings and other gang-related homicides. The National Drug Intelligence Center (NDIC) informs us that "the semiautomatic pistol (especially the 9-millimeter) seems to be the weapon of choice for many street gang members, as opposed to military assault-style weapons" (NDIC 1994, p. 2). None of the studies reviewed here found extensive use of assault weapons by youth gangs. Hutson and his colleagues (1995) found that assault weapons were used in only 3 percent of gang-related homicides in Los Angeles County during the period 1979–1994. In the 1991 study of Los Angeles drive-by shootings, only one of 677 shootings involved an assault weapon (Hutson, Anglin, and Pratts 1994). A handgun (usually a 9 mm) was the most commonly used firearm (in 73 percent of the incidents), and a semiautomatic weapon was used in 31 percent of the incidents.

The next section reviews studies of the connection between youth gang homicides and drug trafficking.

YOUTH GANG HOMICIDES AND DRUG TRAFFICKING

Because the growth in youth gang homicides coincided with the advent of the crack cocaine epidemic in the mid-1980s, the two developments generally were perceived to be interrelated (see Inciardi 1986, 1990; Inciardi and Pottieger 1991; Klein 1995a). A California study (Skolnick 1990, 1992; Skolnick, Correl, Navarro, and Rabb 1988) suggested the connection a decade ago. These researchers contended that the two major Los Angeles gangs, the Crips and Bloods, had become entrepreneurial and were expanding their drug trafficking operations to markets in other cities, and where drug markets appeared, so did violence. This same conclusion was proffered in federal and state governmental reports (Bryant 1989;

California Council on Criminal Justice 1989; Clark 1991; Drug Enforcement Administration 1988; General Accounting Office 1989; Hayeslip 1989; McKinney 1988). These governmental reports suggested that youth gangs were instrumental in the increase in crack cocaine sales and that their involvement in drug trafficking resulted in a growth in youth gang homicides. However, this presumed connection has been questioned by a number of gang researchers (see Decker and Van Winkle 1996; Klein, Maxson, and Cunningham 1991, pp. 623-5; Moore 1990, p. 169). The extent of youth gang involvement in drug trafficking as organizations versus as individual gang members has also been seriously questioned (see Howell and Decker 1999, for a review of studies that address this issue).

Several studies of youth gang homicide and drug trafficking have been conducted in Los Angeles and Chicago. These are reviewed below, followed in turn by summaries of less comprehensive studies or assessments in Boston, Minneapolis, Miami, Houston, and St. Louis.

Los Angeles Studies

Several Los Angeles studies of youth gang homicides have been completed since the crack cocaine epidemic began in the mid-1980s. To test the popular gang drug trafficking-violence hypothesis, Klein and his colleagues (1991) examined Los Angeles homicide investigative files for violence in cocaine incidents during 1984–1985. Two-thirds of the gang homicide cases showed evidence of drug involvement, compared with 56 percent of nongang homicides. Moreover, the proportion of all cocaine sales that involved firearms decreased from 34 percent in early 1984 to 21 percent in late 1985, and the decrease was greater among gang than among nongang cases. Surprisingly, this decrease occurred during the period in which Skolnick and his colleagues contended that gang involvement in drug trafficking was increasing.

Klein and his colleagues (1991) found that drug trafficking was not a primary gang activity, although many of the gang members were involved in crack distribution (in about 25 percent of the arrest instances). Comparison of gang homicide cases with and without drug involvement showed few significant differences with respect to firearm use. The study authors concluded that "the drug/homicide connection . . . is not basically a gang phenomenon. . . . For the period of 1984 and 1985, the initial and major growth period for crack sales in Los Angeles, the purported gang connection seems in most respects to have been considerably overstated," and "the implications for violence similarly seem to have been overstated" (pp. 646-7). "We conclude . . . that the world of crack in Los Angeles belonged principally to the regular drug dealers, not to street gangs" (p. 647).

A subsequent study (Maxson 1995) was conducted in Pasadena and Pomona (midsize suburban cities of Los Angeles) to test the popular perception of a close relationship between gangs, drug sales, and homicide. Violence was present in only 5 percent of the sales incidents. Firearms were involved in only 10 percent of the incidents and showed decreasing prevalence over time. Gang involvement did not increase significantly the violent character of drug sales.

Maxson (1998) recently extended the 1991 study in her examination of a random sample of gang and nongang homicide cases in south central Los Angeles during the 1988–1989 period. Her examination of gang homicide investigative files showed that drug involvement was mentioned in about the same proportion of gang and nongang homicide cases, but the proportion of nongang drug cases increased in comparison with the 1984–1985 period. In 1988–1989, specific mentions of cocaine, and crack cocaine in particular, were more common in nongang than in gang homicides. When Maxson examined only drug-involved cases, however, gang homicides had higher levels of drug sales mentions than did nongang cases. But mentions of drug motives for homicide remained proportionally more common in nongang than in gang homicide cases.

In a study of drive-by shootings in the City of Los Angeles in 1991, Hutson, Anglin, and Pratts (1994) found that a total of 677 children and adolescents were shot at during 1991 (an average of 49 per month). Among the total, 71 percent were gang members. A handgun was the most commonly used firearm (73 percent), and a semiautomatic weapon, usually a 9-mm handgun, was used in 31 percent of the incidents. Analysis of arrest files led Hutson and his colleagues to conclude that "contrary to the general assumption, drug trafficking is not a major causative factor [of drive-by shootings]" (p. 326).

Meehan and O'Carroll (1992) studied the interconnection among gangs, drugs, and homicide toward the end of the period (1980–1988) in which the Los Angeles homicide rate more than doubled the statewide rate. During this period, the proportion of all Los Angeles homicides that were gang related increased from 15 percent to 25 percent. Meehan and O'Carroll tested four hypotheses using police department data from four districts in south central Los Angeles that police said had the highest concentration of youth gang-related homicides. The first study hypothesis, that gang-related homicides are more likely than others to involve narcotics, was rejected. Between 1986 and 1988, only 5 percent of gang-related homicides were narcotics related versus 23 percent of all others. Among victims between the ages of 10 and 19, none of the gang-motivated homicides involved narcotics. However, among victims 25 years and older, homicides that were gang motivated were just as likely to involve narcotics as were homicides that were motivated neither by gangs nor narcotics.

The second study hypothesis, that homicides resulting from conflicts relating to narcotics trafficking are more likely than others to involve gang members, also was rejected. Between 1986 and 1988, only 11 percent of narcotics-motivated homicides involved gangs. Rather, the most common motive for homicides involving gang members was a gang conflict.

The third study hypothesis that Meehan and O'Carroll (1992) examined, that victims of gang-motivated homicides are more likely than others to have been using cocaine before death, likewise was rejected. Victims of gang-motivated homicides in 1987 were significantly less likely than victims of other homicides to have cocaine in their bloodstream.

The fourth study hypothesis, that victims of homicide involving a gang member are more likely to have a history of arrests related to narcotics than are victims of homicides that involved neither gangs nor narcotics, also was rejected. During 1987–1988, victims of gang-involved homicides were no more likely to have a history of narcotics arrests than were victims of homicides that were involved with neither gangs nor narcotics.

Meehan and O'Carroll (1992) concluded that empirical support could not be found in the data they examined for the popular theory that a substantial proportion of the increasing incidence of youth homicides in Los Angeles was attributable to the increasing involvement of gang members in illicit drug trafficking, drug use, or both. Their analysis suggests that gang-motivated homicides do not tend to involve narcotics trafficking or victim drug use and that narcotics-motivated homicides do not tend to involve gangs. They concluded that "gang conflicts that result in a homicide are often independent of narcotics use and trafficking" and recommended that "gang activity and narcotics trafficking or use be addressed as separate, important risk factors for homicide rather than as interrelated cofactors" (p. 687). Meehan and O'Carroll also suggested that "it is quite possible that violence involving traditional youth street gangs that are loosely tied together by neighborhood allegiance is a phenomenon distinct from violence involving more highly organized institutional gangs or networks that exist for the purpose of marketing narcotics" (p. 687).

Hutson and his colleagues (1995) examined gang-related homicides in Los Angeles County during a 16-year period, 1979–1994. Over the entire period, gang-related murders represented 27 percent of all homicides. This figure increased from 18 percent in 1979 to 43 percent in 1994. In their epidemiological analysis, Hutson and his colleagues attempted to isolate factors accounting for the increase in gang-related homicides. Several contributing factors were singled out: an increase in the number of violent street gangs and gang members, increased gang violence, an increase in the use of firearms in gang violence, and other factors. Although some gang-related homicides occurred secondarily to drug trafficking, the study did not find drug transactions to be a major factor (p. 1034). Because the proportion of gang-related homicides involving firearms increased from 71 percent in 1979 to 95 percent in 1994, mainly because of the increased use of handguns, Hutson and his colleagues identified their use as a major factor contributing to the increase in gang-related homicides.

Chicago Studies

Rebecca Block and her colleagues have conducted several studies of gang-motivated homicides in conjunction with the Chicago Homicide Project, an ongoing study of all homicides recorded by police from 1965 to the present. The initial analysis of Chicago homicides during the period 1965–1981 (Block 1985a, 1985b) showed that gang homicides were relatively infrequent. Gang members accounted for 25 percent of all teenage homicides in that period and only 5 percent of all homicides. She also found that almost all of nearly 700 youth gang homicides in the 16-year period were committed in an assault situation.

The second Chicago gang homicide study (Block and Block 1992) covering the 1965–1989 period produced two important findings: first, that "street gang homicides have episodic peaks and troughs in particular neighborhoods" and second, that homicide patterns during the same time frame vary in different community areas of Chicago. Comparing gang-related homicide rates in Black and Latino areas of the city, they found that the patterns of yearly changes were unrelated, suggesting that "successful prevention strategies must target specific homicide syndromes . . . occurring in specific neighborhoods of highest risk and affecting specific demographic groups" (pp. 84-5).

In the third Chicago gang homicide study, Block (1993) observed that "street gang-related homicides are closely concentrated geographically, just as they are concentrated within specific years and specific age groups. They occur in spurts and are clustered in limited areas of the city, probably reflecting periods of intense competition over the expansion and defense of gang territory along a border" (p. 307; see also Klein 1995b). According to Block (1993), "Only about 2% of Chicago street gang-related homicides from 1982 to 1989 involved a drug-related motive, and still fewer involved an offender and a victim who were under the influence of drugs at the time of the incident. In 1989, when Latino street-gang homicides increased, the proportion that were drug-related was even smaller" (p. 317). Thus, she discounted the importance of drug involvement in gang homicide while concluding that "to explain and prevent [gang homicide], we must concentrate on male-on-male homicide—especially among young men and on street gang-related confrontations" (p. 323). Spergel (1995, p. 52) also observed that the connection between gang drug dealing and violence in Chicago during the latter part of the 1980s was "quite tenuous."

A fourth Chicago gang homicide study (Block and Block 1993) made use of detailed Chicago Police Department data files to geographically locate police-recorded offenses and to determine not only the street gang affiliation of the offender and victim but also whether homicides were gang motivated. The study focused on gang-related homicides during the period 1965–1990, particularly the latter three years. Richard and Carolyn Block spatially located offenses within the boundaries of gang turfs based on maps drawn by street gang officers in Chicago's 26 districts. Gang-related neighborhoods were classified into three types: turf hot spots, drug hot spots, or turf and drug hot spots. Separate analyses were conducted on the city's four largest and most criminally active street gangs during the latter period: the Black Gangster Disciples Nation (BGDN), the Latin Disciples, the Latin Kings, and the Vice Lords. The Chicago Police Department estimates that membership in these four gangs numbers about 19,000. From 1987 to 1990, they accounted for 69 percent of all street gang-motivated crimes and for 56 percent of all street gang-motivated homicides, although they represent only about 10 percent of the "major" Chicago youth gangs and 51 percent of the estimated number of street gang members.

More recent data on Chicago homicides reported in the fifth Chicago study show a changing pattern with respect to racial/ethnic involvement, drug-related violence, and homicide trends. Analyses of data for the period 1965–1994 (Block and Christakos 1995) showed that young Black homicide rates increased dramatically during the period 1987–1992, whereas the rate for young Latino males was generally steady. Almost all of the 1987–1992 increase in homicides occurred because of a specific increase in victimizations of 10- to 24-year-old Black males.

Block and Christakos (1995) examined different homicide syndromes to see if changes in them accounted for the 1987–1992 increase. This analysis showed that the increase in street gang-motivated homicides, and possibly also the increase in nonfamily fights and brawls, accounted for the overall growth in Chicago homicides during the late 1980s and early 1990s (based on preliminary analyses, pp. 10–11). From 1990 to 1993, "the number of street gang-related murders in Chicago escalated far more than ever before" (p. 9), accounting for 16 percent of all Chicago homicides in 1993, up from an average of 7 percent per year. The increase occurred mainly from 1989 to 1993. Up until then, street gang murders numbered about 66 per year. The number nearly doubled during the four-year period, to 129 in 1993.

> However, the risk patterns of street gang-motivated homicide can change drastically from year to year. In fact, they are better characterized as following a pattern of spurts rather than a smooth trend. The spurts usually are not citywide but occur in specific neighborhoods and involve specific street gangs. In Chicago, this means that street gang victimization patterns differ by racial/ethnic group. Each peak tends to correspond to a series of escalating confrontations, usually over control of territory (either traditional street gang turf or an entrepreneurial drug market). Thus, overall trends in Chicago street gang homicides since 1965 were a composite of separate patterns of individual gangs and neighborhoods. (Block and Christakos 1995, p. 14)

Analysis of factors related to the increase in Chicago homicides during the late 1980s and early 1990s revealed that the most important development was use of more lethal firearms. From 1988 to 1993, there was a 321 percent increase in the use of fully or semiautomatic weapons in all types of homicides (Block and Christakos 1995, p. 18). In Chicago, from 1987 to 1990, virtually all of the increase in gang-motivated homicides "seems attributable to an increase in the use of high-caliber, automatic, or semiautomatic weapons" (Block and Block 1993, p. 7). In fact, Block and Block (1993) show that although there was no increase in street gang assaults during 1987–1990, there was an increase in gang homicides, indicating that growing lethality (deaths per incident) accounted for the greater number of homicides, not more assaults.

In the most recent analysis of the connection between gang-motivated homicides and drug trafficking in Chicago (Block et al. 1996), Block and her colleagues classified 30 years of gang homicides (1965 to 1994) into four drug-motive categories: to further a drug business, to obtain drugs or money to buy drugs, an altercation over the use of drugs, and other drug motives. Over the 30-year period, drug-motivated gang homicides represented 2 percent of all street gang homicides. Almost all of these occurred in the third decade, but this increase was dwarfed by an increase in nongang drug-motivated homicides. Among the gang-related homicides that occurred after the crack cocaine epidemic began in Chicago (1987–1994), only 3 percent had a drug motive. Block and her colleagues also examined all drug-business homicides from 1990 to 1994 to determine the proportion that involved gangs: only 7 percent did. Street gangs specializing in drug trafficking tended to discourage violence "because it is bad for business" (p. 20). Drug motives may also be underrepresented in gang homicides. Hagedorn (1998) contends that drug-involved gang members might blame gang rivalries in homicide episodes to conceal their personal drug ties that are unrelated to their gang affiliation.

The Chicago studies show the offense specialization of certain gangs in two main categories: turf crimes and entrepreneurial crimes. Small Latino gangs tend to specialize in violent offenses, resulting in very high homicide rates that result almost entirely from turf battles for prominence over the constricted boundaries of small neighborhood areas (Block and Block 1993). From 1987 to 1994, these battles resulted in more than 200 homicides (Block et al. 1996). Nearly half of the Latino gang arrests were for other nonlethal violent crimes. Only one-fourth of their offenses were drug related. In contrast, Chicago's largest African American gangs tend to specialize in entrepreneurial drug offenses. Half or more of the offenses attributed to these gangs from 1987 to 1994 were drug offenses.

Block and Block (1993) made several observations about "typical patterns of street gang activity" in Chicago. First, gangs vary in the type of criminal activities in which they engage. Latino gangs specialize in turf-related violence, whereas African American gangs specialize in drug offenses. Overall, most gang violence is related to emotional defense of one's identity as a gang member, defense of the gang and gang members, defense and glorification of the reputation of the gang, gang member recruitment, and territorial expansion.

Second, according to Block and Block (1993), "the connection between street gangs, drugs, and homicide [is] weak and could not explain the rapid increase in homicide in the late 1980s" (p. 4).

Third, the most lethal areas are along disputed boundaries between small street gangs. These are mainly Latino gangs fighting among themselves in constricted areas.

Fourth, neighborhood characteristics are associated with specific types of gang crime. "Street gangs specializing in instrumental (economic) violence are strongest in disrupted and declining neighborhoods. Street gangs specializing in expressive (interpersonal) violence [are] strongest and most violent in relatively prospering neighborhoods with expanding populations" (Block and Block 1993, p. 8).

Fifth, the most lethal violence (and the highest level of it) occurs in neighborhoods where turf battles occur, not in those where street gang activity focuses on drug offenses.

Sixth, the predominant type of street gang activity in neighborhoods often changed from year to year, or even month to month, and tended to occur sporadically. Finally, the increase in gang deaths is attributed to an increase in the lethality of weapons, mostly high-caliber, automatic, or semiautomatic weapons.

Boston Studies

Miller's (1994) analysis of Boston police arrest data covering 1984 to 1994 produced results similar to the Chicago and Los Angeles studies. Of 138 reported homicides categorized as "probably" or "definitely" gang related, only 10 percent involved drug use or dealing. Among the 138 homicides, only 9 percent of 75 categorized as "definitely" gang related involved drug use or dealing.

Kennedy, Piel, and Braga (1996) examined youth homicides that occurred in Boston from 1990 to 1994. They reviewed the characteristics of 155 young persons (age 21 and younger) who were killed by guns or knives and 125 known homicide offenders who murdered someone with these weapons during the study time frame. Three-fourths of both groups were high-rate offenders. Both victims and offenders had been charged with nearly 10 offenses each, and 60 percent of the homicide victimizations were gang related. Using a very broad gang definition (a "self-identified group of kids who act corporately, at least sometimes, and violently, at least sometimes"), the researchers determined that Boston's high-rate offenders represent a small cadre (about 3 percent) of all youth in Boston neighborhoods with gangs. Kennedy and his colleagues concluded that Boston's adolescent gun problem was not integrally related to drug trafficking. Instead, both gang joining and gun possession and use appeared to be driven by neighborhood fear and the need for protection (see Vigil 1988).

Kennedy and his colleagues (1996) concluded that the gun violence problem in Boston has two main features: first, it is a gang problem that centers on intergang conflicts and second, it is a serious, violent, chronic offender problem.

> A clear picture thus emerges. Most, though not all, of Boston's young homicide victims and offenders emerge from a universe of gang membership and activity; they are high-rate criminal offenders who are known to local authorities, institutionally and personally, and they move in a universe of gang membership, geography, antagonisms, and alliances. (Kennedy et al. 1996, p. 163)

Minneapolis Study

Kennedy and his colleagues conducted a similar analysis of homicide perpetrators and victims in Minneapolis (Kennedy and Braga 1998). As in Boston, Minneapolis's adolescent and young adult homicide problem was predominantly a gang problem involving high-rate serious, violent, and chronic offenders. The high-rate homicide offenders and victims averaged about 7 arrests each. Among the victims age 21 and younger, 63 percent involved a gang-related motive. Again, as in Boston, gang-related homicides in Minneapolis mainly resulted from intergang conflicts and antagonisms.

Miami Study

A connection was made in the Miami media between gang activity and crack dealing and also between homicide and crack distribution among inner-city youth (Inciardi 1990). But

Miami grand juries impaneled in 1985 and again in 1988 (after a substantial increase in the number of gangs) to investigate the apparent increase in gang drug trafficking found that youth gangs were not involved substantially in crack dealing (Dade County District Attorney 1985, 1988). Miami's worst years for murders were in the early 1980s and were primarily due to cocaine wars among adult criminal drug operations (Eddy, Sobogal, and Walden 1988; Gugliotta and Leen 1989).

Houston Study

Brewer et al. (1998) examined both juvenile and adult homicide incidents in Houston from 1990 to 1994. Their analysis showed that only 15 percent of all homicides involving juvenile offenders were either gang related or gang motivated; the percentage for adults was only 4 percent. A larger proportion of them involved drugs: 24 percent of all juvenile homicides and 21 percent of all adult homicides. In contrast, 26 percent of juvenile homicides and 51 percent of adult homicides stemmed from an argument. Brewer and her colleagues reported that Houston police see youth gangs as lacking the organizational structure of organized crime groups, which appears necessary to conduct successful drug distribution operations.

St. Louis Study

In a St. Louis study, Decker and Van Winkle (1996, pp. 185-6) found some gang violence to be related to drug trafficking, mainly drug turf fights. But most St. Louis gang violence, including homicides, had three main sources: (1) violence is a part of their everyday life, apart from the gang, in members' neighborhoods and families; (2) conflict is endemic in youth gangs and differentiates them from other delinquent groups; and (3) violence is integrally related to individual status and role behaviors as gang members.

Decker and Van Winkle (1996) found most gang violence, including homicides, to be expressive, retaliatory, or situationally spontaneous. Although some violence was related to protection of drug turf and disciplining customers, most erupted over seemingly petty acts such as disrespecting the colors of another gang, stepping in front of a rival gang member, flashing gang hand signs at the opposition, and driving through a rival neighborhood.

Exceptions

Although the studies reviewed here consistently show a weak correlation between youth gang-related homicides and drug trafficking, there are exceptions. Block and her colleagues (Block et al. 1996) noted that there could be an indirect relationship among homicides, drug offenses, and gang activity. Many of the gang-related homicides might not have occurred if the drug markets did not exist and routinely bring members of opposing gangs into contact with one another. Such incidents could not be uncovered in Chicago arrest data because of police use of the narrower gang-motivated criterion.

Some youth gangs that are actively involved in street-level drug trafficking, such as Chicago's Vice Lords and the BGDN (Block and Block 1993; Block et al. 1996; Dawley 1992), commit a large number of homicides—many of which could be indirectly related to drug trafficking. These two gangs accounted for nearly 350 homicides in an eight-year period (Block et al. 1996), however, few of them were directly related to drug trafficking.

Some youth gangs engage in drug market wars, although most of these involve adult criminal organizations (Eddy et al. 1988; Gugliotta and Leen 1989). An analysis of gang-motivated drug-business homicides in Chicago from 1987 to 1994 revealed two street gang drug market wars (Block et al. 1996). The first set of episodes involved two "brother" gangs, the BGDN and the Black Disciples, whose clashes resulted in 45 homicides. The second set accounted for 61 homicides, which were associated with an attempt by the Black P Stones to reestablish themselves in the drug market. Together, homicides resulting from these two sets of episodes represented 11 percent of all gang-motivated homicides in the eight-year period. Still, Block and her colleagues (1996) concluded that "gang-related lethal violence is more likely to grow out of turf violence than from drug markets" (p. 23).

Venkatesh (1996) described one of the worst cases of gang drug trafficking and gang violence in Chicago's Robert Taylor Homes, a low-income public housing development. With the advent of crack cocaine, gangs in the housing development were transformed from turf gangs to drug gangs, and an escalation of gang violence resulted. Other studies have documented violent drug trafficking youth gangs (Sanchez-Jankowski 1991; Taylor 1990a, 1990b), and some studies have suggested a somewhat stronger connection between gang drug trafficking and homicide in specific locales (Cohen, Cork, Engberg, and Tita 1998; Cohen and Tita 1998; Hagedorn 1998; Padilla 1992; Sanders 1994; Taylor 1990a, 1990b).

SUMMARY

Some gang homicides are related directly to the business of drug trafficking. Although most gang drug wars appear to involve adult criminal organizations, some do involve youth gangs. These can produce a large number of drug-related homicides, particularly in the case of ongoing warring gangs. Nevertheless, drug-related homicides involving youth gangs appear to represent only a small proportion of all gang-related homicides.

Most of the homicides commonly associated with drug trafficking gangs appear to involve adult criminal organizations formed solely for cocaine and other drug distribution. These have few, if any, of the characteristics of traditional youth gangs (Moore 1990; see also Eddy et al. 1988; Gugliotta and Leen 1989). The interrelationship between drug trafficking and violence is widely revealed in such adult criminal organizations as posses, drug cartels, and prison gangs (see Fagan and Chin 1990; General Accounting Office 1989, 1996; Jackson and McBride 1985; Reiner 1992; Sanchez-Jankowski 1991).

Drug trafficking is an indirect contributor to youth gang homicide. The existence of gang drug markets provides a context in which gang homicides are more likely to occur. Because most youth gang homicides involve intergang conflicts, drug markets bring rival gang members into proximity with one another, thus increasing the likelihood of homicide.

The growth in youth gang homicides over the past decade has been driven by increased access to and use of firearms, particularly lethal weapons (automatic and semiautomatic firearms). The proportion of all youth gang homicides committed with a firearm has been increasing to the point that at the present time almost all of them involve firearms.

Even though many gang homicides occur in areas where drug trafficking is prevalent, this correlation should not be confused with causation of gang homicide. Kennedy and his colleagues (1996) lend support to this view in their conclusion that the majority of the

Boston gang-related homicides were not about drugs, money, or turf; rather, they were usually personal, vendetta-like, and motivated primarily by self-protection. Although gang drug trafficking does not necessarily cause violence, gang participation, drug trafficking, and violence overlap. Thus, it appears that gang involvement and narcotics trafficking should be addressed as separate risk factors for homicide rather than as interrelated cofactors (see Meehan and O'Carroll 1992).

Gang violence has many other sources related to everyday gang social processes (see Anderson 1990; Block and Block 1993; Chin 1996; Horowitz 1983; Howell and Decker 1999; Kennedy et al. 1996; Sanchez-Jankowski 1991). Most youth gang homicides appear to be integrally related to everyday gang life.

Decker (1996) observed in a St. Louis study (see Decker and Van Winkle 1996) how the threat of attack by another group ignites the gang through contagion, increases cohesion, and produces deadly consequences. This is the main collective (i.e., group dynamic) aspect of gang violence. It is contagious and spreads throughout a gang and from one gang to another in a community. Most gang violence is retaliatory, a response to violence—real or perceived—against the gang. Decker (1996) delineated a seven-step process that accounts for the gang violence spurts that Block (1993) discovered (see also Block and Block 1993; Block and Christakos 1995). The process that Decker (1996, p. 262) observed begins with a loosely organized gang:

1. Loose bonds to the gang
2. Collective identification of threat from a rival gang (through rumors, symbolic shows of force, cruising, and mythic violence), reinforcing the centrality of violence that expands the number of participants and increases cohesion
3. A mobilizing event, possibly, but not necessarily, violence
4. Escalation of activity
5. Violent event
6. Rapid deescalation
7. Retaliation

As Horowitz (1983) explains, "In seeking to protect and promote their reputation, gangs often engage in prolonged 'wars,' which are kept alive between larger fights by many small incidents and threats of violence" (p. 94). One gang may claim "precedence, which means that the other group must challenge them if they want to retain their honor and reassert their reputation" (p. 94). "Whatever the 'purpose' of violence, it often leads to retaliation and revenge, creating a feedback loop where each killing requires a new killing" (Decker and Van Winkle 1996, p. 186; see also Fremon 1995).

POLICY AND PROGRAM IMPLICATIONS

Preventing and reducing youth gang homicides should be a top priority in U.S. crime policy. Although the total number of youth gang homicides in the United States is unknown at this time, it is clear that the number has increased significantly since the 1980s and represents a significant proportion of all homicides in certain cities. For example, in the most chronic gang problem cities, Los Angeles and Chicago, youth gang homicides represented nearly half and about one-fourth of all homicides, respectively, in 1995. Public health scientists (Hutson et al. 1995, p. 1031) have observed that "gang-related homicides in Los Angeles County have reached epidemic proportions and are a major health problem." The same condition can be said to exist in Chicago, and the youth gang homicide problem merits attention in other cities that have high rates (see Maxson, 1998).

Because of the complexities of intergang conflicts that characterize youth gang homicides, the development of interventions to prevent and reduce them need to be based on careful analysis of a particular community's gang violence problem (Block and Block 1993). "For example, a program to reduce gang involvement in drugs in a community in which gang members are most concerned with defense of turf has little chance" (Block and Block 1993, p. 9). Similarly, the characteristics of communities can affect the type of gang homicides that are most prevalent. Expressive violence is more common in relatively prospering neighborhoods with expanding populations, whereas acts of instrumental violence (e.g., drug disputes) are more common in disrupted/declining neighborhoods (Block and Block 1993). Richard and Carolyn Block (1993) also caution that "because the predominant type of street gang activity in a neighborhood may change from year to year or month to month, and because the level of street gang-motivated violence tends to occur in spurts, effective intervention strategies must be built on continuously updated information" (p. 9); They are preventable (Block and Block 1993; Hutson, Anglin, and Mallon 1992a, 1992b).

Most youth gang homicides are the result of interactions among gangs. From 1965 to 1994, 86 percent of the victims of nearly 1,000 street gang-related homicides in Chicago were gang members (Block et al. 1996). In Los Angeles, about two-thirds of the victims of gang-related homicides from 1979 to 1994 were gang members (Hutson et al. 1995) and about the same proportion of all gang-related homicides during this period resulted from intergang interactions. Therefore, program interventions that reduce intergang conflicts or prevent them from escalating can reduce gang homicides.

Belonging to a youth gang increases the risk of homicide as much as 1,000 times (Decker and Van Winkle 1996). Thus, preventing youth from joining gangs should be a policy priority. How to do this has not yet been determined, although an antigang school curriculum, the Gang Resistance Education and Training program, shows promise (Esbensen and Osgood 1997).

Firearms are the main instrument used in gang homicides. The growing use of firearms in gang assaults is a major contributor to the growth of gang murders, particularly involving more lethal weapons (automatic and semiautomatic firearms). To be effective in reducing gang homicides, intervention programs must have a gun use reduction component.

Studies to date have identified several other risk factors for gang homicide that can be addressed through social change, economic development, and program interventions. These include racial and class discrimination, immigrant adjustment, changing economic conditions, and drug market conditions (Block and Block 1993); setting and participant characteristics (Maxson et al. 1985); and social disorganization (immigrant resettling) (Block and Block 1993; Hutson et al. 1995; Miller 1982). Programs that improve economic conditions and individual opportunities in gang-ridden neighborhoods would be required to address most of these risk factors. These include community reconstruction (Eisenhower Foundation 1990), Empowerment Zones (revitalization of communities through economic and social services), and Enterprise Communities (promoting physical and human development). The latter two initiatives are large-scale community revitalization programs for selected inner-city areas, funded through the federal Department of Housing and Urban Development (see Office of Juvenile Justice and Delinquency Prevention 1995). Other risk factors can be addressed to some extent with interventions addressed at gang problems in general (see Howell 1997, 1998a, forthcoming, for promising and effective programs). Promising interventions focused on serious youth gang violence and homicides are reviewed next.

Promising Programs

Although none of the gang interventions have been demonstrated to be effective in preventing or reducing homicides, four models aimed at controlling gang violence show promise. The first of these programs is being conducted in the Little Village area of Chicago, a low-income and working-class community with a population that is 90 percent Mexican American (Spergel and Grossman 1997). Called the Gang Violence Reduction Program, it is administered by the Research and Program Development Division of the Chicago Police Department. The program targets mainly the older members (age 17 to 24) of two of the city's most violent Latino gangs, the Latin Kings and the Two Six. These two gangs account for about 70 percent of the gang violence in Little Village.

The Gang Violence Reduction Program is based on the "Comprehensive Community-Wide Approach to Gang Prevention, Intervention, and Suppression Program" that was developed by Spergel and his colleagues (Spergel, Chance, Ehrensaft, Regulus, Kane, Laseter, Alexander, and Oh 1994). The Little Village version consists of two coordinated strategies: (1) targeted control of violent or potentially hard-core violent youth gang offenders, in the form of increased probation department and police supervision and suppression, and (2) provision of a wide range of social services and opportunities for targeted youth to encourage their transition to conventional legitimate behaviors through education, jobs, job training, family support, and brief counseling. Managed by the Neighborhood Relations Unit of the Chicago Police Department, the project is staffed by tactical police officers, probation officers, and community youth workers from the target neighborhood. A new community organization, Neighbors Against Gang Violence, also was established to support the project. This organization is composed of representatives from local churches, a job placement agency, youth service agencies, the Alderman's office, local citizens, and community groups. The program incorporates a comprehensive set of strategies—suppression, social intervention, opportunities provision, and community mobilization—that are integrated and employed simultaneously.

Preliminary evaluation results (after four years of program operations) are positive (Spergel and Grossman 1997; Spergel, Grossman, and Wa 1998; see also Thornberry and Burch 1997). They include a lower level of serious gang violence, including aggravated assaults, among the targeted gangs than among comparable gangs in the area. In addition, there were fewer arrests for serious gang crimes (especially aggravated batteries and aggravated assaults) by members of targeted gangs as compared with control youth from the same gangs and members of other gangs in Little Village. The project also was able to hasten the departure of youth from the gang while reducing their involvement in violence and other crimes. Noted improvement in residents' perceptions of gang crime and police effectiveness in dealing with it also have been observed. These results are attributed to the project's coordinated approach, combining community mobilization, suppression, and social intervention, which appears to be more effective than the traditional suppression-oriented approach (see Spergel and Curry 1990).

A second model, the Boston Gun Project (Kennedy et al. 1996) is based on a careful analysis of Boston's youth (age 21 and younger) violence problem, resulting in the determination that it is gang centered (loosely defined) and neighborhood based. Moreover, an analysis of the criminal history records of homicide offenders and victims revealed that both groups mainly contained gang members and high-rate offenders—mainly charged with property offenses, armed violent offenses, unarmed violent offenses, drug offenses, and firearms offenses (in that order)—led project staff to target gang-involved violent offenders who were known to juvenile justice and criminal justice systems (Kennedy, Braga, and Piehl 1997).

The Boston Gun Project is employing a "coerced use-reduction" strategy, targeting gun violence and violence prevention and the gangs themselves. Using a deterrence strategy, the project aims to prevent gang violence by demonstrating to gang members that "unpleasant consequences" will follow violence and gun use, thus inducing them to change their behavior. To carry out this deterrence strategy, the Boston Police Department's Youth Violence Strike Force uses three techniques. First, probation officers and police officers, patrolling the streets in teams, identify gang members, enforce conditions of probation, and increase sanctions for probation and parole violations. Second, an explicit communication campaign, often carried out face-to-face with gang members, delivers the message that gang violence has provoked the authorities' suppression approach and only an end to gang violence will stop suppression activities. Third, gang mediation specialists are deployed to gang "hot spots," which are generally already known through mapping that shows the overlap of gangs, intergang conflicts, and gun-related crime. Heightened surveillance for shootings, assaults, and other selected incidents will trigger deployment of interagency crisis interventions teams in "swift and comprehensive attention." After this "calming" operation, patrol officers continue to monitor the "hot spot" for reoccurrence of violence.

Simultaneously, the Boston Gun Project aims to interrupt the self-sustaining cycle of fear, weapon use, and violence that appears to be driving youth violence in the city by reducing access to firearms. This strategy, using gun tracing capabilities of the Boston Police Department and the Bureau of Alcohol, Tobacco, and Firearms, entails disrupting the illicit gun market (Kennedy et al. 1996). The rationale supporting the supply-reduction strategy is that disruption of the illicit market will interrupt the dynamics of fear-driven gun acquisition and use, thus reducing gang violence in Boston. Evaluation results are not yet available, although gun homicide victimization among 14- to 24-year-olds in the city is reported to have fallen by two-thirds after the project began (Kennedy 1997). Because homicides were dropping nationwide among this age group when the project began, the evaluation will compare Boston's homicide trends with a sample of other cities. Outcome measurement must also take into account many other youth violence interventions that were operating in Boston during the evaluation period (see U.S. Department of Justice 1996 for a description of some of these interventions).

Both the Chicago and Boston programs target "hot spots" of gang activity. A Chicago police Early Warning System (Block and Block 1993, pp. 54-6) consolidates spatial information and uses automated "hot spot area" identification and other geographic statistics to predict potential crisis areas. Up-to-the-minute information is necessary for targeting specific neighborhoods because of knowledge that gang violence changes over time, following a pattern of provocation, escalation, retaliation, and revenge that often occurs across a spatial border that also changes over time (Block and Block 1993). Information provided by the Early Warning System is used to guide police and community agency interventions to head off the cycle of escalation and retaliation, if possible, through the use of mediation and crisis intervention. One of the discoveries using the Early Warning System is a "marauder" pattern, in which members of rival gangs travel to the central hub of their enemy's territory in search of potential victims (Block et al. 1996, p. 11). Retaliation against leaders of the attacking gang deep inside its territory is common.

The Boston and Chicago projects could be made more comprehensive by adding a hospital emergency room intervention program for injured victims. This is being done in a Minneapolis intervention modeled after Boston's Gun Project for the purpose of warning victims against retaliation (Kennedy and Braga 1998). A gang specialist could be added to Suspected Child Abuse and Neglect Teams now found in many hospitals. This program component would serve to initiate entry of victims into intervention programs to help break the cycle of gang violence (Hutson et al. 1992b). Providing counseling for victims of drive-by shootings could help reduce the traumatic effects of victimization and decrease the likelihood of violent retaliation (Hutson, Anglin, Mallon et al. 1994). The creation of a firearm wounding and fatality reporting system would help in determining the sources of weapons and assist interdiction efforts (American Academy of Pediatrics 1992; Cristoffel 1991).

Other promising gun control interventions can be employed in conjunction with gang homicide strategies. These include restricting access to guns by "dangerous" people (see Cook and Leitzel 1996); supply-reduction (Koper and Reuter 1996); provision of bounties for information leading to the confiscation of an illegal gun (Blumstein and Cork 1996); use of metal detectors in schools (Kamin 1996); obtaining parental permission for warrantless searches (Rosenfeld and Decker 1996); and undercover purchases of firearms, control of supply channels, creation of ammunition scarcity, bilateral buy-back agreements, and nonuse treaties with financial compliance incentives (Zimring 1996).

The third program model, the Tri-Agency Resource Gang Enforcement Team (TARGET), integrates and coordinates the work of the Westminster (California) Police Department, the Orange County District Attorney, and the County Probation Department. TARGET uses intelligence gathering and information sharing to identify and select gang leaders and the most chronic recidivists for prosecution (Capizzi, Cook, and Schumacher 1995). In addition, civil abatement laws are used to suppress the criminal activities of entire gangs.

During its first two years of operation, the TARGET program (1) identified and verified 647 individual gang members; (2) targeted 77 verified gang members for intensive investigation, probation supervision, and prosecution, 69 percent of whom were placed in custody; (3) prosecuted 145 cases involving 168 gang member defendants and achieved a 99 percent conviction rate; (4) supervised an average caseload of 52 probationers regarded as hard-core gang members; and (5) documented a 62 percent decrease in serious gang-related crime (Kent and Smith 1995, p. 295). Begun in Westminster, TARGET is being replicated in six other cities within Orange County. Klein, Maxson, and Miller (1995) suggest that "focused efforts of this type can produce positive effects in smaller gang cities" (p. 292).

The final program model, the Jurisdictions United for Drug Gang Enforcement (JUDGE) program in San Diego, coordinates investigations, prosecutions, and the sanctioning of criminal gang members (Bureau of Justice Assistance 1997). This suppression program, headed by the district attorney's gang unit, targets violent members of drug-trafficking gangs. Several elements are deemed critical to its success: a motivated and reliable informant, a vertical prosecution team that works with investigators from the operation's beginning, a principal prosecutor freed from responsibility for other cases, videotape corroboration of drug transactions using paid informants, coordination with judges, and coordination with a jailer before a sweep to allow preparation for the increased number of detainees. JUDGE also enforces conditions of probation and drug laws and provides vertical prosecution for probation violations and new offenses involving targeted offenders.

Rigorous evaluation will determine whether the increasingly popular gang suppression interventions, such as the Boston Gun Project, have a long-term effect on gang crime. Historically, suppression effects have been short lived (Sherman 1990). Five-year case studies by Weisel and Painter (1997) showed that communities that initially respond to youth gang crime by emphasizing suppression, intelligence gathering, and investigation tend to turn to a more comprehensive approach in a few years, integrating investigations, intelligence gathering, prevention, community policing, and enforcement activities in a collaborative effort with community organizations.

The evidence available to date suggests that police strategies targeting specific gang crimes, locations, and involved gang members can be effective. But long-term proactive investigations of entire gangs is more effective than short-term, reactive investigations of individual gang members (Jackson and McBride 1985). "Gang crimes are viewed by [law enforcement] not as isolated acts, but [as] links in a chain of events that must be broken" (Jackson and McBride 1985, p. 28). It seems unlikely that short-term interventions could have a long-term impact on ongoing gang wars, some of which cover several years duration. These result in a large number of gang homicides.

Thus, it appears that the common or distinctive elements of the most promising interventions for preventing and reducing gang homicides are

- research and assessment of homicides, identifying gang hot spots, supported by automated information systems;
- long-term proactive investigations of entire gangs, supported by intelligence systems;
- gun interdiction;
- arrest, vertical prosecution, and confinement of dangerous gang members who are serious, violent, and chronic offenders;
- community policing and enforcement activities in a collaborative effort with community organizations and juvenile and criminal justice agencies;
- rehabilitation and treatment services in conjunction with graduated sanctions;
- early intervention with potential active gang members and serious, violent, and chronic offenders;
- prevention programs that discourage youngsters from joining gangs; and
- program evaluation.

Comprehensive programs that integrate these program elements can have a significant long-term impact on gang homicide.

QUESTIONS FOR UNDERSTANDING AND CRITICAL THINKING

1. What are some of the distinguishing characteristics of youth gang homicides?
2. What is the difference between a gang-related homicide and a gang-motivated homicide? Why are these distinctions important when examining homicide data?

3. Review and discuss the drug–homicide connection among youth gangs.

4. What are various public policy approaches that could be taken to prevent and reduce youth gang homicides?

5. What are the major components needed for successful gang intervention and prevention programs?

NOTE

1. The term *youth gang* is commonly used interchangeably with *street gang,* referring to neighborhood or street-based youth groups. Motorcycle gangs, prison gangs, racial supremacists, and other hate groups are excluded. Our operational definition for this review coincides closely with Miller's (1982) definition: "A youth gang is a self-formed association of peers, united by mutual interests, with identifiable leadership and internal organization, who act collectively or as individuals to achieve specific purposes, including the conduct of illegal activity and control of a particular territory, facility, or enterprise" (p. 21). Youth gangs are considered to consist of adolescents and young adults, from the approximate ages between 12 and 24. Unfortunately, there is no commonly accepted parameter of either the age range or proportion of individuals below a certain age (i.e., a youth) that can be used to differentiate youth gangs from adult criminal organizations.

REFERENCES

AMERICAN ACADEMY OF PEDIATRICS. 1992. "Firearms and Adolescents." *Pediatrics* 89:784–7.

ANDERSON, ELIJAH. 1990. *Streetwise: Race, Class, and Change in an Urban Community.* Chicago: University of Chicago Press.

BLOCK, CAROLYN R. 1985a. "Lethal Violence in Chicago Over Seventeen Years: Homicides Known to the Police, 1965–1981." Report of the Illinois Criminal Justice Information Authority, Chicago.

BLOCK, CAROLYN R. 1985b. *Specification of Patterns Over Time in Chicago Homicide: Increases and Decreases, 1965–1981.* Chicago: Illinois Criminal Justice Information Authority.

BLOCK, CAROLYN R. 1993. "Lethal Violence in the Chicago Latino Community." Pp. 267–342 in *Homicide: The Victim/Offender Connection,* edited by A. V. Wilson. Cincinnati: Anderson.

BLOCK, CAROLYN R. AND ANTIGONE CHRISTAKOS. 1995. *Major Trends in Chicago Homicide: 1965–1994.* Chicago: Illinois Criminal Justice Information Authority.

BLOCK, CAROLYN R., ANTIGONE CHRISTAKOS, AYAD JACOB, AND ROGER PRZYBYLSKI. 1996. *Street Gangs and Crime: Patterns and Trends in Chicago.* Chicago: Illinois Criminal Justice Information Authority.

BLOCK, RICHARD AND CAROLYN R. BLOCK. 1992. "Homicide Syndromes and Vulnerability: Violence in Chicago Community Areas Over 25 Years." *Studies on Crime and Prevention* 1:61–87.

BLOCK, RICHARD AND CAROLYN R. BLOCK. 1993. "Street Gang Crime in Chicago." *Research in Brief.* Washington, DC: U.S. Department of Justice, National Institute of Justice.

BLUMSTEIN, ALFRED AND DANIEL CORK. 1996. "Linking Gun Availability to Gun Violence." *Law and Contemporary Problems* 59:5–24.

BREWER, VICTORIA E., KELLY R. DAMPHOUSSE, AND CARY D. ADKINSON. 1998. "The Role of Juveniles in Urban Homicide: The Case of Houston, 1990–1994." *Homicide Studies* 2:321–39.

BRYANT, DANIEL. 1989. *Communitywide Responses Crucial for Dealing With Youth Gangs.* Washington, DC: U.S. Department of Justice, Office of Juvenile Justice and Delinquency Prevention.

BUREAU OF JUSTICE ASSISTANCE. 1997. *Urban Street Gang Enforcement.* Washington, DC: U.S. Department of Justice, Bureau of Justice Assistance.

CALIFORNIA COUNCIL ON CRIMINAL JUSTICE. 1989. *Task Force Report on Gangs and Drugs.* Sacramento: California Council on Criminal Justice.

CALIFORNIA DEPARTMENT OF JUSTICE. 1998. "Gang-Related Homicides." *Intelligence Operations Bulletin* 119:1–2.

CAPIZZI, MICHAEL, JAMES I. COOK, AND M. SCHUMACHER, 1995. "The TARGET Model: A New Approach to the Prosecution of Gang Cases." *The Prosecutor* March/April:18–21.

CHIN, KO-LIN, 1996. "Gang Violence in Chinatown." Pp. 157–84 in *Gangs in America,* 2d ed., edited by C. R. Huff. Newbury Park, CA: Sage.

CLARK, C. S. 1991. "Youth gangs." *Congressional Quarterly Research* 22:755–71.

COHEN, JACQUELINE, DANIEL CORK, JOHN ENGBERG, AND GEORGE TITA. 1998. "The Role of Drug Markets and Gangs in Local Homicide Rates." *Homicide Studies* 2:241–62.

COHEN, JACQUELINE AND GEORGE TITA. 1998. "The Drugs-Gangs-Guns Nexus of Homicide in Pittsburgh, 1987–1995." School of Public Policy and Management, Carnegie Mellon University, Pittsburgh, PA. Unpublished manuscript.

COOK, PHILIP J. AND JAMES A. LEITZEL. 1996. " 'Perversity, Futility, Jeopardy': The Dynamics of Gun Events Among Adolescent Males." *Law and Contemporary Problems* 59:55–90.

CRISTOFFEL, K. K. 1991. "Toward Reducing Pediatric Injuries From Firearms: Charting a Legislative and Regulatory Course." *Pediatrics* 88:294–305.

CURRY, G. DAVID, RICHARD A. BALL, AND SCOTT H. DECKER. 1995. "An Update on Gang Crime and Law Enforcement Recordkeeping." University of Missouri, Department of Criminology and Criminal Justice.

CURRY, G. DAVID, RICHARD A. BALL, AND SCOTT H. DECKER. 1996a. "Estimating the National Scope of Gang Crime From Law Enforcement Data." Pp. 21–36 in *Gangs in America,* 2d ed., edited by C. R. Huff. Newbury Park, CA: Sage.

CURRY, G. DAVID, RICHARD A. BALL, AND SCOTT H. DECKER. 1996b. "Estimating the National Scope of Gang Crime From Law Enforcement Data." *Research in Brief.* Washington, DC: U.S. Department of Justice, National Institute of Justice.

CURRY, G. DAVID, ROBERT J. FOX, RICHARD A. BALL, AND DARRYL STONE. 1992. "National Assessment of Law Enforcement Anti-Gang Information Resources." *Research in Brief.* Washington, DC: U.S. Department of Justice, National Institute of Justice.

CURRY, G. DAVID AND IRVING A. SPERGEL. 1988. "Gang Homicide, Delinquency, and Community." *Criminology* 26:381–405.

DADE COUNTY DISTRICT ATTORNEY. 1985. *Dade Youth Gangs.* Circuit Court of the Eleventh Judicial Circuit of Florida in and for the County of Dade. Final report of the Grand Jury, Miami, May 14. Dade County, FL: Dade County District Attorney.

DADE COUNTY DISTRICT ATTORNEY. 1988. *Dade County Gangs-1988.* Circuit Court of the Eleventh Judicial Circuit of Florida in and for the County of Dade. Final report of the Grand Jury, Miami, May 11. Dade County, FL: Dade County District Attorney.

DAWLEY, D. 1992. *A Nation of Lords: The Autobiography of the Vice Lords,* 2d ed. Prospect Heights, IL: Waveland.

DECKER, SCOTT H. 1996. "Collective and Normative Features of Gang Violence." *Justice Quarterly* 13:243–64.

DECKER, SCOTT H. AND BARRIK VAN WINKLE. 1996. *Life in the Gang: Family, Friends, and Violence.* New York: Cambridge University Press.

DRUG ENFORCEMENT ADMINISTRATION. 1988. *Crack Cocaine Availability and Trafficking in the United States.* Washington, DC: U.S. Department of Justice, Drug Enforcement Administration.

EDDY, PAUL, HUGO SOBOGAL, AND SARA WALDEN. 1988. *The Cocaine Wars,* New York: Norton.

EISENHOWER FOUNDATION. 1990. *Youth Investment and Community Reconstruction: Street Lessons on Drugs and Crime for the Nineties.* Washington, DC: Eisenhower Foundation.

ESBENSEN, FINN-AGE AND D. W. OSGOOD. 1997. "National Evaluation of G.R.E.A.T." *Research in Brief.* Washington, DC: U.S. Department of Justice, National Institute of Justice.

FAGAN, JEFFREY AND KO-LIN CHIN. 1990. "Violence as Regulation and Social Control in the Distribution of Crack," Pp. 8–43 in *Drugs and Violence: Causes, Correlates, and Consequences* (NIDA Research Monograph 103), edited by M. De La Rosa, E. Y. Lambert, and B. Gropper, Rockville, MD: U.S. National Institute on Drug Abuse.

FOX, JAMES A. AND MARIANNE ZAWITZ. 1998. *Homicide Trends in the United States.* Washington, DC: U.S. Department of Justice, Bureau of Justice Statistics.

FREMON, CELESTE. 1995. *Father Greg and the Homeboys.* New York: Hyperion.

GENERAL ACCOUNTING OFFICE. 1989. *Nontraditional Organized Crime.* Washington, DC: U.S. Government Printing Office.

GENERAL ACCOUNTING OFFICE. 1996. *Violent Crime: Federal Law Enforcement Assistance in Fighting Los Angeles Gang Violence.* Washington, DC: U.S. Government Printing Office.

GUGLIOTTA, GUV AND JEFF LEEN. 1989. *Kings of Cocaine: Inside the Medellin Cartel.* New York: Simon & Schuster.

HAGEDORN, JOHN M. 1998. "Gang Violence in the Post-Industrial Era." Pp. 365–419, in *Juvenile Violence.* Crime and Justice Series, edited by M. Tonry and M. Moore. Chicago: University of Chicago Press.

HAYESLIP, DAVID W. JR. 1989. "Local-level Drug Enforcement: New Strategies." *Research in Action,* No. 213. Washington, DC: U.S. Department of Justice, National Institute of Justice.

HOROWITZ, RUTH. 1983. *Honor and the American Dream: Culture and Identity in a Chicano Community.* New Brunswick, NJ: Rutgers University.

HOWELL, JAMES C. 1997. "Youth Gang Homicides, Drug Trafficking and Program Interventions." Pp. 115–32 in *Juvenile Justice and Youth Violence.* Thousand Oaks, CA: Sage.

HOWELL, JAMES C. 1998a. "Promising Programs for Youth Gang Violence Prevention and Intervention." Pp. 284–312 in *Serious and Violent Juvenile Offenders: Risk Factors and Successful Interventions,* edited by R. Loeber and D. P. Farrington. Thousand Oaks, CA: Sage.

HOWELL, JAMES C. 1998b. "Youth Gang Drug Trafficking and Homicide: Policy and Program Implications." *Juvenile Justice* 4:9–17.

HOWELL, JAMES C. Forthcoming. "Youth Gang Programs and Strategies." *Bulletin.* Washington, DC: U.S. Department of Justice, Office of Juvenile Justice and Delinquency Prevention.

HOWELL, JAMES C. AND SCOTT H. DECKER. 1999. "The Youth Gangs, Drugs, and Violence Connection." *Bulletin.* Washington, DC: U.S. Department of Justice, Office of Juvenile Justice and Delinquency Prevention.

HUTSON, H. RANGE, DEIRDRE ANGLIN, AND MARC ECKSTEIN. 1996. "Drive-by Shootings by Violent Street Gangs in Los Angeles: A Five-Year Review From 1989 to 1993." *Academic Emergency Medicine* 3:300–3.

HUTSON, H. RANGE, DEIRDRE ANGLIN, DEMETRIOS N. KYRIACOU, JOEL HART, AND KELVIN SPEARS. 1995. "The Epidemic of Gang-related Homicides in Los Angeles County From 1979 Through 1994." *Journal of the American Medical Association* 274:1031–6.

HUTSON, H. RANGE, DEIRDRE ANGLIN, AND WILLIAM MALLON. 1992a. "Injuries and Deaths From Gang Violence: They Are Preventable." *Annals of Emergency Medicine* 21:1234–6.

HUTSON, H. RANGE, DEIRDRE ANGLIN, AND WILLIAM MALLON. 1992b. "Minimizing Gang Violence in the Emergency Department." *Annals of Emergency Medicine* 21:1291–3.

HUTSON, H. RANGE, DEIRDRE ANGLIN, WILLIAM MALLON, AND MICHAEL J. PRATTS. 1994. "Caught in the Crossfire of Gang Violence: Small Children as Innocent Victims of Drive-By Shootings." *Journal of Emergency Medicine* 12:385–8.

HUTSON, H. RANGE, DEIRDRE ANGLIN, AND MICHAEL J. PRATTS. 1994. "Adolescents and Children Injured or Killed in Drive-By Shootings in Los Angeles." *New England Journal of Medicine* 330:324–7.

INCIARDI, JAMES A. 1986. *The War on Drugs: Heroin, Cocaine, Crime, and Public Policy.* Palo Alto, CA: Mayfield.

INCIARDI, JAMES A. 1990. "The Crack-Violence Connection Within a Population of Hard-Core Adolescent Offenders." Pp. 92–111 in *Drugs and Violence: Causes, Correlates, and Consequences* (NIDA Research Monograph 103), edited by M. De La Rosa, E. Y. Lambert, and B. Gropper. Rockville, MD: U.S. National Institute on Drug Abuse.

INCIARDI, JAMES A, AND ANNE E. POTTIEGER. 1991. "Kids, Crack, and Crime." *Journal of Drug Issues* 21:257–70.

JACKSON, ROBERT K. AND WESLEY D. MCBRIDE. 1985. *Understanding Street Gangs.* Placerville, CA: Custom Publishing.

JOHNSON, CLAIRE, BARBARA WEBSTER, AND EDWARD CONNORS. 1995. "Prosecuting Gangs: A National Assessment." *Research in Brief.* Washington, DC: U.S. Department of Justice, National Institute of Justice.

KAMIN, SAM. 1996. "Law and Technology: The Case For a Smart Gun Detector." *Law and Contemporary Problems* 59:221–62.

KENNEDY, DAVID M. 1997. "Pulling Levers: Chronic Offenders, High-Crime Settings, and a Theory of Prevention." *Valparaiso University Law Review* 31:449–84.

KENNEDY, DAVID M. AND ANTHONY A. BRAGA. 1998. "Homicide in Minneapolis." *Homicide Studies* 2:263–90.

KENNEDY, DAVID M., ANTHONY A. BRAGA, AND ANNE M. PIEHL. 1997. "The (Un)Known Universe: Mapping Gangs and Gang Violence in Boston." Pp. 219–62 in *Crime Mapping and Crime Prevention,* edited by K. D. Weisburd and J. T. McEwen. New York: Criminal Justice Press.

KENNEDY, DAVID M., ANNE M. PIEHL, AND ANTHONY A. BRAGA. 1996. "Youth Violence in Boston: Gun Markets, Serious Youth Offenders, and a Use-Reduction Strategy." *Law and Contemporary Problems* 59: 147–96.

KENT, DOUGLAS R. AND PEGGY SMITH. 1995. "The Tri-Agency Resource Gang Enforcement Team: A Selective Approach to Reduce Gang Crime." Pp. 292–96 in *The Modern Gang Reader,* edited by M. W. Klein, C. L. Maxson, and J. Miller. Los Angeles: Roxbury.

KLEIN, MALCOLM W. 1971. *Street Gangs and Street Workers.* Englewood Cliffs, NJ: Prentice Hall.

KLEIN, MALCOLM W. 1995a. *The American Street Gang.* New York: Oxford University.

KLEIN, MALCOLM W. 1995b. "Street Gang Cycles." Pp. 217–36 in *Crime,* edited by J. Q. Wilson and J. Petersilia. San Francisco: Institute for Contemporary Studies.

KLEIN, MALCOLM W. AND CHERYL L. MAXSON, 1989. "Street Gang Violence." Pp. 198–234 in *Violent Crime, Violent Criminals,* edited by M. E. Wolfgang and N. A. Weiner. Newbury Park, CA: Sage.

KLEIN, MALCOLM W., CHERYL L. MAXSON, AND LEA C. CUNNINGHAM. 1991. "Crack, Street Gangs, and Violence." *Criminology* 29:623–50.

KLEIN, MALCOLM W., CHERYL L. MAXSON, AND JODY MILLER. 1995. *The Modern Gang Reader.* Los Angeles: Roxbury.

KOPER, CHRISTOPHER S. AND PETER REUTER. 1996. "Suppressing Illegal Gun Markets: Lessons From Drug Enforcement." *Law and Contemporary Problems* 59:119–46.

MAXSON, CHERYL L. 1995. "Street Gangs and Drug Sales in Two Suburban Cities." *Research in Brief.* Washington, DC: U.S. Department of Justice, National Institute of Justice.

MAXSON, CHERYL L. 1998. "Gang Homicide." PP. 197–219 in *Homicide Studies: A Sourcebook of Social Research,* edited by D. Smith and M. Zahn. Thousand Oaks, CA: Sage.

MAXSON, CHERYL L., G. DAVID CURRY, AND JAMES C. HOWELL. Forthcoming. *Youth Gang Homicides in U.S. Cities.* Tallahassee, FL: National Youth Gang Center.

MAXSON, CHERYL L., MARGARET A. GORDON, AND MALCOLM W. KLEIN. 1985. "Differences Between Gang and Nongang Homicides." *Criminology* 23:209–22.

MAXSON, CHERYL L. AND MALCOLM W. KLEIN. 1990. "Street Gang Violence: Twice As Great, or Half As Great?" Pp. 71–100 in *Gangs in America,* edited by C. R. Huff. Newbury Park, CA: Sage.

MAXSON, CHERYL L. AND MALCOLM W. KLEIN. 1996. "Defining Gang Homicide: An Updated Look At Member and Motive Approaches." Pp. 3–20 in *Gangs in America,* 2d ed., edited by C. R. Huff. Newbury Park, CA: Sage.

MAXSON, CHERYL L., KRISTI J. WOODS, AND MALCOLM W. KLEIN. 1995. "Street Gang Migration in the United States." Washington, DC: Report to the U.S. Department of Justice, National Institute of Justice.

MCKINNEY, KAY C. 1988. "Juvenile Gangs: Crime and Drug Trafficking." *Juvenile Justice Bulletin.* Washington, DC: U.S. Department of Justice, Office of Juvenile Justice and Delinquency Prevention.

MEEHAN, PATRICK J. AND PATRICK W. O'CARROLL. 1992. "Gangs, Drugs, and Homicide in Los Angeles." *American Journal of the Disabled Child* 146:683–7.

MILLER, WALTER B. 1966. "Violent Crimes in City Gangs." *Annals of the American Academy of Political and Social Science* 364:96–112.

MILLER, WALTER B. 1982. *Crime by Youth Gangs and Groups in the United States.* Washington, DC: U.S. Department of Justice, Office of Juvenile Justice and Delinquency Prevention.

MILLER, WALTER B. 1994. "Boston Assaultive Crime." [MRDF]. Boston: Walter B. Miller.

MOORE, JOAN W. 1990. "Gangs, Drugs, and Violence." Pp. 160–76 in *Drugs and Violence: Causes, Correlates, and Consequences* (NIDA Research Monograph 103), edited by M. De La Rosa, E. Y. Lambert, and B. Gropper. Rockville, MD: U.S. National Institute on Drug Abuse.

MOORE, JOAN W. 1991. *Going Down to the Barrio: Homeboys and Homegirls in Change.* Philadelphia: Temple University.

MOORE, JOHN P. 1997. "Highlights of the 1995 National Youth Gang Survey." *Fact Sheet No. 63.* Washington, DC: Office of Juvenile Justice and Delinquency Prevention.

NATIONAL DRUG INTELLIGENCE CENTER. (NDIC). 1994. *NDIC Street Gang Symposium— Selected Findings. Johnstown, PA, November 2–3, 1994.* Washington, DC: National Drug Intelligence Center.

NATIONAL YOUTH GANG CENTER. 1997. *1995 National Youth Gang Survey.* Washington, DC: U.S. Department of Justice, Office of Juvenile Justice and Delinquency Prevention.

OFFICE OF JUVENILE JUSTICE AND DELINQUENCY PREVENTION. 1995. *Matrix of Community-Based Initiatives,* Updated. Washington, DC: U.S. Department of Justice, Office of Juvenile Justice and Delinquency Prevention.

PADILLA, FELIX M. 1992. *The Gang as an American Enterprise: Puerto Rican Youth and the American Dream.* New Brunswick, NJ: Rutgers University.

REINER, IRA. 1992. "Gangs, Crime and Violence in Los Angeles." Office of the District Attorney of the County of Los Angeles. Unpublished manuscript.

ROSENFELD, RICHARD AND SCOTT H. DECKER. 1996. "Consent to Search and Seize: Evaluating an Innovative Youth Firearm Suppression Program." *Law and Contemporary Problems* 59:197–220.

SANCHEZ-JANKOWSKI, MARTIN. 1991. *Islands in the Street: Gangs and American Urban Society.* Berkeley: University of California Press.

SANDERS, WILLIAM B. 1994. *Gangbangs and Drive-bys: Grounded Culture and Juvenile Gang Violence.* New York: Aldine.

SANTE, LUC. 1991. *Low Life: Lures and Snares of Old New York.* New York: Vintage.

SHERMAN, LAWRENCE W. 1990. "Police Crackdowns." *National Institute of Justice Reports.* Washington, DC: U.S. Department of Justice, National Institute of Justice.

SKOLNICK, JEROME H. 1990. "The Social Structure of Street Drug Dealing." *American Journal of Police* 9:1–41.

SKOLNICK, JEROME H. 1992. "Gangs in the Post-Industrial Ghetto." *American Prospect* 8:109–20.

SKOLNICK, JEROME H., THEODORE CORREL, ELIZABETH NAVARRO, AND ROGER RABB. 1988. *The Social Structure of Street Drug Dealing.* Report to the Office of the Attorney General of the State of California, University of California, Berkeley.

SPERGEL, IRVING A. 1984. "Violent Gangs in Chicago: In Search of Social Policy." *Social Service Review* 58:199–226.

SPERGEL, IRVING A. 1995. *The Youth Gang Problem.* New York: Oxford University Press.

SPERGEL, IRVING A., RON CHANCE, KENNETH EHRENSAFT, THOMAS REGULUS, CANDICE KANE, ROBERT LASETER, ALBA ALEXANDER, AND S. OH. 1994. *Gang Suppression and Intervention: Community Models.* Washington, DC: U.S. Department of Justice, Office of Juvenile Justice and Delinquency Prevention.

SPERGEL, IRVING A. AND G. DAVID CURRY. 1990. "Strategies and Perceived Agency Effectiveness in Dealing With the Youth Gang Problem." Pp. 288–309 in *Gangs in America,* edited by C. R. Huff. Newbury Park, CA: Sage.

SPERGEL, IRVING A. AND SUSAN F. GROSSMAN. 1997. "The Little Village Project: A Community Approach to the Gang Problem." *Social Work* 42:456–70.

SPERGEL, IRVING A., SUSAN F. GROSSMAN, AND KWAI M. WA. 1998. *The Little Village Project: A Three Year Evaluation.* Chicago: University of Chicago.

SWEENEY, TERRANCE A. 1980. *Streets of Anger, Streets of Hope: Youth Gangs in East Los Angeles.* Glendale, CA: Great Publishing.

TAYLOR, CARL S. 1990a. *Dangerous Society.* East Lansing: Michigan State University Press.

TAYLOR, CARL S. 1990b. "Gang Imperialism." Pp. 103–15 in *Gangs in America,* edited by C. R. Huff. Newbury Park, CA: Sage.

THORNBERRY, TERENCE P. AND JIM H. BURCH. 1997. "Gang Members and Delinquent Behavior." *Juvenile Justice Bulletin.* Washington, DC: Office of Juvenile Justice and Delinquency Prevention.

U.S. DEPARTMENT OF JUSTICE. 1996. "Youth Violence: A Community-Based Response." Washington, DC: U.S. Department of Justice.

VENKATESH, SUDHIR A. 1996. "The Gang and the Community." Pp. 241–56 in *Gangs in America,* 2d ed., edited by C. R. Huff. Newbury Park, CA: Sage.

VIGIL, JAMES D. 1988. *Barrio Gangs: Street Life and Identity in Southern California.* Austin: University of Texas Press.

WEISEL, DEBORAH L. AND ELLEN PAINTER. 1997. *The Police Response to Gangs: Case Studies of Five Cities.* Washington, DC: Police Executive Research Forum.

ZIMRING, FRANKLIN E. 1996. "Kids, Guns, and Homicide: Policy Notes on an Age-Specific Epidemic." *Law and Contemporary Problems* 59:25–38.

13

Gangs, Drugs, and Neighborhood Change

Jeffrey Fagan

❖

GANGS AND THE URBAN CRISIS

Youth gangs have been part of the urban landscape of North America for well over 200 years. In the late 18th century, gangs such as the Fly Boys, the Smith's Vly gang, and the Bowery Boys were well known in the streets of New York City.[1] As European immigration increased in the early 19th century, gangs such as the Kerryonians (from County Kerry in Ireland) and the Forty Thieves formed in the overcrowded slums of the Lower East Side. Gangs proliferated quickly in that time, with such colorful names as the Plug Uglies, the Roach Guards, the Hide-Binders (comprised mainly of butchers), the Old Slippers (a group of shoemakers' apprentices) and the Shirt Tails.

Illegal income also was a central feature of early gang life, including the illegal trade in alcohol. Many of these gangs were born in the corner groceries that were the business and social centers of the neighborhoods. These groceries also hid the groggeries that were important features of neighborhood life, and guarding them provided a steady income for the gangs. Although not involved in theft, robbery, or the "unsavory" professions of gambling or tavern keeping, these gangs warred regularly over territory with weapons including stones and early versions of the blackjack (Sante, 1991). They occasionally joined forces to defend their neighborhood, and nearly all were united in their opposition to the police.

Throughout the 19th century, gangs emerged in the large cities of the Northeast and in Chicago and other industrial centers of the Midwest. In the early 20th century, gangs also formed in the Mexican immigrant communities of California and the Southwest (Bogardus, 1943). Wherever neighborhoods in large cities were in transition, gangs emerged.

Fagan, J. Gangs, drugs, and neighborhood change. In *Gangs in America,* (1996, 2nd edition). Ed. Huff, CR. Pp. 39–74. Reprinted by permission of Sage Publications, Inc.

The 1,300 street gangs identified by Thrasher (1927/1963) were located in the economically disadvantaged neighborhoods of industrial Chicago in the 1920s. Thrasher interpreted the rise of Chicago's gangs as symptoms of the deteriorating neighborhoods and shifting populations that accompanied the industrialization of the city, and the changing populations that lived in the interstitial areas between the central city and the industrial regions that ringed it.

Like their counterparts in New York and Philadelphia, the Chicago gangs were composed of children of European immigrants, mostly from Poland, Italy, and Ireland, as well as Germany, Russia, and Sweden. Thrasher identified fewer than 8% of the gangs as "Negro," and none were Hispanic. Although ethnic gangs of European descent persisted through the 1960s, gangs composed of African American and Puerto Rican adolescents emerged in the large cities in the years following World War II.

Until the 1970s, the term *gang* was synonymous with the large urban centers of New York, Chicago, Philadelphia, and Los Angeles. That is no longer the case today. Gangs now are present in large and small cities in nearly every state. By 1992, police departments in over 85% of the nation's 250 largest cities reported the presence of street gangs (Klein, 1995a). Gangs today reflect the ethnic and racial diversity of U.S. society. New gangs have formed in small cities in Texas, in the midsize cities of California, and in urban areas throughout the South and the Midwest. Fundamental changes in gangs have accompanied their emergence. Gang members today are likely to remain in the gang longer. Although limited in the past to adolescents, gangs today may range in age from preteen "wanna-bes" to young adults who may remain active beyond their 30th birthday (Klein, 1995a; Moore, 1991).

Traditionally, stealing and other petty economic crimes were the backbone of gang economic life.[2] For some contemporary gangs, however, entrepreneurial goals, especially involving drug selling, have replaced the cultural goals of ethnic solidarity and neighborhood defense that historically motivated gang participation and activities. A few gangs have loose but functional ties to adult organized crime groups (Chin, 1990, 1995a). A few others have become involved in drug selling and developed corporate structures that have replaced the organizations that in the past regulated gang life (see, e.g., Taylor, 1990a, 1990b; but see Moore, 1991).

Gangs no longer are the colorful, turf-oriented groups of adolescents from immigrant or poor neighborhoods. Whereas gangs in the past were likely to claim street corners as their turf, gangs today may invoke the concept of turf to stake claims to shopping malls, skating rinks, school corridors, or even cliques of women. Gangs use graffiti and "tagging" to mark turf and communicate news and messages to other gangs and gang members (Huff, 1989, 1994). The participation and roles of young women in gangs have also changed. Through the 1960s, women were involved in gangs either as auxiliaries or branches of male gangs, or as weapons carriers and decoys for male gang members (Campbell, 1990b). Today, female gangs have emerged that are independent of male gangs, and fighting is common among the new female gangs (Campbell, 1990b; Klein, 1995a). There also is some evidence of sexually integrated gangs, where females fight alongside males (Taylor, 1993).

Gang violence also has changed over the past quarter century. Violence always has been a staple of gang life; fights were common between gangs or between members of a gang. Fights often were rites of initiation or part of the gang's identity and style. But gang violence has become more lethal in the past decade. For nearly 20 years, starting in the mid-1970s, police records show that gang homicides have increased steadily in Chicago, Los Angeles, and the smaller cities surrounding these gang centers (Klein, 1995a). Although making precise estimates is complicated by the different ways that gangs are defined and data are collected, the increase in lethal violence may reflect the increasing number and fire-power of weapons available to gang members. Yet, although gang violence has increased, and gang members continue to be heavily involved in violent acts and other crimes, violence also has increased among nongang youth in the same cities and neighborhoods. Many of these changes in gangs have been diffused into the popular culture through films, music, language and dress styles, and the news media.

Changes in gangs have occurred simultaneously with rapid changes in the social and economic structure of cities and suburbs (Bursik & Grasmick, 1993; Fagan, 1992a, 1992b; Hagedorn, 1988). The expansion of illegal markets and participation of gangs in them, the rise of gangs in small cities as well as large ones, the increasing lethality of gang violence, and the emergence of gangs in small cities are developments that have changed basic knowledge about gangs. What has been poorly understood, however, are the links between changes in gangs and changes in neighborhoods and communities. In this chapter, recent research is reviewed to describe and explain these links. In particular, I analyze the hierarchical influences of political economy, social structure, and neighborhood change as influences on contemporary gangs.

GANGS AND GANGING

Types of Gangs

Heterogeneity between and within gangs has been evident in gang research for over 75 years. Styles of gang membership and gang behaviors vary as do types of gangs. Beginning with Thrasher (1927/1963), gang research has distinguished between "entrepreneurial" gangs concerned with increasing their income through extortion and drug selling, and fighting gangs concerned primarily with increasing their status through violence. These types have been refined and elaborated in various studies.

Cloward and Ohlin (1960) studied gangs in New York City in the 1950s and argued that the type of gang that emerges depends on the balance of legal and illegal opportunities in the surrounding community. *Criminal subcultures* involve gang activity that produces income through illegal means in communities where the gang is well integrated with neighborhood residents. But *conflict subcultures* arise in neighborhoods where the gang is not well integrated with neighbors and where both legal and illegal income opportunities are scarce. Gangs in the conflict subculture are more likely to be violent and to use violence to attain status in the group and in the neighborhood. *Retreatist subcultures* involve gangs with members who, despite living in areas where adolescents are well integrated with neighborhood residents, have failed in both legal and illegal activities. Other retreatist subcultures arise in socially disorganized areas when the gangs fail to achieve status through violence or illegal activities. Cloward and Ohlin contend that these gangs are burdened with the label of "double failure," and they often retreat into heavy drug use (p. 179).

Yet, gang research in other cities has not confirmed the typology offered by Cloward and Ohlin (1960). Short and Strodtbeck (1965/1974), studying Chicago gangs in the 1960s, failed to find either retreatist gangs or criminal subcultures. Hagedorn (1988) studied gangs in Milwaukee in the 1980s and found that they were nearly all "fighting," or conflict gangs. Taylor (1990a, 1990b), studying Detroit gangs in the 1980s, identified three types of gangs. *Scavenger gangs,* which are organizationally unstable and seem to have few goals, are involved in a variety of impulsive petty crimes. *Territorial gangs* seek control of neighborhood and "turf," both for defense from outsiders and for protection of their income-producing activities. They have a discernable leadership structure and share both economic and territorial interests. *Organized, or corporate, gangs* have elaborate and cohesive leadership structures. These gangs exist only to make money, and they mimic businesses in their rules and group dynamics. Instead of turf, they claim markets that may be quite spread out geographically.

In my (Fagan, 1989) research in Chicago, Los Angeles, and San Diego in the 1980s, I identified four types of gangs that were similar to those in Taylor's (1990a, 1990b) typology. Instead of scavenger gangs, I identified *party gangs,* mainly involved in drinking and drug use as well as drug sales, and *social gangs,* which used drugs and committed numerous petty crimes. I also found other gang types (*delinquent gangs, young organizations*) that resembled the territorial and corporate gangs described by Taylor. I noted consistent patterns of the four gang types across the three cities.

Gangs also may evolve over time from one type to another. Some gangs evolved from the break dancing and drill teams that were popular in African American communities in the early 1980s. More recently, conflict and fighting between "tagger" (graffiti) groups suggests their possible development into street gangs (Klein, 1995a). Some of Taylor's (1990a) scavenger gangs evolved into territorial gangs, and some territorial gangs evolved into corporate gangs. Padilla (1992) described the evolution of the "Diamonds," a pseudonym for a Chicago gang, from a street-corner group whose main interests were music and partying, to a fighting gang that also was entrepreneurial. Following the killing of one member by members of a neighborhood gang, the Diamonds consciously decided to use violence to protect their interests and themselves. Later on, some members began selling drugs to increase the gang's income, and the Diamonds developed a formal organizational structure to strengthen their economic and self-defense interests.

Youth Gang Violence

Although violence always has been intrinsic to gang life, data on gang homicides suggest that gang violence has increased. The broader societal problems of youth violence cannot be explained simply by the proliferation of gangs or the involvement of gangs in drug selling, however. The absence of comparable data across periods and locales, as well as the difficulties of classifying gang crimes as gang related, complicates efforts to determine whether the new gang cities have produced higher rates of gang violence. Nevertheless, data on gang homicides in Los Angeles and Chicago suggest real increases, however difficult it may be to measure them.

Not all gang violence is connected with selling drugs or other economic transactions, nor are drug selling and violence causally related within gangs. Moore (1978, 1991, 1992) and Chin (1990, 1995a) found no connection between gang violence and drug dealing among Chicano and Chinese gangs respectively. The African American Milwaukee gangs studied by Hagedorn (1988) and the white gangs in Boston studied by MacLeod (1987) were involved both in violence and (to some extent) in drug selling, but their violence was mostly unrelated to drug selling. Historically, gang violence was evident long before drug selling was a major income source for gangs and gang members.

Several factors may account for the apparent increase in lethal gang violence. First, as the upper age range of gang members expands, the participation of older gang members may contribute to violence. Violence rates increase throughout adolescence, and elevated rates of certain forms of violence—robbery, for example—continue into the early adult years before declining (Farrington, 1985). The involvement of older gang members at ages when they may be more likely to use violence may contribute to overall violence rates. Second, the higher rates of violence between and within gangs may reflect changing community contexts where gangs are active. In socially and economically isolated communities where the exits from gang life are truncated, social controls are weak and gangs may be poorly integrated into communities. Instrumental violence such as robberies by gang members provide a source of income, especially when formal or legal income sources may be unavailable. The social disorganization of the community may also weaken its ability to regulate gangs, removing the social restraints on gang violence.

Third, despite the absence of reliable data, there is broad agreement that the number and firepower of weapons available to gang members has increased. Gang members report that they steal guns from homes or other gun carriers, they buy guns from drug sellers who are trading up in firepower, or they buy them from a vast informal economy of guns (Sheley, Wright, & Smith, 1993). The presence of guns has contributed to changes in the lethality of violence; guns become a part of strategic decisions in settling disputes and challenges to "respect" and "honor" (Klein, 1995a). Guns are carried for self-defense or protection by many gang members, who perceive that others are armed and willing to use their weapons over the smallest interpersonal slight. Thus, some lethal violence is preemptive (Fagan & Wilkinson, in press-a, in press-b).

The need to present a self that is powerful and impenetrable has become an important but dangerous method of commanding respect, honor, or economic advantage (Anderson, 1994; Canada, 1995; Oliver, 1994). Skewed conceptions of power and masculinity have developed in these contexts, fueling a violent response to disputes. Violence and material wealth receive exaggerated attention as the influences of family, work, or school weaken in increasingly poor communities. The strategic importance of violence grows as the isolation of communities increases, cutting off both gang members' exits from gang life and the tempering influences of the broader society.

Nevertheless, violence often is very controlled and used only strategically between many gangs. The corporate gangs in Detroit use violence selectively to enforce organizational discipline or maintain selling territories (Taylor, 1990a). There is little expressive violence or use of violence to attain status in the gang. Chinese gangs are tightly controlled with strong leadership in a complex social order (Chin, 1995a; Chin & Fagan, 1994). Violence that is not sanctioned through the gang's leadership may lead to punishment or expulsion for jeopardizing the gang's extortion rackets or other business activities.

Gangs and Drugs

Drinking and Drug Use

Few phenomena have been stereotyped as easily as gangs, violence, and drug use, especially when they are taken in conjunction. Drug and alcohol use have always been a part of gang life, as has peddling of small quantities of whatever street drugs are popular at the time. Alcohol and marijuana have always been, and continue to be, the most widely used substances among both gang and nongang youth (Fagan, 1989, 1990; Sheley et al., 1993). Drinking and other drugs (primarily marijuana) consistently are mentioned as a common part of gang life throughout the gang literature. For instance, Short and Strodtbeck's (1965/1974) study of Chicago gangs showed that drinking was the second most common activity of gang members of all races, exceeded only by hanging out on the street corner. Although cocaine may be trafficked by many gang members, it is not often used in either its powder or smokable forms (Fagan, 1993).

Ethnographic studies of gang life also show the commonplace occurrence of drinking and its place in a broad pattern of substance use.[3] Dolan and Finney (1984) and Campbell (1990b) illustrated the commonplace role of drug use in gang life among both males and females. Stumphauzer, Veloz, and Aiken (1981) noted that use patterns varied within and between Los Angeles gangs and changed for individuals over time. MacLeod (1987) noted high rates of drinking among white gang members but only occasional beer use among the Brothers, a predominantly black (but somewhat integrated) gang. Sanchez-Jankowski (1991) found that all members of all gangs drank regularly, using gang proceeds for collective purchases. Although they used drugs in varying patterns, alcohol was mentioned consistently. But Sanchez-Jankowski also mentioned that the Irish gangs least often used illicit drugs, because access was controlled by nonwhites who they did not want to engage in business with.

Vigil (1988b) described a variety of meanings and roles of substances among Chicano gang members in East Los Angeles, from social "lubricant" during times of collective relaxation to facilitator for observance of ritual behaviors such as *locura* acts of aggression or violence. In these contexts, drug use provided a means of social status and acceptance as well as mutual reinforcement, and was a natural social process of gang life.[4] Vigil noted how gang members prepared for imminent fights with other gangs by drinking and smoking PCP-laced cigarettes. During social gatherings, the gang members used the same combinations to "kick back" and feel more relaxed among one another. Evidently, gang members had substantial knowledge about the effects of alcohol (and its reactivity to PCP), and they had developed processes to adjust their reactions to the mood and behaviors they wanted.

Feldman, Mandel, and Fields (1985) observed three distinct styles among Latino gangs in San Francisco that in part were determined by the role and meaning of substances in gang social processes. The "fighting" style included males in gangs who were antagonistic toward other gangs. They aggressively responded to any perceived move into their turf by other gangs or any outsider. Drinking and drug use were evident among these gangs but was only situationally related to their violence through territoriality. Violence occurred in many contexts unrelated to drug use or selling and was an important part of the social process of gang affiliation. The "entrepreneurial" style included youth who were concerned with attaining social status by means of money and the things money can buy. They very often were active in small-scale illegal sales of marijuana, pill amphetamines, and PCP. Although fighting and violence were part of this style, it was again situationally motivated by concerns over money or drugs. The last style was evident in gangs whose activities were social and recreational, with little or no evidence of fighting or violence but high rates of drinking and marijuana use.

Padilla (1992), studying a Puerto Rican gang in Chicago, described how alcohol and marijuana often accompanied the rituals of induction and expulsion of gang members. These ceremonies often were tearful and emotional, with strong references to ethnic solidarity. Padilla described how emotions intensified as the ceremony progressed, and drinking was a continuous process during the events.

My (Fagan, 1989) study of gangs in three cities showed diverse patterns of drug and alcohol use among gang members, and differences in the drug-violence relationships between gangs. Heavy drug and alcohol use, but with low levels of gang crime or violence, were reported by two types of gangs. These two types were differentiated only by their involvement in drug selling. Two other gang types used heavy drugs extensively and also were extensively involved in violence. Again, these two gang types also were differentiated by their involvement in drug selling.

Drinking or drug use also is disallowed in some youth gangs, regardless of the gang's involvement in drug selling, especially when it may interfere with drug "business." Chin (1990) found that intoxication was rejected entirely by Chinese gangs in New York City. They used violence to protect their business territories from encroachment by other gangs and to coerce their victims to participate in the gang's ventures. But "angry" violence was rare; violent transactions were limited to instrumental attacks on other gangs. Taylor (1990a) and Mieczkowski (1986) described organizations of adolescent drug sellers in Detroit that prohibited drug use among their members but tolerated drinking. Leaders in these groups were wary of threats to efficiency and security if street-level sellers were high and to the potential for co-optation of business goals if members became involved with consumption of the goods. The gangs were organized around income, and saw drug use (but not alcohol) as detracting from the selling skills and productivity of its members. Expulsion from the gang resulted from breaking this rule, but other violent reprisals also were possible. Gangs in both studies accepted recreational use of substances by members, primarily alcohol, marijuana, and cocaine in social situations not involved with dealing.

In Mieczkowski's (1986) study, the sellers particularly found danger in being high on any drug while on the job, and superiors in the gang enforced the prohibition against heroin use while working by denying runners their consignment and accordingly shutting off their source of income. Violence was occasionally used by superiors (crew bosses) to enforce discipline. Gang members looked down on their heroin-using customers, despite having tried it at some point in their lives, which in part explains the general ideology of disapproval of heroin use.

Buford (1991) depicted crowd violence between loosely knit bands of English football "supporters" as an inevitable consequence of the setting of football matches and the dynamics of crowds of youth. Expectancies of both intoxication and violence preceded the arrival of the "lads" at drinking locations surrounding the stadiums. The expectancies were played out in crowd behavior through rituals that were repeated before each match. Alcohol consumption before and during episodes of unrestrained crowd violence was an integral part of the group dynamic, but Buford does not attribute to alcohol either an excuse function or being a necessary ingredient for relaxation of social norms. In fact, he pointedly notes that the heaviest drinkers were incapacitated by inebriation and were ineffective rioters, whereas the crowd leaders were relatively light drinkers. In this context, alcohol was central but hardly necessary to the attainment of the expected behavior, and the setting itself provided the context and cues for violence.[5]

Drug Selling

Selling small amounts of drugs, especially marijuana, also has been a common feature of gang life for decades. But the cocaine and crack crises of the 1980s created opportunities for gang and nongang youth alike to participate in drug selling and increase their incomes. There is little evidence that gang members have become involved in drug selling more than nongang adolescents. Klein and his colleagues, based on police arrest reports following the appearance of crack in Los Angeles in 1985, found no evidence that gang members were arrested more often than non-gang members for crack sales or that drug-related homicides were more likely to involve gang members than non-gang members (Klein, Maxson, & Cunningham, 1991; Maxson & Klein, 1989).

Among gangs, involvement in the drug trade varies by locale and ethnicity. Chicano gangs in Los Angeles do not sell cocaine but sell small quantities of other drugs (Moore, 1991, 1992; Vigil, 1988a). The crack and cocaine trades in that city are dominated by African American youth, both gang members and nongang youth (Quicker et al., 1992). Crack sales only recently began in Chicago, more than 5 years after Los Angeles gangs began selling drugs. As in Los Angeles, both gang and nongang youth are involved. Crack sales in New York flourished beginning in 1986, but there was no discernable street gang structure that participated in drug selling (Fagan, 1993; Williams, 1989). Instead, loosely affiliated selling crews provided an organizational structure for drug sales (Johnson, Williams, Dei, & Sanabria, 1990). Chinese gangs have remained outside the cocaine and crack trades (Chin, 1990, 1995a), although their members (but not the gangs themselves) have been involved in transporting or guarding heroin shipments from Asia.

Not all gang members sell drugs even in gangs where drug selling is common. Drug-selling cliques within gangs are responsible for gang drug sales. These cliques are organized around gang members who have contacts with drug wholesalers or importers. Among the Diamonds, Padilla (1992) describes how drug selling is a high-status role reserved for gang members who have succeeded at the more basic economic tasks of stealing and robbery. Despite public images of gang members using drug profits for conspicuous consumption of luxury items, drug incomes in fact are quite modest for gang members who sell drugs. Drug incomes are shared within the gang, but the bulk of the profits remain with the clique or gang member who brought the drugs into the gang. The profits from drug selling, combined with the decline in economic exits from gang life, provides some incentive for older gang members to remain in the gang.

Despite the historically uneven relationship between gangs and drug use or selling (Fagan, 1989, 1993; Klein, 1995a; Spergel, 1989, 1995), recent studies contend that the lucrative and decentralized crack markets in inner cities have created a new generation of youth gangs (Skolnick, Correl, Navarro, & Rabb, 1988; Taylor, 1990b). Young drug sellers in these gangs have been portrayed as ruthless entrepreneurs, highly disciplined and coldly efficient in their business activities, and often using violence selectively and instrumentally in the service of profits. This vision of urban gangs suggests a sharp change from the gangs of past decades, and much of the change is attributed to the dynamics of the smokable cocaine market.

But empirical research suggests a different view (Fagan, 1989, 1993; Hagedorn, 1988; Klein et al., 1991; Moore, 1992; Padilla, 1992; Vigil, 1988a; Waldorf, 1992). Drug selling has always been a part of gang life, with diverse meanings tied to specific contexts and variable participation by gangs and gang members (Fagan, in press). For example, I (Fagan, 1989) found diverse patterns of drug selling within and across three cities with extensive, intergenerational gang traditions, and Klein et al. (1991) reported variability within and across Los Angeles gangs in crack selling.[6]

The variability in gang participation in drug use or selling within and across cities suggests that communities vary with respect to their drug markets and the violence that accompanies drug selling. Because gangs have emerged recently in many small cities and gangs in larger cities have expanded or intensified their involvement in drug selling, we also should expect *community change* to explain changes in gang behaviors (Bursik & Gras-mick, 1993; Fagan, 1993; Klein, 1995a; Jackson, 1991; Reiss, 1986b; Shannon, 1986).

What changes have occurred in cities and communities that might explain variation and change in gang participation in drug selling? The social and economic restructuring of cities has reshaped neighborhoods and influenced the natural history of gangs, including the role of drugs within gangs. Two factors in particular have contributed to changes in gangs and the substitution of instrumental and monetary goals for the cultural or territorial affinities that unified gangs in earlier decades. First, cocaine markets changed dramatically in the 1980s, with sharp price reductions. Second, profound changes in the social and economic makeup of cities (Kasarda, 1989; Wacquant & Wilson, 1989) combined to disrupt social controls that in the past mediated gang behavior (Curry & Spergel, 1988). The interaction of these two trends provided ample opportunities for gangs to enter into the expanding cocaine economy of the 1980s. How these social and economic forces fostered gang involvement in drug selling are shown in the sections that follow.

Making Money

There is little reliable information on the economic lives of gang members. Recent studies have focused on gang members' involvement in drug selling, but for many gang members, drug selling is only part of a more complex dynamic of income and expenses (see, e.g., Padilla, 1992). Nevertheless, the importance of illegal work in the developmental sequences leading to gang initiation, gang "careers," and the exits from gang life are evident in ethnographic research on inner-city youth crime. Understanding the economic lives of gang members also requires a perspective beyond the rational economic perspective of costs, returns, and time allocation. It requires an understanding of the attractions of illegal work and its nonmonetary rewards, variables that often are unmeasured in quantitative studies on crime and work (Fagan, 1996; Vicusi, 1986a, 1986b). Economists refer to these variables as tastes and preferences, and a detailed understanding of the motivations and rules of gang life are necessary to include them in a framework of the economic lives of gang members.

Very few studies of gang members provide systematic data on how gang members earn money. Milwaukee reported a wide range of drug incomes (Hagedorn, 1994a). Three in four of the 236 "founding members" of 14 male gangs (72%) had sold cocaine between 1987 and 1991. Of the 90 gang members interviewed, 73 were active drug sellers between 1987 and 1991. About one in four (28.7%) claimed they made no more money from drug selling than they could have made from legal work at the going rates for unskilled labor (about $6 per hour). One in five (20.7%) earned the equivalent of $7 to $12 per hour, and one in four (28.7%) reported drug incomes in the range of $13 to $25 per hour, or $2,000 to $4,000 per month. Few (3 of the 73 sellers) reported "crazy money" (more than $10,000 per month) at any time in their drug selling careers (202). Mean monthly drug sale income was $2,400, or about $15 per hour, compared to legal monthly incomes of $677.[7]

Recent ethnographic work illustrates how the abandonment of legal work has been accompanied by shifts in conceptions of work among young men and women in poor areas. Anderson (1990, 1994) describes how young males in inner-city Philadelphia regard the drug economy as a primary source of employment, and how their delinquent street networks are their primary sources of status and social control. Similar accounts were offered by Hagedorn (1988, 1994a, 1994b), Padilla (1992, 1993), Taylor (1990a, 1990b), and Moore (1991, 1992).

Participants in the illegal economics in inner cities were engaged in a variety of income-producing crimes, including drug selling, fencing, auto theft, petty theft and fraud, commercial extortion, and residential and commercial burglary. In diverse ethnic communities in cities far apart, young men use the language of work ("getting paid," "going to work") to describe their crimes.[8] The confounding of the language of illegal and legal worlds of making money seems to signal a basic shift in the social definition of work. For the young men using this language, money from crime is a means to commodities that offer instrumental value as symbols of wealth and status.

Much of this illegal work is organized within ethnic enterprises combining shared economic and cultural interests. For gangs in these cities, there is less concern than in the past with neighborhood or the traditional "family" nature of gang life. Moore (1991) shows how gang members with limited exits from gang life remained longer in the gang, assuming leadership roles and manipulating the gang for their own economic advantage through perpetuation of gang culture and ideology. Chin and Fagan (1994) and Chin (1995a) describe the complex economic relationship between street gangs and adult social and economic institutions in three Chinatown neighborhoods in New York City. The adult groups, descendants of the *tongs* that were the shadow governments in Chinatowns a century ago, are involved in both legal, well-respected social and business activities *and* a variety of illegal businesses that employ street gangs. The gangs guard territories and act as surrogates in violently resolving conflicts and rivalries between the adult groups. Chin (1995a) concludes that the gangs prosper economically while functionally maintaining the cultural and economic hegemony of these ambiguous adult leadership groups. Moreover, the gangs are involved in a variety of income-producing activities, especially commercial extortion, that are shielded from legal pressures by cultural processes that tolerate and integrate their activities into the social fabric of everyday life in Chinatown (Chin & Fagan, 1994).

Padilla (1992, 1993) describes how the new pattern of exploitation of lower-level workers (street drug-sellers) in the gang was obscured by appeals by older gang members to gang ideology (honor, loyalty to the gang and the neighborhood, discipline, and ethnic solidarity) combined with the lure of income. Taylor (1990a), describing drug gangs in Detroit, and Padilla (1992) also talk about the use of money rather than violence as social control within African American and Latino drug-selling gangs—if a worker steps out of line, he simply is cut off from the business, a punishment far more salient than threats to physical safety. Drug-selling groups in these two studies superficially are ethnic enterprises, but function more substantively as economic units with management structures oriented toward the maintenance of profitability and efficiency. The institutionalization of these sources of illegal work, and their competitiveness with the low-status and low-income legal jobs left behind after deindustrialization, combine to maintain illegal work careers long after they would have been abandoned in earlier generations.

Patterns of illegal work vary in the gang literature. Some gang members abandon legal work after a period of employment, others drift in and out of legal work, and a few seem to choose from the outset exclusive careers in illegal work. There has been little research on how these changes come about, how often they occur, individual differences in shifts, or the decision processes that result in changes. Sanchez-Jankowski (1991), for example, claims to have found an "entrepreneurial spirit" as the "driving force in the work view and behavior of gang members" (p. 101) that pushes them to make rational decisions to engage in the profitable world of drug sales or auto theft.

Hagedorn (1994b) describes how gang members drift in and out of legal work over time, with decisions closely bundled and often reciprocal. Hagedorn claims that the drug labor market vigorously competes with the seemingly more "glamorous" opportunities in the illegal economy, despite the low wages, low status, dangerous and often part-time nature of the legal work. Hagedorn also describes how gang members at times double up between legal and illegal work, holding both types of "jobs" at the same time; at other times, they specialize in drug selling or other illegal work. The hazards and indignity of low-wage, low-status legal jobs cause others to discount the returns from legal work. For example, Bourgois (1989) claims that drug dealers who leave legal jobs to embrace the risks and rewards of drug selling are evidence of a "culture of resistance," preferring the "more dignified workplace" of drug selling than the low wages and "subtle humiliations" of secondary labor markets where racism dominates work conditions and social interactions (p. 641).

The changes in the structure of employment shaped not only job outcomes for young adults but also the outcomes of early legal problems. Sullivan (1989, 1991) tells how early involvement in crimes was normative in three ethnically diverse neighborhoods, but the outcomes of arrest varied by neighborhood. White families helped resolve disputes informally, using family support and job networks to soften the potential stigma of arrest. With high rates of joblessness, nonwhite families had few social buffers or job networks between them and the legal system. Not only did they lack access to job networks, but their families were of little help when their income-producing crimes (robberies) evoked official responses. Their disrupted job networks were unable to mitigate legal problems or ease the school-to-work transition, contributing to the continuity of criminality into early adulthood and adverse legal responses. In contrast, youth in predominantly white neighborhoods were able to make sometimes difficult but successful escapes from adolescent crime networks. Hagan (1993) links this to processes of "social embeddedness" that truncate future options and amplify the adverse effects of adolescent entanglements in the legal system.

GANGS AND DRUG SELLING IN THE WAKE OF DEINDUSTRIALIZATION

The link between gang formation and the social and economic makeup of communities is a consistent theme in the gang literature. Curry and Spergel (1988) showed how gang delinquency rates varied according to the social and economic well-being of particular neighborhoods, reflecting variation in the degree of structural inequality between neighborhoods. During the 1970s, when the decline in manufacturing jobs in large U.S. cities was steepest (Kasarda, 1988, 1989, 1992), gang formation occurred in communities that experienced the most extreme forms of economic disinvestment, labor market contraction, and social dislocation (Jackson, 1991). The location of gangs in low-income neighborhoods and among low-income populations reflects the consistent disadvantage politically of these neighborhoods and their residents compared to people in neighboring communities with greater wealth and access to resources (see Hagedorn, 1994b; McGahey, 1986; Taylor, Taub, & Peterson, 1986; Taylor & Covington, 1988).

These factors are part of the *political* economy of a community because they reflect dimensions of community life that are shaped by forces that lie beyond the control of communities: decisions by bankers and industrialists, technological changes, and the distribution of public resources through political power (Skogan, 1990). The social controls and social organizations that form in communities are the result of the interactions of individuals with the structural features of the community: housing choices constrained by decisions by banks and developers, jobs made available by the decisions of industrialists or banks supporting small businesses and shops, transportation choices that make jobs and other services accessible to neighborhood residents, and the quality and responsiveness of institutions such as police and schools. Accordingly, the social organization of neighborhoods is shaped by social and economic interactions of political decisions with residents' skills, family configurations, and cultural and lifestyle preferences.

Gang formation in neighborhoods reflects disadvantages in these choices: social organizations of adolescents that reflect constrained choices and weak social controls. Although some aspects of the social organization of communities are the result of "consumer" decisions, others are the result of closely guarded institutional practices (Skogan, 1990, p. 173). Job creation is especially critical, for the availability of stable employment at a wage level that can sustain families and small businesses that serve them are critical to maintaining social control within the community.

Gangs can be seen as an adaptive social organization of adolescents that form in response to disadvantages in the political economy of communities. Disinvestment or weak public resources act as constraints on social controls from schools and families. Weak labor market participation attenuates the social control function of older generations with primary roles for socialization and control of children. Accordingly, when social disinvestment destabilizes neighborhoods, the risks of gang formation grow. So too do the risks of drug activity: The constraints on social controls in communities make drug taking more salient, offer little resistance to the development of street-level drug markets, and are ineffective against the violence and disorder in the contexts of those markets. That these factors converge in inner cities offers a partial explanation of the confluence of the growth of gangs and their involvement in drug markets.

We do not know what neighborhood processes translate the effects of political economy into specific forms of social organization and neighborhood dynamics within communities. Social control involves the normative processes and ethics of social interaction that regulate everyday social life (Doyle & Luckenbill, 1991) as well as the mobilization of community that occurs in response to problem behaviors. To the extent that political economic decisions weaken informal and formal social controls and the formation of social capital (Coleman, 1988), these decisions launch processes that give rise to the formation of gangs, the formation of drug markets, and the confluence of the two problems.

In the following section, I analyze the effects of social and economic decisions on the regulatory processes within neighborhoods that seem to be implicated in the growth of drug markets and the formation of gangs. I review examples of the social processes that are launched when people in disadvantaged neighborhoods are exposed to criminogenic structural conditions, especially those factors that lead to gang activity and drug dealing.

The Transformation of the Labor Market and the Growth of Drug Markets

Two factors fundamentally changed the labor market for poor young men and women in urban areas since 1970: the replacement of unskilled and semiskilled blue-collar jobs with "pink-collar" jobs that required higher educational and skill levels, and the growth of the informal economy, especially the illicit economy around drugs (Kasarda, 1989; Wacquant

& Wilson, 1989). The 1970s were a decade marked by surpluses of semiskilled and un-skilled labor in inner cities, created by the relocation of manufacturing and other blue-collar jobs to "satellite cities" in surrounding suburbs. Kasarda (1989) shows that between 1970 and 1980, the number of blue-collar and clerical jobs declined by over 350,000 in New York City but increased by over 75,000 in the surrounding suburbs. Technical and mana-gerial jobs in the city increased by over 250,000 during this time, and by over 400,000 in the suburbs. The net effect for inner city communities was dramatic increases in jobless-ness[9] among young minority men, especially African Americans, since 1970; higher rates of employment among women; and growing dependence on unregulated labor markets for employment and income (Kasarda, 1992).

Traditionally, African Americans have relied heavily on blue-collar jobs in manufac-turing for economic sustenance and social mobility (Farley & Allen, 1987). Beginning in the 1970s, Puerto Ricans and other Latin American and East Asian immigrants "colonized" these jobs (Bourgois, 1995; Tienda, 1989), and African American employment in the manufactur-ing sector of New York declined (Sullivan, 1989). Thus, the economic restructuring of many U.S. cities resulted in large-scale exclusion of their nonwhite residents from constricting la-bor markets that also were transforming from manufacturing to services and shifting spatially from the inner city to the surrounding suburbs (Hochschild, 1989). Similar processes, com-pounded by language and other cultural barriers, created severe economic dislocations for Puerto Ricans, in turn creating conditions of severe impoverishment (Farley, 1987; Kasarda, 1992; Tienda, 1989) and growing dependence on the informal economy (Sassen-Koob, 1989).

Drug selling is an important part of the informal economy in urban areas in the United States (Hunt, 1990; Stepick, 1989) and other countries (Jimenez, 1989; Lanzetta, Castano, & Soto, 1989). Besides the motivation to reap profits, the decline of economic opportuni-ties for labor force participation or licit informal income among inner-city residents strengthened incentives to sell drugs (Bourgois, 1995; Freeman, 1991; Johnson, Williams, Dei, & Sanabria, 1990; Moss & Tilly, 1991; Padilla, 1992; Taylor, 1990b).

Crack appeared in urban neighborhoods that had experienced profound social and economic declines since the 1970s (Fagan, 1992a; Johnson, Hamid, & Sanabria, 1990). For gang members and nongang youth alike, crack distribution became a major part of the in-formal economy where the unemployed could achieve economic returns well beyond the returns of low-wage jobs (see, e.g., Bourgois, 1995; Hamid, 1990; Williams, 1989). The in-troduction of this new and powerful cocaine product, and its popularity among a cohort of young adults with high base rates of drug use, created new demand that exceeded the ca-pacity of established distribution systems (Fagan & Chin, 1990).

In turn, the expansion of the drug economy increased the opportunities for street-level drug selling through improved access to supplies, the availability of entry-level roles in drug distribution with a small capital investment, and the creation of "controlled" selling territo-ries with a guaranteed income (Johnson, Hamid, & Sanabria, 1990; Williams, 1989). The potential for high profits from selling first cocaine and then crack attracted young people into drug dealing in social areas where legitimate economic activity had decreased. The in-formal drug economy offered economic opportunities that replaced formal opportunities lost as capital flowed out of inner-city neighborhoods in the decades preceding the expan-sion of crack and cocaine powder markets.

Before cocaine became widely available, drug distribution was centralized, with a smaller street-level heroin network of users responsible for retail sales (Curtis, 1992; Johnson et al., 1985). After its price declined and cocaine became widely available, the discontinuity in distribution systems across successive drug eras created new opportunities for drug selling and may have encouraged participation in it. The sudden change in cocaine marketing from a restricted and controlled market in the 1970s to a fully deregulated market for crack spawned intense competition for territory and market share (Fagan, 1992a; Williams, 1989). Law enforcement officials in New York City characterized the crack industry as "capitalism gone mad" ("Report from the field," 1989).

In an era of declining formal economic activity, when the traditional exits from gang life were attenuated by a shrinking manufacturing base, drug selling offered strong economic incentives to young men who were largely unskilled workers and either displaced by shifts in the labor markets in the preceding decade or excluded from it due to skill and spatial mismatches. Participation in this sector carried with it considerable risk of arrest and physical victimization, however (Fagan & Chin, 1990). Thus, the new drug markets also offered opportunities to young persons who already had developed careers in the illicit economies through drug selling or violence.

Accordingly, the drug markets may have simply provided "work" for a surplus labor pool of unskilled workers who lacked sufficient human capital for successful involvement in a shrinking formal (legal) labor market and were excluded from it (Freeman, 1991). Alternately, the declining returns from formal work may have increased the salience of the illicit economy of drug selling and attracted people from the formal labor markets. Evidently, the people who benefited most from the expansion of the drug economy had limited employment prospects in the formal economy prior to their involvement with crack or other drugs— they were either unemployed or earning low wages. Perhaps earlier involvement with both crime and drug use adversely affected their labor market entry and participation (Freeman, 1992). Or their skills and mastery of illicit economic activities positioned them to make the most of lucrative opportunities created by the expansion of drug markets (Fagan, 1992a).

The Disruption of Intergenerational Job Networks

The decline of the manufacturing sector within urban centers fostered drug selling among gangs in indirect but important ways. First, it reduced legal economic opportunities that provided exits from gang life. In the past, manufacturing jobs provided entry positions on career ladders for African Americans and Latinos that provided stable if unspectacular earning potential (Farley & Allen, 1987), usually with the expectation of predictable annual increases and a cushion of health and other benefits. More recently, the public sector and jobs fueled by public spending (e.g., health care, social services) served similar functions for nonwhites entering the labor market. These jobs have become marginal as municipal and state fiscal crises worsen.

Second, the manufacturing decline depleted the informal social networks that provided access for each succeeding generation to enter the labor market. Within these networks, older workers (mostly males) provided information and personal contacts for young men to take advantage of job openings or union membership (see Anderson, 1990; Sullivan, 1989, for rich descriptions of how such networks operated). As employment was restructured and opportunities diminished, people with long-standing attachments to local employers both large and small began their exodus (Wilson, 1987, 1991). In turn, the job networks that facilitated each generation's entry into stable employment collapsed or were severely weakened. Both the economic opportunities themselves and the types of people who mediated adolescents' transition into young adulthood no longer were present or effective in the neighborhoods (Fagan, 1993).

Accordingly, economic change broke the intergenerational linkages that in the past helped each generation find its way to stable employment and immersion in conventional life roles. These relationships are critical elements in the social capital of a community (Coleman, 1988, 1990), an asset of the neighborhood that sustains both its economic viability and its social rules across generations. These linkages also are an important part of the informal social controls that mediate the interactions of individuals and the social contexts they live in. These processes play an important part not only in shaping the behavior of children and adolescents but also in mediating their access to economic opportunities and resources (Sampson, 1992).

In the past, the involvement of older residents provided young people with a range of models for adulthood and conveyed a vision of the future (Anderson, 1990). The departure of a generation of men who were the links to work also weakened the stabilizing influence of the remaining "old heads" both as teachers and mediators of adolescent behaviors (Anderson, 1990). Traditionally, old heads in a neighborhood would guide young men as they exited from gang life and entered stable life roles (Anderson, 1990; Moore, 1978; Vigil, 1988a). But the departure of old heads over a one- or two-decade span, or the decline in their influence as their own social situations worsened, created a void in the socialization of the neighborhoods' younger residents. The expectations of young people for the future changed from stable employment (in steady, if unspectacular jobs) to a bleak vision of chronic unemployment or low-wage earnings in low-status jobs where exploitation was common and hostility from Anglo employers was unchecked (see, e.g., Bourgois, 1989; Padilla, 1992).

In some inner-city communities, drug sellers replaced the old heads as the links to employment, role models for younger males and regulators of social and economic behaviors in poor urban neighborhoods (see, e.g., Anderson, 1990). In neighborhoods where gangs were active and influential participants in community life, their influence quickly expanded to fill this void. Gang influence as the dominant informal control and socialization force outweighed the influences of the schools, the licit economy, and legal institutions (see, e.g., Hagedorn, 1988, 1994a, 1994b).

Gang members in particular no longer could use the traditional exits from gang life to assume conventional jobs and instead looked to older gang members for stability of employment and income. Where gang careers in the past evolved through the natural stages of initiation, maintenance, and desistance, the exits from gang life to stable employment and conventional life roles no longer were salient. The pathways out of the gang either were closed off by the shrinking job market or became unattractive alternatives to street life where illicit incomes were available (though at the risk of physical danger or incarceration).

Without a diversity of job networks, the economic and social significance of the drug markets increase. The drug market appears to be an extreme form of labor market segmentation, with vast opportunities for entry in a diversity of roles. Participants in drug selling appear to be long-term participants with weak ties to legal work or newcomers whose weak skills excluded them from work (Fagan, 1992a). They are unskilled workers not well matched to either the service economy or technical jobs and lacking in the human capital necessary for success in the formal economy. They are matched both spatially and in terms of skills for the drug economy.

Although the restoration of intergenerational job networks appears to be essential to provide economically rational alternatives to participation in drug markets, the networks are ineffective without jobs to proffer. The relationships between residential patterns, social networks, and economic diversity are extremely complex and interdependent. And so long as successful residents leave their neighborhoods for better living circumstances, the daily patterns of social interaction that foster these networks of reciprocal social obligations will not develop. Accordingly, patterns of economic life, and the residential and social mobility within neighborhoods that result, are basic to sustaining the social capital that attenuates the allure of the drug economy.

The Institutionalization of Drug Markets

Changes in the economic and social organization of drug markets paralleled the changes in the formal labor market, and these reciprocal changes contributed to the growth of drug markets. The heroin markets from the 1970s were smaller than the crack market both in total volume of sales and the average purchase amount and quantity. Street-level drug selling in New York, for example, was a family centered heroin and marijuana business until the 1980s, when new organizations developed to control distribution of cocaine (Curtis, 1992; Johnson, Hamid & Sanabria, 1990). The psychoactive effects of heroin and methods of administration limited the volume of sales and the number of users. But cocaine was different in every way—a stimulant rather than a depressant, ingested in a variety of ways (nasally, smoked, or injected), and with a shorter half-life for the high. Moreover, it was portrayed for many years as a "safe" drug that was not addictive, did not interfere with other social activities, and the use of which could be easily self-controlled.

Accordingly, as a generation of drug users with favorable definitions of drug use entered the peak years of drug use, both supply and demand for drugs changed in this era, especially cocaine powder (Kozel & Adams, 1985). This fueled a rapid expansion of the drug economy in inner cities (Fagan, 1990; Johnson, Hamid, & Sanabria, 1990). Cheap cocaine became available early in the 1980s, following widespread demand that grew sharply both in inner cities and nationwide. As licit job opportunities declined and informal economic activity grew, involvement in crime generally and drug selling in particular was a natural development in neighborhoods with weakened social controls. Both for gangs and nongang youth, the drug economy provided economic opportunity, although with risks of legal problems and physical danger. The market expanded faster than the ability of existing drug networks to meet demand, creating economic opportunities for both individuals and organizations (Johnson, Hamid, & Sanabria, 1990), but also organizational violence between groups competing for market share and profits (Fagan & Chin, 1990).

The gains from drug selling also far exceeded what could be expected from legitimate work in a shrinking and highly segmented labor market. To the extent that decisions to sell drugs were shaped by the choices available, drug selling was a reasonable if not attractive option for economically marginal inner-city youth. In the closed milieu of these neighborhoods, the tales of extraordinary incomes had great salience and were widely accepted, even if the likelihood of such riches was exaggerated (Bourgois, 1989; Fagan, 1992a, 1993, 1996; MacCoun & Reuter, 1992; Reuter, MacCoun, & Murphy, 1990). The focus of socialization and expectations shifted from disorganized groups of adult males to (what was perceived as) highly organized and increasingly wealthy young drug sellers.

As drug selling expanded into declining local labor markets, it became institutionalized within the local economies of the neighborhoods. Drug selling in storefronts, from behind the counters in bodegas, on street corners, in crack or "freak" houses, and through several types of "fronts" was a common and visible feature of the neighborhoods (Hamid, 1992). Young men and, increasingly, women had several employment options within drug markets: support roles (lookout, steerer), manufacturing (cut, package), or direct street sales (Johnson, Hamid, & Sanabria, 1990). Legendary tales, with some truth, circulated about how a few dollars' worth of cocaine could be turned into several thousand dollars within a short time. These quick riches had incalculable appeal for people in chronic or desperate poverty.

With few conventional social or economic processes to counter it, and in increasingly physically and socially isolated circumstances, drug selling was institutionalized economically and socially within the neighborhoods. Drug selling became a common form of labor market participation, and young men began to talk about drug selling as "going to work" and the money earned as "getting paid" (Padilla, 1992). Many other sellers kept one foot in both licit and illicit work, lending ambiguity to definitions of work and income (Fagan, 1992a; Reuter et al., 1990).

Secondary economies sprang up to service the drug industry (see Taylor, 1990a). As the size and stakes (relative to legitimate income) of the cocaine economy grew, newcomers entered the business and willingly used violence as a regulatory process (Fagan & Chin, 1990). So too were other cultural norms: Exaggerated wealth skewed perceptions of status and achievement. Expectations of time frames for attainment of wealth were truncated based on the skewed tales of instant wealth.

Drug Markets and the Erosion of Social Controls

Just as the economy transformed fundamentally, the social processes that followed transformed too in basic ways. The interdependence of economic and social norms was evident in the social institutionalization of drug selling. In earlier eras, social interactions were organized and reinforced by economic structures. With the advent of drug economies in neighborhoods isolated from other economic and social influences, work and social interactions were now organized around these criminal activities, enforced and regulated increasingly by violence.

Social controls in weakened neighborhoods were overwhelmed by the volatile drug markets or violent crimes such as robbery (Fagan, 1992a; Hamid, 1990). Informal social controls broke down when social networks of neighborhood residents in changing communities were disrupted through high residential mobility or economic disruptions (Sampson, 1987; Skogan, 1990). Violence associated with crack resulted from several parallel processes: competition between sellers and protection of territory (Goldstein, 1989; Goldstein, Brownstein, Ryan, & Belluci, 1989); regulation of employees in new selling organizations (Cooper, 1987; Johnson, Hamid, & Sanabria, 1990; Williams, 1989); the urge for drugs or money to buy it among habitual users (Hamid, 1990; Reinarman, Waldorf, & Murphy, 1989); its liquid value among poor and poorly paid persons (Hamid, 1990); and for a small group, its psychoactive effects (Reinarman et al., 1989; Washton & Gold, 1987).

Collective supervision of youth, a critical source of informal social control and socialization, suffered as intergenerational relationships were disrupted. In turn, as employment in general and male employment in particular declined, the socialization of young people fell disproportionately on women or to formal authorities such as schools and legal institutions. Socialization by older residents of the neighborhoods became a passive or nonexistent process as these traditional forms of informal social control—cohesion among neighbors, social sanctions, group norms—became weaker. Again, these dynamics fostered conditions that facilitated the formation of youth groups into loosely structured gangs.

The Redistributive Function of Drug Selling

Drug selling often plays an important part of the economic context of the region surrounding each neighborhood, and several studies describe a political economy of drug distribution. Increasingly, poor neighborhoods alone could not sustain the dollar amounts and quantities that compose the drug industry (Fagan, 1992a, 1993; Padilla, 1992; Sullivan, 1991; Taylor, 1990a), and buyers from other areas are important contributors to the local drug economy. Accordingly, drug selling serves an important redistributive function in bringing money into the poor neighborhoods and fosters the interdependence between isolated poor neighborhoods and the areas surrounding them.

Drug sellers are suppliers of important goods and services to residents of more affluent areas (Sullivan, 1991), and the vitality of a drug market in a neighborhood is bound up with the relationships within poor neighborhoods and between these neighborhoods and other parts of their cities. To the extent that selling is spatially concentrated in a few areas, the interdependence of those areas with the larger city will sustain a drug market regardless of efforts to improve the material circumstances of its residents.

Class and Cultural Conflicts

One consequence of the structural transformation of urban neighborhoods has been the flight of middle-class residents to neighborhoods, towns, and villages surrounding the urban core (Wilson, 1987). Taking advantage of higher incomes, more stable and better-paying jobs, and the slow erosion of housing segregation in urban and suburban areas, middle-class residents of inner cities often moved out of their old neighborhoods. These former inner-city residents had themselves avoided poverty through ascension to professional, technical, and supervisory jobs in the public and private sector. They left behind the poorer residents in the inner cities, but their jobs often remained there. This was especially true for minorities with public sector jobs, but their only contact with their former inner-city neighbors or the children of those neighborhoods was in official capacities in institutional contexts. Often, these institutions were agencies of social control: welfare, schools, public health, and criminal justice. Class conflict was inevitable between those left behind and those returning as agents of social control.

An important consequence of the flight of the middle class from inner cities is the erosion of the political power that African Americans and other minorities had gained in the 1960s and 1970s (Skogan, 1990; Wilson, 1991). This loss of political power reversed gains made in earlier decades in the allocations of services and budgets. The exodus of middle-class residents of inner-city neighborhoods weakened the efforts of community organizers to fight plant closings, stave off job loss, and counter the trend toward the recentralization of social and health services (Fagan, 1992b).

These losses weigh heavily in poor communities and on adolescents living there. The repair of streets and removal of snow or garbage, the allocations of resources to schools or libraries, and the tenor of legal institutions all reflect the political power of the neighborhood. These important features of urban life also are essential to limiting the effects of community decline (Skogan, 1990), or what Wilson and Kelling (1982) referred to as the "broken windows" syndrome. These political dimensions also interact with social resources to strengthen social controls and increase the personal investments and commitments of the individuals who live there (Reiss, 1986b; Sampson & Groves, 1989).

Isolation and Insulation of Neighborhoods

By 1980, poor urban families were more likely to have poor neighbors than a generation earlier (Wilson, 1987). Although increases in urban poverty per se contributed in part to this trend, residential segregation along racial and economic lines was the primary cause for the growing concentration of poor people in inner cities (Massey, 1990). Together with growing income inequality between African Americans and whites (Moss & Tilly, 1991) and the opening of housing and job opportunities to minorities outside the urban core, poor urban dwellers became increasingly isolated physically, economically, and culturally. Predictably, the concentration of poor people in poor areas has had negative effects on the ability of neighborhoods to shape the lives of their residents. When social norms and values develop in a homogeneously poor context, void of material and social inducements toward conventional norms, the ties of the residents to the social contract are attenuated and deviance is a logical and perhaps inevitable adaptation (Elliott et al., in press).

As the middle-class residents of the urban core left for the better housing and schools of the suburbs or the promise of greater racial tolerance in integrated neighborhoods, the insulation of the neighborhoods was reinforced by the depletion of the housing stock and the flight of basic commercial services. In gang cities including Detroit (Taylor, 1990a) and South Central Los Angeles (Quicker, 1992), thriving commercial districts transformed within a decade into areas dominated by liquor stores and fast-food outlets. In turn, the informal commercial activity that vitalized street life also was weakened. For example, the health food and craft shops in the Caribbean shopping districts in Brooklyn closed down (Hamid, 1990). These services, which often were locally owned, closed or moved elsewhere, removing jobs and the small amount of capital they created. These stores and the traffic they generated were stabilizing parts of both the commercial and the cultural life of the neighborhood. Their departure altered the normative patterns of interaction that constituted "street life," an important part of the social regulation of behaviors for young people.

Social and economic isolation not only may complicate efforts to escape poverty but can foster beliefs that poverty is inevitable and another life is beyond the reach of most inner-city residents. The concentration of poor people within poor neighborhoods, compounded by segregation (Massey & Eggers, 1990) narrows residents' visions of a better life in the near term and changes their expectations for the future.

In Detroit, for example, both racial and income segregation worsened following the devastating 1967 riots (Taylor, 1990a). The spatial patterns of development, especially transit, that had developed there beginning in the 1940s (when the worst U.S. race riots took place) provided a means by which workers could work in Detroit by day and escape each night to the surrounding suburbs. According to Taylor, freeway patterns in Detroit show how the isolation of the neighborhoods was planned and institutionalized: All roads provide entry and exit paths to the suburban ring but no facilitation of an internal traffic flow across city neighborhoods (see Skogan, 1990).

The concentration of poor people in poor neighborhoods, without expectations for improvement, has shaped their social interactions and economic relationships. Their physical and social isolation tends to block out influences from outside the neighborhood, and natural processes such as social comparisons and contagion can become skewed and distorted through a lens of poverty. The social norms that developed in this context are likely to be influenced by the informal and illicit economies, which will confer a disproportionate share of both economic wealth and, in turn, social status when legal work is not an option.

In these circumstances, the significance and social status attached to gang membership in several neighborhoods is obvious. The social isolation of poor neighborhoods skews social norms and ensures that contagion of norms and values will be amplified within a closed social system (Elliott et al., in press; Tienda, 1991). Thus, the social status of drug selling increases when drug income is the primary route to gaining both the material symbols of success and wealth and social standing in the neighborhood. For young men, the drug industry offers many of the benefits of self-determination and economic independence so cherished in the broader culture in Horatio Alger stories or an escape from the petty humiliations and harassment faced by nonwhites in the segmented labor markets for unskilled and manufacturing labor (Bourgois, 1995).

THE FUTURE: THE INSTITUTIONALIZATION OF GANGS

Stability and change characterize street gangs in the United States in the post-World War II era. Stability is evident in the lasting importance of gangs in urban neighborhoods in cities throughout the country. Gangs continue to be developmentally important for adolescents even as the social meaning of adolescence itself changes. The basic "form" of street gangs has endured for decades, even as between-gang variability in gang structures and cohesion continues from era to era (Klein, 1995a; Short, 1996; Spergel, 1995). Ethnicity, fighting, status, getting high, and community are themes as important to gang members today as they were nearly half a century ago.

Change, too, is evident in gangs in the past decade, changes that reflect shifts in the social and economic structure of the United States since the 1960s. Drug selling has become a common part of the economic lives of some gang members. Gang violence has become more lethal, as has violence among adolescents generally. Gangs have emerged in small cities and suburbs, in many cases borrowing the names and reproducing the behaviors of big-city gangs (Klein, 1995a). With the arrival of new ethnic groups in large and small cities, gangs emerge as a natural organizational form for the marginalized among their adolescents (Vigil & Yun, 1990; Vigil, Yun, & Long, 1992). Economic goals now compete with neighborhood defense and ethnic solidarity as motivations for gang participation and conflict, in some cases changing the organizational logic and structure of gangs. Young men and women marginalized from adult social and economic roles now remain in gangs longer, often into their early and middle adult years when in the past they might have left gangs to enter stable careers and start families. In some cases, ties to adult crime groups have become more functional and efficient as prison populations have grown (Moore, 1991; Skolnick et al., 1988).

The structural changes in U.S. society that gave rise to these new forms of gangs and ganging will not easily be undone. If gangs have evolved in a way that responds to the new social, economic, and cultural realities of the late 20th century, then gangs may become a durable and lasting feature of adolescent and neighborhood life—that is, gangs may become institutionalized in U.S. suburbs and cities as a part of the social and cultural ecology of neighborhoods and a career choice for young adolescents that may compete with diminishing jobs and other social roles. What will a future look like when gangs are institutionalized in the social and cultural life of communities and compete with schools and other institutions as sources of opportunity and social control?

Gangs as Work   Illegal markets compete effectively with legal markets in many urban areas, raising the stakes on crime incomes as prospects for legal incomes decline. In the past, the economic returns from hustling and petty crime were a small and often unimportant part of gang life. Today, the increasing importance of the economic dimension of gang life fits well with declining wages for unskilled workers and the changing structure of labor markets. Drug markets have had important impacts on the balance of legal and illegal work and on expectations of young people about the monetary returns from the drug business (see, e.g., Mayer, 1989). As Sullivan (1989) notes, crime will become perceptually interchangeable with legal work.

Just as gangs continue to provide status opportunities, they may also replace the unskilled labor market as a primary source of economic opportunity. As wages for unskilled work remain flat or fall, illegal work becomes more salient and attractive (Fagan, 1996). Thus, the economic opportunity structure of gangs is likely to compete with, or in some cases even replace, the unattractive and shrinking opportunity structure of the legal labor market.[10]

The politics of crime control, the political demand for punishment, and the expansion of the gang enforcement "industry" also will contribute to these trends (Klein, 1995a). Gangs will increasingly become the target of specialized enforcement efforts, fueling an already overheated correctional population. But recall that early incarceration experiences disadvantage adolescents, especially males, as they attempt to enter legal labor markets (Fagan & Freeman, in press; Hagan, 1993; Sampson & Laub, 1993). The weight of mandatory incarceration and longer sentencing policies has fallen disproportionately on nonwhite males in urban areas, especially those involved in drug offenses (Tonry, 1995). Accordingly, the transition to work will be increasingly difficult for young males with criminal histories, contributing to the social and economic attractions of illegal work and the weakening of social control that legal work often provides.

Gang Careers   Longer gang "careers" are one of the important changes in gangs over the past decade (Klein, 1995a). As young adults remain in gangs longer, their own crime and their influence on the crime rates of younger members is likely to increase. If rates of crime and violence increase among adolescents during periods of gang involvement (Thornberry et al., 1993), longer gang careers will mean longer involvement in violence and other crimes. Age grading also is likely to influence the crime rates of younger gang members, as older gang members create more circumstances where violence and other crimes occur.

Gang violence will continue to provide a primary source of status within gangs.[11] As the number of gang cities and gangs increase, clashes between rival gangs in new gang cities may be more likely as new gangs emerge and compete for status and territory. Gang members vying for status in emerging gangs may be sensitive to the challenges to "honor" and "respect" that require a violent response. This may provide motivation for the formation of still newer gangs, incentives for individuals to join them, and opportunities for conflicts to arise between newly formed gangs. Accordingly, one consequence of the growth in gangs and groups such as "tagbangers" (Klein, 1995a) may be an increase in the number of adolescents involved in gangs and an increase in their crime participation.

Like other adolescent violence, gang violence is likely to continue to be lethal. There are several pushes in this direction. For example, the presence and availability of large-caliber automatic weapons changes strategic thinking about violence, and this technology makes participation in lethal violence easier (Zimring & Hawkins, in press). The widespread possession of these weapons creates an "ecology of fear" among gang members, making violence a first and final tactic that preempts retaliation (Fagan & Wilkinson, in press-a, in press-b). As young people "come up" in this climate, their perceptions of danger from other gang members will continue to motivate lethal violence as a means of survival.

Young Women and Gangs   The roles of young women in gangs have changed in the past decade. Today, there is female membership in previously all-male gangs, as well as female gangs (Campbell, 1990b). Not much is known about female gangs, however, and predictions here are especially risky. Women in gangs face a dual fight: conflicts with males over gender roles and conflicts with other gangs (Taylor, 1993). Also, developmental contexts for young women have changed at the same times and in the same ways as have the contexts for males, and the generally weaker social controls provide a context for women to assume social roles that reflect "street life," including street gangs (Anderson, 1994). Hypermasculinity and conflicts between males and females also provide motivation for women to "show heart" to avoid exploitation by men (Taylor, 1993). The motivations for ganging among young women may be weaker and shorter in duration compared to their male counter-parts, however. For example, the barriers to women entering the workforce are weaker than those facing men, easing their transition from adolescence to adult roles and reducing the influence of the gang in their everyday social and economic lives.

Whatever the future of female gangs, the trend toward young women to demand status and respect is likely to continue. Whether this results in the emergence of gangs and groups of women and whether these groups are less cohesive and more transient is too hard to say. Nevertheless, the "traditional" role of female auxiliaries is gone, replaced by women struggling for respect and autonomy against male dominance, both in gangs and outside them.[12]

The Institutionalization of Gangs in Communities

Gangs have been a recurrent criminological problem for centuries. Their importance has varied over different eras, emerging in times of social change to occupy a central role in political conversations about crime and delinquency. Because gangs usually have been transient features of cities and a predictable but finite developmental phase for youth from blue-collar and poor neighborhoods, gangs have not been institutionalized in most places. In a few cities, gangs have been institutionalized for generations. But in other cities, such as Philadelphia and New York, gangs have declined in importance in recent decades or even disappeared.

Gangs have emerged today in more cities than ever before, however, in response to profound social structural changes, fueled by processes of rapid and efficient cultural diffusion, and sustained by a gang enforcement apparatus that itself has diffused to legal institutions across the country. Initially fueled by changes in drug and other illegal markets, the economic function of gangs has become more prominent for gang members and now lives side by side with the traditional motivations of neighborhood and self-defense. Whether gangs will be institutionalized in the social organization of small and large cities, or whether they will continue to be a transient social phenomenon that comes and goes across generations, is as yet unknown.

The future of gangs is tied to the future of urban crises in social control, social structure, labor markets, and cultural processes in a rapidly changing political and economic context. Although gangs will continue to be a part of the urban (and, increasingly, the suburban) landscape, their institutionalization will depend on a series of interdependent tipping points: the threshold of gangs as dominant sources of socialization and social control, the threshold of social and economic marginalization of neighborhoods and communities, the cultural diffusion and reproduction of gangs and ganging, the levels of violence by and against adolescents, and the responses of legal institutions to recurring developmental crises of adolescents in a highly segmented social structure. Of course, gangs may fade as another transient social form, culturally rejected and replaced by some other, as yet unenvisioned, structure of adolescence. This seems unlikely, however. The future of gangs may be uncertain, but recurring social crises in the coming decades are likely to ensure that gangs will be an important part of the future.

QUESTIONS FOR UNDERSTANDING AND CRITICAL THINKING

1. How have gangs evolved over time and how has this altered gang typologies?
2. To what extent are gang members involved in violent crimes, substance use, and drug sales?
3. Review and discuss the various social and economic effects that may be associated with the formation and continuation of contemporary gangs.
4. Will gangs one day become "institutionalized" in our communities?

NOTES

1. See Sante (1991) for a detailed history of gangs in New York beginning in the 18th century.
2. Saint Francis of Assisi commented that nothing gave him greater pleasure than stealing in the company of his friends. English common law in the 13th century accorded especially harsh punishments to the roving bands of youth who moved across the countryside stealing from farmers and merchants. The House of Refuge, the first U.S. institution for delinquent boys, opened in New York City in 1824, largely in response to the unsupervised groups of youth who roamed the city stealing and drinking (Rothman, 1980).
3. Virtually every gang ethnography illustrates this point (see, e.g., Hagedorn, 1988; Campbell, 1990b; Stumphauzer, Veloz, & Aiken, 1981; Vigil, 1988a; Padilla, 1992; Moore, 1978, 1991, 1992; Taylor, 1990a, 1993).
4. Vigil (1988a) notes that these patterns are confined to substances that enhance gang social processes—alcohol, marijuana, PCP, and crack cocaine. There is a sanction against heroin use among Chicano gangs. Heroin involvement is seen as a betrayal of the gang and the barrio: One cannot be loyal to his addiction and the addict ("tecato") culture while maintaining loyalty to the gang.

5. See Burns (1980) for a similar account involving youth in drinking locations in and around Boston.

6. Drug *use* among gang members also is highly variable, ranging from drug use tied to specific so-cial contexts (Vigil, 1988a) to total abstinence (Chin, 1990; Taylor, 1990a). Gang members in my three-city study (Fagan, 1989) also varied in their use of alcohol, marijuana, and more serious drugs. The types of drugs used and the contexts that influence them are as variable for gang mem-bers as they are for nongang youth in cities across the country.

7. To better illustrate the higher expected returns from drug selling, Hagedorn (1994a, pp. 202–203, Table 2) reports, "The *maximum* amount of money earned monthly by any gang member from le-gal income was $2,400, the *mean* for gang drug sales."

8. See Sullivan (1989), Padilla (1992), Taylor, (1990a, 1990b), Waldorf (1992), and Williams (1989). For example, Felix Padilla (1992) describes how gang members in a Puerto Rican Chicago neighborhood regarded low-level drug sellers in their gang as "working stiffs" who were being exploited by other gang members.

9. Official employment statistics are quite limited in portraying trends in unemployment or labor market participation more generally. Jencks (1991) points out that youth unemployment appears to rise during periods when school attendance increases, because students technically are not in the labor force. Fagen (1992b) shows the increase in the residual pool of long-term unemployed and low educated males below 25 years of age since 1970 in the six study cities. Equally impor-tant is the exclusion of "discouraged workers" who drop out of the hunt for work, also participants in the informal economy. Income from crime and drug selling are excluded not only from formal employment but also from most estimates of the informal economy (Sassen-Koob, 1989).

10. One trend we are unlikely to see is the transition of street gangs into adult organized crime groups. For decades, very few gangs have evolved from adolescent street gangs into adult criminal organi-zations. Nevertheless, adult organizations have had a mediating role in the future of gangs in sev-eral studies, from Cloward and Ohlin (1960) to Chin (1995a). Will adult organizations continue to influence gangs and gang youth? There is only weak evidence of gangs generally forming into the types of adult criminal organizations that have been evident among Chinese and Italian street gangs. This is not likely to change. Adult criminal organizations in these two ethnic groups have historical origins in the social structure and culture of their native countries. Moreover, there is little evidence of street gangs developing into adult groups. Chin (1990, 1995a) portrays street gangs as a contract labor force for adult groups who use these economic relationships as a source of social control. "Tal-ented" young gang members may be brought into the adult groups, much in the same way that some college athletes or minor league baseball players are brought into professional sports.

   There are weak parallels for street gangs today. There is some interaction between Chicano street gangs in Southern California and prison gangs, but there remains a disjuncture between the adolescent and adult groups (Moore, 1992b). There is no evidence of adult organized crime groups among other ethnic groups, such as drug gangs, evolving from street gangs or incorpo-rating these gangs into their organizations (Hagedorn, 1994a, 1994b; Klein, 1995a). The transi-tion remains one of individuals, not of groups.

11. This is a consistent theme in gang research (see, e.g., Cohen, 1955; Sanchez-Jankowski, 1991).

12. See, for example, Chesney-Lind, 1993.

REFERENCES

ANDERSON, E. (1990). *Streetwise: Race, class, and change in an urban community.* Chicago: Uni-versity of Chicago Press.

ANDERSON, E. (1994, May). The code of the streets. *Atlantic Monthly,* pp. 81–94.

BOGARDUS, E. (1943). Gangs of Mexican-American youth. *Sociology and Social Research, 28,* 55–66.

BOURGOIS, P. (1989). In search of Horatio Alger: Culture and ideology in the crack economy. *Contemporary Drug Problems, 16*(4), 619–650.

BOURGOIS, P. (1995). *In search of respect: Selling crack in El Barrio*. New York: Cambridge University Press.

BUFORD, B. (1991). *Among the thugs: The experience, and the seduction of, crowd violence*. New York: Norton.

BURNS, T. F. (1980). Getting rowdy with the boys. *Journal of Drug Issues, 10*, 273–286.

BURSIK, R. J., JR., & GRASMICK, H. G. (1993). *Neighborhoods and crime*. New York: Lexington.

CAMPBELL, A. (1990b). *The girls in the gang* (2nd ed.). New Brunswick: Rutgers University Press.

CANADA, G. (1995). *Fist, stick, knife, gun*. Boston: Beacon.

CHESNEY-LIND, M. (1993). Girls, gangs and violence: Anatomy of a backlash. *Humanity and Society, 7*, 321–344.

CHIN, K. (1990). *Chinese subculture and criminality: Non-traditional crime groups in America*. Westport, CT: Greenwood.

CHIN, K. (1995a). *Chinatown gangs*. New York: Oxford University Press.

CHIN, K., & FAGAN, J. (1994). Social order and the formation of Chinese youth gangs. *Advances in Criminological Theory, 6*, 149–162.

CLOWARD, R. A., & OHLIN, L. E. (1960). *Delinquency and opportunity: A theory of delinquent gangs*. Glencoe, IL: Free Press.

COHEN, A. K. (1955). *Delinquent boys: The culture of the gang*. Glencoe, IL: Free Press.

COLEMAN, J. S. (1988). Social capital in the creation of human capital. *American Journal of Sociology, 94*(Suppl.), S95–S120.

COLEMAN, J. S. (1990). *Foundations of social theory*. Cambridge, MA: Harvard University Press.

COOPER, B. M. (1987, December 1). Motor city breakdown. *Village Voice*, pp. 23–35.

CURRY, G. D., & SPERGEL, I. A. (1988). Gang homicide, delinquency, and community. *Criminology, 26*, 381–405.

CURTIS, R. A. (1992). Highly structured crack markets in the southside of Williamsburg, Brooklyn. In J. Fagan (Ed.), *The ecology of crime and drug use in inner cities*. New York: Social Science Research Council.

DOLAN, E. F., & FINNEY, S. (1984). *Youth gangs*. New York: Julian Messner.

DOYLE, D., & LUCKENBILL, D. (1991). Mobilizing law in response to collective problems: A test of Black's theory of law. *Law & Society Review. 25*, 103–116.

ELLIOTT, D., WILSON, W. J., HUIZINGA, D., SAMPSON, R. J., ELLIOTT, A., & RANKIN, B. (in press). The effects of neighborhood disadvantage on adolescent development. *Journal of Research in Crime and Delinquency*.

FAGAN, J. (1989). The social organization of drug use and drug dealing among urban gangs. *Criminology, 27*(4), 633–669.

FAGAN, J. (1990). Social processes of delinquency and drug use among urban gangs. In C. R. Huff (Ed.), *Gangs in America* (1st ed.), Newbury Park, CA: Sage.

FAGAN, J. (1992a). Drug selling and licit income in distressed neighborhoods: The economic lives of drug users and dealers. In G. Peterson & A. Harrell (Eds.), *Drugs, crime and social isolation*. Washington DC: Urban Institute Press.

FAGAN, J. (1992b). The dynamics of crime and neighborhood change. In J. Fagan (Ed.), *The ecology of crime and drug use in inner cities*. New York: Social Science Research Council.

FAGAN, J. (1993). The political economy of drug dealing among urban gangs. In R. Davis, A. Lurigio, & D. P. Rosenbaum (Eds.), *Drugs and community* (pp. 19–54). Springfield, IL: Charles C. Thomas.

FAGAN, J. (1996). Legal and illegal work: Crime, work, and unemployment. In B. Weisbrod & J. Worthy (Eds.), *Dealing with urban crisis: Linking research to action*. Evanston IL: Northwestern University Press.

FAGAN, J. (in press). The dynamics of crime and neighborhood change. In J. Fagan (Ed.), *The ecology of crime and drug use in inner cities*. New York: Social Science Research Council.

FAGAN, J., & CHIN, K. (1990). Violence as regulation and social control in the distribution of crack. In M. de la Rosa, E. Lambert, & B. Gropper (Eds.), *Drugs and violence* (Research Monograph No. 103). Rockville, MD: U.S. Public Health Service, National Institute on Drug Abuse.

FAGAN, J., & FREEMAN, R. (in press). Crime, work, and unemployment. In M. Tonry (Ed.), *Crime and justice: A review of research.* Chicago: University of Chicago Press.

FAGAN, J., & WILKINSON, D. L. (in press-a). Firearms and youth violence. In D. Stoff, J. Breiling, & J. Maser (Eds.), *Handbook of antisocial behavior.* New York: Wiley.

FAGAN, J., & WILKINSON, D. L. (in press-b). The role of scripts in understanding gun violence among adolescents. *Law and Contemporary Problems.*

FARLEY, R., & ALLEN, W. R. (1987). *The color line and the quality of life in America.* New York: Russell Sage.

FARRINGTON, D. P. (1985). Age and crime. In M. Tonry & N. Morris (Eds.), *Crime and justice: An annual review of research* (Vol. 7, pp. 189–250). Chicago: University of Chicago Press.

FELDMAN, H. W., MANDEL, J., & FIELDS, A. (1985). In the neighborhood: A strategy for delivering early intervention services to young drug users in their natural environments. In A. S. Friedman & G. M. Beschner (Eds.), *Treatment services for adolescent substance abusers.* Rockville MD: National Institute or Drug Abuse.

FREEMAN, R. B. (1991). Employment and earnings of disadvantaged young men in a labor shortage economy. In C. Jencks & P. E. Peterson (Eds.), *The urban underclass.* Washington DC: Brookings Institution.

FREEMAN, R. B. (1992). Crime and the economic status of disadvantaged young men. In G. Peterson & A. Harrell (Eds.), *Drugs, crime and social isolation.* Washington DC: Urban Institute Press.

GOLDSTEIN, P. J. (1989). Drugs and violent crime. In N. A. Weiner & M. E. Wolfgang (Eds.), *Pathways to violent crime.* Newbury Park, CA: Sage.

GOLDSTEIN, P. J., BROWNSTEIN, H. H., RYAN, P., & BELLUCI, P. A. (1989). Crack and homicide in New York City, 1989: A conceptually-based event analysis. *Contemporary Drug Problems 16,* 651–687.

HAGAN, J. (1993). The social embeddedness of crime and unemployment. *Criminology, 31,* 465–492.

HAGEDORN, J. M. (1994a). Homeboys, Dope Fiends, Legits, and New Jacks. *Criminology, 32,* 197–219.

HAGEDORN, J. M. (1994b). Neighborhoods, markets, and gang drug organization. *Journal of Research in Crime and Delinquency, 32,* 197–219.

HAGEDORN, J. M. (with Macon, P.). (1988). *People and folks: gangs, crime, and the underclass in a rustbelt city.* Chicago: Lake View Press.

HAMID, A. (1990). The political economy of crack-related violence. *Contemporary Drug Problems, 17*(1), 31–78.

HAMID, A. (1992). Flatbush: A freelance nickels market. In J. Fagan (Ed.), *The ecology of crime and drug use in inner cities.* New York: Social Science Research Council.

HOCHSCHILD, J. L. (1989). Equal opportunity and the estranged poor. *Annals of the American Academy of Political and Social Science, 501,* 143–155.

HUFF, C. R. (1989). Youth gangs and public policy. *Crime & Delinquency, 35,* 524–537.

HUFF, C. R. (1994). Gangs in the United States. In A. Goldstein & C. R. Huff (Eds.), *The gang intervention handbook* (pp. 3–20). Champaign, IL: Research Press.

HUNT, D. (1990). Drugs and consensual crimes: Drug dealing and prostitution. In J. Q. Wilson & M. Tonry (Eds.), *Crime and justice: An annual review of research. Vol. 13: Drugs and crime.* Chicago: University of Chicago Press.

JACKSON, P. I. (1991). Crime, youth gangs, and urban transition: The social dislocations of postindustrial economic development. *Justice Quarterly, 8,* 379–397.

JARRETT, R. (1994). Living poor: Family life among single parent, African-American women. *Social Problems, 41*, 30–49.

JENCKS, C. (1991). Is the American underclass growing? In C. Jencks & P. E. Peterson (Eds.), *The urban underclass*. Washington DC: Brookings Institute.

JIMINEZ, J. B. (1989). Cocaine, informality, and the urban economy in La Paz, Bolivia. In A. Portes, M. Castells, & L. Benton (Eds.), *The informal economy*. Baltimore: Johns Hopkins University Press.

JOHNSON, B. D., HAMID, A., & SANABRIA, H. (1990). Emerging models of crack distribution. In T. Mieczkowski (Ed.), *Drugs and crime: A reader.* Boston: Allyn-Bacon.

JOHNSON, B. D., WILLIAMS, T., DEI, K., & SANABRIA, H. (1990). Drug abuse and the inner city: Impacts of hard drug use and sales on low income communities. In J. Q. Wilson & M. Tonry (Eds.), *Drugs and crime*. Chicago: University of Chicago Press.

KASARDA, J. D. (1988). Jobs, migration and emerging urban mismatches. In M. G. H. McGeary & L. E. Lynn (Eds.), *Urban change and poverty* (pp. 148–198). Washington DC: National Academy Press.

KASARDA, J. D. (1989). Urban industrial transition and the underclass. *Annals of the American Academy of Political and Social Science, 501*, 26–47.

KASARDA, J. D. (1992). The severely distressed in economically transforming cities. In G. Peterson & A. Harrell (Eds.), *Drugs, crime and social isolation*. Washington DC: Urban Institute Press.

KLEIN, M. W. (1995a). *The American street gang: Its nature, prevalence, and control.* New York: Oxford University Press.

KLEIN, M. W., MAXSON, C. L., & CUNNINGHAM, L. C. (1991). "Crack," street gangs, and violence. *Criminology, 29*(4), 623–650.

KOZEL, N. J., & ADAMS, E. H. (Eds.). (1985). *Cocaine use in America: Epidemiological and clinical perspectives* (National Institute of Drug Abuse Research Monograph No. 61). Rockville MD: U.S. Department of Health and Human Services.

LANZETTA, M. DE P., CASTANO, G. M., & SOTO, A. T. (1989). The articulation of formal and informal sectors in the economy of Bogota, Colombia. In A. Portes, M. Castells, & L. Benton (Eds.), *The informal economy*. Baltimore: Johns Hopkins University Press.

MACCOUN, R., & REUTER, P. (1992). Are the wages of sin $30 an hour? Economic aspects of street-level drug dealing. *Crime & Delinquency, 38*, 477–491.

MACLEOD, J. (1987). *Aint no makin it: Leveled aspirations in a low-income neighborhood*. Boulder, CO: Westview.

MASSEY, D. S. (1990). American apartheid. *American Journal of Sociology, 96*, 329–357.

MAXSON, C. L., & KLEIN, M. W. (1989). Street gang violence. In N. A. Weiner & M. E. Wolfgang (Eds.), *Pathways to criminal violence*. Newbury Park, CA: Sage.

MAYER, J. (1989, September 8). In the war on drugs, toughest foe may be that alienated youth. *Wall Street Journal*, p. 1.

MCGAHEY, R. (1986). Economic conditions, neighborhood organization and urban crime. In A. J. Reiss, Jr., & M. Tonry (Eds.), *Communities and crime* (pp. 231–270). Chicago: University of Chicago Press.

MIECZKOWSKI, T. (1986). Geeking up and throwing down: Heroin street life in Detroit. *Criminology, 24*, 645–666.

MOORE, J. W. (1978). *Homeboys: Gangs, drugs and prison in the barrics of Los Angeles*. Philadelphia: Temple University Press.

MOORE, J. W. (1991). *Going down to the barrio: Homeboys and homegirls in change*. Philadelphia: Temple University Press.

MOORE, J. W. (1992). Institutionalized youth gangs: Why white fence and El Hoyo Maravilla change so slowly. In J. Fagan (Ed.), *The ecology of crime and drug use in inner cities*. New York: Social Science Research Council.

Moss, P., & Tilly, C. (1991). *Why black men are doing worse in the labor market: A review of supply-side and demand-side explanations* (Paper prepared for the Social Science Research Council, Committee on Research on the Urban Underclass, Subcommittee on Joblessness and the Underclass). New York: Social Science Research Council.

Padilla, F. (1992). *The gang as an American enterprise*. New Brunswick, NJ: Rutgers University Press.

Padilla, F. (1993). The working gang. In S. Cummings & D. J. Monti (Eds.), *Gangs* (pp. 173–192). Albany: State University of New York Press.

Quicker, J. (with Galeai, Y. N., & Batani-Khalfani, A). (1992). Bootstrap or noose? Drugs, gangs, and violence in South Central Los Angeles. In J. Fagan (Ed.), *The ecology of crime and drug use in inner cities*. New York: Social Science Research Council.

Reinarman, C., Waldorf, D., & Murphy, S. (1989, November). *The call of the pipe: Freebasing and crack use as norm-bound episodic compulsion*. Paper presented at the Annual Meeting of the American Society of Criminology, Reno, NV.

Reiss, A. J., Jr. (1986b). Why are communities important in understanding crime? In A. J. Reiss, Jr., & M. Tonry (Eds.), *Communities and crime* (pp. 1–33). Chicago: University of Chicago Press.

Report from the field on an endless war. (1989, March 12). *New York Times*, Sec. 4, p. 1.

Reuter, P., MacCoun, R., & Murphy, P. (1990). *Money from crime* (Report R-3894). Santa Monica, CA: RAND.

Rothman, D. J. (1980). *Conscience and convenience: The asylum and its alternatives in progressive America*. Boston: Little, Brown.

Sampson, R. J. (1987). Urban black violence: The effect of male joblessness and family disruption. *American Journal of Sociology, 93*(2), 348–382.

Sampson, R. J. (1992). Family management and child development: Insights from social disorganization theory. In J. McCord (Ed.), *Facts, forecasts, and frameworks* (pp. 63–92). New Brunswick, NJ: Transaction.

Sampson, R. J., & Groves, W. B. (1989). Community structure and crime: Testing social disorganization theory. *American Journal of Sociology, 94*, 774–802.

Sampson, R. J., & Laub, J. H. (1993). *Crime in the making: Pathways and turning points through life*. Cambridge, MA: Harvard University Press.

Sanchez-Jankowski, M. (1991). *Islands in the street: Gangs and American urban society*. Berkeley: University of California Press.

Sante, L. (1991). *Low life: Lures and snares of old New York*. New York: Farrar, Giroux and Straus.

Sassen, S. (1991). The informal economy. In J. H. Mollenkopf & M. Castells (Eds.), *Dual city: Restructuring New York*. New York: Russell Sage.

Sassen-Koob, S. (1989). New York City's informal economy. In A. Portes, M. Castells, & L. A. Benton (Eds.), *The informal economy: Studies in advanced and less developed countries* (pp. 60–77). Baltimore: Johns Hopkins University Press.

Shannon, L. W. (1986). Ecological effects of the hardening of the inner city. In R. M. Figlio, S. Hakim, & G. F. Rengert (Eds.), *Metropolitan crime patterns* (pp. 27–54). Monsey NY: Criminal Justice Press.

Sheley, J., Wright, J., & Smith, M. D. (1993, November-December). Kids, guns and killing fields. *Society*, pp. 84–87.

Short, J. F., Jr., & Strodtbeck, F. L. (1965/1974). *Group process and gang delinquency*. Chicago: University of Chicago Press.

Short, J. F. Personal, gang & community careers. (1996). In: C. R. Huff (Ed.), *Gangs in America* (2nd ed., pp. 221–240). Newbury Park, CA: Sage.

Skogan, W. (1990). *Disorder and decline*. New York: Free Press.

SKOLNICK, J. H., CORREL, T., NAVARRO, E., & RABB, R. (1988). *The social structure of street drug dealing* (monograph). Sacramento: Office of the Attorney General, State of California.

SPERGEL, I. A. (1988). *Report of the Law Enforcement Youth Gang Symposium.* Chicago: School of Social Service Administration, University of Chicago.

SPERGEL, I. A. (1989). Youth gangs: Continuity and change. In N. Morris & M. Tonry (Eds.), *Crime and justice: An annual review of research* (Vol. 12). Chicago: University of Chicago Press.

SPERGEL, I. A. (1995). *The youth gang problem: A community approach.* New York: Oxford University Press.

STEPICK, A. (1989). Miami's two informal sectors. In A. Portes, M. Castells, & L. Benton (Eds.), *The informal economy.* Baltimore: Johns Hopkins University Press.

STUMPHAUZER, J. S., VELOZ, E. V., & AIKEN, T. W. (1981). Violence by street gangs: East Side story? In R. B. Stuart (Ed.), *Violent behavior: Social learning approaches to prediction, management, and treatment* (pp. 68–82). New York: Brunner-Mazel.

SULLIVAN, M. (1989). *Getting paid: Youth crime and unemployment in three urban neighborhoods.* New York: Cornell University Press.

SULLIVAN, M. (1991). Crime and the social fabric. In J. Mollenkopf & M. Castells (Eds.), *The dual city.* New York: Russell Sage.

TAYLOR, C. S. (1990a). *Dangerous society.* East Lansing: Michigan State University Press.

TAYLOR, C. S. (1990b). Gang imperialism. In C. R. Huff (Ed.), *Gangs in America* (1st ed.). Newbury Park, CA: Sage.

TAYLOR, C. S. (1993). *Girls, gangs, women, and drugs.* East Lansing: Michigan State University Press.

TAYLOR, D. G., TAUB, R. P., & PETERSON, B. L. (1986). Crime, community organization, and causes of neighborhood decline. In R. M. Figlio, S. Hakim, & G. F. Rengert (Eds.), *Metropolitan crime patterns.* Monsey NY: Willow Tree Press.

TAYLOR, R., & COVINGTON, J. (1988). Neighborhood changes in ecology and violence. *Criminology, 26,* 553–590.

THORNBERRY, T., KROHN, M., LIZOTTE, A., & CHARD-WIERSCHEM, D. (1993). The role of juvenile gangs in facilitating delinquent behavior. *Journal of Research in Crime and Delinquency, 30*(1), 55–87.

THRASHER, F. M. (1963). *The gang: A study of 1313 gangs in Chicago.* Chicago: University of Chicago Press. (Abridged ed.; Original work published 1927; Rev. ed., 1936)

TIENDA, M. (1989). Puerto Ricans and the underclass debate. *Annals of the American Academy of Political and Social Science, 501,* 105–119.

TIENDA, M. (1991). Poor people and poor places: Deciphering neighborhood effects on poverty outcomes. In J. Huber (Ed.), *Macro-micro linkages in sociology* (pp. 244–262). Newbury Park, CA: Sage.

TONRY, M. (1995). *Malign neglect: Race, crime and punishment in America.* New York: Oxford University Press.

VICUSI, W. K. (1986a). Market incentives for criminal behavior. In R. B. Freeman & H. J. Holzer (Eds.), *The black youth unemployment crisis* (pp. 301–346). Chicago: University of Chicago Press.

VICUSI, W. K. (1986b). The risks and rewards of criminal activity: A comprehensive test of criminal deterrence. *Journal of Labor Economics, 4,* 317–340.

VIGIL, J. D. (1988a). *Barrio gangs: Street life and identity in Southern California.* Austin: University of Texas Press.

VIGIL, J. D. (1988b). Group processes and street identity: Adolescent Chicano gang members. *Ethos, 16,* 421–445.

VIGIL, J. D., & YUN, S. C. (1990). Vietnamese youth gangs in southern California. In C. R. Huff (Ed.), *Gangs in America* (1st ed., pp. 146–162). Newbury Park, CA: Sage.

VIGIL, J. D., YUN, S., & LONG, J. M. (1992). Youth gangs, crime, and the Vietnamese in Orange County, California. In J. Fagan (Ed.), *The ecology of crime and drug use in inner cities*. New York: Social Science Research Council.

WACQUANT, L. D., & WILSON, W. J. (1989). The costs of racial and class exclusion in the inner city. *Annals of the American Academy of Political and Social Science, 501*, 8–25.

WALDORF, D. (1992). *When the Crips invaded San Francisco: Gang migration*. (Technical Report, Grant 5 R01 DA06486, National Institute on Drug Abuse). San Francisco: Institute for Scientific Analysis.

WASHTON, A., & GOLD, M. (1987). Recent trends in cocaine abuse as seen from the "800-cocaine hotline." In A. M. Washton & M. Gold (Eds.), *Cocaine: A clinician's handbook*. New York: Guilford Press.

WILLIAMS, T. (1989). *The cocaine kids: The inside story of a teenage drug ring*. Redding, MA: Addison-Wesley.

WILSON, J. Q., & KELLING, G. (1982, February). Broken windows. *Atlantic Monthly*, pp. 46–52.

WILSON, W. J. (1987). *The truly disadvantaged: The inner city, the underclass, and public policy*. Chicago: University of Chicago Press.

WILSON, W. J. (1991). Studying inner-city social dislocations: The challenge of public agenda research. *American Sociological Review, 56*, 1–14.

ZIMRING, F. E., & HAWKINS, G. (in press). *American violence*. New York: Oxford.

14

Legitimating Drug Use

A Note on the Impact of Gang Membership and Drug Sales on the Use of Illicit Drugs

Scott H. Decker

A good deal is known about gang members' involvement as sellers of drugs. We know little, however, about the extent to which gang members are involved in the drug market as users, and about the role that involvement in drug sales plays in the use of drugs. This paper presents data from an 11-city survey of arrestees that includes a substantial number of gang members, to explore the relationship between demographic characteristics such as age and race, gang membership, drug sales, and drug use. In addition, the gang members views' regarding drug use by their associates are explored. The contrast between the drug-using behavior and norms designed to control such behavior is examined in the group context of adolescent gang membership.

One recurrent theme of contemporary gang research is the nexus between street gangs and drug sales. Though this relationship is not new (Yablonsky 1966; Short and Strodbeck 1965), it has gained significance in recent years. The reemergence of street gangs in the 1980s (Curry, Ball, and Decker 1996; Huff 1991; Klein 1995) coincided with the explosion of crack cocaine sales in American cities. These parallel developments have been linked in the minds of the public, in policy statements (Conley 1993), and in some research

Decker, S.H. (2000). Legitimating drug use: A note on the impact of gang membership and drug sales on the use of illicit drugs. *Justice Quarterly,* 17, 393–410. Reprinted by permission of the Academy of Criminal Justice Sciences.

(Mieczkowski 1986; Sanchez-Jankowski 1991; Skolnick 1990; Taylor 1990). Although the validity of the conclusion that street gangs control drug sales has been questioned (Decker and Van Winkle 1995; Klein and Maxson 1994; Sanders 1994), one fact remains clear: gang members are involved substantially in drug markets.

This involvement occurred at a time when a variety of public health (National Institute on Drug Abuse 1994a, 1994b), law enforcement (National Institute of Justice 1995), and survey indicators (Office of National Drug Control Policy 1997) documented an increase in cocaine use. None of these indicators, however, provides a measure of the relationship between involvement in drug sales and drug use. Gang members' involvement in drug sales has been well documented, but their role as users is not well understood. In this paper we examine the relationship between drug sales and drug use among gang members by combining the results of a large survey of arrestees in 11 cities with in-depth qualitative interviews conducted in two of those cities. The triangulation of multiple data sources provides a unique opportunity to examine both the patterns of behavior and the justifications offered for those patterns by research subjects. Throughout this paper, we document the extent to which involvement in drug sales is linked to drug use, and the role of gang membership in that relationship.

This analysis raises two specific conceptual issues. First, we examine the concordance between the gang's normative stance regarding drug use by members and their actual behavior in this regard. A key issue in the contemporary understanding of gangs is the "fit" between what gangs profess to be and their actual behavior. There is debate about the extent to which gang norms and structure actually influence and control a member's behavior. According to formal-rational view, the gang belief system is enforced and maintained by a gang structure that involves strong leaders, rules, and discipline among members. The alternative view stresses the gang members' independence and the gang's inability— through normative or structural means—to regulate conduct among members. From this perspective, the informal and associational ties of membership play a larger role in determining gang behavior, and are less effective.

In addressing the second conceptual issue, we examine norms that regulate drug use and the specific circumstances under which it occurs. Here we study the variation in such norms by drug type and social context as well as by individual characteristics such as age and gender. Particularly interesting is the effect of drug sales on drug use. Taken together, these issues increase our understanding of the gang as an effective mechanism for controlling its members' behavior.

THE LINKS BETWEEN GANGS AND DRUGS

The research focus on the link between gang members and drug sales primarily has examined gang members as sellers of drugs (Decker and Van Winkle 1996; Hagedorn 1988; Klein, Maxson, and Cunningham 1991; Padilla 1992). Most research has demonstrated that gang members sell drugs as individuals, and that gangs exert little instrumental control over the patterns of sales and the profits made by their members. The concept of a market, however, implies both sellers and buyers; little is known about gang members' involvement as users of drugs, and what relationship, if any, exists between involvement as a seller and the subsequent use of drugs. It is important to expand these details of the gang member-drug market link to provide a more complete picture of the nexus between gangs and drugs, and to understand more clearly how proximity to drugs as a seller affects choices to use drugs. Gang structures may be weaker than peer norms, particularly in the face of easy access to drugs. The combination of a ready supply of drugs and peer norms that either support or are ambivalent toward drug use may lead many gang members to indulge.

Several ethnographies (Hagedorn 1988, 1994, 1998a; Moore 1978, 1991; Padilla 1992; Vigil 1988) suggest the plausibility of a relationship between drug sales and drug use among gang members. These studies underscore the ever-present nature of drug use, especially minor forms of drug use such as marijuana. In addition, many gang members interviewed during these investigations were heavily involved in drug sales. Moore and Vigil document this relationship, particularly for use of opiates and marijuana among Hispanic gang members in Los Angeles. Hagedorn (1998a) argues that in the 1980s gang members were both sellers and users of cocaine, but that use of cocaine declined as cocaine sales became a means of generating income. Despite this, he reports that 42 percent of cocaine sellers are presently using the drug. These studies, however, provided no comparison group of nongang members; thus we were less able to more fully document the relationship between gang membership, drug sales, and drug use.

Four broadly based youth surveys clarify the relationships between drug sales and drug use among gang members. Fagan (1989) surveyed inner-city youths in high-crime neighborhoods in San Diego, Los Angeles, and Chicago. He identified four distinct types of gangs: social gangs, party gangs, serious delinquents, and cohesive and organized gangs. Examining patterns of drug use and drug sales across these four types of gangs, Fagan concluded that involvement in drug sales is correlated positively with drug use at the aggregate level. That is, gangs with high levels of drug sales also use drugs at high levels. This relationship is true for marijuana as well as for serious drugs, such as cocaine, heroin, and PCP.

The second study (Esbensen and Huizinga 1993) examined data from the Denver Youth Study, based on the selection of "socially disorganized" clusters of block groups. The prevalence of drug use other than alcohol (including marijuana, crack, cocaine, heroin, and PCP) was higher among gang members than nongang members. In addition, gang members reported that their gang was heavily involved in drug sales, though only one in five reported selling drugs themselves.

Battin et al. (1998) used data from the Seattle Development Project to assess how extensively gang involvement contributed to delinquency over and above involvement with delinquent friends. They examined the impact of gang status at age 14 on behavior at 15, and the effects of gang status of fifteen-year-olds on behavior at 16. When the authors compared gang members to youths with delinquent friends and to youths with nondelinquent friends, they found that gang members were more likely than the other groups to use marijuana, and (among 15-year-olds) more likely to have used more serious drugs in the past year. In addition, both 14- and 15-year-old gang members were more likely than the other youths to be involved in drug sales.

Thornberry (1998) and Bjerregaard and Smith (1995) used data from the Rochester Youth Development Study, where 30 percent of the sample reported gang membership. Thornberry reported that a large percentage of gang members reported drug use (61%) and drug sales (70%) across the nine waves of data collection. Bjerregaard and Smith reported that more than one-third of gang boys (38%) and 44 percent of gang girls admitted marijuana use. Lizotte et al. (1997) reported that gun carrying among urban youths tended to be "sporadic," but that involvement in gangs and drug selling were correlates of such behavior. In particular, they found that as subjects aged, they were less attached to their gangs and more involved in drug sales, though this research did not report direct measures of the impact of drug sales on drug use.

Waldorf (1993) studied this issue most directly; he examined the pattern of use and sales among 300 gang members in San Francisco. His results point to a marked difference in patterns of sale and use by drug type. The majority of Waldorf's respondents who reported that they sold powder cocaine, opiates, and marijuana also reported using those drugs. The relationship between the sale and the use of crack cocaine, however, was quite different than for powder cocaine. Fewer than one in five (18%) crack sellers reported using that drug in the month preceding their interview. As the reasons for avoiding crack cocaine use, most gang members cited the addictive nature of the drug and the harmful effects on profits. These results may reflect what Hagedorn (1998a, 1998b) observed regarding gangs in Milwaukee: crack cocaine has achieved a decidedly negative reputation on the street, associated with images of degenerate individuals bereft of all vestiges of self-respect (Jacobs 1999). Hagedorn concluded however, that gang membership "is indisputably a risk factor for drug use" (1998b:128).

THE PRESENT STUDY

In this research note we explore the nature and levels of drug use in a sample of gang and nongang arrestees, and the impact of drug sales on drug use. Gang members' drug use is compared with that of nongang peers matched on age and gender. These comparisons are designed to determine the use of drugs by gang members, specifically prevalence levels and drug preferences, and the extent to which gang involvement and drug sales influence drug use. We also examine gang members' perspectives regarding drug use, based on two separate field studies of gang members. By triangulating qualitative and quantitative data measures, we can illuminate both the patterns of use and the gang norms that form a context for use.

The study employs data from two sources. We use data from the 1995 Drug Use Forecasting (DUF) Gun Addendum (Decker, Pennell, and Caldwell 1996) to measure gang membership, drug use, and drug sales. DUF is a research platform of the National Institute of Justice, designed to gain information on arrestees' drug use, treatment needs, and drug trends.[1] Subjects in the DUF sample represent a middle point between offenders who have been convicted and imprisoned, and those still at large on the streets. Because of the large volume of arrests in big cities, arrestees may be more representative of the broader group consisting of weakly motivated offenders. During the first two quarters of 1995, a gun addendum was administered to all arrestees interviewed by DUF staff members in 11 cities: Atlanta, Chicago, Detroit, Indianapolis, New Orleans, Phoenix, Los Angeles, Miami, St. Louis, San Diego, and the District of Columbia. These cities were chosen because of their high levels of firearm violence, because juveniles are interviewed there as part of the DUF protocol, and because they have provided reliable, valid interview data as part of the DUF program. Gang membership is a low-prevalence behavior, even among arrestees; thus it makes sense to combine the 11 cities to produce a large enough N to permit statistical analyses. Also, because the field studies come from two of the 11 cities, the comparative value of combining the data is enhanced.

---

[1] For a description of the data collection techniques, see National Institute of Justice (1998).

Measurement issues of concern in this context are gang membership, drug sales, and drug use. In these data, gang membership is measured by self-reports, a robust technique for determining whether a given individual is indeed a gang member (Esbensen and Huizinga 1993; Klein 1995). Curry and Spergel (1992) found that self-reported measures of gang membership were highly correlated with behaviors indicative of this association, including having friends in the gang, involvement in gang fights, and arrests with gang members. Measures of drug sales are also difficult to validate. The DUF data, however, is a well-established data collection system. Because drug possession is illegal and because drug use often stigmatizes individual users, its measurement is problematic (Wish and Gropper 1990). As a consequence, drug use is often underreported, sometimes substantially so (Rosenfeld and Decker 1993). Thus the use of urinalysis helps to circumvent this measurement problem. We do not know, however, whether or not underreporting is correlated with age, gender, or gang membership.

The second source of data is interviews with gang members; these interviews come from two different studies. The first was conducted by Decker and Van Winkle (1996) in St. Louis. In this study the authors used field techniques to contact and interview 99 active gang members between 1990 and 1993. The St. Louis sample was recruited from gang members who were at large on the street. The second study is based on data from interviews conducted with gang members in Chicago (Decker, Bynum, and Weisel 1998) during 1995. These interviews were held with imprisoned gang members and gang probationers from the black and Hispanic gangs identified as most highly organized, the Gangster Disciples (GDs) and the Latin Kings. The use of these data is intended to identify the modal categories of responses regarding drug use among gang members, and to illustrate the dimensions of the categories. The data have the additional virtue of coming from cities included in the DUF sample. Chicago and St. Louis are also useful comparison cities: Chicago is a "chronic" gang city, and St. Louis is an "emerging" gang city (Spergel and Curry 1993). When a field study from each of the major types of gang cities is used, the responses are more representative of the breadth of gang members' norms regarding drug use. The combination of quantitative and qualitative data permits triangulation, a rare occurrence in criminological research.

THE DUF GUN ADDENDUM SAMPLE

Between January 1995 and June 30, 1995, 8,038 arrestees were interviewed regarding drug use, gun possession, and gang membership. The descriptive characteristics of this sample are presented in Table 14–1. Most of the interviews were conducted with adult males (58%), followed by adult females (23%), juvenile males (17%), and juvenile females (2%). Seven percent of all interviewees reported that they were currently gang members, and 22 percent said they had sold drugs in the past year. A large fraction of the sample (64%) tested positive for any illegal drug; cocaine (37%) and marijuana (37%) were by far the leading categories.

Survey participants had been charged with a variety of offenses. The modal category was violent crime (32% of respondents were charged with a UCR-defined violent crime), followed closely by property crime (30%). Eighteen percent of the arrestees were charged with a drug crime—either sales, possession, or possession with intent to sell. Fourteen percent were charged with a consensual crime such as prostitution, and 5 percent were charged with a probation or parole violation.

TABLE 14–1   Characteristics of the DUF Sample. (*N*= 8,038)

	Percentage	(Number)
Age/Gender		
Adult males	58	(4,640)
Adult females	23	(1,870)
Juvenile males	17	(1,352)
Juvenile females	2	(176)
Gang Membership		
Currently a member	7	(550)
Ever a Member	11	(792)
Drug Sales		
Sold drugs in the past year	22	(1,526)
Drug Positive		
Any drug	64	(5,147)
Cocaine	37	(2,956)
Marijuana (50ng)	37	(2,971)
Opiates	6	(503)
Two or more drugs	21	(1,676)
Amphetamines	4	(375)
Charge		
Violent Crime	32	(2,359)
Property Crime	30	(2,238)
Consensual Crime	14	(1,074)
Drug Crime	18	(1,355)
Probation/Parole Violation	5	(372)

FINDINGS

Survey Data

The pattern of drug use by gang and nongang members is presented in Table 14–2.[2] We first examine the relationship between gang status and drug use, by comparing the percentage of each group that tested positive for any drug, two or more drugs, and any one of four separate drugs (cocaine, marijuana, opiates, and PCP). The first observation to be made from this table is that a large fraction of each group tested positive for an illicit drug: 65 percent of nongang members and 58 percent of gang members. Even so, there are interesting patterns of drug use that distinguish the two groups. Nongang members were substantially

---

[2] Because of the size and the nonrandom nature of the sample, tests of significance are not presented.

TABLE 14–2   Drug Use by Gang Status (Percentages)

	Nongang Members	Gang Members
Any Drug	65	58
Two or More	21	21
Cocaine	38	24
Marijuana	36	44
Opiates	6	5
PCP	2	4
(N)	(550)	(7,166)
Cocaine		
Juvenile male	8	12
Adult male	42	38
Marijuana		
Juvenile male	51	51
Adult male	38	38
(N)	(550)	(7,166)

more likely to test positive for cocaine use (38%) than were gang members (24%), while gang members tested positive for marijuana at higher percentages (44%) than did nongang members (36%). We observed no differences between the groups for polydrug use, and levels of opiate use and PCP use were very low for both groups. These findings suggest that gang members prefer marijuana and use less cocaine than nongang arrestees.

These patterns of use, however, may reflect other underlying demographic characteristics such as age or gender. The second panel in Table 14–2 disaggregates each of the two groups (gang and nongang members) into the two age/gender categories that account for the overwhelming majority of gang members: juvenile males and adult males.[3] A larger fraction of adult males, both gang and nongang members, tested positive for cocaine than did their juvenile counterparts. Interestingly, among juvenile males, gang members tested positive for cocaine at higher rates than did their nongang counterparts, although by only 4 percent. These levels of cocaine use among adult male gang members are very close to that reported by Hagedorn (1998a, 1998b) in Milwaukee. For cocaine, age rather than gang status affects levels of use among arrestees. A similar finding is observed for marijuana use: equal percentages of gang and nongang members tested positive for marijuana within each age/gender group. That is, among juvenile males, the same percentage of nongang members as of gang members tested positive for marijuana. The same finding was observed for adult males, but at lower levels. The results for cocaine and marijuana, taken together, indicate that among males, age is a more important correlate of drug use than is gang membership.

---

[3] Indeed, there were too few female gang members for analysis.

TABLE 14–3   The Impact of Gang Membership and Drug Sales on Drug Use (Percentages)

	Sellers (N= 1,526)		Nonsellers (N= 6,187)	
	Gang Member (224)	Nongang Member (995)	Gang Member (250)	Nongang Member (4,270)
Drug Urine Analysis Positive				
Any Drug				
Total	64	68	53	64
Juvenile	57	53	47	50
Adult	59	63	65	67
Cocaine				
Total	25	38	23	38
Juvenile	8	11	8	14
Adult	44	39	42	38
Marijuana				
Total	48	39	41	36
Juvenile	55	51	47	51
Adult	40	39	37	38
Multiple Drugs				
Total	22	22	20	21
Juvenile	17	14	14	14
Adult	23	24	29	23

In Table 14–3, we first control for drug sales in the relationship between gang membership and drug use among males. We do so by comparing the percentage of gang and nongang members who test positive for four drug types among those who reported drug sales in the 12 months before the survey and those who reported that they had not sold drugs in that period. Next, we control for age to determine whether the relationship holds under more fully specified subcategories. One of the hypotheses guiding this research is that regardless of gang status, involvement in drug sales will be associated with higher levels of drug use because drug sales facilitate drug use. We also posit that if the gang is an effective mechanism for controlling its members' behavior, this will be seen in generally lower levels of drug use among gang members. Each of these effects should operate independent of age. If, for example, juveniles were more likely to test positive for a certain drug regardless of gang status or experience in drug sales, arguments about the impact of these variables would be less viable.

The results shown in Table 14–3 generally support the assumption that those involved in drug sales, regardless of gang status, are more likely to use drugs. This is particularly true for marijuana use. For cocaine, however, nongang members were more likely to test positive, regardless of whether they sold drugs. Overall, drug sellers were more likely to test positive for the use of any illicit drug than were those who reported no drug sales. Within each category of drug sales, a lower percentage of gang members tested positive for any illicit drug—except marijuana—than did nongang members. These results seem to support the expectation regarding the effect of gang membership and drug sales on use.

A different picture emerges, however, when we consider the panels of Table 14–3 that control for age. The pattern for any drug use is specified by introducing age as a control (Hirschi and Selvin 1968). Among adults, a higher percentage of those who did not sell drugs tested positive for any illicit drug. The pattern for juveniles, however, is the reverse: those who did not sell drugs were less likely to test positive. This suggests that drug types may well show variation that is linked to age. Indeed, the difference between the results for cocaine use and for marijuana use helps to disentangle these findings. Within each of the four categories created by the intersection of gang status and drug sales, adults were three to five times more likely than juveniles to test positive for cocaine. This pattern reverses for marijuana, albeit at a lower level: regardless of gang status/drug sales category, a higher percentage of juveniles than of adults tested positive for marijuana use. These results indicate that age rather than behavior was the most salient factor in accounting both for the choice of drug and for level of use.

The quantitative data, however, do not provide a clear pattern regarding the impact of gang membership on drug use and drug sales. This suggests that gang membership may not exert the dominant effect on these behaviors that is suggested in many previous field studies. This question calls for data that explore in greater depth the motivations for, and prohibitions against, drug use among gang members. We undertake such an analysis in the following section, using the results of interview data from two of the survey cities, Chicago and St. Louis.

Interview Data

Several themes were evident in gang members' comments about drug use by fellow members. First, most gang members who use drugs made a clear distinction between "bad" drugs and drugs that are "okay" to use. This distinction rests on the perception that some drugs are debilitating while others are simply recreational. The use of "drug type" in this distinction is crucial because "acceptable drug use" is more consistent with the pattern of juvenile drug use in the general population. In the case of marijuana, it appears that gang norms have acceded to those of youth culture, which normalize marijuana use. A second set of accounts revealed in the interviews is the status of formal rules among members regarding drug use. Here we examine the extent to which rules exist regarding drug use among gang members, are followed, and, if violated, carry punishments. A third view comes from gang members who report that abstinence is the only acceptable stance regarding drugs because drug use leads to problems with the money made from drug sales. Finally, some gang members report that heavy use of controlled drugs is acceptable but that individuals are responsible for themselves.

"Stay away from bad drugs, but weed is okay."

In the first category of responses regarding drug use, gang members drew a line between drugs that were acceptable for use and those which were unacceptable. Marijuana was identified as "acceptable" for use because it was believed to be nonaddictive, was part of life in the gang, and was thought not to interfere with gang members' judgment. Bluntly put, marijuana is the most popular illicit drug among juveniles, perhaps because of the group context associated with the use of this drug. Indeed, many gang members distinguished between marijuana and "real" drugs. This distinction reflects in part the role that marijuana has come to play in youth culture as a drug that allows retreat from the world while maintaining a hip or cool image. Marijuana is associated with the life of a "player" on the street, and is perceived as allowing its users to retain control over their use of the drug.

> No members are to sell or inject any drugs that are addictive. That was any drugs at first, and it was loosely understood that we didn't count marijuana. And they amended it to you could snort cocaine. (Imprisoned GD)[4]
>
> We were not allowed to shoot drugs and stuff like that. You can get high, but that dope fiend stuff, no. (Imprisoned GD)
>
> And drugs, they don't supposed to use them. Let me rephrase that, they not supposed to use no heavy drugs. Like alcohol, marijuana, they don't really consider that heavy. As far as that other stuff, you get caught using that, you out of there. (GD on probation)
>
> You can't smoke crack, you can't do cocaine, you can't do heroin, just smoke weed and drink. (GD on probation)
>
> Right now, the most important rules is us Latin Kings, we can't smoke no cocaine, we can't smoke no PCP or snort it. There are a lot of guys that get into these drugs. It's all right to do a couple of lines of cocaine and smoke a joint or something, but as far as China white goes. . . (Latin King on probation)
>
> You can drink. You can't do drugs. You can smoke weed and everything but you can't do crack or nothing major because here you are with nothing, just standing there as a target. (Latin King on probation)
>
> Are a lot of members using drugs?
>
> Naw, just smoke weed, that's all. (St. Louis Crenshaw Mafia Gangster Blood)
>
> Do most of your members use drugs?
>
> Naw, I told you, don't nobody do that stuff.
>
> Except for marijuana?
>
> Yeah, marijuana, that's all.
>
> You don't toot no blow or nothing?
>
> Them older guys might do that. I done did it twice, it was half a button, I did it twice but I ain't really never did it. (St. Louis Thundercat)
>
> Yeah. Smoke Primos, sniff heroin, smoke some weed, you know. They don't smoke no rock, but they smoke Primos, smoke weed, and drink Michelob. (St. Louis 6th Street Hoover Crip)

"You know you can't use, and we will fuck you up if you do"

The second category of responses emphasized the harmful effects of drug use and proposed a rapid, punitive response to such use. This group of gang members identified a number of responses to drug use, including marijuana, by gang members. Some included mild forms of social disapproval such as shunning or ostracizing; others threatened physical violence. Older gang members generally held this set of prohibitions, which reflected the core values of those who had moved beyond the pulls of youth culture.

> You can't use your own drugs. If we catch a guy that is smoking rock in our gang, that's an automatic violation. (GD on probation)

---

[4] GD stands for Gangster Disciple.

We are not supposed to use. They have started to allow us to sell, but at one time, we weren't supposed to sell either.

We are definitely not supposed to use. That is a strict violation. (Imprisoned Latin King)

What happens to gang members who use drugs?

People don't hang with them very much.

How come.

Because they be doing drugs and we don't be doin' it. (St. Louis Hoover Crip)

No cocaine smoking at all. You get caught smoking cocaine you an outcast, black sheep. You got no more friends, you just married a pipe. (St. Louis Compton Gangster)

What happens to people in the gang who use drugs?

If you get caught, you get beat up. (St. Louis Piru 104 Blood)

We might smoke every once in a while but no cocaine, no Primos. I know what that shit can do to you and if I catch anybody, like one of my boys, he used to sell dope and he turned into a smoker, I beat the piss out of that man. I said, You in violation, you lucky you don't get capped (shot). (St. Louis Insane Gangster Disciple)

"You can't use, it fucks up the money"

A third category of responses to gang drug use emphasized abstinence for instrumental reasons. Simply put, using drugs was viewed as incompatible with good business practices because users could not be trusted to be accurate with the money and to avoid dipping into their own stash. Repeated experiences with drug users have led gang members to these conclusions.[5] For many gang members, making money is important enough to generate prohibitions and severe penalties for transgressions. The violence associated with rule breaking is consistent with Decker and Van Winkle's (1996) finding that gang members are willing to employ excessive violence in many situations, beyond what is necessary to achieve the end in mind.

Why aren't there rock stars (heavy crack users) in the gang?

I don't play that, they be messin up money, become short then. (St. Louis Thundercat)

Not (using drugs) heavily but you got to use your mind, your mind is strongest in your power, mentally and physically. You can't have too many (members) doing it because I can give a man so much amount of this stuff and I ask him to knock it off and he wind up smoking half of it. That's not making a good profit. (St. Louis North Side Crip)

We'll tell them don't take no losses. You wait until you finish selling and then you can buy whatever you want to buy with your own money, but don't fuck up our profits. You mess our things up, we going to mess up you thing. We will beat his motherfucking ass. (St. Louis 107 Hoover Crip)

If somebody in the gang and we find out you smoke rocks or anything, we beat you up and make you check yourself into a Care-Unit or something cause we just hate to see one of our boys go out. We know fiends that look bad and we don't want none of our friends to go out like that. (St. Louis Compton Gangster)

What happens to people in the gang who start using cocaine and crack?

Probably get killed.

By somebody in the gang?

Yeah, because they messing up the profits. (St. Louis Inglewood Bounty Hunters)

---

[5] Although all of the examples in this and the next section are taken from St. Louis gang members, gang members from the Chicago interviews expressed similar sentiments.

"If you use, it is O.K., but you must be crazy"

A final category of responses acknowledges drug use but expresses some concern over the need to maintain distance from users. Gang members who chose to use drugs, however, were simply tolerated by a number of gang members. None of the Chicago gang respondents were included in this category, a reflection of their more organized nature and their ability to exercise control over members' behavior.

> Some of them (gang members) smoke cocaine and snort boy (heroin). (St. Louis North County Crip)
>
> Yeah, there's a whole lot of gang members like about 20 or 25 of them are using drugs like coke. (St. Louis 23rd Street Hoover Crip)
>
> Well we don't (use drugs). It's something that we know is wrong for a change. We know drugs is bad, but if you want to buy it from us of course we are going to give it to you. (St. Louis Gangster Disciple)
>
> People I know are not involved in drug use. If anybody was, I wouldn't be with them. (St. Louis Rolling 60's Crip)
>
> What would happen if somebody in your gang gets on crack?
>
> We would think he crazy or something. (St. Louis 88th Street Mob)

CONCLUSION

In this paper we have examined the link between gang membership, drug sales, and drug use. Using an 11-city survey of arrestees, we found high levels of drug use among both gang and nongang members. Although a lower proportion of gang members than of nongang members tested positive for illegal drugs (except marijuana), we found different patterns of use based on membership. Nongang members were more likely than gang members, to test positive for cocaine; this pattern was reversed for use of marijuana. We also found strong age differences: older members of the sample (regardless of gang status or drug sales) were more likely to test positive for cocaine; younger members (again, regardless of gang status or drug sales) were more likely to test positive for marijuana. Because we lack trend data, we cannot establish the time order for gang membership, drug sales, and drug use.

These high levels of drug use among gang members conflict with reports provided to ethnographers regarding gang norms guiding drug use. Such reports emphasize the harmful effects of drug abuse, and stress the role of the gang in enforcing discipline against drug users. Despite such legends, drug use among gang members—including more serious drugs such as cocaine—remains high. Gang members interviewed in Chicago and St. Louis revealed four categories of responses on their gangs' views of drug use by members. These views ranged from assigning individual responsibility to gang members who chose to use drugs, to professing a system of strict punishments for members who engage in drug use.

The results reported here contrast with ethnographic studies which consistently find that gangs emphasize abstinence. Those field-based studies report that except for marijuana, most gang members repudiate drug use. To reiterate, we found considerable drug use among gang members: a considerable fraction of gang members tested positive for serious illicit drugs, and most of the interview subjects acknowledged at least tacit acceptance of some drug use by members, particularly marijuana. Perhaps these differences are linked to the differences in the sources of data used in this research note: probationers, arrestees in custody, inmates, and gang members at large on the street. We believe, however, that the explanation lies elsewhere, namely in the discontinuity between the gang belief system and actual behavior, particularly among adolescents.

Various factors account for the discontinuity between the lore of gang drug use and the results presented here. First, Klein (1971) points to the role of the "gang myth system" within gangs. This system promulgates a set of beliefs regarding gang behavior and actions which is often inconsistent with reality. As Klein notes, this belief system, based as it is on a fictitious set of beliefs, supports an ideal of the gang that rarely has a basis in fact. An image of serious drug abuse is inconsistent with gang members' image of themselves as controlling their own fate and being ever ready to deal with the dangers of life in the gang. Gang members' denial of drug use is also consistent with a view of gangs that reinforces myths about the positive effects of gangs and gang members in their communities.

Second, gang members make it clear that they distinguish between "real" and recreational drug use. With this distinction, marijuana and (under some circumstances) cocaine are acceptable, while the use of other drugs is not. The distinction appears to be based on the associational aspects of youth culture in general, and on gang life specifically. Marijuana enjoys considerable popularity among young people and is a regular part of "hanging out" on the street. Therefore it is no coincidence that young male arrestees, whether involved with gangs or not, distinguish marijuana use from use of more serious drugs such as crack cocaine and heroin. Thus marijuana use is legitimated by the group context in which it occurs. Juvenile males' use of marijuana has increased considerably in the last decade (Johnston, O'Malley, and Bachman 1998), and perhaps has increased the legitimacy of this drug. Our results may reflect the broader acceptance of marijuana among adolescents.

Third, this analysis calls into question the gangs' ability to control their members' behavior. The majority of gang researchers conclude that gangs are not effective in doing this (Decker and Van Winkle 1996; Hagedorn 1988; Klein 1971; Vigil 1988). If gangs are ineffective mechanisms for controlling the money made by their members or for organizing their members for criminal activity, it is unlikely that they can dictate what members do in their private lives. After all, gang members engage in a considerable amount of crime; these actions, in themselves, are evidence of their unwillingness to be governed by rules, particularly rules that are not backed up by sanctions. Therefore it is unlikely that gang members would allow much regulation of their private lives, particularly in regard to drug use. Thus it appears that neither the gang structure nor the gang belief system is effective in controlling this aspect of many members' lives. This point suggests that some aspects of youth culture, such as independence and thrill seeking, may transcend gang membership.

Finally, the sale of drugs has an interesting effect on drug use. One of the key issues addressed here is the role of sales for use. Although a higher percentage of sellers than of nonsellers tested positive for any illicit drug, we found no pattern for the impact of drug sales on cocaine or marijuana use. Selling drugs does not increase the likelihood that individuals will test positive for drugs, regardless of gang status. Age is a more important determinant of drug use and drug type than is either gang status or selling drugs. A major component of gang behavior reflects the focal beliefs and practices of adolescents, the age group that participates most often in gangs. Our findings diminish the significance of gang status and drug selling for drug use, and indicate the importance of age in determining the choice of drug and the level of use.

QUESTIONS FOR UNDERSTANDING AND CRITICAL THINKING

1. To what extent are gang members involved in the drug market as users?
2. How does the nature and extent of drug use differ for gang members versus nongang members?
3. Do drug sales facilitate drug use regardless of gang status?
4. Review and discuss the discontinuity between the gang belief system and gang behavior among juveniles.

REFERENCES

BATTIN, S., K. HILL, R. ABBOTT, R. CATALANO, AND J. D. HAWKINS. 1998. "The Contribution of Gang Membership to Delinquency Beyond Delinquent Friends." *Criminology* 36:93–115.

BJERREGAARD, B. AND C. SMITH. 1995. "Gender Differences in Gang Participation, Delinquency, and Substance Abuse." Pp. 93–105 in *The Modern Gang Reader,* edited by M. Klein, C. Maxson, and J. Miller. Los Angeles, CA: Roxbury.

CONLEY, C.H. 1993. *Street Gangs: Current Knowledge and Strategies.* Washington, DC: U.S. Department of Justice.

CURRY, G.D., R.A. BALL, AND S.H. DECKER. 1996. *Estimating the National Scope of Gang Crime from Law Enforcement Data.* Washington, DC: National Institute of Justice.

CURRY, G.D. AND I. A. SPERGEL. 1992. "Gang Involvement and Delinquency among Hispanic and African American Adolescent Males." *Journal of Research on Crime and Delinquency* 29:273–91.

DECKER, S.H., T.S. BYNUM, AND D.L. WEISEL. 1998. "Gangs as Organized Crime Groups: A Tale of Two Cities." *Justice Quarterly* 15:395–423.

DECKER, S.H., S. PENNELL, AND A. CALDWELL. 1996. *Arrestees and Guns: Monitoring the Illegal Firearms Market.* Washington, DC: National Institute of Justice.

DECKER, S.H. AND B. VAN WINKLE. 1995. "Slingin' Dope: The Role of Gangs and Gang Members in Drug Sales." *Justice Quarterly* 11:1001–22.

_____. 1996. *Life in the Gang: Family, Friends, and Violence.* New York: Cambridge University Press.

ESBENSEN, F. AND D. HUIZINGA. 1993. "Gangs, Drugs and Delinquency in a Survey of Urban Youth." *Criminology* 31:565–90.

FAGAN, J. 1989. "The Social Organization of Drug Use and Drug Dealing among Urban Gangs." *Criminology* 27:633–70.

HAGEDORN, J. 1988. *People and Folks: Gangs, Crime and the Underclass in a Rustbelt City.* Chicago, IL: Lake View Press.

_____. 1994. "Homeboys, Dope Fiends, Legits, and New Jacks: Adult Gang Members, Drugs, and Work." *Criminology* 32:197–219.

_____. 1998a. "The Business of Drug Dealing in Milwaukee." *Wisconsin Policy Research Institute Report* 11:1–30.

_____. 1998b. "Cocaine, Kicks and Strain: Patterns of Substance Abuse in Milwaukee Gangs." *Contemporary Drug Problems* 25:113–47.

HIRSCHI, T. AND H. SELVIN. 1968. *Delinquency Research: An Appraisal of Analytic Methods.* New York: Free Press.

HUFF, R. 1991. *Gangs in America.* Thousand Oaks, CA: Sage.

JACOBS, B. A. 1999. *Dealing Crack: The Social World of Streetcorner Selling.* Boston, MA: Northeastern University Press.

JOHNSTON, L., P. O'MALLEY, AND J. BACHMAN. 1998. *National Survey Results on Drug Use from the Monitoring the Future Study, 1975–1997.* Vol. 1, *Secondary School Students.* Washington, DC: U.S. Department of Health and Human Services, National Institute on Drug Abuse.

KLEIN, M. 1971. *Street Gangs and Street Workers.* Englewood Cliffs, NJ: Prentice-Hall.

_____. 1995. *Street Gangs in America.* New York: Oxford University Press.

KLEIN, M. AND C. MAXSON. 1994. "Gangs and Cocaine Trafficking." Pp. 42–58 in *Drugs and Crime: Evaluating Public Policy Initiatives,* edited by D. MacKenzie and C. Uchida. Thousand Oaks, CA: Sage.

KLEIN, M., C. MAXSON, AND L. CUNNINGHAM. 1991. "'Crack,' Street Gangs, and Violence." *Criminology* 29:623–50.

LIZOTTE, A. J., G. J. HOWARD, M. D. KROHN, AND T. P. THORNBERRY. 1997. "Patterns of Illegal Gun Carrying among Urban Males." *Valparaiso University Law Review* 31:375–93.

MIECZKOWSKI, T. 1986. "Geeking Up and Throwing Down: Heroin Street Life in Detroit." *Criminology* 26:645–55.

MOORE, J. 1978. *Homeboys.* New Brunswick, NJ: Rutgers University Press.

_____. 1991. "Going Down to the Barrio: Homeboys and Homegirls in Change." Philadelphia, PA: Temple University Press.

NATIONAL INSTITUTE OF JUSTICE. 1995. *Drug Use Forecasting Annual Report, 1994.* Washington, DC: U.S. Department of Justice.

_____. 1998. *1997 Annual Report on Adult and Juvenile Arrestees.* Washington, DC: U.S. Department of Justice.

NATIONAL INSTITUTE ON DRUG ABUSE. 1994a. *Annual Emergency Room Data 1992. Data from the Drug Abuse Warning Network DAWN.* Series 1, Number 12-A. Washington, DC: U.S. Government Printing Office.

_____. 1994b. *Annual Medical Examiner Data 1992. Data from the Drug Abuse Warning Network DAWN.* Series 1, Number 12-B. Washington, DC: U.S. Government Printing Office.

OFFICE OF NATIONAL DRUG CONTROL POLICY. 1997. *Pulse Check: National Trends in Drug Abuse.* Washington, DC: Executive Office of the President.

PADILLA, F. 1992. *The Gang as an American Enterprise.* New Brunswick, NJ: Rutgers University Press.

ROSENFELD, R. AND S. DECKER. 1993. "Discrepant Values, Correlated Measures: Cross-City and Longitudinal Comparisons of Self-Reports and Urine Tests of Cocaine Use among Arrestees." *Journal of Criminal Justice* 21:223–30.

SANCHEZ-JANKOWSKI, M. 1991. *Islands in the Street: Gangs and Urban American Society.* Berkeley, CA: University of California Press.

SANDERS, W. 1994. *Drive-Bys and Gang Bangs: Gangs and Grounded Culture.* New York: Aldine.

SHORT, J. S. AND F. STRODTBECK. 1965. *Group Process and Gang Delinquency.* Chicago, IL: University of Chicago Press.

SKOLNICK, J. 1990. "The Social Structure of Street Drug Dealing." *American Journal of Police* 9:1–41.

SPERGEL, I. AND G.D. CURRY. 1993. "The National Youth Gang Survey: A Research and Development Process." Pp. 359–400 in *Gang Intervention Handbook,* edited by A. Goldstein and C. R. Huff. Champaign-Urbana, IL: Research Press.

TAYLOR, C. 1990. *Dangerous Society.* East Lansing, MI: Michigan State University Press.

THORNBERRY, T. 1998. "Membership in Youth Gangs and Involvement in Serious and Violent Offending." Pp. 147–66 in *Serious and Violent Juvenile Offenders: Risk Factors and Successful Interventions,* edited by R. Loeber and D. P. Farrington. Thousand Oaks, CA: Sage.

VIGIL, D. 1988. *Barrio Gangs.* Austin, TX: University of Texas Press.

WALDORF, D. 1993. "Don't Be Your Own Best Customer: Drug Use of San Francisco Gang Drug Sellers." *Crime, Law and Social Change* 19:1–15.

WISH, E. D. AND B. A. GROPPER. 1990. "Drug Testing by the Criminal Justice System: Methods, Research, and Applications." Pp. 321-91 in *Drugs and Crime,* edited by M. Tonry and J.Q. Wilson. Chicago, IL: University of Chicago Press.

YABLONSKY, L. 1966. *The Violent Gang.* New York: Penguin.

PART VI

Gang Victimization

15

Youth Maltreatment and Gang Involvement

Kevin M. Thompson and Rhonda Braaten-Antrim

Although childhood maltreatment has been found to contribute to a variety of youth problem behaviors, the implications of being maltreated on gang involvement remain unclear. This research examines whether physical and sexual maltreatment raises the risk of gang involvement among secondary school students. Findings show that being maltreated increases the probability of gang involvement, independent of demographic factors. When youth are subjected to extreme levels of maltreatment, their odds of participating in gang activities differ only slightly from youth who report occasional maltreatment, suggesting that prevalence measures may be better predictors of gang involvement than incidence measures. When youth are beaten physically and molested sexually, their odds of gang involvement are four times higher than youth who do not experience maltreatment. Finally, being maltreated is a much more robust correlate of gang involvement than the level of support, communication, educational interest, and supervision youth receive from their parents.

Childhood maltreatment has been empirically implicated in a variety of youth problem behaviors (Bolton, Reich, & Gutierres, 1977; Smith & Thornberry, 1995; Trickett & McBride-Chang, 1995; Widom, 1989; Zingraff, Leiter, Myers, & Johnson, 1993). Research has linked childhood maltreatment to delinquency (Smith & Thornberry, 1995; Widom, 1989; Zingraff et al., 1993), status offenses (Rotheram-Borus, Mahler, Koopman, & Langabeer, 1996; Widom, 1996), eating disorders (Schaaf & McCanne, 1994), teenage pregnancy (Boyer & Fine, 1992), substance abuse (Pedersen & Skrondal, 1996), and suicide (Yama, Tovey, Fogas, & Morris, 1995). When panel or retrospective designs have been employed,

---

Authors' Note: We appreciate the useful comments of the anonymous reviewers.

Thompson, K.M. and Braaten-Antrim, R. Youth maltreatment and gang involvement. *Journal of Interpersonal Violence,* 13 (1998). Pp. 328–345. Reprinted by permission of Sage Publications, Inc.

childhood maltreatment has been found to contribute to long-term behavioral disorders in adulthood as well (Johnsen & Harlow, 1996; Simpson, Westerberg, Little, & Trujillo, 1994; Slavik, Carlson, & Sperry, 1995; Widom, 1989).

One potential consequence of childhood maltreatment that has received less coverage is gang involvement. Although family influences on gang involvement have received ample attention (Chin, 1990; Thrasher, 1927; Vigil, 1988), it is unclear whether maltreatment has implications for the probability of gang involvement. This issue merits attention for several reasons. First, there is reason to believe that maltreatment will contribute more robustly to the probability of gang involvement than family variables such as neglect-supervision (Brownfield, Thompson, & Sorenson, 1997; Knox et al., 1995), parental support (Chang, 1996), and family structure (Knox et al., 1996). For the most part, studies have not established that these family variables are even modest predictors of gang involvement, leading some gang scholars to conclude that defective family structure and process variables may not be important precursors to gang involvement (Jankowski, 1991; D. Joe & Robinson, 1980; Rutter & Giller, 1983; Spergel, 1995). Consequently, it is important to determine if it is premature to abandon family process variables as precursors to gang involvement. Second, the pathway from being maltreated to gang involvement appears more straightforward than the relationship between gang involvement and other family variables. Social learning-theory assumptions suggest that youth will mimic resolutions to disputes that they experience in the home (Akers, 1994). Because gangs have been found to afford youth with ample opportunity to act out violently (Klein, 1995; Miller, 1975; Tracy, 1979) it seems reasonable to assume that youth will participate in groups that reinforce tendencies manifested by their family. This article tests this assumption by examining the relationship between physical and sexual maltreatment and gang involvement in a large sample of secondary school students.

YOUTH MALTREATMENT AND GANG INVOLVEMENT

Estimates of the prevalence of physical maltreatment suggest that anywhere from 40% to 60% of children suffer at least one violent act from their parents (National Center on Child Abuse and Neglect, 1988; Straus & Gelles, 1986). Slightly more than 1 in 10 children experience severe violence in which they are hit with a fist, kicked, or assaulted with a weapon (Straus & Gelles, 1986). Estimates of the range of sexual abuse vary more widely. National representative samples indicate that 6% of girls and 2% of boys suffer from at least one bout of sexual abuse (Finkelhor, Hotaling, Lewis, & Smith, 1990). In a Los Angeles survey, Wyatt (1985) found a sexual abuse prevalence rate of more than 50% among young women in the sample. Although it may be difficult to get a precise handle on the self-reported level and nature of child maltreatment, there is mounting evidence that child practitioners and public health officials are seeing more youth and adults with serious adverse consequences from physical and sexual abuse (Dembo et al., 1989).

One consequence of maltreatment may be participation in groups that embrace similar methods for handling conflict. One such group is the youth gang. Gangs frequently advocate violence against rival gangs (Block & Block, 1993; Miller, 1975; Spergel, 1984) and are not reluctant to physically and sexually violate their own members (Jankowski, 1991; Knox, 1996; Spergel, 1995). Research has repeatedly demonstrated that gang members commit a higher proportion of violent acts than nongang delinquents (Esbensen, Huizinga, & Weiher, 1993; Klein, 1995; Maxson, Gordon, & Klein, 1985), and many gang members promote themselves as warriors, combat veterans, and guerrilla warfare fighters to highlight their violent nature (Knox, 1994).

Why youth join gangs and seem so eager to resort to gang violence can be traced to their treatment within the family. Regrettably, the link between maltreatment and gang involvement has received much less publicity than the relationship between maltreatment and delinquency. When maltreatment has been examined as a precursor to gang involvement, firm conclusions have been limited by the nature of the samples. Most of the quantitative studies surveyed gang members in custody (Chang, 1996; Evans & Mason, 1996; Knox et al., 1996), thereby limiting generalizations to gang members who had been adjudicated by the courts. Several of these studies suggest that maltreatment makes an important contribution to gang involvement. Other studies direct our attention to alternative correlates. Most of the qualitative studies provide rich descriptions of gang life but by design prevent us from making correlational assertions about maltreatment and gang involvement (Campbell, 1984; Hagedorn, 1988).

In her ethnography of gang girls in New York City, Campbell (1984) noted that the home lives of these girls were frequently marked by physical and sexual abuse. In interviews with Milwaukee gang members, Hagedorn (1988) identified the often violent home life faced by these youth, leading to shame and resentment among gang members. K. A. Joe and Chesney-Lind's (1995) study of 48 gang youth in Hawaii found that more than one half of the boys and three fourths of the girls had been the victims of physical abuse. Of the girls, 62% were victims of sexual abuse or sexual assault, as well. Although maltreatment appears to be an important precursor to gang involvement in these studies, the lack of a nongang comparison group and uncontrolled confounding variables suggest that we accept this relationship cautiously.

Quantitative analyses of the relationship between maltreatment and gang involvement have usually relied on surveys of incarcerated youth. Rhodes and Fischer (1993) surveyed youth participating in a court diversion program and found that neither physical nor sexual abuse differentiated gang from nongang members. In a study of adjudicated youth, Evans and Mason (1996) noted that physical and sexual abuse was an insignificant correlate of male gang involvement. Among girls, sexual abuse was a significant predictor of *nongang* involvement. Chang (1996) examined data from female detainees in Illinois and found that a history of child abuse was weakly, but significantly, related to gang membership. Experiencing family violence was predictive of gang membership among girls but not boys in Campbell's (1984) study. Finally, in their recent large, national survey of incarcerated juveniles, Knox and colleagues (1996) found that having physically violent parents was a weak but significant correlate of gang membership.

The preceding studies suggest that the relationship between youth maltreatment and gang involvement is at best unclear. When maltreatment is implicated empirically in gang involvement, the bivariate effects appear to be weak. Controls for demographic characteristics seem to further temper these effects. Moreover, none of these studies provide much information on whether extreme levels of maltreatment affect gang involvement over and above being occasionally maltreated. We also need better information on how maltreatment relates to gang involvement vis-à-vis more traditional family influences (e.g., supervision, support, communication). Only a few multivariate analyses have compared the effects of maltreatment on gang involvement alongside family relationship variables (Chang, 1996; Evans & Mason, 1996).

Because of the nature of these samples, it is also unclear whether being maltreated increases the probability of gang involvement among samples of noncustodial youth. The weak correlations observed in these studies may largely be a function of sampling youth in custody, thereby restricting variation on the independent variables. Finally, it is important to know whether gang involvement is affected more through physical or sexual abuse and whether being both physically and sexually abused further increases a youth's odds of gang involvement. Consequently, the following questions will be posed in this investigation:

1. Does physical and sexual maltreatment contribute significantly to the probability of gang involvement, independent of demographic characteristics?
2. Do youth who are exposed to more frequent maltreatment risk greater odds of gang involvement than youth who are only occasionally maltreated?
3. Are youth who suffer both physical and sexual maltreatment at greater risk for gang involvement than youth who experience one form of maltreatment?
4. How do the effects of maltreatment on gang involvement contrast with the effects of traditional family relationship variables?

These questions will be addressed using a self-report survey of noncustodial secondary school students. The study did not preselect youth on the basis of maltreatment or gang involvement, and the instrument included a number of demographic variables and numerous measures of the quality of the family relationship.

METHOD

The data for this study were gathered in 1994 by a private research firm for a school district in a medium-sized, midwestern city (Search Institute, 1994). The study gathered information from students on a variety of at-risk behaviors. Consequently, the questionnaire included items about suicide, gang involvement, substance use, and delinquency.

Sample

The target population for the study was students attending 6th through 12th grades in the school district. School staff members administered the questionnaire with explicit instructions to assure students of anonymity. Of the approximately 2,600 students in the sampling frame, 2,468 completed the questionnaire. Due to inconsistent responding, missing data on 40 or more items, or reports of unrealistically high levels of at-risk behaviors, 110 survey forms were then discarded. Thus, the sample size included 2,358 students.

Table 15–1 shows the sampling distribution based on grade, gender, and race/ethnicity. Students were somewhat equally distributed across grade and gender. The sample, however, was heavily White, with Hispanics comprising the largest ethnic minority group.

Measures

Gang Involvement

The questionnaire included an item labeled "gang fights," in which students were asked to respond to the following question: "During the last 12 months, how many times have you taken part in a fight where a group of your friends were against another group?" The response categories ranged from *never* (1) to *5 or more times* (5). This definition is somewhat

TABLE 15–1   Demographic Characteristics of Sample

	N	Percentage of Total Sample
Grade		
6	370	16
7	439	19
8	348	15
9	313	13
10	348	15
11	306	13
12	231	10
Gender		
Male	1,195	51
Female	1,149	49
Race/ethnicity		
American Indian	52	2
Asian or Pacific Islander	47	2
Black	18	1
Hispanic	110	5
White	2,092	89

consistent with the implicative method of defining gangs, as proposed by Hagedorn (1988). Gangs in this definition are defined by their commitment to defending one another, their territory, and the gang name in the status-setting fights that occur in school and on the street. Although this emic definition has been subject to debate (see Ball & Curry, 1995), it embodies the often fleeting nature of gang involvement, in which many peripheral members are called on for fighting purposes (Yablonsky, 1959). This definition yields an estimate of 522 youth who participated in a gang fight in the past year. This estimate of gang involvement approximates local law enforcement estimates of youth gang participation in the city.[1] Moreover, the distribution of the gang involvement item is correlated in a direction and magnitude with previously known correlates of self-reported gang involvement (Conly, Kelly, Mahanna, & Warner, 1993; Knox, 1994; Knox et al., 1996; Thompson, Brownfield, & Sorenson, 1996). In the sample, males are more than twice as likely as females to participate in gang fights (gamma = .345), ethnic minorities engage in significantly more gang fights than Whites (gamma = .478), and gang fighting is more common among youth residing in single-parent families (gamma = .174).

Youth Maltreatment

There were two items in the questionnaire that tapped the more serious forms of youth maltreatment as delineated in the Cicchetti and Barnett (1991) classification scheme. In one question, students were asked, "Have you ever been physically abused by an adult (that is, where an adult caused you to have a scar, black and blue marks, welts, bleeding, or a broken bone)?" This item is consistent with the definition of physical abuse in which an individual knowingly and willfully inflicts unnecessarily severe corporal punishment or unnecessary physical suffering on a child (Widom, 1989). Sexual abuse refers to unwanted sexual contact between a minor and an adult when the minor is being used for sexual stimulation. Incidents that occur within the family unit are referred to as incest. Sexual abuse by people outside the family is called sexual molestation (Hartman & Burgess, 1989). For this item, students were asked, "Have you ever been sexually abused by someone (that is, someone in your family, or someone else, did sexual things to you that you did not want or forced you to touch them sexually)?" Respondents were asked to report these incidents on a 5-point Likert-type scale from *never* to *more than 10 times.* For the analyses, we will employ three separate maltreatment measures: (a) a prevalence measure contrasting maltreated with nonmaltreated youth, (b) a combined maltreatment scale in which we contrast youth who are both physically and sexually maltreated with those who suffer from one form of abuse or are not maltreated, and (c) an ordinal measure of maltreatment in which we contrast youth who are nonmaltreated, occasionally maltreated (one to three incidents of abuse), and frequently maltreated (more than three incidents of abuse).

One limitation of this cross-sectional design is the difficulty in ferreting out the temporal ordering of variables. This is somewhat important because we are treating gang involvement as the dependent variable in this analysis. It is plausible that early gang involvement could trigger physical abuse (but not likely sexual abuse) by a parent, particularly if gang involvement leads to official intervention. One argument against this assumption is that most maltreatment occurs prior to adolescence and begins to desist when youth are physically more equipped to defend themselves, at about 12 to 13 years of age (Bahr, 1989; Garbarino, Schellenbach, & Sebes, 1986). Because our gang-fight item restricts responses to incidents occurring in the past 12 months, the only level for which reported incidents of gang fighting might precede physical abuse would be among 6th graders. An examination of the empirical relationship between physical maltreatment and gang fighting among 6th graders shows the direction and magnitude of this relationship to be similar to the other grades. For sexual abuse to regularly succeed gang involvement, we would need to demonstrate that a high proportion of youngsters are molested during their adolescent years. However, Crewdson (1988) reports that 75% of randomly sampled adults report that their first incident of sexual abuse occurred before the age of 12. Urquiza and Keating (1990) surveyed males and found that 83% of abuse incidents occurred before the age of 13. With most published accounts of gang involvement showing a commencement age of about 13 (Klein, 1995; Knox et al., 1995; Miller, 1982; Spergel, 1984), we are confident that most of these maltreatment episodes preceded gang involvement.

Family Relationship Variables

The instrument included several indicators of the nature of the youth's relations with parents. Parental supervision refers to how closely parents monitor their child's freedom. This was measured by the item, "How much of the time do your parents ask you where you are going or with whom you will be?" Response categories ranged from *all of the time* (1) to *never* (5). Parental support refers to the degree of warmth and understanding provided by parents. The item "My parents give me help and support when I need it" seemed to reflect this concept. How well respondents communicated with parents was measured by the item, "I have lots of good conversations with my parents." Both of these items were measured along a 5-point Likert-type scale. A measure of the level of parental interest in the youth's educational experiences was captured by the item, "How often does one of your parents talk to you about what you are doing in school?" Response categories ranged from *very often* (1) to *never* (5).

Control Variables

Several variables will be controlled in the logistic regression analysis due to their relationship to youth maltreatment and gang involvement (Smith & Thornberry, 1995; Widom, 1989). These variables include gender, race/ethnicity, grade, and family structure. Family structure was measured by whether the respondent lived all or most of the time in a single-parent family (as opposed to not living in a single-parent family). All analyses are conducted using the Statistical Package for the Social Sciences (SPSS) for Windows software.

RESULTS

Table 15–2 presents the cross tabulations (expressed as percentages) of youth maltreatment by grade, gender, race/ethnicity, and family structure. Overall, 14.5% of the sample reported that they had been physically abused by an adult to the point of receiving some type of injury. This prevalence rate resembles rates reported in studies employing either official records or self-reported measures of physical abuse (Smith & Thornberry, 1995; Trickett & McBride-Chang, 1995). Slightly more than 8% of the sample reported being sexually abused. This figure is slightly higher than the prevalence rate reported in national surveys (Finkelhor et al., 1990) but is markedly lower than estimates reported elsewhere (Boudewyn & Liem, 1995; Dickinson & Leming, 1995; Wyatt, 1985).

The distribution of physical and sexual maltreatment in this sample resembles the demographic distributions reported in other studies (Boudewyn & Liem, 1995; Pedersen & Skrondal, 1996; Salmon & Calderbank, 1996; Silverman, Reinherz, & Giaconia, 1996). Ninth graders were more likely than students in other grades to report being physically and sexually abused, although grade was a weak correlate of both forms of maltreatment. Gender is a weak correlate of physical maltreatment but is a strong correlate of sexual maltreatment. Girls in this study were eight times more likely than boys to experience sexual abuse. Being from a single-parent family almost doubles the bivariate odds of being physically and sexually maltreated. Finally, American Indians, Hispanics, and Blacks experienced greater odds of being both physically and sexually abused than Whites or Asians, although the small number of Blacks in the sample restricts confident comparisons with members of other racial/ethnic groups.

Youth Maltreatment and Gang Involvement

Does being maltreated in childhood increase a youth's odds of gang involvement? Table 15–3 presents the relationship between youth maltreatment and gang involvement for both the prevalence of gang involvement (Panel A) and the frequency of gang involvement (Panel B). The top of Panel A displays the bivariate relationships between youth maltreatment and the prevalence of gang involvement. Of the youth who were physically maltreated, 37% engaged in gang fighting compared with 20% for nonmaltreated youth. Expressed as odds, physically maltreated youth were 2.35 times more likely to be gang involved than nonmaltreated youth. For sexual maltreatment, the bivariate differences are smaller. Of those youth who were sexually

TABLE 15–2   Prevalence of Youth Maltreatment by Demographic Characteristics (in percentages)

	Physical Maltreatment		Sexual Maltreatment	
	Yes	No	Yes	No
Total sample Grade[a]	14.5	85.5	8.3	91.7
6	10.3	89.7	4.1	95.9
7	12.6	87.4	7.6	92.4
8	13.9	86.1	6.1	93.9
9	20.1	79.9	14.4	85.6
10	15.0	85.0	9.5	90.5
11	15.7	84.3	9.2	90.8
12	15.7	84.3	8.7	91.3
Gender[a]				
Male	12.2	87.8	2.0	98.0
Female	16.9	83.1	14.9	85.1
Race/ethnicity[a]				
American Indian	28.8	71.2	19.6	80.4
Asian	12.8	87.2	6.4	93.6
Black	50.0	50.0	27.8	72.2
Hispanic	18.2	81.8	11.9	88.1
White	13.4	86.6	7.5	92.5
Family structure[a]				
Intact family	12.9	87.1	7.0	93.0
Single-parent family	21.8	78.2	13.0	87.0

[a] Likelihood ratio value < .05 (2-tailed).

maltreated, 32% reported gang fighting compared with 21% of nonmaltreated youth. Here, the odds of gang involvement were 1.77 times higher for sexually maltreated than sexually nonmaltreated youth. All of these bivariate relationships are significant at the .05 level.

The bottom part of Panel A presents the multivariate relationships, controlling for grade, gender, race/ethnicity, and family structure. The regressions were run with both forms of maltreatment in the equation. Both logistic regression coefficients are significant, indicating that maltreatment has an effect on gang involvement over and above the effects of the control variables. By using the mean of the dependent variable, we can apply a simple transformation that allows us to determine the proportional effect of being maltreated on the probability of gang involvement, net of the control variables.[2] For physical maltreatment, this effect is .427 × .173 = .074. For sexual maltreatment, this effect is .363 × .173 = .063. Consequently, being physically maltreated raises a youth's odds of gang involvement by about 7.5% relative to being nonphysically maltreated. For sexual maltreatment, these odds rise by a little more than 6%. That means that the control variables reduce by 7% the effect of phys-

TABLE 15–3   Relationship Between Physical and Sexual Maltreatment and Gang Involvement

	Physical Maltreatment		Sexual Maltreatment	
	Yes	No	Yes	No
Panel A				
Prevalence of gang involvement (%)	36.7	19.7	32.3	21.2
Logistic regression coefficient $(b)^a$	.478[*]		.485[*]	
Standard error	.069		.094	
Change in probability[b]	.083		.084	
Constant	−.371		−.253	
Panel B				
Frequency of gang involvement	1.72	1.31	1.58	1.35
Ordinary least squares b coefficient[a]	.361[*]		.213[*]	
Standard error	.049		.066	
Constant	2.29			

[a] Controlling for grade level, gender, race/ethnicity, and family structure.
[b] The change in the probability of gang involvement is assessed at the mean of the dependent variable.
[*] $p < .05$, one-tailed test.

ical maltreatment on gang involvement and by 3.8% the effect of sexual maltreatment on gang involvement. Although these effects appear to be relatively small, being maltreated rivals the effect of gender, which contributes a net effect of 8.2% to gang involvement.[3] Furthermore, the explained variance contribution of maltreatment to gang involvement in this data set resembles the variance contribution of maltreatment to delinquency in other studies (see Tarter, Hegedus, Winsten, & Alterman, 1984; Widom, 1989; Zingraff et al., 1993).

We also examined the effects of a maltreatment scale in which physical and sexual maltreatment scores were combined. The bivariate results show that the odds of gang involvement are four times higher for youth who suffer both forms of maltreatment than youth who are not maltreated. When entered into the logistic regression equation, we note that being both physically and sexually maltreated raises the probability of gang involvement by roughly 13% over experiencing no maltreatment.[4]

Panel B examines the effect of being maltreated on the frequency of gang involvement. Physically maltreated youth engaged in an average of 1.72 gang fights in the past year compared with 1.31 gang fights for nonmaltreated youth. This relationship is sustained when the control variables are entered into the equation ($b = .36, p < .05$). The mean number of gang fights for sexually maltreated youth was 1.58. For youth who were not sexually maltreated, the mean was 1.35. This difference was also significant independent of the control variables ($b = .21, p < .05$).

The results in this table allow us to firmly state that being physically or sexually maltreated increases a youth's odds of gang involvement and also influences how frequently youth will participate in gang fights. These effects operate independently of the confounding variables.

Occasional Versus Frequent Maltreatment

If being physically and sexually maltreated has implications for the probability of gang involvement, does being the frequent recipient of maltreatment increase the probability of gang involvement over and above suffering occasional episodes of maltreatment? The contingency analysis shows that the odds of participating in gang fighting are two times higher for youth who are occasionally physically maltreated compared with youth who experience no maltreatment (likelihood ratio = 45.1, $p < .001$). Being frequently maltreated increases the odds of gang involvement by 1.34 times over youth who are occasionally abused. As in the logistic regression analysis, the effects of sexual abuse on gang involvement are weaker (likelihood ratio = 12.0, $p < .01$). Moreover, the odds of gang involvement in which the frequent group is compared with the occasional group is 1.15, suggesting that being sexually abused has roughly the same effect on gang involvement as suffering from numerous incidents.

These effects were also examined for the frequency of gang involvement. The results of the analyses of variance and Scheffé tests resemble the findings for the contingency tables. The mean differences are greater between the nonmaltreated group and the occasional maltreated group than between the occasional and frequent groups, and the differences are larger for physical maltreatment ($F = 48.3$, $p < .001$) than for sexual maltreatment ($F = 7.5$, $p < .01$).

Maltreatment Versus the Effects of Family Relationship Variables

We have already observed that the effects of maltreatment on gang involvement are much stronger than the impact of single parenting on gang involvement. This section examines whether maltreatment contributes more strongly to the probability of gang involvement than parental support, communication, supervision, and educational neglect. We previously noted that many gang researchers have argued that family relationship variables are typically weak correlates of gang involvement. Table 15–4 depicts the relationship between these six parenting factors and gang involvement, controlling again for demographic characteristics. The data show that none of the four parental relationship variables contributes significantly to the probability of gang involvement nor does their presence in the multivariate regression analysis weaken the effects of maltreatment on gang involvement. These findings are even more convincing if we consider that the four parent interaction variables are worded in a way that makes them more time simultaneous to gang involvement than the maltreatment variables. When these variables are transformed to their original continuous properties, the results are unchanged. Hence, we can conclude that being maltreated increases the probability that youth will participate in gangs independent of other parenting deficits that youth may experience.

DISCUSSION

We began this investigation by stating that the relationship between youth maltreatment and gang involvement is unclear. Findings to date have been mixed, mostly with samples of court-confined youth. This study departs from previous studies by examining self-reported maltreatment among nonconfined youth. The use of survey data also enables us to conduct multivariate analyses, thereby avoiding some of the shortcomings of much of the qualitative work in this area.

TABLE 15–4   Relationship Between Parenting Factors and Gang Involvement[a]

	Logistic Regression Coefficient (b)	Standard Error
Parental support	.047	.100
Parental communication	.008	.079
Parental supervision	.076	.091
Parental education neglect	.056	.127
Physical maltreatment	.429[*]	.074
Sexual maltreatment	.335[*]	.098
Constant	3.78	

[a] Controlling for grade, gender, race/ethnicity, and family structure.
[*] $p < .05$.

Our data firmly demonstrate that youth maltreatment has implications for the probability of gang involvement. Although physical maltreatment contributes slightly more variance to the probability of gang involvement than sexual maltreatment, the additive effects of the two on gang involvement are alarming. Youth who are both physically and sexually abused are about four times more likely to participate in a gang than youth who are not maltreated. In logistic regression terms, this difference translates to an increase of 13% in the probability of gang involvement.

We also find that suffering from one or a few episodes of maltreatment seems sufficient to trigger gang involvement, because youth who are repeatedly abused increase their odds of gang involvement only slightly more than occasionally abused youth. This means that prevention is likely more critical to offsetting the effects of maltreatment on gang involvement than is intervention. By the time child protection professionals discover that a child has been abused, it may be too late to avert gang involvement. Consequently, educating tomorrow's parents regarding the harm of abuse is critical.

Finally, the data confirm suspicions by several researchers regarding the effects of family relationship variables on gang involvement. Unlike maltreatment, parental supervision, support, communication, and educational interest were all unrelated to gang involvement. Nevertheless, we would argue against suspending discussion about the relationship between family interaction variables and gang involvement. We agree with Spergel (1995) that certain family factors may be interlocked with distinctive cultural and/or racial-ethnic factors in contributing to gang involvement. Identifying these factors requires exploration, because their discovery may hold one key to reducing gangs and gang-related activities.

Regrettably, the nature of this sample limits us from generalizing these findings to larger communities and those that have larger ethnic minority populations. We would encourage researchers to test these assumptions in other geographic locations and on more ethnically diverse samples. Also, although we are confident that our gang item provides a reliable and valid measure of gang involvement, we would encourage researchers to test these assumptions in which youth are asked whether they are members of a gang. We would also encourage researchers to determine whether gang participation increases the probability of physical maltreatment in the home. Although research suggests that most physical mal-treatment occurs prior to adolescence (Bahr, 1989; Garbarino et al., 1986), it is possible that gang participation could exacerbate an already troubled home situation. A test of this as-sumption requires time-ordered data.

We believe we have found one key as to why youth participate in gangs. Neverthe-less, our research stops short of identifying the intervening mechanisms that increase gang involvement among maltreated youth. Social learning theory assumptions direct us to the modeling of violence thesis, in which youth who are physically mistreated seek out groups that practice similar methods for resolving disputes. In this way, gangs mirror the familial experiences of maltreated youth. Smith and Thornberry (1995) believe, however, that being maltreated goes beyond the learning of principles for dispute resolution. They suggest a range of variables that potentially mediate the maltreatment-gang relationship. These in-clude lowered self-esteem, development of faulty attributions, maladaptive coping styles, and changes in physiological responses. Future research may wish to test whether these mechanisms help us to understand why beaten and molested youth are at greater risk for gang involvement. Solving this puzzle might assist agents and practitioners in taking a proactive, preventive stance to crack the cycle of violence.

QUESTIONS FOR UNDERSTANDING AND CRITICAL THINKING

1. To what extent does childhood abuse/maltreatment increase the risk of gang involvement?
2. Does this relationship differ if a youth had been sexually abused versus physically abused?
3. How do the effects of abuse on gang involvement differ from the effects of family re-lationship variables, i.e., parental supervision, support, and communication and gang involvement?
4. If abused youth have a greater risk for gang involvement, what kind of proactive, pre-vention strategies need to be examined and implemented?

NOTES

1. The sheriff in the county has repeatedly claimed that there are roughly 600 to 700 youth gang members in the county. Because the city comprises about 85% of the population of the county, our estimate approaches proportionately the number we would expect in the city proper.
2. This is done by multiplying the parameter estimate (b) by the variance of the dependent dichotomy.
3. The coefficients for the control variables are not presented because the focus is on the effect of the maltreatment variables. These coefficients are available on request.
4. The unstandardized coefficient for physical + sexual maltreatment was .751 when compared with the reference category for no maltreatment. Hence, .751 × .173 = .129, controlling for the effects of demographic variables.

REFERENCES

AKERS, R. L. (1994). *Criminological theories.* Los Angeles: Roxbury.
BAHR, S. J. (1989). *Family interaction.* New York: Macmillan.
BALL, R. A., & CURRY, G. D. (1995). The logic of definition in criminology: Purposes and meth-ods for defining "gangs." *Criminology, 33,* 225–246.

BLOCK, R., & BLOCK, R. (1993). *Street gang crime in Chicago* (Research in brief, National Institute of Justice, Office of Justice Programs, U.S. Department of Justice). Washington, DC: U.S. Government Printing Office.

BOLTON, F. G., REICH, J. W., & GUTIERRES, S. E. (1977). Delinquency patterns in maltreated children and siblings. *Victimology, 2,* 349–357.

BOUDEWYN, A. C., & LIEM, J. H. (1995). Childhood sexual abuse as a precursor to depression and self-destructive behavior in adulthood. *Journal of Traumatic Stress, 8,* 445–459.

BOYER, D., & FINE, D. (1992). Sexual abuse as a factor in adolescent pregnancy and child maltreatment. *Family Planning Perspectives, 24,* 4–11.

BROWNFIELD, D., THOMPSON, K. M., & SORENSON, A. M. (1997). Correlates of gang membership: A test of strain, social learning, and social control theories. *Journal of Gang Research, 4,* 11–22.

CAMPBELL, A. (1984). *The girls in the gang.* Oxford, UK: Basil Blackwell.

CHANG, J. (1996). A comparative study of female gang and non-gang members in Chicago. *Journal of Gang Research, 4,* 9–18.

CHIN, K. (1990). *Chinese subculture and criminality: Non-traditional crime groups in America.* New York: Greenwood.

CICCHETTI, D., & BARNETT, D. (1991). Toward the development of a scientific nosology of child maltreatment. In W. Grover & D. Cicchetti (Eds.). *Thinking clearly about psychology: Essays in honor of Paul E. Meehl. Vol. 2: Personality and psychopathology* (pp. 346–377). Minneapolis: University of Minnesota Press.

CONLY, C. H., KELLY, P., MAHANNA, P., & WARNER, L. (1993). *Street gangs: Current knowledge and strategies* (Report by the U.S. Department of Justice, Office of Justice Programs). Washington, DC: U.S. Government Printing Office.

CREWDSON, J. (1988). *By silence betrayed.* New York: Little, Brown.

DEMBO, R., WILLIAMS, L., LA VOIE, L., BERRY, E., GETREU, A., WISH, E. D., & SCHMEIDLER, J. (1989). Physical abuse, sexual victimization, and illicit drug use: Replication of a structural analysis among a new sample of high risk youths. *Violence and Victims, 4,* 121–138.

DICKINSON, G. E., & LEMING, M. R. (1995). *Understanding families: Diversity, continuity, and change.* Orlando, FL: Harcourt Brace.

ESBENSEN, F., HUIZINGA, D., & WEIHER, A. (1993). Gang and non-gang youth: Differences in explanatory factors. *Journal of Contemporary Criminal Justice, 9,* 94–116.

EVANS, W., & MASON, A. (1996). Factors associated with gang involvement among incarcerated youth. *Journal of Gang Research, 3,* 31–40.

FINKELHOR, D., HOTALING, G., LEWIS, I. A., & SMITH, C. (1990). Sexual abuse in a national survey of adult men and women: Prevalence, characteristics, and risk factors. *Child Abuse and Neglect, 14,* 19–28.

GARBARINO, J., SCHELLENBACH, C., & SEBES, J. (1986). *Understanding families at risk: Adolescent mistreatment.* Hawthorne, NY: Aldine.

HAGEDORN, J. (1988). *People and folks: Gangs, crime, and the underclass in a rust belt city.* Chicago: Lake View Press.

HARTMAN, C. R., & BURGESS, A. W. (1989). Sexual abuse of children: Causes and consequences. In D. Cicchetti & V. Carlson (Eds.), *Child maltreatment: Theory and research on the causes and consequences of child abuse and neglect* (pp. 95–128). Cambridge, UK: Cambridge University Press.

JANKOWSKI, M. S. (1991). *Islands in the street: Gangs and American urban society.* Berkeley: University of California Press.

JOE, D., & ROBINSON, N. (1980). Chinatown's immigrant gangs. *Criminology, 18,* 337–345.

JOE, K. A., & CHESNEY-LIND, M. (1995). Just every mother's angel: An analysis of gender and ethnic variations in youth gang membership. *Gender and Society, 9,* 408–431.

JOHNSEN, L. W., & HARLOW, L. L. (1996). Childhood sexual abuse linked with adult substance use, victimization, and AIDS-risk. *AIDS Education and Prevention, 8,* 44–57.

KLEIN, M. W. (1995). *The American street gang. Its nature, prevalence, and control.* New York: Oxford University Press.

KNOX, G. W. (1994). *An introduction to gangs.* Bristol, IN: Wyndham Hall Press.

KNOX, G. W. (1996). Gang profile: The Black Disciples. *Journal of Gang Research, 3,* 45–65.

KNOX, G. W., HARRIS, J. M., McCURRIE, T. F., ELDER, A. P., TROMANHAUSER, E. D., & LASKEY, J. A. (1996). *Achieving justice and reversing the problem of gang crime and gang violence in America today: Preliminary results of the Project GANGFACT.* Chicago: Chicago State University, National Gang Crime Research Center.

KNOX, G. W., MARTIN, B. J., ELDER, A. P., HOLMES, S. R., MORRIS, R. E., & AQUINO, K. (1995). *Gang prevention and gang intervention: Preliminary results from the 1995 Project GANGPINT.* Chicago: National Needs Assessment Gang Research Task Force, Chicago State University, National Gang Crime Research Center.

MAXSON, C. L., GORDON, M. A., & KLEIN, M. W. (1985). Differences between gang and nongang homicides. *Criminology, 23,* 209–222.

MILLER, W. B. (1975). *Violence by youth gangs and youth groups as a crime problem in major American cities.* (Technical report of the National Institute for Juvenile Justice and Delinquency Prevention, Office of Juvenile Justice and Delinquency Prevention, U.S. Department of Justice). Washington, DC: U.S. Government Printing Office.

MILLER, W. B. (1982). *Crime by youth gangs and groups in the United States* (Technical report of the National Institute for Juvenile Justice and Delinquency Prevention, U.S. Department of Justice). Washington, DC: Office of Juvenile Justice and Delinquency Prevention.

NATIONAL CENTER ON CHILD ABUSE AND NEGLECT. (1988). *Study findings: Study of national incidence and prevalence of child abuse and neglect.* Washington, DC: U.S. Department of Health and Human Services.

PEDERSEN, W., & SKRONDAL, A. (1996). Alcohol and sexual victimization: A longitudinal study of Norwegian girls. *Addiction, 91,* 565–581.

RHODES, J. E., & FISCHER, K. (1993). Spanning the gender gap: Gender differences in delinquency among inner city adolescents. *Adolescence, 28,* 879–889.

ROTHERAM-BORUS, M. J., MAHLER, K. A., KOOPMAN, C., & LANGABEER, K. (1996). Sexual abuse history and associated multiple risk behavior in adolescent runaways. *American Journal of Orthopsychiatry, 66,* 390–400.

RUTTER, M., & GILLER, H. (1983). *Juvenile delinquency: Trends and perspectives.* New York: Guilford.

SALMON, P., & CALDERBANK, S. (1996). The relationship of childhood physical and sexual abuse to adult illness behavior. *Journal of Psychosomatic Research, 40,* 329–336.

SCHAAF, K. K., & McCANNE, T. R. (1994). Childhood abuse, body image disturbance, and eating disorders. *Child Abuse and Neglect, 18,* 607–615.

SEARCH INSTITUTE. (1994). *Profiles of student life: Attitudes and behaviors.* Minneapolis, MN: Author.

SILVERMAN, A. B., REINHERZ, H. Z., & GIACONIA, R. M. (1996). The long-term sequelae of child and adolescent abuse: A longitudinal community study. *Child Abuse and Neglect, 20,* 709–723.

SIMPSON, T. L., WESTERBERG, V. S., LITTLE, L. M., & TRUJILLO, M. (1994). Screening for childhood physical and sexual abuse among outpatient substance abusers. *Journal of Substance Abuse Treatment, 11,* 347–358.

SLAVIK, S., CARLSON, J., & SPERRY, L. (1995). Extreme lifestyles of adults who have experienced sexual abuse. *Individual Psychology, 51,* 358–374.

SMITH, C. S., & THORNBERRY, T. P. (1995). The relationship between childhood maltreatment and adolescent involvement in delinquency. *Criminology, 33,* 451–481.

SPERGEL, I. A. (1984, June). Violent gangs in Chicago: In search of social policy. *Social Service Review,* 201–202.

SPERGEL, I. A. (1995). *The youth gang problem: A community approach.* New York: Oxford University Press.

STRAUS, M. A., & GELLES, R. J. (1986). Societal change and change in family violence from 1975 to 1985 as revealed by two national surveys. *Journal of Marriage and the Family, 48,* 465–479.

TARTER, R. E., HEGEDUS, A. M., WINSTEN, N. E., & ALTERMAN, A. I. (1984). Neuropsychological, personality, and familial characteristics of physically abused delinquents. *Journal of the American Academy of Child Psychiatry, 23,* 668–674.

THOMPSON, K. M., BROWNFIELD, D., & SORENSON, A. (1996). Specialization patterns of gang and nongang offending: A latent structure analysis. *Journal of Gang Research, 3,* 25–35.

THRASHER, F. M. (1927). *The gang: A study of 1,313 gangs in Chicago.* Chicago: University of Chicago Press.

TRACY, P. E. (1979). *Subcultural delinquency: A comparison of the incidence and seriousness of gang and nongang member offensivity.* Philadelphia: University of Pennsylvania, Center for Studies in Criminology and Criminal Law.

TRICKETT, P. K., & MCBRIDE-CHANG, C. (1995). The developmental impact of different forms of child abuse and neglect. *Developmental Review, 15,* 311–337.

URQUIZA, A. J., & KEATING, L. M. (1990). The prevalence of sexual victimization of males. In M. Hunter (Ed.), *The sexually abused male.* Lexington, MA: Lexington Books.

VIGIL, J. D. (1988). *Barrio gangs: Street life and identity in Southern California.* Houston: University of Texas Press.

WIDOM, C. S. (1989). Child abuse, neglect, and violent criminal behavior. *Criminology, 27,* 251–271.

WIDOM, C. S. (1996). Childhood sexual abuse and its criminal consequences. *Society, 33,* 47–53.

WYATT, G. E. (1985). The sexual abuse of Afro-American and White-American women in childhood. *Child Abuse and Neglect, 9,* 507–519.

YABLONSKY, L. (1959). The delinquent gang as a near-group. *Social Problems, 7,* 108–117.

YAMA, M. F., TOVEY, S. L., FOGAS, B. S., & MORRIS, J. (1995). The relationship among childhood sexual abuse, parental alcoholism, family environment and suicidal behavior in female college students. *Journal of Child Sexual Abuse, 4,* 79–93.

ZINGRAFF, M. T., LEITER, J., MYERS, K. A., & JOHNSON, M. C. (1993). Child maltreatment and youthful problem behavior. *Criminology, 31,* 173–202.

16

Gender and Victimization Risk Among Young Women in Gangs

Jody Miller

Research has documented the enhancement effects of gang involvement for criminal offending, but little attention has been given to victimization. This article examines how gang involvement shapes young women's risks of victimization. Based on interviews with active gang members, the author suggests that (1) gang participation exposes youths to victimization risk and (2) it does so in gendered ways. Young women can use gender to decrease their risk of being harmed by rival gangs or other street participants by not participating in "masculine" activities such as fighting and committing crime. However, the consequence is that they are viewed as lesser members of their gangs and may be exposed to greater risk of victimization within their gangs. The author suggests that more research is needed to examine whether and how gang involvement enhances youths' exposure to victimization risk, and that researchers should maintain a recognition of the role of gender in shaping these processes.

An underdeveloped area in the gang literature is the relationship between gang participation and victimization risk. There are notable reasons to consider the issue significant. We now have strong evidence that delinquent lifestyles are associated with increased risk of victimization (Lauritsen, Sampson, and Laub 1991). Gangs are social groups that are or-

An earlier version of this article was presented as a paper at the 1997 National Research and Evaluation Conference, Washington, DC. Thanks to David Curry, Kathy Daly, Scott Decker, Janet Lauritsen, Cheryl Maxson, Richard Wright, and anonymous *Journal of Research in Crime and Delinquency* reviewers for constructive remarks on earlier versions of this article. This work was supported by a grant from the National Institute of Justice (grant 951642394). Opinions expressed are those of the author and do not necessarily reflect those of the funding agency.
Miller, J. Gender and victimization risk among young women in gangs. *Journal of Research in Crime and Delinquency,* 35 (1998). Pp. 429–453. Reprinted by permission of Sage Publications, Inc.

ganized around delinquency (see Klein 1995), and participation in gangs has been shown to escalate youths' involvement in crime, including violent crime (Esbensen and Huizinga 1993; Esbensen, Huizinga, and Weiher 1993; Fagan 1989, 1990; Thornberry et al. 1993). Moreover, research on gang violence indicates that the primary targets of this violence are other gang members (Block and Block 1993; Decker 1996; Klein and Maxson 1989; Sanders 1993). As such, gang participation can be recognized as a delinquent lifestyle that is likely to involve high risks of victimization (see Huff 1996:97). Although research on female gang involvement has expanded in recent years and includes the examination of issues such as violence and victimization, the oversight regarding the relationship between gang participation and violent victimization extends to this work as well.

The coalescence of attention to the proliferation of gangs and gang violence (Block and Block 1993; Curry, Ball, and Decker 1996; Decker 1996; Klein 1995; Klein and Maxson 1989; Sanders 1993), and a possible disproportionate rise in female participation in violent crimes more generally (Baskin, Sommers, and Fagan 1993; but see Chesney-Lind, Shelden, and Joe 1996), has led to a specific concern with examining female gang members' violent activities. As a result, some recent research on girls in gangs has examined these young women's participation in violence and other crimes as offenders (Bjerregaard and Smith 1993; Brotherton 1996; Fagan 1990; Lauderback, Hansen, and Waldorf 1992; Taylor, 1993). However, an additional question worth investigation is what relationships exist between young women's gang involvement and their experiences and risk of victimization. Based on in-depth interviews with female gang members, this article examines the ways in which gender shapes victimization risk within street gangs.

GENDER, VIOLENCE, AND VICTIMIZATION

Feminist scholars have played a significant role in bringing attention to the overlapping nature of women's criminal offending and patterns of victimization, emphasizing the relationships of gender inequality and sexual exploitation to women's participation in crime (Arnold 1990; Campbell 1984; Chesney-Lind and Rodriguez 1983; Daly 1992; Gilfus 1992). In regard to female gang involvement, recent research suggests that young women in gangs have disproportionate histories of victimization before gang involvement as compared with non-gang females (Miller 1996) and gang males (Joe and Chesney-Lind 1995; Moore 1991). Moreover, there is evidence that young women turn to gangs, in part, as a means of protecting themselves from violence and other problems in their families and from mistreatment at the hands of men in their lives (Joe and Chesney-Lind 1995; Lauderback et al. 1992).

This is not surprising, given the social contexts these young women face. Many young women in gangs are living in impoverished urban "underclass" communities where violence is both extensive and a "sanctioned response to [the] oppressive material conditions" associated with inequality, segregation, and isolation (Simpson 1991:129; see also Sampson and Wilson 1995; Wilson 1996). Moreover, violence against *women* is heightened by the nature of the urban street world, where gendered power relations are played out (Connell 1987), crack markets have intensified the degradation of women (Bourgois and Dunlap 1993; Maher and Curtis 1992), and structural changes may have increased cultural support for violence against women (Wilson 1996).

The social world of adolescence is highly gendered as well (Eder 1995; Lees 1993; Thorne 1993). It is a period in which peer relationships increase in significance for youths, and this is magnified, especially for girls, with increased self-consciousness and sensitivity to others' perceptions of them (Pesce and Harding 1986). In addition, it is characterized by a "shift from the relatively asexual gender system of childhood to the overtly sexualized gender systems of adolescence and adulthood" (Thorne 1993:135). Young women find themselves in a contradictory position. Increasingly, they receive status from their peers via their association with, and attractiveness to, young men, but they are denigrated for their sexual activity and threatened with the labels *slut* and *ho* (Eder 1995; Lees 1993). The contexts of adolescence and the urban street world, then, have unique features likely to make young women particularly vulnerable to victimization. Thus, for some young women, gang involvement may appear to be a useful means of negotiating within these environments.

However, as Bourgois (1995) notes, actions taken to resist oppression can ultimately result in increased harm. Among young women in gangs, an important question to examine is how participation in gangs itself shapes young women's risk of victimization, including the question of whether gang involvement places girls at higher risks of victimization because of a potential increased involvement in crime. Lauritsen et al. (1991) found that "adolescent involvement in delinquent lifestyles strongly increases the risk of both personal and property victimization" (p. 265). Moreover, gender as a predictor of victimization risk among adolescents decreases when participation in delinquent lifestyles is controlled for (Lauritsen et al. 1991). That is, much of young men's greater victimization risk can be accounted for by their greater participation in offending behaviors. Among gang members, then, involvement in crime is likely associated with increased risk for victimization. Gang girls' participation in crime is thus an important consideration if we hope to understand the relationship between their gang membership and victimization risk.

GIRLS, GANGS, AND CRIME

Research comparing gang and nongang youths has consistently found that serious criminal involvement is a feature that distinguishes gangs from other groups of youths (Bjerregaard and Smith 1993; Esbensen and Huizinga 1993; Esbensen et al. 1993; Fagan 1989, 1990; Klein 1995; Thornberry et al. 1993; Winfree et al. 1992). Until recently, however, little attention was paid to young women's participation in serious and violent gang-related crime. Most traditional gang research emphasized the auxiliary and peripheral nature of girls' gang involvement and often resulted in an almost exclusive emphasis on girls' sexuality and sexual activities with male gang members, downplaying their participation in delinquency (for critiques of gender bias in gang research, see Campbell 1984, 1990; Taylor 1993).

However, recent estimates of female gang involvement have caused researchers to pay greater attention to gang girls' activities. This evidence suggests that young women approximate anywhere from 10 to 38 percent of gang members (Campbell 1984; Chesney-Lind 1993; Esbensen 1996; Fagan 1990; Moore 1991), that female gang participation may be increasing (Fagan 1990; Spergel and Curry 1993; Taylor 1993), and that in some urban areas, upward of one-fifth of girls report gang affiliations (Bjerregaard and Smith 1993; Winfree et al. 1992). As female gang members have become recognized as a group worthy of criminologists' attention, we have garnered new information regarding their involvement in delinquency in general, and violence in particular.

Recent research on female gang involvement indicates that the pattern of higher rates of criminal involvement for gang members holds for girls as well as their male counterparts (Bjerregaard and Smith 1993; Esbensen and Winfree forthcoming; Thornberry et al. 1993).

The enhancement effect of gang membership is most noticeable for serious delinquency and marijuana use (Thornberry et al. 1993). Bjerregaard and Smith (1993) summarize:

> The traditional gang literature has generally suggested that gang membership enhances delinquent activity, and particularly serious delinquent activity for males, but not for females. In contrast, our study suggests that for females also, gangs are consistently associated with a greater prevalence and with higher rates of delinquency and substance use. Furthermore, the results suggest that for both sexes, gang membership has an approximately equal impact on a variety of measures of delinquent behavior. (P. 346)

An interesting counterpart is provided by Bowker, Gross, and Klein (1980), who suggest there is evidence of "the structural exclusion of young women from male delinquent activities" within gangs (p. 516). Their (male) respondents suggested that not only were girls excluded from the planning of delinquent acts, but when girls inadvertently showed up at the location of a planned incident, it was frequently postponed or terminated. Likewise, Fagan (1990) reports greater gender differences in delinquency between gang members than between nongang youths (pp. 196–97). Male gang members were significantly more involved in the most serious forms of delinquency, whereas for alcohol use, drug sales, extortion, and property damage, gender differences were not significant.

However, Fagan also reports that "prevalence rates for female gang members exceeded the rates for non-gang males" for all the categories of delinquency he measured (see also Esbensen and Winfree 1998). Fagan (1990) summarizes his findings in relation to girls as follows:

> More than 40% of the female gang members were classified in the least serious category, a substantial difference from their male counterparts [15.5 percent]. Among female gang members, there was a bimodal distribution, with nearly as many multiple index offenders as petty delinquents. Evidently, female gang members avoid more serious delinquent involvement than their male counterparts. *Yet their extensive involvement in serious delinquent behaviors well exceeds that of non-gang males or females.* (P. 201, my emphasis)

Few would dispute that when it comes to serious delinquency, male gang members are involved more frequently than their female counterparts. However, this evidence does suggest that young women in gangs are more involved in serious criminal activities than was previously believed and also tend to be more involved than nongang youths—male or female. As such, they likely are exposed to greater victimization risk than nongang youths as well.

In addition, given the social contexts described, it is reasonable to assume that young women's victimization risk within gangs is also shaped by gender. Gang activities (such as fighting for status and retaliation) create a particular set of factors that increase gang members' victimization risk and repeat victimization risk—constructions of gender identity may shape these risks in particular ways for girls. For instance, young women's adoption of masculine attributes may provide a means of participating and gaining status within gangs but may also lead to increased risk of victimization as a result of deeper immersion in delinquent activities. On the other hand, experiences of victimization may contribute to girls' denigration and thus increase their risk for repeat victimization through gendered responses and labeling—for example, when sexual victimization leads to perceptions of sexual availability or when victimization leads an individual to be viewed as weak. In addition, femaleness is an individual attribute that has the capacity to mark young women as "safe" crime victims (e.g., easy targets) or, conversely, to deem them "off limits." My goal here is to examine the gendered nature of violence within gangs, with a specific focus on how gender shapes young women's victimization risk.

METHODOLOGY

Data presented in this article come from survey and semistructured in-depth interviews with 20 female members of mixed-gender gangs in Columbus, Ohio. The interviewees ranged in age from 12 to 17; just over three-quarters were African American or multiracial (16 of 20), and the rest (4 of 20) were White. The sample was drawn primarily from several local agencies in Columbus working with at-risk youths, including the county juvenile detention center, a shelter care facility for adolescent girls, a day school within the same institution, and a local community agency.[1] The project was structured as a gang/nongang comparison, and I interviewed a total of 46 girls. Gang membership was determined during the survey interview by self-definition: About one-quarter of the way through the 50+ page interview, young women were asked a series of questions about the friends they spent time with. They then were asked whether these friends were gang involved and whether they themselves were gang members. Of the 46 girls interviewed, 21 reported that they were gang members,[2] and an additional 3 reported being gang involved (hanging out primarily with gangs or gang members) but not gang members. The rest reported no gang involvement.

A great deal of recent research suggests that self-report data provide comparatively reliable and valid measures of youths' gang membership (see Bjerregaard and Smith 1993; Fagan 1990; Thornberry et al. 1993; Winfree et al. 1992). This research suggests that using more restrictive measures (such as initiation rituals, a gang name, symbolic systems such as colors or signs) does not change substantive conclusions concerning gang members' behaviors when comparing self-defined gang members to those members who meet these more restrictive definitions. Although most researchers agree that the group should be involved in illegal activities in order for the youth to be classified as a gang member (see Esbensen et al. 1993; Esbensen and Huizinga 1993; Fagan 1989), other research that has used self-nomination without specifying crime as a defining feature has nonetheless consistently found serious criminal involvement as a feature that distinguishes gangs from other groups of youths (Fagan 1990; Thornberry et al. 1993; Winfree et al. 1992). All the gang members in my sample were members of groups they described as delinquent.

Cooperation from agency personnel generally proves successful for accessing gang members (see Bowker et al. 1980; Fagan 1989; Short and Strodtbeck 1965). However, these referrals pose the problem of targeting only officially labeled gang youth. I took several steps to temper this problem. First, I did not choose agencies that dealt specifically with gang members, and I did not rely on agency rosters of "known" gang members for my sample. As a result of the gang/nongang comparative research design, I was able to avoid oversampling girls who were labeled as gang members by asking agency personnel to refer me not just to girls believed to be gang involved but also any other girls living in areas in Columbus where they might have contact with gangs. Second, although I was only moderately successful, throughout the project I attempted to expand my sample on the basis of snowball techniques (see Fagan 1989; Hagedorn 1988). I only generated one successful referral outside of the agency contexts. However, I was successful at snowballing *within* agencies. Several girls I interviewed were gang involved but without staff knowledge, and they were referred to me by other girls I interviewed within the facilities. Thus, in a limited capacity, I was able to interview gang members who had not been detected by officials. Nonetheless, my sample is still limited to youths who have experienced intervention in some capacity, whether formal or informal, and thus it may not be representative of gang-involved girls in the community at large.

The survey interview was a variation of several instruments currently being used in research in a number of cities across the United States and included a broad range of questions and scales measuring factors that may be related to gang membership.[3] On issues related to violence, it included questions about peer activities and delinquency, individual delinquent involvement, family violence and abuse, and victimization. When young women responded affirmatively to being gang members, I followed with a series of questions about the nature of their gang, including its size, leadership, activities, symbols, and so on. Girls who admitted gang involvement during the survey participated in a follow-up interview to talk in more depth about their gangs and gang activities. The goal of the in-depth interview was to gain a greater understanding of the nature and meanings of gang life from the point of view of its female members. A strength of qualitative interviewing is its ability to shed light on this aspect of the social world, highlighting the meanings individuals attribute to their experiences (Adler and Adler 1987; Glassner and Loughlin 1987; Miller and Glassner 1997). In addition, using multiple methods, including follow-up interviews, provided me with a means of detecting inconsistencies in young women's accounts of their experiences. Fortunately, no serious contradictions arose. However, a limitation of the data is that only young women were interviewed. Thus, I make inferences about gender dynamics, and young men's behavior, based only on young women's perspectives.

The in-depth interviews were open-ended and all but one were audiotaped. They were structured around several groupings of questions. We began by discussing girls' entry into their gangs—when and how they became involved, and what other things were going on in their lives at the time. Then, we discussed the structure of the gang—its history, size, leadership, and organization, and their place in the group. The next series of questions concerned gender within the gang; for example, how girls get involved, what activities they engage in and whether these are the same as the young men's activities, and what kind of males and females have the most influence in the gang and why. The next series of questions explored gang involvement more generally—what being in the gang means, what kinds of things they do together, and so on. Then, I asked how safe or dangerous they feel gang membership is and how they deal with risk. I concluded by asking them to speculate about why people their age join gangs, what things they like, what they dislike and have learned by being in the gang, and what they like best about themselves. This basic guideline was followed for each interview subject, although when additional topics arose in the context of the interview, we often deviated from the interview guide to pursue them. Throughout the interviews, issues related to violence emerged; these issues form the core of the discussion that follows.

SETTING

Columbus is a particular type of gang city. Gangs are a relatively new phenomenon there, with their emergence dated around 1985 (Maxson, Woods, and Klein 1995). In addition, it is thriving economically, experiencing both population and economic growth over the last decade (Rusk 1995). As such, it is representative of a recent pattern of gang proliferation into numerous cities, suburbs, and towns that do not have many of the long-standing problems associated with traditional gang cities, such as deindustrialization, population loss, and the deterioration of social support networks (see Curry et al. 1996; Hagedorn 1988; Klein 1995; Maxson et al. 1995; Spergel and Curry 1993). Even as Columbus has prospered, however, its racial disparities have grown (Columbus Metropolitan Human Services Commission 1995:17). In fact, in relative terms (comparing the gap between African Americans and Whites), racial disparities in measures such as income and percentage poverty in Columbus are equal to or even greater than in many cities experiencing economic and population declines.[4]

According to recent police estimates, Columbus has about 30 active gangs, with 400 to 1,000 members (LaLonde 1995). Most of these groups are small in size (20 or fewer members) and are either African American or racially mixed with a majority of African American members (Mayhood and LaLonde 1995). Gangs in Columbus have adopted "big-city" gang names such as Crips, Bloods, and Folks, along with the dress styles, signs, and graffiti of these groups, although gangs are and have been primarily a "homegrown" problem in Columbus rather than a result of organized gang migration (Huff 1989). Local police view these groups as criminally oriented, but not especially sophisticated. On the whole, gangs in Columbus seem to match those described in other cities with emergent gang problems—best characterized as "relatively autonomous, smaller independent groups, poorly organized and less territorial" than in older gang cities (Klein 1995:36).

The young women I interviewed described their gangs in ways that are very much in keeping with these findings. All 20 are members of Folks, Crips, or Bloods sets.[5] All but 3 described gangs with fewer than 30 members, and most reported relatively narrow age ranges between members. Half were in gangs with members who were 21 or over, but almost without exception, their gangs were made up primarily of teenagers, with either one adult who was considered the OG ("Original Gangster," leader) or just a handful of young adults. The majority (14 of 20) reported that their gangs did not include members under the age of 13.

Although the gangs these young women were members of were composed of both female and male members, they varied in their gender composition, with the vast majority being predominantly male. Six girls reported that girls were one-fifth or fewer of the members of their gang; 8 were in gangs in which girls were between a quarter and a third of the overall membership; 4 said girls were between 44 and 50 percent of the members; and 1 girl reported that her gang was two-thirds female and one-third male. Overall, girls were typically a minority within these groups numerically, with 11 girls reporting that there were 5 or fewer girls in their set.

This structure—male-dominated, integrated mixed-gender gangs—likely shapes gender dynamics in particular ways. Much past gang research has assumed that female members of gangs are in auxiliary subgroups of male gangs, but there is increasing evidence—including from the young women I spoke with—that many gangs can be characterized as integrated, mixed-gender groups. For example, from interviews with 110 female gang members in three sites (Boston, Seattle, and Pueblo, Colorado), Curry (1997) found integrated mixed-gender gangs to be the predominant gang structure of female gang members, with 57.3 percent of girls describing their gangs as mixed-gender.[6] It is likely that gang structure shapes both status orientations and criminal involvement among gang members (Brotherton 1996), and that these differences may also be mediated by ethnicity (Brotherton 1996; Joe and Chesney-Lind 1995; Moore and Hagedorn 1996). Generalizability beyond mixed-gender, predominantly African American gangs in emergent gang cities, then, is questionable.

GENDER, GANGS, AND VIOLENCE

Gangs as Protection and Risk

An irony of gang involvement is that although many members suggest one thing they get out of the gang is a sense of protection (see also Decker 1996; Joe and Chesney-Lind 1995; Lauderback et al. 1992), gang membership itself means exposure to victimization risk and even a willingness to be victimized. These contradictions are apparent when girls talk about what they get out of the gang, and what being in the gang means in terms of other members' expectations of their behavior. In general, a number of girls suggested that being a gang member is a source of protection around the neighborhood. Erica,[7] a 17-year-old African American, explained, "It's like people look at us and that's exactly what they think, there's a gang, and they respect us for that. They won't bother us. . . . It's like you put that intimidation in somebody." Likewise, Lisa, a 14-year-old White girl, described being in the gang as empowering: "You just feel like, oh my God, you know, they got my back. I don't need to worry about it." Given the violence endemic in many inner-city communities, these beliefs are understandable, and to a certain extent, accurate.

In addition, some young women articulated a specifically gendered sense of protection that they felt as a result of being a member of a group that was predominantly male. Gangs operate within larger social milieus that are characterized by gender inequality and sexual exploitation. Being in a gang with young men means at least the semblance of protection from, and retaliation against, predatory men in the social environment. Heather, a 15-year-old White girl, noted, "You feel more secure when, you know, a guy's around protectin' you, you know, than you would a girl." She explained that as a gang member, because "you get protected by guys . . . not as many people mess with you." Other young women concurred and also described that male gang members could retaliate against specific acts of violence against girls in the gang. Nikkie, a 13-year-old African American girl, had a friend who was raped by a rival gang member, and she said, "It was a Crab [Crip] that raped my girl in Miller Ales, and, um, they was ready to kill him." Keisha, an African American 14-year-old, explained, "If I got beat up by a guy, all I gotta do is go tell one of the niggers, you know what I'm sayin'? Or one of the guys, they'd take care of it."

At the same time, members recognized that they may be targets of rival gang members and were expected to "be down" for their gang at those times even when it meant being physically hurt. In addition, initiation rites and internal rules were structured in ways that required individuals to submit to, and be exposed to, violence. For example, young women's descriptions of the qualities they valued in members revealed the extent to which exposure to violence was an expected element of gang involvement. Potential members, they explained, should be tough, able to fight and to engage in criminal activities, and also should be loyal to the group and willing to put themselves at risk for it. Erica explained that they didn't want "punks" in her gang: "When you join something like that, you might as well expect that there's gonna be fights. . . . And, if you're a punk, or if you're scared of stuff like that, then don't join." Likewise, the following dialogue with Cathy, a White 16-year-old, reveals similar themes. I asked her what her gang expected out of members and she responded, "to be true to our gang and to have our backs." When I asked her to elaborate, she explained,

> *Cathy:*   Like, uh, if you say you're a Blood, you be a Blood. You wear your rag even when you're by yourself. You know, don't let anybody intimidate you and

be like, "Take that rag off." You know, "you better get with our set." Or something like that.

JM: Ok. Anything else that being true to the set means?

Cathy: Um. Yeah, I mean, just, just, you know, I mean it's, you got a whole bunch of people comin' up in your face and if you're by yourself they ask you what's your claimin', you tell 'em. Don't say "nothin'."

JM: Even if it means getting beat up or something?

Cathy: Mmhmm.

One measure of these qualities came through the initiation process, which involved the individual submitting to victimization at the hands of the gang's members. Typically this entailed either taking a fixed number of "blows" to the head and/or chest or being "beaten in" by members for a given duration (e.g., 60 seconds). Heather described the initiation as an important event for determining whether someone would make a good member:

> When you get beat in if you don't fight back and if you just like stop and you start cryin' or somethin' or beggin' 'em to stop and stuff like that, then, they ain't gonna, they'll just stop and they'll say that you're not gang material because you gotta be hard, gotta be able to fight, take punches.

In addition to the initiation, and threats from rival gangs, members were expected to adhere to the gang's internal rules (which included such things as not fighting with one another, being "true" to the gang, respecting the leader, not spreading gang business outside the gang, and not dating members of rival gangs). Breaking the rules was grounds for physical punishment, either in the form of a spontaneous assault or a formal "violation," which involved taking a specified number of blows to the head. For example, Keisha reported that she talked back to the leader of her set and "got slapped pretty hard" for doing so. Likewise, Veronica, an African American 15-year-old, described her leader as "crazy, but we gotta listen to 'im. He's just the type that if you don't listen to 'im, he gonna blow your head off. He's just crazy."

It is clear that regardless of members' perceptions of the gang as a form of "protection," being a gang member also involves a willingness to open oneself up to the possibility of victimization. Gang victimization is governed by rules and expectations, however, and thus does not involve the random vulnerability that being out on the streets without a gang might entail in high-crime neighborhoods. Because of its structured nature, this victimization risk may be perceived as more palatable by gang members. For young women in particular, the gendered nature of the streets may make the empowerment available through gang involvement an appealing alternative to the individualized vulnerability they otherwise would face. However, as the next sections highlight, girls' victimization risks continue to be shaped by gender, even within their gangs, because these groups are structured around gender hierarchies as well.

Gender and Status, Crime and Victimization

Status hierarchies within Columbus gangs, like elsewhere, were male dominated (Bowker et al. 1980; Campbell 1990). Again, it is important to highlight that the structure of the gangs these young women belonged to—that is, male-dominated, integrated mixed-gender gangs—likely shaped the particular ways in which gender dynamics played themselves out. Autonomous female gangs, as well as gangs in which girls are in auxiliary subgroups, may be shaped by different gender relations, as well as differences in orientations toward status, and criminal involvement.

All the young women reported having established leaders in their gang, and this leadership was almost exclusively male. While LaShawna, a 17-year-old African American, reported being the leader of her set (which had a membership that is two-thirds girls, many of whom resided in the same residential facility as her), all the other girls in mixed-gender gangs reported that their OG was male. In fact, a number of young women stated explicitly that only male gang members could be leaders. Leadership qualities, and qualities attributed to high-status members of the gang—being tough, able to fight, and willing to "do dirt" (e.g., commit crime, engage in violence) for the gang—were perceived as characteristically masculine. Keisha noted, "The guys, they just harder." She explained, "Guys is more rougher. We have our G's back but, it ain't gonna be like the guys, they just don't give a fuck. They gonna shoot you in a minute." For the most part, status in the gang was related to traits such as the willingness to use serious violence and commit dangerous crimes and, though not exclusively, these traits were viewed primarily as qualities more likely and more intensely located among male gang members.

Because these respected traits were characterized specifically as masculine, young women actually may have had greater flexibility in their gang involvement than young men. Young women had fewer expectations placed on them—by both their male and female peers—in regard to involvement in criminal activities such as fighting, using weapons, and committing other crimes. This tended to decrease girls' exposure to victimization risk comparable to male members, because they were able to avoid activities likely to place them in danger. Girls *could* gain status in the gang by being particularly hard and true to the set. Heather, for example, described the most influential girl in her set as "the hardest girl, the one that don't take no crap, will stand up to anybody." Likewise, Diane, a White 15-year-old, described a highly respected female member in her set as follows:

> People look up to Janeen just 'cause she's so crazy. People just look up to her 'cause she don't care about nothin'. She don't even care about makin' money. Her, her thing is, "Oh, you're a Slob [Blood]? You're a Slob? You talkin' to me? You talkin' shit to me?" Pow, pow! And that's it. That's it.

However, young women also had a second route to status that was less available to young men. This came via their connections—as sisters, girl-friends, cousins—to influential, high-status young men.[8] In Veronica's set, for example, the girl with the most power was the OG's "sister or his cousin, one of 'em." His girlfriend also had status, although Veronica noted that "most of us just look up to our OG." Monica, a 16-year-old African American, and Tamika, a 15-year-old African American, both had older brothers in their gangs, and both reported getting respect, recognition, and protection because of this connection. This route to status and the masculinization of high-status traits functioned to maintain gender inequality within gangs, but they also could put young women at less risk of victimization than young men. This was both because young women were perceived as less threatening and thus were less likely to be targeted by rivals, and because they were not expected to prove themselves in the ways that young men were, thus decreasing their participation in those delinquent activities likely to increase exposure to violence. Thus, gender inequality could have a protective edge for young women.

Young men's perceptions of girls as lesser members typically functioned to keep girls from being targets of serious violence at the hands of rival young men, who instead left routine confrontations with rival female gang members to the girls in their own gang. Diane said that young men in her gang "don't wanna waste their time hittin' on some little girls. They're gonna go get their little cats [females] to go get 'em." Lisa remarked,

> Girls don't face much violence as [guys]. They see a girl, they say, "we'll just smack her and send her on." They see a guy—'cause guys are like a lot more into it than girls are, I've noticed that—and they like, well, "we'll shoot him."

In addition, the girls I interviewed suggested that, in comparison with young men, young women were less likely to resort to serious violence, such as that involving a weapon, when confronting rivals. Thus, when girls' routine confrontations were more likely to be female on female than male on female, girls' risk of serious victimization was lessened further.

Also, because participation in serious and violent crime was defined primarily as a masculine endeavor, young women could use gender as a means of avoiding participation in those aspects of gang life they found risky, threatening, or morally troubling. Of the young women I interviewed, about one-fifth were involved in serious gang violence: A few had been involved in aggravated assaults on rival gang members, and one admitted to having killed a rival gang member, but they were by far the exception. Most girls tended not to be involved in serious gang crime, and some reported that they chose to exclude themselves because they felt ambivalent about this aspect of gang life. Angie, an African American 15-year-old, explained,

> I don't get involved like that, be out there goin' and just beat up people like that or go stealin', things like that. That's not me. The boys, mostly the boys do all that, the girls we just sit back and chill, you know.

Likewise, Diane noted,

> For maybe a drive-by they might wanna have a bunch of dudes. They might not put the females in that. Maybe the females might be weak inside, not strong enough to do something like that, just on the insides. . . . If a female wants to go forward and doin' that, and she wants to risk her whole life for doin' that, then she can. But the majority of the time, that job is given to a man.

Diane was not just alluding to the idea that young men were stronger than young women. She also inferred that young women were able to get out of committing serious crime, more so than young men, because a girl shouldn't have to "risk her whole life" for the gang. In accepting that young men were more central members of the gang, young women could more easily participate in gangs without putting themselves in jeopardy—they could engage in the more routine, everyday activities of the gang, like hanging out, listening to music, and smoking bud (marijuana). These male-dominated mixed-gender gangs thus appeared to provide young women with flexibility in their involvement in gang activities. As a result, it is likely that their risk of victimization at the hands of rivals was less than that of young men in gangs who were engaged in greater amounts of crime.

Girls' Devaluation and Victimization

In addition to girls choosing not to participate in serious gang crimes, they also faced exclusion at the hands of young men or the gang as a whole (see also Bowker et al. 1980). In particular, the two types of crime mentioned most frequently as "off-limits" for girls were drug sales and drive-by shootings. LaShawna explained, "We don't really let our females [sell drugs] unless they really wanna and they know how to do it and not to get caught and everything." Veronica described a drive-by that her gang participated in and said, "They wouldn't let us [females] go. But we wanted to go, but they wouldn't let us." Often, the exclusion was couched in terms of protection. When I asked Veronica why the girls couldn't go, she said, "so we won't go to jail if they was to get caught. Or if one of 'em was to get shot, they wouldn't want it to happen to us." Likewise, Sonita, a 13-year-old African American, noted, "If they gonna do somethin' bad and they think one of the females gonna get hurt they don't let 'em do it with them. . . . Like if they involved with shooting or whatever, [girls] can't go."

Although girls' exclusion from some gang crime may be framed as protective (and may reduce their victimization risk vis-à-vis rival gangs), it also served to perpetuate the devaluation of female members as less significant to the gang—not as tough, true, or "down" for the gang as male members. When LaShawna said her gang blocked girls' involvement in serious crime, I pointed out that she was actively involved herself. She explained, "Yeah, I do a lot of stuff 'cause I'm tough. I likes, I likes messin' with boys. I fight boys. Girls ain't nothin' to me." Similarly, Tamika said, "girls, they little peons."

Some young women found the perception of them as weak a frustrating one. Brandi, an African American 13-year-old, explained, "Sometimes I dislike that the boys, sometimes, always gotta take charge and they think, sometimes, that the girls don't know how to take charge 'cause we're like girls, we're females, and like that." And Chantell, an African American 14-year-old, noted that rival gang members "think that you're more of a punk." Beliefs that girls were weaker than boys meant that young women had a harder time proving that they were serious about their commitment to the gang. Diane explained,

> A female has to show that she's tough. A guy can just, you can just look at him. But a female, she's gotta show. She's gotta go out and do some dirt. She's gotta go whip some girl's ass, shoot somebody, rob somebody or something. To show that she is tough.

In terms of gender-specific victimization risk, the devaluation of young women suggests several things. It could lead to the mistreatment and victimization of girls by members of their own gang when they didn't have specific male protection (i.e., a brother, boyfriend) in the gang or when they weren't able to stand up for themselves to male members. This was exacerbated by activities that led young women to be viewed as sexually available. In addition, because young women typically were not seen as a threat by young men, when they did pose one, they could be punished even more harshly than young men, not only for having challenged a rival gang or gang member but also for having overstepped "appropriate" gender boundaries.

Monica had status and respect in her gang, both because she had proven herself through fights and criminal activities, and because her older brothers were members of her set. She contrasted her own treatment with that of other young women in the gang:

> They just be puttin' the other girls off. Like Andrea, man. Oh my God, they dog Andrea so bad. They like, "Bitch, go to the store." She like, "All right, I be right back." She will go to the store and go and get them whatever they want and come back with it. If she don't get it right, they be like, "Why you do that bitch?" I mean, and one dude even smacked her. And, I mean, and, I don't, I told my brother once. I was like, "Man, it ain't even like that. If you ever see someone tryin' to disrespect me like that or hit me, if you do not hit them or at least say somethin' to them. . . ." So my brothers, they kinda watch out for me.

However, Monica put the responsibility for Andrea's treatment squarely on the young woman: "I put that on her. They ain't gotta do her like that, but she don't gotta let them do her like that either." Andrea was seen as "weak" because she did not stand up to the male members in the gang; thus, her mistreatment was framed as partially deserved because she did not exhibit the valued traits of toughness and willingness to fight that would allow her to defend herself.

An additional but related problem was when the devaluation of young women within gangs was sexual in nature. Girls, but not boys, could be initiated into the gang by being "sexed in"—having sexual relations with multiple male members of the gang. Other members viewed the young women initiated in this way as sexually available and promiscuous, thus increasing their subsequent mistreatment. In addition, the stigma could extend to female members in general, creating a sexual devaluation that all girls had to contend with.

The dynamics of "sexing in" as a form of gang initiation placed young women in a position that increased their risk of ongoing mistreatment at the hands of their gang peers. According to Keisha, "If you get sexed in, you have no respect. That means you gotta go ho 'in' for 'em; when they say you give 'em the pussy, you gotta give it to 'em. If you don't, you gonna get your ass beat. I ain't down for that." One girl in her set was sexed in and Keisha said the girl "just do everything they tell her to do, like a dummy." Nikkie reported that two girls who were sexed into her set eventually quit hanging around with the gang because they were harassed so much. In fact, Veronica said the young men in her set purposely tricked girls into believing they were being sexed into the gang and targeted girls they did not like:

> If some girls wanted to get in, if they don't like the girl they have sex with 'em. They run trains on 'em or either have the girl suck their thang. And then they used to, the girls used to think they was in. So, then the girls used to just come try to hang around us and all this little bull, just 'cause, 'cause they thinkin' they in.

Young women who were sexed into the gang were viewed as sexually promiscuous, weak, and not "true" members. They were subject to revictimization and mistreatment, and were viewed as deserving of abuse by other members, both male and female. Veronica continued, "They [girls who are sexed in] gotta do whatever, whatever the boys tell 'em to do when they want 'em to do it, right then and there, in front of whoever. And, I think, that's just sick. That's nasty, that's dumb." Keisha concurred, "She brought that on herself, by bein' the fact, bein' sexed in." There was evidence, however, that girls could overcome the stigma of having been sexed in through their subsequent behavior, by challenging members that disrespect them and being willing to fight. Tamika described a girl in her set who was sexed in, and stigmatized as a result, but successfully fought to rebuild her reputation:

> Some people, at first, they call her "little ho" and all that. But then, now she startin' to get bold. . . . Like, like, they be like, "Ooh, look at the little ho. She fucked me and my boy." She be like, "Man, forget y'all. Man, what? What?" She be ready to squat [fight] with 'em. I be like, "Ah, look at her!" Uh huh. . . . At first we looked at her like, "Ooh, man, she a ho, man." But now we look at her like she just our kickin' it partner. You know, however she got in that's her business.

The fact that there was such an option as "sexing in" served to keep girls disempowered, because they always faced the question of how they got in and of whether they were "true" members. In addition, it contributed to a milieu in which young women's sexuality was seen as exploitable. This may help explain why young women were so harshly judgmental of those girls who were sexed in. Young women who were privy to male gang members' conversations reported that male members routinely disrespect girls in the gang by disparaging them sexually. Monica explained,

> I mean the guys, they have their little comments about 'em [girls in the gang] because, I hear more because my brothers are all up there with the guys and everything and I hear more just sittin' around, just listenin'. And they'll have their little jokes about "Well, ha I had her," and then and everybody else will jump in and say, "Well, I had her, too." And then they'll laugh about it.

In general, because gender constructions defined young women as weaker than young men, young women were often seen as lesser members of the gang. In addition to the mistreatment these perceptions entailed, young women also faced particularly harsh sanctions for crossing gender boundaries—causing harm to rival male members when they had been viewed as nonthreatening. One young woman[9] participated in the assault of a rival female gang member, who had set up a member of the girl's gang. She explained, "The female was supposingly goin' out with one of ours, went back and told a bunch of [rivals] what was goin' on and got the [rivals] to jump my boy. And he ended up in the hospital." The story she told was unique but nonetheless significant for what it indicates about the gendered nature of gang violence and victimization. Several young men in her set saw the girl walking down the street, kidnapped her, then brought her to a member's house. The young woman I interviewed, along with several other girls in her set, viciously beat the girl, then to their surprise the young men took over the beating, ripped off the girl's clothes, brutally gang-raped her, then dumped her in a park. The interviewee noted, "I don't know what happened to her. Maybe she died. Maybe, maybe someone came and helped her. I mean, I don't know." The experience scared the young woman who told me about it. She explained,

> I don't never want anythin' like that to happen to me. And I pray to God that it doesn't. 'Cause God said that whatever you sow you're gonna reap. And like, you know, beatin' a girl up and then sittin' there watchin' somethin' like that happen, well, Jesus that could come back on me. I mean, I felt, I really did feel sorry for her even though my boy was in the hospital and was really hurt. I mean, we coulda just shot her. You know, and it coulda been just over. We coulda just taken her life. But they went farther than that.

This young woman described the gang rape she witnessed as "the most brutal thing I've ever seen in my life." While the gang rape itself was an unusual event, it remained a specifically gendered act that could take place precisely because young women were not perceived as equals. Had the victim been an "equal," the attack would have remained a physical one. As the interviewee herself noted, "we coulda just shot her." Instead, the young men who gang-raped the girl were not just enacting revenge on a rival but on a *young woman* who had dared to treat a young man in this way. The issue is not the question of which is worse—to be shot and killed, or gang-raped and left for dead. Rather, this particular act sheds light on how gender may function to structure victimization risk within gangs.

DISCUSSION

Gender dynamics in mixed-gender gangs are complex and thus may have multiple and contradictory effects on young women's risk of victimization and repeat victimization. My findings suggest that participation in the delinquent lifestyles associated with gangs clearly places young women at risk for victimization. The act of joining a gang involves the initiate's submission to victimization at the hands of her gang peers. In addition, the rules governing gang members' activities place them in situations in which they are vulnerable to assaults that are specifically gang related. Many acts of violence that girls described would not have occurred had they not been in gangs.

It seems, though, that young women in gangs believed they have traded unknown risks for known ones—that victimization at the hands of friends, or at least under specified conditions, was an alternative preferable to the potential of random, unknown victimization by strangers. Moreover, the gang offered both a semblance of protection from others on the streets, especially young men, and a means of achieving retaliation when victimization did occur.

Lauritsen and Quinet (1995) suggest that both individual-specific heterogeneity (unchanging attributes of individuals that contribute to a propensity for victimization, such as physical size or temperament) and state-dependent factors (factors that can alter individuals' victimization risks over time, such as labeling or behavior changes that are a consequence of victimization) are related to youths' victimization and repeat victimization risk. My findings here suggest that, within gangs, gender can function in both capacities to shape girls' risks of victimization.

Girls' gender, as an individual attribute, can function to lessen their exposure to victimization risk by defining them as inappropriate targets of rival male gang members' assaults. The young women I interviewed repeatedly commented that young men were typically not as violent in their routine confrontations with rival young women as with rival young men. On the other hand, when young women are targets of serious assault, they may face brutality that is particularly harsh and sexual in nature because they are female—thus, particular types of assault, such as rape, are deemed more appropriate when young women are the victims.

Gender can also function as a state-dependent factor, because constructions of gender and the enactment of gender identities are fluid. On the one hand, young women can call upon gender as a means of avoiding exposure to activities they find risky, threatening, or morally troubling. Doing so does not expose them to the sanctions likely faced by male gang members who attempt to avoid participation in violence. Although these choices may insulate young women from the risk of assault at the hands of rival gang members, perceptions of female gang members—and of women in general—as weak may contribute to more routinized victimization at the hands of the male members of their gangs. Moreover, sexual exploitation in the form of "sexing in" as an initiation ritual may define young women as sexually available, contributing to a likelihood of repeat victimization unless the young woman can stand up for herself and fight to gain other members' respect.

Finally, given constructions of gender that define young women as nonthreatening, when young women do pose a threat to male gang members, the sanctions they face may be particularly harsh because they not only have caused harm to rival gang members but also have crossed appropriate gender boundaries in doing so. In sum, my findings suggest that gender may function to insulate young women from some types of physical assault and lessen their exposure to risks from rival gang members, but also to make them vulnerable to particular types of violence, including routine victimization by their male peers, sexual exploitation, and sexual assault.

This article has offered preliminary evidence of how gender may shape victimization risk for female gang members. A great deal more work needs to be done in this area. Specifically, gang scholars need to address more systematically the relationships between gang involvement and victimization risk rather than focusing exclusively on gang members' participation in violence as offenders. My research suggests two questions to be examined further, for both female and male gang members. First, are gang members more likely to be victimized than nongang members living in the same areas? Second, how does victimization risk fluctuate for gang members before, during, and after their gang involvement? Information about these questions will allow us to address whether and how gang involvement has an enhancement effect on youths' *victimization,* as well as their delinquency.

With the growing interest in masculinities and crime (see Messerschmidt 1993; Newburn and Stanko 1994), an important corollary question to be examined is how masculinities shape victimization risk among male gang members. The young women I interviewed clearly associated serious gang violence with the enactment of masculinity and used gender constructions to avoid involvement in those activities they perceived as threatening. Young men thus may be at greater risk of serious physical assaults, because of their greater involvement in serious gang crime and violence, and because gender constructions within the gang make these activities more imperative for young men than for young women.

QUESTIONS FOR UNDERSTANDING AND CRITICAL THINKING

1. Review and discuss the relationship between gang involvement and victimization.
2. How does gang involvement of young women expose them to greater risks of victimization both within the gang and in absence of the gang?
3. What types of victimization risks do female gang members encounter and by whom?
4. What types of protective factors may minimize risk of victimization?

NOTES

1. I contacted numerous additional agency personnel in an effort to draw the sample from a larger population base, but many efforts remained unsuccessful despite repeated attempts and promises of assistance. These included persons at the probation department, a shelter and outreach agency for runaways, police personnel, a private residential facility for juveniles, and three additional community agencies. None of the agencies I contacted openly denied me permission to interview young women; they simply chose not to follow up. I do not believe that much bias resulted from the nonparticipation of these agencies. Each has a client base of "at-risk" youths, and the young women I interviewed report overlap with some of these same agencies. For example, a number had been or were on probation, and several reported staying at the shelter for runaways.
2. One young woman was a member of an all-female gang. Because the focus of this article is gender dynamics in mixed-gender gangs, her interview is not included in the analysis.
3. These include the Gang Membership Resistance Surveys in Long Beach and San Diego, the Denver Youth Survey, and the Rochester Youth Development Study.
4. For example, Cleveland, Ohio provides a striking contrast with Columbus on social and economic indicators, including a poverty rate double that found in Columbus. But the poverty rate for African Americans in Cleveland is just over twice that for Whites, and it is more than three times higher in Columbus.
5. The term *set* was used by the gang members I interviewed to refer to their gangs. Because they adopted nationally recognized gang names (e.g., Crips, Bloods, Folks), they saw themselves as loosely aligned with other groups of the same name. This term was used to distinguish their

particular gang (which has its own distinct name, e.g., Rolling 60s Crips) from other gangs that adopted the broader gang name. I will use the terms *set* and *gang* interchangeably.

6. This was compared to 36.4 percent who described their gangs as female auxiliaries of male gangs, and only 6.4 percent who described being in independent female gangs (Curry 1997; see also Decker and Van Winkle 1996).

7. All names are fictitious.

8. This is not to suggest that male members cannot gain status via their connections to high-status men, but that to maintain status, they will have to successfully exhibit masculine traits such as toughness. Young women appear to be held to more flexible standards.

9. Because this excerpt provides a detailed description of a specific serious crime, and because demographic information on respondents is available, I have chosen to conceal both the pseudonym and gang affiliation of the young woman who told me the story.

REFERENCES

ADLER, PATRICIA A. AND PETER ADLER. 1987. *Membership Roles in Field Research.* Newbury Park, CA: Sage.

ARNOLD, REGINA. 1990. "Processes of Victimization and Criminalization of Black Women." *Social Justice* 17(3): 153–66.

BASKIN, DEBORAH, IRA SOMMERS, AND JEFFREY FAGAN. 1993. "The Political Economy of Violent Female Street Crime." *Fordham Urban Law Journal* 20:401–17.

BJERREGAARD, BETH AND CAROLYN SMITH. 1993. "Gender Differences in Gang Participation, Delinquency, and Substance Use." *Journal of Quantitative Criminology* 4:329–55.

BLOCK, CAROLYN REBECCA AND RICHARD BLOCK. 1993. "Street Gang Crime in Chicago." Research in Brief. Washington, DC: National Institute of Justice.

BOURGOIS, PHILIPPE. 1995. *In Search of Respect: Selling Crack in El Barrio.* Cambridge, UK: Cambridge University Press.

BOURGOIS, PHILIPPE AND ELOISE DUNLAP. 1993. "Exorcising Sex-for-Crack: An Ethnographic Perspective from Harlem." Pp. 97–132 in *Crack Pipe as Pimp: An Ethnographic Investigation of Sex-for-Crack Exchanges,* edited by Mitchell S. Ratner. New York: Lexington Books.

BOWKER, LEE H., HELEN SHIMOTA GROSS, AND MALCOLM W. KLEIN. 1980. "Female Participation in Delinquent Gang Activities." *Adolescence* 15 (59): 509–19.

BROTHERTON, DAVID C. 1996. " 'Smartness,' 'Toughness,' and 'Autonomy': Drug Use in the Context of Gang Female Delinquency." *Journal of Drug Issues* 26(1): 261–77.

CAMPBELL, ANNE. 1984. *The Girls in the Gang.* New York: Basil Blackwell.

_____. 1990. "Female Participation in Gangs." Pp. 163–82 in *Gangs in America,* edited by C. Ronald Huff. Beverly Hills, CA: Sage.

CHESNEY-LIND, MEDA. 1993. "Girls, Gangs and Violence: Anatomy of a Backlash." *Humanity & Society* 17 (3): 321–44.

CHESNEY-LIND, MEDA AND NOELIE RODRIGUEZ. 1983. "Women under Lock and Key: A View from the Inside." *The Prison Journal* 63 (2): 47–65.

CHESNEY-LIND, MEDA, RANDALL G. SHELDEN, AND KAREN A. JOE. 1996. "Girls, Delinquency, and Gang Membership." Pp. 185–204 in *Gangs in America,* 2d ed., edited by C. Ronald Huff. Thousand Oaks, CA: Sage.

COLUMBUS METROPOLITAN HUMAN SERVICES COMMISSION. 1995. *State of Human Services Report—1995.* Columbus, OH: Columbus Metropolitan Human Services Commission. March, Orlando, FL.

CONNELL, R. W. 1987. *Gender and Power.* Stanford, CA: Stanford University Press.

CURRY, G. DAVID. 1997. "Selected Statistics on Female Gang Involvement." Paper presented at the Fifth Joint National Conference on Gangs, Schools, and Community, March, Orlando, FL.

Curry, G. David, Richard A. Ball, and Scott H. Decker. 1996. Estimating the National Scope of Gang Crime from Law Enforcement Data. Research in Brief. Washington, DC: National Institute of Justice.

Daly, Kathleen. 1992. "Women's Pathways to Felony Court: Feminist Theories of Lawbreaking and Problems of Representation." *Review of Law and Women's Studies* 2 (1): 11–52.

Decker, Scott H. 1996. "Collective and Normative Features of Gang Violence." *Justice Quarterly* 13 (2): 243–64.

Decker, Scott H. and Barrik Van Winkle. 1996. *Life in the Gang.* Cambridge, UK: Cambridge University Press.

Eder, Donna. 1995. *School Talk: Gender and Adolescent Culture.* New Brunswick, NJ: Rutgers University Press.

Esbensen, Finn-Aage. 1996. Comments presented at the National Institute of Justice/Office of Juvenile Justice and Delinquency Prevention Cluster Meetings, June, Dallas, TX.

Esbensen, Finn-Aage and David Huizinga. 1993. "Gangs, Drugs, and Delinquency in a Survey of Urban Youth." *Criminology* 31 (4) 565–89.

Esbensen, Finn-Aage, David Huizinga, and Anne W. Weiher. 1993. "Gang and Non-Gang Youth: Differences in Explanatory Factors." *Journal of Contemporary Criminal Justice* 9 (2): 94–116.

Esbensen, Finn-Aage and L. Thomas Winfree. 1998. "Race and Gender Differences between Gang and Non-Gang Youth: Results from a Multi-Site Survey." *Justice Quarterly* 15 (3): 505–25.

Fagan, Jeffrey. 1989. "The Social Organization of Drug Use and Drug Dealing among Urban Gangs." *Criminology* 27(4): 633–67.

_____. 1990. "Social Processes of Delinquency and Drug Use among Urban Gangs." Pp. 183–219 in *Gangs in America,* edited by C. Ronald Huff. Newbury Park, CA: Sage.

Gilfus, Mary E. 1992. "From Victims to Survivors to Offenders: Women's Routes of Entry and Immersion into Street Crime." *Women and Criminal Justice* 4 (1): 63–89.

Glassner, Barry and Julia Loughlin. 1987. *Drugs in Adolescent Worlds: Burnouts to Straights.* New York: St. Martin's.

Hagedorn, John M. 1988. *People and Folks: Gangs, Crime and the Underclass in a Rustbelt City.* Chicago: Lake View Press.

Huff, C. Ronald. 1989. "Youth Gangs and Public Policy." *Crime and Delinquency* 35 (4): 524–37.

_____. 1996. "The Criminal Behavior of Gang Members and Nongang At-Risk Youth." Pp. 75–102 in *Gangs in America,* 2d ed., edited by C. Ronald Huff. Thousand Oaks, CA: Sage.

Joe, Karen A. and Meda Chesney-Lind. 1995. "Just Every Mother's Angel: An Analysis of Gender and Ethnic Variations in Youth Gang Membership." *Gender & Society* 9(4): 408–30.

Klein, Malcolm W. 1995. *The American Street Gang: Its Nature, Prevalence and Control.* New York: Oxford University Press.

Klein, Malcolm W. and Cheryl L. Maxson. 1989. "Street Gang Violence." Pp. 198–231 in *Violent Crime, Violent Criminals,* edited by Neil Weiner and Marvin Wolfgang. Newbury Park, CA: Sage.

LaLonde, Brent. 1995. "Police Trying to Contain Gang Problem." *The Columbus Dispatch,* September 3, p. 2A.

Lauderback, David, Joy Hansen, and Dan Waldorf. 1992. " 'Sisters Are Doin' It for Themselves': A Black Female Gang in San Francisco." *The Gang Journal* 1 (1): 57–70.

Lauritsen, Janet L. and Kenna F. Davis Quinet. 1995. "Repeat Victimization among Adolescents and Young Adults." *Journal of Quantitative Criminology* 11 (2): 143–66.

Lauritsen, Janet L., Robert J. Sampson, and John H. Laub. 1991. "The Link between Offending and Victimization among Adolescents." *Criminology* 29 (2): 265–92.

Lees, Sue. 1993. *Sugar and Spice: Sexuality and Adolescent Girls.* New York: Penguin.

MAHER, LISA AND RICHARD CURTIS. 1992. "Women on the Edge of Crime: Crack Cocaine and the Changing Contexts of Street-Level Sex Work in New York City." *Crime, Law and Social Change* 18:221–58.

MAXSON, CHERYL L., KRISTI WOODS, AND MALCOLM W. KLEIN. 1995. Street Gang Migration in the United States. Final Report to the National Institute of Justice.

MAYHOOD, KEVIN AND BRENT LALONDE. 1995. "A Show of Colors: A Local Look." *The Columbus Dispatch,* September 3, pp. 1–2A.

MESSERSCHMIDT, JAMES W. 1993. *Masculinities and Crime: Critique and Reconceptualization of Theory.* Lanham, MD: Rowman and Littlefield.

MILLER, JODY. 1996. "The Dynamics of Female Gang Involvement in Columbus, Ohio." Paper presented at the National Youth Gang Symposium, June, Dallas, TX.

MILLER, JODY AND BARRY GLASSNER. 1997. "The 'Inside' and the 'Outside': Finding Realities in Interviews." Pp. 99–112 in *Qualitative Research,* edited by David Silverman. London: Sage.

MOORE, JOAN. 1991. *Going Down to the Barrio: Homeboys and Homegirls in Change.* Philadelphia: Temple University Press.

MOORE, JOAN AND JOHN M. HAGEDORN. 1996. "What Happens to Girls in the Gang?" Pp. 205–18 in *Gangs in America,* 2d ed., edited by C. Ronald Huff. Thousand Oaks, CA: Sage.

NEWBURN, TIM AND ELIZABETH STANKO. 1994. *Just Boys Doing Business?: Men, Masculinities and Crime.* New York: Routledge.

PESCE, ROSARIO C. AND CAROL GIBB HARDING. 1986. "Imaginary Audience Behavior and Its Relationship to Operational Thought and Social Experience." *Journal of Early Adolescence* 6 (1): 83–94.

RUSK, DAVID. 1995. *Cities without Suburbs.* 2d ed. Washington, DC: The Woodrow Wilson Center Press.

SAMPSON, ROBERT J. AND WILLIAM JULIUS WILSON. 1995. "Toward a Theory of Race, Crime, and Urban Inequality." Pp. 37–54 in *Crime and Inequality,* edited by John Hagan and Ruth D. Peterson. Stanford, CA: Stanford University Press.

SANDERS, WILLIAM. 1993. *Drive-Bys and Gang Bangs: Gangs and Grounded Culture.* Chicago: Aldine.

SHORT, JAMES F. AND FRED L. STRODTBECK. 1965. *Group Process and Gang Delinquency.* Chicago: University of Chicago Press.

SIMPSON, SALLY. 1991. "Caste, Class and Violent Crime: Explaining Differences in Female Offending." *Criminology* 29 (1): 115–35.

SPERGEL, IRVING A. AND G. DAVID CURRY. 1993. "The National Youth Gang Survey: A Research and Development Process." Pp. 359–400 in *The Gang Intervention Handbook,* edited by Arnold P. Goldstein and C. Ronald Huff. Champaign, IL: Research Press.

TAYLOR, CARL. 1993. *Girls, Gangs, Women and Drugs.* East Lansing: Michigan State University Press.

THORNBERRY, TERENCE P., MARVIN D. KROHN, ALAN J. LIZOTTE, AND DEBORAH CHARD-WIERSCHEM. 1993. "The Role of Juvenile Gangs in Facilitating Delinquent Behavior." *Journal of Research in Crime and Delinquency* 30 (1): 75–85.

THORNE, BARRIE. 1993. *Gender Play: Girls and Boys in School.* New Brunswick, NJ: Rutgers University Press.

WILSON, WILLIAM JULIUS. 1996. *When Work Disappears: The World of the New Urban Poor.* New York: Knopf.

WINFREE, L. THOMAS, JR., KATHY FULLER, TERESA VIGIL, AND G. LARRY MAYS. 1992. "The Definition and Measurement of 'Gang Status': Policy Implications for Juvenile Justice." *Juvenile and Family Court Journal* 43:29–37.

PART VII

Gang Prevention and Intervention

17

Promising Programs for Youth Gang Violence Prevention and Intervention

James C. Howell

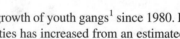

The United States has seen rapid growth of youth gangs[1] since 1980. During this period, the number of youth gang problem cities has increased from an estimated 286 with over 2,000 gangs and nearly 100,000 members (Miller, 1982) to about 2,000 cities, towns, and counties with more than 23,000 gangs and membership totaling nearly 665,000 in 1995 (National Youth Gang Center, 1997). The 1995 National Youth Gang Survey covered over 4,000 law enforcement agencies in the United States, 58% of which reported gang youth problems in their jurisdiction, using their own definition (National Youth Gang Center, 1997).

Preventing and controlling youth gangs is important because recent studies show that gang members, who represent a minority of adolescent samples, account for the majority of all self-reported offenses among urban juveniles in gang problem cities, and from about half to over two thirds of all serious and violent offenses committed by adolescents in Denver (Esbensen & Huizinga, 1993), Rochester (Thornberry, 1998), and Seattle (Battin, Hill, Abbott, Catalano, & Hawkins, 1998). Moreover, studies in all three of these sites

AUTHOR'S NOTE: Preparation of this chapter was supported in part by an Office of Juvenile Justice and Delinquency Prevention award (#95-JD-MU-K001) to the National Youth Gang Center, Institute for Intergovernmental Research (IIR). I am grateful to Rolf Loeber, David Farrington, David Altschuler, Jim Short, Walter Miller, John Moore, Bruce Buckley, Joan Moore, Cheryl Maxson, David Curry, and Rebecca Block for helpful comments on earlier drafts.

Howell, J.C. Promising programs for youth gang violence prevention and intervention. In *Serious and Violent Juvenile Offenders: Risk Factors and Successful Interventions,* (1998), Eds. Loeber, R. and Farrington, D.P. pp. 284–312. Reprinted by permission of Sage Publications, Inc.

show an increase in the incidence of serious and violent offending while adolescents are active gang members (Esbensen & Huizinga, 1993; Hill, Hawkins, Catalano, Kosterman, Abbott, & Edwards, 1996; Thornberry, Krohn, Lizotte, & Chard-Wierschem, 1993). In Rochester, nearly two thirds of chronic violent offenders self-reported gang membership at some point in their adolescent years (Thornberry, Huizinga, & Loeber, 1995).

Can the youth gang problem be solved? Miller (1974) suggests:

> It happens that great nations engage in national wars for almost identical reasons [that gangs do] . . . personal honor, prestige, and defense against perceived threats to one's homeland. . . . When a solution to this problem [of fighting nations has been found], we will at the same time have solved the problem of violent crimes in city gangs. (p. 112)

Is there basis for more optimism than Miller expresses?

The history of efforts to solve the youth gang problem in the United States is largely filled with frustration and failure. Early in our nation's history, youth gang work emphasized prevention. These programs were followed by interventions designed to reintegrate particular gangs into conventional society. Then a major shift occurred as programs, led by the police, aimed to suppress youth gangs. Currently, a mixture of approaches is being tried across the nation, predominantly police suppression programs (Spergel & Curry, 1993). None of these approaches has been demonstrated conclusively through rigorous research to be effective. Two factors appear to account for this: the difficulties associated with gang intervention work and the complexity of program evaluation in this area.

Youth gang intervention is a very formidable enterprise. Because we lack a clear understanding of why and how youth gangs form, preventing their formation is problematic. Gang interventions rarely are based on theoretical assumptions. This lack of knowledge impedes efforts to disrupt existing gangs and divert youth from them. Gangs dissolve and disappear for reasons that are poorly understood. In some cities, youths who join gangs leave them within about 1 year. Yet we do not understand why. Future youth gang research must address the formation of gangs, disruptive forces, and factors that account for diversion of youths from gangs.

Evaluation of youth gang interventions is an equally complex undertaking. Not only must gang formation, dissolution, and diversion be shown but also delinquency prevention or reduction. Because each youth gang is unique and each community is different in some respects, obtaining comparable comparison groups or communities is difficult. Measurement problems abound. There is no commonly accepted definition of a youth gang; therefore, comparing study results is problematic. Most important, very few rigorous evaluations of youth gang programs have been undertaken.

With these caveats in mind, we review the existing literature. Evaluations of youth gang programs and new approaches for preventing and reducing youth gang problems are reviewed. A youth gang prevention and intervention program strategy is recommended based on this review. The general questions guiding this review are: What can we learn from what has been tried? What has failed? What looks promising? In the next section, we review gang program evaluations. That section is followed by recommended approaches our review suggests. Three strategies are recommended: targeting gang problems directly; targeting gang problems within a comprehensive strategy for dealing with serious, violent, and chronic juvenile delinquency; and targeting gang-related (and gang-motivated) homicides. Our third program recommendation is based in part on the Epidemiology of Youth Gang Homicides at the end of this chapter (Table17–2).

A REVIEW OF GANG PROGRAM EVALUATIONS

Space limitations here preclude a detailed review of all gang program evaluations. See Table 17–1 for summary information on selected evaluations.

Prevention and Intervention Programs

Prevention

The early history of gang programming in the United States emphasized preventing both gang emergence and joining, based on the gang and delinquency research conducted by Shaw (1930), with his colleague, McKay (Shaw & McKay, 1931), and Thrasher (1927/1963). The Chicago Area Project (CAP), created in 1934 by Clifford Shaw, was designed to implement the community organization theory he and his colleagues developed on "social disorganization," proffering the notion that community organization could be a major tool for reducing crime and gang problems. CAP was designed to involve local community groups, that is, indigenous community organizations, in improving neighborhood conditions that Shaw believed permitted the formation of youth gangs. "Tying informal community structures to formal agencies—schools, enforcement, welfare—would provide the social structure for healthy socialization and vitiate the need for gangs and other forms of deviance" (Klein, 1995, p. 139). CAP invented "detached workers" (agency representatives detached from their offices and assigned to communities). CAP also originated the community gang worker role. "Indeed, the concept of 'detached workers' or 'gang workers'. . . became the more narrow essence of major gang projects for decades to come" (Klein, 1995, p. 140).

CAP was a massive program. Because its influence and program activities extended throughout Chicago, one must wonder if it could be evaluated except in comparison with another similar city. Nevertheless, Kobrin's (1959) 25-year retrospective assessment concluded that the project had been successful, on "logical and analytical" grounds (see Alinsky, 1946; Klein, 1995, pp. 139–140). Claims of the success of the CAP program continue to be publicized (Sorrentino, 1959; Sorrentino & Whittaker, 1994) despite the absence of rigorous evaluation results. The program is still operating, which says something about views of its value among Chicago officials.

More important, CAP created a legacy in gang programming in its emphasis on the role of the community and its private organizations. As Witmer (quoted in Klein, 1995) put it, CAP demonstrated:

> Local residents can organize themselves with effective mechanisms for dealing with youth problems. Such organizations can endure over long periods of time. Local talent can be discovered and enlisted in the battle. One need not be dependent on existing bureaucratic entities. (p. 141)

Literally hundreds of community committees were formed, which emphasized different community concerns (Klein, 1995, p. 140). Local workers became the staff of community programs. Local programs sponsored recreation opportunities, community self-renewal, mediation, and advocacy before government agencies, especially school, probation, and parole officials (Schlossman & Sedlak, 1983a, 1983b). Most of these efforts were directed at

TABLE 17–1   Selected Gang Program Evaluations: 1936–1997

Program	Study	Design	Type of Intervention	Results
New York City Boys Club	Thrasher (1936)	Descriptive and case study	Prevention—general delinquency	Negligible impact
Community Area Project	Kobrin (1959); Schlossman and Sedlak (1983a, 1983b)	Descriptive and case study	Prevention—community organization	Indeterminable
Total Community Delinquency Control Project (Midcity Project)	Miller (1962)	Field observation and quasi-experimental	Prevention—community organization, family services, and detached worker	Negligible impact
Chicago Youth Development Project	Caplan, Deshaies, Suttles, and Mattick (1967); Gold and Mattick (1974); Mattick and Caplan (1962)	Quasi-experimental community comparison	Prevention—detached worker and community organization	No differential impact
Chicago YMCA Program for Detached Workers	Short (1963); Short and Strodtbeck (1965)	Field observation and quasi-experimental observation	Prevention—detached worker	Early results encouraging; no final results; evaluation suspended
Group Guidance Program	Klein (1969, 1971)	Quasi-experimental	Prevention—detached worker	Significant increase in gang delinquency
Ladino Hills Project	Klein (1968)	Quasi-experimental	Prevention—detached worker	Significant reduction in gang delinquency
Community Action Program (Woodlawn Organization)	Spergel, Turner, Pleas, and Brown (1969); Spergel (1972)	Descriptive statistical trends	Social intervention	Ineffective
Wincroft Youth Project (United Kingdom)	Smith, Farrant, and Marchant (1972)	Quasi-experimental	Prevention—detached worker	No differential impact
Gang Violence Reduction Program	Torres (1981, 1985)	Quasi-experimental	Suppression and crisis intervention	Declines in gang homicides and intergang violence
House of Umoja	Woodson (1981, 1986)	Descriptive, case study, statistical trends	Prevention, crisis intervention, and social intervention	Effected truce among warring gangs; reduced homicides; sanctuary

Program	Study	Design	Type of Intervention	Results
Operation Hardcore	Dahmann (1981)	Quasi-experimental (process)	Suppression (vertical prosecution)	Successful gang prosecution process
San Diego Street Youth Program	Pennell (1983)	Quasi-experimental community comparison	Prevention—detached worker	Indeterminable
Crisis Intervention Services Project	Spergel (1986)	Quasi-experimental community comparison	Crisis intervention and suppression	Some reduction in serious and violent crimes
Gang prevention curriculum	Thompson and Jason (1988)	Quasi-experimental school comparison	Prevention—discouraging adolescents from joining gangs	Marginal reduction
Youth Gang Drug Prevention Program (ACYF)	Cohen, Williams, Bekelman, and Crosse (1994)	Quasi-experimental treatment and control comparison	Prevention—discouraging adolescents from joining gangs; community mobility	Little/no effects on gang involvement; some delinquency reduction
Aggression Replacement Training	Goldstein and Glick (1994)	Quasi-experimental treatment and control comparison	Skill streaming, anger control, and moral education	Preliminary results with members of 10 gangs positive
General Reporting Evaluation and Tracking (GREAT) system	Kent and Smith (1995)	Quasi-experimental (process)	Suppression—targeting gang members for prosecution and supervision	Successful targeting process
Gang Violence Reduction Program	Spergel and Grossman (1995, 1996, 1997)	Quasi-experimental community comparison	Prevention, social intervention, and suppression	Preliminary results positive; best results with combined approach
Youth Gang Drug Intervention and Prevention Program for Female Adolescents	Curry, Williams, and Koenemann (1996, 1997)	Quasi-experimental (in Pueblo, Colorado; Boston; Seattle)	Prevention and social intervention	Pueblo program showed positive results with culture-based program for Mexican American females
Gang Resistance Education and Training (G.R.E.A.T.) program	Esbensen and Osgood (1997)	Quasi-experimental treatment and control comparison	Prevention—discouraging adolescents from joining gangs	Preliminary results are positive

community improvements, securing services for residents, and organizing direct intervention in delinquency and gang activity (Klein, 1995, p. 140).

Another community-based gang program that, like CAP, relied on indigenous community organizations was established much later. The House of Umoja began operating in Philadelphia during the 1970s (Spergel, 1995). It consists of a residential and nonresidential program for gang and other delinquent youths, providing a sanctuary for them from street life while assisting target youths through a comprehensive program that included educational development, career development, employment assistance, and individual counseling. The House of Umoja is a unique grassroots program initiated by community residents (David and Falaka Fattah). Based on the extended family concept and a "new concept of peace," the program organized a gang summit, resulting in a gang warfare truce (Spergel, 1995; Woodson, 1981, 1986). Woodson's (1981) assessment concluded that the truce and other House of Umoja activities were instrumental in reducing the number of gang deaths in the city from an average of 39 per year in 1973, to 6 in 1976, and to only 1 in 1977. Although other programs claimed credit for part of this reduction in gang homicides, there is no doubt that House of Umoja played a key role. The 1974 gang summit leading to the truce drew 500 members from 75% of the city's gangs (Fattah, 1987). No gang members died during the 60-day truce that resulted.

Only one program designed to prevent youths from joining gangs has been evaluated rigorously and shown to have promise. It was a component of Project Broader Urban Involvement and Leadership Development (BUILD) (Brewer, Hawkins, Catalano, & Neckerman, 1995; Ribisl & Davidson, 1993). The prevention component consisted of a gang prevention curriculum and an afterschool program. The school gang prevention curriculum consisted of 12 classroom sessions conducted over 12 weeks that focused on background information on gangs, gang violence, and substance abuse in gangs; gang recruitment strategies and methods of resisting gang recruitment; consequences of gang membership; and values clarification. Most classroom sessions were led by project staff; others were led by a prosecuting attorney and by ethnic minority guest speakers who held various positions in the community. The curriculum was taught to eighth-grade students in Chicago middle schools located in lower-and lower-middle-class areas with high levels of gang activity. Following completion of the curriculum component, youths from the classrooms considered to be at high risk for joining a gang were invited to participate in an afterschool program. It provided recreational activities, job skills training workshops, educational assistance programs, and social activities. At-risk youth were identified by teachers and project staff (using gang rosters compiled by detached street gang workers on the basis of interviews with gang members). The selected youth were not already gang members, to the best knowledge of project staff and teachers.

Thompson and Jason's (1988) evaluation of the program incorporated a "nonequivalent comparison group" design, in which three pairs of public middle schools were matched on the basis that the same gang actively recruited members from both schools in a pair. One school in each pair was randomly assigned to be an experimental school, and the other was designated as a comparison school. The researchers assessed gang membership again at the end of the school year using the same method as was used to select at-risk youth. All of the at-risk youth received the school curriculum, and 51% of them participated in at least one of the several afterschool activities. Results showed that experimental youth were less likely to join a gang than comparison youth, but the difference was only marginally statistically significant. The evaluation was limited by the short-term follow-up period and the relatively small sample size (74 experimental youth and 43 comparison youth), given the low prevalence of gang membership (4 of the 43 comparison youth had joined gangs by the end of the school year and only 1 of the 74 experimental youth had). This kind of intervention appears to hold promise for preventing adolescents from joining gangs. A more recent evaluation of a gang prevention curriculum produced a stronger basis for curricular approaches.

Evaluation of the Bureau of Alcohol, Tobacco, and Firearms' Gang Resistance Education and Training (G.R.E.A.T.) program, initiated in 1991 by Phoenix law enforcement agencies, has shown positive preliminary results (Esbensen & Osgood, 1997). The G.R.E.A.T. program is a school-based intervention gang program in which uniformed law enforcement officers teach a 9-week curriculum to middle school students. These weekly sessions consist of nine lessons:

1. Introduction—acquainting students with the G.R.E.A.T. program and the presenting officer
2. Crime/victims and your rights—students learn about crimes, their victims, and their impact on the school and neighborhood
3. Cultural sensitivity/prejudice—teaching students how cultural differences affect their school and neighborhood
4. and 5. Conflict resolution (two lessons)—students learn how to create an atmosphere of understanding that would enable all parties to better address interpersonal problems and work together on solutions
6. Meeting basic needs—teaching students how to satisfy their basic social needs without joining a gang
7. Drugs/neighborhoods—students learn how drugs affect their school and neighborhood
8. Responsibility—students learn about the diverse responsibilities of people in their school and neighborhood
9. Goal setting—teaching students the need for personal goal setting and how to establish short- and long-term goals

Police instructors are trained in the G.R.E.A.T. curriculum in a management training session. They are taught how to use role-playing techniques and group exercises. This teacher training includes learning how to prepare students to present a lesson in the G.R.E.A.T. program, preparing them for later teaching in their own classrooms. The G.R.E.A.T. curriculum concludes with a graduation ceremony.

Evaluation of the G.R.E.A.T. program incorporated a quasi-experimental research design (Esbensen & Osgood, 1997). A cross-sectional survey of nearly 6,000 students in 315 classrooms in 42 different schools was conducted in 11 geographically and population-representative sites after the G.R.E.A.T. curriculum was administered. Because the G.R.E.A.T. program was taught in the seventh grade, eighth-grade students were surveyed to allow for a 1-year follow up, while guaranteeing that none of the sample was currently enrolled in the program. Two ex post facto comparison groups were created to allow for evaluation of program effects. Because preventing adolescents from joining gangs and engaging in criminal activity were the major goals of the program, a self-reported measure of gang joining and involvement in illegal activity was included in the cross-sectional survey.

Creation of the two comparison groups of students in the 42 schools (one group that received the G.R.E.A.T. curriculum and another that did not receive it) resulted in non-equivalent comparison groups. Comparison of sex, race, age, family status, and family education background characteristics of students in the two samples revealed that they differed on race and family socioeconomic status. Therefore, analyses controlled for between-school differences. Schools also were found to vary substantially in terms of the number of students who completed the G.R.E.A.T. program. Therefore, all analyses were replicated, limiting the total sample to a restricted sample of 28 schools in which there were at least 15 participants and nonparticipants. This procedure tended to strengthen the magnitude of the programmatic effect.

Students who completed the G.R.E.A.T. program reported lower levels of gang affiliation and self-reported delinquency, including drug use, minor offending, property crimes, and crimes against persons. Compared to the control group, the treatment group reported more positive attitudes to the police, more negative attitudes about gangs, having more friends involved in prosocial behavior, higher levels of perceived guilt at committing deviant acts, more commitment to school, higher levels of attachment to both mothers and fathers, more communication with parents about their activities, fewer friends involved in delinquent activity, less likelihood of acting impulsively, lower likelihood of engaging in risky behavior, and lower levels of perceived blockages to academic success.

The study authors caution that these results are preliminary and need to be viewed with caution. First, significant differences existed between the two groups. Second, a quasi-experimental design has been implemented in the longitudinal phase of the evaluation, in a prospective panel design at six representative sites. Both pre- and posttest measures have been obtained. Adding strength to this design, postprogram measures will be obtained in a planned 3-year follow-up.

Interventions using detached workers

A significant shift in youth gang program approaches, from prevention through community organization to interventions relying almost exclusively on detached workers, occurred in the late 1940s with the establishment of the New York City Youth Board (1960). Created to combat the city's growing number of fighting gangs, this city-run program relied on detached workers to transform street gangs, most of which was to be done in the streets, where gangs met, played, and hung out. Worker activities included going fishing with gang members, securing health care, employment counseling, advocacy work with the police and court, and most any other action that might transform gangs or woo juveniles away from them (Geis, 1965). The Youth Board's gang program "lost the community focus [of the Chicago CAP] and developed instead a rather narrowly focused worker program which, nonetheless, became the model for future street work programs" (Klein, 1995, p. 142). Although the program was never evaluated, it served as a forerunner of detached worker programs.

The Boston detached worker program was evaluated (Miller, 1962), in perhaps the most rigorous gang program evaluation ever conducted. For 3 years, project staff in the Mid-city Project (established in Roxbury, Boston in 1954) worked with 400 members of 21 corner gangs, providing intensive services to 7 gangs. This "total community" project consisted of three major program components: community organization, family service, and gang work. The project aimed to open channels of access to legitimate opportunities, especially in the education and employment areas. The project plan was comprehensive and unusually well implemented. However, Miller's (1962) evaluation proved the project to be ineffective. All of his measures of delinquency—disapproved actions, illegal behavior, during-project court appearances, before-during-after court appearances, and control group court appearances—provided consistent support for a finding of "negligible impact" (p. 187). The results were very disappointing to the field because of the quality of the program.

Evaluation of a California detached worker program brought into even more serious question the value of this approach. The Group Guidance Program of the Los Angeles Probation Department was evaluated by Klein (1969, 1971, 1995). The program, begun in 1961, was designed to employ "group guidance" by street workers in an attempt to intervene in the emergence of Black gangs in South-Central Los Angeles. Group activities, including weekly club meetings, sports activities, tutoring, individual counseling, and advocacy with community agencies and organizations, were designed to "de-isolate" gang members from their community institutions. Klein found that officially recorded arrests of gang members increased during the project period. He concluded that "increased group programming leads to increased cohesiveness (both gang growth and gang 'tightness'), and increased cohesiveness leads to increased gang crime" (Klein, 1995, p. 145).

The Ladino Hills Project, created in South-Central Los Angeles in 1961, was an experiment Klein (1968, 1971, 1995) designed to test his gang cohesiveness hypothesis, that if gang cohesiveness could be reduced through nongroup interventions, then gang delinquency would be reduced. Project staff, working with a gang that had the highest rate of commitments to correctional facilities of any gang in Los Angeles County, were to work individually with gang members. Interventions included helping gang members get jobs, tutoring, recreation in established agencies, and individual therapy. Program implementation was relatively successful. Klein's (1968) evaluation showed that gang cohesiveness was reduced by about 40%. Although individual arrest rates remained relatively constant, an overall reduction of 35% in gang member arrests was observed (attributed mainly to fewer members). However, several years later, the gang reassumed its preproject, gang-ridden character. Klein (1995) concluded that "we had affected the [gang members] but not their community. The lesson is both obvious and important. Gangs are by-products of their communities: They cannot long be controlled by attacks on symptoms alone; community structure and capacity must also be targeted" (p. 147). Because of the success of his experiment, Klein has repeatedly warned practitioners against any activities that might contribute to gang cohesion, because these might increase gang delinquency. However, his findings have been challenged (J. W. Moore, 1978). Several other detached worker programs have been evaluated, generally with negative results (see Table 17–1).

Although there is disagreement concerning the effectiveness of detached worker programs (see Bursik & Grasmick, 1993; Goldstein & Glick, 1994), we must conclude that this program model, in its original concept, has not produced positive results. Indeed, evaluation of a Chicago detached worker program (Caplan, Deshaies, Suttles, & Mattick, 1967; Gold & Mattick, 1974; Mattick & Caplan, 1962) and another one in Los Angles (Klein, 1969) showed that they may have increased delinquency. Numerous reasons have been offered to account for the ineffectiveness of this strategy. Klein (1971; see also Spergel, 1966) suggests that it was unclear whether these programs were designed to control gangs, treat gang member personality problems, provide access to social and cultural opportunities, transform values, or prevent delinquency. Conflicting program objectives made evaluation difficult.

Spergel (1995) contends that a detached worker strategy by itself is inadequate to deal with complex problems such as remedial education, job preparation and development, and community issues. Perhaps this is why the detached worker concept has been expanded over the past 30 years to incorporate other interventions (Fox, 1985), including temporary shelters for low-income youths, mentoring programs, activity centers, postsentencing social services, drug treatment programs, and intergang mediation (Spergel & Curry, 1990). Detached worker programs with these augmentations have not been evaluated, although one modified approach (gang transformation within a comprehensive youth services program) has shown positive results (Goldstein & Glick, 1994) in an initial trial. The authors believe the positive results they observed are attributable to the combination of skill streaming (a broad array of interpersonal and daily living skills), anger control, and moral reasoning. However, important details of the evaluation are not presented, such as how the treatment and control samples were selected and their comparability. The significance of the results is also dampened by small samples.

Crisis Intervention

In the next era of youth gang programming, detached workers were put in vehicles and sent to "hot spots" of gang activity. Philadelphia's Crisis Intervention Network (CIN), established in 1974, pioneered the new approach assigning gang workers to areas, not gangs. They were to patrol hot spots in radio-dispatched cars, attempting to defuse potentially violent situations. Although the CIN was not evaluated, it was acclaimed to be successful, though this conclusion has been challenged (Klein, 1995; Needle & Stapleton, 1983; Spergel, 1995).

Spergel (1986) evaluated the Crisis Intervention Services Project (CRISP) (see Ribisl & Davidson, 1993), which operated in a gang-ridden section of Chicago. Spergel (1995) described the program as a "mixed social intervention or crisis intervention approach, with strong deterrent and community involvement characteristics." Staff patrolled areas where gang violence was likely to erupt during evening and late-night hours, attempting to mediate conflicts. Secondary components of the program included intensive counseling for gang youth and their families referred from juvenile court, mobilization of local neighborhood groups, and establishment of a neighborhood advisory group that oversaw the project. The program focused on several target areas in four police precincts characterized by high levels of gang activity.

The evaluation (Spergel, 1986) compared the number and type of gang incidents in the target area with a matched set of nontarget areas. Offenses were categorized as Type I, serious violent crimes (homicide, robbery) and Type II, less serious violent crimes (simple assault, intimidation, gang recruitment). Spergel's evaluation showed that gang crimes and overall crime increased in both the target and comparison areas. However, he found a significant reduction in the rate of increase in Type I offenses in the project areas compared to the control areas, comparing the preproject period with the project period. Little difference in Type II offenses was found between the experimental and control areas. Comparisons within the target areas suggested that the positive effects of the program were greater in the areas where program implementation closely followed the original design. The program appeared to be more effective for juveniles than for young adults, but it appeared to have little effect on nongang crime. Nevertheless, these were the most encouraging gang intervention results to date.

Gang Suppression Programs

The use of gang suppression techniques originated in the Philadelphia CIN program, with its deployment of mobile units to gang crisis areas. California criminal justice officials soon expanded the concept (Klein, 1995) in prosecution and police programs. Operation Hardcore, a prosecutorial gang suppression program, was created by the Los Angeles District Attorney's Office in 1979 and is still operational today (Genelin, 1993). It was the first prosecution program to target serious, violent, juvenile gang-related offenses (Klein, Maxson, & Miller, 1995). Modeled after "major crime units" established in other cities' district attorney's offices, its distinctive features include vertical prosecution, reduced caseloads, additional investigative support, and resources for assisting victims.

An independent evaluation of the program (Dahmann, 1981) compared handling of defendants and cases by Operation Hardcore with other cases in Los Angeles handled by nonprogram attorneys both before and during program operations. It showed that Operation Hardcore had more convictions, fewer dismissals, more convictions to the most serious charge, and a higher rate of state prison commitments than the normal prosecutorial process. Dahmann concluded that "these results suggest that selective prosecution has been an effective strategy in Los Angeles and that the Operation Hardcore program has obtained demonstrable improvements in the criminal justice handling of gang defendants and their cases" (p. 303). Operation Hardcore remains a highly regarded program. Evaluation of the program has not examined its impact on gang crimes (Klein, 1995).

Police gang suppression programs (see Klein, 1995) drew impetus from the apparent growth of youth gang problems in the Southwest in the early 1980s. Gang Units (see Jackson & McBride, 1985) were created in law enforcement departments, carrying out gang intelligence, investigation, suppression, and prevention functions (Klein, 1995). Deliberate suppression tactics employed by the Los Angeles Police Department's CRASH (Community Resources Against Street Hoodlums) operations took the form of "gang sweeps," "hot spot targeting," and "intensified patrol" to apply "excruciating pressure" on gangs. Other terms used to characterize police "crackdowns" include saturation, special surveillance, zero tolerance, and caravanning (cruising neighborhoods in a caravan of patrol cars) (Klein, 1995).

In contrast, law enforcement suppression activities can be incorporated in a balanced approach, such as in the activities of the Los Angeles Sheriff Department's Operation Safe Streets (OSS). Based on gang crime statistics, it appears that the OSS has done a more effective job in combating gang violence than CRASH (Klein, 1995). This could be expected, given that police crackdowns have shown limited effectiveness, generally short term (Sherman, 1990). In contrast, OSS employs "street-level intelligence, carefully nurtured" (Klein, 1995). OSS officers employ tactics attuned to the nature of gangs. They often work in the same community many years, know the gangs and their members very well, and thus are better able to diffuse volatile situations (see Jackson & McBride, 1985).

Operation Hammer, perhaps the worst example of a police suppression program, is described by Klein (1995). It was a Los Angeles Police Department CRASH antigang street sweep, launched in the South-Central section of the city in 1988. It consisted of a force of 1,000 police officers who swept through the area on a Friday night and again on Saturday, arresting likely gang members on a wide variety of offenses, including already existing warrants, new traffic citations, gang-related behaviors, and observed criminal activities. A total of 1,453 arrests resulted. All those arrested were taken to a mobile booking operation adjacent to the Memorial Coliseum. Most of the arrested youths were released without charges. Almost half were not gang members. There were only 60 felony arrests, and charges were filed in only 32 instances (Spergel, 1995). "This remarkably inefficient process was repeated many times, although with smaller forces—more typically one hundred or two hundred officers" (Klein, 1995, p. 162).

The newest gang suppression strategy is gun control. The Boston Gun Project (Kennedy, Piehl, & Braga, 1996) consists of a coordinated strategy based on analysis of the city's youth violence problem and illicit gun market. Research on Boston's youth violence problem has centered on youth gangs and their use of firearms. Mapping of gang territories and homicides revealed the central role gangs play in the city's youth gun problem. The Gun Project working group developed use-reduction and gun market disruption schemes that are being implemented and evaluated. Coerced use-reduction targeting gang members is the main strategy.

In sum, suppression programs have not been rigorously evaluated; therefore, their effectiveness is unknown. Following his review of the basic tenets of deterrence theory and tests of its viability, Klein (1993) concluded:

> It is not so much that suppression does or does not "work": evidence one way or another is sorely lacking. There are logical, as well as experiential, reasons to believe that suppression programs can have deterrent effects and thus, by our reasoning, can contribute substantially to gang and drug activity prevention. (p. 100)

Several researchers have noted that youth gang problems have not decreased in the areas where suppression programs have been implemented (Klein, 1995; J. W. Moore, 1978, 1991; Spergel, 1995). However, as Jackson and McBride (1985) note, gangs accept punishment when it is justified.

Legislative Approaches

A recent summary by the National Conference of State Legislatures (NCSL, 1995; see also Hunzeker, 1993) indicates that enforcement suppression has been a predominant theme in new legislation over the past few years (see also Johnson, Webster, & Connors, 1995). States including California, Nevada, Florida, Georgia, Illinois, and Louisiana have enhanced penalties for crimes carried out in participation with or at the direction of gangs. The California Street Terrorism Enforcement (STEP) Act of 1988 (California Penal Code, sec. 186.22) has served as a model for emulation by Florida, Georgia, Illinois, and Louisiana. A unique notification process is used to inform persons that they can be prosecuted under the STEP Act (Klein, 1995): Police and/or prosecutors gather evidence that a targeted gang fits the act's definition. This information is presented to the court, resulting in an enabling judicial order. Known gang members are then notified in writing that they are members of such a group. Following such notice, the act can then be applied to these members, enhancing penalties for subsequent offenses.

A number of states have enacted new youth gang prevention measures (NCSL, 1995). Florida created gang prevention councils in 1990 through which judicial circuits develop strategies to reduce gang activities. The state of Washington enacted a Youth Gang Reduction Act in 1991 that targets elementary and secondary students. Oregon enacted a statute in 1995 that provides tax credits for employers who hire gang-involved or gang-affected youth. A 1995 Texas law provides for the establishment of a gang information system. Hawaii also established legislatively a comprehensive program in 1991 that includes a statewide law enforcement task force on youth gangs, prosecution efforts that target career gang criminals, school-based prevention programs, and parks and recreation programs. A two-pronged strategy is embodied in the Hawaii Youth Gang Response System: prosecution of hard-core gang criminals, and reducing the growth of gangs through prevention and education focused on younger kids. Although preliminary results of a process evaluation of Hawaii's program are encouraging, outcome results are yet preliminary (Chesney-Lind et al., 1995a, 1995b; Chesney-Lind, Marker, Stern, Song, et al., 1992; Chesney-Lind, Marker, Stern, Yap, et al., 1992). These statutory changes show some states' interest in a combination of prevention and intervention approaches, although most of the recent legislation favors suppression tactics. Gang suppression legislation has not been evaluated.

National Assessment of Youth Gang Programs

Only one national survey of youth gang programs has been conducted. Spergel and his colleagues (Spergel, 1991; Spergel & Curry, 1993) conducted a nationwide assessment of youth gang prevention, intervention, and suppression programs under Office of Juvenile Justice and Delinquency Prevention (OJJDP) support. The assessment (conducted in 1988) included a survey of 254 respondents in 45 communities and 6 special program sites regarding strategies they employed and their perception of the most effective strategies they used. All surveyed sites were jurisdictions that had a youth gang problem and an organized response to the problem. Responses were categorized into the major program types that Spergel (1991) identified in his literature review of gang programs: community organization, social intervention, opportunities provision, and suppression. A fifth response category was added by the survey team: organizational change and development.

Suppression was the most frequently employed strategy in the 51 jurisdictions (44%), followed by social intervention (31%), organizational change and development (11%), community organization (9%), and opportunities provision (5%). "Chronic gang problem" cities tended to combine suppression, social intervention, and community organization strategies, whereas "emerging gang problem cities" favored singular approaches, either community organization, organizational development, or suppression (Spergel, Curry, et al., 1994). Respondents were also asked to assess the effectiveness of the approaches they had tried. Provision of social opportunities was perceived to be most effective in chronic gang problem cities. Community organization (mobilization) was also believed to be an effective strategy, but only when social opportunities were also provided. In contrast, respondents in emerging gang problem cities saw community organization (mobilization) as the most effective strategy. Overall, respondents were not confident that their antigang efforts were particularly productive. Only 23% of the police and 10% of all other respondents believed their community's gang situation improved between 1980 and 1987.

Spergel and Curry (1993) conducted a validity check on respondents' perceived effectiveness of program interventions by comparing responses to actual changes in five empirical indicators—numbers of gangs, gang members, gang-related homicides, gang-related assaults, and gang-related narcotics incidents—in a random sample of 21 cities in the survey. Their analysis of the data (which were reasonably complete for most of the variables) showed that perceptions correlated perfectly with the empirical indicators, whether there was improvement or deterioration in the gang situation.

In another component of the national assessment, in seven of the study sites, Curry (1990) surveyed a sample of current and former gang members who were identified through service agency contacts with them. According to client reports, the most commonly received services were recreation and sports. These services, together with job placement, were viewed as most helpful in curtailing gang activity. Service recipients were mainly males under age 21. Although Hispanic youth reported receiving fewer services than other youths, they rated the services they received as more helpful than black or white recipients toward achieving their employment goals.

As a result of the national assessment, Spergel and his colleagues developed the Comprehensive Community-Wide Approach to Gang Prevention, Intervention, and Suppression Program that consists of 12 program models for police, prosecutors, judges, probation, parole, corrections, schools, youth employment, community-based youth agencies, and a range of grassroots organizations (Spergel, Chance, et al., 1994). Two of the models, general community design and community mobilization, are cross-cutting systemwide models that encompass planning and coordination efforts. Each of the 12 models identifies program rationales, policies, procedures, and leadership roles appropriate for implementing each of them. Spergel and his colleagues also recommended that communities create a community-based youth agency to provide a continuum of services to gang and gang-prone youth.

Because gang migration is an important aspect of the youth gang problem, law enforcement views of programs that might work are valuable. In the course of their national gang migration study, Maxson, Woods, and Klein (1996) conducted interviews with law enforcement representatives in 211 cities that have experienced street gang migration, and community representatives in about one fourth of these cities. Respondents were asked to assess the use and effectiveness of several gang policies and practices. Most respondents said operational coordination with local, state, and federal law enforcement agencies was relatively common. However, few law enforcement officers viewed this as effective in reducing gang migration or illegal activities. Selective law violations (e.g., narcotics laws) were targeted in three fourths of the surveyed departments, but only 42% of them viewed this strategy as effective. Enforcement of specific gang laws (e.g., STEP) was not viewed as a particularly effective response. About 40% of the surveyed law enforcement agencies used gang sweeps and other suppression strategies, which were believed to be effective by a majority of officers. Almost two thirds of the 211 street gang migration cities employed community collaboration strategies, and over half believed these to be effective.

In sum, the only strategies perceived to be effective by a majority of law enforcement respondents were community collaboration (54%), crime prevention activities (56%), and street sweeps (62%) or other suppression tactics (63%). Interviews with community respondents did not identify any innovative or promising strategies to address gang migration. Most respondents cited collaborative approaches that targeted overall gang activity or youth crime in general as holding promise.

Klein (1995) cites five reasons for the current tendency to embrace suppression as the favored approach to youth gangs: (a) the lack of demonstrated success of the community organization and detached worker programs, (b) the proliferation of gangs in more and more cities, (c) the perceived increase in gang violence and victimization of innocent bystanders, (d) the crack cocaine epidemic and the purported involvement of gangs in drug trafficking, and (e) the swing of the sociopolitical pendulum to more conservative philosophies. Yet Klein has noted the resurfacing of community organization approaches that target weaknesses in community structures including employment, schools, social services, health programs, and the like. He believes that improvements in these areas hold much more promise than suppression because "street gangs are by-products of partially incapacitated communities. Until we dedicate the state and federal resources necessary to alter these community structures, gangs will continue to emerge despite value transformation, suppression, or other community efforts" (Klein, 1995, p. 153).

Klein contends that much of the interest in community-centered approaches that seek improvements in social and economic systems is emanating from the law enforcement community. For example, he cites Los Angeles Sheriff Sherman Block, who said: "As long as gang cultures exist, we are chasing our tails. Law enforcement cannot break the cycle, only social improvements can break it" (quoted in Sahagun, 1990, cited in Klein, 1995, p. 152) and Los Angeles Undersheriff Robert Edmunds: "Our experience is illsuited to preventing the emergence of new gangs or the increased membership of existing gangs. . . . Obviously, we miscalculated the solution. . . . What is needed are partnerships involving all segments of our society" (quoted in Sahagun, 1990, cited in Klein, 1995, p. 152).

There is considerable disagreement over the issue of whether social improvements through community organization can be achieved, although the importance of social conditions to gang organization and violence is not disputed. Short (1990) reminds us that, like individuals, "communities, too, have careers in delinquency" (p. 224). In addition to community factors, Short's (1990, 1995a, 1995b, 1996) analysis of the critical features of the youth gang problem specifies individual characteristics and group processes that must be taken into account in developing gang prevention and intervention programs. Short contends that community factors that contribute to gang delinquency and violence consist of both macro- and microlevel influences. Macrolevel forces that produce youth gangs include the spread of gang culture, youth culture, and a growing underclass (Short, 1995b, 1996).

> More than ever before in history, young people, targeted for commercial exploitation and isolated from mainstream adult roles and institutions, confront economic conditions beyond their control. Economic decline, severe unemployment, and the unavailability of "good jobs," are associated not only with street gangs, but with their transformation into "economic gangs" (including drug gangs), and with ethnic, racial, and class-related antagonisms that lead to other types of collective violence. These same forces alter both intergang relationships and relationships between gangs and their communities. (Short, 1995b, p. 19)

Quantifying these forces and connecting them to gang problems is difficult. Group processes operate at the microlevel (individual, peer group), influenced by the macrolevel (community) forces, and interact to produce gang violence (Short, 1990, 1995b, 1996). Thus, Short urges development of comprehensive programs targeting both levels (such as the CAP) and multifaceted early-intervention programs such as the Beethoven Project in the Chicago Robert Taylor Homes, a public housing community (Center for Successful Child Development, 1993).

Miller (1993) argues that the primary target of change should be the behavior of individuals rather than institutions, organizations, or structural features of the larger society, such as the employment situation, income distribution, health delivery systems, and the like. Not that these social system features are less important; changes in them should be supported, but are outside the scope of his specific proposal. Second, efforts to alter the balance between procrime and anticrime incentives should be directed not at the general category of criminal behavior, but at specific offenses such as theft, armed robbery, and assault. Third, incentives to commit crimes derive from the community subculture. He argues that a substantial reduction in criminal behavior could be achieved by interrupting the intergenerational transmission of subcultural features in the lower class. If this intergenerational transmission (of criminal culture) could be interrupted or modified, the incentive balance could shift toward strengthening anticrime incentives.

Miller (1993) proposes a four-component program focused on the strategy of weakening procrime incentives and strengthening anticrime incentives: (a) reducing procrime incentives at the community subcultural level, (b) increasing anticrime incentives at the community level, (c) reducing procrime incentives at the national level, and (d) increasing anticrime incentives at the national level. He contends that "incentives that appear to be clearly related to motivation for crime appear to be amenable to change, and can be feasibly acted on become the high priority targets for change" (p. 14). Miller suggests that this strategy could be implemented and tested most easily in small or medium-size cities, in high-gang neighborhoods. The first-priority target group would be preschool children (aged 1–5), then preadolescent (6–11), and adolescents (12–19). He suggests that program interventions could be added to or made part of programs already involving the target groups, such as Boys and Girls Clubs, afterschool programs, Head Start, and so on. Because there is some evidence that the provision of incentives to high-risk youth can enhance academic success (see, e.g., Greenwood, Model, Rydell, & Chiesa, 1996; Taggart, 1995), Miller's proposed approach merits testing.

We have reviewed in this section the results of the only national survey of youth gang programs and a national survey of law enforcement agencies. To these results, we added the perspectives of several experienced gang researchers. None of these information sources prescribes interventions for particular types of gangs (e.g., violent, nonviolent) or specific gang crimes (e.g., drug sales, assault, robbery). The state of the art of gang programming has not been advanced to the level of linking program interventions to specific gang types and criminal patterns. In the next section, we recommend three gang intervention strategies that the literature reviewed in this section suggests might work in combating gang problems in general.

RECOMMENDED STRATEGIES AND PROGRAMS

No single program has been demonstrated through rigorous evaluation to be effective in preventing or reducing gang violence. There are several reasons for this. Like many other social problems, youth gang problems remain unsolved (Miller, 1990). The complexity of gang problems makes prevention and intervention difficult. Finally, as we saw in the last section, few rigorous evaluations of gang interventions have been conducted.

Nevertheless, our literature review suggests that youth gang problems can be ameliorated, that is, reduced in prevalence and severity (Miller, 1990). Three promising gang program strategies are recommended based on this review. The first one targets gang problems directly. The second one targets gang problems within a comprehensive strategy for dealing with serious, violent, and chronic juvenile delinquency. The third approach targets gang-related (and gang-motivated) homicides.

Comprehensive Community-Wide Approach to Gang Prevention, Intervention, and Suppression Program

This program model (see earlier discussion) was designed specifically to target youth gang problems, as the product of a nationwide assessment of youth gang prevention, intervention, and suppression programs in the late 1980s (Spergel, 1991, 1995; Spergel & Curry, 1993; Spergel, Curry, et al., 1994). As already mentioned, 12 program components developed by Spergel and his colleagues (Spergel, Chance, et al., 1994) are available for the design and mobilization of community efforts by police, prosecutors, judges, probation and parole officers, corrections officers, schools, employers, community-based agencies, and a range of grassroots organizations (Spergel, Chance, Ehrensaft, Regulus, Kane, & Alexander, 1992). Technical assistance manuals are available to support local program development (Spergel, Chance, Ehrensaft, Regulus, Kane, & Laseter, 1992). Variations of these models are currently being implemented and tested in Bloomington, Illinois; Mesa, Arizona; Tucson, Arizona; Riverside, California; and San Antonio, Texas. An independent evaluation is being conducted by the University of Chicago.

The most promising gang violence prevention and intervention program is being conducted in the Little Village area of Chicago, a low-income and working-class community of about 90% Mexican Americans (Spergel & Grossman, 1994, 1995, 1996). Called the Gang Violence Reduction Program, it is administered by the Research and Program Development Division of the Chicago Police Department. The program targeted over 200 of the "shooters," "influentials," or gang leaders (aged 17–24) of two of the city's most violent Latino gangs. These two gangs account for almost 70% of the gang homicides and other violent gang crimes in the community.

The Gang Violence Reduction Program consists of two coordinated strategies: (a) targeted control of violent or potentially hardcore violent youth gang offenders, in the form of increased probation department and police supervision and suppression, and (b) provision of a wide range of social services and opportunities for targeted youth, to encourage their transition to conventional legitimate behaviors through education, jobs, job training, family support, and brief counseling. Managed by the Neighborhood Relations Unit of the Chicago Police Department, the project is staffed by tactical police officers, probation officers, community youth workers (from the University of Chicago), and workers in Neighbors Against Gang Violence, a new community organization established to support the project. The program incorporates a complement of prevention, intervention, and suppression strategies, based on a comprehensive model Spergel and his colleagues developed (Spergel, Chance, et al., 1994). These multiple strategies are "employed interactively" (Spergel & Grossman, 1995, p. 3).

Preliminary evaluation results (after 4 years of program operations) are positive (Spergel & Grossman, 1996). Program interventions "have been associated with a decline, or at least a reduction in the rate of increase in gang violence" (p. 24). Overall, gang-motivated violence arrests increased by 32% in Little Village, compared to an increase of 77% in the control area (p. 28). Compared to nontargeted gangs, the two gangs targeted in the program were still responsible for the preponderance of serious and violent gang crimes in the area, but generally experienced a smaller combined rate of increase in number of offenders involved in gang homicides and other violent crimes. Examination of arrests among program clients in both gangs showed an increase in the average number of arrests over a

3-year period (Spergel & Grossman, 1997). However, reductions were observed for gang members over 19 years of age. Thus, by this measure, the project was much more successful with older gang members.

Self-reported measures among program subjects showed significant reductions in both violent and property-related crimes between the first time interval and the last one. Among program clients, reductions in total crime and violence were almost twice as great for those who received services or contacts from both police and gang workers compared to youth who did not receive such coordinated contacts. The reduction in drug selling was more than eight times greater for youth receiving combined services from police and gang workers, compared to program youth receiving noncoordinated or alternate forms of services (Spergel & Grossman, 1996).

In sum, the Little Village Gang Violence Reduction Program appears to have been successful in reducing gang crime, during a period in which gang violence was increasing significantly in the Little Village area. The success of the program is much more evident by self-reported measures than by arrest data. However, Spergel and Grossman (1996) note that arrest increases may partially be accounted for by a change in police data collection practices instituted in 1993, and by organizational policy changes in police practices resulting in more emphasis on suppression activities.

OJJDP's Comprehensive Strategy for Serious, Violent, and Chronic Juvenile Offenders

Targeting gang problems within a community's comprehensive strategy for dealing with serious, violent, and chronic juvenile offenders is the second recommended approach. OJJDP's Comprehensive Strategy for Serious, Violent, and Chronic Juvenile Offenders (Wilson & Howell, 1993) provides a framework for strategic community planning and program development. OJJDP's *Guide for Implementing the Comprehensive Strategy for Serious, Violent, and Chronic Juvenile Offenders* (Howell, 1995) is a resource for carrying out the OJJDP Comprehensive Strategy. It contains numerous promising and effective program models that will help prevent and reduce gang problems while targeting serious, violent, and chronic juvenile offenders.

The theoretical foundation of the Comprehensive Strategy is the "social development model" (Catalano & Hawkins, 1996; Hawkins & Weis, 1985), a risk-focused approach to delinquency that identifies risk factors contributing to delinquency, prioritizes them, and specifies ways to buffer and reduce those risks. The Comprehensive Strategy consists of prevention and graduated sanctions components, encompassing the entire juvenile justice and human service fields. The graduated sanctions component uses structured decision-making tools (risk and needs assessments) to achieve the best match between public safety risks and offenders' present and treatment needs in a continuum of sanctions and program options.

Because separate causal pathways to gang participation versus nongang serious and violent offending have not been identified, programs found to be effective or promising for preventing and reducing serious and violent delinquency in general may hold promise in combating gang delinquency and violence. Promising programs that might be included in a comprehensive youth gang program follow. These address known risk factors for gang participation.

Prevention Component

The prevention component of the Comprehensive Strategy incorporates a risk- and protective-factor approach for systematically assessing community risk factors, identifying and prioritizing the most prevalent risk factors, then selecting from promising and effective interventions those that best target the priority risk factors and strengthen protective factors. Communities That Care (Hawkins & Catalano, 1992) is a structured process for analysis of risk factors and the development of approaches that reduce them and buffer their negative effects by increasing protective factors. The major risk factors for gang involvement are found in the individual, family, school, peer group, and community domains (Thornberry, 1998). Promising programs that seek to reduce these risk factors are noted below.

A public education campaign is needed to educate national, state, and local leaders, parents, children, and adolescents about the risks associated with gang participation. This educational campaign should be based on the elevated risk of homicide among gang members—60 times the risk of homicide among the general population (Morales, 1992)—and focus particularly on inner cities and low-income areas.

Discouraging children and young adolescents from joining gangs is the most cost-effective approach to reducing serious gang crime (National Drug Intelligence Center, 1994). As we saw earlier, two gang prevention curricula (Project BUILD and G.R.E.A.T.) have showed positive results (Esbensen & Osgood, 1997; Thompson & Jason, 1988).

A number of promising *family-based* early-intervention programs have been identified (see Hawkins, Catalano, & Brewer, 1995b, pp. 52–60; Horne, 1993), including: pre- and perinatal medical care, intensive health education for the mother, child immunizations, parent training, child cognitive development activities, home visitation (Olds, Henderson, Tatelbaum, & Chamberlin, 1988), and home-based parent training and skills training for juveniles (Tremblay, Vitaro, et al., 1992). These aim mainly to strengthen family management and can reduce the likelihood that offspring will join gangs (see Yoshikawa, 1995).

Promising *school* programs include the Perry Preschool Project (Schweinhart, Barnes, & Weikart, 1993); the Syracuse University Family Development Research Program (Lally, Mangione, & Honig, 1988); a variety of classroom organization, management, and instructional interventions, including school-based behavioral interventions (for a review and summary, see Brewer et al., 1995); graduation incentives for high-risk youths (Taggart, 1995; see also Greenwood et al., 1996); and an antibullying program (Olweus, 1992).

Promising *peer group* and *individual-focused* programs include manhood development (Watts, 1991); employment training, education, and counseling (Corsica, 1993); conflict resolution and peer mediation in tandem (Hawkins, Farrington, & Catalano, in press); alternatives to gang participation (Klein, 1995); equipping peers to help one another (Goldstein & Glick, 1994); and techniques for separating youths from gangs (Hunsaker, 1981; Kohn & Shelly, 1991).

Community programs must increase social and economic alternatives to gang involvement. Promising programs include community reconstruction (Eisenhower Foundation, 1990), Empowerment Zones (revitalization of communities through economic and social services), and Enterprise Communities (promoting physical and human development). Empowerment Zones and Enterprise Communities are large-scale programs supported through the federal Department of Housing and Urban Development (see OJJDP, 1995c) that aim to reconstruct selected inner-city areas. Other programs are needed that help improve social and economic conditions in impoverished communities, providing "social capital" for young people (Short, 1995b), enabling them to reach turning points such as gainful employment in pathways to success outside gangs (Sampson & Laub, 1993a). Community norms supporting gang crime and violence must also be changed. Strengthening anticrime incentives and weakening procrime incentives may work (Miller, 1993).

Promising programs designed to prevent gang problems in particularly low-income areas and public housing projects include the Beethoven Project in Chicago's Robert Taylor Homes (Center for Successful Child Development, 1993); Neutral Zone (Thurman, Giacomazzi, Reisig, & Mueller, 1996); Community Outreach Program (Kodluboy & Evenrud, 1993); and Boys and Girls Clubs: Targeted Outreach (Feyerherm, Pope, & Lovell, 1992).

Community policing is an essential component of a comprehensive gang prevention program. Several community policing programs appear to have realized some success in dealing with youth crime problems (see Cronin, 1994, for three promising models). One of these is the Norfolk Police Assisted Community Enforcement (PACE) program, focused in low-income housing areas. Although the PACE program has not been evaluated, crime has decreased by an estimated 29% in the targeted neighborhoods (Cronin, 1994). Police report fewer service calls and a significant drop in on-street drug trafficking and gunfire in the targeted areas. One key to the apparent success of the PACE program is the formation of partnerships between police and neighborhood organizations, empowering neighborhoods through community mobilization to develop in concert with the police and other city agencies solutions to gang and other crime problems. These solutions include social and human service needs.

Another community policing model that specifically targets youth gangs is the Reno, Nevada, program (Weston, 1995). Through the formation of the Community Action Team (CAT), the Reno Police Department involves minority neighborhoods, community service agencies, and political leaders in a community solution to the city's serious youth gang problem. The CAT program, developed in response to gang problems, had two strategies: (a) creation of a highly specialized team of officers to target the top 5% of violent gang members in a repeat offender program, and (b) a prevention and early intervention program that targeted the city's estimated 80% of local gang members who were not involved in criminal activity and not considered to be hard core. Neighborhood advisory groups provide feedback from community residents, and an interagency group coordinates prevention and intervention resources. Although the program has not been independently evaluated, Weston (1995) reports that "it would appear that limited violence and limited growth in gang membership is related to the many success stories resulting from intervention efforts" (p. 300). Neighborhood block watch also appears to be a useful community crime prevention technique (Lindsay & McGillis, 1986; Rosenbaum, Lewis, & Grant, 1986).

Successful prevention of gang problems cannot be accomplished without involving community leaders and neighborhood organizations, because of the integral relationship between gangs and community conditions and dynamics (Spergel, Chance, et al., 1994). Thus, community mobilization is a key component of a comprehensive gang prevention program. It is a process of consciousness raising, objective identification of gang problem dimensions, and developing a community commitment to take action. "The essence of the community mobilization process is to reinvigorate or reorganize community structures so that community energies and resources are developed to address the youth gang problem, and these resources are integrated and targeted on the gang problem" (Spergel, Chance, et al., 1994, p. 6).

It is also critical that gang prevention program developers solicit input from gang members. Gang leaders have identified program strategies they believe would be most valuable in their communities. These included gutting and burning abandoned structures, building counseling centers and recreation areas, beautification of the neighborhood, renovation of educational facilities, tutoring programs, health care facilities, replacement of welfare programs with state-sponsored employment, economic development programs, and an increased role for residents in law enforcement activities (Bursik & Grasmick, 1993, p. 178).

Graduated Sanctions Component

The graduated sanctions component should consist of structured sanctions, including priority arrest, adjudication, intensive probation, incarceration, and aftercare for juvenile offenders (Krisberg & Howell, 1998). Vertical prosecution of older, chronic, serious and violent gang offenders should be pursued in the criminal justice system (Genelin, 1993; Weston, 1995). A continuum of juvenile corrections treatment options should be provided in an intensive supervision program (Krisberg, Neuenfeldt, Wiebush, & Rodriguez, 1994).

Interpersonal skills training appears to hold promise for improving social skills, reducing anger, and possibly violence reduction among street gang youth and with institutionalized populations, some of which have included gang members (Goldstein, 1993; Goldstein & Glick, 1994). In a recent experiment, Aggression Replacement Training (ART) was tested as a gang intervention program with 10 aggressive juvenile gangs in New York City. Goldstein and Glick (1994) report a reduction in arrest rates, as well as other evaluation results, supporting the effectiveness of a 2-year project using the ART intervention approach. In an 8-month followup, 13% of the ART group were rearrested, compared to 52% of the control group. On other measures, compared to the control group, the ART group showed significant improvements in community functioning, and slightly better improvements in interpersonal skills and anger control. The ART model teaches gang members anger control and other skills, and it attempts to turn their real-world reference group, the gang, from an antisocial group into a prosocial one (Goldstein & Glick, 1994).

The multisystemic therapy (MST) program appears to be a promising treatment and rehabilitation program for gang members even though it has not specifically targeted them. MST has been found to be effective in treating multiple problems of serious and violent juvenile offenders in different settings (Henggeler, Melton, & Smith, 1992; Henggeler, Melton, Smith, Schoenwald, & Hanley, 1993). A Columbia, Missouri program (Borduin et al., 1995) targeted chronic serious juvenile offenders referred to the project by juvenile court personnel. Two hundred families were randomly assigned to the treatment program or to the control group. Therapeutic interventions were based on the multisystemic approach to the prevention and treatment of childhood and adolescent behavioral problems (Henggeler & Borduin, 1990). The follow-up (4 years later) showed that 22% of MST youth were rearrested, compared to 72% of youths who received individual counseling and 87% of youths who refused either treatment (Borduin et al., 1995).

MST incorporates a socioecological view in which antisocial behavior in youth is seen as linked to multiple systems in which the youth is embedded, that is, the key characteristics of youth and the family, peer, school, and neighborhood systems. MST uses interventions that are present focused and action oriented, directly addressing intrapersonal (i.e., cognitive) and systemic (i.e., family, peer, school) factors known to be related to adolescent antisocial behavior. Empowering parents with the skills and resources to independently address the difficulties of rearing adolescents is an overriding treatment goal. Although multiple systems may be involved, MST involves a single therapist for each client, providing brief (about 4 months) but intensive treatment, generally in the home or in community locations (e.g., school or recreation center) (Borduin et al., 1995).

MST appears to have applicability as a juvenile justice system rehabilitation approach for youth gang members. Treatment groups in various MST experiments have included gang members. This discovery provided the basis for fielding an experiment specifically targeting gang members. Thus, the MST model is currently being tested in Galveston, Texas in the Second Chance program, which targets gang-involved youth (Thomas, 1996).

The "8% Solution" program (also known as the 8% Early Intervention Program) in Orange County, California, implements the graduated sanctions component of the Comprehensive Strategy. The program is based on an analysis of court referrals showing that 8% of referred adolescents account for more than half of all repeat offenses in the county (Kurz & Moore, 1994). Risk assessment and analysis of the characteristics of the 8% group (who had four or more court referrals in the following 3 years) showed that four factors correctly classified 70% of the chronic recidivists who were under 16 years of age: (a) school performance, (b) family problems, (c) substance abuse, and (d) antisocial behavior (stealing, running away, gang affiliation). Thus, the 8% Solution program targets initial court referrals under age 16 with these characteristics because they are at risk of becoming chronic juvenile offenders (and adult offenders as well, 53% in a 6-year follow-up). Potential 8% cases are initially identified during probation intake and verified through a comprehensive assessment process.

Once youths are admitted to the 8% Solution program, the initial goal is to bring their behavior under control and in compliance with probation terms and conditions while working to achieve stability in the adolescent's home (Orange County Probation Department, 1995). From that point a broad range of sanctions options (from day reporting to community confinement) are used in conjunction with a continuum of program options for the juvenile and family members to achieve habilitation goals while providing intensive case supervision. These options include individual incentives, family problem assessment and intervention services, family preservation and support services (including home-based intervention, respite care, and parent aids), individualized treatment for particular problem behaviors (e.g., mental health, drug and alcohol abuse), and a wide range of community service opportunities for the project clients.

A preliminary evaluation comparing a pilot group of program clients with the original study group shows about a 50% reduction in new offenses, court petitions, probation violations, and subsequent correctional commitments among the 8% program group in a 12-month follow-up (Orange County Probation Department, 1996). An independent assessment of the 8% program (Greenwood et al., 1996) concluded that it is cost-effective. Greenwood and his colleagues estimate (p. 38) that the program costs about $14,000 per serious crime prevented (about 70 serious crimes per million dollars). The California legislature recently appropriated funds for replication and testing of the program in six other counties within the state.

The gang component of the 8% Solution program targets gang leadership and the most chronic recidivists through a coordinated program of gang interdiction, apprehension, and prosecution (Capizzi, Cook, & Schumacher, 1995). These three strategies are integrated and coordinated by TARGET (Tri-Agency Resource Gang Enforcement Team), consisting of the Westminster Police Department, the Orange County District Attorney, and the County Probation Department. The Gang Incident Tracking System (GITS) identifies and tracks gang members, providing the information base for the TARGET program, which supports gang interdiction, apprehension, and prosecution. TARGET uses intelligence gathering and information sharing to identify and select appropriate gang members and gangs for intervention. Civil abatement procedures are used to suppress the criminal activities of entire gangs.

During its first 2 years of operation, the TARGET program (a) identified and verified 647 individual gang members; (b) targeted 77 verified gang members for intensive investigation, probation supervision, and prosecution, 69% of whom were placed in custody; (c) prosecuted 145 cases involving 168 gang member defendants and achieved a 99% conviction rate; (d) supervised an average caseload of 52 probationers regarded as hard-core gang members; and (e) documented a 62% decrease in serious gang-related crime (Kent & Smith, 1995). Begun in Westminster, TARGET is being replicated in six other cities within Orange County. Klein et al. (1995) suggest that "focused efforts of this type can produce positive effects in smaller gang cities."

Effective police and agency interventions can be enhanced by sound, current gang information. The Chicago Early Warning System (Block & Block, 1991) is a model for this purpose, and it can be replicated in other jurisdictions. This system, stimulated by earlier research in Chicago (see Curry & Spergel, 1988) is based on a statistical model that consolidates spatial information and uses automated "hot spot area" identification and other geographic statistics to predict potential crisis areas. The Early Warning System is used in the Chicago Police Department's Police Area Four project, in which the police identify problem areas, then target prevention efforts in those areas. Up-to-the-minute information is necessary for targeting specific neighborhoods, because of knowledge that gang violence changes over time, following a pattern of escalation, retaliation, and revenge that often occurs across a spatial border that also changes over time (Block & Block, 1993). Information provided by the Early Warning System is used to inform police and community agency interventions to head off the cycle of retaliation and retribution, if possible, through the use of mediation and crisis intervention. The Chicago Early Warning System effectively supports the Little Village project (discussed previously) by providing timely information on criminal gang activity (see Spergel & Grossman, 1997).

The main target crime in the Police Area Four project is gang-related homicides. Although conventional wisdom suggests that homicide cannot be prevented, the Blocks disagree (Block & Block, 1991). They contend that homicides can be prevented by targeting efforts on (a) the "specific Homicide Syndromes [e.g., expressive] that are the most dangerous and have the highest chance of successful prevention, (b) specific neighborhoods in which the risk of being murdered is especially high, and (c) specific groups who are at the highest risk of victimization" (p. 57).

These conclusions are supported by extensive gang homicide research the Blocks have conducted in Chicago, principal findings of which Block and Block (1993) summarized as follows:

First, most of Chicago's street gang crime can be identified with the city's four largest gangs. From 1987 to 1990, they accounted for 69% of all street gang-motivated crimes and for 56% of all street gang-motivated homicides, although they represent only about 10% of the "major" Chicago youth gangs and 51% of the estimated number of street gang members.

Second, gangs varied in the types of criminal activities in which they engaged. Some specialized in instrumental crimes. Most gang violence was emotional defense of one's identity as a gang member, defense of the gang and gang members, defense and glorification of the reputation of the gang, gang member recruitment, and territorial expansion. Except for the Vice Lords, a majority of street gang offenses for all other gangs in the city were turf related.

Third, "the connection between street gangs, drugs, and homicide was weak and could not explain the rapid increase in homicide in the late 1980s" (p. 4). Only 3% of gang-motivated homicides between 1987 and 1990 were related to drugs.

Fourth, the most lethal areas were along disputed boundaries between small street gangs. These were mainly Latino gangs fighting among themselves over limited turfs.

Fifth, neighborhood characteristics were associated with specific types of gang crime. "Street gangs specializing in instrumental violence were strongest in disrupted and declining neighborhoods. Street gangs specializing in expressive violence were strongest and most violent in relatively prospering neighborhoods with expanding populations" (p. 8).

Sixth, the most lethal violence (and highest level) occurred in neighborhoods where turf battles occurred, not in those where street gang activity focused on drug offenses.

Seventh, although street gang assaults did not increase during the period, and gang-related homicides did, the increase in deaths was attributed to an increase in the lethality of weapons, mostly high-caliber, automatic or semiautomatic weapons.

Eighth, many areas that had high levels of gang-related homicides had low levels of other types of homicide.

Ninth, the predominant type of street gang activity in neighborhoods often changed from year to year, or even month to month, and tended to occur sporadically.

Gun access and use reduction is an essential component of a comprehensive strategy. Recent studies have shown the proliferation and use of firearms among youth gangs (Block & Block, 1993; Maxson, Gordon, & Klein, 1985). Gang members are significantly more likely than nonmembers to own a gun illegally (Bjerregaard & Lizotte, 1995). Adolescents who own guns for protection are more likely to be involved in gangs and to commit serious crimes (Lizotte, Tesoriero, Thornberry, & Krohn, 1994). Therefore, limiting gun access and use is an important means of reducing lethal gang violence.

Numerous proposals for firearms reduction have been made that merit testing (Cook, 1981a, 1981b, 1991; Cook & Nagin, 1979; Newton & Zimring, 1969; Zimring, 1985, 1993, 1996; Zimring & Hawkins, 1987). Several approaches suggested recently have particular applicability to the youth gang firearm problem. Police seizures of illegally carried guns in hot spot areas have been found to reduce gun crimes, homicides and drive-by shootings, though not significantly (Sherman, Shaw, & Rogan, 1995). "Coerced use reduction" may be effective (Kennedy, Peihl, & Braga, 1996). Undercover purchases of firearms from adolescents, control of the supply channels, creation of ammunition scarcity, bilateral buy-back agreements, and nonuse treaties with financial compliance incentives hold promise (Zimring, 1996). Interdicting supply channels may be more feasible than commonly assumed because of the newness of guns used in gang homicides and their purchase within the state (Kennedy et al., 1996; Zimring, 1976). Equally important, research is needed on the relationship between firearms and violent street gang activity, on the extent of youth gun ownership and use, and patterns of acquisition of guns by minors in the gang gun inventory environment (Zimring, 1993, 1995).

Multiagency coordination of investigations, prosecutions, and sanctioning criminal gang members is important for effective and efficient law enforcement. One model, JUDGE (Jurisdictions United for Drug Gang Enforcement), targets drug-involved gang members in San Diego. The multiagency task force enforces conditions of probation and drug laws and provides vertical prosecution for probation violations and new offenses involving targeted offenders. Evaluation of JUDGE showed vertical prosecution to be a cornerstone for successful implementation and the advantages of a multiagency approach (Office of Justice Programs, 1996).

The gang program model that holds the most promise is likely to contain multiple components, incorporating prevention, social intervention, treatment, suppression, and community mobilization approaches. Involvement of all sectors of the community is essential (Bursik & Grasmick, 1993). To work, gang program components must be integrated in a collaborative approach, supported by a management information system.

A Strategy to Prevent and Reduce Youth Gang-Related (or Gang-Motivated) Homicides

Because of recent increases in gang homicides (see Howell, 1997), a third gang program strategy for targeting them is recommended. Of course, reducing youth gang-related (or gang-motivated) homicides should be a priority wherever they occur. But studies in Chicago and Los Angeles indicate that these two cities disproportionately account for gang-related homicides[2] in the United States. In Chicago, the number of street gang-motivated homicides increased almost fivefold between 1987 and 1994, from 51 to 240 (Block, Christakos, Jacob, & Przybylski, 1996). Gang-related homicides in Los Angeles County more than doubled from 1987 to 1992, from 387 to 803 (Klein, 1995). Chicago and Los Angeles alone accounted for nearly 1,000 gang homicides in 1992. Hutson, Anglin, Kyriacou, Hart, and Spears (1995) concluded that "gang-related homicides in Los Angeles County have reached epidemic proportions and are a major health problem" (p. 1031).

The Epidemiology of Youth Gang Homicides (Table 17–2) summarizes demographic information and research on risk factors for gang homicides. The major risk factors are community conditions (weapon availability/lethality, social disorganization, racial and class discrimination, immigrant adjustment, changing economic situation, drug market conditions), communities where gangs and gang violence are most prevalent, and where gangs are involved in turf disputes in closely concentrated geographical areas within specific years and specific age groups. Consideration of these risk factors with available knowledge of promising and effective programs suggests a strategy that may work to prevent and reduce youth gang-related homicides. They are preventable (Block & Block, 1993; Hutson, Anglin, & Mallon, 1992).

Chicago's Gang Violence Reduction Program appears to be a promising program model for targeting gang-motivated violence and homicides (Spergel & Grossman, 1995, 1996, 1997). It should be replicated and tested in other Chicago communities, in specific Los Angeles communities, and in other cities experiencing significant levels of gang homicides. One key to its success is the Early Warning System Geoarchive of the Illinois Criminal Justice Information Authority, which provides up-to-date information on hot spots of gang violence for targeted intervention efforts by the police and other agencies.

This literature review has identified other promising interventions that should be considered in designing a comprehensive gang homicide prevention and reduction program: a hospital emergency room intervention program for injured victims that could be established by adding a gang specialist to the Suspected Child Abuse and Neglect Team—SCAN—now found in many hospitals (Morales, 1992), serving to initiate entry into programs to break the cycle of gang violence (Hutson et al., 1995), and counseling for victims of drive-by shootings

TABLE 17–2 Epidemiology of Youth Gang Homicides

I. The United States is one of the most violent countries in the world, 5th among 41 countries.[a]

Has the highest homicide rate in the world.[b]

A. Prevalence	Gang members are 60 times more likely to die of homicide than are members of the general population (600 per 100,000 gang members.)[c]
	Gang homicide rate in St. Louis is 1,000 times higher than U.S. rate.[d]
	In 1989–1993, 33% of L.A. gang-related homicides were drive-bys.[e]
	In 1985–1994, 7% of Chicago gang-motivated homicides were drive-bys.[f]
B. Incidence	Chicago had 240 street gang-motivated homicides in 1994.[f]
	Los Angeles County had just under 800 gang-related homicides in 1994.[g]
C. Victim/offender	75% of Chicago gang-related homicides are intergang. 14%, nongang victims, and 11% intragang.[f]
	Peak age of homicide offenders is 18.
	64% of Chicago gang-related homicide victims are age 15–19.[f]
	82% of juvenile gang homicides in L.A. are intraracial.[b]
	63% of gang homicides in L.A. result from intergang interactions.[b]
	23% of L.A. drive-by shooting victims are innocent bystanders.[e]
	64% of gang homicide victims are gang members.[b]
D. Weapons	Firearms are used in 95% of gang-related homicides[b]; use of fully automatic or semiautomatic weapons increased 13-fold in Chicago from 1987 to 1994.[f]

II. Risk factors: In addition to the risk factors for gang membership, fatalities are mainly related to:

Turf disputes in closely concentrated geographical areas within specific years and specific age groups.[h]

Expressive violence in relatively prospering neighborhoods with expanding populations, acts of instrumental violence (e.g., drug disputes) in disrupted/declining neighborhoods.[i]

Racial and class discrimination, immigrant adjustment, changing economic situation, drug market conditions.[i]

Setting and participant characteristics.[j]

Weapon availability/lethality, more gangs and gang violence.[k]

Social disorganization (immigrant resettling.)[l]

Drug trafficking is not strongly correlated with youth gang homicides.[m]

a. Rosenberg and Mercy (1986).
b. Hutson, Anglin, Kyriacou, Hart, and Spears (1995).
c. Morales (1992).
d. Decker and Van Winkle (1996).
e. Hutson, Anglin, and Eckstein (1996).
f. Block, Christakos, Jacob, and Przybylski (1996).
g. Maxson, in press.
h. Block (1993).
i. Block and Block (1993).
j. Maxson, Gordon, and Klein (1985).
k. Block and Block (1993); Hutson et al. (1995); Miller (1982).
l. Curry and Spergel (1988).
m. Block (1993); Block and Block (1993); Hutson et al. (1994, 1995); Kennedy et al., 1996; Klein, Maxson, and Cunningham (1991); Hutson et al. (1994); Meehan and O'Carroll (1992); Miller (1994).

to reduce the traumatic effects of victimization and discourage retaliation (Groves, Zuckerman, Marans, & Cohen, 1993; Hutson, Anglin, & Pratts, 1994; Pynoos & Nader, 1988).

Access to firearms by violent street gangs should be reduced by legislation, regulation, and community education and by removing illegal guns from the possession of gang members. A number of promising strategies have been recommended (Block & Block, 1993; Cook, 1981a, 1981b, 1991; Cook & Nagin, 1979; Hutson et al., 1995; Kennedy et al., 1996; Sheley & Wright, 1993; Sherman et al., 1995; Wright, 1995; Zimring, 1976, 1993, 1996; Zimring & Hawkins, 1987). A firearm wounding and fatality reporting system should be established to determine sources of weapons and assist interdiction efforts (Teret, Wintemute, & Beilenson, 1992; see also American Academy of Pediatrics, 1992; Cristoffel, 1991; Kellerman, Lee, Mercy, & Banton, 1991).

Effective program strategies must be built on continuously updated information, because of the frequently changing patterns (Block & Block, 1993). Short-term successes can be realized by targeting the causes of acute escalation in violence levels (Block & Block, 1993). As the Blocks have shown, programs must take into account the instrumental and expressive characteristics of gang violence. "For example, a program to reduce gang involvement in drugs in a community in which gang members are most concerned with defense of turf has little chance" (Block & Block, 1993, p. 9). Because juveniles tend to shoot others of their own ethnic group (Hutson, Anglin, & Eckstein, 1996), prevention programs must be culture specific (Soriano, 1993) and age appropriate (Block & Christakos, 1995; Centers for Disease Control, 1990; Hutson et al., 1994; Hutson et al., 1995; Klein & Maxson, 1989).

Several studies have refuted the supposed strong correlation between gang-related homicides and drug trafficking. Analyses of arrests in Boston (Miller, 1994), Chicago (Block & Block, 1993; Block et al., 1996), Miami (Dade County Grand Jury, 1985, 1988; Inciardi, 1990), and Los Angeles (Hutson et al., 1995; Klein, Maxson, & Cunningham, 1991; Maxson, 1995, Meehan & O'Carroll, 1992) have consistently shown a low correlation between gang-related homicides and drug trafficking (see Howell, 1997, for a detailed review). Therefore, gang homicides and narcotics trafficking involving adolescents and young adults should be addressed as separate risk factors for homicide rather than as interrelated cofactors (Meehan & O'Carroll, 1992).

SUMMARY

This review of the gang program literature suggests that comprehensive gang programs can be structured in two ways. One method involves gearing them specifically toward gang problems; the other one aims to reduce gang delinquency within a broader strategy aimed at serious, violent, and chronic juvenile offenders. The program model that proves to be most effective is likely to contain multiple components, incorporating prevention, social intervention, treatment, suppression, and community mobilization approaches. Gang program components must be integrated in a collaborative approach with full interagency coordination, supported by a management information system and rigorous program evaluation.

The Comprehensive Community-Wide Approach to Gang Prevention, Intervention, and Suppression Program developed by Spergel and his colleagues targets gang problems. It emphasizes community change as its main theoretical approach. The original model contains 12 program components for the design and mobilization of community efforts by police, prosecutors, judges, probation and parole officers, corrections officers, schools, employers, community-based agencies, and a range of grassroots organizations. Technical assistance manuals are available to support local program development. Variations of these models are currently being implemented and tested in five sites under OJJDP support. Another version of this comprehensive model, the Gang Violence Reduction Program, has been implemented in Chicago and is showing very promising results.

The second approach, reducing gang delinquency by targeting serious, violent, and chronic delinquency, is accomplished by implementing the OJJDP Comprehensive Strategy for Serious, Violent, and Chronic Juvenile Offenders. A number of program options are suggested, based on this literature review. This chapter organized these options under the prevention and graduated sanctions components of the Comprehensive Strategy. Its theoretical underpinnings are grounded in the social development model, a risk- and protection-factor approach, fashioned after the public health model. The graduated sanctions component uses risk and needs assessments as management tools to place offenders in a continuum of graduated sanctions and treatment options.

The 8% Solution program implements the graduated sanctions component of the OJJDP Comprehensive Strategy for Serious, Violent, and Chronic Juvenile Offenders. Assessment of gang involvement is included in the criteria for early-intervention services. The gang component of the 8% Solution program targets gang leadership and the most chronic recidivists. The program uses intelligence gathering and information sharing to identify and select appropriate gang members and gangs for intervention.

Finally, a strategy to prevent and reduce youth gang-related (or gang-motivated) homicides is recommended. It incorporates program strategies that look promising for preventing and reducing gang homicides. The central program intervention is the Chicago Gang Violence Reduction Program. To be effective, it must be supported by up-to-date information on hot spots of gang violence for targeted intervention efforts by the police and other agencies. Replication of the Early Warning System Geoarchive of the Illinois Criminal Justice Information Authority is recommended for this purpose. It is recommended that the proposed homicide reduction strategy be implemented in specific Chicago and Los Angeles communities, where gang homicides have reached epidemic proportions.

SOME RECENT FINDINGS

Boston's anti-gang strategy (see Kennedy et al., 1996) has received a great deal of national attention. Although evaluation results are not yet available, a reduction in juvenile homicides of some 80% from 1990 to 1995 in the city has been reported (DOJ, 1997), and none has been recorded for 1996 or through September 1997 (Harden, 1997). Other official data indicate lower juvenile arrest rates for aggravated assault and battery with a firearm (1993-1995) and fewer violent crimes in public schools from 1995 to 1996 (DOJ, 1996).

QUESTIONS FOR UNDERSTANDING AND CRITICAL THINKING

1. What types of gang prevention and intervention programs appear to be more successful than others? Explain.

2. Review and discuss gang suppression approaches and their continuance as a popular policy approach.

3. How could programs be developed by members of an entire community?

4. What types of elements should be included in a more comprehensive, holistic approach to gang prevention and intervention?

5. How would such programs be evaluated?

NOTES

1. The term *youth gang* is commonly used interchangeably with *street gang,* referring to neighborhood or street-based youth groups. Motorcycle gangs, prison gangs, racial supremists, and other hate groups are excluded. Our operational definition for this review coincides closely with Miller's (1982) definition: "A youth gang is a self-formed association of peers, united by mutual interests, with identifiable leadership and internal organization, who act collectively or as individuals to achieve specific purposes, including the conduct of illegal activity and control of a particular territory, facility, or enterprise" (p. 21).

2. Law enforcement agencies in Los Angeles and Chicago define *gang homicides* differently (see Maxson & Klein, 1990). In Los Angeles, the basic element is evidence of gang membership on the side of either the suspect or the victim. Maxson and Klein call this a "gang member" definition (p. 77). In Chicago, a homicide is considered gang related only if the preponderance of evidence indicates that the incident grew out of a street gang function, that is, gang-motivated (Block et al., 1996).

REFERENCES

ALINSKY, S. D. (1946). *Reveille for radicals.* Chicago: University of Chicago Press.

AMERICAN ACADEMY OF PEDIATRICS. (1992). Firearms and adolescents. *Pediatrics, 89,* 784–787.

BATTIN, S. R., HILL, K. G., ABBOTT, R. D., CATALANO, R. F., & HAWKINS, J. D. (1998). The contribution of gang membership to delinquency beyond delinquent friends. *Criminology, 36,* 93–115.

BJERREGAARD, B., & LIZOTTE, A. J. (1995). Gun ownership and gang membership. *Journal of Criminal Law and Criminology, 86,* 37–58.

BLOCK, C. (1993). Lethal violence in the Chicago Latino community. In A. V. Wilson (Ed.), *Homicide: The victim/offender connection* (pp. 267–342). Cincinnati, OH: Anderson.

BLOCK, C. R., & BLOCK, R. B. (1991). Beginning with Wolfgang: An agenda for homicide research. *Journal of Crime and Justice, 14,* 31–70.

BLOCK, C. R., & CHRISTAKOS, A. (1995). Major trends in Chicago homicide: 1965–1994. *Research Bulletin.* Chicago: Illinois Criminal Justice Information Authority.

BLOCK, C. R., CHRISTAKOS, A., JACOB, A., & PRZYBYLSKI, R. (1996). Street gangs and crime: Patterns and trends in Chicago. *Research Bulletin.* Chicago: Illinois Criminal Justice Information Authority.

BLOCK, R., & BLOCK, C. R. (1993). Street gang crime in Chicago. *Research in brief.* Washington, DC: U.S. Department of Justice, National Institute of Justice.

BORDUIN, C. M., CONE, L. T., MANN, B. J., HENGGELER, S. W., FUCCI, B. R., BLASKE, D. M., & WILLIAMS, R. A. (1995). Multisystemic treatment of serious juvenile offenders: Long-term prevention of criminality and violence. *Journal of Consulting and Clinical Psychology, 63,* 569–578.

BREWER, D. D., HAWKINS, J. D., CATALANO, R. F., & NECKERMAN, H. J. (1995). Preventing serious, violent, and chronic juvenile offending: A review of evaluations of selected strategies in childhood, adolescence, and the community. In J. C. Howell, B. Krisberg, J. D. Hawkins, & J. J. Wilson (Eds.), *Sourcebook on serious, violent, and chronic juvenile offenders* (pp. 61–141). Thousand Oaks, CA: Sage.

BURSIK, R. J., JR., & GRASMICK, H. G. (1993). *Neighborhoods and crime: The dimensions of effective community control.* New York: Lexington Books.

CAPIZZI, M., COOK, J. I., & SCHUMACHER, M. (1995, Fall). The TARGET model: A new approach to the prosecution of gang cases. *The Prosecutor,* pp. 18–21.

CAPLAN, N. S., DESHAIES, D. J., SUTTLES, G. D., & MATTICK, H. W. (1967). The nature, variety, and patterning of street club work in an urban setting. In M. Klein & B. G. Myerhoff (Eds.), *Juvenile gangs in context* (pp. 194–202). Englewood Cliffs, NJ: Prentice Hall.

CATALANO, R. F., & HAWKINS, J. D. (1996). The social development model: A theory of antisocial behavior. In J. D. Hawkins (Ed.), *Delinquency and crime: Current theories* (pp. 149–197). New York: Cambridge University Press.

CENTER FOR SUCCESSFUL CHILD DEVELOPMENT. (1993). *Beethoven's fifth: The first five years of the Center for Successful Child Development* (Executive summary). Chicago: Ounce of Prevention Fund.

CENTERS FOR DISEASE CONTROL. (1990). Forum on youth violence in minority communities: Setting the agenda for prevention. *Public Health Report, 106,* 225–279.

CHESNEY-LIND, M., LEISEN, M. B., ALLEN, J., BROWN, M., ROCKHILL, A., MARKER, N., LIU, R., & JOE, K. (1995a). *Crime, delinquency, and gangs in Hawaii: Evaluation of Hawaii's Youth Gang Response System: Part I.* Honolulu: University of Hawaii, Manoa, Social Science Research Institute, Center for Youth Research.

CHESNEY-LIND, M., LEISEN, M. B., ALLEN, J., BROWN, M., ROCKHILL, A., MARKER, N., LIU, R., & JOE, K. (1995b). *The Youth Gang Response System. A process evaluation: Part II.* Honolulu: University of Hawaii, Manoa, Social Science Research Institute, Center for Youth Research.

CHESNEY-LIND, M., MARKER, N., STERN, I. R., SONG, V., REYES, H., REYES, Y., STERN, J., TAIRA, J., & YAP, A. (1992). *An evaluation of Act 189: Hawaii's response to youth gangs.* Honolulu: University of Hawaii, Manoa, Social Science Research Institute, Center for Youth Research.

CHESNEY-LIND, M., MARKER, N., STERN, I. R., YAP, A., SONG, V., REYES, H., REYES, Y., STERN, J., & TAIRA, J. (1992). *Gangs and delinquency in Hawaii.* Honolulu: University of Hawaii, Manoa, Social Science Research Institute, Center for Youth Research.

COHEN, M. I., WILLIAMS, K., BEKELMAN, A. M., & CROSSE, S. (1994). Evaluation of the National Youth Gang Drug Prevention Program. In M. W. Klein, C. Maxson, & J. Miller (Eds.), *The modern gang reader* (pp. 266–275). Los Angeles: Roxbury.

COOK, P. J. (Ed.). (1981a). Gun control. *Annals of the American Academy of Political and Social Science, 455,* 1–167.

COOK, P. J. (1981b). The "Saturday night special": An assessment of alternative definitions from a policy perspective. *Journal of Criminal Law and Criminology, 72,* 1735–1745.

COOK, P. J. (1991). The technology of personal violence. In M. Tonry (Ed.), *Crime and justice: An annual review* (Vol. 14, pp. 1–71). Chicago: University of Chicago Press.

COOK, P. J., & NAGIN, D. (1979). *Does the weapon matter?* Washington, DC: Institute of Law and Social Research.

CORSICA, J. Y. (1993). Employment training interventions. In A. Goldstein & C. R. Huff (Eds.), *The gang intervention handbook* (pp. 301–317). Champaign, IL: Research Press.

CRISTOFFEL, K. K. (1991). Toward reducing pediatric injuries from firearms: Charting a legislative and regulatory course. *Pediatrics, 88,* 294–305.

CRONIN, R. (1994). *Innovative community partnerships: Working together for change.* Washington, DC: U.S. Department of Justice, Office of Juvenile Justice and Delinquency Prevention.

CURRY, G. D. (1990). *Client evaluation of youth gang services.* Report to the U.S. Department of Justice, Office of Juvenile Justice and Delinquency Prevention.

CURRY, G. D., & SPERGEL, I. A. (1988). Gang homicide, delinquency, and community. *Criminology, 26,* 381–405.

CURRY, G. D., WILLIAMS, K., & KOENEMANN, L. (1996, November). *Structure, culture, and delinquency in female gang involvement.* Paper presented at the annual meeting of the American Society of Criminology, Chicago.

CURRY, G. D., WILLIAMS, K., & KOENEMANN, L. (1997, March). *Race and ethnic differences in female gang involvement.* Paper presented at the annual meeting of the Academy of Criminal Justice Sciences, Lexington.

DADE COUNTY GRAND JURY. (1985). *Dade youth gangs.* Final report of the Grand Jury, Miami.

DADE COUNTY GRAND JURY. (1988). *Dade County gangs.* Final report of the Grand Jury, Miami.

DAHMANN, J. (1981). *Operation Hardcore, a prosecutorial response to violent gang criminality: Interim evaluation report.* Washington, DC: Mitre Corporation. Reprinted in M. W. Klein, C. L. Maxson, & J. Miller (Eds.). (1995). *The modern gang reader* (pp. 301–303). Los Angeles: Roxbury.

DECKER, S. H., & VAN WINKLE, B. (1996). *Life in the gang: Family, friends, and violence.* New York: Cambridge University Press.

DEPARTMENT OF JUSTICE. (1996). *Youth violence: A community-based response.* Washington, DC: U.S. Department of Justice.

EISENHOWER FOUNDATION. (1990). *Youth investment and community reconstruction: Street lessons on drugs and crime for the nineties.* Washington, DC: Author.

ESBENSEN, F., & HUIZINGA, D. (1993). Gangs, drugs, and delinquency in a survey of urban youth. *Criminology, 31,* 565–589.

ESBENSEN, F., & OSGOOD, D. W. (1997). National evaluation of G.R.E.A.T. *Research in brief.* Washington, DC: U.S. Department of Justice, National Institute of Justice.

FATTAH, D. (1987). The House of Umoja as a case study for social change. *Annals of the American Academy of Political and Social Science, 494,* 37–41.

FEYERHERM, W., POPE, C., & LOVELL, R. (1992). *Youth gang prevention and early intervention programs.* Report to the U.S. Department of Justice, Office of Juvenile Justice and Delinquency Prevention.

FOX, J. R. (1985). Mission impossible? Social work practices with black urban youth gangs. *Social Work, 30* 25–31.

GEIS, G. (1965). *Juvenile gangs.* Report to the President's Committee on Youth Crime. Washington, DC: Government Printing Office.

GENELIN, M. (1993). Gang prosecution: The hardest game in town. In A. Goldstein & C. R. Huff (Eds.), *The gang intervention handbook* (pp. 417–426). Champaign, IL: Research Press.

GOLD, M., & MATTICK, H. (1974). *Experiment in the streets: The Chicago Youth Development project.* Ann Arbor: University of Michigan, Institute for Social Research.

GOLDSTEIN, A. P. (1993). Interpersonal skills training interventions. In A. Goldstein & C. R. Huff (Eds.), *The gang intervention handbook* (pp. 87–157). Champaign, IL: Research Press.

GOLDSTEIN, A. P., & GLICK, B. (1994). *The prosocial gang: Implementing aggression replacement training.* Thousand Oaks, CA: Sage.

GREENWOOD, P. W., MODEL, K. E., RYDELL, C. P., & CHIESA, J. (1996). *Diverting children from a life of crime: Measuring costs and benefits.* Santa Monica, CA: RAND.

GROVES, B. M., ZUCKERMAN, B., MARANS, S., & COHEN, D. J. (1993). Silent victims: Children who witness violence. *Journal of the American Medical Association, 269,* 262–264.

HARDEN, (1997). Boston's approach to juvenile crime encircles youths, reduces slayings. *The Washington Post, D October 23, p. A3.*

HAWKINS, J. D., & CATALANO, R. F. (1992). *Communities that care.* San Francisco: Jossey-Bass.

HAWKINS, J. D., CATALANO, R. F., & BREWER, D. D. (1995b). Preventing serious, violent, and chronic offending: Effective strategies from conception to age 6. In J. C. Howell, B. Krisberg, J. D. Hawkins, & J. J. Wilson (Eds.), *Sourcebook on serious, violent, and chronic juvenile offenders* (pp. 36–60). Thousand Oaks, CA: Sage.

HAWKINS, J. D., FARRINGTON, D. P., & CATALANO, R. F. (in press). Reducing violence through the schools. In D. S. Elliott, B. A. Hamburg, & K. R. Williams (Eds.), *Youth violence: New perspectives for schools and communities.* Cambridge: Cambridge University Press.

HAWKINS, J. D., & WEIS, J. G. (1985). The social development model: An integrated approach to delinquency prevention. *Journal of Primary Prevention, 6*(2), 73–97.

HENGGELER, S. W., & BORDUIN, C. M. (1990). *Family therapy and beyond: A multisystemic approach to treating the behavior problems of children and adolescents.* Pacific Grove, CA: Brooks/Cole.

HENGGELER, S. W., MELTON, G. B., & SMITH, L. A. (1992). Family preservation using multisystemic therapy: An effective alternative to incarcerating serious juvenile offenders. *Journal of Consulting and Clinical Psychology, 60,* 953–961.

HENGGELER, S. W., MELTON, G. B., SMITH, L. A., SCHOENWALD, S. K., & HANLEY, J. H. (1993). Family preservation using multisystemic treatment: Long-term follow-up to a clinical trial with serious juvenile offenders. *Journal of Child and Family Studies, 2,* 283–293.

HILL, K. G., HAWKINS, J. D., CATALANO, R. F., KOSTERMAN, R., ABBOTT, R., & EDWARDS, T. (1996, November). *The longitudinal dynamics of gang membership and problem behavior: A replication and extension of the Denver and Rochester gang studies in Seattle.* Paper presented at the annual meeting of the American Society of Criminology, Chicago.

HORNE, A. M. (1993). Family-based interventions. In A. Goldstein & C. R. Huff (Eds.), *The gang intervention handbook* (pp. 189–218). Champaign, IL: Research Press.

HOWELL, J. C. (Ed.). (1995). *Guide for implementing the comprehensive strategy for serious, violent, and chronic juvenile offenders.* Washington, DC: U.S. Department of Justice, Office of Juvenile Justice and Delinquency Prevention.

HOWELL, J. C. (1997). Youth gang homicides, drug trafficking, and program interventions. In J. C. Howell, *Juvenile justice and youth violence* (pp. 115–132). Thousand Oaks, CA: Sage.

HUNSAKER, A. (1981). The behavioral-ecological model of intervention with Chicano gang delinquents. *Hispanic Journal of Behavioral Sciences, 3,* 225–239.

HUNZEKER, D. (1993). Ganging up against violence. *State legislatures.* Denver, CO: National Conference of State Legislatures.

HUTSON, H. R., ANGLIN, D., & ECKSTEIN, M. (1996). Drive-by shootings by violent street gangs in Los Angeles: A five-year review from 1989 to 1993. *Academic Emergency Medicine, 3,* 300–303.

HUTSON, H. R., ANGLIN, D., KYRIACOU, D. N., HART, J., & SPEARS, K. (1995). The epidemic of gang-related homicides in Los Angeles County from 1979 through 1994. *Journal of the American Medical Association, 274,* 1031–1036.

HUTSON, H. R., ANGLIN, D., & MALLON, W. (1992). Injuries and deaths from gang violence: They are preventable. *Annals of Emergency Medicine, 21,* 1234–1236.

HUTSON, H. R., ANGLIN, D., & PRATTS, M. J. (1994). Adolescents and children injured or killed in drive-by shootings in Los Angeles. *New England Journal of Medicine, 330,* 324–327.

INCIARDI, J. A. (1990). The crack-violence connection within a population of hard-core adolescent offenders. In M. De La Rosa, E. Y. Lambert, & B. Gropper (Eds.), *Drugs and violence: Causes, correlates, and consequences* (pp. 92–111). NIDA Research Monograph No. 103. Rockville, MD: U.S. National Institute on Drug Abuse.

JACKSON, R. K., & MCBRIDE, W. (1985). *Understanding street gangs.* Plackerville, CA: Custom.

JOHNSON, C., WEBSTER, B., & CONNORS, E. (1995). Prosecuting gangs: A national assessment. *Research in brief.* Washington, DC: U.S. Department of Justice, National Institute of Justice.

KELLERMAN, A. L., LEE, R. K., MERCY, J. A., & BANTON, J. (1991). The epidemiologic basis for the prevention of firearm injuries. *Annual Review of Public Health, 12,* 17–40.

KENNEDY, D. M., PIEHL, A. M., & BRAGA, A. A. (1996). Youth violence in Boston: Gun markets, serious youth offenders, and a use-reduction strategy. *Law and Contemporary Problems, 59,* 147–196. [Special issue]

KENT, D. R., & SMITH, P. (1995). The Tri-Agency Resource Gang Enforcement Team: A selective approach to reduce gang crime. In M. W. Klein, C. L. Maxson, & J. Miller (Eds.), *The modern gang reader* (pp. 292–296). Los Angeles: Roxbury.

KLEIN, M. W. (1968). *The Ladino Hills Project: Final report.* Los Angeles: University of Southern California, Youth Studies Center.

KLEIN, M. W. (1969). Gang cohesiveness, delinquency, and a street-work program. *Journal of Research in Crime and Delinquency, 6,* 135–166.

KLEIN, M. W. (1971). *Street gangs and street workers.* Englewood Cliffs, NJ: Prentice Hall.

KLEIN, M. W. (1993). Attempting gang control by suppression: The misuse of deterrence principles. *Studies on Crime and Prevention, 2,* 88–111.

KLEIN, M. W. (1995). *The American street gang: Its nature, prevalence, and control.* New York: Oxford University Press.

KLEIN, M. W., & MAXSON, C. L. (1989). Street gang violence. In N. A. Weiner & M. E. Wolfgang (Eds.), *Violent crime, violent criminals* (pp. 198–234). Newbury Park, CA: Sage.

KLEIN, M. W., MAXSON, C. L., & CUNNINGHAM, L. C. (1991). Crack, street gangs, and violence. *Criminology, 29,* 623–650.

KLEIN, M. W., MAXSON, C. L., & MILLER, J. (1995). *The modern gang reader.* Los Angeles: Roxbury.

KOBRIN, S. (1959). The Chicago Area Project—A twenty-five year assessment. *Annals of the American Academy of Political and Social Science, 322,* 19–29.

KODLUBOY, D. W., & EVENRUD, L. A. (1993). School-based interventions: Best practices and critical issues. In A. Goldstein & C. R. Huff (Eds.), *The gang intervention handbook* (pp. 257–299). Champaign, IL: Research Press.

KOHN, G., & SHELLY, C. (1991, August). *Juveniles and gangs.* Paper presented at the annual convention of the American Psychological Association, Washington, DC.

KRISBERG, B. & HOWELL, J. C. (1998). The impact of the juvenile justice system & prospects for graduated sanctions in a comprehensive strategy. In R. Loeber & D. Farrington (Eds.). *Serious & Violent Juvenile Offenders: Risk Factors & Successful Interventions.* (pp. 346–366). Thousand Oaks, CA: Sage.

KRISBERG, B., NEUENFELDT, D., WIEBUSH, R., & RODRIGUEZ, O. (1994). *Juvenile intensive supervision: Planning guide.* Washington, DC: U.S. Justice Department, Office of Juvenile Justice and Delinquency Prevention.

KURZ, G. A., & MOORE, L. E. (1994). *The "8% problem": Chronic juvenile offender recidivism.* Santa Ana, CA: Orange County Probation Department.

LALLY, J. R., MANGIONE, P. L., & HONIG, A. S. (1988). The Syracuse University Family Development Research Project: Long-range impact of an early intervention with low-income children and their families. In D. R. Powell (Ed.), *Annual advances in applied developmental psychology* (Vol. 3, pp. 79–104). Norwood, NJ: Ablex.

LINDSAY, B., & MCGILLIS, D. (1986). Citywide community crime prevention: An assessment of the Seattle program. In D. P. Rosenbaum (Ed.), *Community crime prevention: Does it work?* (pp. 46–67). Beverly Hills, CA: Sage.

LIZOTTE, A. J., TESORIERO, J. M., THORNBERRY, T. P., & KROHN, M. D. (1994). Patterns of adolescent firearms ownership and use. *Justice Quarterly, 11,* 51–73.

MATTICK, H., & CAPLAN, N. S. (1962). *Chicago Youth Development Project: The Chicago boys club.* Ann Arbor, MI: Institute for Social Research.

MAXSON, C. L. (1995, September). Street gangs and drug sales in two suburban cities. *Research in brief.* Washington, DC: U.S. Department of Justice, National Institute of Justice.

MAXSON, C. L. (in press). Gang homicide. In M. D. Smith & M. A. Zahn (Eds.), *Homicide studies: A sourcebook of social research.* Thousand Oaks, CA: Sage.

MAXSON, C. L., GORDON, M. A., & KLEIN, M. W. (1985). Differences between gang and nongang homicides. *Criminology, 23,* 209–222.

MAXSON, C. L., & KLEIN, M. W. (1990). Street gang violence: Twice as great, or half as great? In C. R. Huff (Ed.), *Gangs in America* (pp. 71–100). Newbury Park, CA: Sage.

MAXSON, C. L., WOODS, K., & KLEIN, M. W. (1996. February). Street gang migration: How big a threat? *National Institute of Justice Journal, 230,* 26–31.

MEEHAN, P. J., & O'CARROLL, P. W. (1992). Gangs, drugs, and homicide in Los Angeles. *American Journal of the Disabled Child, 146,* 683–687.

MILLER, W. B. (1962). The impact of a "total community" delinquency control project. *Social Problems, 10,* 168–191.

MILLER, W. B. (1974). American youth gangs: Past and present. In A. Blumberg (Ed.), *Current perspectives on criminal behavior* (pp. 410–420). New York: Knopf.

MILLER, W. B. (1982). *Crime by youth gangs and groups in the United States.* Washington, DC: U.S. Department of Justice, Office of Juvenile Justice and Delinquency Prevention. (Rev. 1992)

MILLER, W. B. (1990). Why the United States has failed to solve its youth gang problem. In C. R. Huff (Ed.), *Gangs in America* (pp. 263–287). Newbury Park, CA: Sage.

MILLER, W. B. (1993). *Critique of "Weed and Seed" project with a proposal for a new prevention initiative.* Report to the U.S. Department of Justice, Office of Juvenile Justice and Delinquency Prevention.

MILLER, W. B. (1994). *Boston assaultive crime* [Memorandum].

MOORE, J. W. (1978). *Homeboys: Gangs, drugs and prison in the barrios of Los Angeles.* Philadelphia: Temple University Press.

MOORE, J. W. (1991). *Going down to the barrio: Homeboys and homegirls in change.* Philadelphia: Temple University Press.

MORALES, A. (1992). A clinical model for the prevention of gang violence and homicide. In R. C. Cervantes (Ed.), *Substance abuse and gang violence* (pp. 105–118). Newbury Park, CA: Sage.

NATIONAL CONFERENCE OF STATE LEGISLATURES. (1995). *Special analysis of 1995 juvenile justice gang related enactments for the National Youth Gang Center.* Denver, CO: Author.

NATIONAL DRUG INTELLIGENCE CENTER. (1994). *NDIC Street Gang Symposium* [Proceedings]. Washington, DC: Author.

NATIONAL YOUTH GANG CENTER. (1997). *The 1995 National Youth Gang Survey.* Washington, DC: U.S. Department of Justice, Office of Juvenile Justice and Delinquency Prevention.

NEEDLE, J., & STAPLETON, W. V. (1983). *Police handling of youth gangs.* Washington, DC: U.S. Department of Justice, Office of Juvenile Justice and Delinquency Prevention.

NEW YORK CITY YOUTH BOARD. (1960). *Reaching the fighting gang.* New York: Author.

NEWTON, G. D., & ZIMRING, F. E. (1969). *Firearms and violence in American life: A staff report to the National Commission on the Causes and Prevention of Violence.* Washington, DC: Government Printing Office.

OFFICE OF JUSTICE PROGRAMS, WORKING GROUP ON GANGS. (1996). *A report to the assistant attorney general.* Washington, DC: U.S. Department of Justice, Office of Justice Programs.

OFFICE OF JUVENILE JUSTICE AND DELINQUENCY PREVENTION. (1995c). *Matrix of community-based initiatives.* Washington, DC: Author.

OLDS, D. L., HENDERSON, C. C. R., TATELBAUM, R., & CHAMBERLIN, R. (1988). Improving the life-course development of socially disadvantaged mothers: A randomized trial of nurse home visitation. *American Journal of Public Health, 78,* 1436–1445.

OLWEUS, D. (1992). Bullying among school children: Intervention and prevention. In R. D. Peters, R. J. McMahon, & V. L. Quinsey (Eds.), *Aggression and violence throughout the life span* (pp. 100–125). Newbury Park, CA: Sage.

ORANGE COUNTY PROBATION DEPARTMENT. (1995). *8% Early Intervention Program: Program design and preliminary field test results.* Santa Ana, CA: Author.

ORANGE COUNTY PROBATION DEPARTMENT. (1996). *8% Early Intervention Program field test results (12 months).* Santa Ana, CA: Author.

PENNELL, S. (1983). *San Diego Street Youth Program: Final evaluation.* San Diego, CA: Association of Governments.

PYNOOS, R. S., & NADER, K. (1988). Psychological first aid and treatment approach to children exposed to community violence: Research implications. *Journal of Traumatic Stress, 1,* 445–473.

RIBISL, K. M., & DAVIDSON, W. S., II. (1993). Community change interventions. In A. Goldstein & C. R. Huff (Eds.), *The gang intervention handbook* (pp. 333–355). Champaign, IL: Research Press.

ROSENBAUM, D. P., LEWIS, D. A., & GRANT, J. A. (1986). Neighborhood-based crime prevention: Assessing the efficacy of community organization in Chicago. In D. P. Rosenbaum (Ed.), *Community crime prevention: Does it work?* (pp. 109–133). Beverly Hills, CA: Sage.

ROSENBERG, M. L., & MERCY, J. A. (1986). Homicide epidemiologic analysis at the national level. *Bulletin of the New York Academy of Medicine, 62,* 382–390.

SAHAGUN, L. (1990, November 11). Fight against gangs turns to social solution. *Los Angeles Times,* p. A3.

SAMPSON, R., & LAUB, J. (1993a). *Crime in the making: Pathways and turning points through life.* Cambridge, MA: Harvard University Press.

SCHLOSSMAN, S., & SEDLAK, M. (1983a). *The Chicago Area Project revisited.* Report prepared for the U.S. National Institute of Education. Santa Monica, CA: RAND.

SCHLOSSMAN, S., & SEDLAK, M. (1983b). The Chicago Area Project revisited. *Crime & Delinquency, 29,* 398–462.

SCHWEINHART, L. J., BARNES, H. V., & WEIKART, D. P. (1993). *Significant benefits: The High/Scope Perry Preschool study through age 27.* Ypsilanti, MI: High/Scope.

SHAW, C. R. (1930). *The Jack Roller: A delinquent boy's own story.* Chicago: University of Chicago.

SHAW, C. R., & MCKAY, H. D. (1931). *Social factors in juvenile delinquency: Report on the causes of crime* (Vol. 2). National Commission on Law Observance and Enforcement. Washington, DC: Government Printing Office.

SHELEY, J. F., & WRIGHT, J. D. (1993). Gun acquisition and possession in selected juvenile samples. *Research in brief.* Washington, DC: National Institute of Justice, Office of Juvenile Justice and Delinquency Prevention.

SHERMAN, L. W. (1990, March-April). Police crackdowns. In *National Institute of Justice reports.* Washington, DC: U.S. Department of Justice, National Institute of Justice.

SHERMAN, L. W., SHAW, J. W., & ROGAN, D. P. (1995, January). The Kansas City gun experiment. *Research in brief.* Washington, DC: U.S. Department of Justice, National Institute of Justice.

SHORT, J. F., JR. (1963). Street corner groups and patterns of delinquency: A progress report. *American Catholic Sociological Review, 28,* 13–32.

SHORT, J. F., JR. (1990). New wine in old bottles? Change and continuity in American gangs. In C. R. Huff (Ed.), *Gangs in America* (pp. 223–239). Newbury Park, CA: Sage.

SHORT, J. F., JR. (1995a). *Poverty, ethnicity, and violence.* Boulder, CO: Westview.

SHORT, J. F., JR. (1995b, November). *Youth collectives (including gangs) and adolescent violence.* Paper presented at the annual meeting of the American Society of Criminology, Boston.

SHORT, J. F., JR. (1996). *Gangs and adolescent violence.* Boulder, CO: Center for the Study and Prevention of Violence.

SHORT, J. F., JR., & STRODTBECK, F. L. (1965). *Group process and gang delinquency.* Chicago: University of Chicago Press.

SMITH, C. S., FARRANT, M. R., MARCHANT, H. J. (1972). *The Wincroft Youth Project.* London: Tavistock.

SORIANO, F. I. (1993). Cultural sensitivity and gang intervention. In A. Goldstein & C. R. Huff (Eds.), *The gang intervention handbook* (pp. 441–461). Champaign, IL: Research Press.

SORRENTINO, A. (1959). The Chicago Area Project after twenty-five years. *Federal Probation, 23,* 40–45.

SORRENTINO, A., & WHITTAKER, D. W. (1994, May). The Chicago Area Project: Addressing the gang problem. *FBI Law Enforcement Bulletin,* pp. 7–12.

SPERGEL, I. A. (1966). *Street gang work: Theory and practice.* Reading, MA: Addison-Wesley.

SPERGEL, I. A. (1972). Community action research as a political process. In I. A. Spergel (Ed.), *Community organization: Studies in constraint* (pp. 231–262). Beverly Hills, CA: Sage.

SPERGEL, I. A. (1986). The violent youth gang in Chicago: A local community approach. *Social Service Review, 60,* 94–131.

SPERGEL, I. A. (1991). *Youth gangs: Problem and response.* Report to the U.S. Department of Justice, Office of Juvenile Justice and Delinquency Prevention.

SPERGEL, I. A. (1995). *The youth gang problem: A community approach.* New York: Oxford University Press.

SPERGEL, I. A., CHANCE, R. L., EHRENSAFT, K. E., REGULUS, T., KANE, C., & ALEXANDER, A. (1992). *Prototype/models for gang intervention and suppression.* Report to the U.S. Department of Justice, Office of Juvenile Justice and Delinquency Prevention.

SPERGEL, I. A., CHANCE, R. L., EHRENSAFT, K., REGULUS, T., KANE, C., & LASETER, R. (1992). *Technical assistance manuals.* Report to the U.S. Department of Justice, Office of Juvenile Justice and Delinquency Prevention.

SPERGEL, I. A., CHANCE, R., EHRENSAFT, K., REGULUS, T., KANE, C., LASETER, R., ALEXANDER, A., & OH, S. (1994). *Gang suppression and intervention: Community models.* Washington, DC: U.S. Department of Justice, Office of Juvenile Justice and Delinquency Prevention.

SPERGEL, I. A., & CURRY, G. D. (1990). Strategies and perceived agency effectiveness in dealing with the youth gang problem. In C. R. Huff (Ed.), *Gangs in America* (pp. 288–309). Newbury Park, CA. Sage.

SPERGEL, I. A., & CURRY, G. D. (1993). The National Youth Gang Survey: A research and development process. In A. Goldstein & C. R. Huff (Eds.), *The gang intervention handbook* (pp. 359–400). Champaign, IL: Research Press.

SPERGEL, I. A., CURRY, D., CHANCE, R., KANE, C., ROSS, R., ALEXANDER, A., SIMMONS, E., & OH, S. (1994). *Gang suppression and intervention: Problem and response.* Washington, DC: U.S. Department of Justice, Office of Juvenile Justice and Delinquency Prevention.

SPERGEL, I. A., & GROSSMAN, S. F. (1994, November). *Gang violence and crime theory: Gang Violence Reduction Project.* Paper presented at the American Society of Criminology Annual Meeting, Miami, FL.

SPERGEL, I. A., & GROSSMAN, S. F. (1995, July). *Little Village Gang Violence Reduction Program.* Paper presented at the annual conference on Criminal Justice Research and Evaluation, Washington, DC.

SPERGEL, I. A., & GROSSMAN, S. F. (1996). *Evaluation of a gang violence reduction project: A comprehensive and integrated approach.* Chicago: University of Chicago, School of Social Service Administration.

SPERGEL, I. A., & GROSSMAN, S. F. (1997). *Evaluation of the Little Village Gang Violence Reduction Project* Chicago: University of Chicago, School of Social Service Administration.

SPERGEL, I. A., TURNER, C., PLEAS, J., & BROWN, P. (1969). *Youth manpower: What happened in Woodlawn.* Chicago: University of Chicago, School of Social Service Administration.

TAGGART, R. (1995). *Quantum Opportunity Program.* Philadelphia: Opportunities Industrialization Centers of America.

TERET, S. P., WINTEMUTE, G. J., & BEILENSON, P. L. (1992). The firearm fatality reporting system: A proposal. *Journal of the American Medical Association, 267,* 3073–3074.

THOMAS, C. R. (1996, June). *The Second Chance Program.* Paper presented at the National Youth Gang Symposium. Dallas, TX.

THOMPSON, D. W., & JASON, L. A. (1988). Street gangs and preventive interventions. *Criminal Justice and Behavior, 15,* 323–333.

THORNBERRY, T. P. (1998). Membership in youth gangs and involvement in serious & violent offending. In R. Loeber & D. Farrington (Eds.), Serious & Violent juvenile offenders: *Risk factors & successful interventions.* (pp. 147–166). Thousand Oaks, CA: Sage.

THORNBERRY, T. P., HUIZINGA, D., & LOEBER, R. (1995). The prevention of serious delinquency and violence: Implications from the Program of Research on the Causes and Correlates of Delinquency. In J. C. Howell, B. Krisberg, J. D. Hawkins, & J. J. Wilson (Eds.), *Sourcebook on serious, violent, and chronic juvenile offenders* (pp. 213–237). Thousand Oaks, CA: Sage.

THORNBERRY, T. P., KROHN, M. D., LIZOTTE, A. J., & CHARD-WIERSCHEM, D. (1993). The role of juvenile gangs in facilitating delinquent behavior. *Journal of Research in Crime and Delinquency, 30,* 55–87.

THRASHER, F. M. (1936). The boys' club and juvenile delinquency. *American Journal of Sociology, 41,* 66–80.

THRASHER, F. M. (1963). *The gang: A study of 1,313 gangs in Chicago.* Chicago: University of Chicago Press. (Original work published 1927)

THURMAN, Q. C., GIACOMAZZI, A. L., REISIG, M. D., & MUELLER, D. G. (1996). Community-based gang prevention and intervention: An evaluation of the Neutral Zone. *Crime & Delinquency, 42,* 279–295.

TORRES, D. M. (1981). *Gang Violence Reduction Project 3rd evaluation report.* Sacramento: California Department of the Youth Authority.

TORRES, D. M. (1985). *Gang Violence Reduction Project: Update.* Sacramento: California Department of the Youth Authority.

TREMBLAY, R. E., VITARO, F., BERTRAND, L., LE BLANC, M., BEAUCHESNE, H., BOILEAU, H., & DAVID, L. (1992). Parent and child training to prevent early onset of delinquency: The Montreal Longitudinal-Experimental Study. In J. McCord & R. E. Tremblay (Eds.), *Preventing antisocial behavior: Interventions from birth through adolescence* (pp. 117–138). New York: Guilford.

WATTS, R. J. (1991, June). *Manhood development for African-American boys: Program and organization development.* Paper presented at the American Society for Community Research and Action, Tempe, AZ.

WESTON, J. (1995). Community policing: An approach to youth gangs in a medium-sized city. In M. W. Klein, C. L. Maxson, & J. Miller, *The modern gang reader* (pp. 297–300). Los Angeles: Roxbury.

WILSON, J. J., & HOWELL, J. C. (1993). *A comprehensive strategy for serious, violent, and chronic juvenile offenders: Program summary.* Washington, DC: U.S. Department of Justice, Office of Juvenile Justice and Delinquency Prevention.

WOODSON, R. L. (1981). *A summons to life: Mediating structures and the prevention of youth crime.* Cambridge, MA: Ballinger.

WOODSON, R. L. (1986). *Gang mother: The story of Sister Falaka Fattah.* Elmsford, NY: Pergamon.

WRIGHT, J. D. (1995, March-April). Ten essential observations on guns in America. *Society,* pp. 63–68.

YOSHIKAWA, H. (1995). Long-term effects of early childhood programs on social outcomes and delinquency. *Future of Children, 5,* 51–75.

ZIMRING, F. E. (1976). Street crime and new guns: Some implications for firearms control. *Journal of Criminal Justice, 4,* 95–107.

ZIMRING, F. E. (1985). Violence and firearms policy. In L. A. Curtis (Ed.), *American violence and public policy* (pp. 133–152). New Haven, CT: Yale University Press.

ZIMRING, F. E. (1993). Policy research on firearms and violence. *Health Affairs, 12,* 109–121.

ZIMRING, F. E. (1996). Kids, guns, and homicide: Policy notes on an age-specific epidemic. *Law and Contemporary Problems, 59,* 25–37. [Special issue]

ZIMRING, F. E., & HAWKINS, G. (1987). *The citizen's guide to gun control.* New York: Macmillan.

18

Gang Prevention and Intervention Strategies of the Boys and Girls Clubs of America

Carl E. Pope and Rick Lovell

Abstract

This article summarizes an evaluation of youth gang prevention and intervention programs across 33 Boys and Girls Clubs which were designed to implement strategies and techniques for reaching and mainstreaming at-risk youth or those on the fringe of gang involvement. Thirty Boys and Girls Club sites were funded as prevention program sites (of which eight received additional funds to develop youth gang prevention consortiums) and three were funded as intervention program sites.

This study, conducted from April 1991 to February 1992, was designed as a process evaluation, summarizing what happened across the club sites. The information collected and used for evaluation contained basic demographic descriptors, indicators of at-risk factors, and indicators of school performance. The evaluation was based on data obtained from case management information collected by Club personnel at all sites, on-site observations, and interviews by members of the research team.

The evaluation centered on actual program implementation in order to draw inferences concerning the degree to which gang prevention and intervention program objectives were achieved. In addition, the descriptive data suggests that some outcome objectives were achieved; however, the evaluation was not designed as a scientific outcome study. Overall, the results of this evaluation demonstrate that these programs were effective in reaching targeted youth and that some of the efforts implemented deserve consideration by those planning future prevention and/or intervention undertakings.

Pope C. E. and Lovell, R. (1997). Gang prevention and intervention strategies of the boys and girls clubs of America. *Free Inquiry in Creative Sociology,* 25, 117–126. Reprinted by permission of the University of Oklahoma.

INTRODUCTION

The constellation of problems related to gang and group delinquency in the United States is growing. Besides direct costs to victims resulting from violent and property offenses, "the community as a whole" is paying significant monies for law enforcement, trials and other judicial proceedings, secure confinement, and correctional programs (Thompson, Jason 1988). Further, large numbers of America's youth, especially in public housing and inner city areas, are slipping into a quagmire from which return is extremely difficult.

With inner city conditions rapidly deteriorating, hundreds of thousands of young persons face desperate and largely hopeless lives. The problems one sees in inner city areas are coming home to all Americans either directly or indirectly as they emerge geographically, economically, politically and socially. Factors such as unemployment, under-employment, poverty, and the like have at one time or another been linked to increasing or decreasing rates of crime, delinquency, and gang activity. Often unable to subsist within the legal economy, many take refuge in the illegal subeconomy—engaging in prostitution, gambling, drugs and the like—and often express frustration in acts of expressive and instrumental violence as witnessed in the recent resurgence of youth gang activity (Hagedorn 1988; Huff 1990; Jankowski 1991; Klein, Maxson 1989; Vigil, Yun 1990). As a result, members of the underclass comprise the bulk of juvenile and adult institutionalized populations. Thus, a significant number of American youth, especially inner city youth, are "at risk." In a country where tens of millions partake of abundance, these youth live in conditions where their access to developmental opportunities is much different than that of their more well-situated "peers."

STRATEGIC INITIATIVES: THE ROLE OF MEDIATING STRUCTURES

The problems of inner city poverty and deterioration are long-standing and complex. Obviously, attempts to address inner city conditions must proceed in several dimensions. Over the last several decades two strategic approaches have predominated in efforts to deal with inner city gang problems. As pointed out by Spergel and Curry,

> the predominant strategy for dealing with the gang problem during the 1950's and 1960's was social intervention, whereas the predominant strategy during the 1970's and 1980's was suppression. (1993)

Elements of both strategies have carried forward into the 1990's (very heavy on suppression); however, there is increasing recognition of the need for strategic initiatives of a different sort.

As Spergel and Curry also inform us,

> analysis of the data from the National Youth Gang Survey [Spergel 1991] produced little evidence of the efficacy of either approach [social intervention or suppression] as a primary strategy for either chronic or emerging gang problem cities. (Spergel, Curry 1993)

Considering this, Spergel and Curry point to the need for "appropriate and complementary strategies," especially

> the need for various community organizations, including law enforcement and youth agencies, to play important interactive and collective roles in both emerging and chronic problem cities. (1993)

Spergel's and Curry's analysis essentially results in a call for community mobilization. Introducing the basic notion that increasing gang activity may signify "a progressive weakening of the basic institutions of socialization, especially the family, but also the schools and other community organizations," they indicate that

> secondary institutions in the community, particularly police, schools, and youth agencies must assume additional support and control functions that perhaps formerly were fulfilled by families. (1993)

In the image conveyed, there would be a need for a coordinated collective effort which may constitute a strategic dimension of initiatives to transcend suppression and/or social intervention "to nurture a coherent community in which problematic or at-risk youth can play a constructive and meaningful role."

More than fifty years ago, F. M. Thrasher (1927) described the work of voluntary organizations, such as ethnic clubs, churches, and others, in helping to shape the behaviors of gang members. Attention to the roles and potential of various primary and secondary organizations may have been diminished over time by emphases on mega-initiatives of relatively short-term duration. Studies and analyses of what has occurred/is occurring in inner city areas lead to the understanding that when essential primary institutions deteriorate, external mega-initiatives may miss, or perhaps more importantly, may misspecify their targets. A void is then present which must be filled in order to "carry out those functions critical to the youth socialization process," (Spergel, Curry 1993) as well as to integrate efforts and essentially create a more stable, if not empowered, neighborhood or community.

The notion of "mediating structures" has been around for some time (Berger, Neuhaus 1977). Applied to consideration of 1990's strategic initiatives, one is directed to search for mechanisms by which support may be channeled to fill the void, utilizing organizations which contribute stability to neighborhoods or communities, provide an interface with larger institutions, and have the capacity to link local needs to initiatives of promise.

WEED AND SEED

While there have been some efforts at developing mediating structures to address the inner cities dilemma, little has been done with the focus and scope of Operation Weed and Seed. Operation Weed and Seed has involved a multi-dimensional strategy with a primary emphasis on addressing the problems of gangs, drugs, violence, crime and community recovery from drug problems and violent gang activity. The thrust of the overall strategy was based upon an awareness that in various communities a coordinated comprehensive approach was needed. The idea was to form partnerships among governmental and private organizations to significantly reduce criminal activity (the "weed" part) and promote community recovery (the "seed" part).

The four strategies of Weed and Seed included:

1. suppression—enforcement, adjudication, prosecution, and supervision targeting those "who account for a disproportionate percentage of criminal activity."
2. community-oriented policing—providing a "bridge" between law enforcement activities and "neighborhood reclamation and revitalization activities."

3. prevention, intervention, intervention, and treatment—focusing on "youth services, school programs, community and social programs, and support groups."

4. neighborhood reclamation and revitalization—focusing on "economic development activities designed to strengthen legitimate community institutions."

The overall idea was to concentrate resources in designated areas to provide a comprehensive approach.

BOYS AND GIRLS CLUBS

As noted in a recent report:

> For more than 130 years the Boys Clubs of America has been working to prevent juvenile delinquency and develop productive citizens and leaders among our Nation's most vulnerable youth. . . The Clubs provide youth with alternatives to the streets that include activities that develop their sense of belonging, competence, usefulness and influence. (Sweet 1991)

With over 1400 local clubs operating in every major metropolitan area, Boys and Girls Clubs of America (BGCA) was an ideal partner to Weed and Seed efforts. Clubs typically provide recreational programming for youth as well as other services such as tutorial programs; field trips; craft programs; mentoring positive enhancements, such as SMART MOVES (a programming strategy which provides focused group discussions tailored to teens concerning such topics as drug use, sexual relations, and other matters); and the like. Moreover, BGCA has proven to be effective in servicing disadvantaged youth, with local club facilities often located adjacent to or within public housing (Feyerherm, Pope, Lovell 1992).

An evaluation conducted by researchers from Columbia University and the American Health Foundation (Schinke, Cole, Orlandi 1991) noted the following:

> Social support services are critical for youth in public housing. Yet comprehensive and sensitive services for young people in public housing are practically nonexistent. Public housing communities urgently need the kind of attention, community organization, and carefully designed intervention programs that Boys and Girls Clubs offer.

The emphasis must be on coordinated efforts at community organization and recovery.

Similarly, a 1986 Louis and Harris Associates survey underscored the fact the BGCA have a positive impact on our nation's youth, especially those from disadvantaged families. Club experiences lay a strong foundation for success in later life. As noted by Sweet (1991), Boys and Girls Clubs has a lengthy and "strong record of positive involvement with children at particular risk—those in declining neighborhoods and in public housing. . . " As part of Weed and Seed, BGCA engaged in a targeted outreach program in order to reach those youth at risk of becoming involved in gangs and gang-related activity (eg. drugs, violence, and crime generally). The results reported here represent an evaluation of this targeted outreach program. The main aims were to 1) assess the implementation of the programs, including a determination of efforts which worked well and could be replicated, as well as those efforts which fell short of expectations (problem areas) and 2) assess, to the degree possible, the programs' effectiveness.

METHODOLOGY

The methodology utilized here was designed to accomplish the objectives noted and consisted of a "process" evaluation. As Patton (1980) observed:

> Process evaluations are aimed at elucidating and understanding the internal dynamics of program operations. Process evaluations focus on the following kinds of questions: What are the factors that come together to make the program what it is? What are the strengths and weaknesses of the program? How are the clients brought into the program and how do they move through the program once they are participants? What is the nature of staff-client interactions?

Central to a process evaluation is a detailed description of program operations which is ideally suited to a qualitative design. Thus, the assessment relied heavily on qualitative interviews and observations, which were supplemented by a limited quantitative component involving data drawn from case records.

BGCA PROGRAM OPERATIONS

The BGCA project involved 30 Clubs selected and funded as gang prevention sites, with a commitment to provide case management and services for 35 youth. Through a special grant from the Office of Health and Human Services, eight of these sites were selected to network with other community organizations or youth gang consortia to reach an additional 100 at-risk youth through community-wide events. In each of the sites *prevention* meant implementation of strategies to deter youth primarily aged 7 to 11, from becoming involved in gang or gang related activities. Three additional Clubs were selected as intervention sites. These Clubs received substantially more funding and were to develop and implement strategies to serve at risk youth (typically those on the fringes of gangs or "wanna-bes") in the primary target ages of 12 to 16. At least 50 youth were to be served in each gang intervention site.

All the participating local Clubs were selected through a process which included submission of an application for funding and a detailed plan for implementation. A committee comprised of directors of BGCA reviewed the proposals and made the actual decisions concerning which local Clubs would be funded. As implemented, the BGCA efforts fall within the general rubric of prevention.

Prevention and Consortium Programs

Fifteen of the prevention and consortium sites were included in the evaluation. For the prevention sites, the evaluation was based in part on data obtained from case management information collected by Club personnel at each site. All available program records were used to provide an assessment as comprehensive as possible. Using the case management data, analysis was conducted to provide information on demographic characteristics of youth served. In addition, site visits to selected programs were accomplished. On-site observation was combined with interviews of various persons arranged through the auspices of the local Clubs. These interviews were conducted with program directors, Club staff directly involved with prevention programming, program participants, school officials, local justice officials, and parents when possible. The evaluation cen-

TABLE 18–1   Gender and Race/Ethnicity Distribution of Program Youth

	Prevention		Consortium		Intervention		All Programs	
	N	%	N	%	N	%	N	%
Gender								
Female	251	29	196	29	71	19	518	27
Male	593	68	468	70	301	81	1362	71
Missing	33	4	4	1	0	0	37	2
Total	877	100	668	100	372	100	1917	100
Race/Ethnicity								
White	94	11	130	19	25	7	249	13
African American	593	68	361	54	152	41	1106	58
Hispanic	114	13	151	23	167	45	432	23
Asian	18	2	25	4	22	6	65	3
Native American	0	0	8	1	1	0	9	0
Other Races	3	0	3	0	2	1	8	0
Missing	55	6	0	0	3	1	58	3
Total	877	100	668	100	372	100	1917	100

tered on actual program implementation in order to determine strengths of implementation and areas of implementation needing improvement, and, draw inferences concerning the degree to which program plans were achieved. The consortium sites were approached in the same manner—one visit was made to each of the selected sites by one member of the research team.

Intervention Programs

All three intervention sites were included in the evaluation. As with the prevention programs, available case management information was analyzed to provide demographic information, indicators of at-risk factors such as past and current school performance, as well as gang and justice system involvement. In addition, each of the intervention sites was visited twice by two members of the research team. Again, on-site observations were combined with interviews of various persons, as indicated. In both the prevention and intervention program interviews, the evaluators use semi-structured interview schedules to obtain information on such issues as:

- the nature of the gang problem in the area
- club activities as part of the prevention/intervention efforts
- relationship to other Club programs and activities
- efforts in mainstreaming of participants and, among other items
- relationships with other youth-serving agencies

TABLE 18-2   Factors Placing Program Youth at Risk of Gang Involvement

	Prevention		Consortium		Intervention		All Programs	
	N	%	N	%	N	%	N	%
At-Risk Factors								
"Wanna-Be"	85	10	0	0	19	5	105	5
Family Gang Involved	5	1	0	0	36	10	41	2
School Behavioral Problem	338	39	422	63	33	9	793	41
Failing School	309	35	246	37	37	10	592	31
Truant	133	15	136	20	15	4	284	15
Runaway	27	3	5	1	66	18	122	6
Abuse/Neglect	164	19	64	10	4	1	232	12
Substance Abuse	26	3	5	1	52	14	83	4
Parental Substance Abuse	177	20	98	15	4	1	279	15
In Custody	43	5	63	9	94	25	200	10
Other	84	10	113	17	98	26	295	15

TABLE 18-3   Discipline and Rewards for Program Youth

	Prevention		Consortium		Intervention		All Programs	
	N	%	N	%	N	%	N	%
Disciplinary Actions	229	26	121	18	7	2	357	19
Accomplishments								
In-Club	421	48	192	29	23	6	636	33
Outside	117	13	79	12	11	3	207	11
Volunteer	236	27	153	23	102	27	491	26
Other	51	6	3	0	183	49	237	12

Beyond this, interviews were conducted with program participants for the three intervention programs using semi-structured interview schedules developed by the evaluation team.

FINDINGS

Selected Descriptive Information

A total of 1,917 youth were served by the project: 877 were served by the 22 prevention sites, 668 by the eight prevention consortium sites, and 372 by the three intervention sites. Schools served as the largest referral source (45%), followed by youth walk-ins (23%), juvenile justice agencies (9%), and youth agencies (9%). As defined in the program design, the prevention and consortium sites served youth between ages 7 and 11 (98%), while the intervention sites focused on older youth (85% were 12 through 18 years of age).

A substantial number of girls participated in the program, especially at the prevention and consortium sites (29% of all participants). At the three intervention sites, girls made up 19 percent of the total served. The greatest number of youth served by the project were African-American (58%), followed by Hispanic (23%) and Caucasian youth (13%). Asian youth accounted for 3 percent, while Native Americans and others made up 1 percent.

The greatest at-risk factors identified were school-related. Forty-one percent of the youth exhibited behavioral problems in school, 31 percent were failing school, and 15 percent were chronically truant. Parental substance abuse and abuse/neglect were next in significance (15% and 12% respectively), followed by "other" factors at 15 percent (defined by Club staff as environment/neighborhood factors).

Once enrolled at the Clubs, most youth attended regularly. Ninety percent of the youth attended once a week or more, with 26 percent attending daily, 19 percent attending half of the available hours, and 19 percent attending at least twice a week. One third received recognition for in-club accomplishments, while 26 percent received recognition for volunteer work outside of the Club. Project staff used other agencies as referral sources, with 41 percent of all youth involved in the project receiving some form of referral to one or more community agencies.

Referrals to outside agencies for other services were highest among youth at intervention sites (73% of all intervention youth), followed by consortium sites (56%) and prevention sites (15%). It would be expected that the intervention sites would require the greatest level of referral services due to the focus of the efforts.

Although this was a process evaluation, the descriptive data did suggest trends in the educational arena. School behavior showed the greatest level of improvement among the school risk factors, with 48 percent of the participants showing improvement; the highest (62%) were among the consortium sites where the established relationships with the schools was the strongest. Over one-third of the youth showed improved grades and another one-third improved their attendance. Less than six percent of the youth showed declines in any of the school risk factors during program involvement.

Strengths in Program Implementation

BGCA's and OJJDP's expectations of "success" for the various programs centered on accomplishing networking activities, actually implementing the specified efforts, recruiting and retaining the targeted at-risk youth, maintaining case management records, and attempting to "mainstream" the targeted youth during the program time period in order to 1) bring them together with other Club members for positive associations and 2) encourage the targeted youth to remain involved in the Clubs and other positive activities beyond the project time period. The various programs were envisioned as "demonstrations," with a relatively short-term focus and a primary interest in implementation. Little attention was given to conceptualizing, operationalizing, or measuring effects beyond those already described, or to any follow-up other than the one-shot evaluation immediately following program implementation and termination.

All programs met their overall goals to serve the designated numbers of targeted youth. This required each participating Club to staff its effort (for the prevention and consortium programs this generally meant real-locating time and duties for existing staff, and for the intervention efforts this meant both reallocating time and duties for existing staff and hiring new staff), engage in initial coordination with schools and other local agencies, and engage in recruiting targeted youth. As noted earlier, schools were the sources from which the largest number of youth were recruited. Across programs, recruitment was a program strength. Specific efforts varied, but most involved identifying at-risk youth directly through liaison with school or other agency personnel; then contacting youth and parents, parent, or responsible adult; explaining the program and participation in the program; and formally enrolling those youth who desired to participate and whose parent(s) or responsible adult(s) consented. The structured, formal recruitment process supported directly the notion of targeted outreach and was a key feature of all programs.

Retention of youth in the programs was excellent over the project time period. More than ninety percent of those initially enrolled remained officially enrolled throughout the project period. As noted above, however, a sizable percentage (36%) attended sporadically, while a smaller percentage (26%) attended each day, 19 percent attended regularly and more than half of the available hours, and 19 percent attended regularly and approximately twice per week. In all programs, staff attempted both to motivate the targeted youth and to promote attendance through incentives. These incentives included awards and recognition based on accumulating hours and/or points for various activities, as well as other incentives such as special parties for targeted youth (e.g., pizza parties). Staff also sought to interest and motivate the targeted youth by mainstreaming them into general Club activities.

Mainstreaming, or integrating the targeted youth into the general Club population and activities, was an essential feature of all programs and was a strength of implementation. Mainstreaming required program staff to balance provision of specified activities to the targeted youth with ensuring that the youth could be integrated without identification as targeted youth. Across the programs, staff were sensitive to these requirements and generally were able to meet them by 1) keeping records separate and confidential to the extent possible and 2) providing explanations to targeted youth and other Club youth as necessary. Mainstreaming was essential, as well, in extending program resources. All programs utilized general Club resources in this way to supplement program funding. Actually, absent this strategy it would have been very difficult for most Clubs to provide sufficient activities and staffing to operate the programs. With this strategy, the efforts were viable.

Networking, building or utilizing relationships with other organizations and agencies, was a strong point in all programs, especially those designated to build a consortium.

Networking is an integral feature of Boys and Girls Clubs operations on a continuing basis, and it was not surprising to find that Club staff were skilled and knowledgeable in this area. Each Club was able to capitalize on established relationships, and many formed new sets of relationships relevant to their specified efforts. Across all sites there were strong efforts to establish or utilize existing relationships with schools (especially those immediately adjacent to the housing areas in which targeted youth resided and those they attended), law enforcement, juvenile court and juvenile probation agencies, and others. In some instances, the local Clubs were the only viable alternatives available within the program area. Even in these instances, staff coordinated and shared information with other organizations.

Eight programs were to build consortium efforts. All focused on building partnerships, especially with schools and other organizations capable of working together with the local Club to deliver activities and services and/or to directly support activities and services. Typically, program partnerships with schools involved development of a school liaison to assist in monitoring progress and determining needs for after-school tutorials and educational enhancements. The educational enhancements would involve such activities as computer-assisted learning and other learning activities to supplement classroom activities. The central idea would be to provide interesting, motivational learning activities which extended and supported classroom activities rather than simply retracing classroom activities. This focus was important and participants reported that their interest in both school and after-school learning activities increased as a result.

There were several other notable partnership ventures. Two were exemplary. In one of these, a local Club joined with an element of the United States Army from a nearby military installation to create and implement a leadership-training program for targeted youth. The program included a ten-week cycle of weekend instruction and activities in which military personnel provided seminar-type classroom activities and outdoor-skills activities such as map reading, compass orienting, and outdoor overnight camping and learning activities. The military personnel also obtained the participation of cadets from a nearby university R.O.T.C. detachment to act as volunteers at the local Club for an array of additional activities. This partnership deserves careful consideration because of the possibilities for future efforts to bring to bear resources not usually included in designing or planning for gang prevention programs.

As well, the second exemplary effort involved a creative and very useful partnership. The local Club joined with an advertising agency in the area to develop what eventually became an award-winning print and television ad campaign against gangs. The ad agency provided guidance, technical expertise, and production facilities, as well as commitment of individuals from the agency to work with the targeted youth. The targeted youth creatively designed both the print ads and the television ads (30-second and 1-minute commercials) and were the actors in the television ads. These ads were powerful and showed the creative capabilities of the youth, given guidance and opportunity. It would be a large understatement to point out that the participants were motivated by this partnership—the targeted youth, the agency personnel, and the Club staff. Such partnerships may be possible in many areas and deserve careful consideration by those designing or planning gang prevention and intervention efforts.

Among other specified efforts across programs, basketball leagues and trips beyond central city neighborhoods were strengths of implementation. Boys and Girls Clubs operate with the rubric of recreation to provide activities designed to interest youth as the prerequisite for engaging youth with developmental opportunities. Basketball leagues were a staple across the programs, and these were designed to serve two obvious purposes. They were organized and operated to provide alternatives to the streets at times of day when youth typically are "hanging out" on the streets, and they were aimed at maintaining the participation of targeted youth by providing an activity of special interest to many of the program participants. All evidence indicated that both these purposes were achieved for most participating youth across the programs.

Trips beyond central city neighborhoods were another staple across programs. Those familiar with America's inner cities realize that many youth do not travel beyond their neighborhoods to see directly what many more well-situated youth take for granted. Trips to museums, state and national parks, and other places of interest were utilized to maintain the interest of participants and to expand their first-hand knowledge of what things are like beyond their own usual horizons. The broader aim was to provide youth the beginnings of a way to locate themselves beyond a central city neighborhood. The project period was limited, but such activities should receive careful consideration by those designing more long-term efforts.

The intervention programs were implemented by three Clubs in which the usual scope of operations included reaching teenage youth. Even among Boys and Girls Clubs, reaching and retaining teens is known to be difficult, requiring experienced staff and efforts tailored to teens and the local situations in which teens are living. Not all Clubs extend their efforts to include teens. Among the noted difficulties is that of concurrently providing programming of interest to younger children and programming which will hold the interest of teens. Also among noted difficulties is the matter of providing space, staff, and time sufficient to provide programming and enough separation so that teens (especially) and younger children feel a distinction in age and activities.

The three intervention programs were very strong. The participating Clubs employed combinations of established programming (e.g., SMART MOVES) and creative activities of interest to teens. A normal policy of Boys and Girls Clubs is implementation of a guiding principle stressing that a Club is to be a safe haven from violence and any other undesirable conditions in the surrounding environment. The intervention programs were located in areas where actual gang activity and other problems, such as instrumental use of youth by adults as participants in drug dealing, were pervasive. Under sometimes difficult conditions, staff in these programs had maintained the Clubs as safe havens. The value of this situation is immeasurable, but its importance must be understood. Just as it is ridiculous to expect hungry children to function and learn at full capacity, it is unreasonable to expect youth to receive positive messages in situations which may be volatile. The intangible "respect" must be present. Across all the programs, staff observed and implemented the safe haven principle and adhered to the notion of "respect." With the intervention programs and attempts to deal with teens, establishing the threshold conditions appeared to be of great importance.

A final strength of note in the implementation of these efforts was the commitment of the various Clubs' staff to retaining the targeted youth beyond the project period. In each program evaluated, this aim was expressed and actions were observed which showed the research team that the commitment was genuine. With no follow-up and a one-shot evaluation of limited duration it is impossible to determine the extent to which this aim was fulfilled. Boys and Girls Clubs have demonstrated their long term commitment to central city areas by being there for the long haul. "Programs" come and go, usually with limited project time periods of 12 months, 18 months, 24 months, or whatever. "Programs" often are implemented by organizations which come and go. Central city residents who are the objects of such "programs" understand this, realize that expectations may be created and then ended on project termination day, and often are reluctant to become involved. Long term commitment is necessary. The long term commitment of Boys and Girls Clubs to be there and continue their efforts beyond a discrete project period, to undertake more projects, and to genuinely attempt to retain youth in a developmental strategy provided the platform for this project and was the main strength of implementation.

Difficulties in Implementation

Each of the program staffs faced difficulties unique to their efforts. Most of these were overcome in creative ways. There were several ubiquitous difficulties in implementing these projects, and not all could be overcome. Four of these deserve direct attention by those designing or planning future efforts. These are not presented here to diminish the efforts of the Boys and Girls Clubs; rather, they are intended here to bring reality to thinking about such efforts.

First, each of the programs was required to keep extensive records regarding the targeted youth, their involvement, and their progress. Some programs managed to do more than others, but all programs had difficulty with this requirement. None of the programs had the luxury of providing staff personnel whose main duty would be record-keeping. Program staff all had an array of duties, and few program staff were assigned only to duties involving the specified project. Beyond this, program staff had to cover more than one usual shift during days at work and were required to have some means for monitoring activities and progress of 35 or more targeted youth who might at any given time be involved in activities in different places, perhaps supervised by staff or persons other than the program staff. The expectations for record-keeping, given the program staffing, were unrealistic. The data recorded were minimal in most cases, although program staff made genuine efforts. Consequently, data regarding the youth was inconsistent. Those planning future efforts should attend to developing case management realistically in line with staffing capacity. If there is to be evaluation, evaluators or the evaluation should be included in planning with the aim of specifying essential data collection relevant to the questions to be asked.

Second, all programs experienced difficulties in obtaining involvement from the parents of participating youth. At best, the involvement of parents for the duration of the project was very limited (i.e., a very few parents were involved consistently for the duration, most often where they were included as members of a program advisory committee). At worst, parental involvement was very limited and sporadic or nonexistent. Staff across the programs employed a variety of approaches to enlist and retain the involvement of parents. These approaches included home visits (which require a large amount of time for staff); regular meals held at Club facilities with parents and, most often, the participating youth invited, and, among other approaches, attempts to include a role for parents in ongoing program activities. Parental involvement is important, especially so because youth need encouragement and conditions at home which support positive activities taking place elsewhere. The problem of obtaining parental involvement is not unique to the programs undertaken by the Clubs. The problem is ubiquitous, one to be faced in the implementation of any effort targeting youth.

Third, across the programs there was one particular difficulty with school liaison. Liaisons were established, and these were a strength. However, those planning future efforts may expect to find, as with these programs, that issues of privacy and confidentiality of records require creativity and cooperation of school officials in providing substantive information for monitoring and determining progress of participating youth. This was not insurmountable for the Clubs in program implementation but did require development of viable working agreements. This situation deserves careful consideration as a practical reality issue in designing efforts which require information on school progress.

Fourth, in some locations the Boys and Girls Club implementing the program was the primary resource in the area and was unaffected by other organizations and other efforts in its implementation. In some areas, "turf" became an issue and required the program staff to negotiate working agreements with other groups or organizations also operating programs or implementing efforts. With some groups, the working agreements required periodic negotiation and relations were often strained. Turf was an issue in regard to some resident associations in some housing developments where these resident associations wanted actual control of program resources and decisions or where these associations were committed to other ventures and the implementation of the Club's program was not initially welcomed. Also, some Clubs experienced a situation in which several organizations were all attempting to implement funded efforts targeting the same inner city population and were all attempting to make claims on or obtain resources from the same set of local agencies (i.e., schools, law enforcement, housing authority, among others.). Where these difficulties arose, program staff eventually overcame them, but these affected the nature and levels of implementation in some instances. Those designing or planning future efforts should attend to the context and politics of implementation in particular areas.

CONCLUSIONS AND RECOMMENDATIONS

The overall conclusion of this evaluation effort was that the youth gang prevention and early intervention initiative of the Boys and Girls Clubs of America was both sound and viable in its approach. The neighborhoods and communities where many of the 1,450 Clubs are located, as well as the nature of the Clubs' programming, place them in position to serve the needs of youth at risk of gang involvement. All sites evaluated dealt with youth who were clearly at risk of gang involvement. As planned, the prevention sites clearly targeted a younger population, in which the risk factors were more along the lines of early warning signals (poor school performance, discipline problems, etc.). The intervention programs dealt with an older population, with a greater number of youth with justice system contacts, substance abuse histories, and the like.

The level of attendance and involvement served as a clear indicator of the ability of Clubs to provide viable programming and activities which attract at-risk youth, bring them into the Clubs, and maintain their interest and participation in regular Club programming. Boys and Girls Clubs of America stands out as an exemplar of a national network of youth-serving organizations with the commitment to a nationwide offensive to counteract the problem of youth gangs in America. Given the scope of the gang problem nationally, and the need to reach youth before they become involved in gangs, more comprehensive, long-term efforts should be initiated utilizing organizations such as Boys and Girls Clubs as the committed core.

This evaluation showed the need for long term efforts rather than short term programs. It also showed the need for multi-stage "full service" efforts in which youth are given a commitment from early years through teenage years, maintaining contact and providing developmental opportunities to escape the conditions in which they started. This requires changes in national priorities and in the prevailing strategy of funding many programs of short duration. Coordinated efforts with national scope, flexible enough to be tailored to local needs, with a "full service" developmental approach are necessary. This requires organizations such as BGCA and the affiliated Clubs—many more of them, and a reassessment of the role played by federal agencies. If, as a nation, we are not going to take the steps necessary to reverse the deterioration of inner city areas, then we at least must make it a national priority to support and expand the set of organizations and efforts in there for the long haul.

QUESTIONS FOR UNDERSTANDING AND CRITICAL THINKING

1. What types of gang prevention and intervention strategies have dominated program development?
2. How can community mobilization more effectively tackle gang problems?

3. Review and discuss how the Boys and Girls Clubs of America approach gang problems in their respective communities.

4. Should such programs be targeted only to "at-risk" youth and if so, how are these youth defined?

REFERENCES

BERGER PL, RJ NEUHAUS 1977 *To Empower People: The Role of Mediating Structures in Public Policy* Washington, DC: American Enterprise Institute for Policy Research

FEYERHERM W, CE POPE, R LOVELL 1992 Youth Gang Prevention and Early Intervention Programs. Final Report. Boys and Girls Clubs of America

HAGEDORN J 1988 *People and Folks: Gangs, Crime, and the Underclass in a Rustbelt City* Chicago: Lake View

HUFF CR 1990 *Gangs in America* Newbury Park, CA: Sage

JANKOWSKI MS 1991 *Islands in the Street: Gangs and American Urban Society* Berkely, CA: U California Press

KLEIN MW, CL MAXSON 1989 Street gang violence. In NA Weiner, ME Wolfgang eds *Violent Crime. Violent Criminals* Newbury Park, CA: Sage

PATTON MQ 1980 *Qualitative Evaluation Methods* Beverly Hills, CA: Sage

SCHINKE SP, KC COLE, MA ORLANDI 1991 The Effects of Boys and Girls Clubs on Alcohol and Other Drug Use and Related Problems in Public Housing. Final Research Report. Boys and Girls Clubs of America

SPERGEL IA, GD CURRY 1993 The National Youth Gang Survey: a research and development process. In CR Huff, AP Goldstein eds *The Gang Intervention Handbook.* Champaign, IL: Research Press

SWEET RW 1991 OJJDP and Boys and Girls Clubs of America: Public Housing and High-Risk Youth. *Juvenile Justice Bulletin.* Office of Juvenile Justice and Delinquency Prevention. U.S. Department of Justice

THOMPSON D, L JASON 1988 Street gangs and preventive interventions *Criminal Justice Behavior* 15 323–333

THRASHER FM 1927 *The Gang: a Study of 1,313 Gangs in Chicago* Chicago: U Chicago Press

VIGIL JD, SC YUN 1990 Vietnamese youth gangs in southern California. In CR Huff ed *Gangs in America* Newbury Park, CA: Sage

Index

❖

A

Abbott, R., 265, 317, 318

abstinence, emphasis on, 274

abuse. *See* Maltreatment and Victimization

"acceptable" drug use, notions of, 271–272

Adams, E.H., 248, 259

Adkinson, C.D., 208

Adler, P.A., 24, 301

adolescent-limited delinquents, 123

agency towns, growth of, 125, 133

Aggression Replacement Training, 321, 337

aggressive gang response programs, use of, 20

Aiken, T.W., 238, 261

Akers, R.L., 282

alcohol, gangs and use of, 59, 122, 130, 135, 237–239

Alegado, D., 151, 152

Alexander, A., 223, 333

alienation, 97, 115

Alinsky, S.D., 319

Allen, W.R., 245, 246, 258

Alterman, A.I., 289

ambiguity of the term gang, 4

American Indian gangs. *See* Navajo youth gangs

Anderson, E., 96, 102, 115, 196, 197, 201, 221, 237, 241, 246, 247, 254

Anglin, D., 210, 211, 212, 214, 215, 222, 225, 341, 343

antisocial behavior, role of, 123, 124, 130, 131, 134

Apter, T., 52

Aquino, K., 286

Arnette, J.L., 188, 196, 197, 201

Arnold, R., 171, 185, 297

Ary, D.V., 174, 186

Aryan Brotherhood, 161

Asbury, H., 74

Asian Car Thieves, 152

athletic clubs, 5

Atkinson, P., 173, 185

attachment, desire for a sense of, 51

Auman, A., 143

B

Baca Zinn, M., 98

Bachman, J., 275

Backstrom, T., 74, 76, 92

Bahr, S.J., 286, 292

Ball, R.A., 14, 24, 25, 49, 73, 74, 206, 263, 285, 297, 302

Banton, J., 343

Barker, J., 97

Barlas, S., 188, 199, 201

Barnes, H.V., 335

Barnett, D., 285

Baron, S., 49

barrio and gangs. *See also* Race and ethnicity

adult perspectives on gangs and the community, 103–104

cultural expectations, 109

die, willingness to, 114–115

economic influences, 104–105

families, role of, 112

heterogeneity of life experiences, 103

immigration, role of, 108